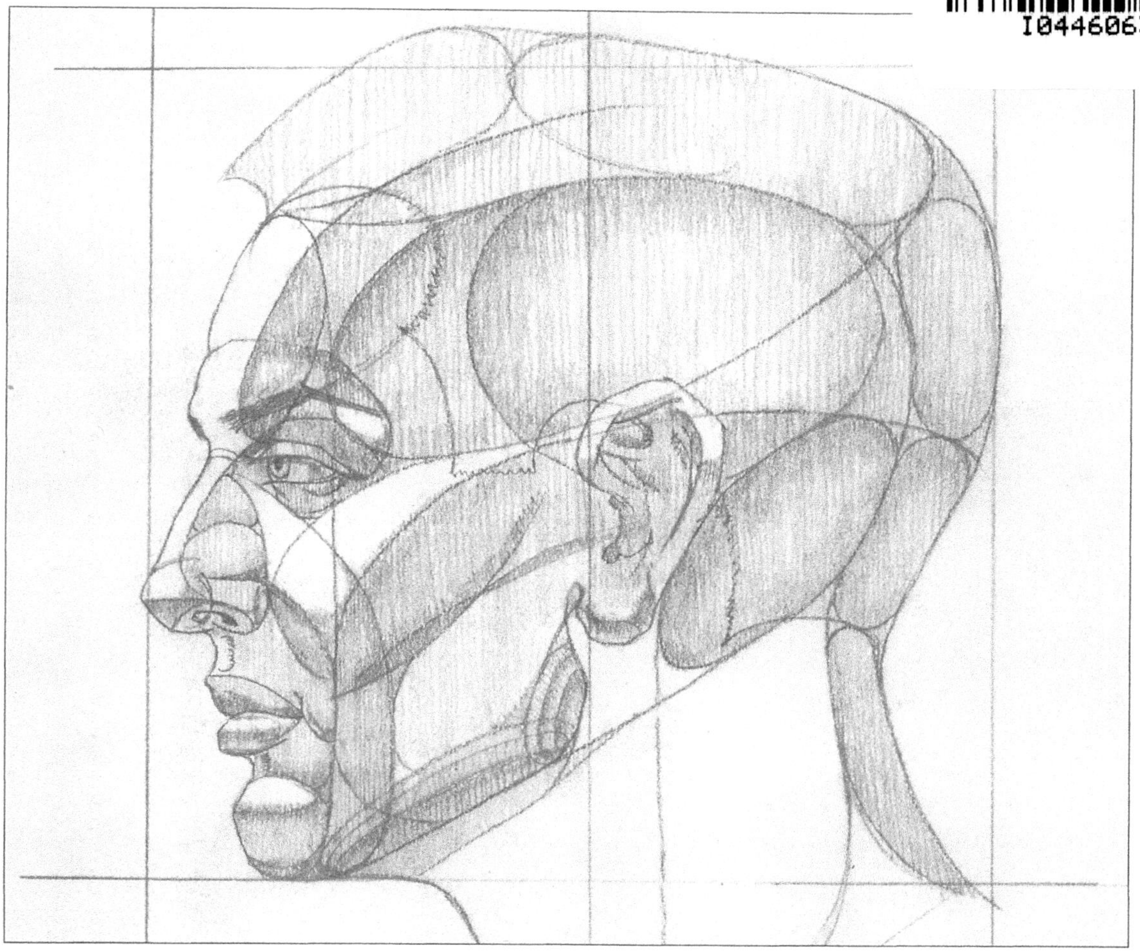

Mastering Drawing
THE HUMAN FIGURE
From Life, Memory & Imagination

Jack Faragasso

DOVER PUBLICATIONS
Garden City, New York

ACKNOWLEDGEMENTS

I must first acknowledge my great debt to Frank J. Reilly, for this book would not have been possible without his teaching and inspiration. I am also indebted to my students, for as the old Roman saying goes, "as we teach we learn." I have learned much from them.

Credit must be given to Peter J. De Weerdt for his comprehensive layout of the book and his advice and help in its production. I would also like to thank Karen Bonacorda for the typing of the manuscript as well as for her intelligent editorial comments. Thanks also to Joan Reutershan, Susan Grosse and Julie Hannibal for their help in proofing the manuscript. I wish to acknowledge the work of Hans J. De Weerdt for his advice and guidance on computer technology without which this book would not be possible.

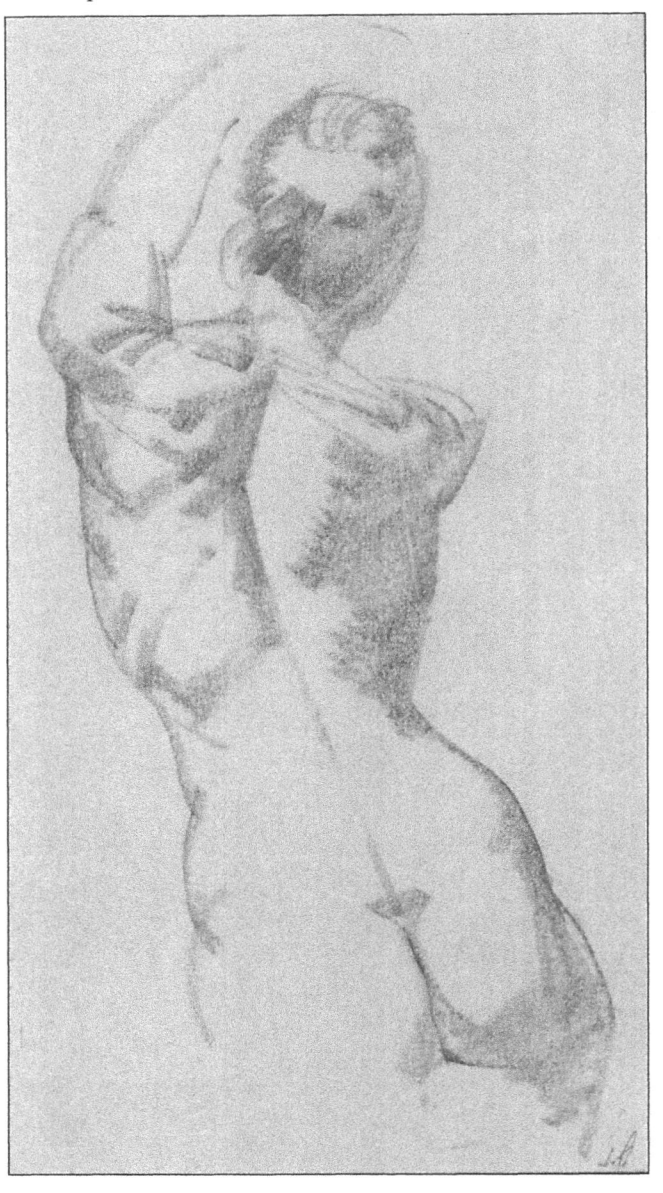

Bibliographical Note

This Dover edition, first published in 2020, is an unabridged republication of the edition published by Stargarden Press, New York, in 2004.

Library of Congress Cataloging-in-Publication Data

Names: Faragasso, Jack, author.
Title: Mastering drawing the human figure : from life, memory and imagination / Jack Faragasso.
Description: Garden City, New York : Dover Publications, 2020. | Series: Dover art instruction | "This Dover edition, first published in 2020, is an unabridged republication of the edition published by Stargarden Press, New York, in 2004"— Colophon. | Summary: "Complete handbook by veteran instructor of the Art Students League, suitable for all: novices, students, professionals. Covers basic structure of head and body, light and shade, conveying action, depicting drapery, more"—Provided by publisher.
Identifiers: LCCN 2019050719 | ISBN 9780486841243 (trade paperback)
Subjects: LCSH: Figure drawing—Technique. | Human figure in art.
Classification: LCC NC765 .F318 2020 | DDC 743.4—dc23
LC record available at https://lccn.loc.gov/2019050719

All drawings by the author.
Layout and design by Peter J. De Weerdt

Printed in Canada
84124307   2024
www.doverpublications.com

DEDICATED TO THE MEMORY OF
FRANK J. REILLY
WHO TAUGHT SO MANY

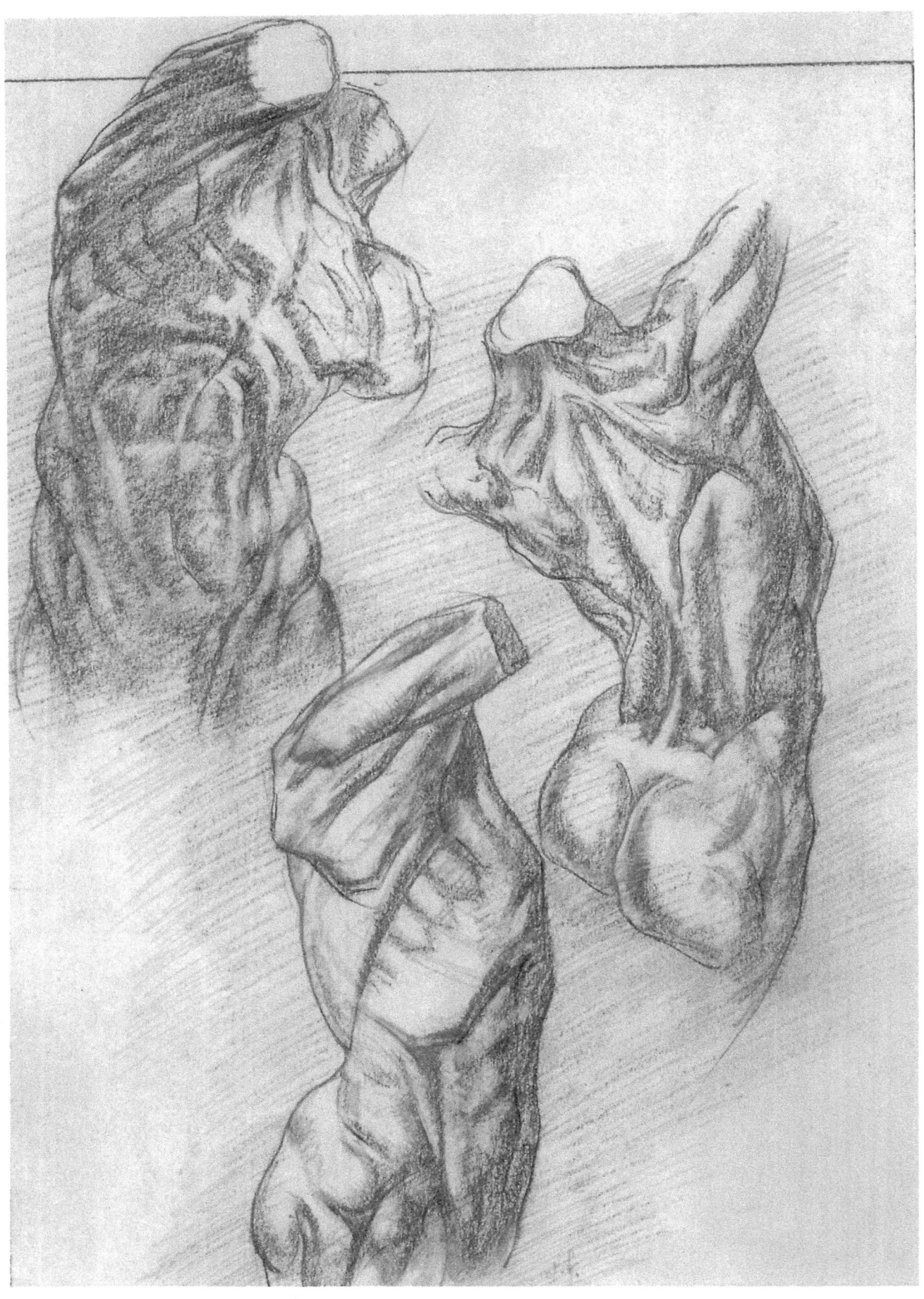

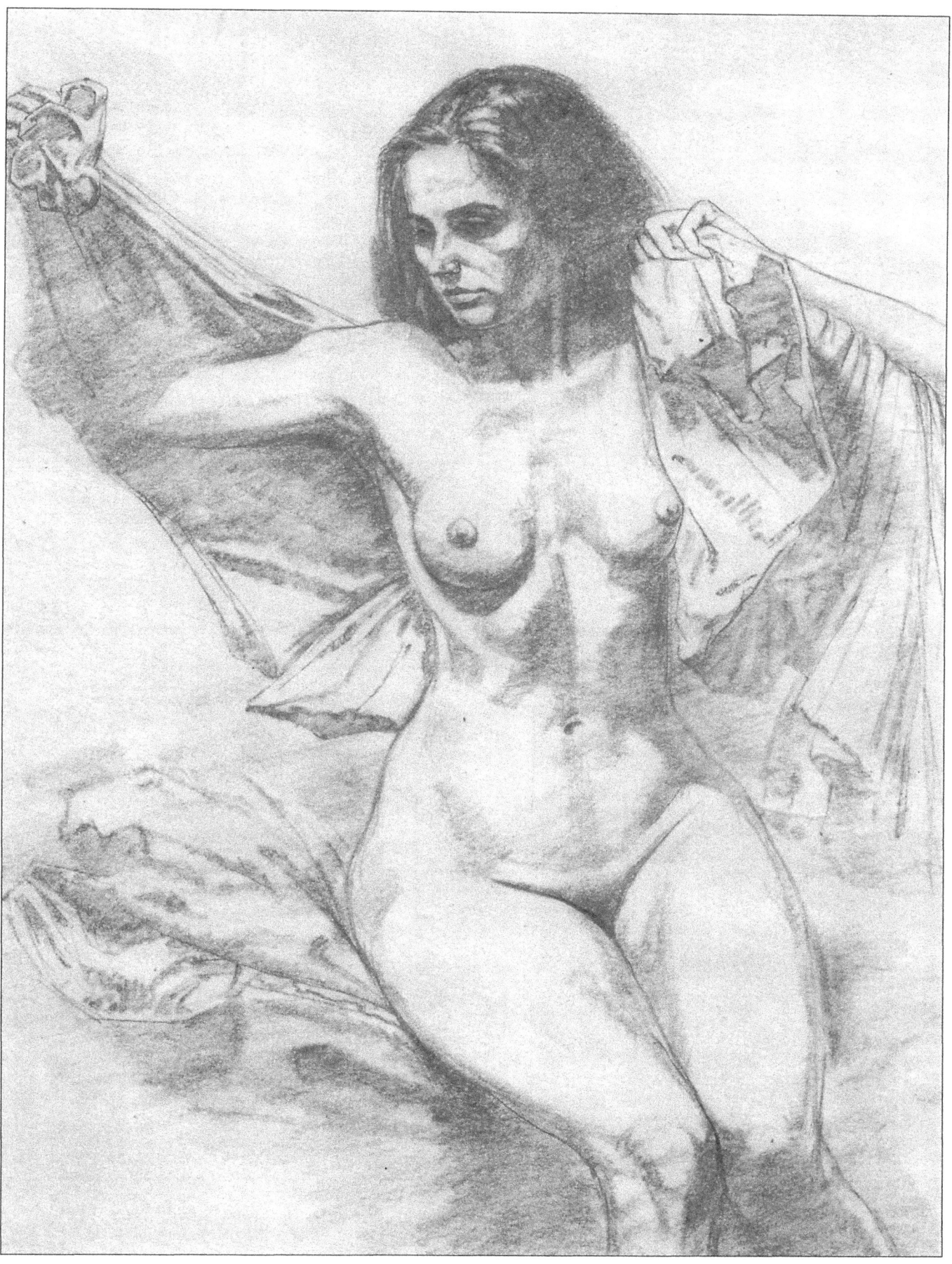

TABLE OF CONTENTS

INTRODUCTION

WHO THIS BOOK IS FOR

This book is for all of those who love to draw the human form. It is for those who have never drawn a line, for those who are students who can draw to a certain degree, and for those professional artists who are proficient in drawing. It is also, of course, for those who teach drawing.

Of the above mentioned groups it is most likely the beginner who can most easily assimilate these lessons for his mind is clear and as yet uncluttered with many obscure, conflicting and ofttimes erroneous ideas.

Those who are studying at art schools usually read, and have read, many books on drawing by many different artists desperately seeking to find out as many facts and "secrets" that will help them draw well. This is understandable of course but it can cause much confusion and hinders rather than accelerates progress.

Those who are professional artists can use what is taught within these pages to confirm the truthfulness of their work or remedy some defect – for all of us have defects in our work. It is a fact that one can find errors of drawing by the best and most famous artists who ever lived.

BACKGROUND

"One can see farther sitting on the shoulders of a giant." Old proverb.

What is contained in these pages is based mainly on the teachings of Frank J. Reilly who I studied with and knew personally for many years, plus many of my own ideas on the subject of drawing which have evolved from my, at this point, 30 years of teaching at the Art Students League of New York. I have organized this knowledge to the best of my ability with regard to ease of learning and clarity.

At one point in his life Mr. Reilly came to the conclusion that he would not go down in history as a great artist, but he believed he could be known as one of the greatest teachers of drawing, painting and "picture making," as he termed it.

Many who studied with him, and there were thousands, would agree he succeeded, for no one, with the exceptions of Frank Vincent Dumond and George Bridgemen, also teaching at the Art Students League, produced so many professional artists in all branches of the art world.

Unfortunately for Mr. Reilly he was teaching how to draw and paint in a representational manner while the world of art was mainly abstract expressionist – as well as containing dozens of other "isms." His students had no recourse, if they wanted to make a living with their art, other than to go into the illustration field – the only avenue open to them that still used a great deal of representational art. Here dozens and dozens of Mr. Reilly's students excelled. Many years passed and eventually all the "isms" were exhausted and many came to dead ends. Slowly but surely the pendulum started to swing back to representational painting. At this point many of his students who were now top notch illustrators abandoned that field, joined galleries and became firmly established as "fine artists," especially in the western and southwestern states. Unfortunately, Mr. Reilly died before he could see the fulfillment, truthfulness and blossoming of his teaching ideas.

Clearly Mr. Reilly was doing something right in his teaching. He claimed he took what was regarded as the best ideas of the best artists in the best periods of art – organized it, added to it and presented it in a unified, orderly and related manner which was to lead to the best results in the quickest possible way. He claimed anyone could learn to draw provided he really wanted to and worked hard. Frankly I did not believe this when I first started teaching for I saw many who seemed hopeless but over a period of time I was amazed at how they improved through following instructions and by doing many, many drawings and paintings.

HOW TO USE THIS BOOK

The beginner should first read this book rapidly from beginning to end. Just skimming over the pages will do. This is so you may see how the theories and ideas evolve and where they lead you to. The next step is to read the book slowly – this time really trying to comprehend what is presented. The third step is to read the book from the beginning again this time making drawings of the diagrams shown. Complete one chapter at a time. Do not go any further until you can draw the basic figure structure diagrams from memory. I want you to build on a firm foundation mastering one thing pretty much before going on to the next one – an idea incidentally that da Vinci stressed well over 400 years ago. If you find this difficult put tracing paper over the diagrams and copy them over and over again. Lastly you will draw from the live model using these structural diagrams as your guide. If you still are unsure about yourself and are apprehensive about drawing from life, practice first by drawing your structure lines over photographs, available by the hundreds in catalogues and magazines, with a Pentel type pen that marks on a glossy surface. In this way you can prove to yourself the usefulness and truthfulness of the structure system and be better prepared to draw from the living model. You will have blueprints impressed on your mind to guide you as you work.

The material in this book is presented in the order it should be learned as much as is possible – for it is impossible to learn anything in exact order. First learn the basic structure system as it applies to the head and the figure, then study forms and planes, what and where they are, and lastly how light and shade falls on these planes and forms. All of this, combined with the proper use of line, the concept of action and with the infusion of your feeling produces drawings of the fullest most complete sense.

Eventually when you can draw fairly well you may do away with any and all structure lines you deem unnecessary and let yourself go in complete freedom – but if you get into trouble you can always go back to your basic structure lessons to solve your problems. Drawing from memory and imagination, which should always be practiced wherever you are, will come more easily to you after you absorb these basic lessons of drawing.

Color, the next step for the artist, is not treated here but is covered quite extensively in my previous book, The Student's Guide to Painting, which was published in 1980 by North Light.

A WORD OF CAUTION

Teaching drawing for many years has made me aware of certain pitfalls that I feel I must warn against. One of them is that of placing too much reliance on what one perceives as a foolproof method of drawing – that it can be followed one thousand percent and that one does not have to think on one's own…thinking *is* required as well as using your imagination to expand and embellish upon what you're learning. The student must not assume that he can draw every pose or every head in exactly the same sequence. There are too many variables involved. For instance as when I say always start drawing the figure by starting with the head as that is your basic unit of measurement. This is valid most of the time but there are many instances when the head is not visible. In this case the recommended procedure has to be slightly altered, the approach varied depending on the pose. Another instance is when the model is lying on a flat surface. Here you have to relate the model to the surface first – before you start completing the figure. Failure to do so results in the many drawings in which the model seems to go into or below the flat surface, an impossibility of course. When drawing the model seated in a chair or on a stool or any other kind of furniture then the two have to be considered as one, for they relate directly to each other and should be drawn accordingly.

It would be nice and convenient to be able to draw every pose using the same exact procedure but unfortunately – or perhaps fortunately – things do not always work the way we want them to. There are times when one must draw a big outside shape first to contain a complex arrangement of anatomical forms and relationships – or perhaps one needs to put down a long sweeping directional line of a certain angle on the outside contours of the model to force all the structural lines to their proper places.

Try to stick as much as possible to the basic recommended procedure along with the other aids which will be presented on the following pages.

A word of caution also to students who get too involved with structural diagrams. Occasionally one will get so wrapped up in drawing these diagrams that he or she may never get to a point of making a life-like drawing – producing instead what looks like a road map. Of course this is not the purpose of the structure system.

One must also realize that the forms and planes of the head and figure are of an infinite variety, that the light and shade on them can come from angles of an infinite variety and that your viewing positions in relation to them can be countless. These three conditions, therefore, produce an infinite variety of structure lines which, of course, cannot all be put in a book. What is necessary is to absorb the underlying theories of what is taught here and use them with your rational intelligence as well as your feeling. In this way you should be able to handle any situation.

A FURTHER WARNING

Too much reliance is placed on copying the model, but after all, how would a beginning student know any better? Copying the model will lead to a dull, stiff looking drawing or painting. The model is a living, breathing entity always in subtle movement – not a lifeless plaster cast. The only benefits of copying casts are to study light and shade somewhat and to learn a little about proportions. If the student bases his future productions on solely copying casts he will never produce anything worthwhile. If he tries learning to draw by copying the model he will be constantly frustrated or produce an uninspired work. He will not be able to infuse his own creativity into the drawing. One must approach the drawing or painting of the model with concepts and skill. Our concepts are of structure – structure within action – growth and empathy. Remember we reconstruct from nature. We do not copy.

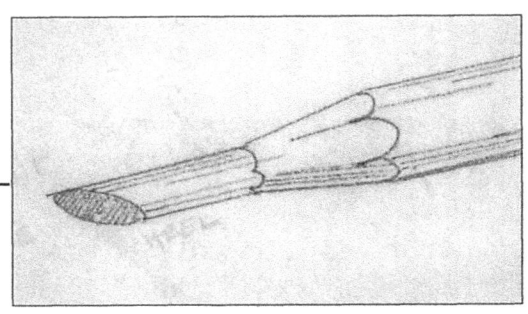

CHAPTER ONE

MATERALS

Masterful drawings can be produced with ordinary newsprint paper and a charcoal or Wolff's carbon pencil. You will have to draw and throw away hundreds of drawings before you have to start worrying about their longevity and passing into museum collections so do not worry about not drawing on expensive acid-free archival paper for a while.

Remember, whenever you change the type of paper you draw on you generally have to change the pencil you draw with – and if you change your pencil you will generally have to change the paper. In most cases it will take time to adjust to a different kind or degree of pencil. Be patient and do not despair as this is normal.

You will find that one combination of pencil and paper will work better for you than another depending on your purpose. As an example you will have to use a hard pencil if you are making a linear drawing and a much softer one if you're doing a full value rendering.

What we are looking for is maximum control – we do not want the pencil to slip and slide all over the paper. We want a combination of pencil and paper that will produce a slight drag. We want a pencil that makes a line that we can go over and alter another line or value without slipping – a line that can vary from a hairline to a broad stroke in one sweep – one that will respond to our every thought and nuance of touch. For these reasons paper with a slick surface and graphite pencils are not recommended for our learning drawings.

The act of drawing should be approached with love, energy and enthusiasm. It should be enjoyable not drudgery.

You will not learn as much if you draw with a bored attitude or are uninterested in what you're doing. The paper or pad should be clipped onto and backed by a hard stiff board, such as masonite, that does not bend. You cannot have maximum control holding your pad in your hand or resting your paper on a wobbly bent surface. Don't make problems for yourself.

Your pencil should be sharpened with a single-edged razor blade and given a wedge with a sandpaper block. Before the model starts posing you should be practicing many strokes and variations of strokes, much in the way musicians practice on their instruments before performances. These warm-up exercises will loosen you up and aid you in making skillful lines when you get into the actual drawing.

ABOUT MATERIALS

PENCILS: There are dozens of name brand pencils on the market, some very old, some new. I think on the whole pencils were much better in the past. This is probably due to today's increased production costs and the conformance to environmental laws which prohibit certain manufacturing processes. Today you may buy a top-rated brand pencil and find all of a sudden it feels like you are drawing with a cinder of coal. There is also less consistency in their designations.

Pencils are designated "H" for hard and "B" for soft. The basic grades of General's charcoal pencils are H, HB, 2B, 4B and 6B, 6B being the softest. Wolff's carbon pencils which have been used by draughtsmen and artists for generations range from H the hardest to BBB the softest. Graphite pencils, which are not recommended for our type of learning drawing range all the way from 9B the softest to 9H the hardest. The range is 9B, 8B, 7B, 6B, 5B, 4B, 3B, 2B, B, F, H, 2H, 3H, 4H, 5H, 6H, 7H, 8H and 9H.

The designations for hard and soft pencils are not universally standardized so an HB, say in the Ritmo brand, may be the equivalent to a 4B in the General's charcoal brand.

The pencils I prefer most for the learning drawings and drawings in general are Wolff's BB or BBB, General's charcoal 2B, 4B or 6B and Ritmo HB and 3B. These work very well on ordinary newsprint. You will have to try out many pencils to find the one that suits you best and that will change as you progress in your work.

Do not drop pencils as they will crack throughout and will be difficult and in many cases impossible to sharpen. Keep your pencils, razor blades and erasers in a small box where they cannot bounce around.

I have previously mentioned that it is important to keep your interest and enthusiasm up when drawing and for that reason you may want to try drawing with a sanguine or sepia pencil or a combination of sanguine and charcoal pencil for a change, but only after you are sufficiently advanced.

PAPER: For all practical purposes use a fairly smooth newsprint. Avoid a heavily textured newsprint as it might hinder your pencil stroke. I prefer the student use an 11″ x 14″ size pad. I suggest you make one drawing to a page as you will be better able to concentrate on proportions, shapes and proper placement. You should also have a 9″ x 12″ newsprint pad for making smaller studies of individual parts of the figure and drapery

DRAWING BOARD: Your drawing pad or paper should be firmly clipped to a piece of 1/4″ thick masonite at least 18″ x 16″ or any other convenient size. This will give you maximum control. If you are drawing on separate sheets of paper you will get better results by using several sheets together rather than one sheet over the masonite. In this way you will have some "give" on the surface of the paper which allows for better strokes.

SHARPENER: Use a single-edged razor blade or a multipurpose snap-off cutter to sharpen your pencils. Single-edged razor blades are much cheaper when purchased in a box of a large quantity.

ERASER: Make sure to purchase a kneaded rubber eraser, not a plastic one. The kneaded rubber eraser is good for rubbing out large areas and can be molded to a point to take out small areas. It is especially useful when making a full-value charcoal drawing to create tones and highlights.

SANDPAPER BLOCK: A sandpaper block is needed to refine your pencil point and to put a wedge on it – which is recommended in this book for the execution of learning drawings.

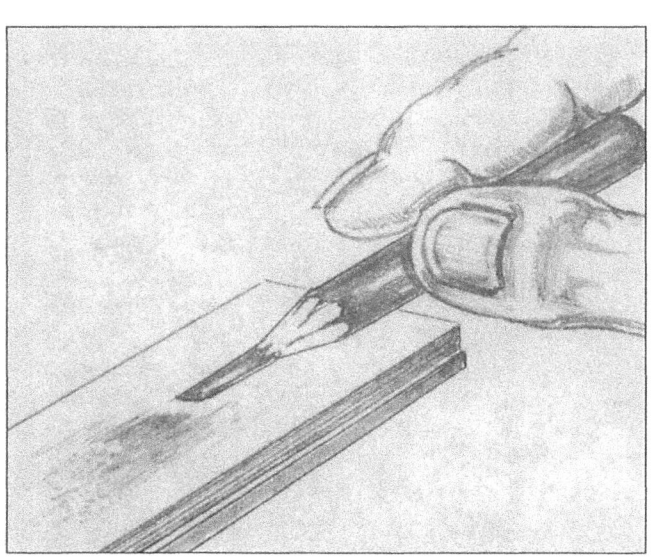

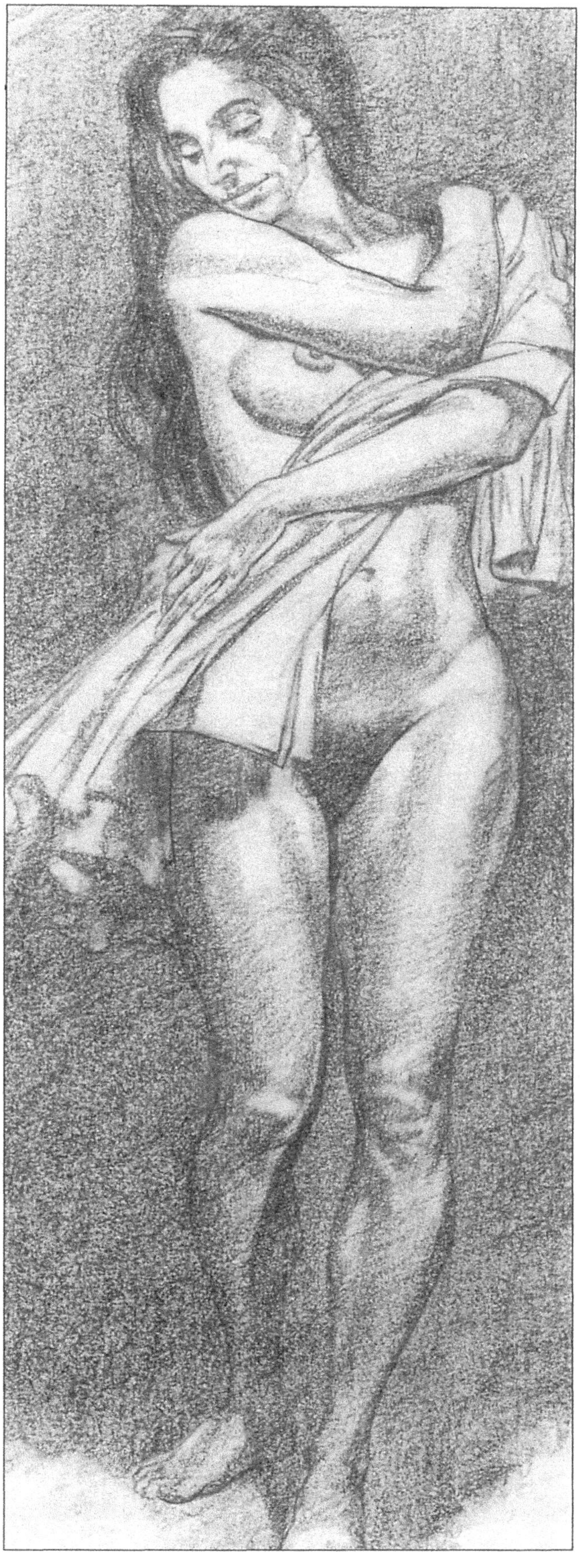

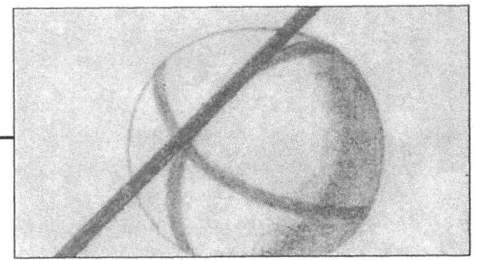

CHAPTER TWO

LINE

There is much to be learned about the use of line and how it can be achieved with an ordinary pencil. Simply sharpening a pencil to a point and drawing with it will not give you the maximum potential of line.

Figs. 1a.b.c.d. and e. show how the pencil is prepared for our type of learning drawing as well as many other types of drawing. You will have greater control and variety of line with a short pencil and therefore it is advisable to cut the pencil in half. A short pencil can be contained in the palm of your hand held by your thumb and forefinger. In this way the pencil can be twisted or turned to make a great variety of lines and strokes.

Fig. 1a. Lay the pencil on a flat, solid surface. Gently push an industrial type single-edge razor blade into the pencil at the halfway mark.

Fig. b. With the razor blade still into the pencil roll it back and forth until the cut encircles the entire pencil. Do not make this cut too deep.

Fig. c. Using a razor blade or knife and starting about 1/2 inch behind your cut line cut a wedge down to the carbon or charcoal, stopping at the cut line. Do this all around the pencil.

Fig. d. Now, holding the entire pencil down with the palm of your hand use your razor blade to cut completely through. You now have two short pencils. Continue to sharpen the pencil to a fine point and then sharpen the other half pencil.

Fig. e. You now have a sharp pencil point. Rub it on a sandpaper block at an angle to create a wedge. This wedge is what one draws with, and the angle of it will gradually adjust itself to each individual.

Fig. f. Typical lines made with the wedge-like point. The first line is a wide line made with the flatness of the wedge and by pressing more on the "heel" of the wedge. This produces a line which is soft on one side and hard on the other side at the same time. The second example is a thin line which can be made with either the edge or point of the wedge.

Figs. 2a.b.c.d. and e. show five examples of some of the many varieties of lines that can be made with a wedge-like point.

Fig. a. A hard and sharp line grading to wide and soft.

Fig. b. All soft grading from narrow to wide.

Fig. c. All narrow.

Fig. d. A wide line grading to a narrow line.

Fig. e. An all wide line. It can be light or dark.

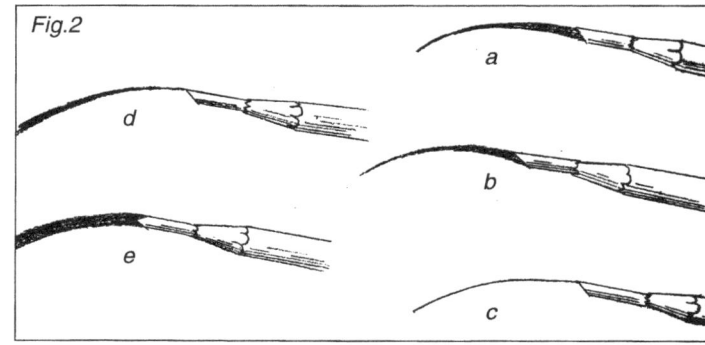

Fig.2

Fig. 3. To develop your linear skills repeat the direction, flow and weight of the line many times with your pencil *without* touching the paper. Do this rapidly and confidently. You will soon visualize an afterimage of where the line is to go – then lower the pencil to the paper and execute the line.

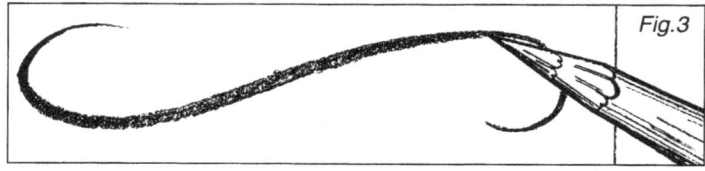

Fig.3

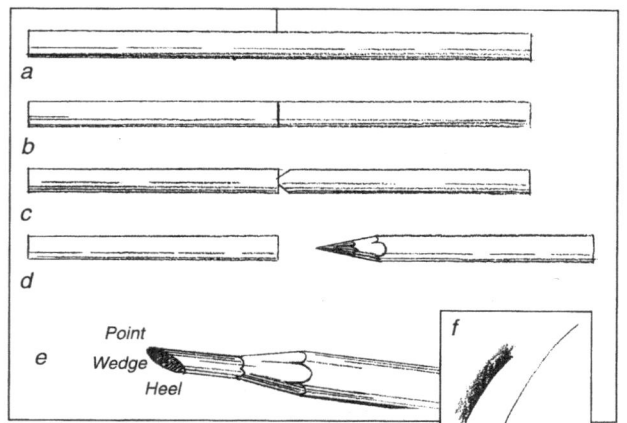

Fig.1

a

b

c

d

e

Point
Wedge
Heel

f

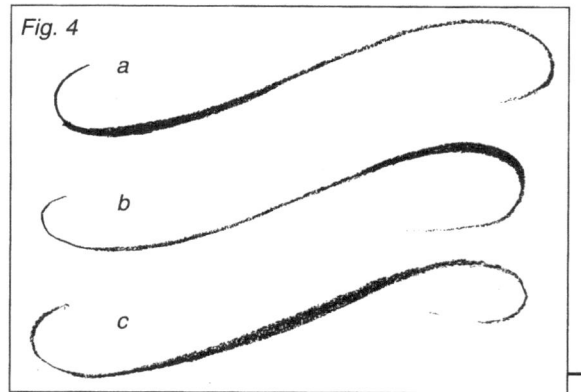

Fig. 4

a

b

c

Figs. 4a.b.c. These are three examples of practice lines to be made with the pencil's wedge point.

Fig. a. Heavy on the left end, light on the right end.

Fig. b. Light on the left end, heavy on the right end.

Fig. c. Light on both ends, heavy in the middle.

Fig. 5. Lines are light or dark, thick or thin or hard or soft. Shown are six examples of various lines. Generally lines that are light, thin and hard are on the light side of the form and lines that are dark, thick and soft are on the shadow side. Hard lines that are thin project and are used on bony projections. Soft lines recede both in the light and shadow but are used mainly on the shadow side especially on soft, fleshy areas.

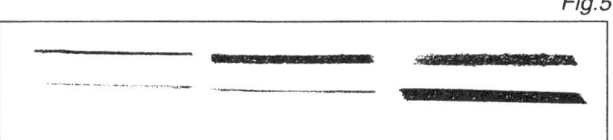

Fig.5

Figs. 6a.b.c. Three examples demonstrating how the use of hard and soft lines makes forms project or recede.

Fig. a. If lines are all the same the horizontal line of the background will stay on the same plane of the circle which represents a form.

Fig. b. To make a form project, which is represented by the circle, harden its outline, especially where it approaches the horizontal and soften the horizontal line as it approaches the outline of the circle.

Fig. c. The reverse can also be true, as evidenced quite clearly by looking at any painting by Vermeer. By softening the contours of a form or a foreground plane and by sharpening background edges you will force the eye to look at the sharp edges. This automatically forces a foreground form or a plane of foreground forms with softened contours to appear out of focus and nearer to the eye.

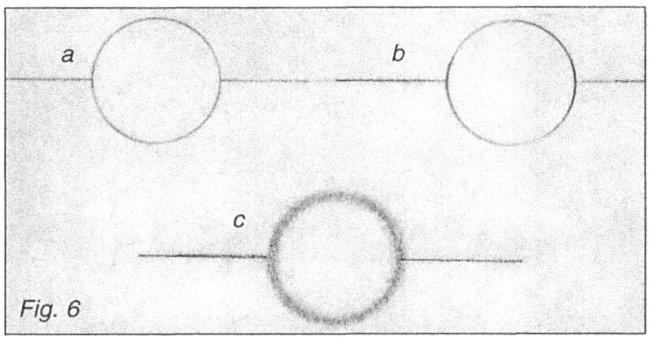

Fig. 6

Fig. 7a. When starting a drawing of the figure start with a soft, light line. This is the "action" start line.

Fig. b. To emphasize the action bear down on the pencil to produce a slightly darker effect towards the center of the line.

Fig. c. Use light to dark lines to express forms in light and shadow. By the simple use of a thin and thick line a circle appears to be a sphere with a shadow.

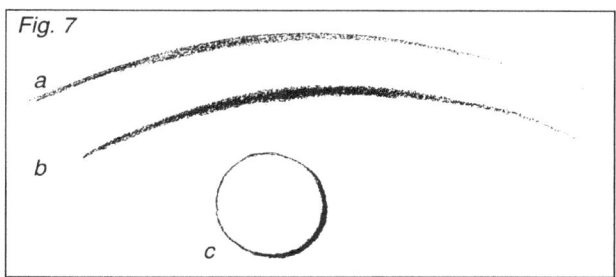

Fig. 7

Fig. 8a. Execute any line for your thought in the beginning. *Remember a line should be thought of as coming from somewhere and going somewhere.*

Fig b. If the line is not to your liking do not rub it out but use it for comparison and execute another one.

Fig. c. If the second line is not right it might be possible to try again and succeed. However if this fails rub it out and start all over again.

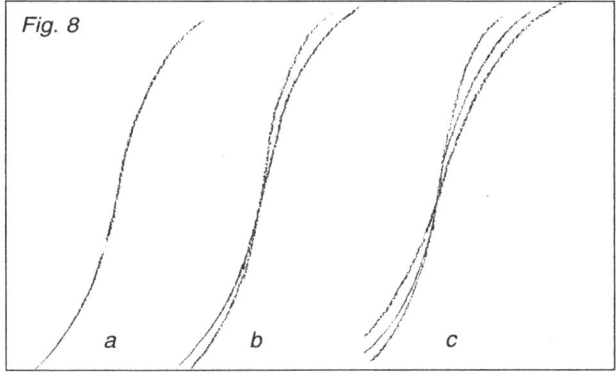

Fig. 8

Fig. 9. A typical type of line to practice with your pencil wedge. Aim for quality and accuracy of line. Start the line lightly, heavy up on it as you progress and fade it off as you end it. It is my opinion that a well executed line that goes to a slightly wrong place is better than a badly executed line that goes to the right place.

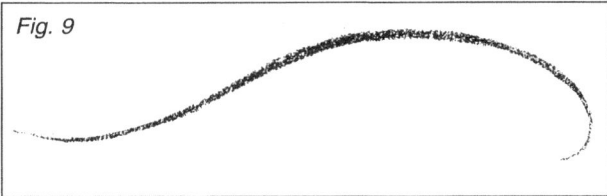

Fig. 9

Fig. 10. The drawing shows a sphere behind a plane of glass. The pane of glass is a flat plane. Shown is a straight line on the pane; it is casting a shadow on the sphere. *Straight lines are on flat planes. All lines on forms must appear as going completely around the forms.*

Fig.10

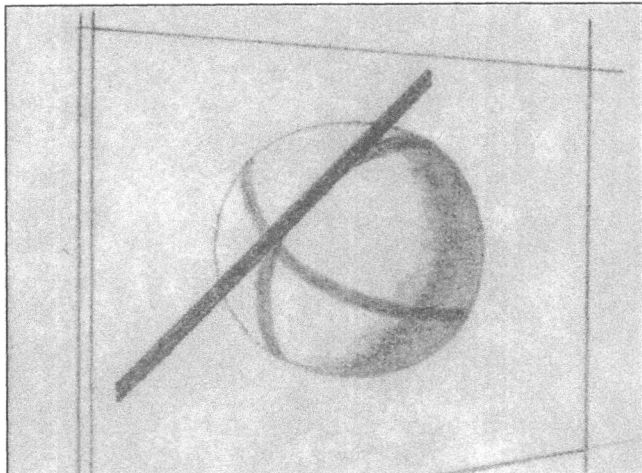

Figs. 11a.b. Two more examples of lines going around forms. It is a good idea to draw these lines as if you could see through the object to continue the lines.

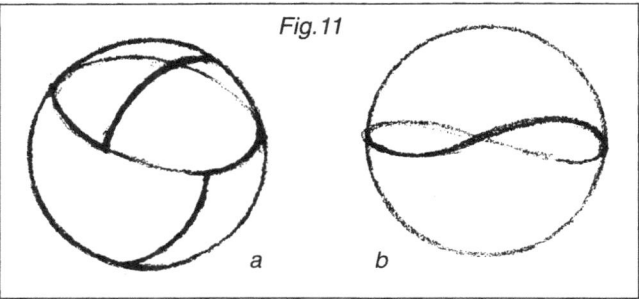

Figs. 12a.b.c. To draw the figure from the standpoint of structure we use "idea" lines. The idea line comes first. On this line the forms are drawn. *In almost all cases the shapes of the forms stay on top of, on the outside of the idea line.* The drawing on the left, *Fig. a.,* shows a curved idea line with overlapping forms upon it. The center drawing, *b.,* shows an angled idea line with forms of different sizes. The drawing on the right, *Fig. c.,* shows a rare instance where the forms cause indentations in the idea line.

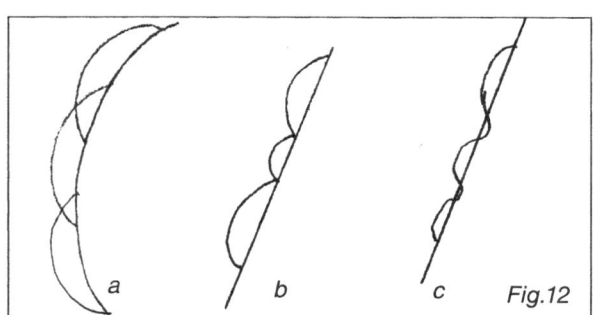

Figs. 13a.b.c. Three drawings demonstrating straight and curved idea lines with forms upon them.

Fig. 13

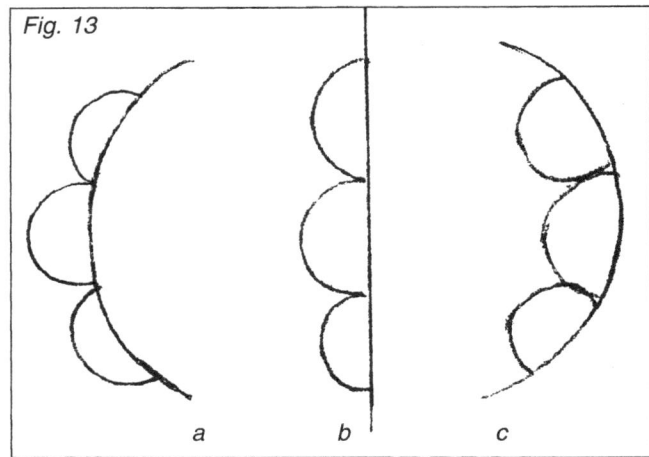

Figs. 14a.b.c. Curved surfaces of forms are sometimes difficult to get in the right place. To solve this problem I recommend the following procedure. Draw a straight line of a certain angle connecting two points. Make sure this angle is as accurate as possible. Next draw a curved line going from point to point. Observe where the greatest bulge of the form occurs.

Fig. 14

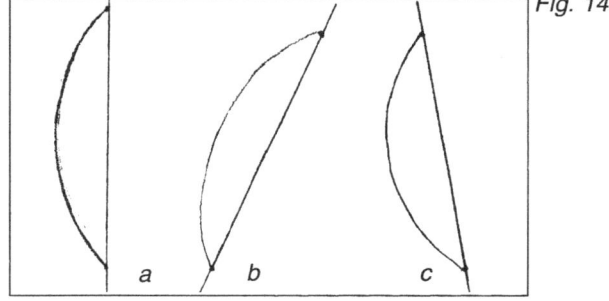

Figs. 15a.b.c.d. These drawings show the different types of curvatures of forms. Shown left to right, a form that has its greatest bulge on the top of the curve, *Fig. a.,* one that has the greatest curvature in the middle, *Fig. b.,* and one where the greatest part of the bulge is at the bottom, *Fig. c.* The fourth drawing, *Fig. d.,* shows two overlapping forms, one with the highest bulge towards the top and another with the greatest bulge at the bottom. Anatomical forms are seldom if ever as simple as these examples but the principles are the same.

Fig. 15

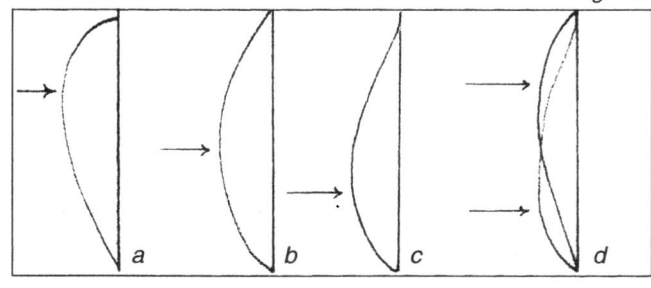

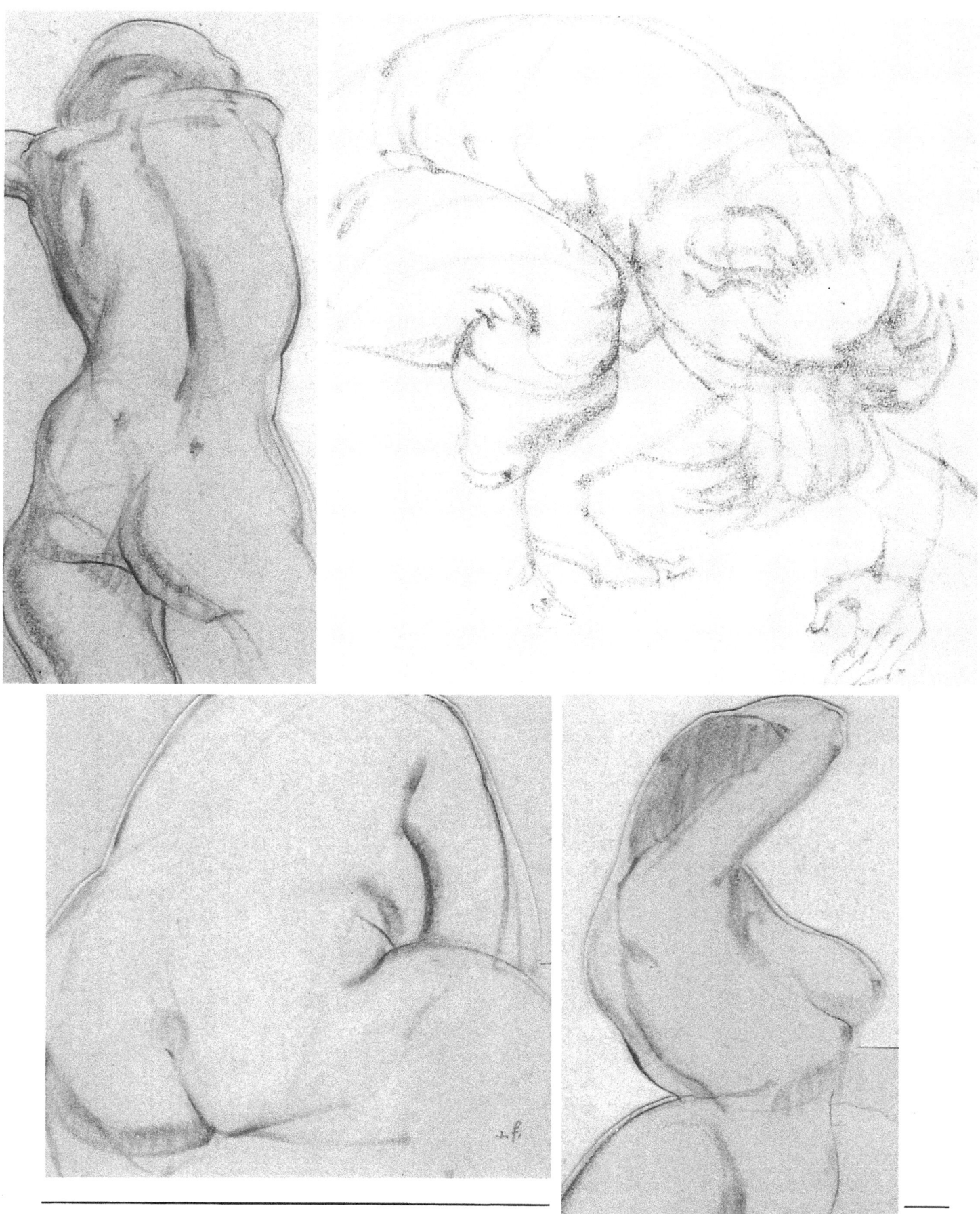

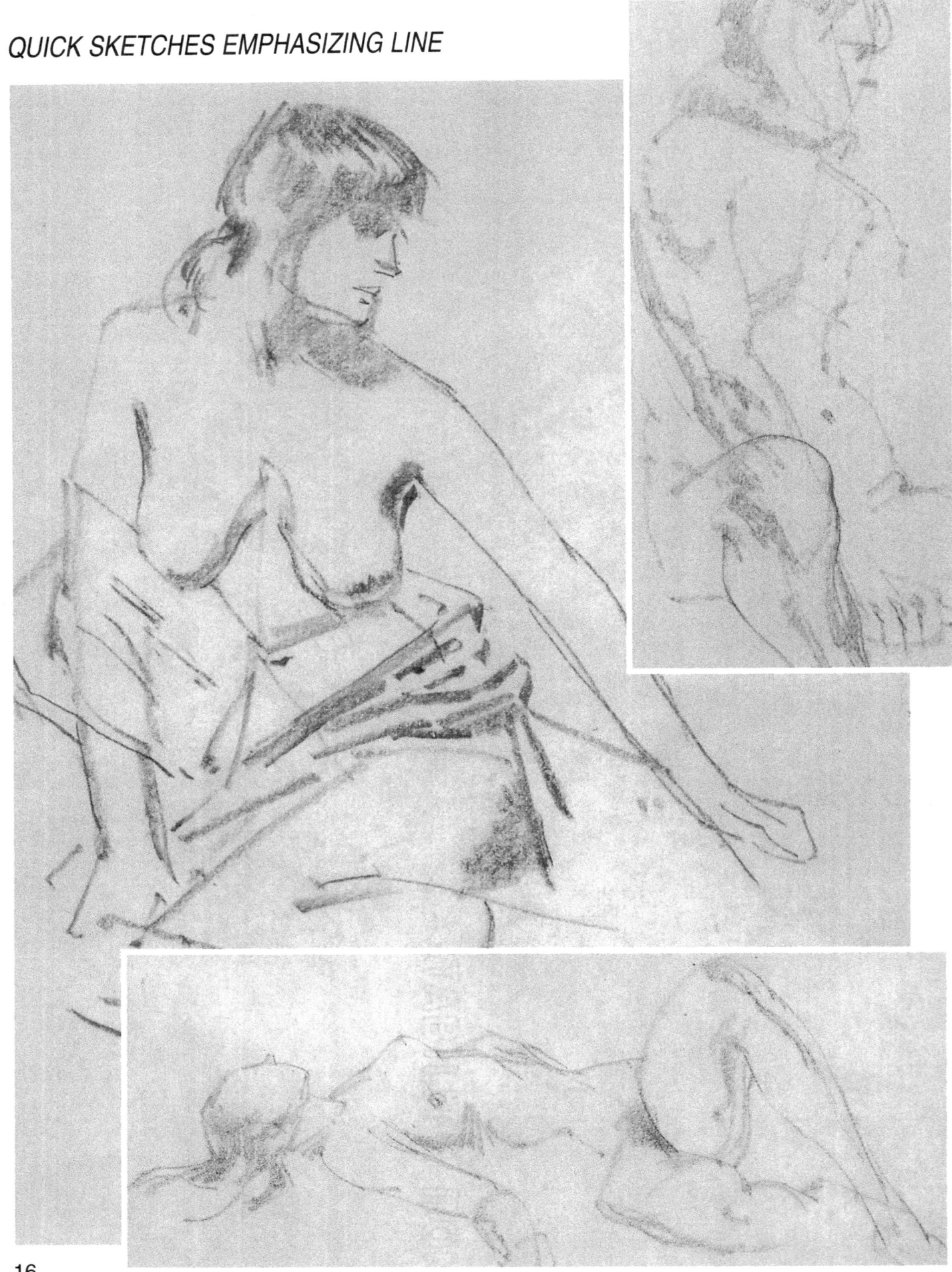

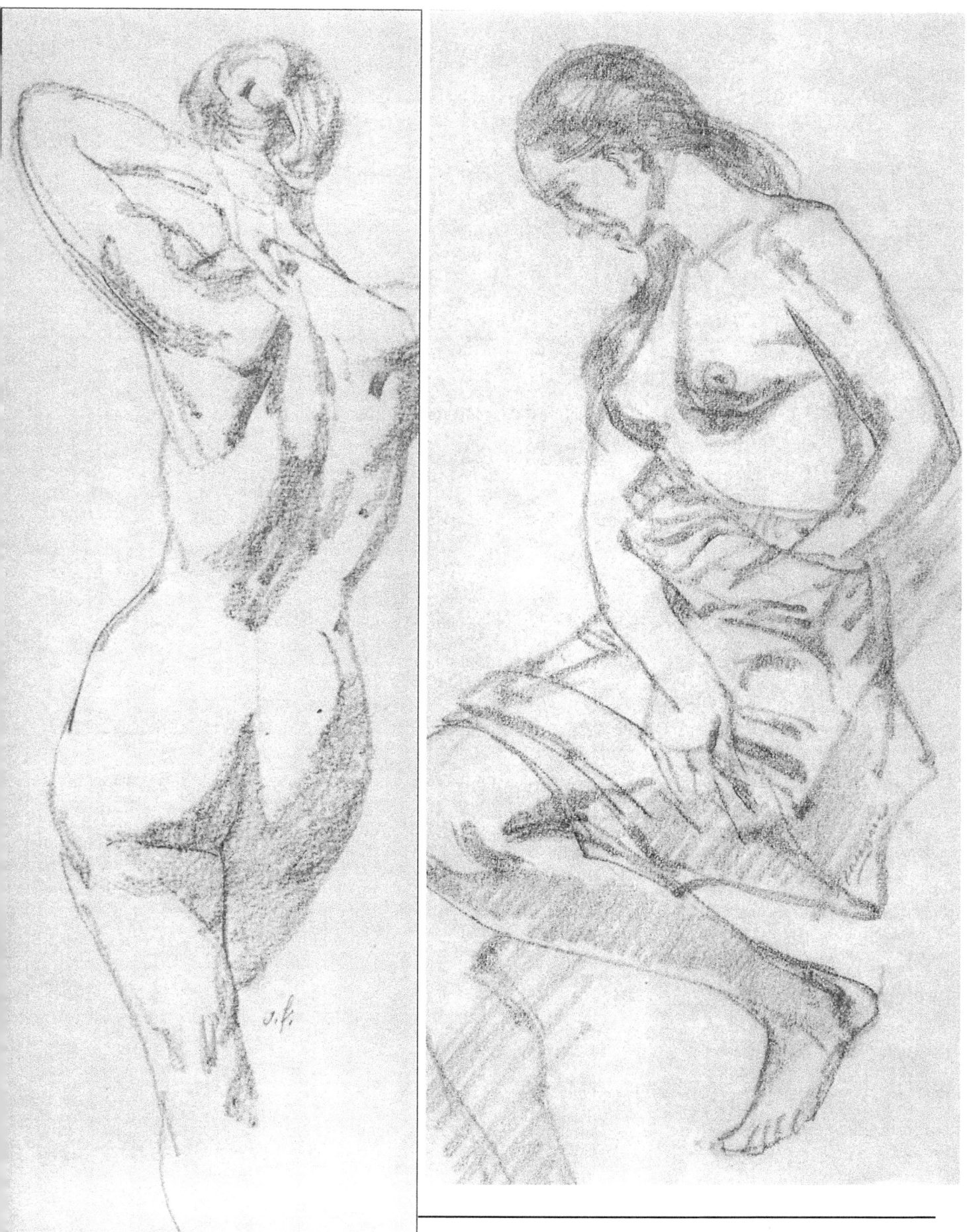

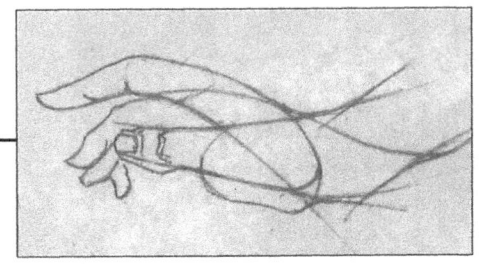

CHAPTER THREE

RELATIONSHIPS

WHAT ARE RELATIONSHIPS?

A relationship, in our terms, is anything that ties two things together. It flows through objects and unifies nature. It is an idea which many things hinge upon. Seek out the relationships of what you're drawing.

WHY RELATIONSHIPS?

The first line you put down is always correct – it usually becomes incorrect when you draw the second line. Why you may ask? Most likely because it does not correctly relate to the first line. In a good drawing lines will relate either visually or physically or both. When we look at a drawing and feel it is correct and beautifully done it is because all the relationships of line and light and shade are accurate and have the proper relative emphasis. It is important, therefore, to develop a sense of these relationships. First one must seek them in a broad sense, then in a finer more complete sense. Lastly one should develop one's own personal sense of unity of relationships as regards drawing, painting and picture-making.

Drawing with and seeking out relationships aids in recognition, ease and thoroughness of learning. They are also an aid to memory which in turn aids in speed of execution. They are, therefore, of the utmost importance. All this is in contrast to the beginner who tries to remember and copy scores of isolated facts, missing the larger more important things and thereby not achieving success of his aims.

Some relationships, such as the anatomical ones, are basic, such as the head which relates to the neck, which relates to the rib cage which relates to the pelvis. Or muscles which relate to tendons that relate to bones. Other relationships are strictly visual, dependent on your position to the model and the pose and light and shade on the model.

LINEAR RELATIONSHIPS

Regarding the relationships of lines, they can relate basically in three different ways. One way is from the outside of one side of a form to the opposite outside of a form; second is from the outside of a form to the inside of a form and the third way is for an inside line to relate to another inside line, (see Fig. 1.).

A line can also relate to another line on the edge of a light and shade division. If you cannot find a relationship, *force the line to relate somewhere.* Michelangelo did this occasionally as well as other good artists and is allowable. Among the following drawings on page 20 is one that is completely made up and full of anatomical mistakes yet you will probably not notice anything wrong with it the reason being that everything is completely related. See if you can find it.

To draw using relationships this way requires the mind to be one step ahead of the hand, (sorry about that), at least in your learning period. You must ask yourself, *where is the line coming from and where is it going?* Judgements should always be made from a known quantity at one end and an estimated quantity at the other end. The line is then to be drawn with swiftness and sureness as discussed in the previous chapter on Line.

Fig. 1. shows a simplified drawing of a leg which explains some of the ways a line can relate. The line *a* to *a1* is a line going from the inside of the leg to the outside of the leg. Line *a1* continues from the outside to the inside of the leg and back to the outside of the leg near the ankle at *a2*. Line *b* to *b1* goes from the outside to the outside of the gastrocnemius form. Line *c* goes from the outside of the leg to *c1*, the outside of the knee form, and *d* to *d1* is an inside line relating to an inside line.

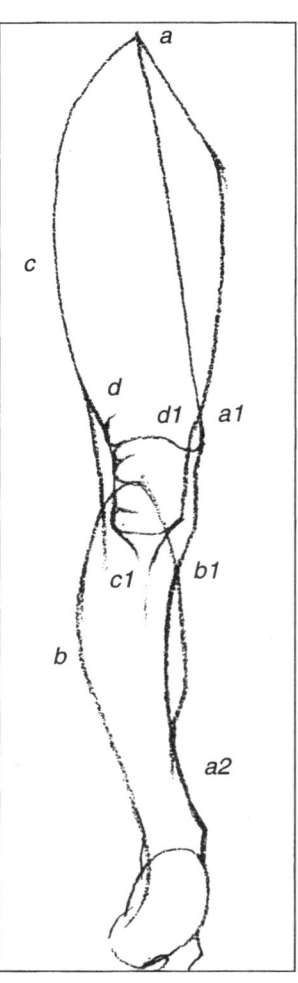

Fig.1

Fig. 2. shows how one relationship line, in this case a visual one, can connect edges, corners and centers of many forms. Always try to see seemingly unrelated objects connected somehow with one or more relationship lines.

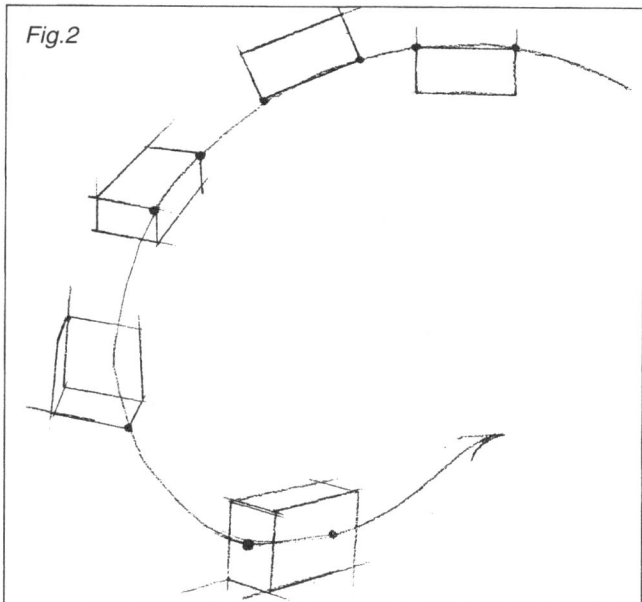
Fig.2

Fig. 3. A schematic showing some of the many ways forms can relate. Note the alignment of the right side edge of the top square to the left side edge of the square below it. The bottom of this square aligns with the top of the square to the left of it. The bottom of the square on the far left aligns with the tops of the two bottom squares. Try to use these principles with whatever you're drawing whether it be apples, humans or man-made objects.

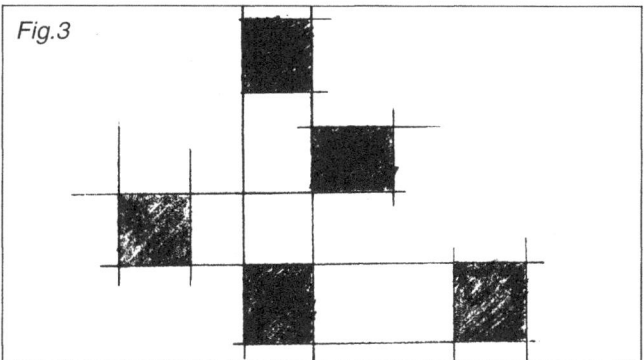
Fig.3

Fig. 4. A series of drawings showing some of the many ways edges and corners of forms can be related.

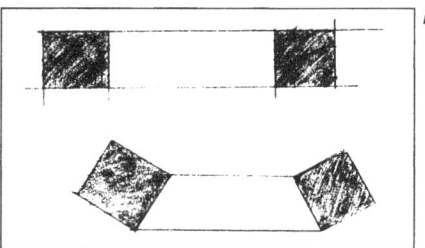
Fig.4

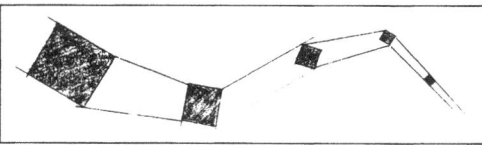
Fig.4a

Fig. 5. When drawing a series of objects, such as the spheres shown, one should draw a line describing what the forms are doing first. Once the desired movement or curvature is attained then the forms are added.

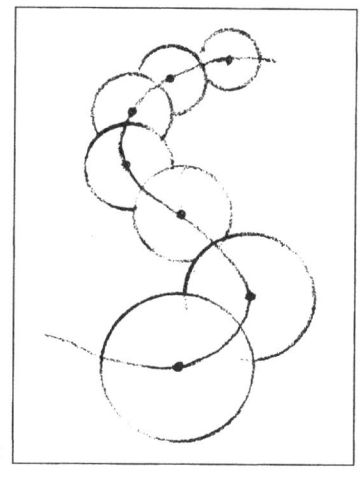
Fig.5

Figs. 6a.b.c.d. This series of four drawings prepares you for the complexities of the relationships of line and line combined with light and shade, especially as regards the human figure. The first drawing, *Fig. a.*, shows a simple alignment of the outside boundaries of the two forms. The second drawing, *Fig. b.*, shows an alignment of the opposite boundaries of the forms. In drawing *Fig. c.*, the right side boundary of the upper form aligns with the center of the bottom form and its central axis aligns with the left side boundary of the lower form. In the last drawing, *Fig. d.*, the outside border of the shadow area on the right side of the top form aligns with the inside border of the shadow area on the lower form. The inside edge of the shadow border on the upper form aligns with the inside edge of the halftone area of the lower form, and the inside of its halftone border aligns with the left outside edge of the lower form. There can be an endless variety of these arrangements. If you look for them you will find them

Fig. 6

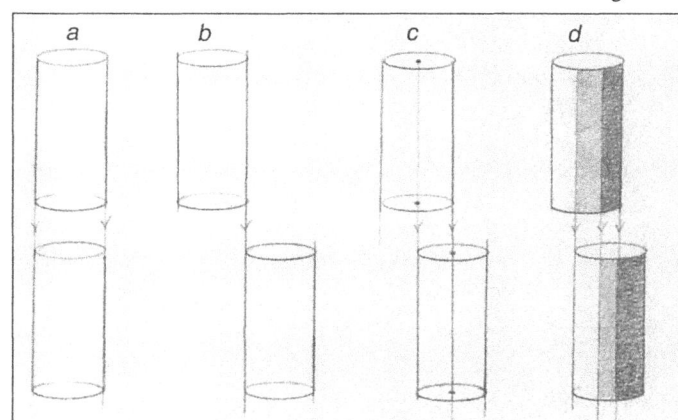

Figs. 7a.b.c. Here we have two partial drawings of an arm and one of a back showing a more concrete application of the previous highly simplified examples. The drawings show relationships of lines to lines, lines to borders of light and shade patterns and borders of light and shade patterns to other light and shade patterns and borders

Fig.7

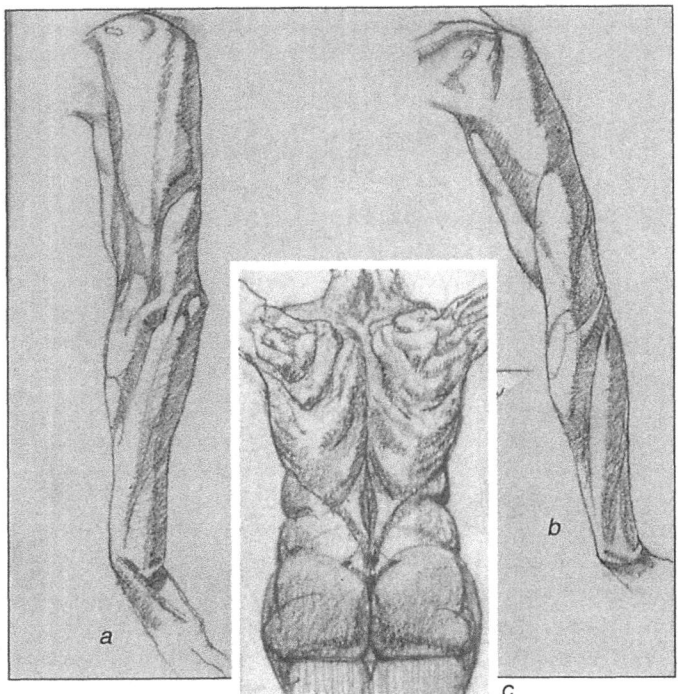

Fig. 8.
Another example
of relating lines
forming planes
and forms

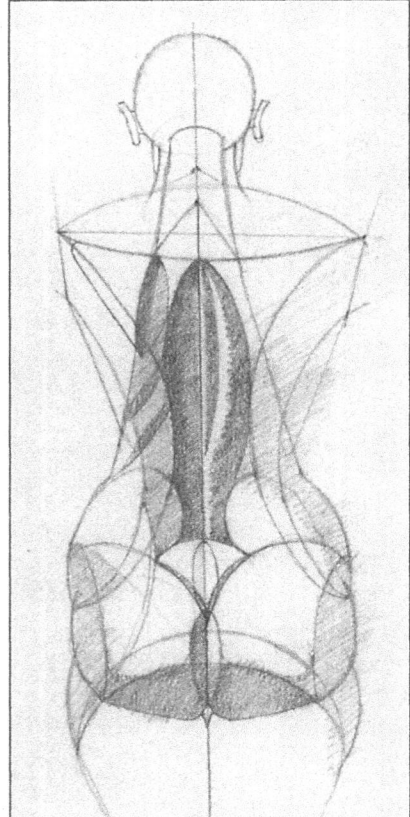

Fig.8

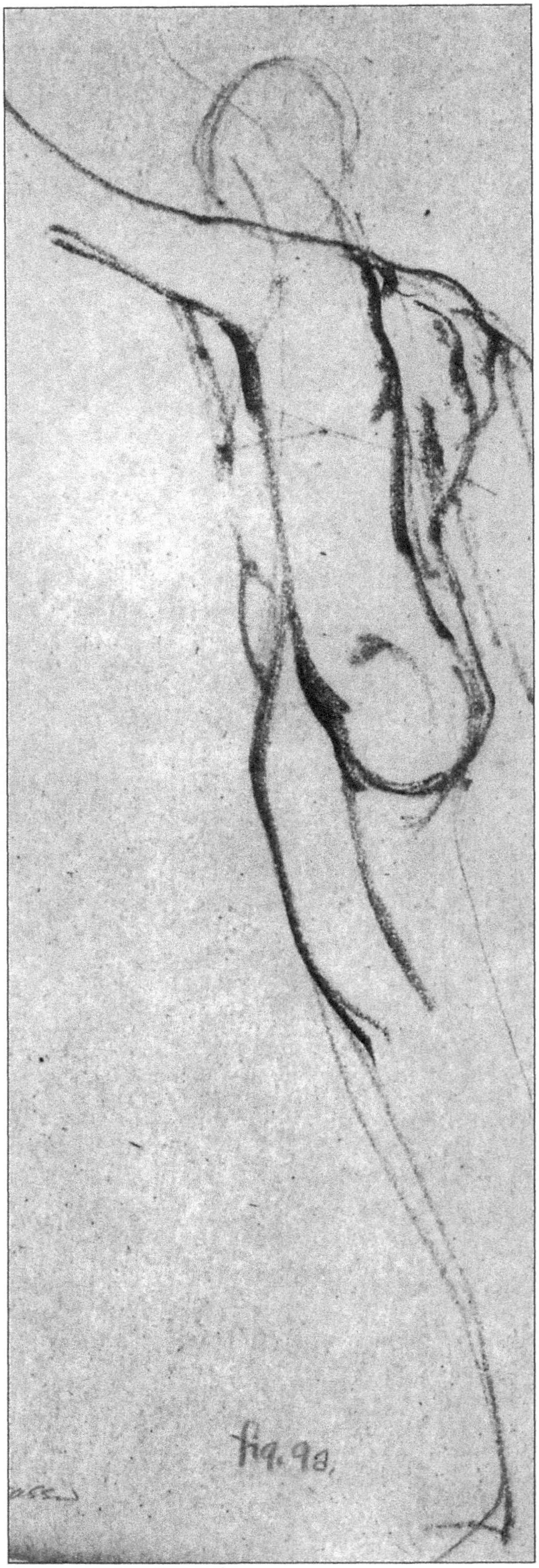

Figs. 9a. and b. emphasize the longest relationship lines of the figure in action. These long relation-ship lines must always be sought out and stated at the start.

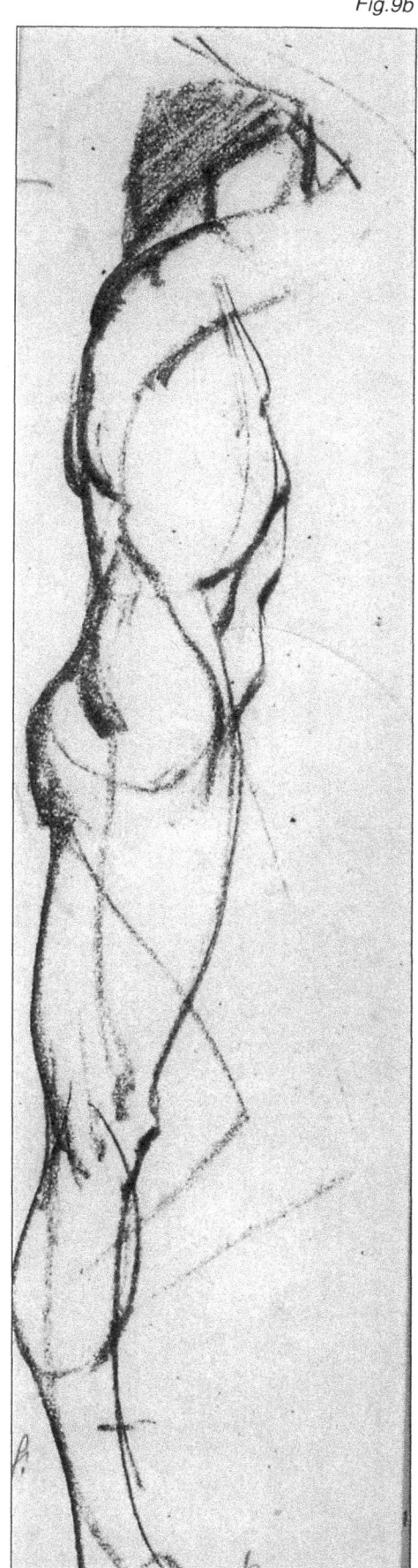

Fig. 10. Showing the relationship from the top of the knee to the edge of the gastrocnemius muscle.

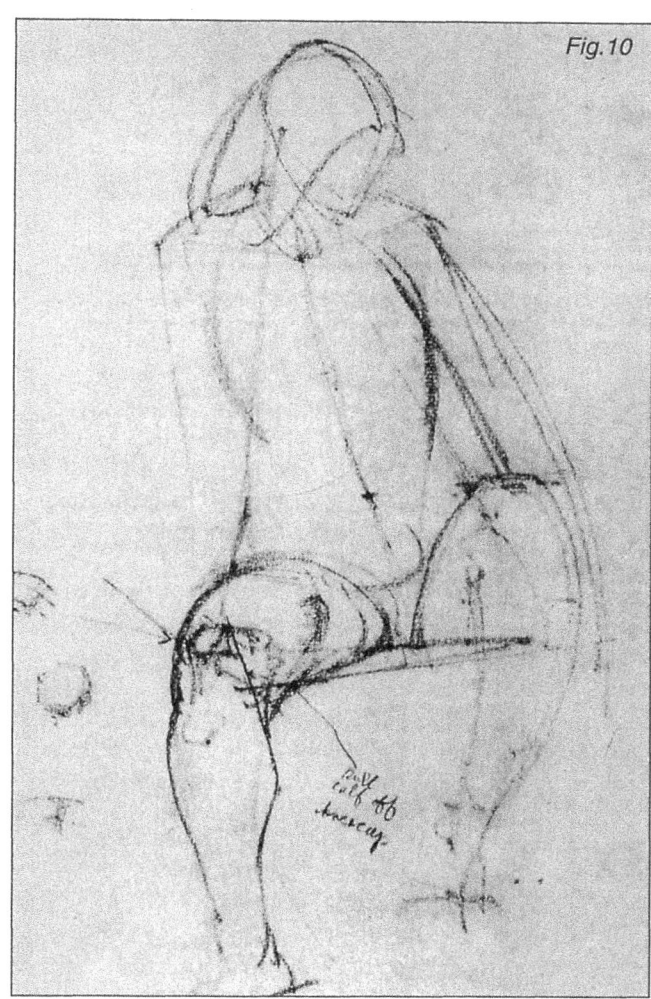

A WORD OF ADVICE

One should always draw in the direction of the action of the form or figure. *These lines should delineate the largest forms first.* Always work from the largest forms to the smaller forms and from the smaller forms to the smallest forms. In this way things will fall in their proper place and be more accurate. *Do not emphasize lines that cut across the direction of the action* even though they are apparent to the eye. Underplay them or eliminate them altogether.

Pay particular attention to which line of a form cuts in front of the line of another form. This will give the impression that a particular form is in front of another which is behind it. The line that delineates the form that is in front of another form should be harder than the line which delineates the form which is behind it. This produces what is called "conceptual" drawing and requires trained powers of observation, a little knowledge of anatomy and considerable skill in handling a pencil.

CHAPTER FOUR

GROWTH

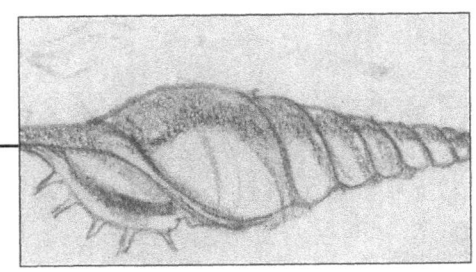

In order to draw a thing well, whether it be animal, vegetable or mineral, either from life or from memory, it is important to understand the nature of its growth – for all living things as well as some non-living things, such as crystals and snowflakes, grow according to certain principles.

All forms of life have a growth pattern from the simplest to the most complex pattern and from the simplest form to the most complex part of the most complex form. Fundamentally, this is the life force asserting itself from within the form outwards in any and all directions according to its inherent instructions.

Drawing with the principles of growth in mind aids in recognition of form and character as well as accuracy of drawing and memorization. These, in turn, will allow you to obtain a more life-like quality of whatever the thing is. It "draws" out the innate nature of the thing. It allows you to project the direction and in many cases the size and shape of anything when you know which way it will grow. Drawing with the feeling of the way a thing grows will also import a greater life-like quality to your work and emphasize its uniqueness.

Imagine yourself as a plant or tree and feel the petals or branches growing outwards, upwards and downwards according to a certain design. Travel with the spiraling forms around a sea shell with your mind. *Utilizing the principles of growth will also help strengthen your instincts of rightness and wrongness, a most valuable addition to your drawing skills.*

The many drawings of plants, trees, bushes, water and other natural phenomena by Leonardo da Vinci are excellent examples of drawings made with the principle of growth in mind. They are, therefore, drawings of a greater truth.

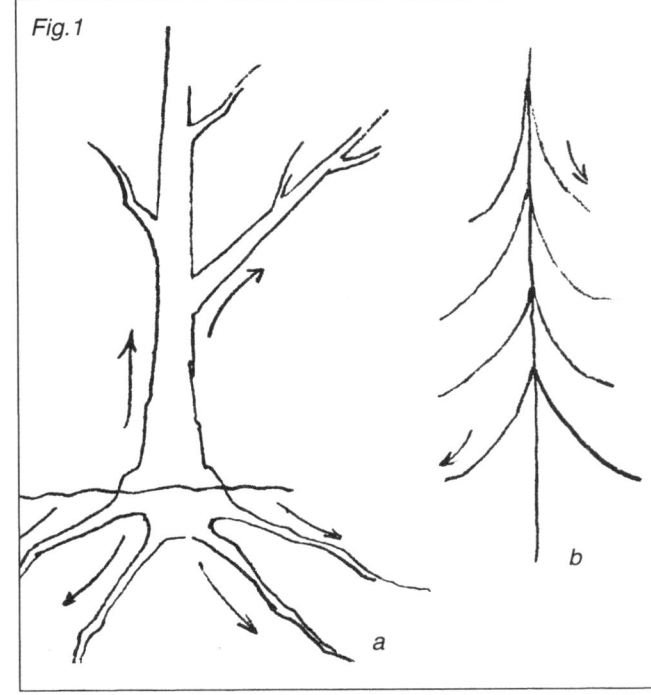

Figs. 1a.b.c.d.e.f.g.h. show the growth patterns of trees, their roots and branches and of leafs. Drawings should be done as shown in the direction of the arrows for greater feeling.

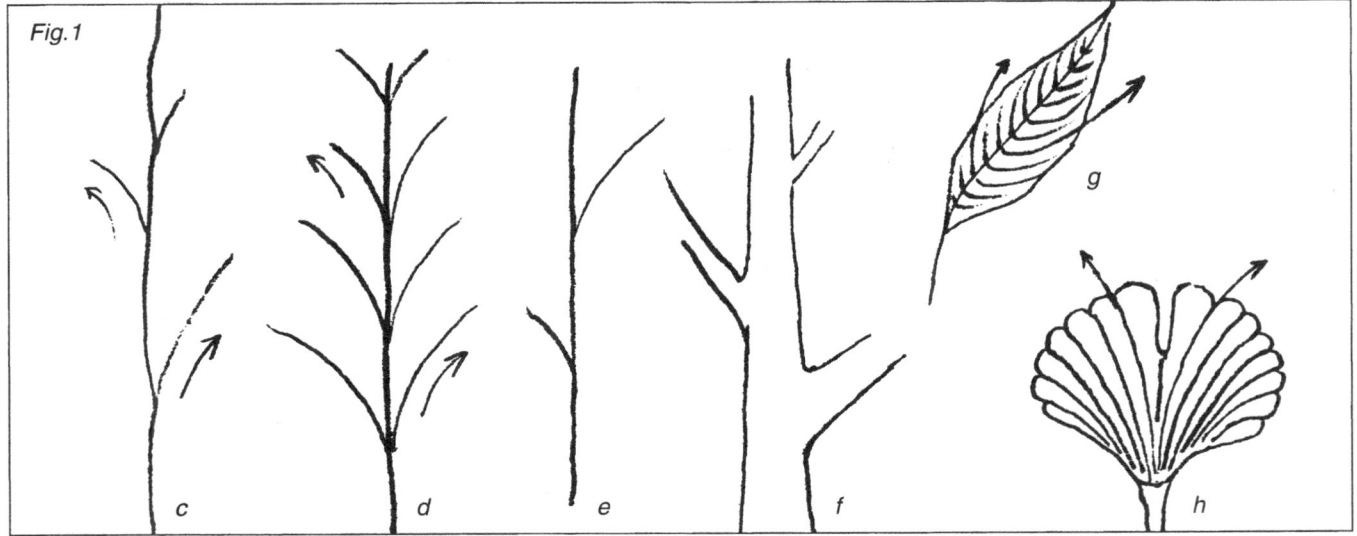

THE GOLDEN SECTOR

A little knowledge of the "golden sector" or "golden mean" would be helpful in recognizing certain intervals or distances within forms. The mathematical equivalent of many of the shapes found in nature such as the curves of sea shells, designs of plants and their leaf systems, galaxies and even some crystals conform to the golden sector.

The mathematics of the golden sector dates back to antiquity and was used by the ancient Romans, Greeks and Egyptians in their architecture and music. It eventually passed into oblivion and was later rediscovered by Leonardo Fibonacci of Florence, Italy in the 13th century. The mathematics of the golden sector is roughly a series of numbers: 1, 2, 3, 5, 8, 13, 21, 34, 55, 89, etc. Simply add the two previous numbers to obtain the next one.

Fig. 2a. shows the growth pattern of man, *2b.c. and e.* that of sea shells, *2d.* a starfish and *2f.* a bird showing the growth pattern of the wings and legs.

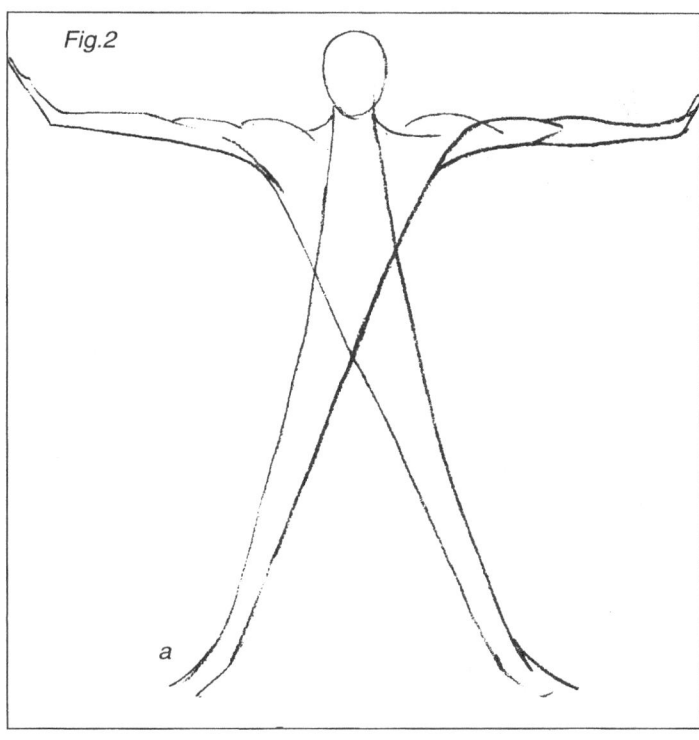

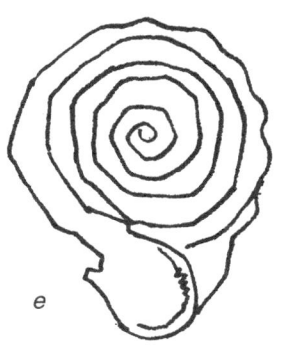

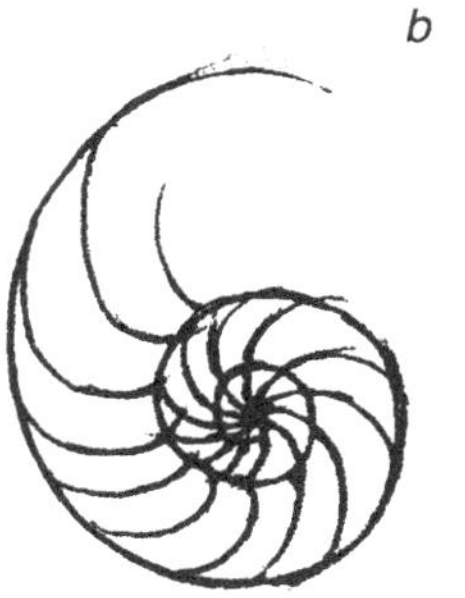

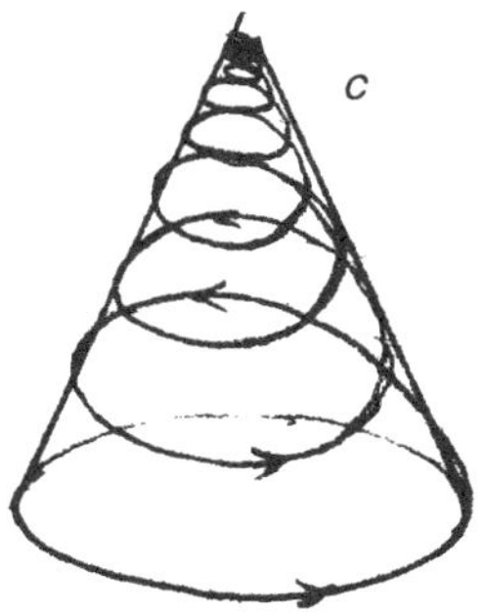

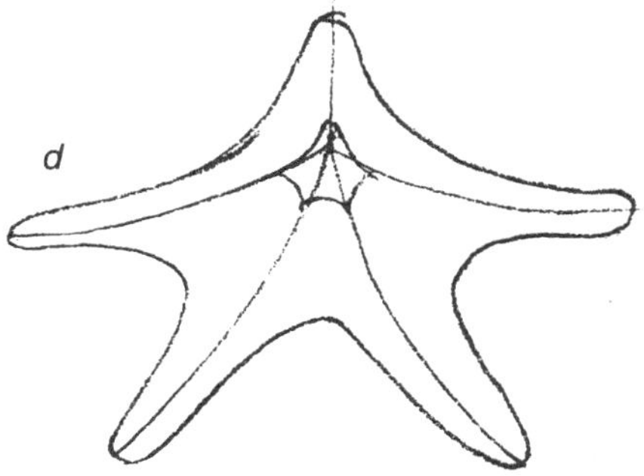

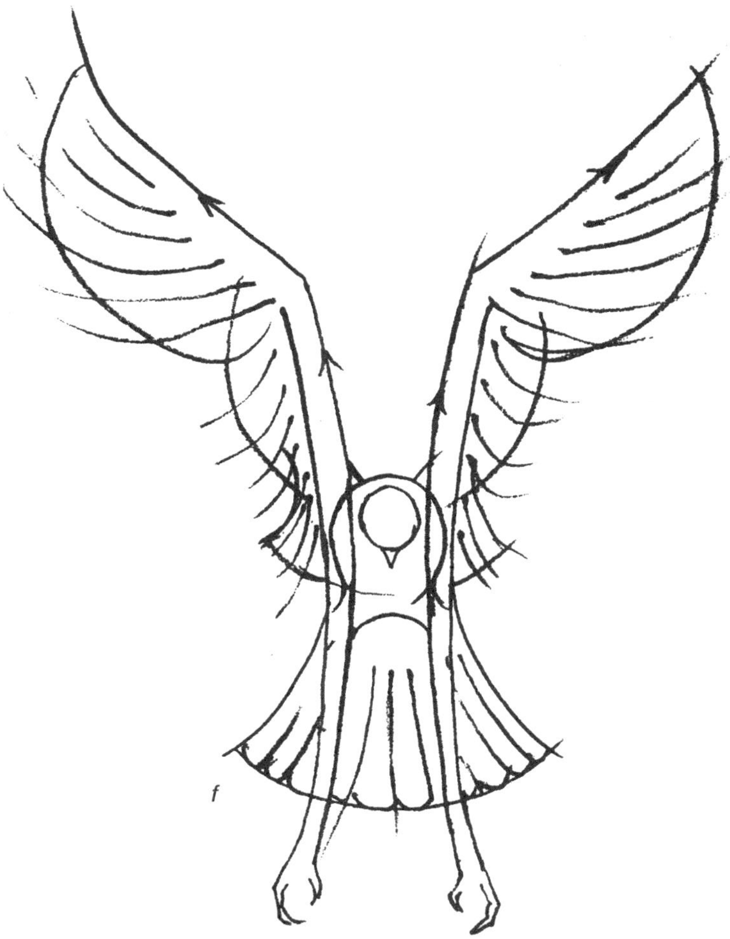

Figs. 3a.b.c. are three examples of the directional anatomical growth of the human being.

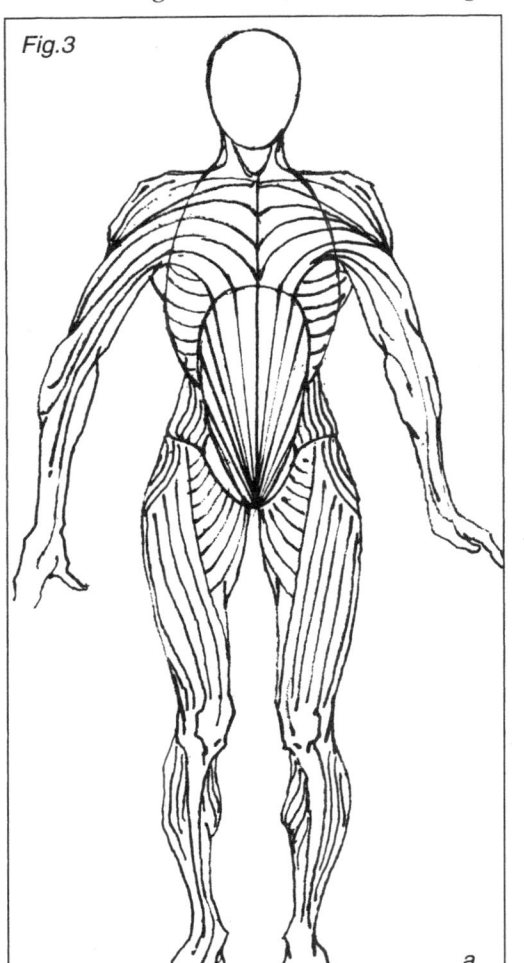

Fig.3

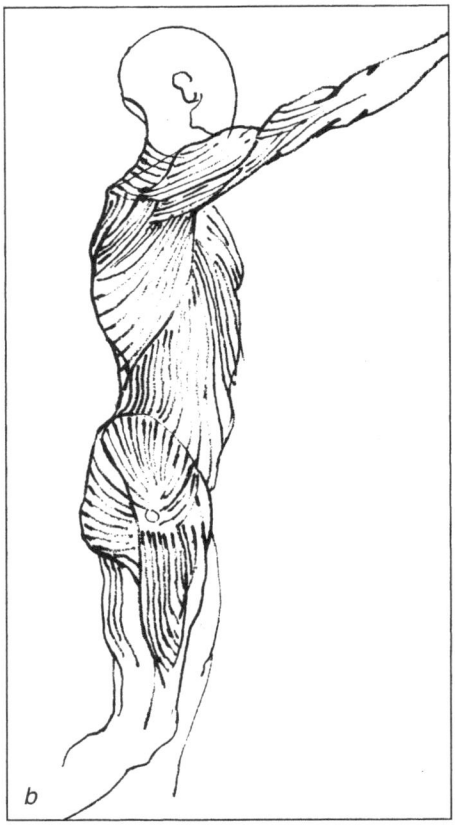

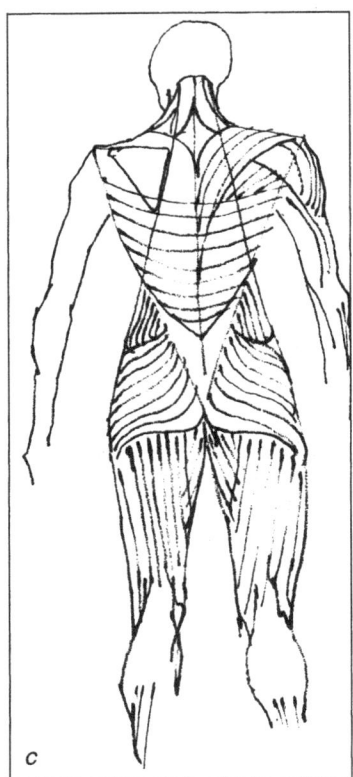

a

b

c

Figs. 4a.b.c.d.e.f.g.h.i. Some drawings of animals and birds drawn with the principle of growth in mind.

Fig.4

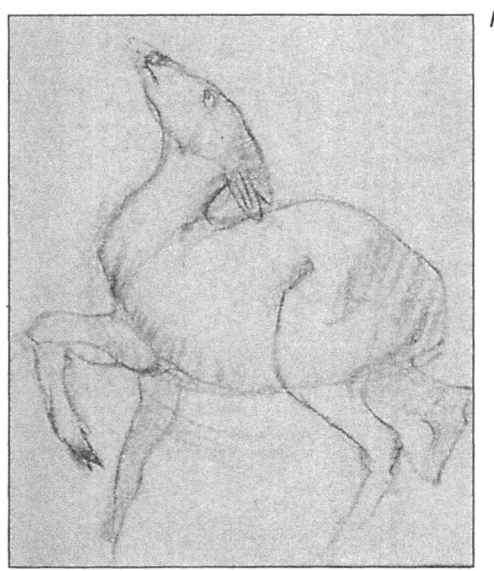

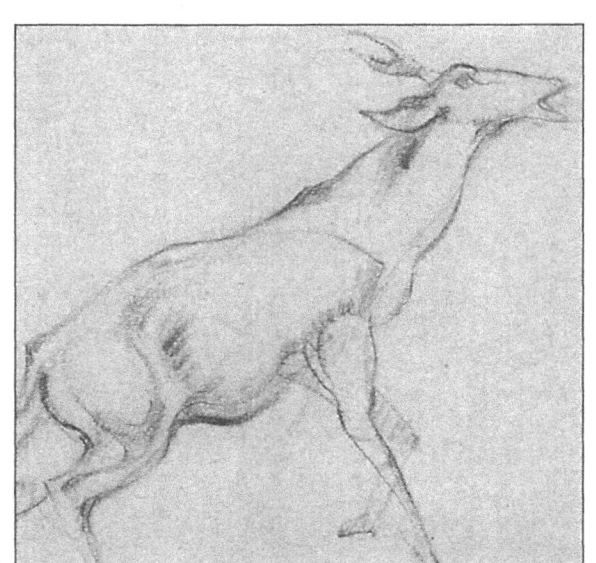

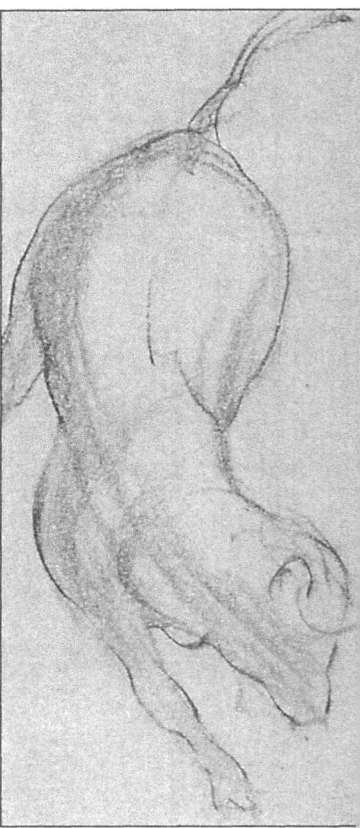

a

b

c

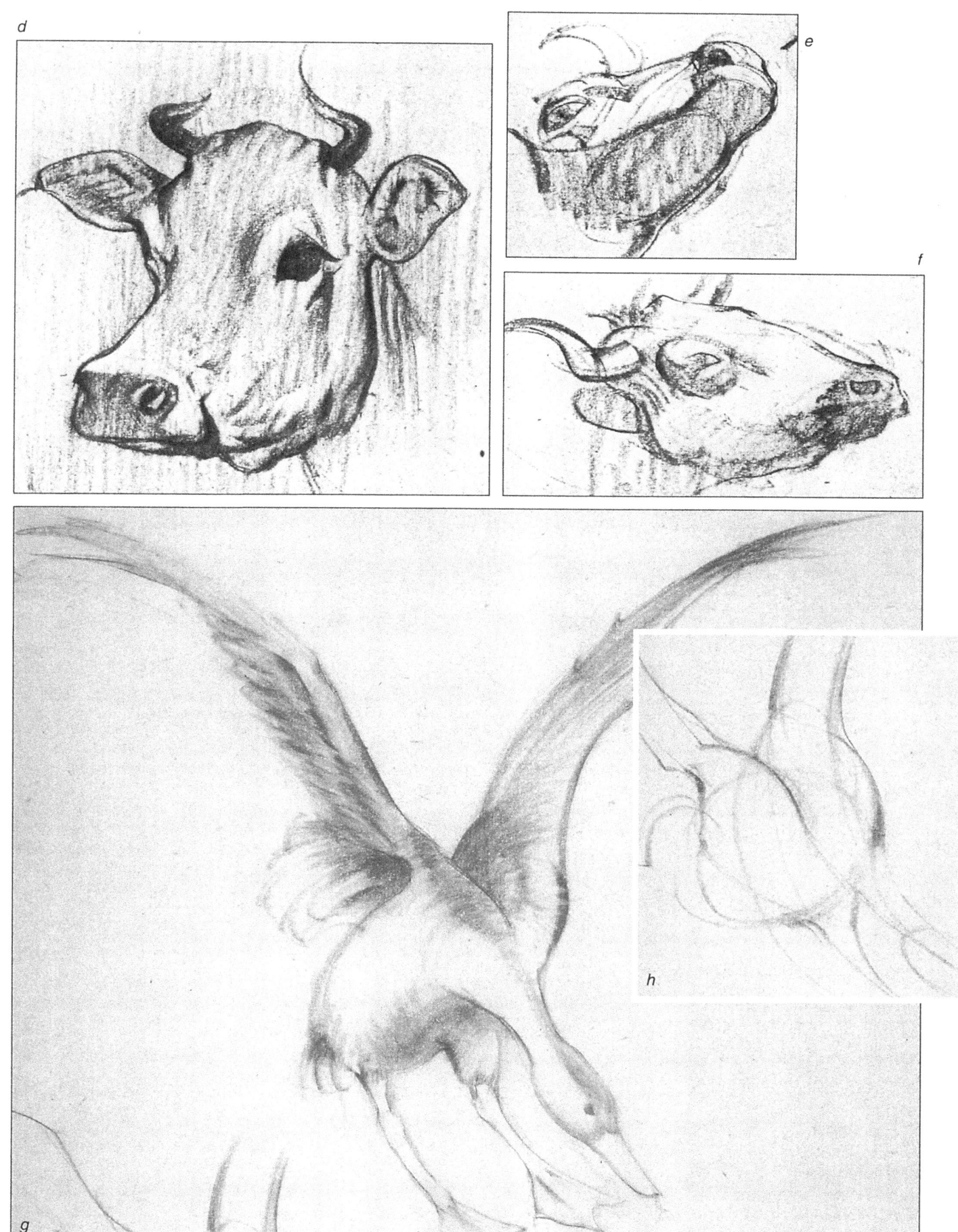

d

e

f

g

h

CHAPTER FIVE

FORM

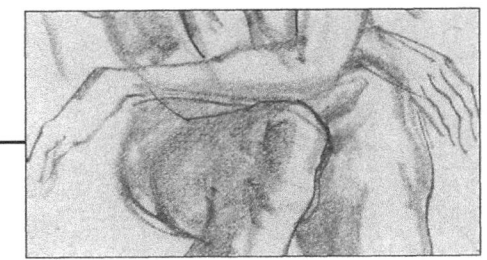

A thorough knowledge of form and planes as well as light and shade is essential to anyone who aspires to be a good artist – for what we draw or paint is form – form in space. The procedure of study should be to study forms and what they are first, secondly the nature of planes and lastly how light and shade falls on these forms and planes. *The character of the form is due to its planes not its details.*

I have always maintained that the difference between a first rate artist and a mediocre one is the former always draws and paints the planes on the forms precisely where they should be with, of course, the right light and shade on them. The weaker artist does not have the knowledge or perception to do this. Forgeries, copies and imitations usually fall short of fine works of art for the same reason.

Forms come in an infinite variety of sizes and shapes. Examples of simple forms are an egg, a cube, a cone, sphere or cylinder. A form has a boundary, an axis, a cross-section and usually a shadow. In short, a form is a solid shape that has bulk and volume. Since forms are usually opaque they have light and shade on them. However some forms can be translucent or transparent such as a balloon or a bottle. Forms also have texture which can be of a glossy, matte or nap nature.

It is important to think of the figure in terms of its major forms as it is these first forms that affect the outside shape the most.

The secondary forms sometimes affect the outside shape and the tertiary forms seldom affect the outside shape. The big forms of the body are the head, the torso, the entire leg and the entire arm. Examples of secondary forms are the rib cage, the breasts and the buttocks. Some examples of tertiary forms are the nipples of the breasts, the ball of the nose and the kneecap to name a few.

Do not underestimate the value of the study of forms. In representational drawing and painting the large forms must be perceived, understood and maintained. And the smaller forms must always be subordinated to the larger ones

Some examples of basic forms are shown in *Figs. 1a.b.c.d.e.f.g.h.i.j and k.* Shown starting at the top left are an egg-shaped form, a cone, a brick shape, a sphere, a square and a pyramid shape. *Figs. j. and k.* show two long forms, one twisted. The drawings at the bottom of the page, *Figs. g.h. and i.,* are three examples of bent and twisted forms. Notice how these can resemble the human torso.

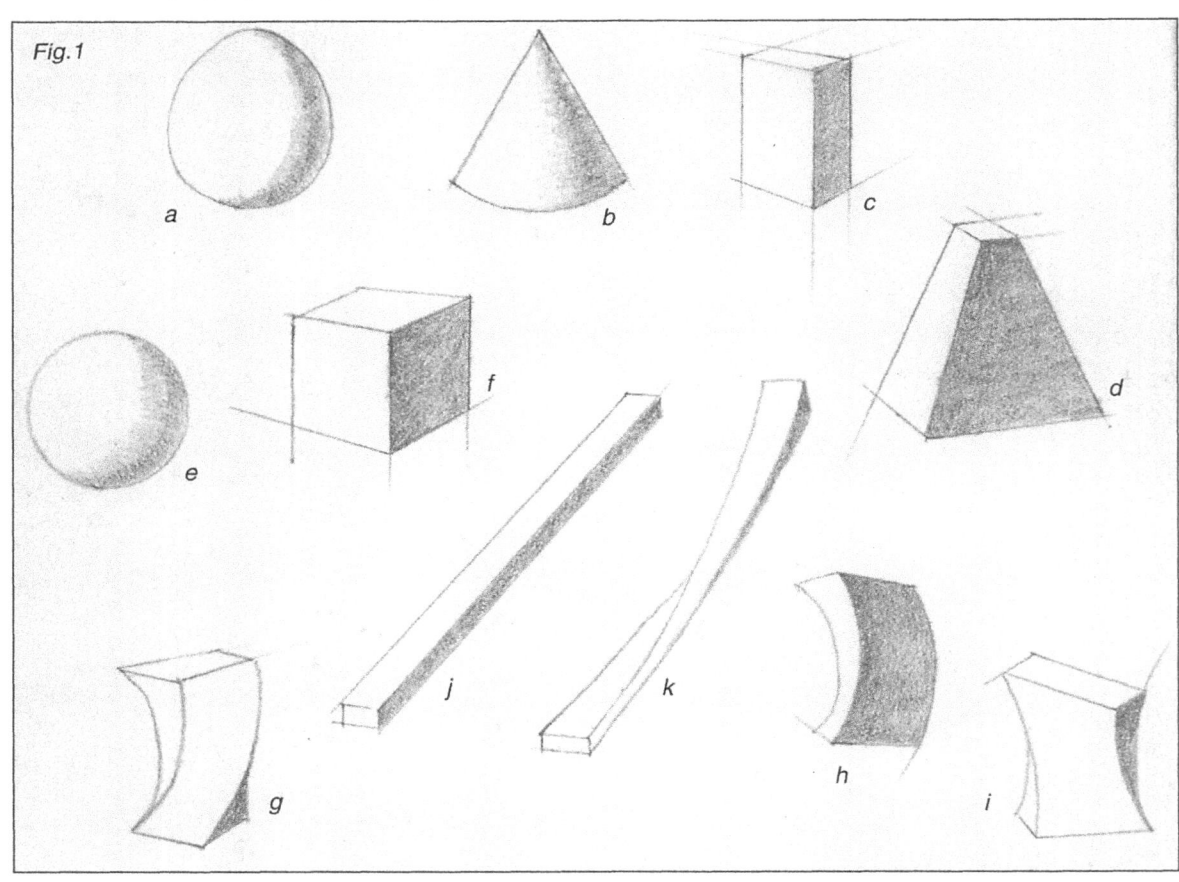

Fig. 1

Forms can be found in many configurations. Here we see in *Figs. 2a.b.c.d.* forms touching one another and overlapping one another. *Fig. 2e.* shows two forms connected by a third form, *Fig. 2f.* forms on top of forms and *Fig. 2g.* two dissimilar overlapping forms unified with a shadow pattern.

Figs. 4a.b.c., show three examples of large torso forms shown in profile.
Figs. d.and e. The large forms of the leg and the arm are shown divided into two smaller forms – the upper and lower halves. These smaller forms are then divided into smaller and smaller forms.

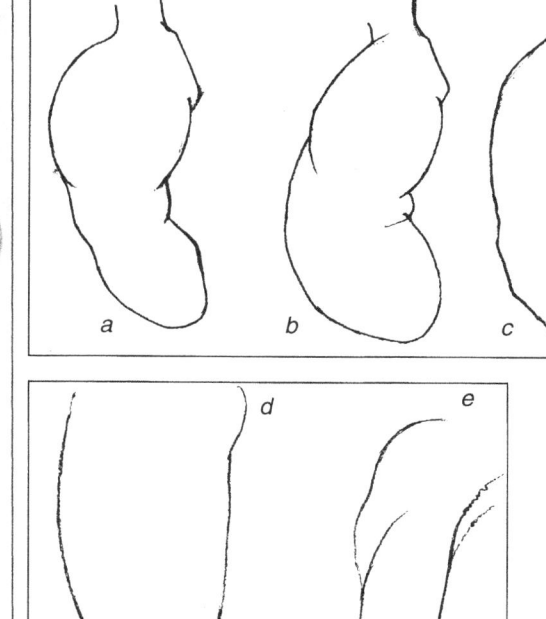

Fig.4

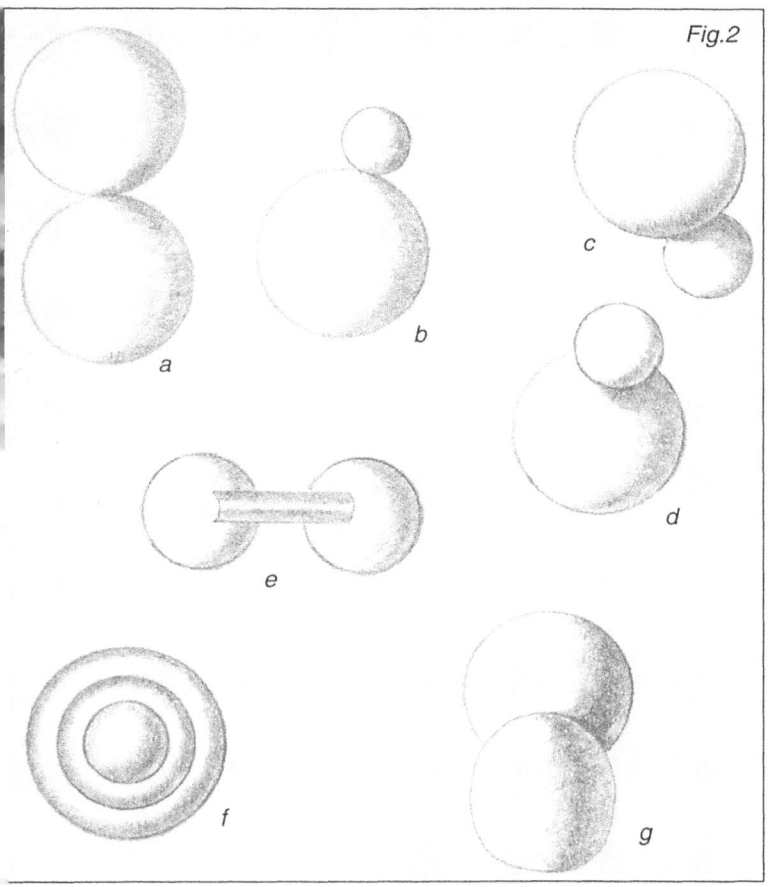

Fig.2

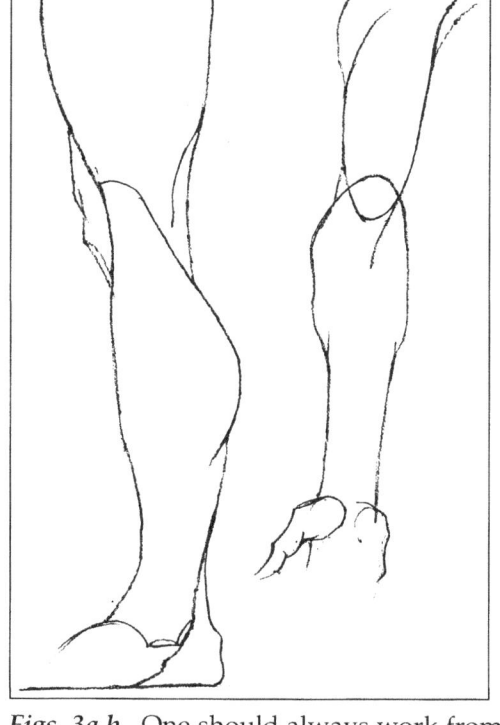

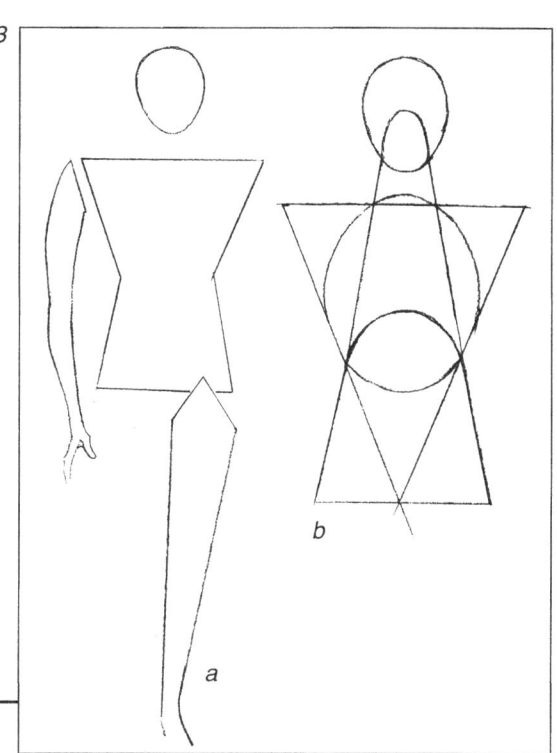

Fig.3

Figs. 3a.b. One should always work from the larger form to the smaller forms whether in drawing or painting. Shown on the top left, *Fig. a.,* are the first largest forms of the human figure which are the head, torso, arm and leg. The diagram on the right, *Fig. b.,* shows some secondary forms such as the muzzle on the skull, the rib cage and the combined pelvic-abdominal form. Note how the muzzle overlaps the skull form and the combined pelvic-abdominal form overlaps the rib-cage form. The bottom drawings,

Figs. 5a.b.c.d. Regarding human anatomy forms come in an infinite variety of shapes and sizes. We can have forms that are vertically divided or forms that are horizontally divided as shown in **Figs. 5a. and b.** Many of these larger forms are divided into smaller forms in different ways. Shown at **Fig. c.** is a vertically divided form such as the gastrocnemius muscles of the lower leg. **Fig. d.** is a multi-horizontally divided form as the large form of the abdominal muscle.

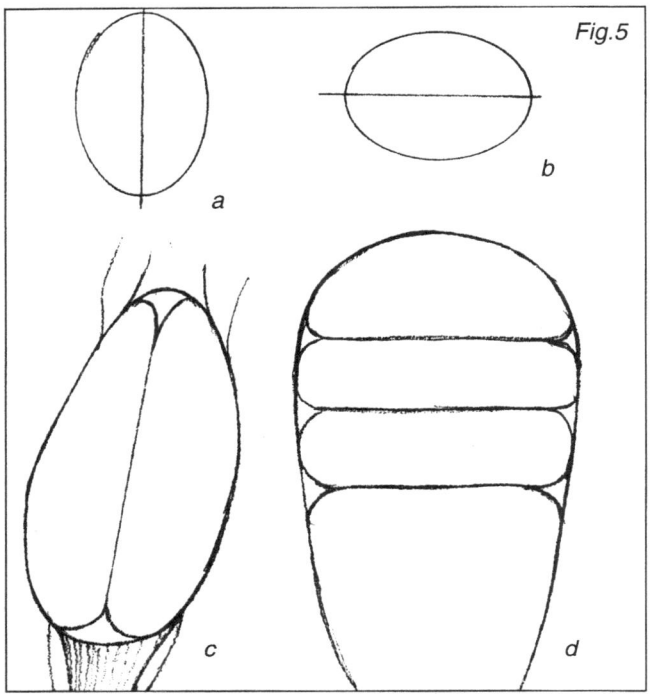

Below these are drawings, **Figs. 6a.b.,** showing simplified, stylized forms of the lower leg. Seek out these large forms and their planes before putting in smaller details. Stylize the forms slightly rather than copying every little bump.

If there are two forms of the same type they should first be drawn as one form as shown in

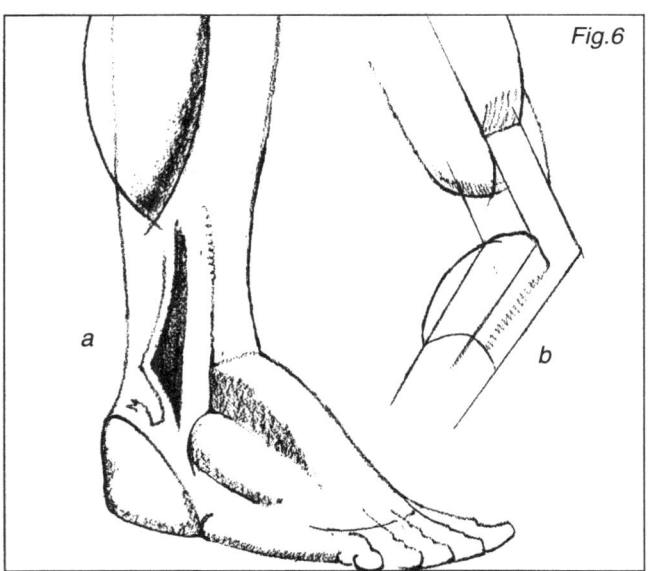

Fig. 7a. and then divided or separated from one another as in **Figs. 7b. and c.** This will give symmetry and unity of line and light and shade to the drawing.

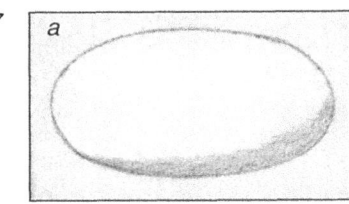

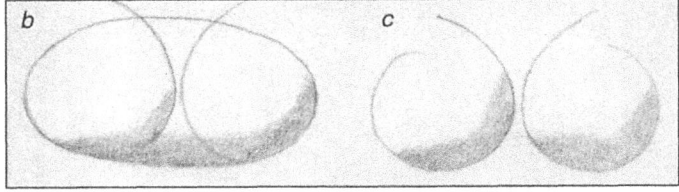

Figs. 7d.e.f. show light and shade on overlapping forms such as the breasts and on the muzzle which overlaps the skull form. The drawings on the bottom of the page,

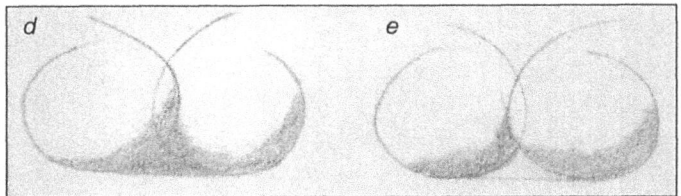

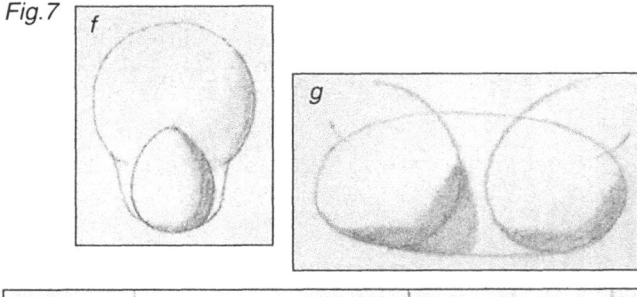

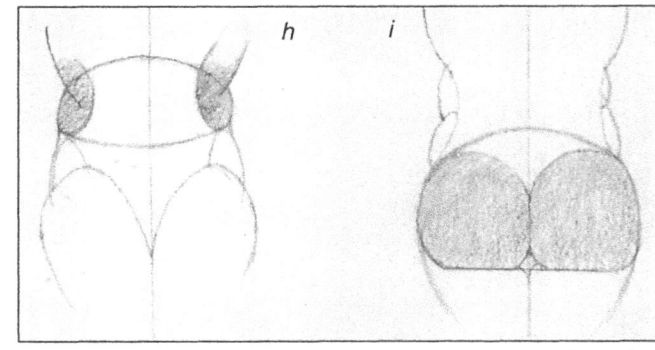

Figs. 7g.h.i., are examples of parted forms such as the breasts, the external obliques and the buttocks.

Fig. 8. A highly stylized drawing emphasizing the major forms of the torso. These are more important than the many smaller forms and should be looked for first.

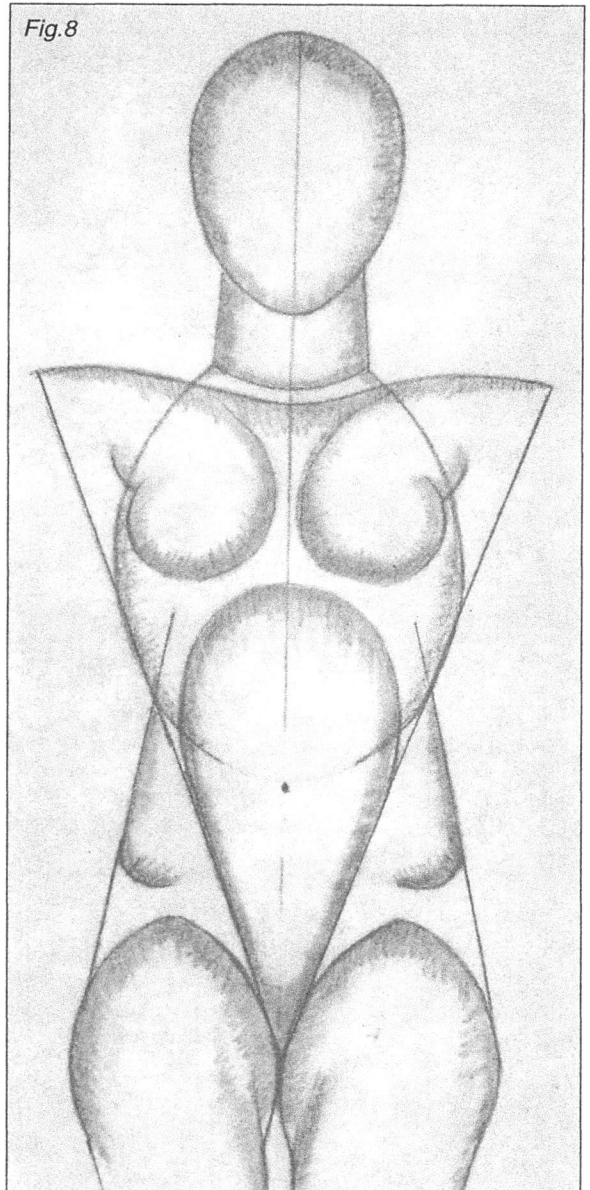

Fig.8

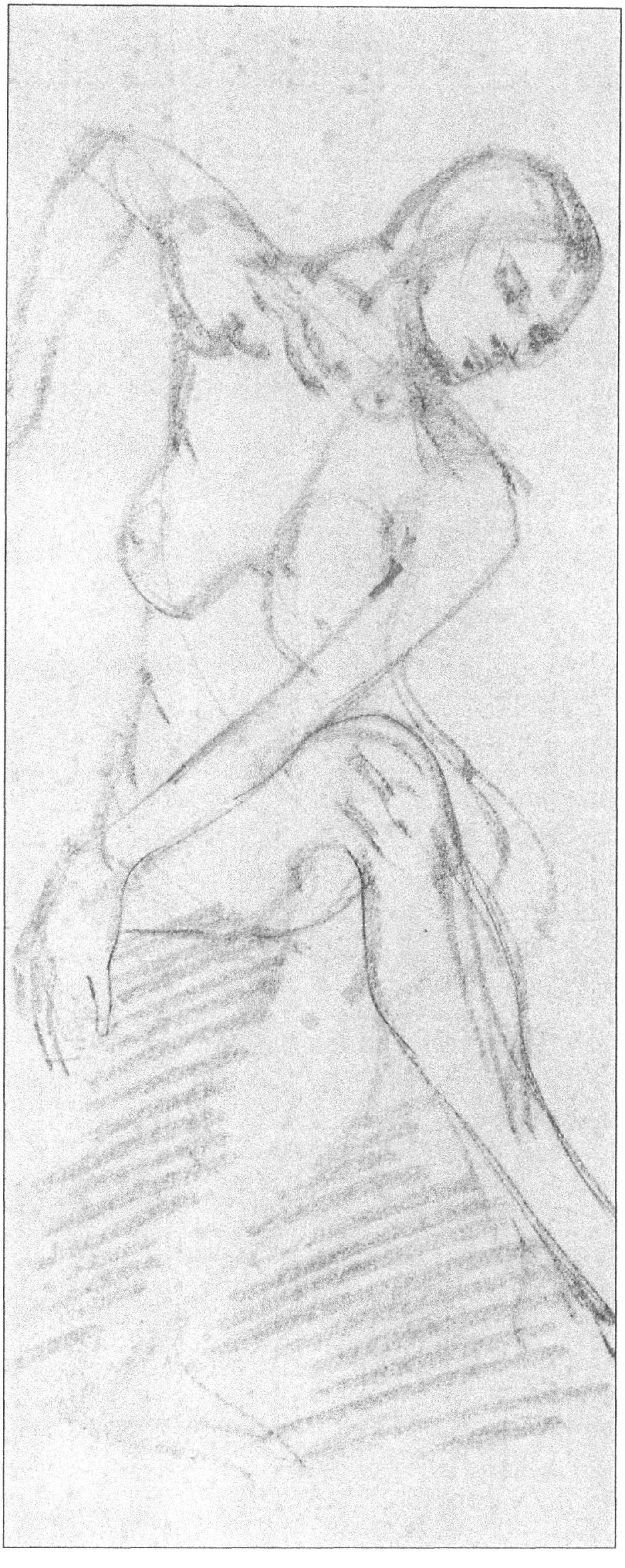

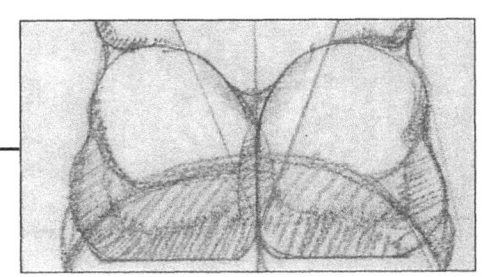

CHAPTER SIX

PLANES

Once you have an understanding of forms you should familiarize yourself with what planes are. A plane is a flattened area of a form – as a facet on a diamond. A simple way of thinking about a plane is this: take a peeled hard boiled egg, (a form), and slice a piece off of it with a sharp knife. You have now made two planes, one on the egg, the other on the part you sliced off.

The human being is an extremely complicated arrangement of forms and planes. For example the entire nose is one large form. The flat plane of the nasal bone wedges into the ball of the nose which is a smaller form. The bottom of the ball of the nose flattens into bottom planes, both front bottom and side bottom. *(see Chapter 18)*. In drawing the nose shading of various degrees must be exactly where the planes are and fused or blended or left separate as the case may be.

Planes help us create the illusion of form. They appeal to the sense of touch and are actually more important than the features in obtaining character. Planes are naturally more defined in thin bony people, less so in obese people or rounded objects.

One should learn all the planes of the head and figure even though certain ones will be seen at any given time depending on the position of the light to the model as well as the model relative to your eye. Observe the symmetry of the planes of the head and figure; what's on one side is on the other side.

Planes do such things as connect corners of form, (very important), make tangent with other planes or can be atop other planes. They can be horizontal or vertical, repeat themselves and vary in widths and angles to each other (See the explanatory drawings on the following pages.).

Once you understand what forms and planes are you should place tracing paper over the many illustrations of planes and forms of the head and figure shown in this book and shade them in the different areas. Later you may want to make more finished drawings from the photographs of the cast shown on page 172. Lastly you should draw from the living model and apply all that you have learned. You will be amazed how differently you perceive nature now.

Figs. 1a.b. Examples of planes on two forms. Notice how the degree of light and darkness changes on each plane.

Fig.1

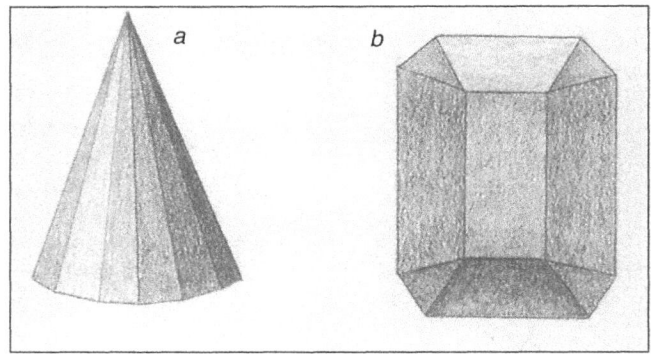

Figs. 2a.b.c.d. Fig. 2a. is a simple form. *Fig. b.* shows a section of this form sliced off thereby creating a plane. *Fig. c.* Planes created by slicing top and bottom of the form. *Fig. d.* Another example of the many different ways planes can be made on a form.

Fig.2

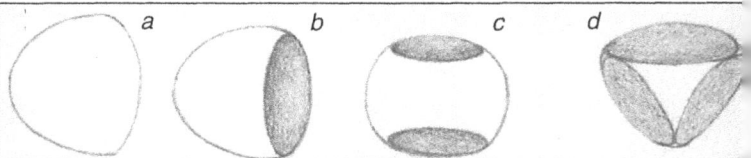

Figs. 3a.b.c. Different arrangements of planes and forms. *Fig. 3a.* shows a rounded form atop what is left of a larger form after four planes have been made.

Fig.3

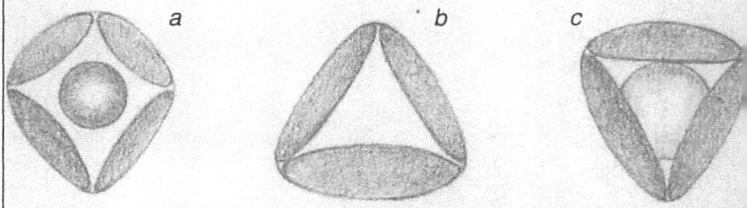

Figs. 4a.b. Always draw the large form first before making the planes. *Fig. a.* shows planes that originate on a horizontal axis, and b. shows planes that originate on a vertical axis.

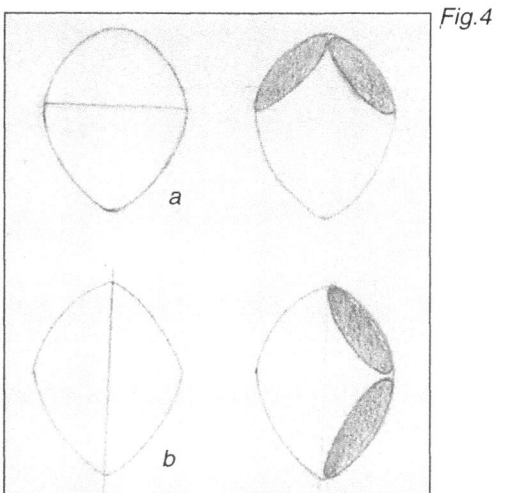

Fig.4

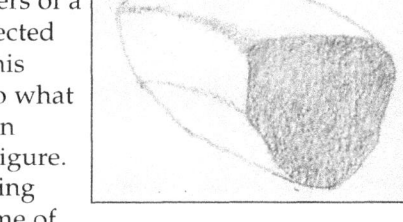

Fig.5

Fig. 5. An example of outside corners of a form that are connected creating planes. This example is closer to what you will draw when drawing from the figure.

The following drawings show some of the many different types of planes and how they interrelate with forms.

Figs. 6a.b.c.d.e.f.g.h. Fig. 6a. Two sided symmetrical, very common on the head and torso. *Fig. b.* Vertical planes running parallel to each other. *Fig. c.* An example of variations of width within planes. *Fig. d.* An example of planes touching planes. Here we see two sideplanes and a top plane touching a front plane. *Fig. e.* One plane overlapping another plane which eliminates part of a plane. *Fig. f.* An example of planes on planes, front view. *Figs. g.h.* These drawings show horizontal repeat planes. The curvature of the planes should show the perspective of the form.

There are many combinations of planes and forms. The following drawings show some of the many ways that they can inter-relate. Refer to the drawings of the planes of the head where these ideas are carried further.

Fig. 7a. A sideplane overlapping a form, in this case the muzzle of the face.

Fig. b. Two planes touching two forms. The inner sideplane is touching the smaller nose form and the outer sideplane is touching what we refer to as the form of the "tooth cylinder."

Fig. c. A form on a plane.

Fig. d. A form shown touching the bottom of another form.

Fig. e. A small form touching the top of another form, (the muzzle).

Fig. f. This drawing shows a form interlocking with two crossing sideplanes.

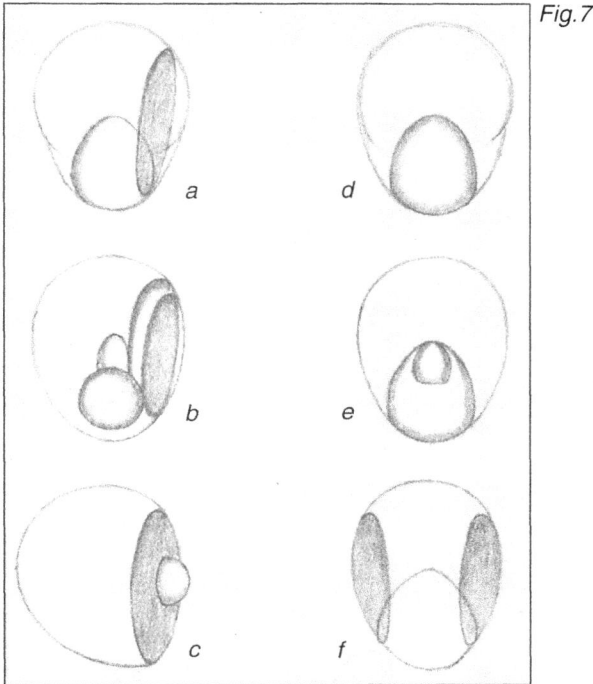

Fig.7

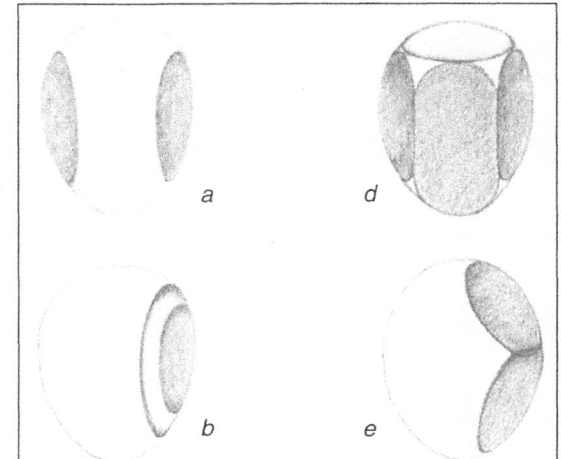

Fig.6

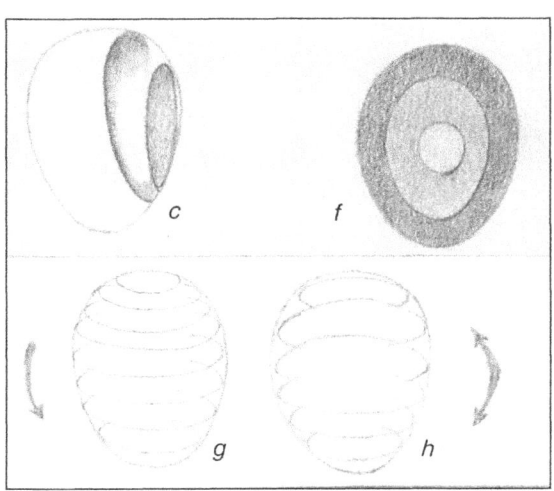

Fig.6

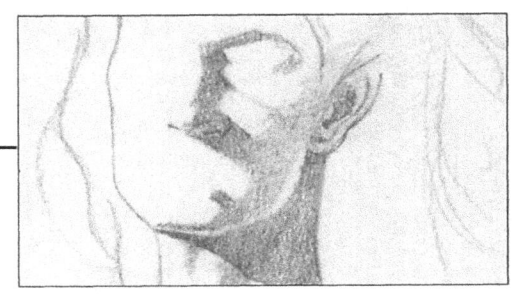

CHAPTER SEVEN

LIGHT AND SHADE ON FORM AND PLANES

The typical beginning students' drawings consist of mainly disjointed unrelated scribbly lines and some crude attempt at shading. They don't have the slightest idea about how to use light and shade on their drawings to produce lighting effects, forms and action. However there are also many who have been drawing and painting for many years who still make many mistakes in the use of light and shade. The subject is vast and seemingly complicated but in reality when studied methodically reveals itself to be simple as it conforms to rules and laws which are easy to learn, comprehend and apply.

The student just learning to draw, however, should not concern himself too much with light and shade until he thoroughly understands just what is a form, what is a plane and how they are drawn to express the action of the figure.

Light and shade on form should clearly show from what direction the light source is coming and what the shape and surface of the form or plane is. All of this will be clearly explained on the following pages. Let us start at the beginning by studying Fig. 1., which shows a sphere in light and shade.

Fig. 1. A sphere in simple light and shade. The shadow is always at right angles to the source of light. In front of the shadow is the halftone. In front of the halftone are at least three distinguishable values of light. The highlight is at the cresting of the area of lightest light.

The shadow cast by the sphere is of two major parts, the umbra and penumbra. The umbra is the darkest part of the shadow. The penumbra is lighter than the umbra, it is a "half shadow." It is soft edged that becomes even softer as it recedes from the object's edges. The umbra also becomes soft edged as it recedes from the object and eventually merges into the penumbra. Not shown is the darkest dark, commonly called the accent. The accent is only where no light can enter, such as where the object touches the surface. Since we are looking down on the sphere we cannot see this aspect of it. However, it would be readily discernible in a side view.

The shadow shape is the most discernable shape of value on the model as it is simple. A shadow is opposite the light source having no direct illumination on it and reveals both form and plane. At the start of the drawing the shadow and cast shadows should be massed and stated in as one for the sake of unity. Later they will be separated by slight value differences.

Fig. 1

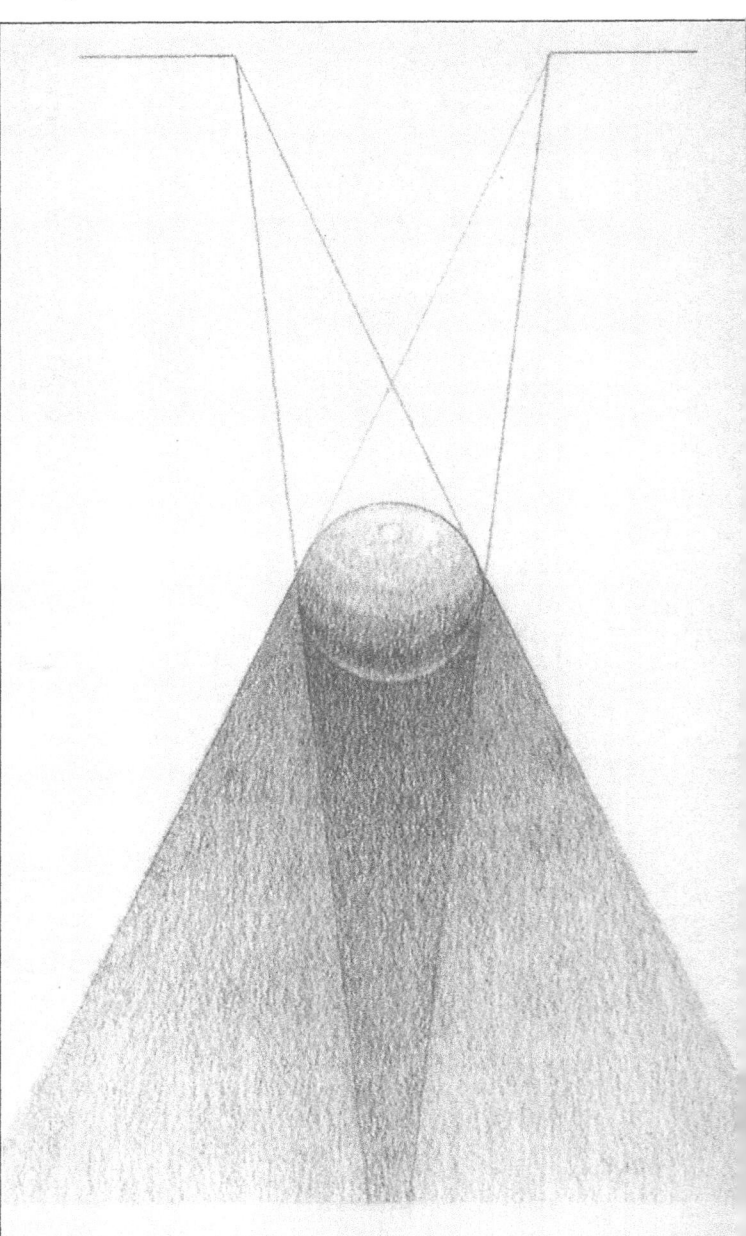

Fig. 2a. shows a division on light and shade which is hard edged. This means that there is a flat corner on the form and is one extreme. Therefore whenever you draw objects with flat corners you should use a hard edge at the light and shade division. Drawing, *Fig. b.,* shows a cylinder with a soft graduation of light and shade, and it is the opposite extreme. There are an infinite amount of edge gradations between these two extremes.

The five circular drawings in the center of page 33, *Figs. c.d.e.f. and g.,* illustrate how shadows are at right angles to the source of light. Visualize a straight line from the center of the light source to the model. The shadow plane will be at right angles to it.

The two bottom drawings, *Figs. 2h. and i.* illustrate how the shadows of many forms should be connected into one shadow shape for simplicity, unity and to avoid spottiness. *Fig. 2h.* shows a form overlapping a form and *Fig.2i.* shows a form on a form, both unified by one shadow shape.

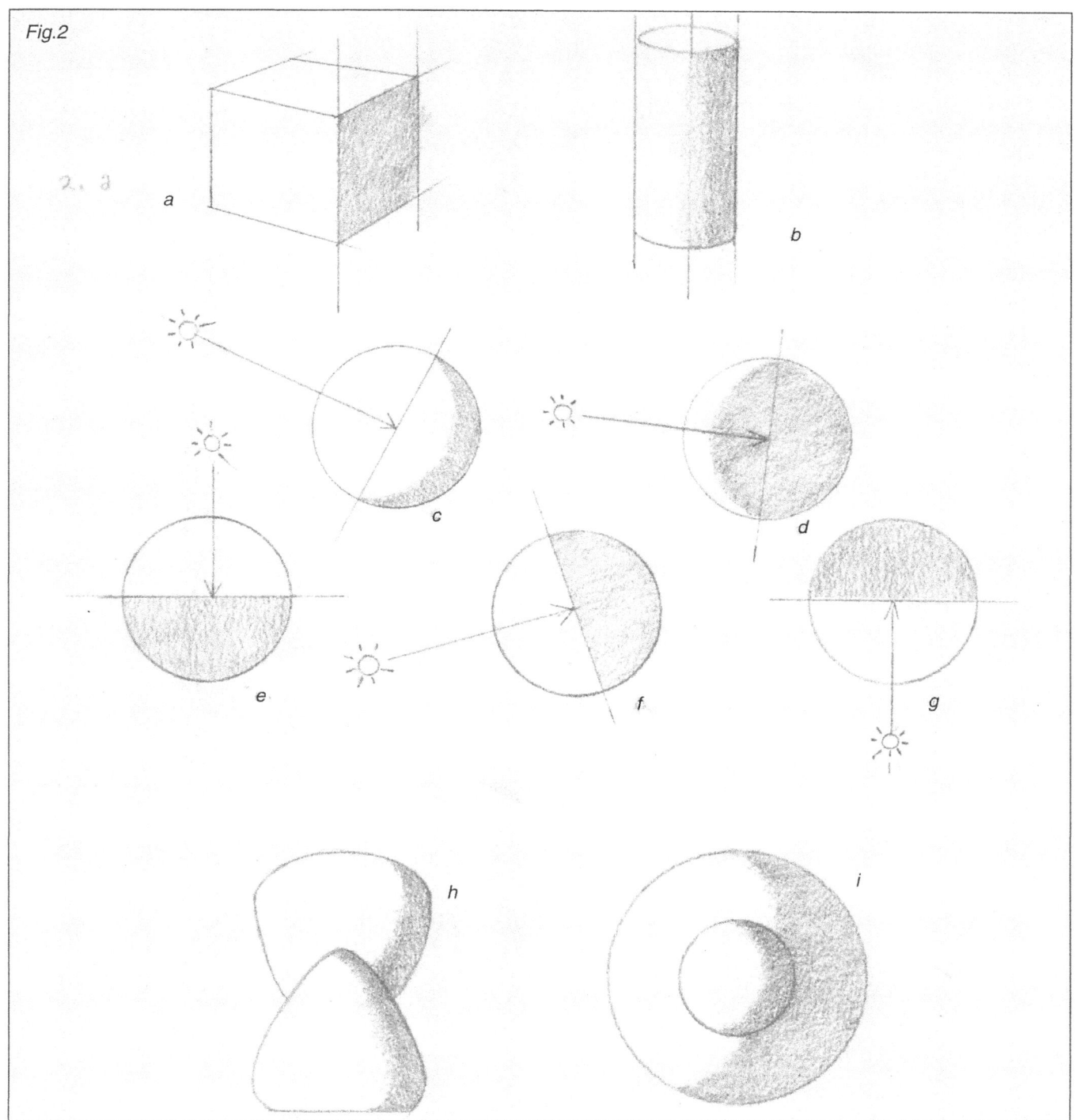

The beginner is usually bewildered as to how to put many small forms into light and shade and therefore treats each form individually. This is a mistake as the large light and shade patterns are overlooked and lost. Drawing *Fig. 3a.* shows how to simplify the light and shade when there are many small forms involved. They are to be treated as one. One should always search out and state the big light and shade patterns, then model the smaller forms. You can see this principle applied over and over again in the many Old Master portraits which have a white ruff around their necks.

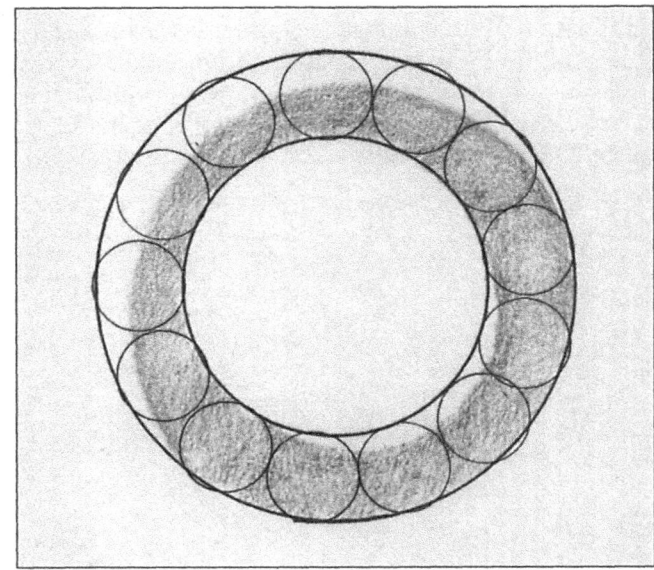

Fig.3a

The drawings below this, *Figs. 3b.c. and d.*, show, both in profile and straight on how to treat a form that is in various degrees of detachment from a flat surface. At the left, *Fig. 3b.*, where the object, a slightly bulging form, is on a flat wall all the edges of the object are hard. In the second example, *Fig. c.*, the form is bulging further from the wall. A cast shadow now appears and all the edges are rendered equally soft. Lastly, in *Fig. d.*, a sphere is almost completely detached from the flat surface. All the edges are soft but the shadow and cast shadow edges are even softer.

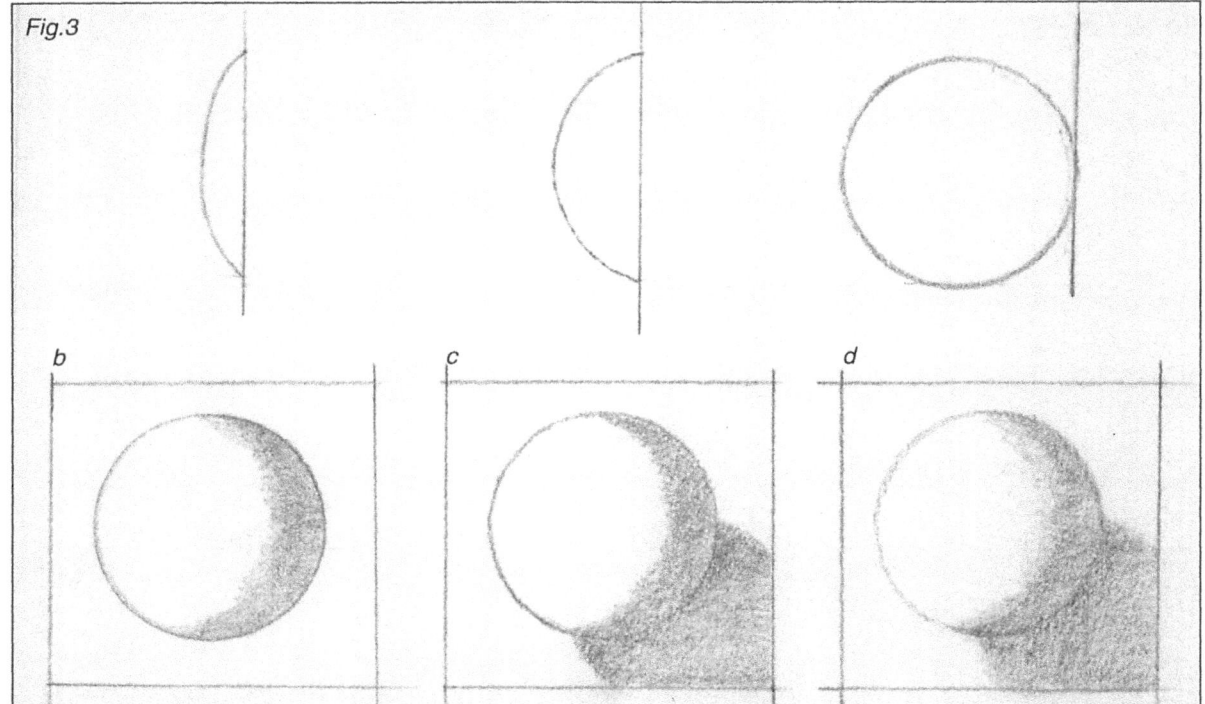

Fig.3

b

c

d

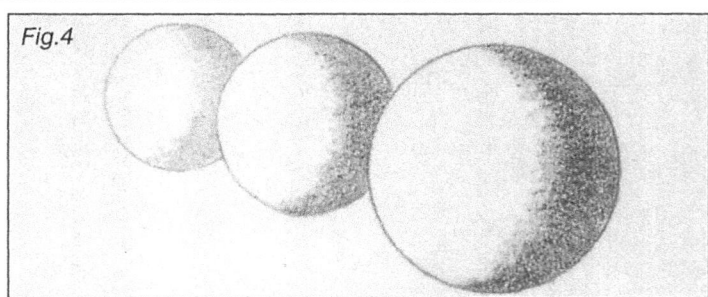

Fig.4

Fig. 4. shows how forms can be made to recede in space. The foremost form should have the greatest degree of contrast of light and shade. The middle object should have less contrast of light and shade and the distant object even less contrast of light and shade. This coupled with hard edges on the front form and softer edges as well as reduction of size on the background forms will produce the illusion of depth.

SHADOW PATTERNS OF THE FIGURE

Shadows go with the action, usually a top to bottom direction, more so than the lights. One should search for the main action relationship of the shadow pattern and state it in first as shown in *Fig. 5a.* Drawing *Fig. 6.* shows the same principle except now the shadow pattern is shown skipping over large forms. Note how they are visually connected; an easy fact to overlook. It is a little less obvious when actually drawing from life but the relationships are there nonetheless.

The right hand drawing, *Fig. 8.* is a portion of an arm showing a shadow pattern crossing diagonally over many forms. This will in no way change the projecting or receding of the form.

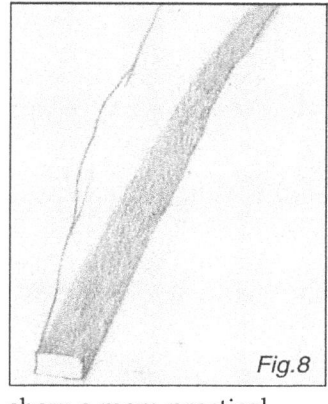

Fig.8

Figs. 9 a.b.c. and d. show a more practical application of shadow patterns. We start with merely two structure lines, starting at the widest points of an arm or leg to the narrowest points of the limbs, such as the wrists or ankles *(Fig. 7a.).* In the second drawing, *Fig. b.*, one draws the forms over these lines, judging their shapes and sizes by how much they deviate from the two basic structure lines. In the third drawing, *Fig. c.*, a large simple shadow pattern is added going with the action. Lastly in *Fig. d.* the shadow pattern is broken up into individual forms and further defined. Outlines are then adjusted.

Fig.5

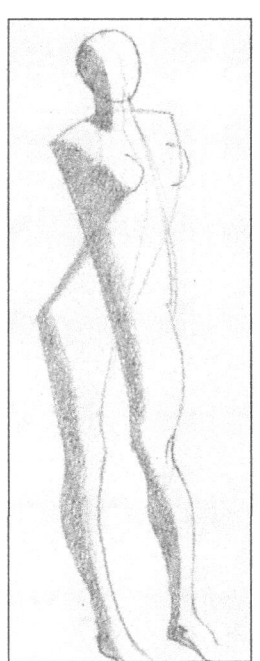

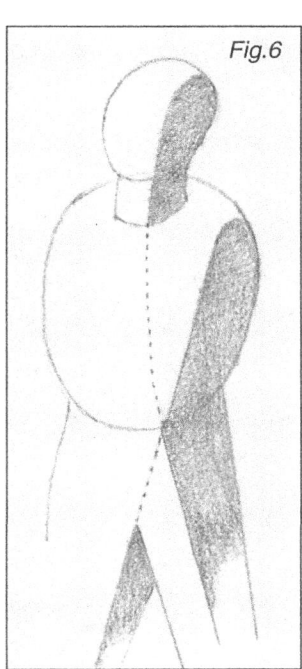

Fig.6

Fig. 7. shows the massing of the shadows and cast shadows at the head, neck and shoulder. Note the shadow on the torso which connects many forms such as the breasts, abdominal muscles, external obliques, etc. Lower down the figure we have one united shadow mass covering the two lower legs. Occasionally you will find a cast shadow in the light which cuts across the action. This is hurtful to good drawing and should be underplayed or left out altogether.

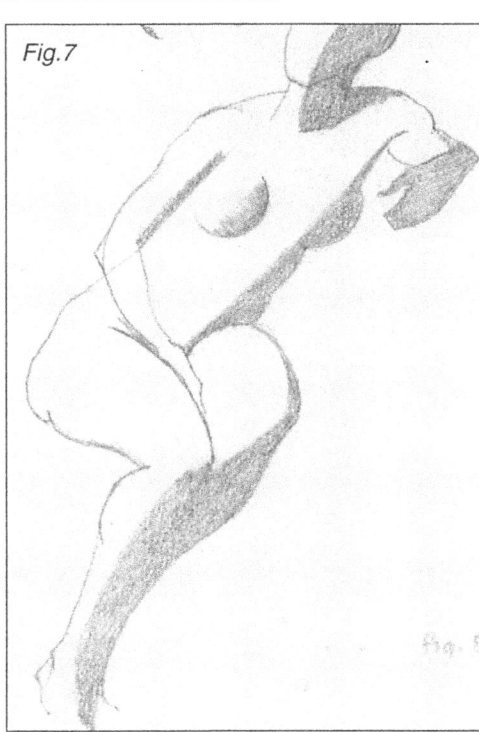

Fig.7

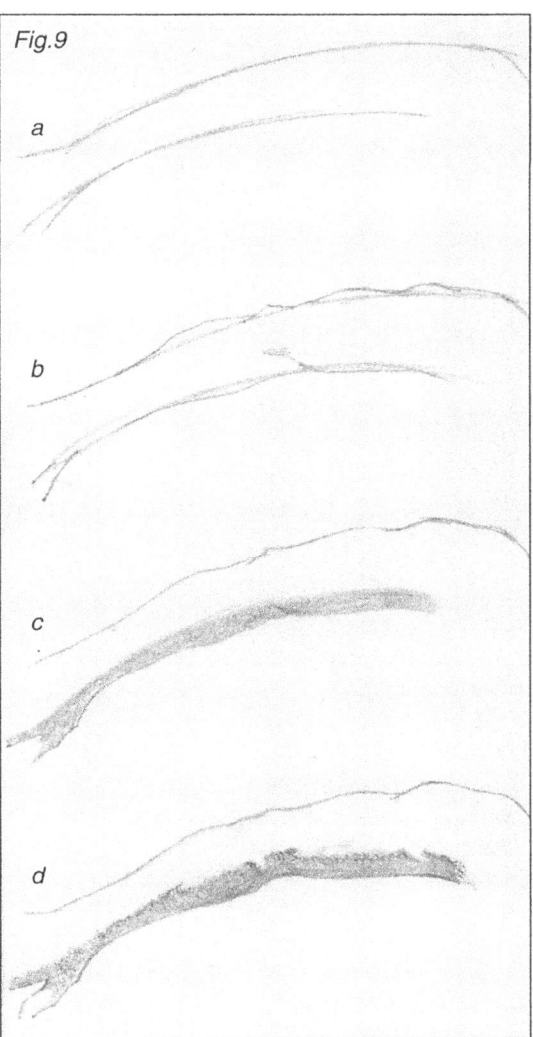

Fig.9

a

b

c

d

CAST SHADOWS

Cast shadows are frequently overlooked or not drawn as well as regular shadows by most students. There are many things to learn about cast shadows. In the first place the cast shadow should show the shape of the object that casts it. A little knowledge of perspective is sometimes needed here. Drawings **Figs. 10a.b. and c.** show some simple shaped objects and their cast shadows. The cast shadow should also show the shape of the object that it is cast on. **Figs. 10d. and e.** show cast shadows describing the forms they fall on. One should keep this in mind when drawing the forms of the head and the figure.

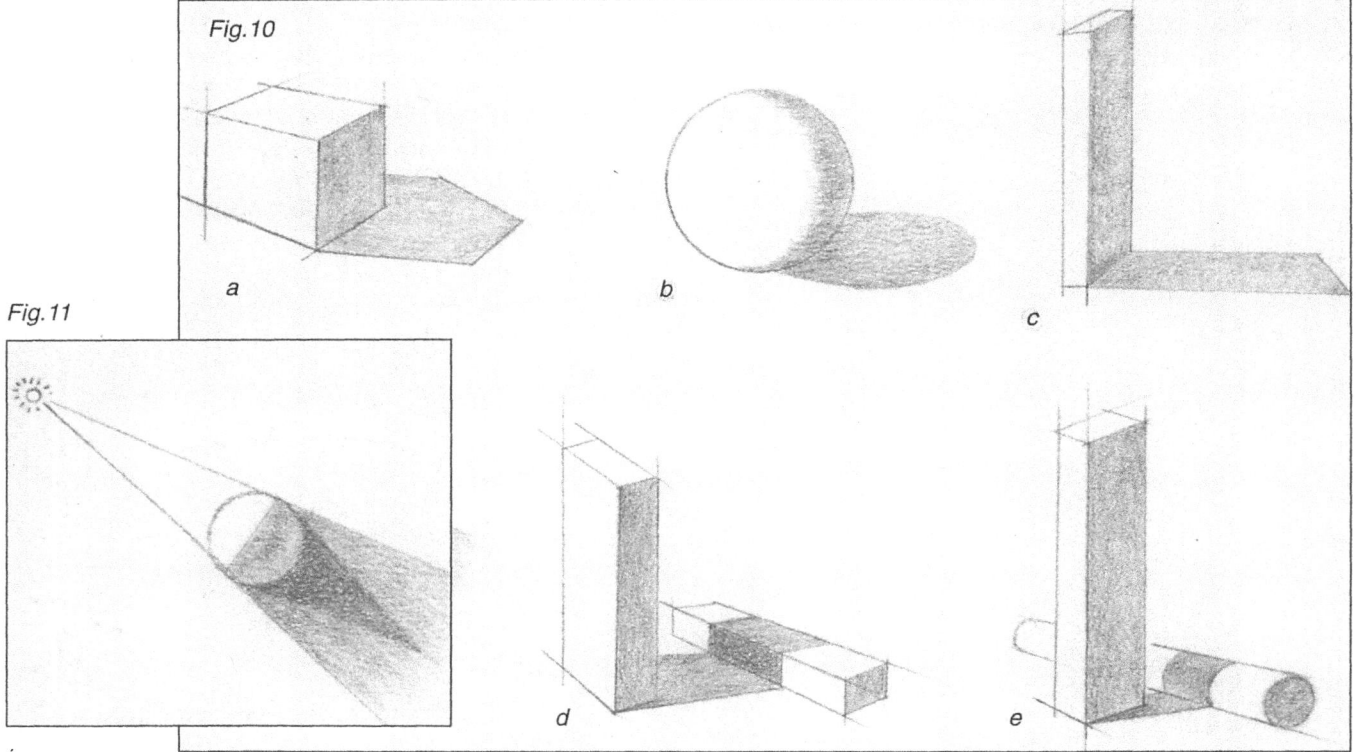

Fig.10

a

b

c

Fig.11

d

e

Fig.11. shows how the cast shadow goes with the direction of the light. The darker part of the cast shadow is called the umbra. The lighter gray area outside the umbra is called penumbra

The directions of the cast shadows will vary on how far the light source is from the object that is casting them. **Fig. 12a.** shows cast shadows radiating away from the light source in many directions and angles. This happens when the light source is close to the object or objects. When the light source is a great distance away, such as the sun, all cast shadows will appear parallel, see **Fig. b.**

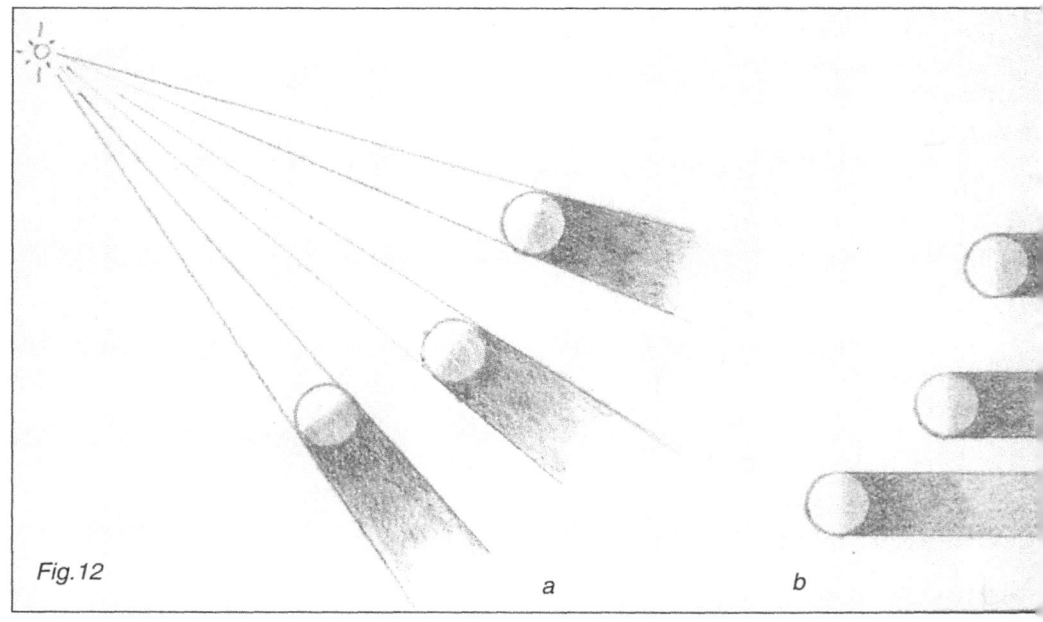

Fig.12

a

b

Figs. 13a.b.c.d.e.f. shows six examples of how cast shadows draw the complex anatomical forms of the neck as well as some of the skull. The cast shadows reveal the direction of the source of light as well as the size and shape of each form or groups of forms. This is frequently overlooked or not paid much attention to but is very, very important to good drawing and painting. Knowledge of anatomy is helpful here as long as the student understands he must draw the massed groups of muscles with their many different planes.

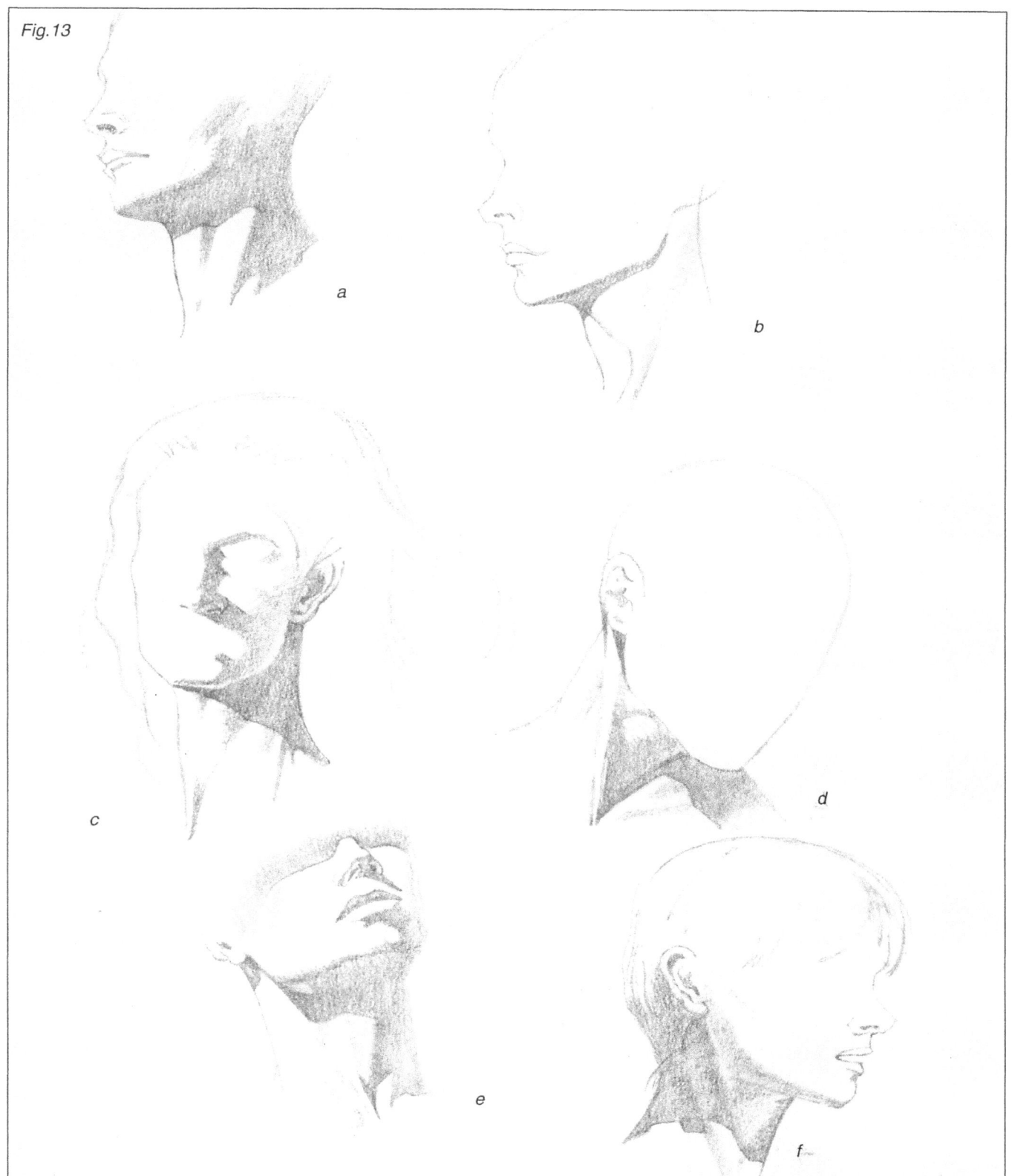

Fig.13

The simplified schematic drawing, *Fig. 14.* represents a model casting a shadow on a background and platform. Where the model touches the wall will be the darkest part of the cast shadow, the accent.

As the space between the model and the background increases the cast shadow will become lighter, due of course to more light entering into it. In general, cast shadows will become lighter as they depart from their starting point. Notice how the cast shadows cast by the feet and legs grade from very dark, immediately behind the foot, to lighter as they recede towards the wall.

Care should be taken with the rendering of the edges of the cast shadows. These edges will range from very hard to very soft – almost non-existent. The hardest edges will be where the cast shadow is the darkest and, naturally, closest to the model. Keep a feeling of "air" in the cast shadow.

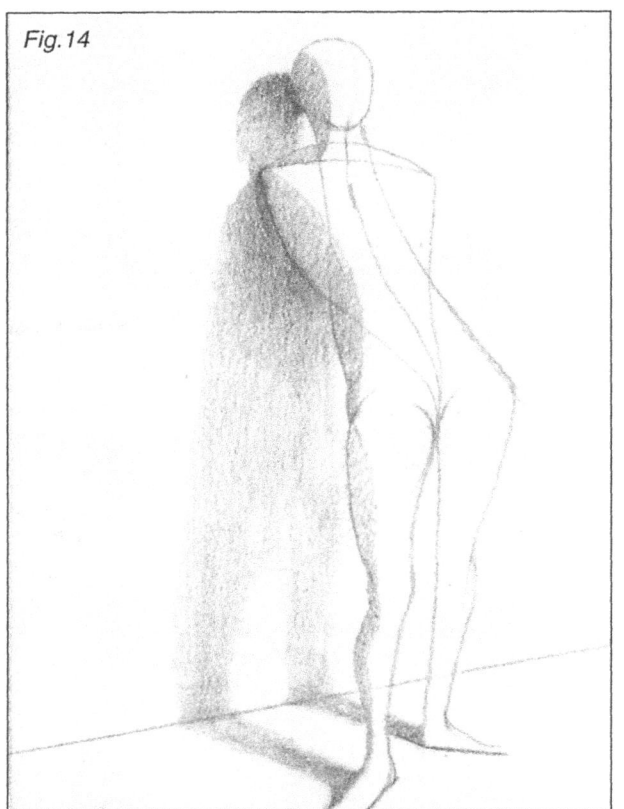

Fig.14

LIGHT AND SHADE ON FORM AND BACKGROUND

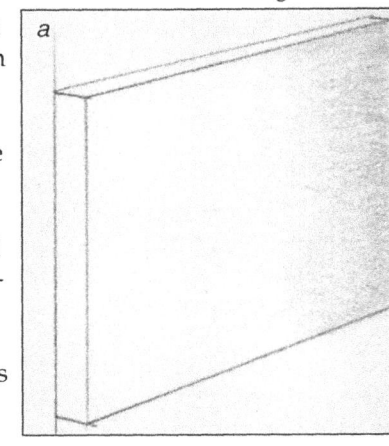

Fig. 15

a

There must be a consistency of lighting on the model or form and the background. This is almost overlooked by the beginner as he or she is concerned with painting a "head" or a "figure" all by itself completely unrelated to the background with regard to light and shade. The two examples at the top of the page, *Figs. 15a. and b.* show how value gradations will affect the flatness or curvature of the background. The use of very little value gradation produces a flat background as show in *Fig. a.* If too much value gradation is used the flat background will now appear as having a deep curvature as seen in *Fig. b.* Of course you may want this effect at certain times.

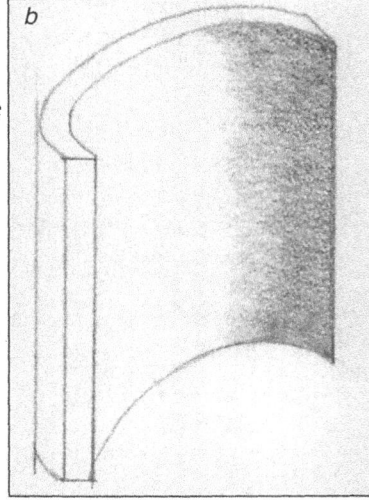

b

The three drawings below these show how unity of lighting on the object and the background should be properly represented. Note the consistency of the lighting on the model and background. *Fig. 16a.* shows the light source coming from the upper left hand side. In *Fig. b.* the light source is on the right side and center and in *Fig. c.* the lighting is coming from below. Note how the shadow pattern is at right angles to the source of light. This is also explained diagrammatically in *Figs. 2c.d.e.f. and g.*

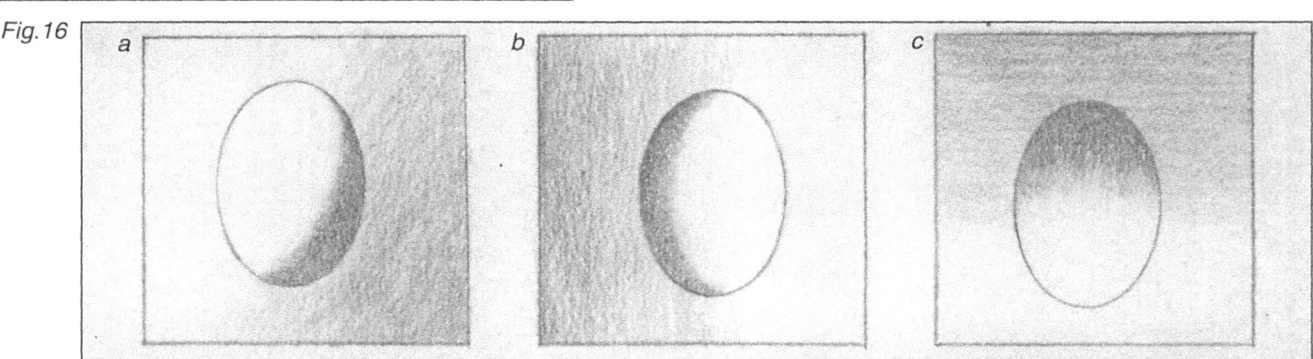

Fig.16 *a* *b* *c*

CONCERNING LIGHT SOURCES

Light sources are ultimately of two kinds, commonly referred to as diffused or point. A diffused source of light is, for example, an overall grey day sky or light from a studio window that faces north. This light is cool, soft and diffused with very subtle gradations. Because of this subtlety an example is not shown. The drawing, *Fig. 17.* shows how a typical point source of light, in this case coming from the upper left hand corner, produces gradations of values on a background. These gradations of light will radiate outwards from the area of lightest light gradually becoming darker in value and larger in area in a geometric ratio. Typical point sources of light are, of course, a spotlight, the sun and the moon.

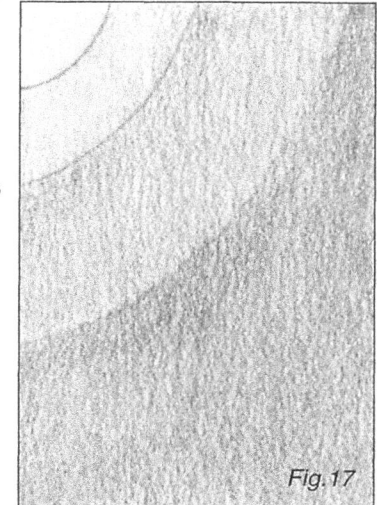

Fig. 17

THE CENTER-LIGHT OR CREST LIGHT

The typical "learning" drawing is not a full value drawing. What it is is a drawing made on white or off white paper consisting of variations of line, accents, shadow values, halftone values and a value that is a little lighter than the halftone for defining forms in the light. When this type of drawing is made on a grey toned or tinted paper then one may use white chalk for highlights but most sparingly. In the above-mentioned types of drawings there is no rendering of a crest light or center-light. This type of lighting is used only when making a fully modeled, full value drawing. Without it the form, particularly in the light areas, will appear flat.

The center-light is so called because it is found in or is rather on the area where the form crests. Since this is usually near the center of the form it is called the center-light. The center-light is always soft edged on all sides. It blends imperceptibly into the surrounding areas. It does not exist on a flat surface.

Do not confuse the center-light with the highlight. The highlight, if any, is much smaller than the center-light and is many times found within it. Portions of the highlight may blend into the center-light but usually there is one part of it that stays quite distinct. *Highlights are commonly found on corners or ridges of forms.* Therefore if a form crests to such a degree as to form a corner rather than a rounded surface, the light atop that corner could be called a highlight. Try to visualize the cross-section of any form you draw in order to get a better idea of the size, shape and position of the center-light; *see Figs. 18.a.b.c.*

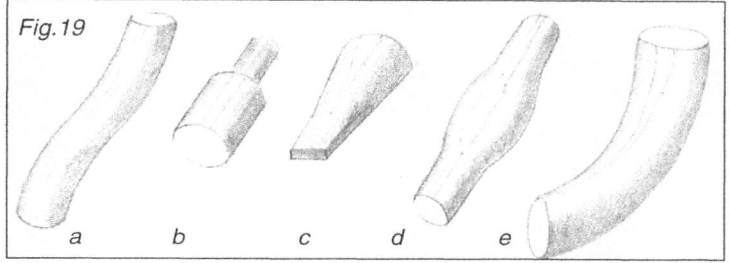

Fig. 19

a   b   c   d   e

Figs. 19a.b.c.d.e. show how the shape of the center-light conforms to the form it is on. All of these examples will help you understand the modeling of the forms of the human figure as well as many other forms in nature. In *Fig. 19a.* we see a narrow center-light following the curvature of the form. *Fig. b.* has two cylindrical forms, one wide, one narrow. Notice that the center-light of the narrower cylinder is narrow and the one on the wider cylinder, wider. *Fig. c.* shows a wide center-light tapering and disappearing as it enters into the flat surface. Two examples shown in *Figs. d. and e.* demonstrate how the widths of the crest lights change as the shape of the form changes.

One should not put the same degree of center-light modeling on all the planes for it may defeat our purpose to draw or paint form in space. The drawing, *Fig. 20.* represents, in an abstract way, three common forms of the figure. The top part represents the front forms we look into, the middle part represents top plane forms that come forward and the lower part represents shadow forms in recession.

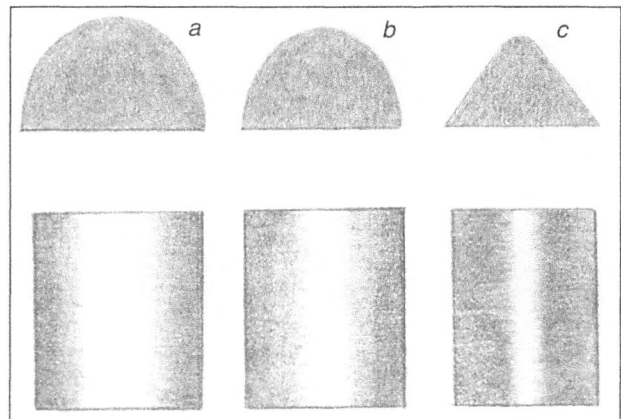

Fig. 18

a   b   c

Fig. 20

39

The front forms should receive the greatest degree of center-lighting. Modeling should be restrained on the top planes that come forward so as to not hurt their feeling of receding. The center-lighting on the forms in the shadow area should be modeled the last of all so as to not hurt the unity of the shadows. You don't want to have the feeling of too much progression and recession within the shadows either in drawing or painting.

The three drawings at the right side of the page, *Figs. 21a.b. and c.* show how the center-light changes direction on three major forms of the arm when the arm is turned. You will find three center-lights following the shape and direction of forms throughout the whole figure.

If you have difficulty seeing center-lighting, squint very hard or look at the model through a darkened glass. Values will become more apparent then.

LIGHT AND SHADE IN MODELING

Forms of the human being, indeed of all living creations, are seldom if ever perfectly round or perfectly square. Forms, as we have discussed before, have flattened areas called planes. These planes, when seen in light and shade, become part of the light, halftone or shadow areas, depending on the angle of the light to them. *Fig. 22a.* shows a typical illustration of a cylinder with a halftone which is massing with the light. The next cylinder, *b.,* shows a cylinder with a flattened surface (plane). This plane is of a darker halftone value than that which is shown in the previous example. It is not massing with either the light or the shadow, which incidentally seldom occurs on the face or figure. The third drawing, *Fig. c.,* shows a cylinder with a flattened halftone surface at the bottom which becomes rounded at the top. Here this halftone plane, at the bottom, may or may not mass with the shadow. As we ascend towards the top of the cylinder its roundness takes over producing a light halftone which masses with the light. Somewhere in the center of this halftone plane it may stay distinct, not massing with

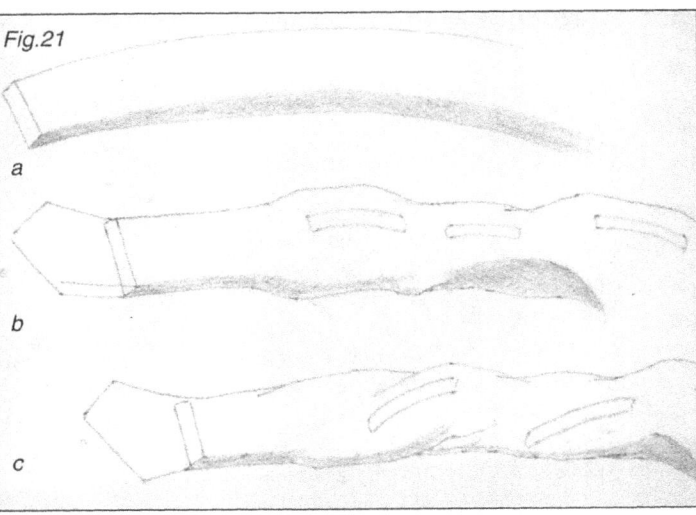

Fig.21

Fig.22

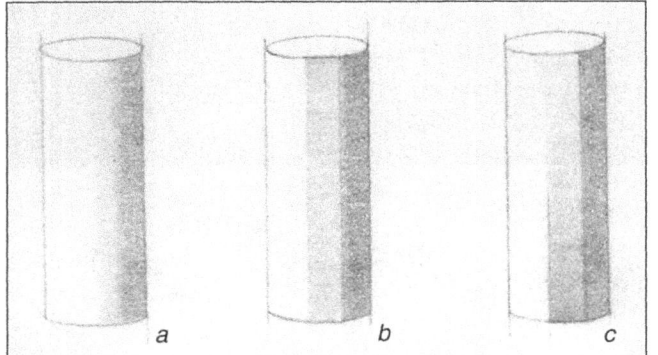

either the light or shadow. These three simple drawings should help you understand and solve much of the mystery of modeling form in light and shade.

THE CORRECT USAGE OF LIGHT AND SHADE ON THE FIGURE

One cannot correctly render form unless one can perceive forms, planes and values. The previous chapters and illustrations have explained much about forms and planes and the way light reveals them.

The drawings on page 41 show three examples of light and shade on the same torso. The first drawing on the left, *Fig. 23a.* may look good to you but has many mistakes regarding values. This type of rendering is usually done by a fairly advanced student who copies what he *thinks he sees.* It is a drawing without a correct concept. It has to be pointed out over and over again that darks in the light *appear darker* than they really are and that the lights in the shadow area *appear lighter* than they really are. This is an illusion and is due to the fact that a small dark area surrounded by a large area of light will appear darker than it is. Conversely a small light area surrounded by a large area of darkness will appear lighter than it is. Because of this darks in the light should be made lighter than they appear and lights in the dark areas should be made lower in value than they appear.

In the first drawing, *Fig. 23a.* we see many darks in the light area and many lights in the shadow area. The result is a lack of a feeling of a strong directional light on the model. Darks "punch holes" in the figure and lights "jump out" thereby destroying the unity of light on form.

The second drawing *Fig. b.* shows the correct way to render the same torso in a *form-lighting condition.* Here the light area, the halftone area and the

Fig.23   a   b   c

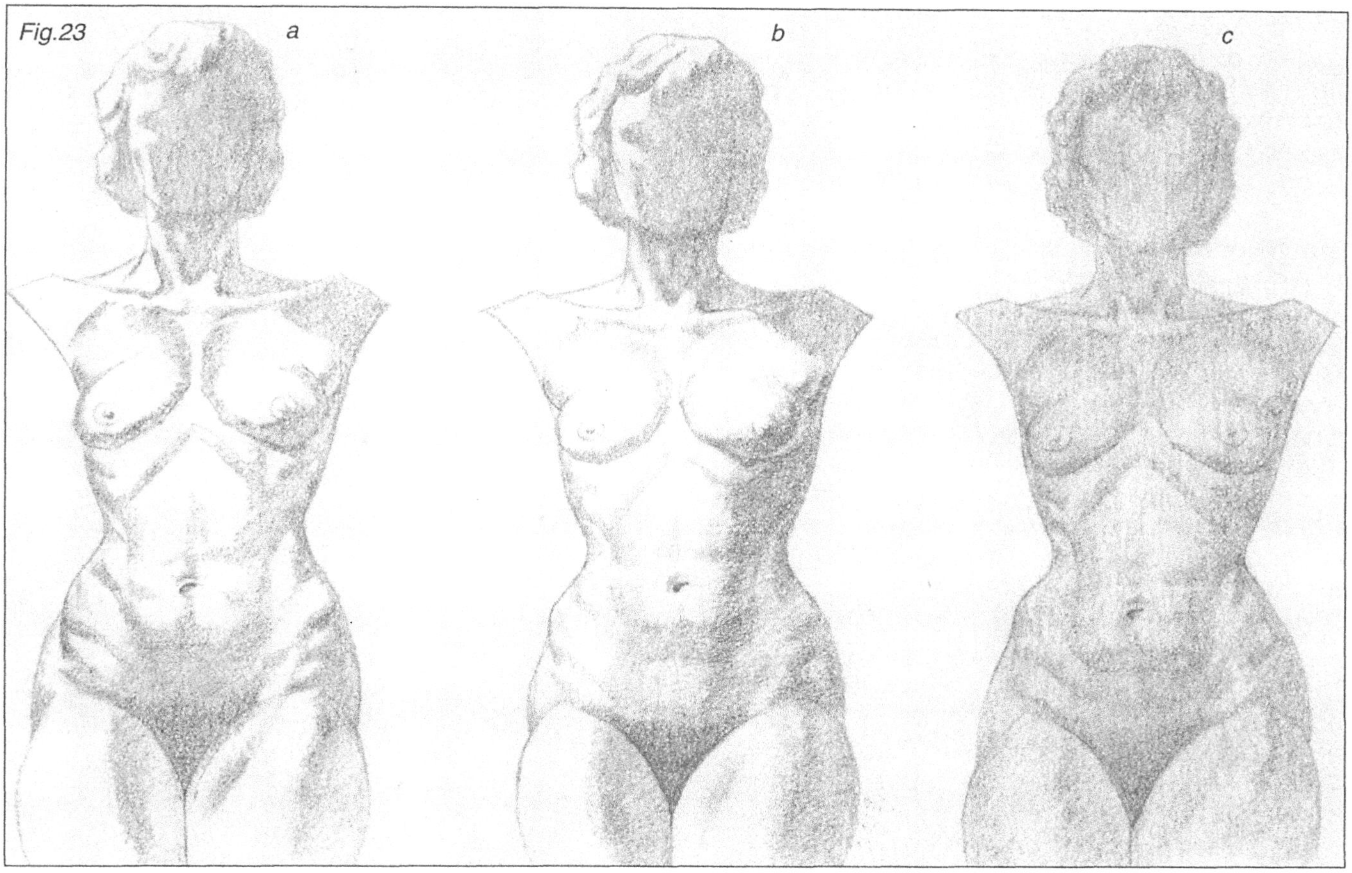

shadow area are quite distinct and separate. Of course they merge into one another here and there but initially they were stated separately. Note that the darks in the light area do not approach the degree of the values of the halftone and shadow. The lights within the halftone and shadow area should be and are darker in value than any of those in the light area. There is nothing in the light area which is as dark as the shadow value. Modeling in this manner correctly expresses the light and shade. If you want to make a lighter form within the shadow plane do not go lighter but rather *go darker on the underplanes first.* In this manner you will achieve your lighter form and still maintain the unity of the shadow plane. If this does not produce the desired effect then go lighter but only slightly so.

  Drawing, *Fig. c.,* the third example, shows an advanced student's idea of rendering form, which is very good, but completely lacking in light effect. He or she doesn't have the slightest idea of how to achieve it. The entire torso is shaded with the same values and therefore appears to have no light of any degree of strength from any direction on it.

  The three rectangles within *Fig. 24.* show the basic tones that are commonly used for modeling the form of learning drawings. The first rectangle shows the light tones, the second the halftones, and the third the shadow tones. Note that the light area values do not approach the darker halftone values,

which in turn do not approach the even darker shadow area values. At the bottom of these three basic tones are slightly darker values which would be used for bottom planes and sideplanes within the respective tones. The dark line at the bottom of the shadow underplane is an accent – the darkest line of the drawing. These three tones and their subtle gradations coupled with the skillful use of line are enough to make a masterful drawing.

Fig.24

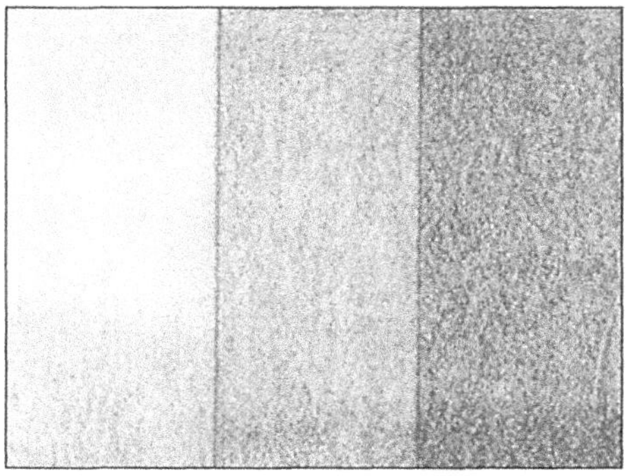

The four rectangles, *Figs. 25a.b.c.d.* show some of the many different value arrangements that are used to convey the weakness or strength of the light on the model. You can safely use the ones shown as a guide. In the first example, *Fig. 25a.* we see three areas of values, one of light, one of halftone and one of shadow. Within the shadow is a darker area representing an underplane or sideplane within it. The shadow is followed by an even darker line representing an accent – the darkest line in your drawing. One should not use a shadow tone in the light area or a light tone in the shadow area. To make more complete form you go slightly darker in value within these three areas but do not go so dark as to approach the value of the next darker area.

The second drawing, *Fig. b.* shows the lighting that should be used in what I refer to as a "learning drawing." Basically it is achieved with variations of outline, a very light tone for modeling in the light (shown in the center of the light area), a darker tone for the halftone and an even darker tone for the shadow. As in all cases, there is a darker tone in the shadow and an accent.

Fig. c. is an example of a lighting arrangement that should be used when you want to represent a stronger lighting effect on the model. To achieve this you will need, besides line, a very light tone to model form in the light, again shown in the center of the light area. The halftone band which follows is made narrower and lighter than ordinary, for the stronger the light the narrower and lighter the halftone band becomes. This is followed by the usual shadow area with its darker underplane value and accent.

The fourth example *Fig. d.* represents a full value rendering on grey paper. Here one uses the grey paper as the average skin tone of the model and gradually goes darker and darker for the halftones and shadows. Do not try to do large areas of modeling by smudging white chalk all over your drawing. Highlights and center-lights are made with white chalk which is softened into the grey paper at certain areas.

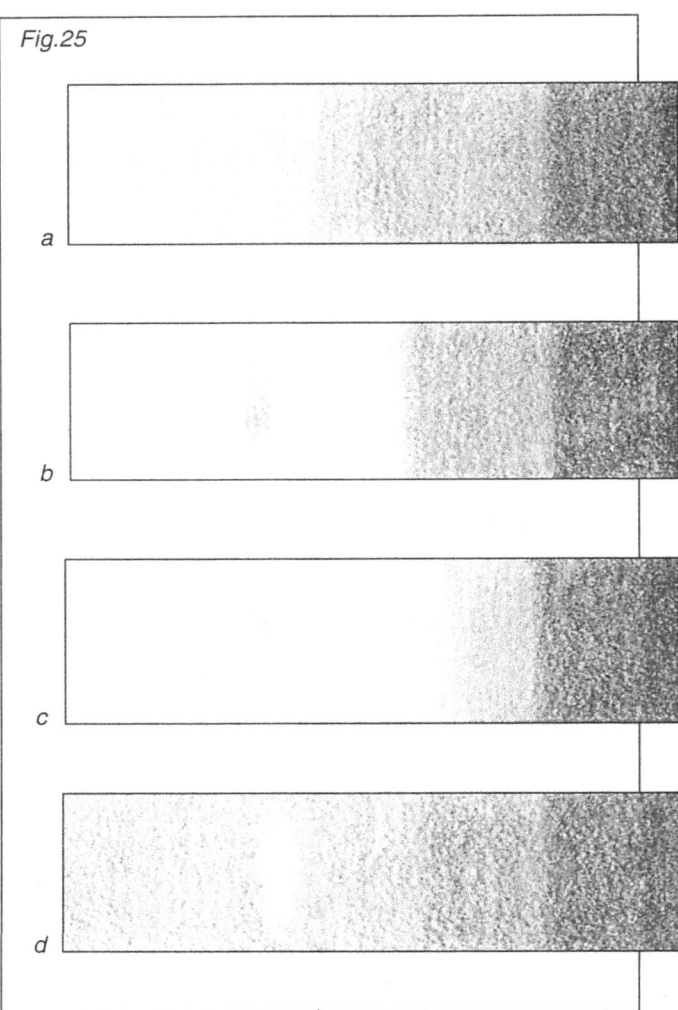

Fig.25

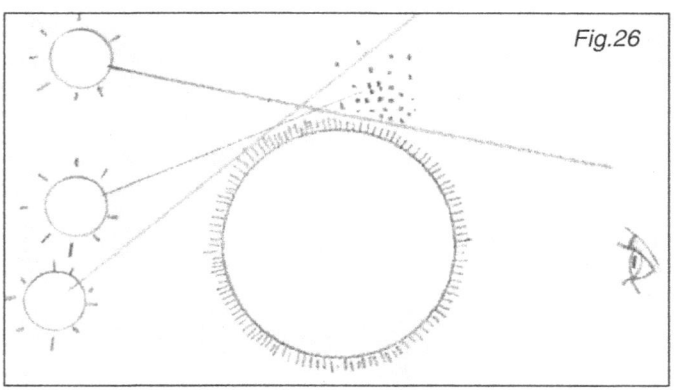

Fig.26

HALATION

If one is making a full value charcoal drawing that includes a background, then one might have to consider the aspect of halation. This is a narrow band of light surrounding certain parts of the model caused by the scattering of light by thousands of tiny hairs or fibers. There can be no halation without texture and back lighting. Therefore, halation is seen most frequently around hair, garments, drapes, etc. The more the light source, which is behind the model, lines up with the eye the greater the halation appears. *Fig. 26.* explains this phenomenon diagrammatically.

HIGHLIGHTS

One uses a highlight on a drawing in only two cases. One is when the drawing is made on a toned paper, grey or any other color, and the other is when one makes a full value charcoal rendering. When drawing on a toned paper I advise using a good quality white chalk pencil such as Conte or General's. These can be sharpened to any type of point or wedge, assuring full control. As I feel the highlight be put on last with sureness and accuracy I suggest you study your drawing well before you place them. Once you've made a decision

Do not confuse this type of charcoal drawing with the commonly seen fully rendered academic drawings of the French Academy at the turn of the century. These usually had no background tone only the figure being fully modeled. This modeling on the figure was made with very fine strokes of charcoal going first from the white of the paper to the lightest tones of the skin and from there to darker and darker tones until the drawing was finished. Blending tones with a paper stump is considered in bad taste from time to time; you have to use your own judgement. Chalk highlights are generally not used or needed in this type of drawing.

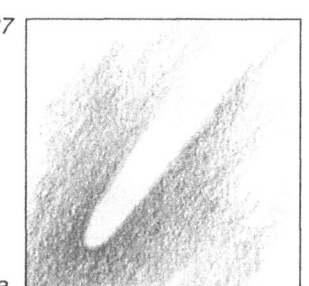

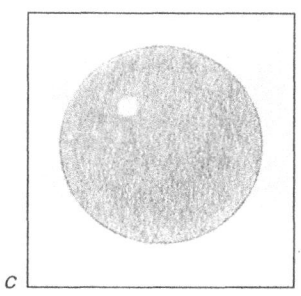
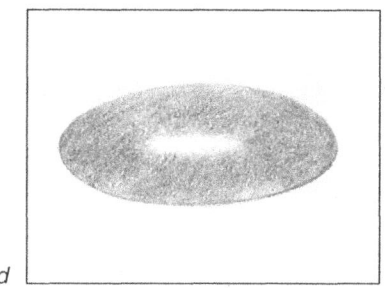

Fig.27

a   b   c   d

make the stroke swiftly and surely, bearing down hard on the chalk where you start and lifting up on it as you complete the stroke. This will cause the white chalk to blend into the grey tone of the paper as shown in *Fig. 27a.*

When one makes a full value charcoal drawing the entire white surface of the paper is covered with a light charcoal tone. This may be evened out with a chamois cloth. After a few outlines one proceeds to make form by going darker and darker with the charcoal. The highlights and some center-lights are made with a kneaded rubber eraser molded to a convenient point. Here the highlight will blend more softly into the surrounding tones than in the previously described drawing *(see Fig. 27b.).*

The highlight on a spherical form will appear as a soft edged round dot as is shown in *Fig. 27c.* This is mostly the case if the highlight is caused by a round light source. However if the source of the highlight is a window then the shape of the highlight will be the shape of the window, curved of course to follow the curvature of the sphere. Highlights will conform to the shape of the form they're on as seen in *Fig. 27d.*

THE ACCENT

The highlight, the lightest element of the drawing is opposed by the accent, the darkest line in the drawing. Accents are only where no light enters – such as where a foot touches the floor or between creases of flesh. Four examples of accents are shown and you will find them all on the model when you're drawing.

An accent almost always has form blending into it from one side or the other. The first example, *Fig. 28a.,* shows an accent with the form blending into it from the left side. The right side stays distinct and hard. This effect can be gotten with one stroke of the flat part of the wedge of your pencil while bearing down on the heel of the wedge. The second example, *Fig. b,.* is similar; only the form is blending into the accent from the right hand side with the left hand side staying distinct. Form can also blend into the accent from both sides as shown in *Fig. c.* Lastly *Fig. d.* shows how a reflected light can be made automatically by simply going darker within the tone and stopping before one reaches the line of the accent.

Fig.28

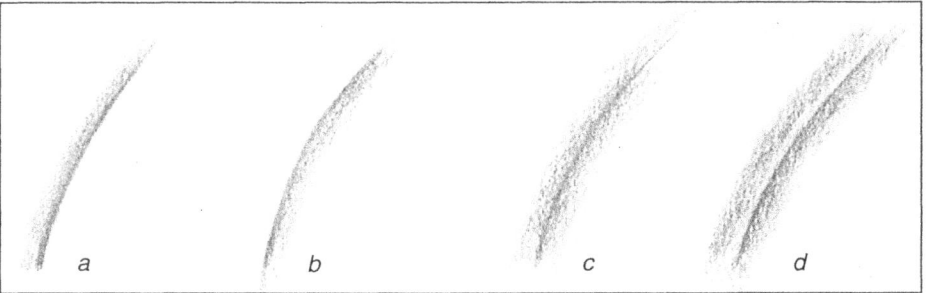

a   b   c   d

FOCUS

There can be only one area of sharp focus on the model and that is where you're looking. To create a greater illusion of depth and reality the model should be drawn and even painted with the area of greatest interest in the sharpest focus. Everything else will be more or less out of focus. Of course this applies to drawings that contain value gradations more so than those that are strictly line.

The two illustrations, *Figs. 29a.b.* graphically show the area that is in sharpest focus, number 1 in a circle. Numbers 2 and 3 in the ovals represent the areas that are going more and more out of focus both in horizontal and vertical directions. Of course you can put your sharpest focus anywhere you wish and follow the same principle.

Fig.29

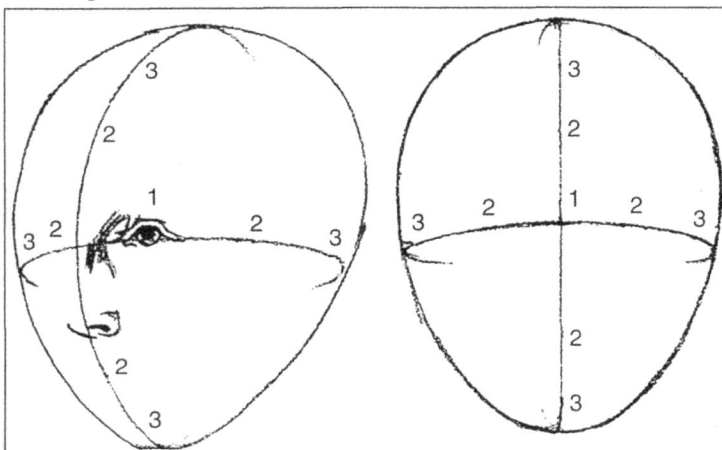

Fig. 30. shows a more concrete, practical application of this idea in the drawing of a pair of lips. Note the sharpness of line on the right side grading to the softness on the left side. This causes the lips to appear as though they are turning and going away from you.

Fig.30

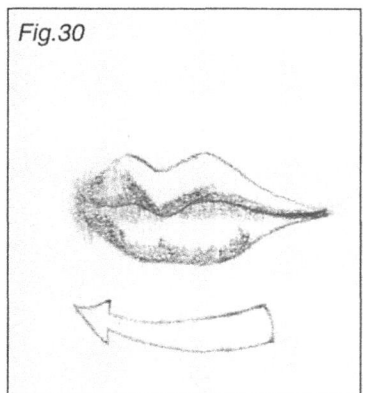

QUICK SKETCH STUDIES DEMONSTRATING LIGHT AND SHADE ON FORM

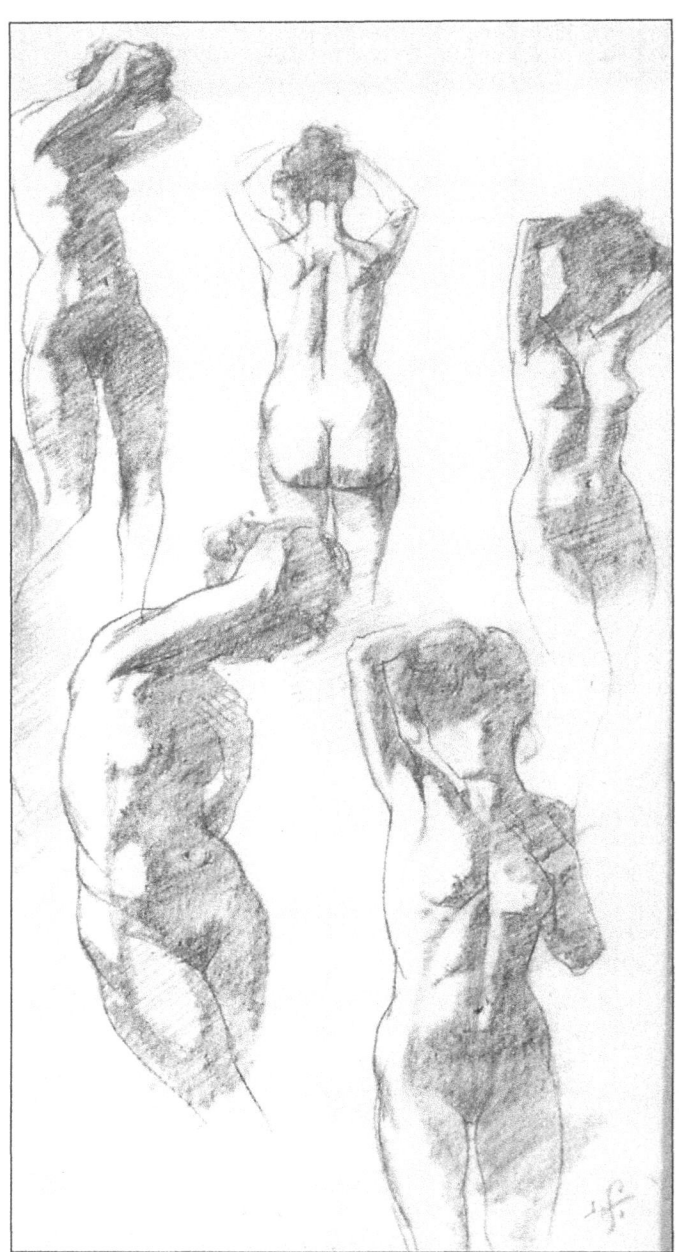

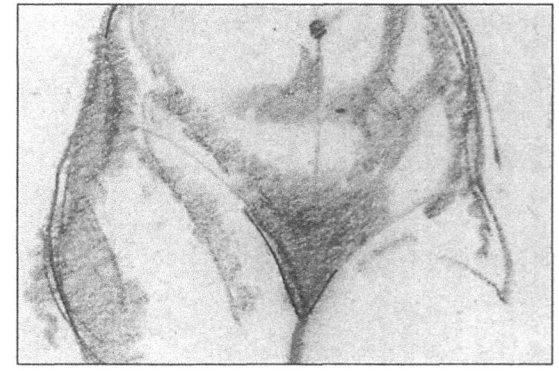

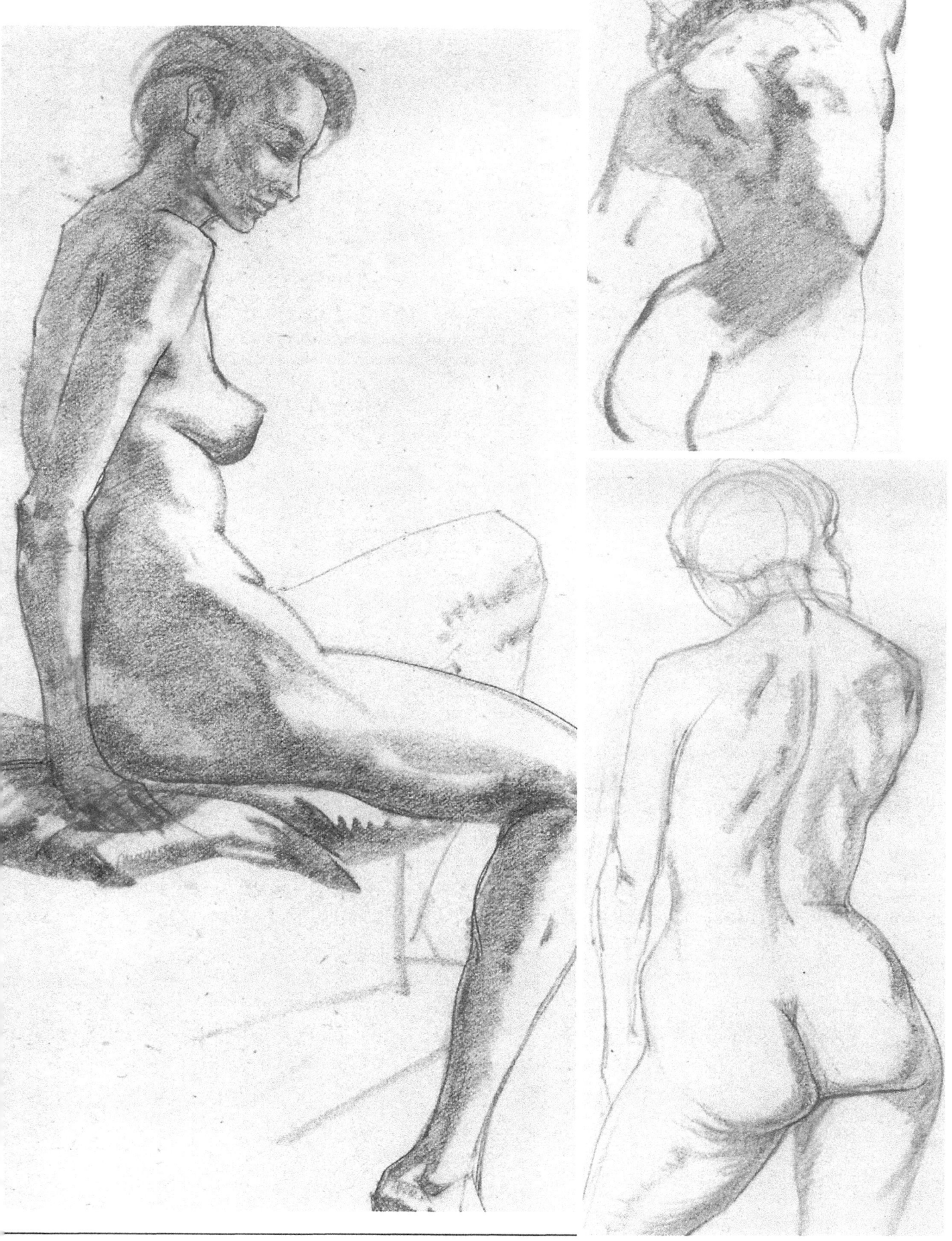

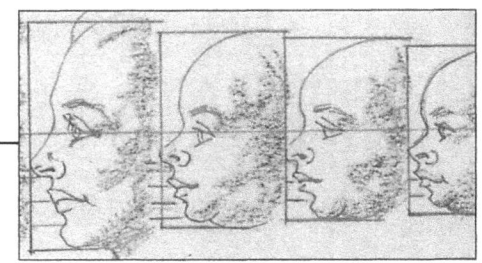

CHAPTER EIGHT

PROPORTIONS

"Perfection comes about little by little by many numbers." Polykleitos 450 B. C.
"The world is number." Pythagoras 4th century B. C.

It is quite possible that the first artists did not concern themselves with proportions, at least not consciously so. As time went on works of art and architecture increased and kept on increasing. It was now that people could make judgements as to what looked better or what looked worse. For some reason not yet known to us certain proportions were regarded as being more beautiful or truthful than others – or simply looked more "right." At this point it was simple for artists to take measurements of what was regarded as the best proportions and use them in their works. The ancient Greek philosophers went a step further. They intuitively reasoned an "ideal" world where there existed "ideal" perfect images of earthly things – and they sought to express this in their works of art rather than merely copying things as they appeared to their senses.

One of the many reasons for the start of the Renaissance in Italy was the unearthing of these ancient Greek statues and a revival of interest in their ancient philosophies, ideals and theories. Inspired by these works of art they made many measurements of people and animals that they considered "beautiful" or "correct" and sought mathematical relationships within these proportions. Using these as a springboard they produced a wealth of great art that flooded the entire civilized world for centuries.

Let me state here, however, that there is no such thing as perfect proportions for everyone, for proportions vary with different people at different times and different places. A survey of any two dozen authorities on proportions will reveal many differences among their conclusions – although I consider them minor. Proportions also vary with your point of sight to the model and have to usually be altered quite a bit for compositional and expressive purposes.

So why do we need to know proportions? For one thing we need a starting point, and as I have previously mentioned, we have many fine works of art upon which to base our conclusions. Unknown quantity can be better judged by known quantities. Proportions give us a simple way to estimate what is right or wrong, at least to the majority of people in this culture at this time. We could not have come to the conclusions we have if this were not so.

There have always been many ways to measure the human figure, such as the length of a hand, a foot or a head. The head is almost universally used for this measurement. Its length is commonly used as the basic unit of measurement of the figure. When using this length of the head the average male would measure 7 1/2 heads high, the "ideal" or "picture male" would measure 8 heads high, heroic figures 9 heads high and fashion figures 9 or even 10 heads high.

One should not make a drawing adhering dogmatically to recommended proportions as they might produce a static, lifeless drawing. A sight measurement utilizing proportions, relationships and your feeling about what the size and shape of things should be will result in a better drawing. For instance, after drawing an oval for the head, draw a line through its center to the pit of the neck. Extend this line downward through the navel to the crotch. Next draw a line through the pit of the neck to the widest points of the shoulders. By connecting these widest points to the point of the crotch you will form a triangular shape which will automatically give you the correct size of the rib cage form. All of this will be explained quite thoroughly in the chapter on structure. Drawing with a procedure of this kind will give you accurate measurements without having to measure too much – and your drawing will look correct because of the proper relationships of things to one another. Proportions should be considered just another aid in helping you draw well.

ADJUSTING FOR PHOTOGRAPHIC DISTORTION

A knowledge of ideal proportions is very important if you intend to make drawings or paintings from photographs. I have noticed that almost no one questions the proportions of a figure in a photograph as they feel that the camera never lies. The truth of the matter is that proportions in photographs are almost always distorted, many times terribly so. To prove this to yourself place a piece of tracing paper over a photograph that appears normal to you and trace the outline of the figure with a Pentel type pen or a pencil. When you remove the paper from the photograph and look at the outline you have drawn you may be shocked at how wrong this outline will seem.

If you intend to work from the photograph you should make alterations based on ideal proportions on the tracing paper. When you are satisfied with the look of the revised drawing you may trace this onto paper or canvas and proceed to render or paint it.

Following are captions for the drawings showing proportions of the figure.

Fig. 1. A quick simple way to set up the basic proportions of the "ideal" figure. The six examples show the basic measurements in halves, quarters and eighths.

Fig. 1a. At the top of this line is a division which represents the length of the head. Eight of these units will be the full length.

Fig. b. The full length divided in half. The crotch is at the halfway point.

Fig. c. Dividing the length into quarters gives the position of the nipples of the breasts and the bottom of the knees.

Fig. d. The full eight head division.

Fig. e. The basic figure abstraction.

Fig. f. This drawing shows the upper division of the torso divided into thirds. The first third is from the top of the head to the top of the shoulder line. The second division is from the shoulder line to the waist and the third is from the waist to the line of the hips. Notice that the waist line is where the lines from the shoulders to the crotch are intersected by those from the hips to the neck.

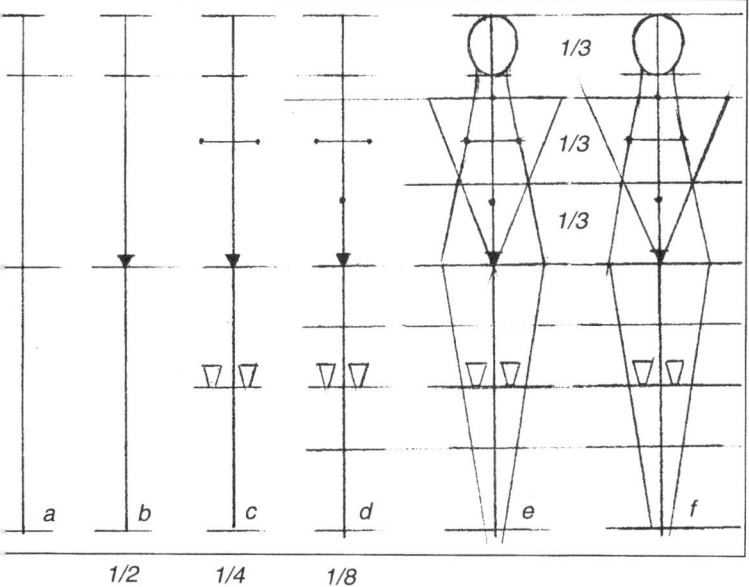

Fig. 1

a b c d e f

1/2 1/4 1/8

Fig. 2a. A more complete basic figure abstraction of ideal proportions. This torso is 8 heads tall or 7 foot lengths or 10 hand lengths. If we use the length of the head as our basic unit of measurement the following measurements will be approximate.

4 heads distance – Top of forehead to the crotch, crotch point to bottom of the feet.

3 heads distance – The length of the spine. The pit of the arm to the fingertips from the top of the head to the navel.

2 heads distance – The width of the shoulders of the female from the clavicle to the top of the iliac crest.

2 1/3 heads distance – Width of the shoulders of the male.

2 heads distance – The femure bone. From the elbow to the fingertips. From the bottom of the knee to the bottom of the feet. From the bottom of the knee to the crotch.

2 1/2 heads distance – The length of the upper leg when seated from the back of the buttocks to the front of the knee.

2 1/3 heads distance – From the bottom of the foot to the top of the knee.

3/4 heads distance – The sternum, clavicle, scapula, hand.

1/2 heads distance – Length of middle finger.

1 hand distance – From the bottom of the chin to the top of the forehead.

Fig.2a

Elbow at Waist Line

Wrist, Trocanter Crotch

Midway Crotch to Bottom of knee

Bottom of Knee

47

Figs. 2a.b. and c. show some variations of the basic proportions.

Fig. b. Variations on the width of the hips from a "normal" width, inside lines to very wide hips, outside lines.

Fig. c. The crotch point is not always exactly four heads distance from the top of the head. Shown are a higher than normal and lower than normal crotch point.

Fig. d. A comparison of the lengths of legs. The drawing in the center is in the proportions of the "picture man," the ideal type. To the left of it is the more common, average length of the lower leg – it is usually one half a head shorter than the upper leg. It is usually the lower leg that most varies in size.

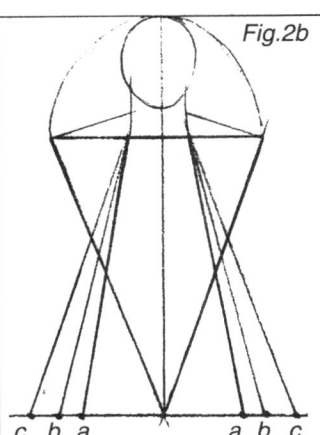

Fig.2b

Figs. 3a. and b. demonstrate the normal resting positions of the arms both in front and back views.

Figs. 4a.b. Adult male "real life" proportions. The drawing on the left is a composite of front and back views to show comparative positions of major forms.

Figs. 5a.b. Adult male proportions of "picture man," or idealized figure.

Figs. 6a.b.c. Front, side and back views of idealized male figure. Assuming the head 9 inches in height then 8 times 9 equals 72 inches or 6 feet.

Fig. 7. Proportions of the idealized man with outstretched arms

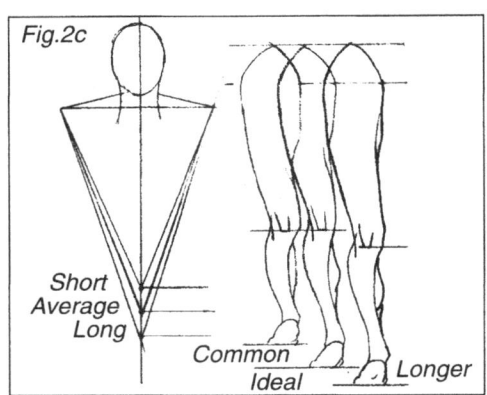

Fig.2c

Short
Average
Long

Common
Ideal
Longer

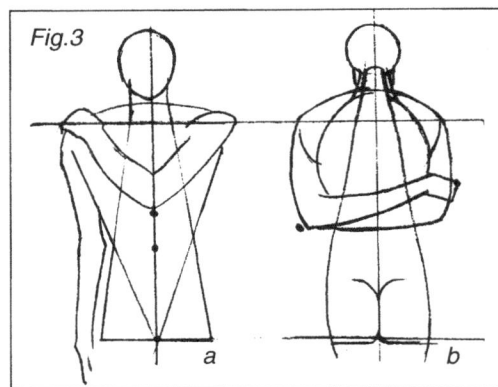

Fig.3

a   b

Front-Back-"Real Life" Proportions

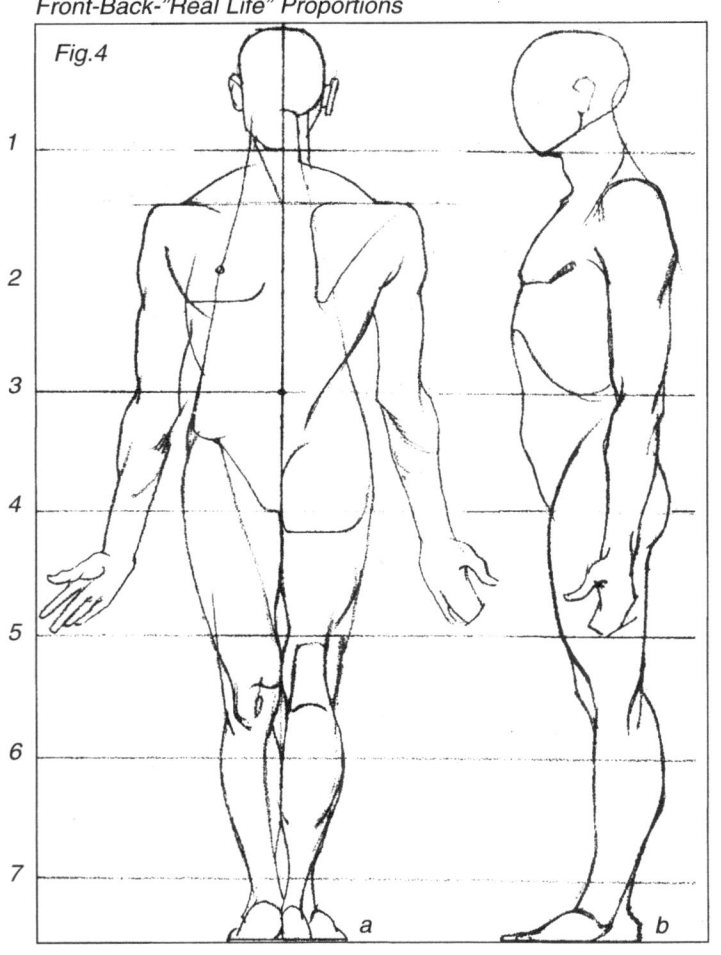

Fig.4

a   b

Picture Man Proportions

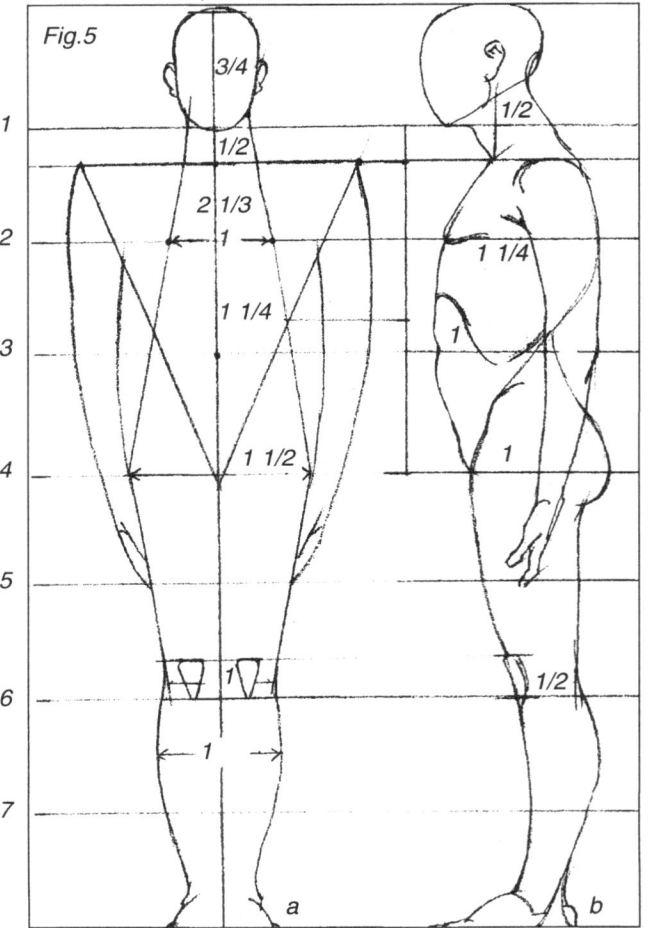

Fig.5

a   b

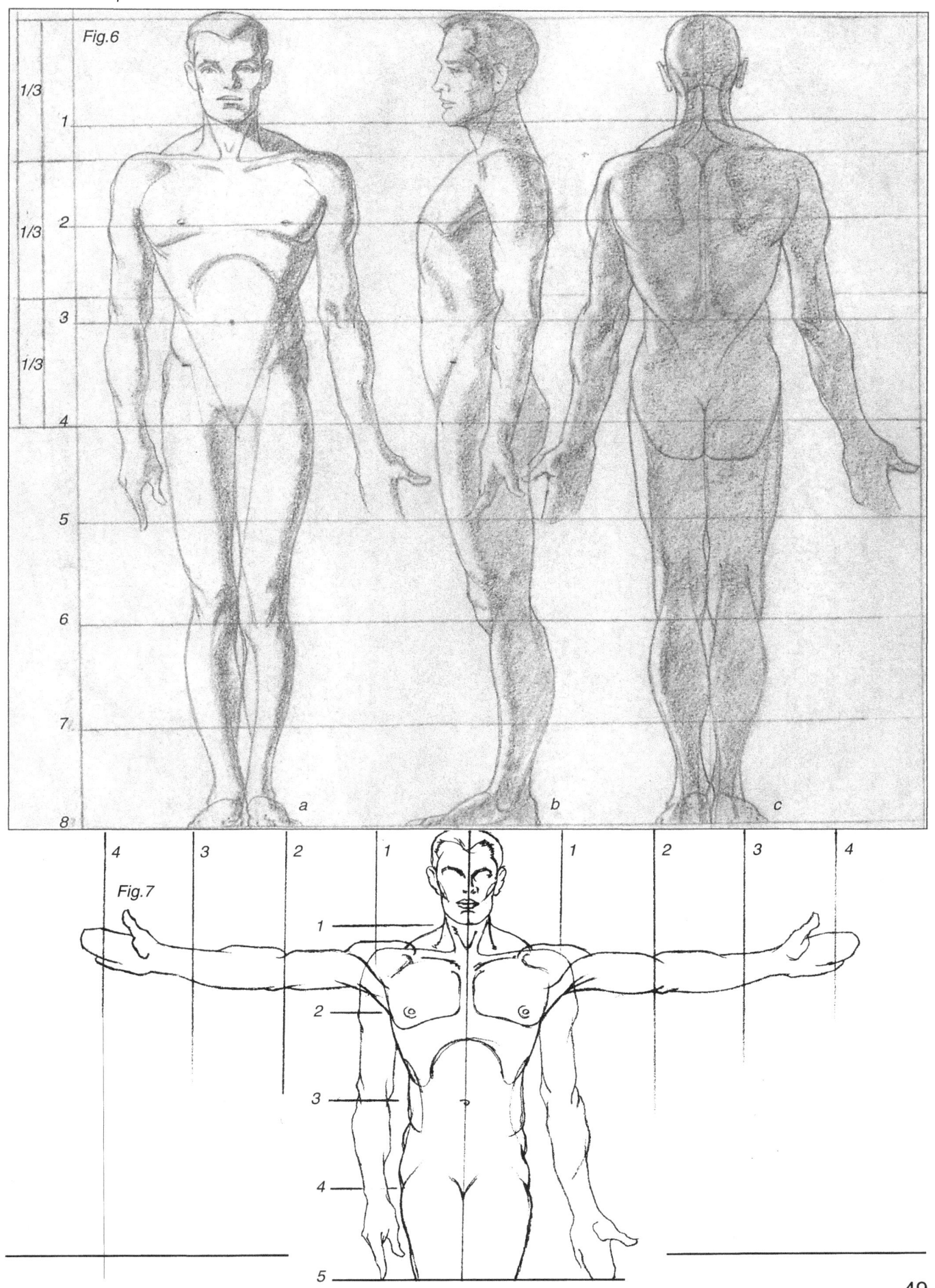

Fig.6

Fig.7

Fig.8

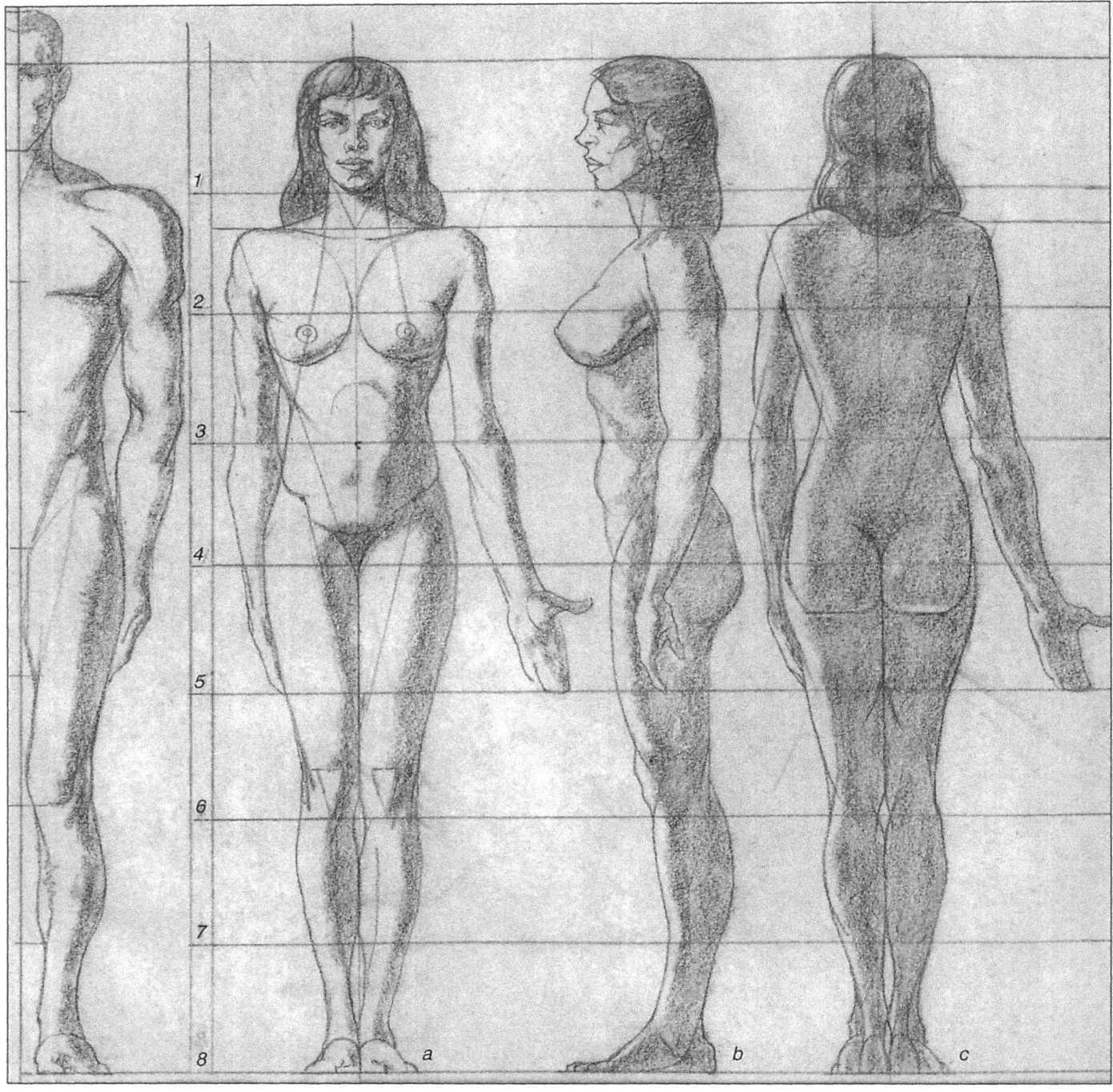

Figs. 8a.b.c. Front, side and back views of an 8 head female figure show
n with partial male figure for comparison.

Fig. 9. Relative proportions and measurements of figures in different positions. A figure sitting on a chair is 6 heads high, the same as a kneeling one. A figure sitting on a floor is 4 1/4 heads high. The average table is from 28 to 30 inches high and the average chair is 18 inches high.

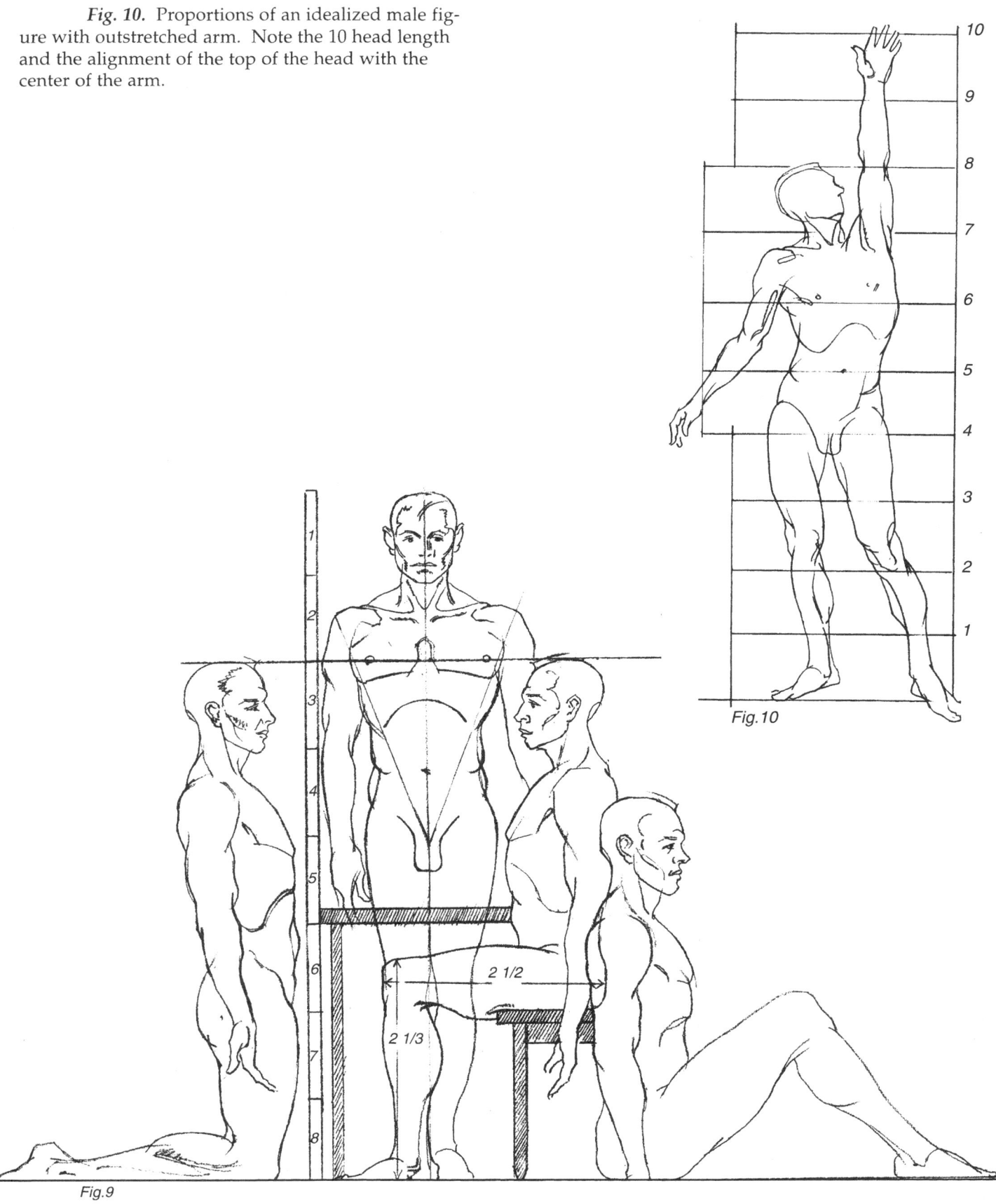

Fig. 10. Proportions of an idealized male figure with outstretched arm. Note the 10 head length and the alignment of the top of the head with the center of the arm.

Fig.10

2 1/2

2 1/3

Fig.9

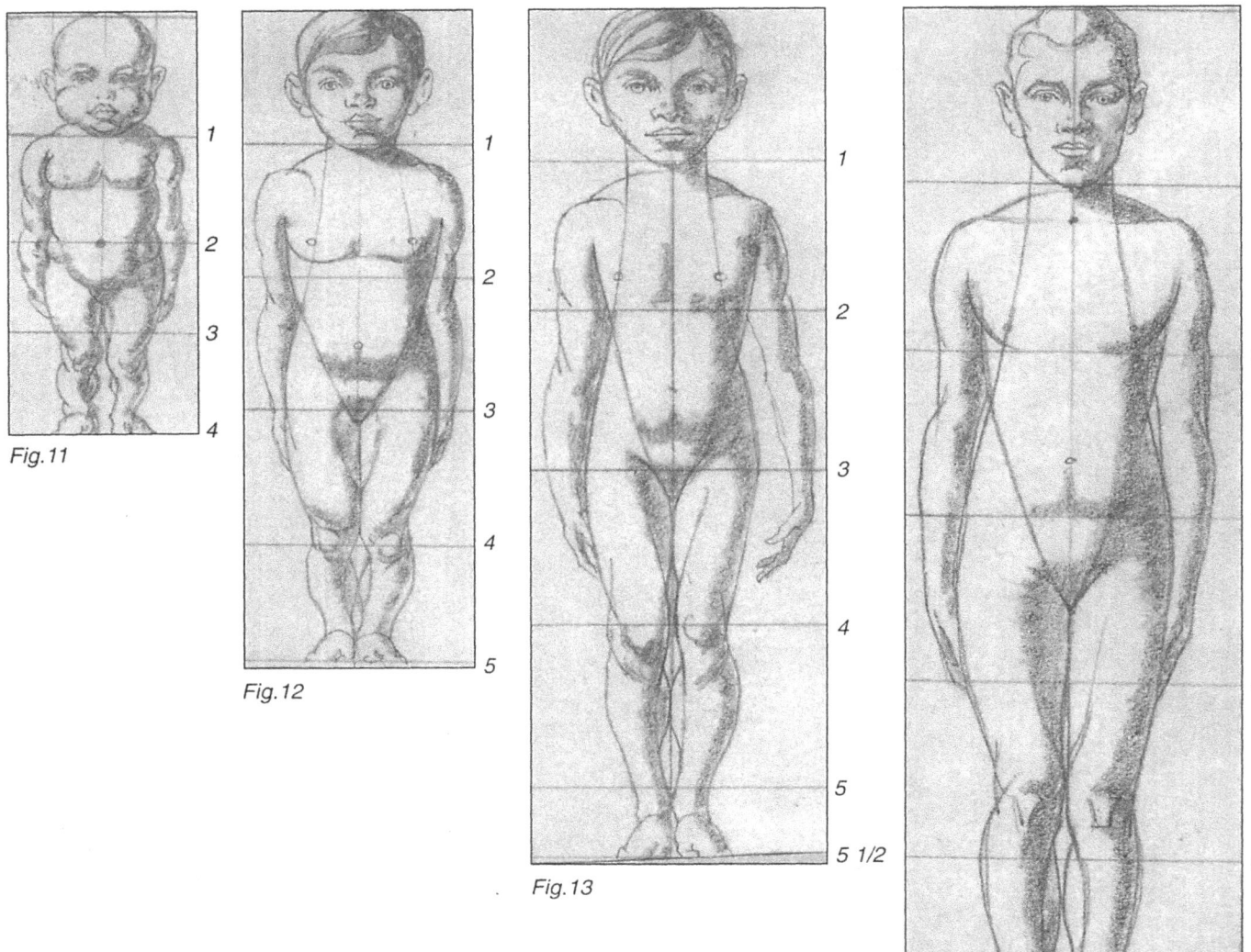

Fig. 11

Fig. 12

Fig. 13

Fig. 14

The following series of drawings show the proportions and how they change from infant to adult. You can use them as they are but, as they're based on a consensus of opinions by many authorities, they can be altered slightly one way or the other.

Fig. 11. An infant is 4 heads high. The center of the figure is not at the crotch as in an adult but at the navel which is two heads distance from the top or bottom of the infant.

Fig. 12. At two years of age the child is 5 heads high.

Fig. 13. At five years of age the child is 5 1/2 heads high.

Fig. 14. At the age of 7 1/2 years the child is 6 1/2 heads.

Fig. 15. Several years later, at the age of 12 years, the child is still 6 1/2 heads high but he is taller.

Fig. 16. At the age of 15 years the body is 7 heads high. Notice that the crotch is still not at the halfway point of the torso.

Fig. 17. A full grown adult of 20 years, 7 1/2 heads high. The crotch is now at the center of the body.

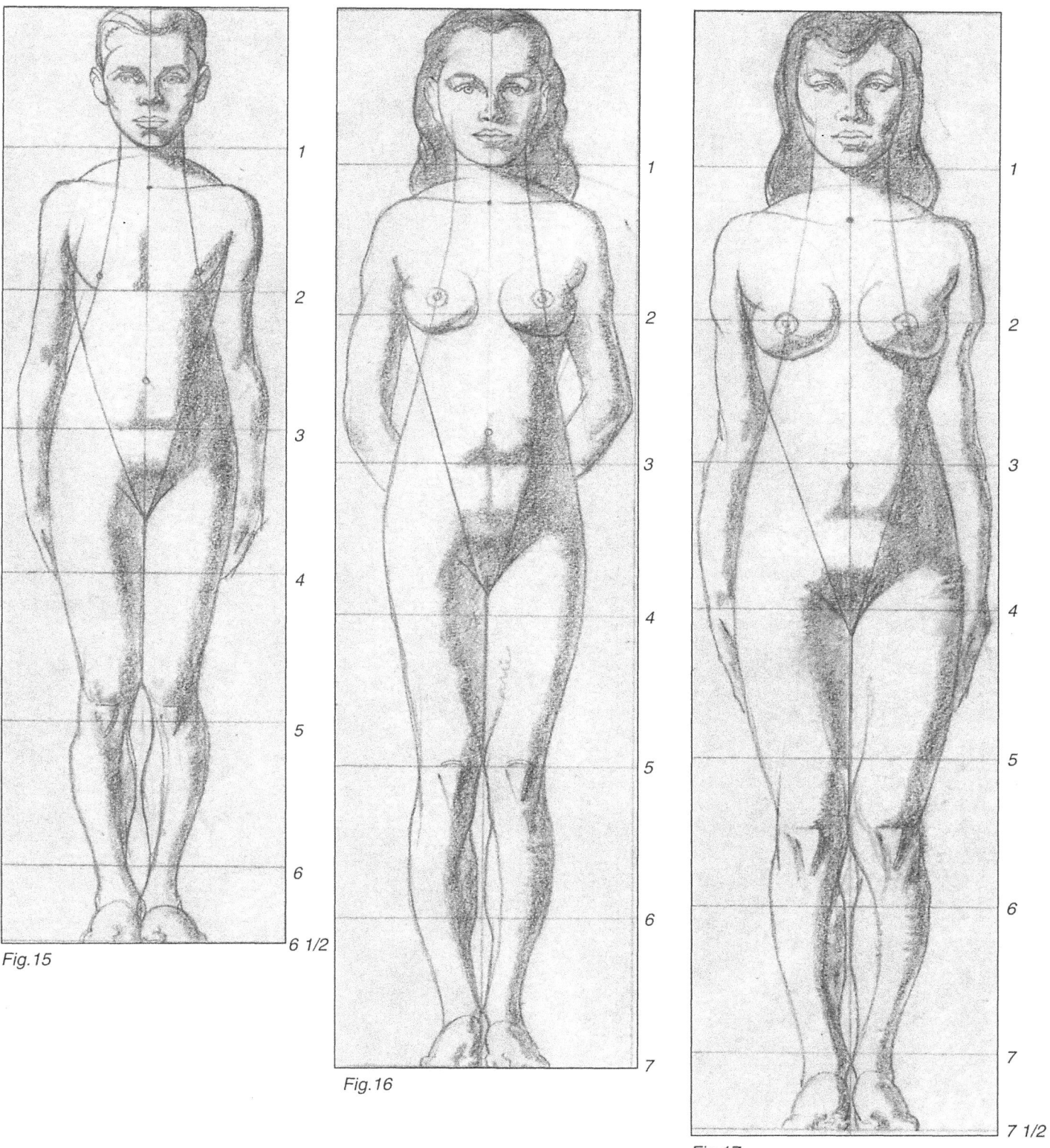

Fig.15

Fig.16

Fig.17

53

Fig. 18

Fig. 19

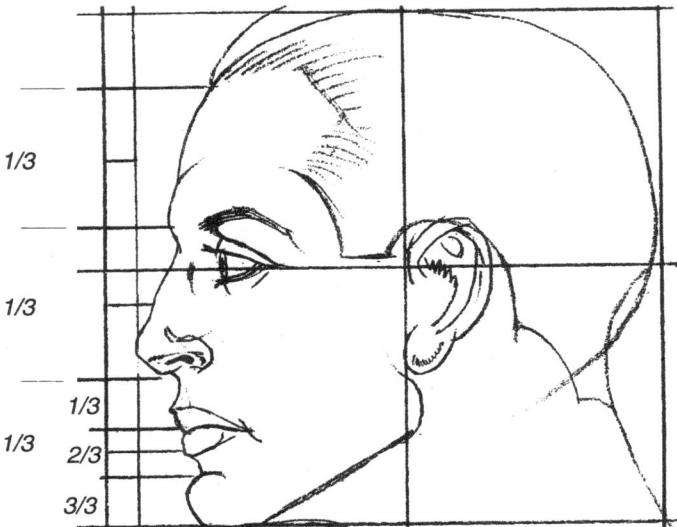

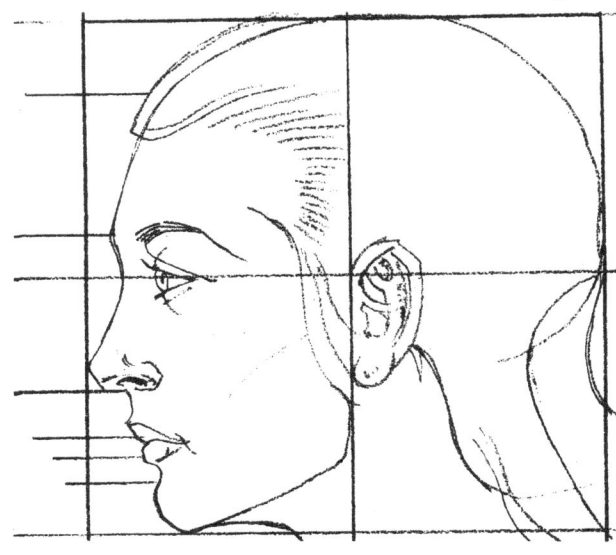

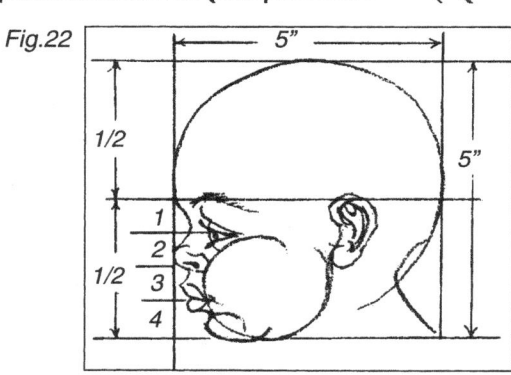

Fig. 22

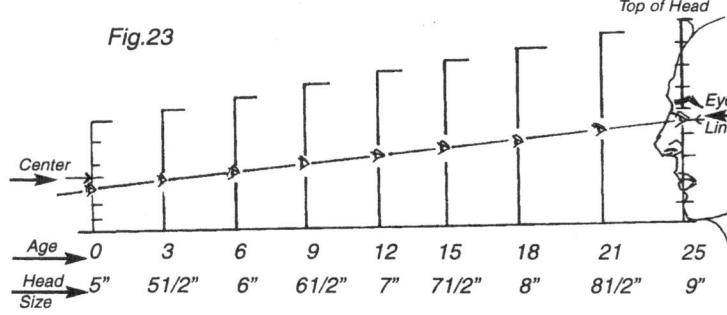

Fig. 23

The head in profile fits in a square. A horizontal line dividing the head in half will pass through the eye, generally through the lower part. A vertical line dividing the head in half will mark where the ear starts, and will end at the pit of the neck.

Everyone varies in the basic proportions of the head but you need a starting point to make judgements. The head is generally divided into thirds. One third is from the top of the forehead, (near the hairline), to the eyebrow. The second third is from the top of the eyebrow to the bottom of the nose and the third third is from the bottom of the nose to the bottom of the chin. The bottom third is again divided into thirds. Ideally there is one third distance from the bottom of the nose to the center of the lip line and one third distance from the lip line to the top of the chin.

There is a tremendous variation in the basic three thirds division of the head and it is one of the first things you must look for. For instance one may have a disproportionately large forehead area, a smaller area between the eyebrow and the bottom of the nose and again a larger area between the nose and the bottom of the chin.

Fig. 18. Ideal male head proportions.

Fig. 19. Ideal female head proportions.

Fig. 20. Average old man's head proportions.

Fig. 21. Comparison of young and old man. Shrinkage of the skull on an old man is mainly on the bottom part.

Fig. 22. A child's head fits in a 5-inch square. Note the comparison with the 9-inch square which is the average size of the male head in profile. A horizontal line drawn through the middle of the head will be atop the eyebrow ridge and top of the ear. The lower half of the face is divided into quarters. The bottom of the first quarter would be at the eye,

the bottom of the second quarter at the bottom of the nose and the bottom of the third quarter at the center of the lips. The bottom of the chin is, of course, at the bottom of the fourth quarter.

Fig. 23. The graph explains the increase of the size of the head as the age increases, from 0 years to 25 years of age. Note how at birth the child's eye is below the center line of the face and gradually rises to the center of the head at the age of 25.

Fig. 24. A series of heads from the adult to the infant showing their relative sizes and proportions.

Figs. 25a.b.c. Front, side and back of the average female figure. *Figs. 26a.b.c.* Front, side and back of the idealized "picture man."

Fig.20

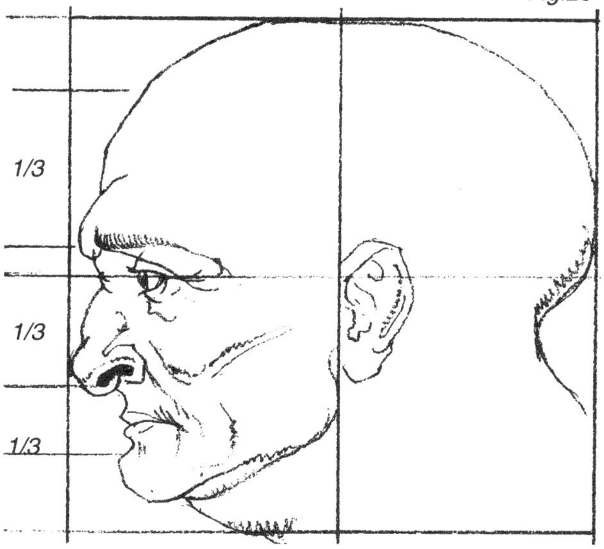

Fig.21

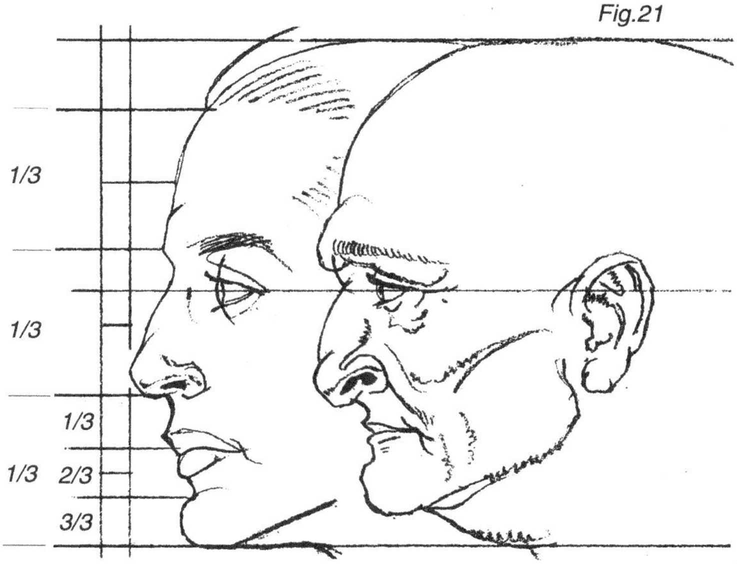

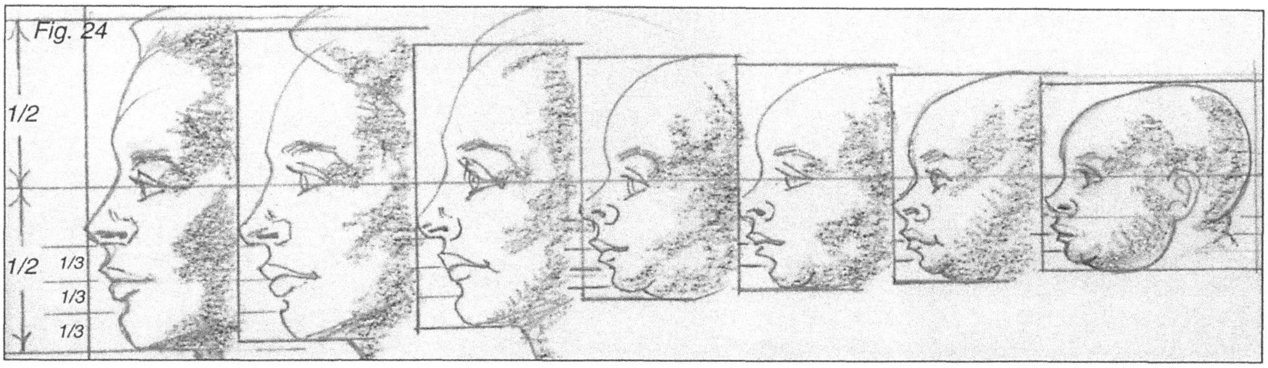

1/3
1/3
1/3

1/3
1/3
1/3 1/3
1/3 2/3
3/3

Fig. 24

1/2
1/2 1/3
1/3
1/3

Adult Man   Adult Woman   12 Years Old   3 Years Old   1 Year Old   4 Months Old   Infant

Fig.25

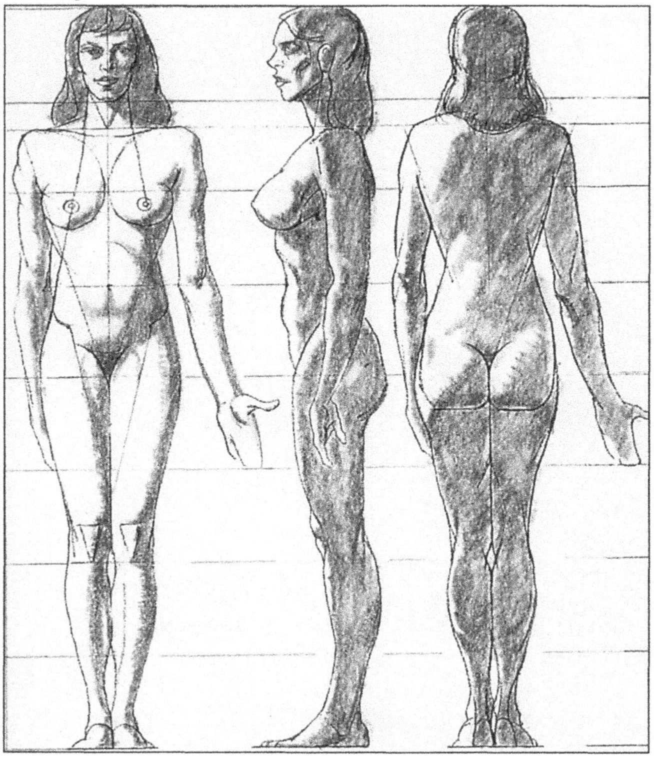

Fig.26

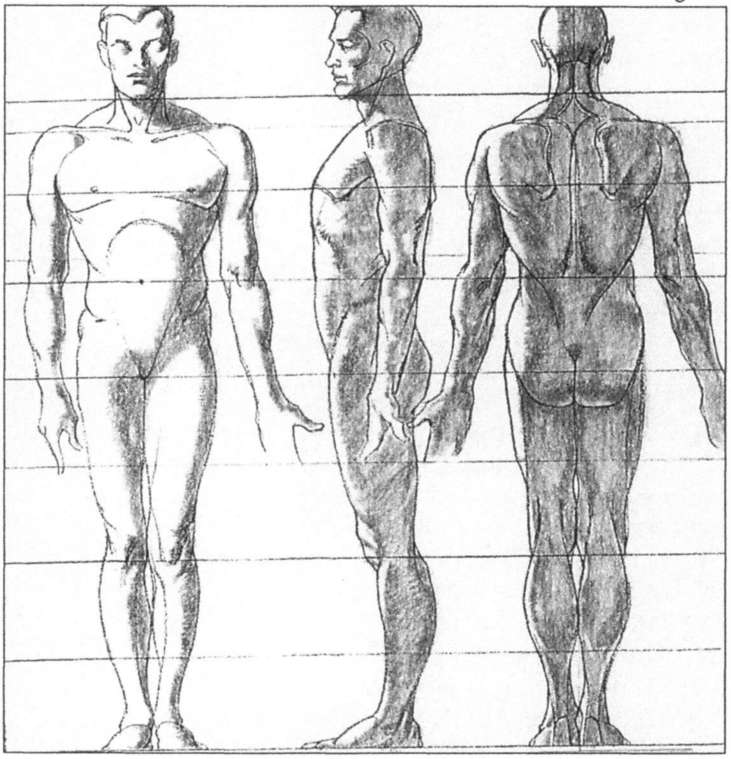

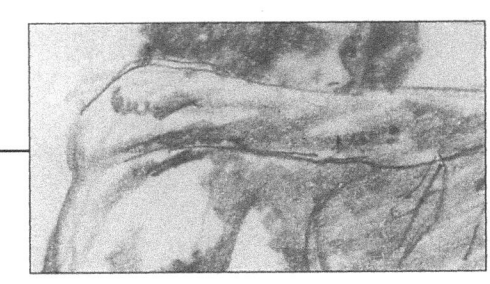

CHAPTER NINE

THE CONCEPT OF ACTION

To be a good draughtsman one must not copy the model but draw with concepts. One of the most important concepts of drawing is the concept of what we shall term "action." Drawing with the concept of action differentiates a drawing from one that is copied – for a copied drawing is dull, static and lifeless. That which is executed with the concept of action in mind produces a vital lifelike drawing and allows one to draw from memory and imagination, and that is what we should aspire to do. It would be impossible to make creative compositions if drawings were made by merely copying the model. Great drawing is produced with knowledge, skill, feeling, imagination and the concepts of growth and action.

WHAT IS MEANT BY THE TERM "ACTION"

It is the imbalance of the three major forms, the head, the cage and the pelvis which produces a flowing action. It is the turning and tilting of these forms to the left or right or the tipping of the forms frontwards or backwards. An action therefore is a movement of these forms in a certain manner.

If the model is perfectly balanced, say standing erect with equal weight on both legs, then there is no action to speak of. However, if there is even the slightest shift of weight, say to one leg, then the hip above that leg will rise and be higher than the other hip. The crotch point will shift off center and the angle of the shoulder line will be in opposition to the angle of the hip line. We now have what is called an "action" of the figure.

The easiest way to decide what the action of the model is is to first ask yourself "what is the model doing?" Then answer yourself. For instance say, "The model is standing on the left leg and leaning heavily on the right hand." The action in this case flows from the right hand up the arm and diagonally down the torso to the opposite left leg and foot. The action will flow to where the weight is.

The principles of the concept of action are not difficult to understand and will be fully explained and discussed. There is a problem, however, when working from the living model and that is after a few moments the model will shift or settle into a slightly different pose. The way to overcome this is to *anticipate* what will happen with the pose and *exaggerate* the action. For instance, if the model starts out with only a slight amount of weight on one leg, the model will lean more and more on that leg as time goes on. That hip then will rise, the crotch will

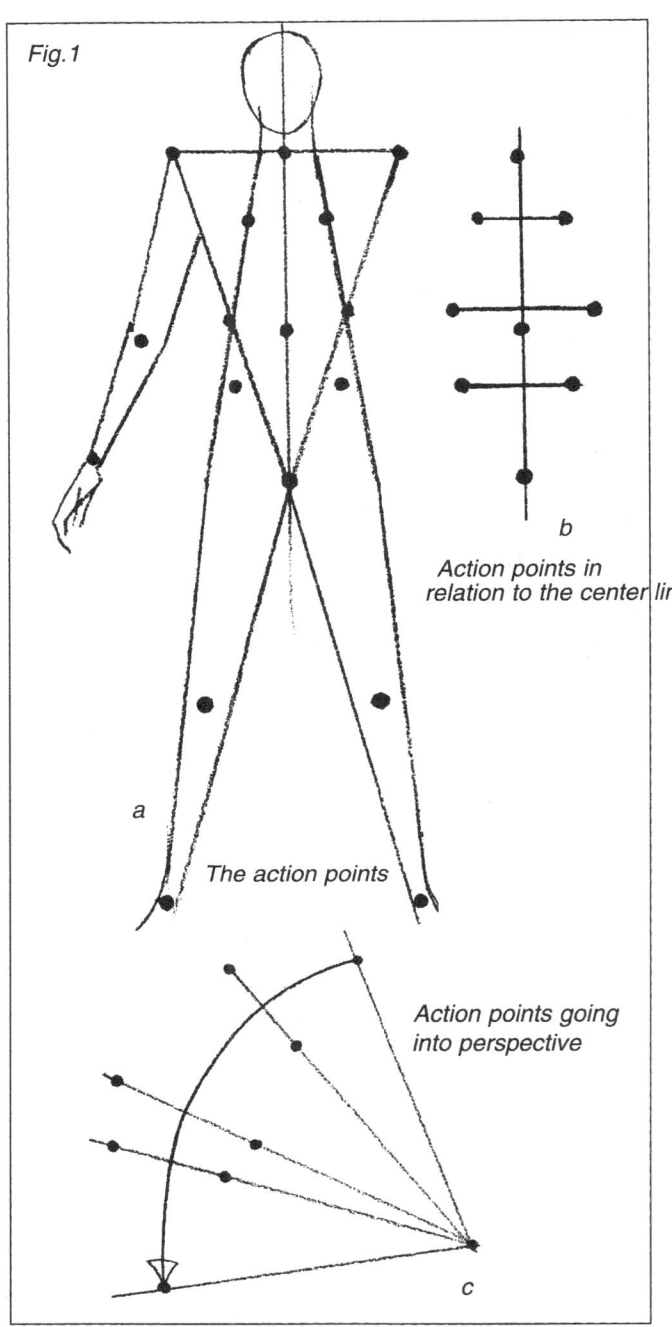

Fig.1

Action points in relation to the center line

b

The action points

a

Action points going into perspective

c

move over towards that leg and the opposite shoulder will rise. If you draw with this understanding the model will eventually fall into a pose that looks like what you're drawing and you won't be so concerned about the model moving. This anticipation of course requires much experience of drawing from the model. You must be patient and draw from the living model every chance you can get.

PROCEDURE

In order to obtain the correct action of the figure one always starts with the oval of the head and ascertains its angle. Draw a center line around this oval to the pit of the neck. This is where the sterno-mastoid muscles meet. Continue this line through the pit of the neck downwards through the center of the breasts to the navel and then onto the crotch point. This is the most important line of your drawing for if it goes in the wrong direction your drawing will be wrong. The chances are that you will not draw this center line correctly at first. Do not erase it but draw one or two more center lines using the first one for comparison. There are many times you will have to continue this center line past the crotch point down the inside of the leg to the bottom of the foot. One should always look for the longest lines to obtain the unity and action of the drawing.

The center line in profile will pass the same points as in the frontal view but will draw the profile of a particular torso. On the back view the center line will still be drawn around the skull to the seventh cervical vertebra and continue down the center of the spine to the crease of the buttocks.

The drawings on the following pages will explain the principles of action and are further elaborated upon in the chapter on Structure.

Fig. 1a. The black dots on the basic figure abstraction represent what are called "action points." These points are, starting at the top of the figure, at the widest points of the shoulders, the pit of the neck, the nipples of the breasts, the waist, the navel, the crests of the iliac, the crotch, the knees and the ankles. Action points are also shown at the elbow and wrist.

Fig. 1b. The action points shown in relationship to the center or action line. Note that the pit of the neck, the navel and the crotch point lie on this line. It is important to note that horizontal lines connecting the nipples of the breasts and the crests of the iliac are always at right angles to the center line.

Fig. 1c. An example showing the action points going into perspective when the action line is curved. Always keep this in mind when drawing figures in foreshortening and perspective.

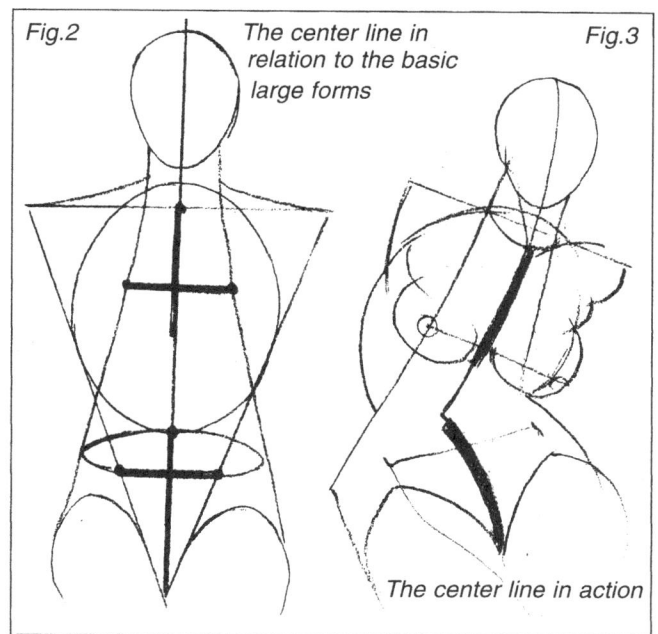

Fig. 2. A more concrete example of the figure showing the large forms of the head, the rib cage and the pelvic area. Notice the center line aligning the pit of the neck, navel and crotch and how the lines connecting the nipples of the breasts and crests of the iliac are at right angles to this line. The drawing, *Fig. 3.*, shows the same idea within a more complex pose.

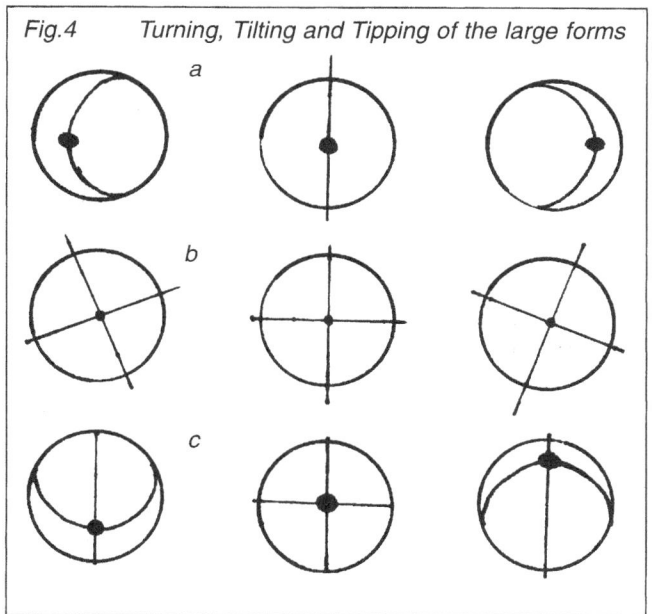

Figs. 4a.b.c. The circles can represent the head form, the rib cage form or the pelvic form. *Row a.* represents the form turning to the right and left. *Row b.* shows the form tilting to the right and left and *Row c.*, bottom, represents the form tipping forwards and backwards. These directional lines should be established first, that is before any details are drawn.

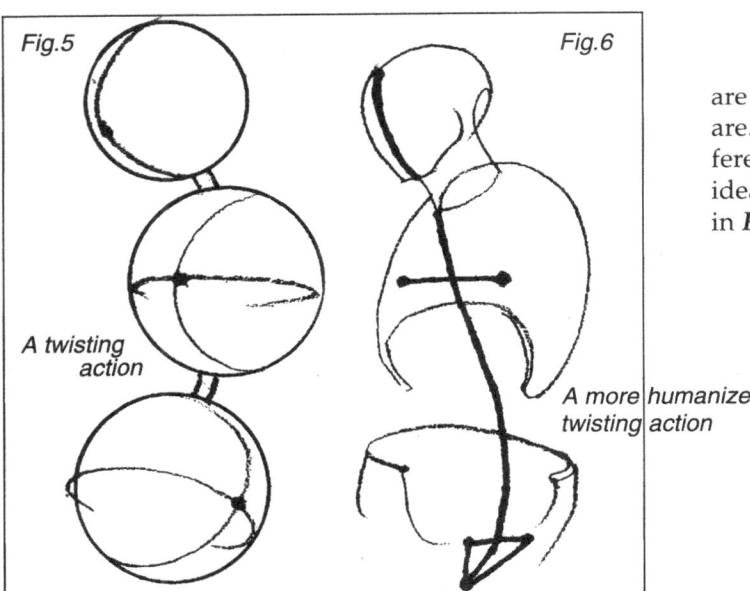

Fig. 5. The head, rib cage and pelvic forms are not always lined up exactly; in fact they seldom are. The three spheres shown here are each in a different position causing a twisting action. The same idea applied to simplified anatomical forms is shown in *Fig. 6.*

A twisting action

A more humanized twisting action

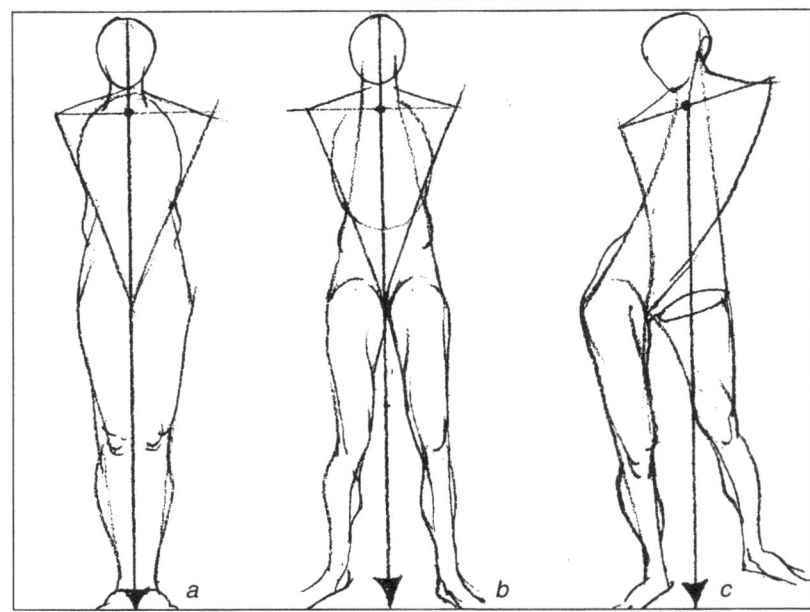

Center of Balance — Fig.8

The imbalance of forms

Figs. 7a.b. It is the imbalance of forms which produces a flowing action. Note how the large forms are in opposition to each other.

Fig. b. is a more humanized version of this idea.

Figs. 8a.b.c. The center of balance of the figure is estimated by dropping a perpendicular line from the pit of the neck. If the figure rests on one foot, then the shoulder on that side will be lower than the other; the center line will shift towards the ankle of that foot.

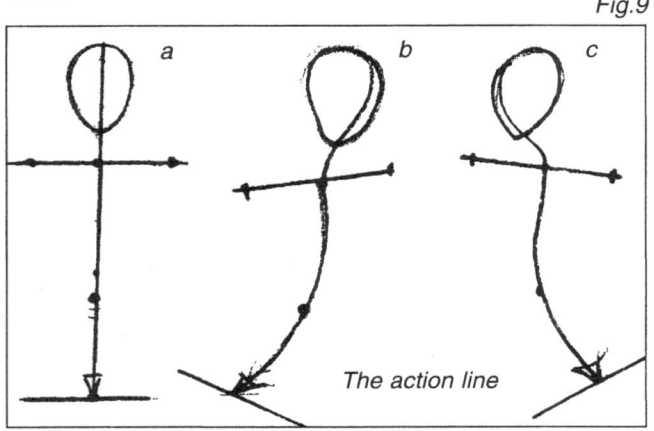

The action line

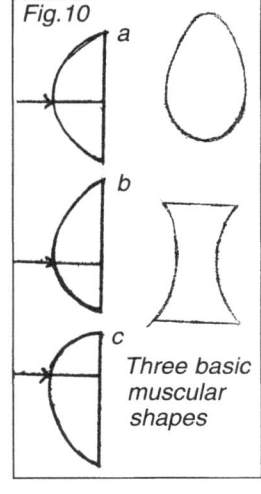

Three basic muscular shapes

Figs. 9a.b.c. The proper action of the figure is determined by the accurate placement of the center line which goes from the pit of the neck to the crotch.

Figs. 10a.b.c. Three examples showing, in a simplified way, the difference between the shapes of muscles. Top, *Fig. a.*, shows no action, *Fig. b.*, relaxed or hanging and *Fig. c.*, rigid and tense.

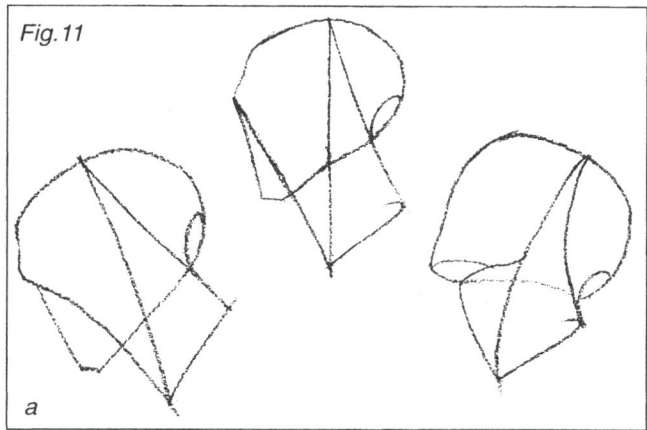

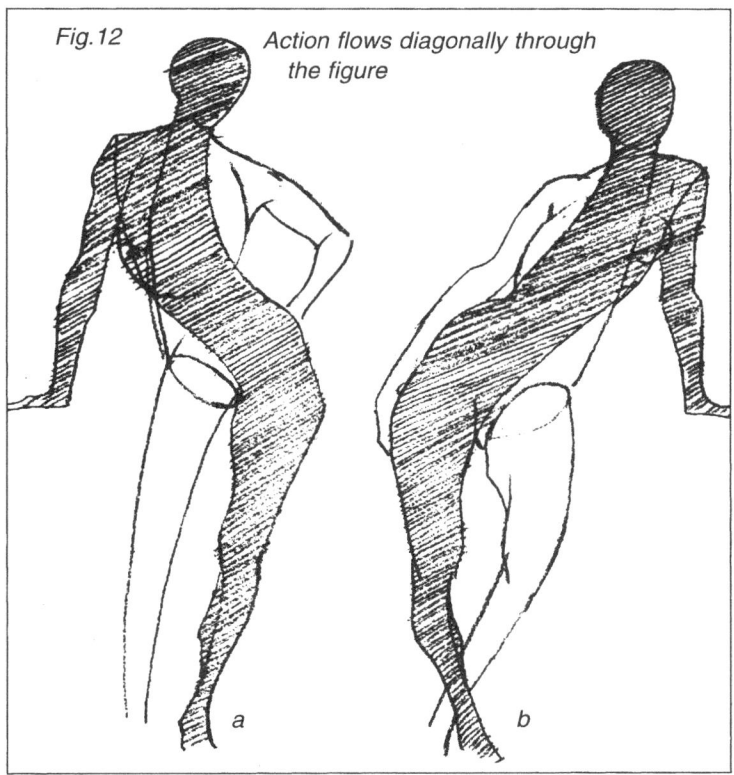

Figs. 11a.b. To determine the "action" of the head draw a line from the pit of the neck to a point on top of the skull which meets a line from the back of the neck. **Fig a.,** shows the head bending forward, upright and bending backwards. **Fig b.** shows the head tilting to the left, upright and tilting to the right. The direction of the center line is all important here.

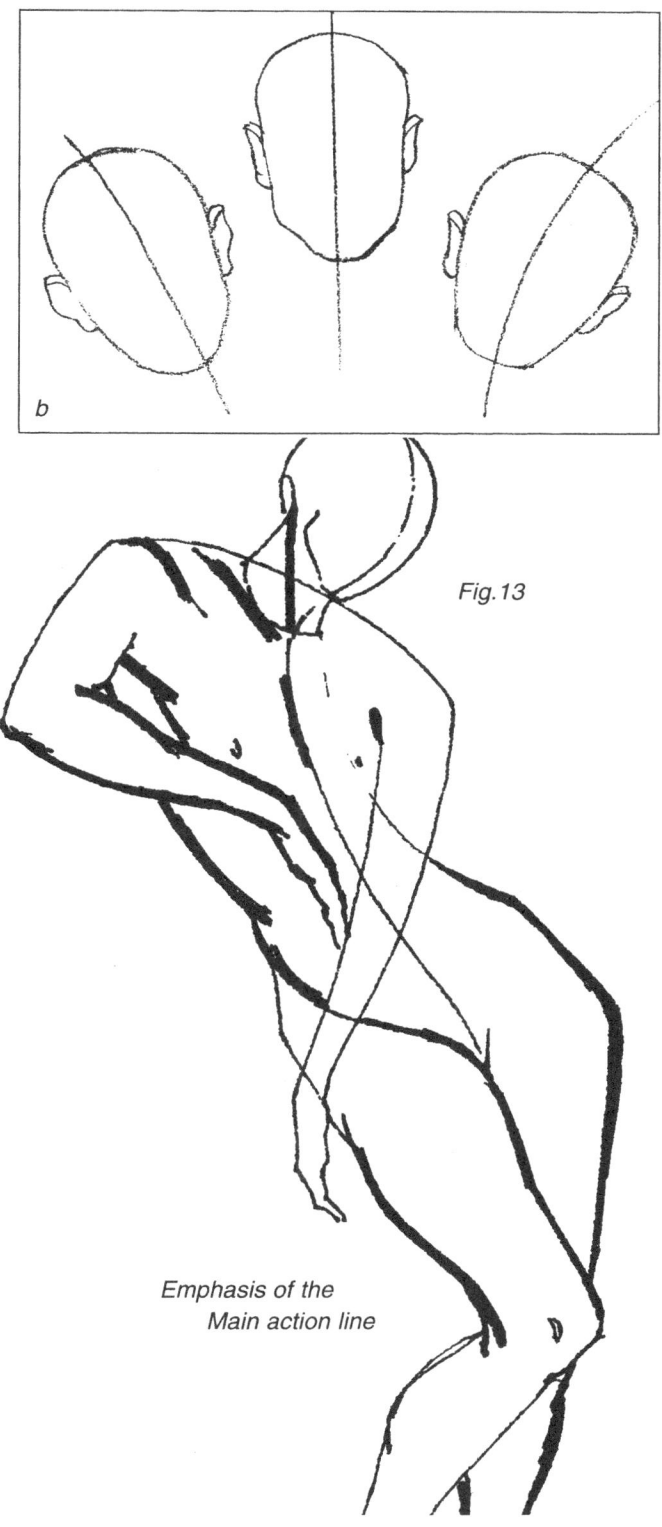

Figs. 12a.b. The shaded portions of the above drawings a. and b. show how the action of the body flows diagonally across the figure. When drawing the basic structure lines decide where the weight is and draw from the opposite side to that point.

Fig. 13. The main action relationship lines of the pose should be searched out and emphasized. Every pose has such lines. The bold lines on the above drawing emphasize the lines that stress the action of the figure. The lines of the left arm are deliberately underplayed for if they were given equal emphasis they would interfere with the flow of the action.

Figs. 14a.b. Two diagrams showing the counter balancing of the large masses of the upper torso and the leg.

Figs. 15a.b.c. Three contrasting drawings of the figure, one extremely strained and one extremely relaxed. In the drawing of the strained figure the muscular shapes are more pronounced, angular and bumpier. In the drawing of the relaxed figure the forms are simpler, rounder and more relaxed. They give the impression of gravity pulling on them.

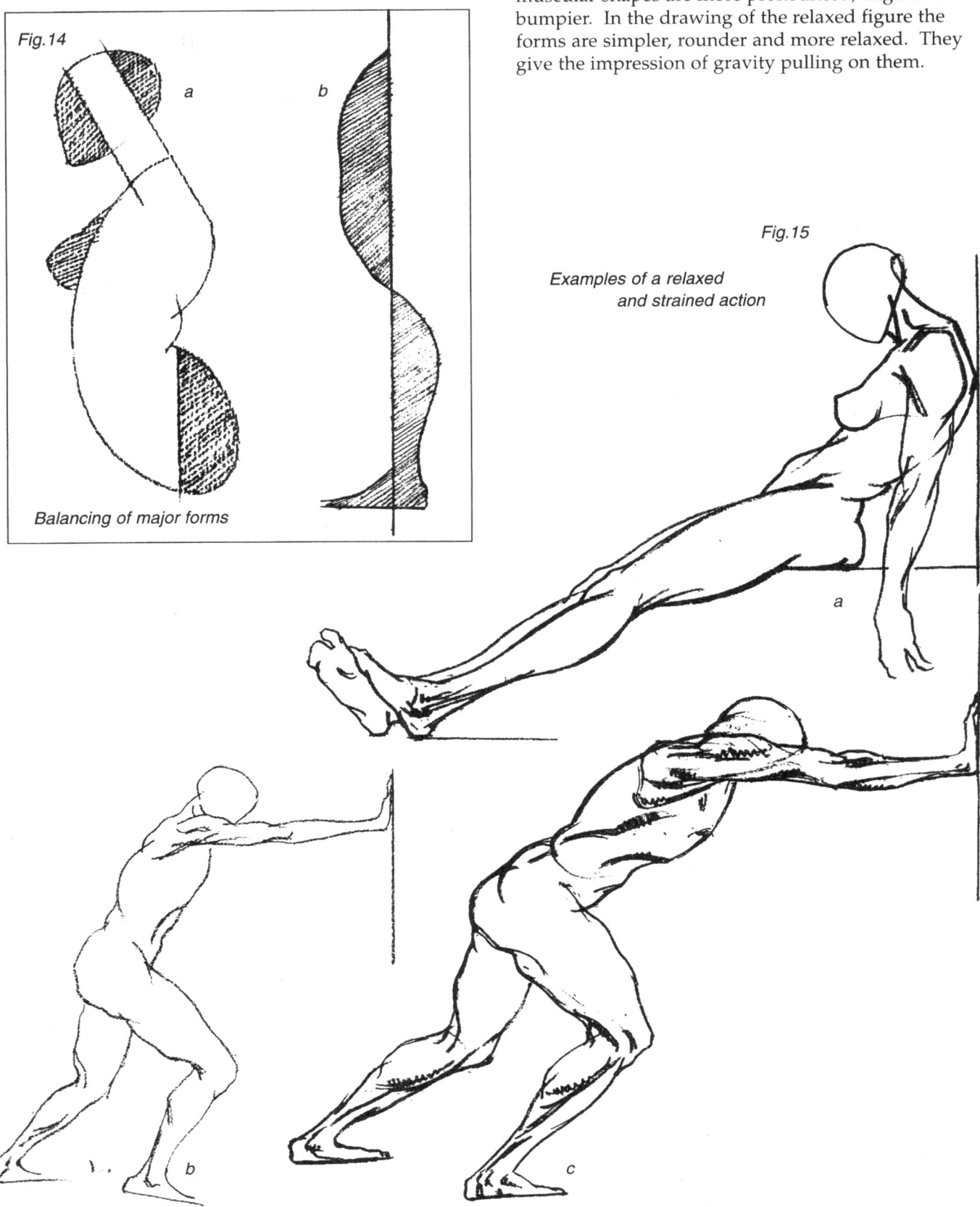

Fig.14

a

b

Balancing of major forms

Fig.15

Examples of a relaxed and strained action

a

b

c

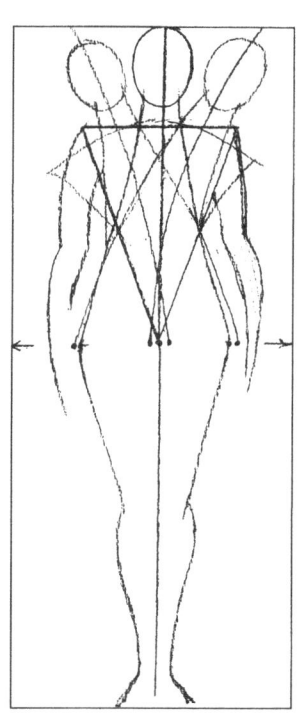

The static frontal showing shifting of crotch and hip points, tilting to the left and tilting to the right

Fig.16

Figs. 16a.b.c. The following drawings will show the shift of the crotch point and the hips when the body tilts to the right or left as long as the feet stay together. In this case the shaded area shows the basic static frontal view.

Fig. b. The shaded portion shows the figure tilting to the right. The crotch point and hip move to the left.

Fig. c. The shaded portion shows the figure tilting to the left. The crotch point and hip move to the right.

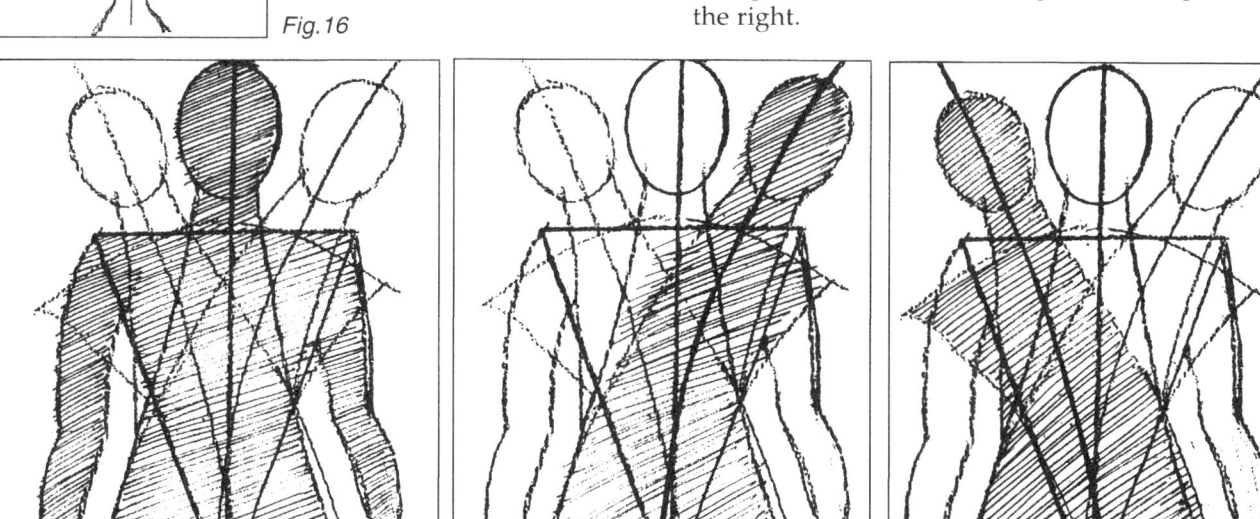

a

b

c

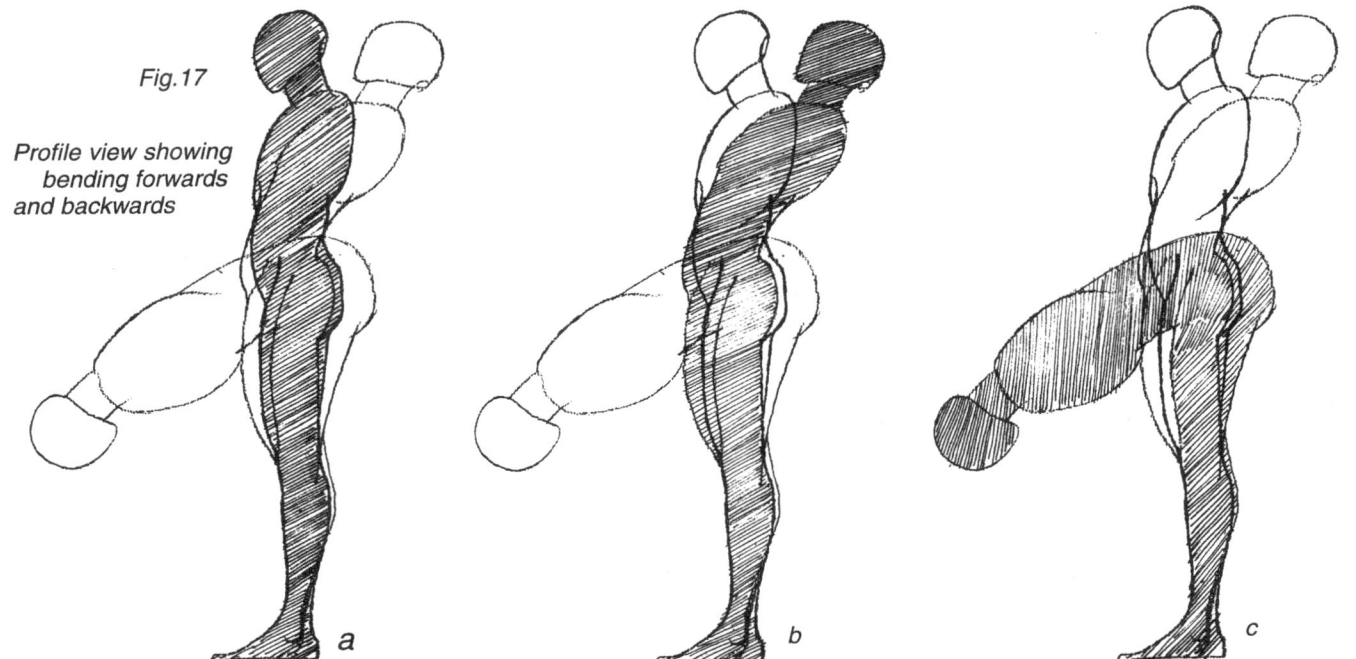

Fig.17

Profile view showing bending forwards and backwards

a

b

c

Fig. 17a. Profile, bending forwards and backwards. The heavily outlined figure, shown shaded is in upright profile view. Notice that the foot and lower leg and foot are stationary.

Fig. b. The profile figure bending backwards. Although the lower leg and foot stay the same the abdomen and buttocks project forward.

Fig. c. The shaded portion shows the profile figure bending forward. Again, the foot remains where it was but the buttocks and upper leg move backwards.

Figs. 18a.b.c.d.e.f.g.h.i.j.k.l. The drawings on this and the following pages show how the approximate positions of the limbs can be arrived at. The black dots within the limbs represent what is called a "pivot point." Place the point of the compass on a pivot point and the pencil end of the compass at the bottom of the foot or the tips of the fingers. Now swing the compass in whatever direction you wish, creating an arc. The limb can be drawn to a position anywhere on the arc.

These measurements are not to be taken as a thousand percent accurate as the proportions will have to be varied due to, among other things, the position of the limb. For instance, in sculpture, if one leg is firmly planted on the ground and the other high in the air, the raised one would have to be made a little fatter and longer than what one would normally think. This is due to the fact that the light bending around it as well as the air surrounding it will make it look smaller in size. Likewise, in a painting, many things have to be altered for compositional purposes.

The shaded portions of the drawings, **Figs. 18a.b.c.d.e.f.g.h.i.j.k.l.** show a standing figure in profile with a full leg swinging forwards and backwards, raised with the lower leg moving forwards and backwards, and the lower limb swinging backwards and upwards.

Showing how to arrive at the many different positions of the legs

Fig.18

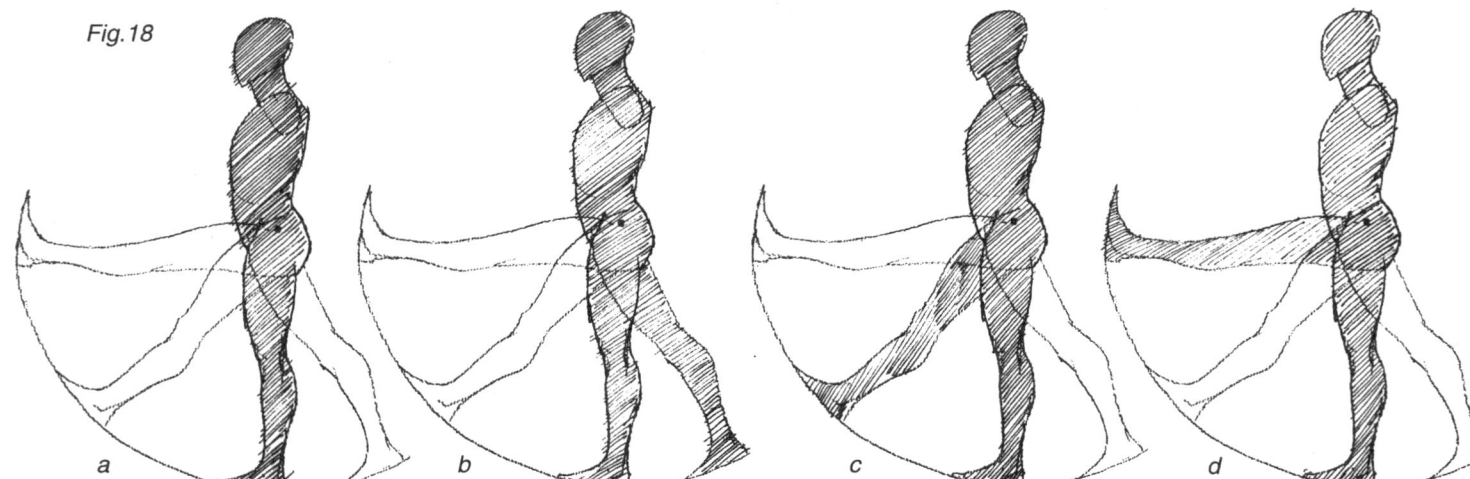

a

b

c

d

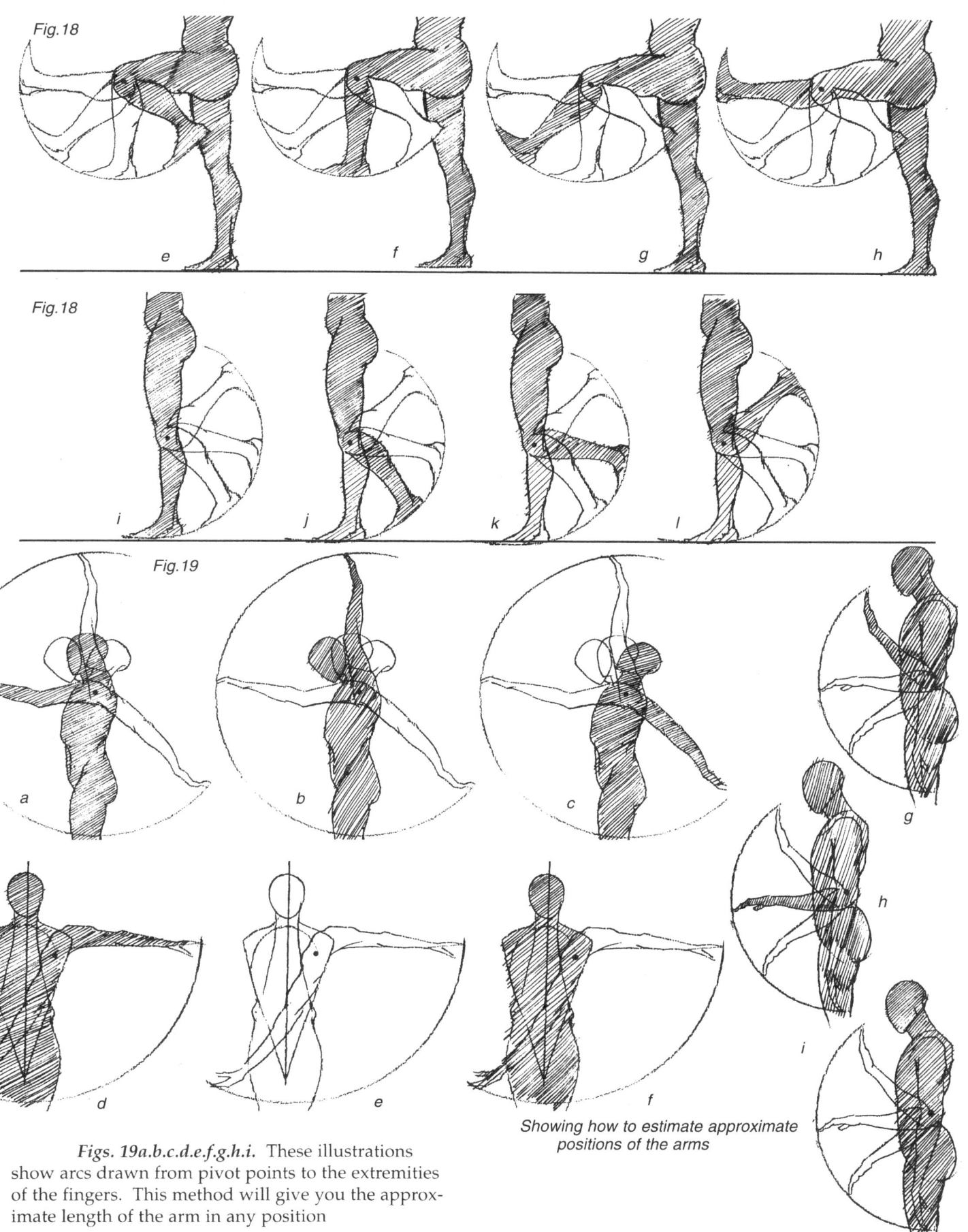

Fig.18

Fig.18

e   f   g   h

i   j   k   l

Fig.19

a   b   c

d   e   f

g

h

i

Showing how to estimate approximate positions of the arms

Figs. 19a.b.c.d.e.f.g.h.i. These illustrations show arcs drawn from pivot points to the extremities of the fingers. This method will give you the approximate length of the arm in any position

A PORTFOLIO OF DRAWINGS
OF THE FIGURE IN ACTION

The drawings on the following pages are drawings that stress the action of the figure made in accordance with the principles described and explained in the previous chapters. They have been made from memory, imagination and from life. Some took only a few seconds and some a few minutes. The shorter the time you have to make a drawing the more quickly you get down the line or lines that most completely express the action. *Actually, every drawing you do, no matter how long you intend to work on it, should be started quickly.*

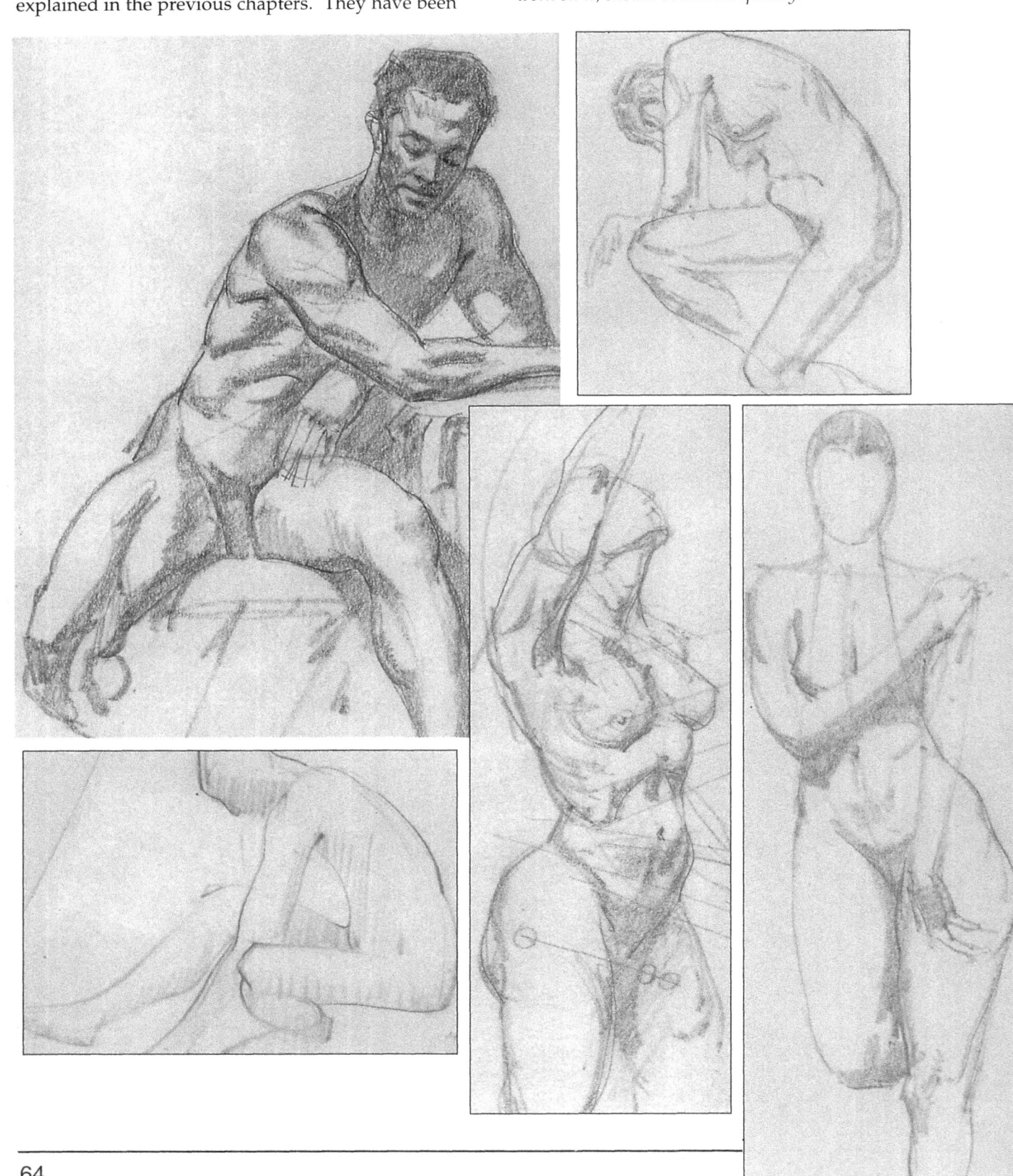

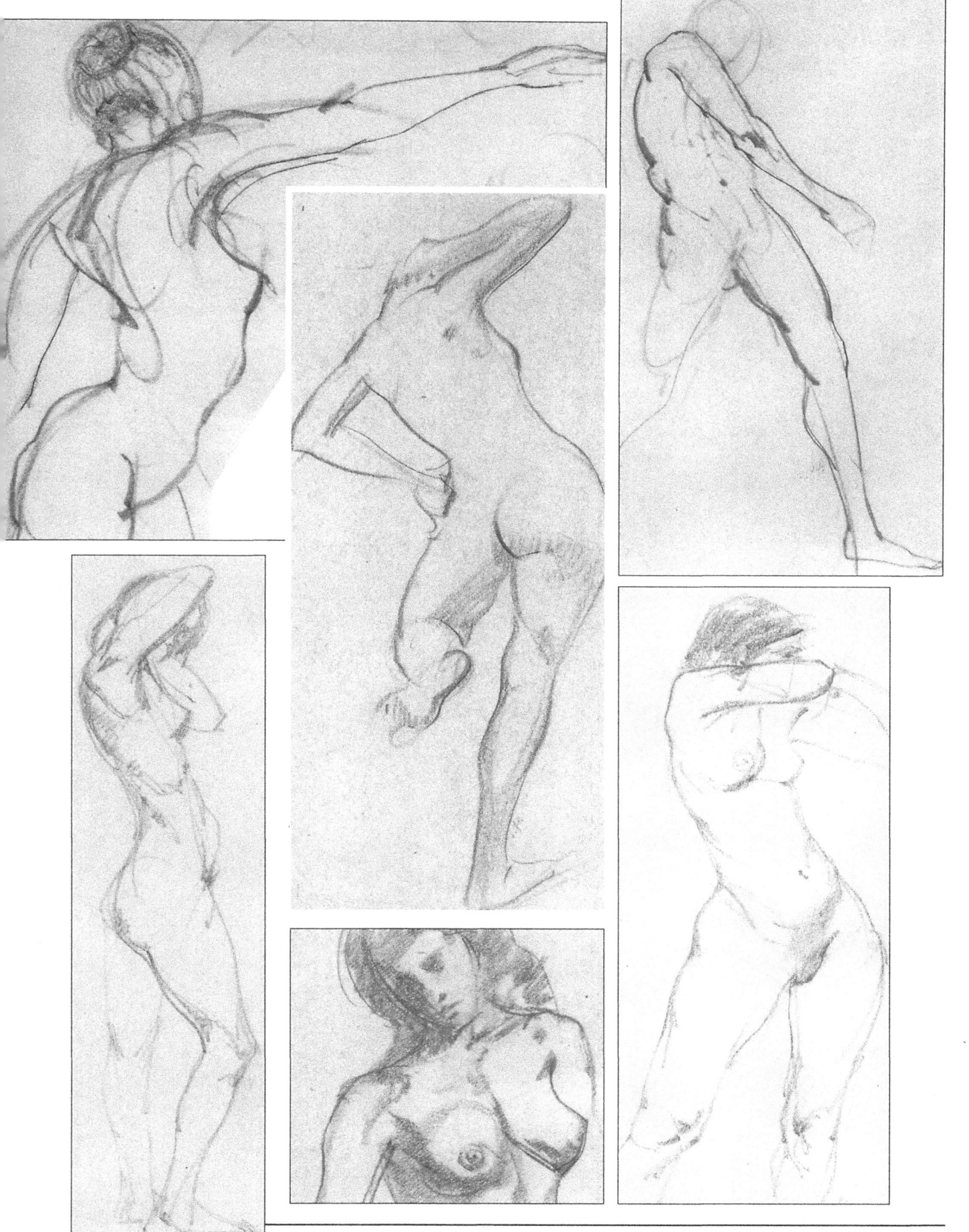

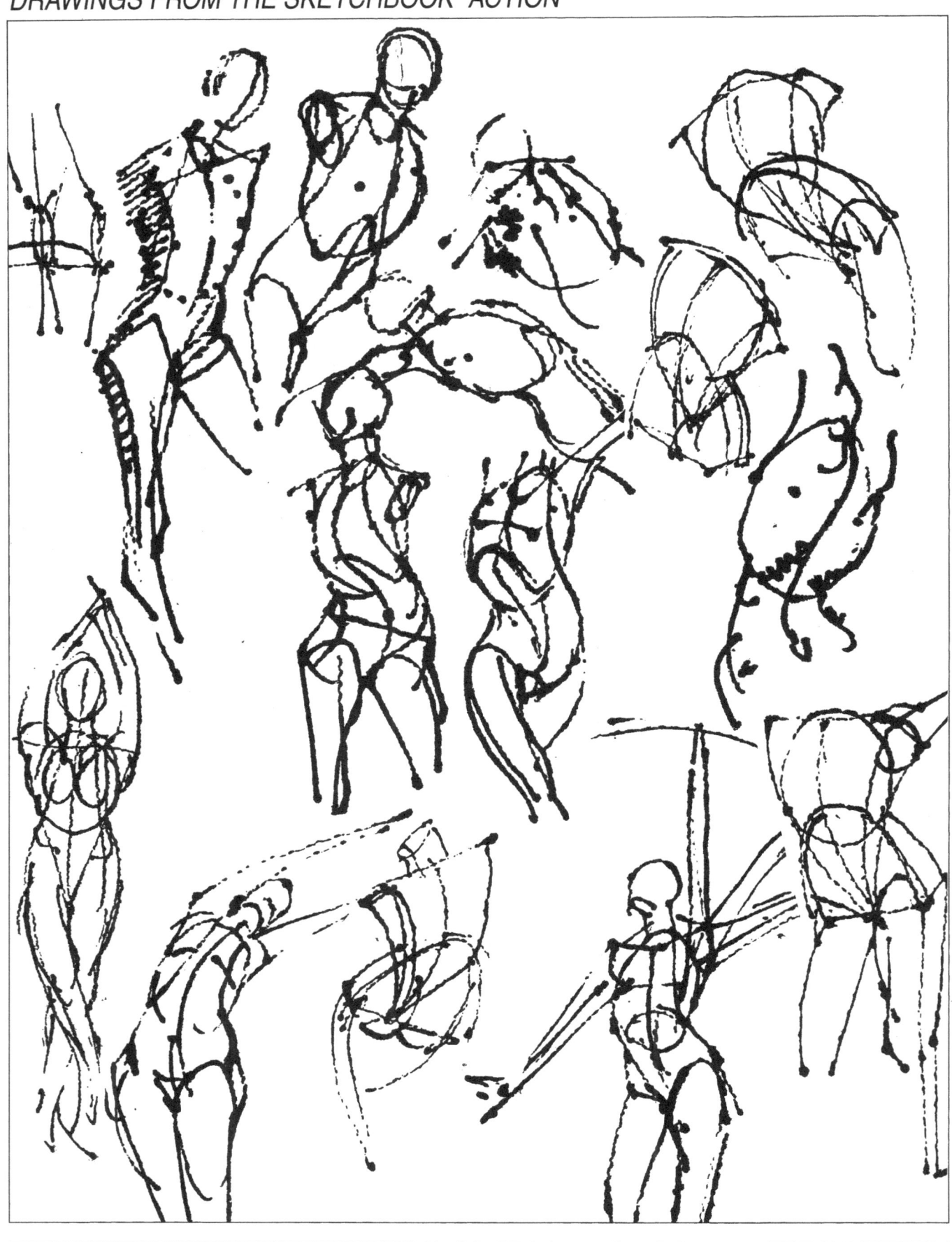

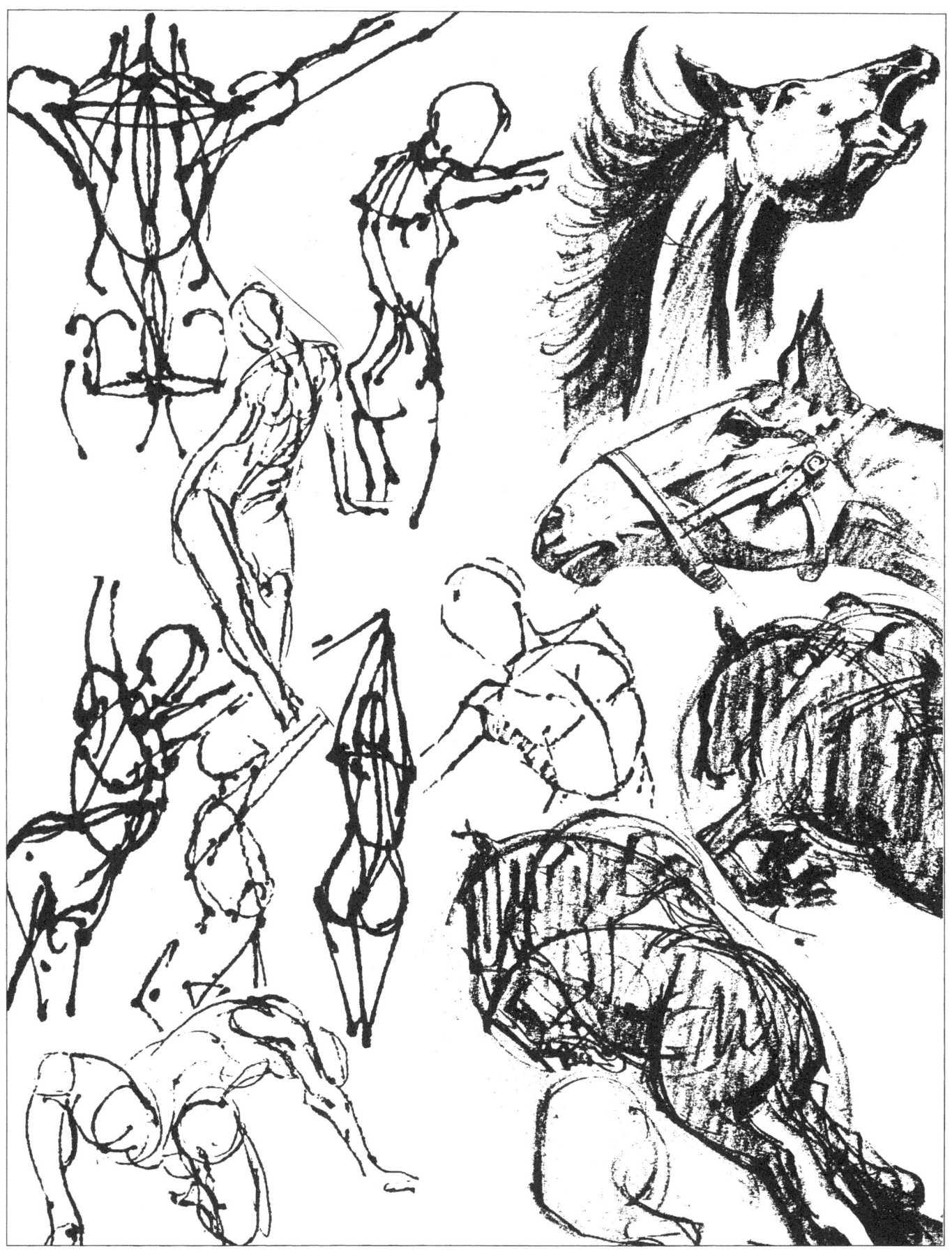

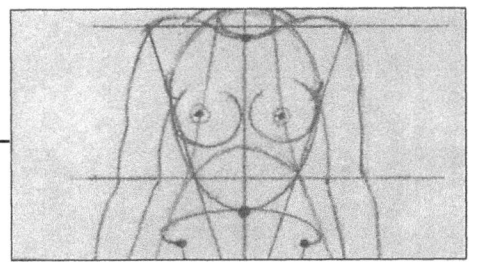

CHAPTER TEN

BASIC STRUCTURE OF THE FIGURE

We now come to the most important part of the system of "structure," that is its use in the drawing of the figure. At this point I must digress a bit.

The unified system of drawing, painting and "picture making" with the use of structure was formulated and taught by Mr. Frank J. Reilly for over thirty years at the Art Students League of New York and elsewhere. He evolved it from many sources as well as from his own investigations and efforts. After his untimely death in 1967 I assumed teaching his ideas and methods at his school which was at Steinway Hall and at the Art Students League. At this point in time I have been teaching for thirty years. Therefore what you see being taught on these pages has been continuously taught for almost sixty years.

In his early years of teaching Mr. Reilly did not have his material and lectures as well organized as he did later on. Being extremely busy with so many students he would give lectures at different intervals for different lengths of time. Consequently, if you missed a session in which a three hour lecture was given on a certain topic, you missed quite a lot. You had to study with him steadily for at least three years before things "came together" in your mind. Since few students studied so intently, few could

have a complete grasp of Mr. Reilly's ideas, although many did remarkably well as illustrators, portrait painters and fine artists. I could list at least fifty names of students who I have personally known who became some of the nation's top illustrators, painters and landscape artists. There are of course many, many others.

Students left the class and went out to the outside world armed with large notebooks filled with notes concerning figure drawing, landscape, drapery, perspective, etc., etc. Unfortunately no one had complete notes and everyone wished Mr. Reilly would write a book or books. But it never happened and with his death in 1967 all hope was lost. Over the years dribs and drabs of Mr. Reilly's teaching leaked out in various publications. Unfortunately these writings were in no way complete or accurate, leading to a great disservice to Mr. Reilly.

Only one who studied with Mr. Reilly for at least four years and knew him personally so as to fully understand his thinking and ideas, and most importantly taught with these ideas, could be truly qualified to put together a definitive work. I believe in all modesty, that this book is as close to the teaching and thinking processes of Mr. Reilly as you will ever get. Over the years I have organized the material, corrected it, embellished and added to it and most of all taught it – as I still do.

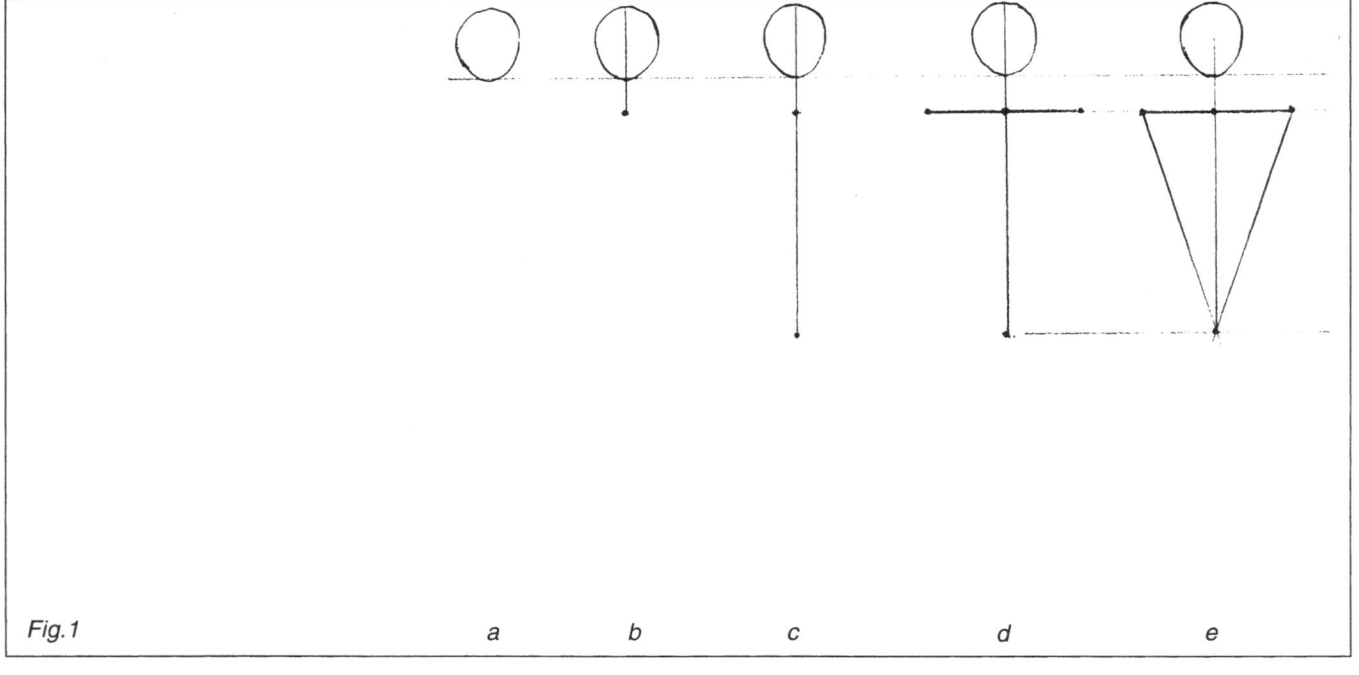

Fig. 1   a   b   c   d   e

Teaching is necessary to prove things out. You learn what is important and what is not important. You learn all the pitfalls that the student faces. You learn the order in which something is to be taught, for learning is more easily accomplished when things are taught in a certain order.

You must build on a firm foundation to obtain good results – so it is with building a home and so it is with learning how to draw and paint.

These instructions, drawings and diagrams are your foundation. They will guide you towards good work, towards creativeness – towards your own visual, graphic explanation of nature.

BASIC STRUCTURE OF THE FIGURE, FRONT AND BACK

Although one cannot proceed exactly the same way in every instance there is a logical way to approach drawing the figure from the standpoint of "structure." The following series of drawings show the logical sequence of figure construction starting with a few simple lines to which are added the large main forms. Remember we are to always work from the big to the small and from the small to the smaller.

These structure lines should be thoroughly learned. They are of extreme importance for as we shall see all the forms and planes of the body which we shall cover later depend on and are directly related to these basic structure lines. Following is an example of the procedure to follow and commit to memory.

Fig. 1a. We start with the head shape, a simple oval.

Fig. b. A center line is drawn down the center of the oval to the pit of the neck.

Fig. c. The center line is continued from the pit of the neck to the crotch point.

Fig. d. A shoulder axis line is drawn through the pit of the neck to the widest points of the shoulders.

Fig. e. Connect the widest points of the shoulders with lines to the crotch point forming an inverted triangle.

Fig. f. Draw an axis line through the crotch point to the widest points of the hips. The crotch and the widest points of the hips are on this line.

Fig. g. Now draw lines from beneath the ears down the neck to the widest points of the hips. You have now established the basic large form of the torso. At this stage you may also draw the structural lines of the legs which are simply two tapering lines from the widest points, where the leg begins, to the narrowest points, the width of the ankle. It seems easier, and works better, if when drawing a leg to start with the inside line of the leg. This line starts at the crotch point and goes to the inside of the ankle. Next draw a line from the widest point of the hip to the outer point of the width of the ankle. Continue these two lines to anywhere they may relate on the feet.

Fig. h. The shape of the neck hole and rib cage form are added. *Note how the rib cage form stays within the confines of the inverted triangle and connects to the back of the neck hole.* The rib cage form will always connect to the back of the neck hole no matter what position the person is in. This form can sometimes extend a little outside the triangle but not by much. It should never be such a smallish oval shape that it doesn't touch the lines of the inverted triangle. At

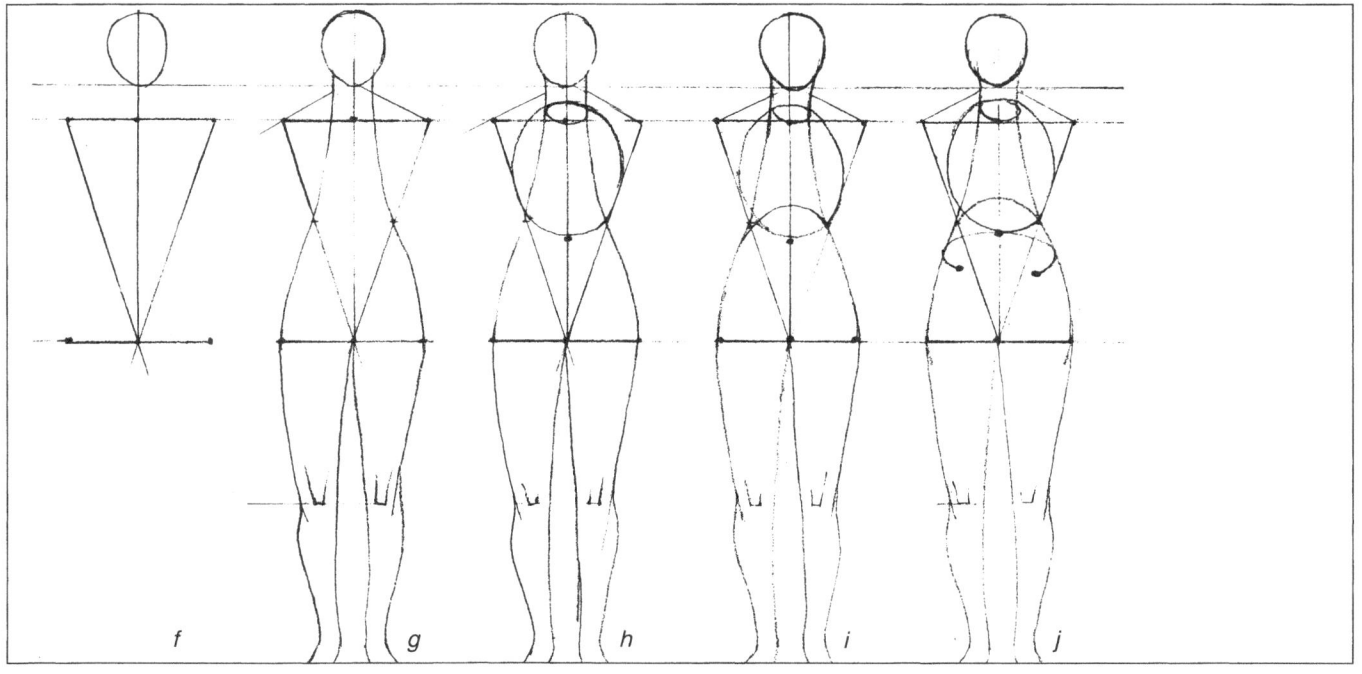

f   g   h   i   j

the bottom of the rib cage form will be the position of the navel in the male, a little lower in the female.

Fig. i. Connect the widest points of the hips with an arching line. This creates the combined pelvic abdominal form which overlaps the rib cage form. These combined forms make the torso.

Fig. j. Using the navel as a starting point draw an incomplete semicircle. This semicircle describes, in a simplified manner, the top of the pelvis and ends at the anterior superior iliac spine. It is at this point that the sartorius muscle originates.

Fig. k. The breast forms are added. Think of them as originating from the widest points of the shoulders heading towards the center line. At this point one draws the leg forms inserting into the torso.

Fig. l. Draw the sartorius muscles from the points on the iliac to the insides of the knee forms.

Fig. m. The abdominal form is now added. Notice how it stays within the confines of the inverted triangle. Now continue the line of the sartorius muscle around the inside of the knee form downward following the curve of the shinbone to the ankle and then to the bottom of the foot. From the bottom of the inner ankle arc a line to the outer ankle which draws the instep of the foot. Remember the inner ankle is always higher than the outer ankle. The sterno-mastoid muscles are added within the neck form.

Fig. n. The forms of the arms are added completing the basic figure.

Fig. o. This drawing shows the rear or back view of the basic figure. The seventh cervical vertebra of the neck is the equivalent of the pit of the neck in the front view. Note the triangular shapes of the scapulae hanging on a curved line, which goes to the widest points of the shoulders, and the way the neck muscles insert into the base of the skull. *Note also that the line at the bottom of the buttock forms is below the crotch point of the front.*

The combination of the width of the shoulders together with the width of the hips along with the distance from the pit of the neck to the crotch determines the particular individual. There are innumerable combinations of these measurements and probably no two people have exactly the same ones.

This is one of the first things you must get correct in your drawing, for that will give you the individual person. If you miss these ratios you miss the individual and everything else you draw will be wrong, for the drawing is based on a wrong foundation. The following drawings show some of the basic combinations. Practice making dozens of similar drawings to familiarize yourself with the idea.

Fig. 2a. Narrow shoulders, wide hips. *Fig. b.* Wide shoulders, narrow hips. *Fig. c.* Wide shoulders, wide hips. *Fig. d.* Wide shoulders, average hips. *Fig. e.* Wide shoulders, bony, box-like hip shape. *Fig. f.* The crotch point can be lower or higher than the average. This drawing shows a higher than average crotch point, and an average and lower than average crotch point. *Fig. g.* shows variations of the width of the shoulders. The outer points designate wider than average shoulders, the middle points average width and the inner points designate narrower than average shoulders. The combinations of *Figs. 2f. and g.* would cover the dimensions of almost all the torsos of humanity as regards shoulder width and length of the crotch from the pit of the neck.

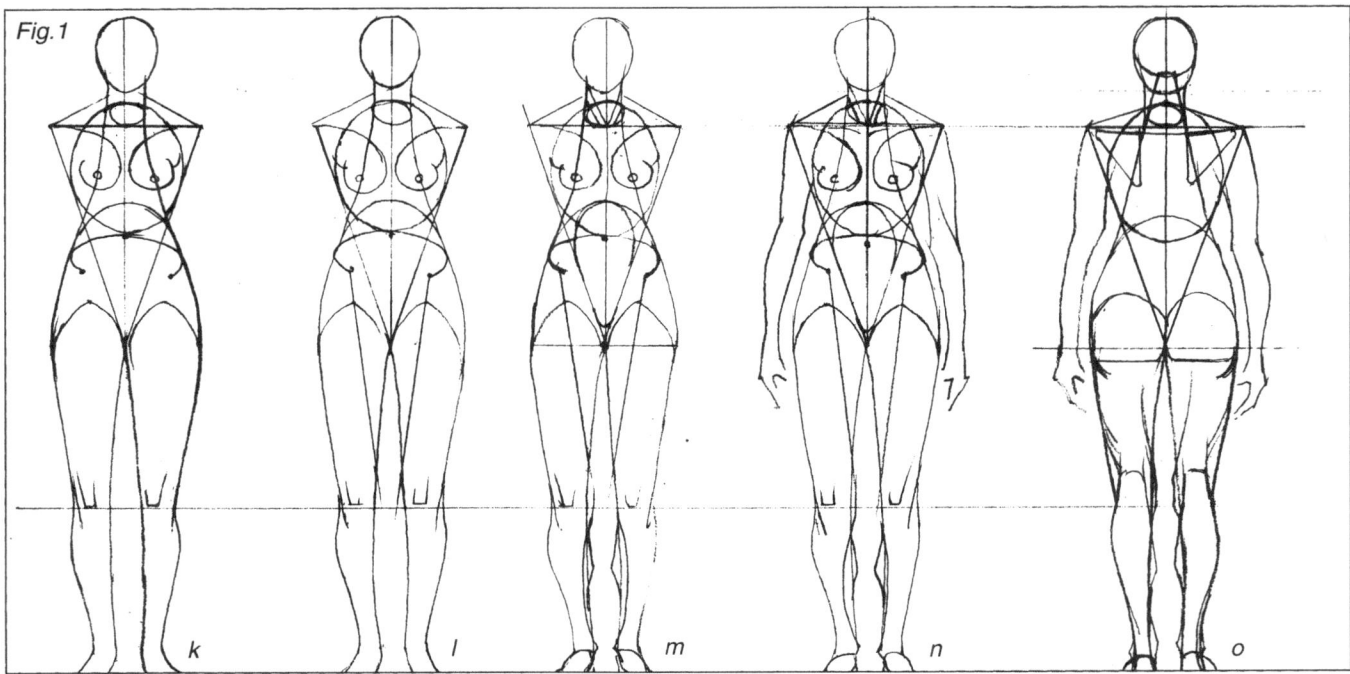

Fig. 1

k   l   m   n   o

Fig.2

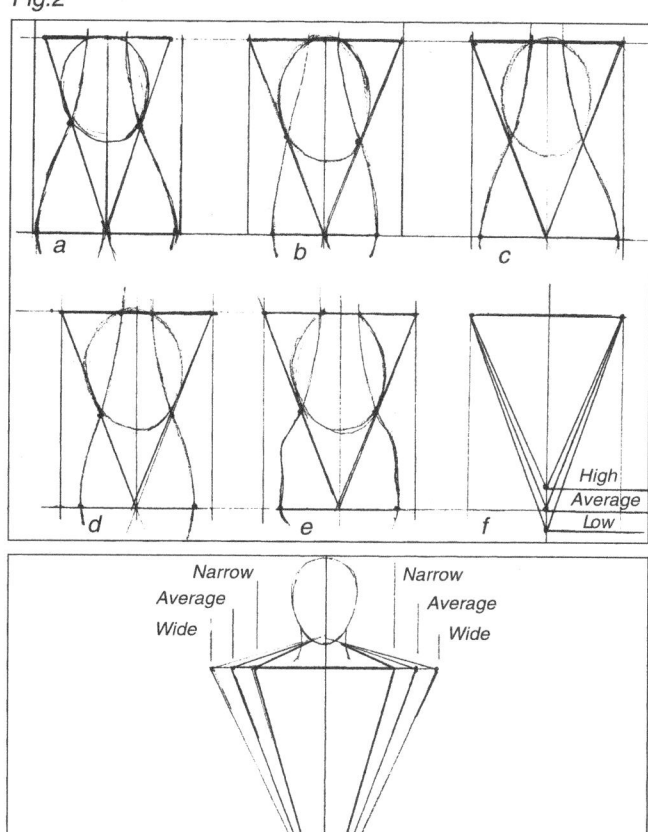

a   b   c

d   e   f

High
Average
Low

Narrow   Narrow
Average   Average
Wide   Wide

g

BASIC STRUCTURE OF THE FIGURE, PROFILE

The five drawings shown explain the use of structure lines in drawing the profile view. In the profile view the shape of the head is very important as it determines the width of the neck which in turn determines how the rib cage attaches to it. It also determines one of the points of balance, the pit of the neck.

After the shape of the skull is determined one takes a looping line off the base of the back of the skull and ends it at the seventh cervical vertebra. This line also creates an underplane of the skull and is *always* shorter than the line of the front of the neck which ends at the pit of the neck. A perpendicular line drawn through the center of the skull, in front of the ear, through the pit of the neck and on to the front of the ankle determines the center of balance in profile. By drawing an oval connecting the front and the back of the lines of the neck you complete the neck form. The rib cage form will attach to the oval of this neck form.

Fig. 3a. Draw an accurate shape of the skull, although highly simplified. Next drop a vertical which is halfway within the skull and at the beginning of the ear. This line will pass through the pit of the neck and terminate in front of the ankle. Mark off your proportions on this line – in this case the figure is eight heads in height. The center line still begins at the pit of the neck but now it *draws the contour of the individual* as it ends at the crotch point.

Fig. b. The neck hole, rib cage and combined pelvic, abdominal and buttocks forms are added.

Fig. c. The leg must be properly related to the upper torso. To accomplish this one always takes a line from the *back of the rib cage form* across to the iliac crest thence out to the front of the leg making tangent with the line of balance. The back of the leg is now added by looping a line from the bottom of the buttocks down to the width of the back of the ankle form.

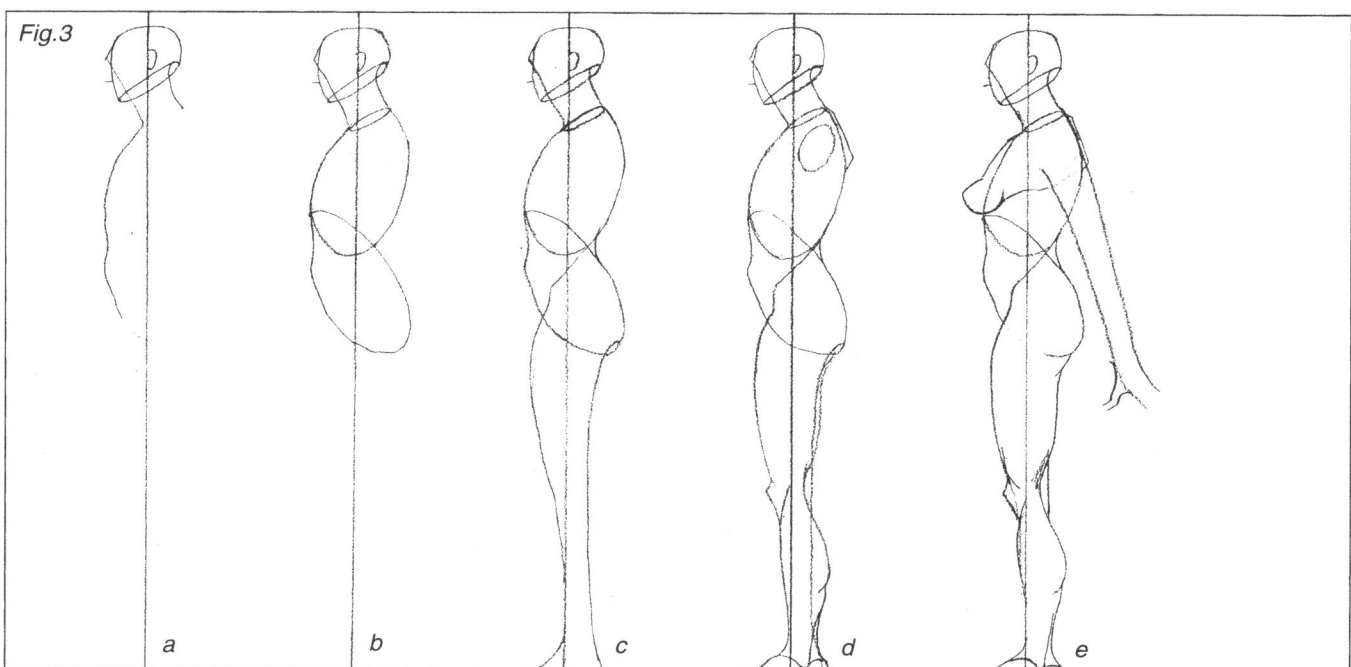

Fig.3

a   b   c   d   e

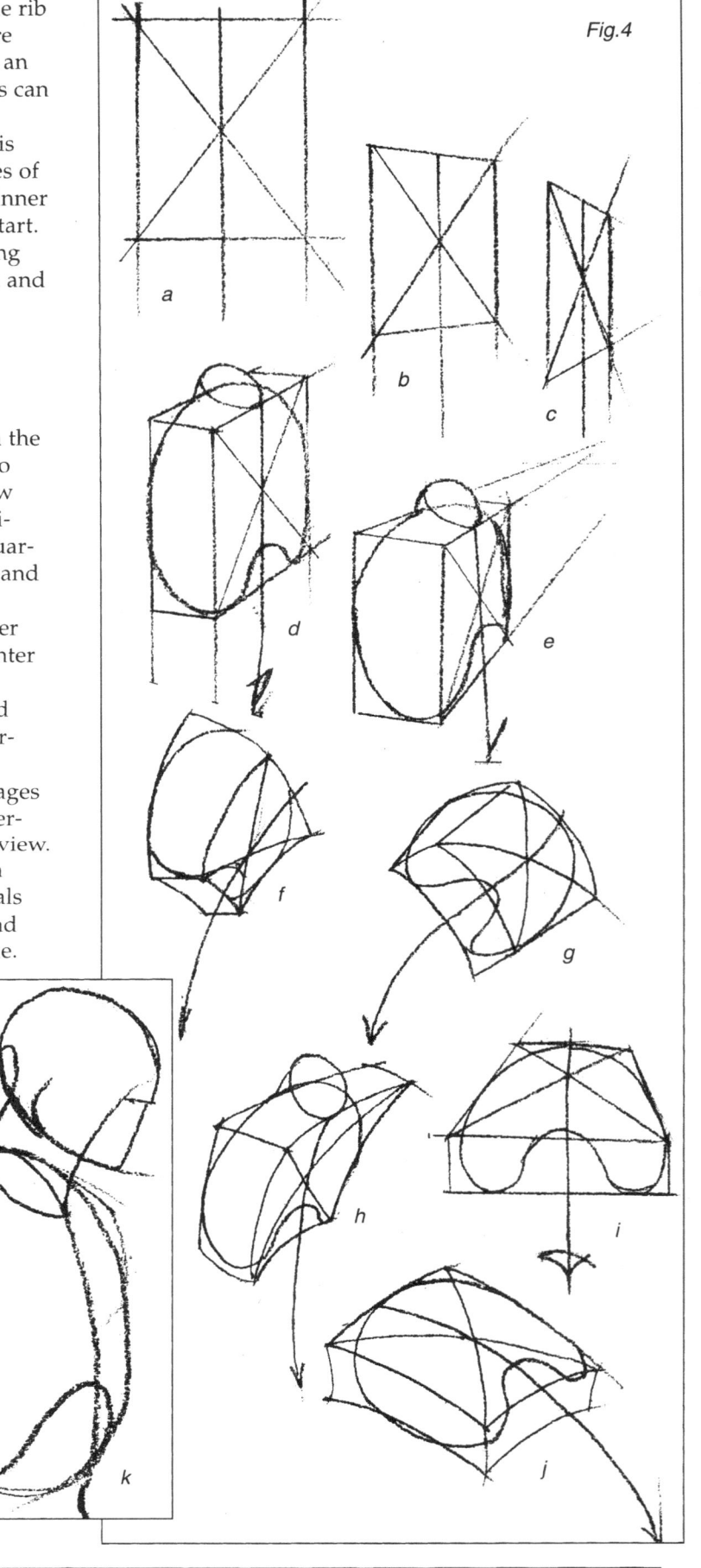

Fig. 4

Fig. d. A flat scapula form is added to the rib cage form. The large forms of the leg and foot are added to the basic structure lines. Shown also is an "arm hole" from which an arm of many positions can be drawn.

Fig. e. The addition of a breast and arm is added. In perfect profile the inner and outer lines of the arm will visually line up with the outer and inner lines of the neck. At least this is a good way to start. The bottom line of the breast should have a feeling that it goes around the rib cage towards the back and the bottom of the scapula.

BASIC STRUCTURE OF THE FIGURE, THE THREE-QUARTER VIEW

Most of the figures you draw will be in the three-quarter position. It is essential, therefore, to understand how to use the structure lines to draw these many seemingly complex and difficult positions. Basically the structure lines of the three-quarter view positions are a combination of the front and side views.

The key to drawing a correct three-quarter view depends on the proper placement of the center line and the correct shape of the rib cage form. Because this rib cage form is basically egg shaped students have difficulty putting it into proper perspective.

The drawings shown on the following pages help explain how one puts this form in correct perspective, essential for drawing the three-quarter view.

Fig. 4a. A rectangular shape represents a front view of the chest area. By drawing diagonals from corner to corner you find its center point and through this center point you draw the center line.

Fig. b. and c. As the rectangle goes into perspective the center line moves, its position still determined by drawing diagonals.

Figs. d. and e. Sides of various widths are added, making a box-like shape. This box is now put into perspective and a center line drawn in the usual way. The center line gives you the pit of the neck where you may draw the neck hole. The rib cage form is now drawn to fill up the box-like shape.

Figs. f.g.h.i. and j. These drawings show how the many different positions of the rib cage form may be drawn.

Fig. k. The start of a drawing of a figure in three-quarter view using the principles explained and shown.

Figs. 5a.b.c. These drawings help explain the position of the center line. In the back view, Fig. a., the center line extends from the seventh cervical vertebra to the center of the buttocks. Drawing b. shows an arching center line connecting the rib cage form with the pelvic form.

Fig. c. The center line of the figure can be thought of as existing in three different positions. First on the front of the figure, second as running through the center of the entire torso and third on the back starting at the seventh cervical vertebra. If you imagine this drawing turned towards you so it is all frontal all three center lines would line up and appear as one.

METHOD OF CONSTRUCTION

The five following steps explain how to draw the figure in three-quarter view. They should be followed as much as is possible, in almost all cases, in the order shown.

Fig. 6a. One starts with a correct skull shape in its approximate position. Next draw a center line around the skull and continue it to the pit of the neck. Draw lines to represent the front and the back of the neck and connect them with an oval. This completes the neck form. Note how the back of the neck is shorter than the front of the neck. This is always the case. Continue the center line through the pit of the neck, through the navel, to the crotch.

Fig. b. Here you will have to do some visual estimating. First, estimate how far the outside edge of the rib cage form is from the center line and place a dot. The next dot should be placed at the point where the flatness of the front plane ends and the side of the rib cage begins. This is usually at the point of the nipple of the pectoral muscle. Last, place a dot at the outer edge of the rib cage form, the back.

Fig.5

Fig. c. Connect the outside points with an oval going to the back of the base of the neck hole. The rib cage form is now complete. Draw a line through the base of the neck hole to the widest points of the shoulders.

Fig. d. This drawing shows lines drawn from the widest points of the shoulders to the crotch. The line from the point of the left shoulder will pass through the point of the nipple of the pectoral. The line from the shoulder on the right will pass through the outer point of the rib cage form. You may want to draw the shape of the bottom of the rib cage now. The next step is to drop a line from below the ear through the point on the pectoral to a point which is at the widest point of the widest part of the front of the leg. From this point extend a line to what you feel is the proper width of the side of the leg and place another point. A line is now drawn from the neck, or a place on the neck form, to this point, thereby making the side of the torso.

Fig. e. You are now ready to complete the figure. Add the arm holes and shoulder forms. Draw a semicircle, which represents the top of the pelvis, to terminate at points which are on the lines

Fig.6

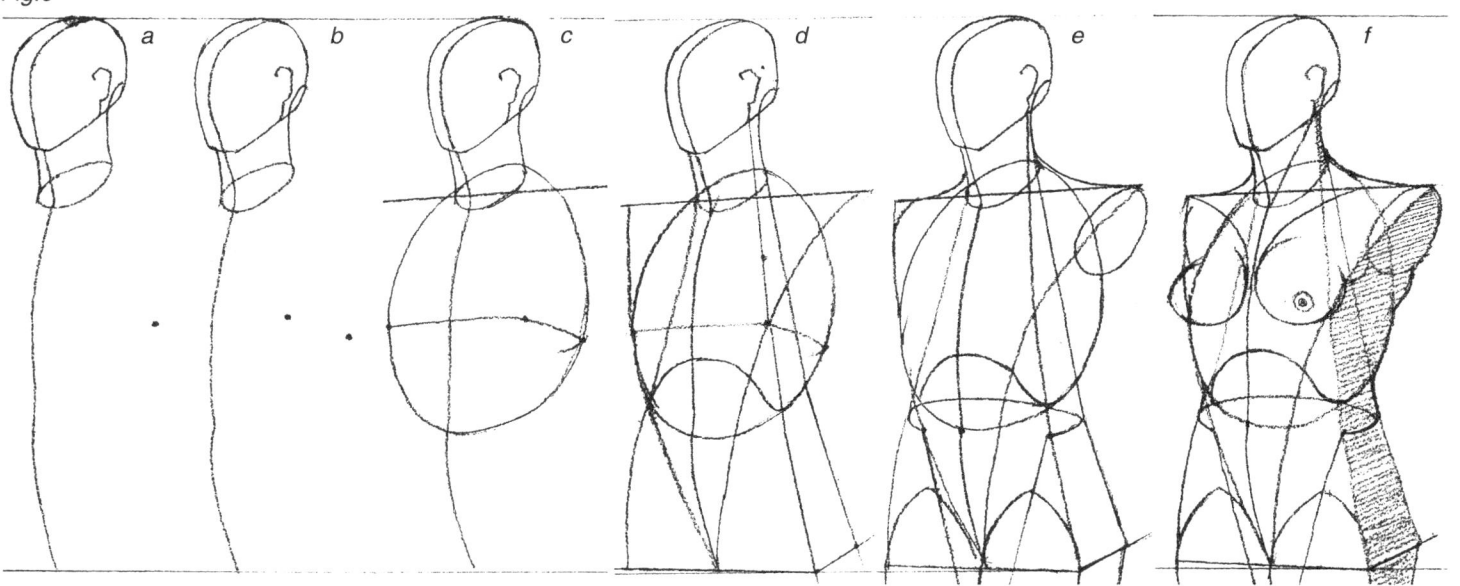

which were extended from the ear to the point of the width of the front of the leg. Diagonal lines coming from these points represent the sartorius muscle which will extend downwards and wrap around the inside of the knee. Shown here also are the forms of the upper legs inserting into the torso.

Fig f. This drawing shows, in a simplified way, how the shading of the sideplane conforms to our structure lines.

Figs. 7a.b.c.d. These drawings show how the center line should follow the contour of the figure to help you better understand the form. To confirm the accurate placement of this line you may want to drop a straight line from the pit of the neck to the crotch point. The angle of a straight line is easier to determine than one that bumps and curves.

Fig. a. The center line in profile view is emphasized here.

Figs. b. and c. The center lines of these three-quarter views follow the contours of the figure. It is important that it is in the center of the individual forms in perspective. Note also how the outer structure line follows the general shape of the structure line.

Fig. d. This drawing shows the simplest, easiest way to start drawing the figure in a twisting three-quarter action.

OTHER CONSIDERATIONS CONCERNING STRUCTURE

The drawings on this page are to further clarify the ideas of the structure system.

Fig. 8a. Back view. The lines with the arrowheads run along the tops of the scapula forms. They can be at different angles depending on which shoulder is higher than the other.

Fig. b. Front view. The same idea except the directional lines are running along the tops of the clavicles at different angles.

Fig. c. The shoulder girdle and back muscle group added to the basic rib cage form.

Fig. d. Showing the position of the large form of the abdominal muscles in relation to the inverted triangle.

Fig. e. Notice the bow shape of the clavicle forms and where the breast forms originate. Note also the external oblique forms, how they come off the line of the sideplane and how they are related.

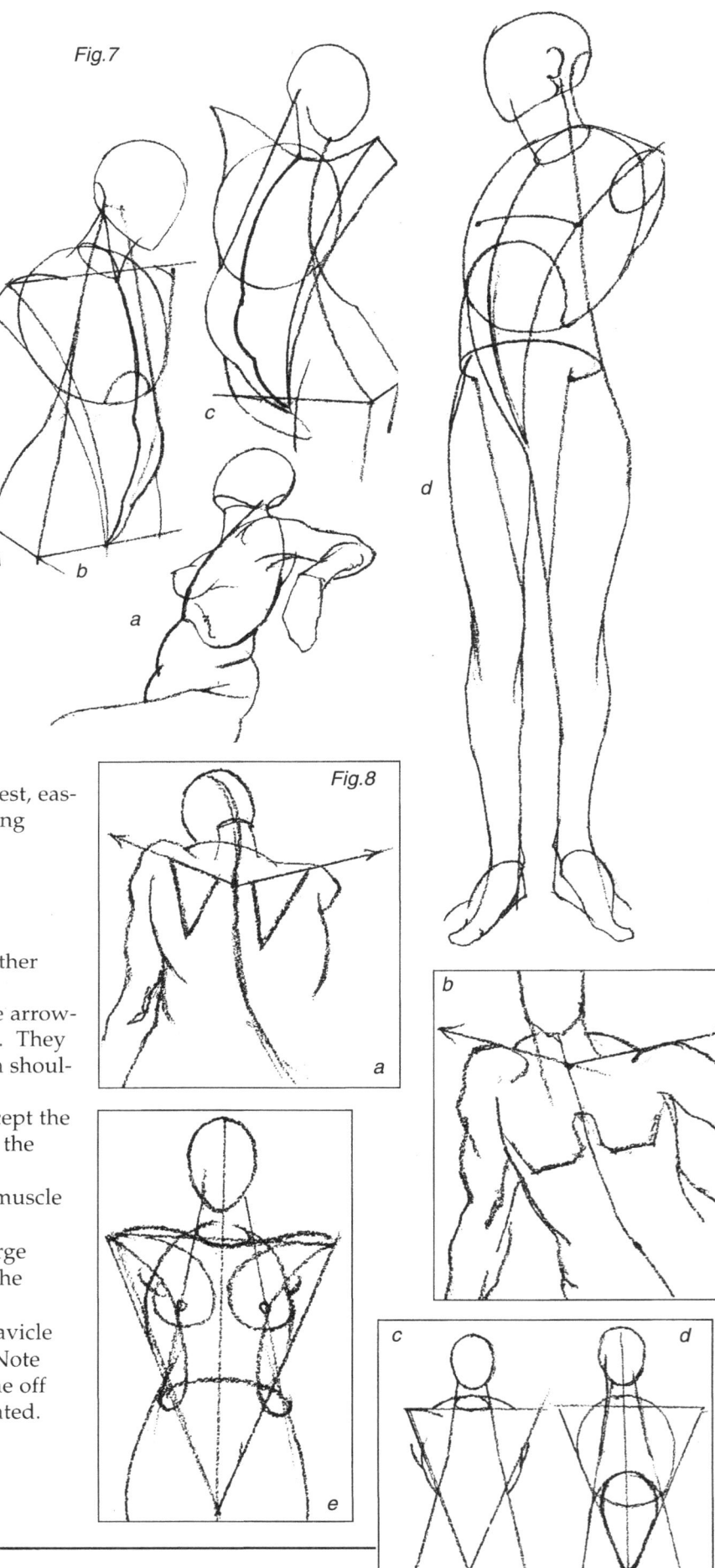

Fig.7

Fig.8

SIMPLIFIED CONCEPTIONS OF THE LARGE FORMS IN ACTION

Since most beginners start drawing by making an outline, they completely miss the twisting, bending or tipping of the major forms of the torso. These drawings always lack the three dimensional aspect of form in action.

Before you put down the first stroke of your drawing take a few seconds to analyze the pose. Ask yourself, "What is the model doing?" "What are the major forms doing?" The simplified drawings shown here are a powerful aid in getting your drawing right in the beginning.

Figs. 9a.b. and c. represent the torso as, *Fig. a.*, bending, *Fig. b.*, turning and, *Fig. c.*, tipping forwards and backwards. Following these examples are combinations of two of the movements. Drawing *Fig. ab.* is a combination of *Fig. a. and Fig. b.;* drawing *Fig. bc.* is a combination of *Fig. b. and Fig. c.;* drawing *Fig. ac.* is a combination of *Fig. a. and Fig. c.* Below these are imaginary drawings made up of various combinations of the three basic movements in different positions. See how many you can invent by yourself.

Fig.9

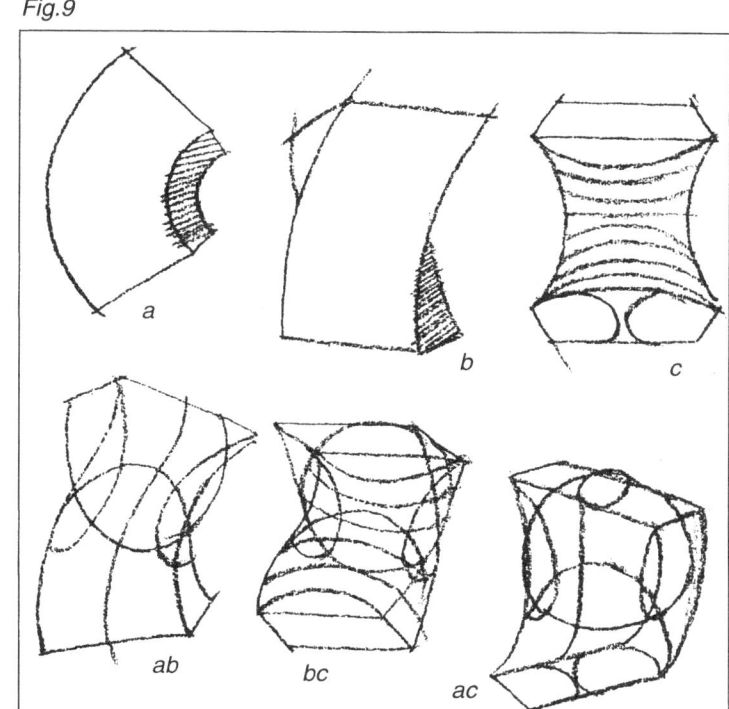

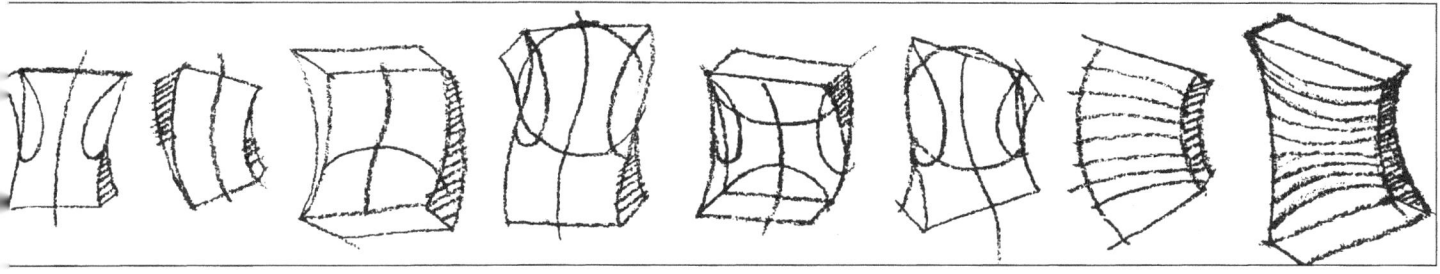

SIMPLIFIED STRUCTURE

The six drawings, *Figs. 10a.b.c.d.e. and f.* demonstrate the simplest and quickest possible way to use the structure lines when drawing the legs in different positions of perspective. There can be many variations of these lines but the main thing to remember is that you must overlook almost all the anatomical forms and draw only the biggest things about the leg – that is, where it starts, where it ends and what is the large general shape. Carrying these ideas to completion will be shown later on in this chapter.

Fig.10

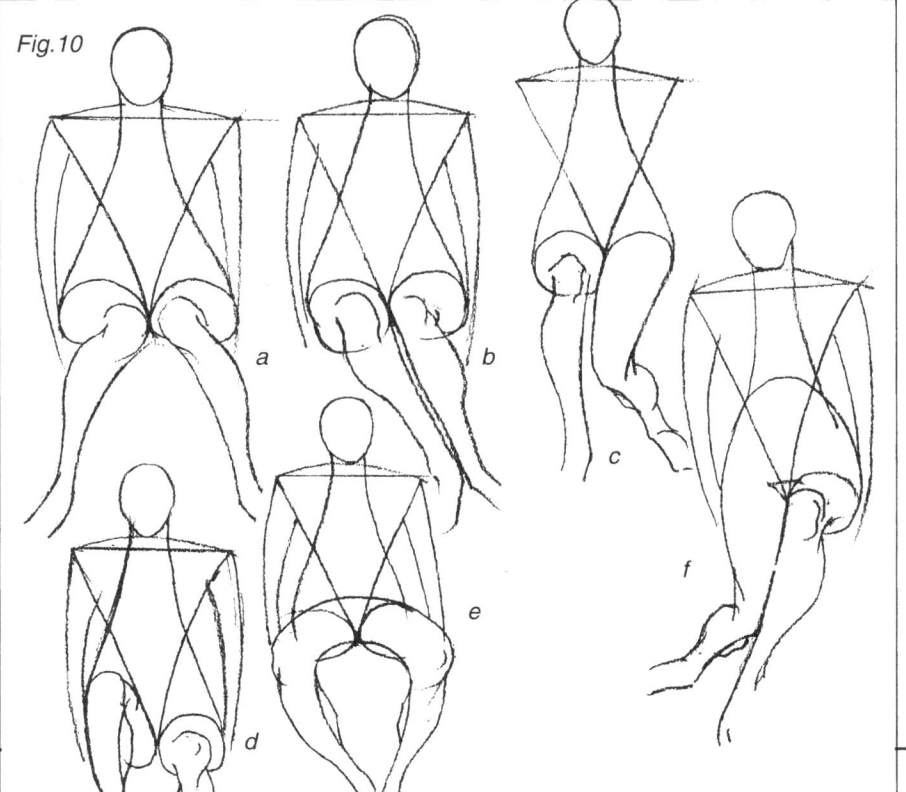

Drawings *Figs. 11a.b.c. and d.* explain how the structure lines are used to capture the pose of the figure in action. One should always start with the head, then the center line to the crotch point. This center line, or action line, should always continue down the inside of the leg that the weight is on. In all cases the structure lines should be drawn first to the leg that the weight is on. The structure lines of the other leg can thus be easily estimated. All structure lines should be biased in the direction of the action.

    Figs. 12a.b.c. Determine the balance of the figure by dropping a perpendicular from the pit of the neck. Check where it ends in relation to the ankles of the feet. Notice how far away it is from the navel or the crotch and if it lines up with the inside of a leg. I would, however, not try to be too precise with this idea all the time as it is more important that the life-like action of the figure be achieved and maintained.

    Drawings Figs. 13a. and b. show the beginning of developing forms over the basic simple structural framework. Note the relationship of the head to the neck hole and the rib cage form to the back of the neck hole. Note also the two lines from beneath the ears to the widest points of the hip and the abdominal forms. *Fig. b.* shows the start of shading over simple structure lines

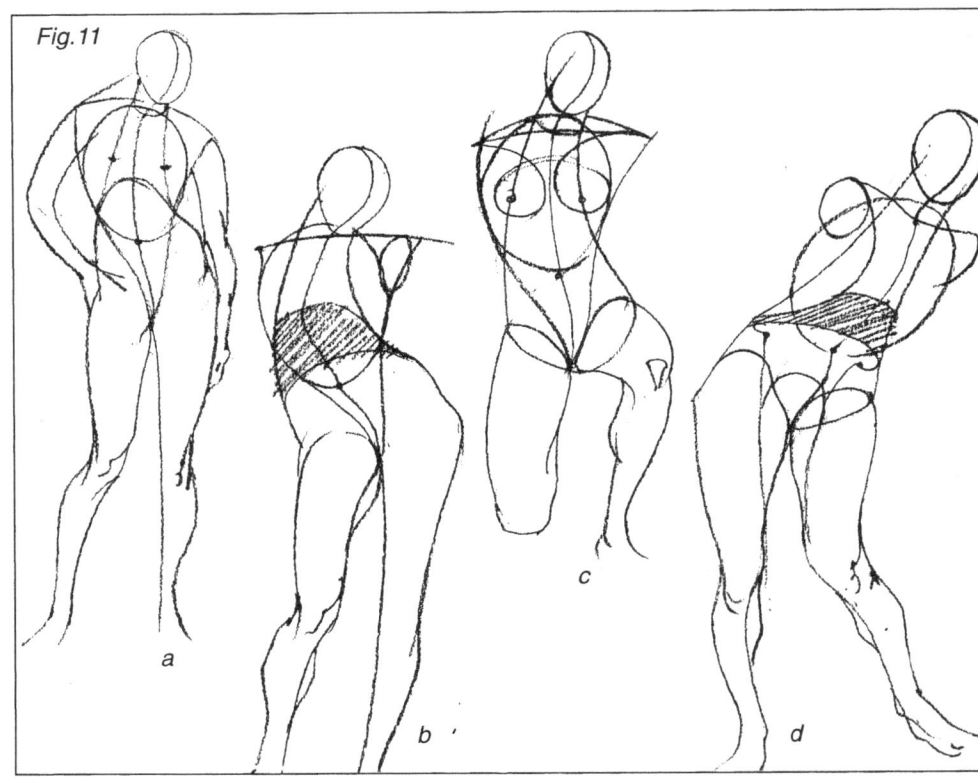

Fig.11

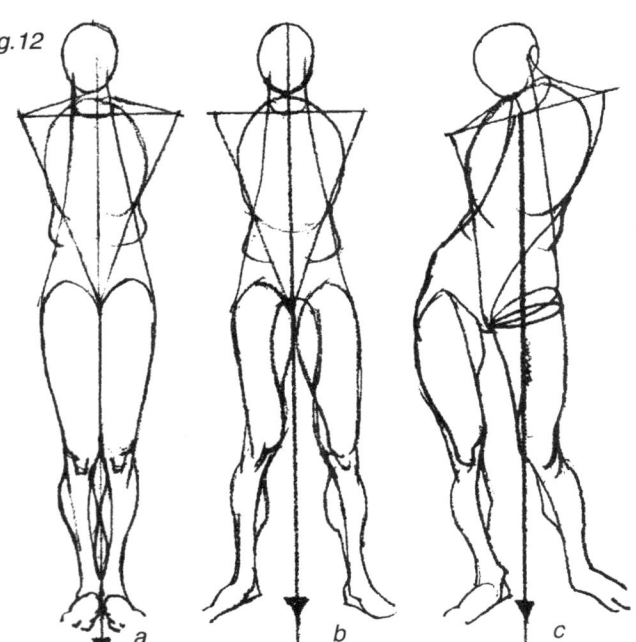

Fig.12

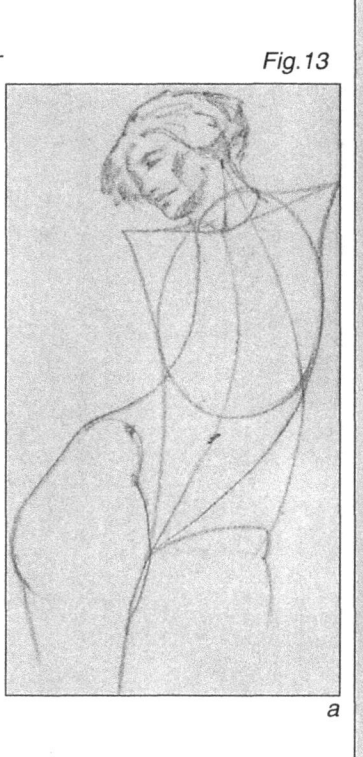

Fig.13

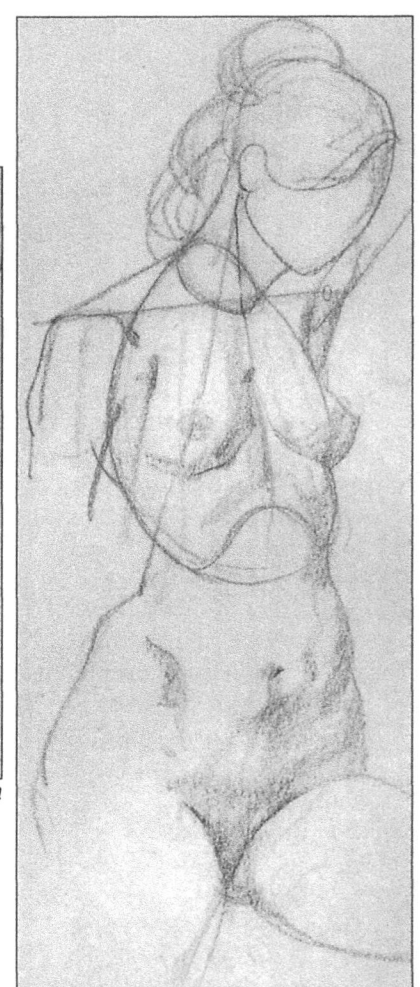

76

SWEEPING RELATIONSHIP LINES

Long sweeping relationship lines are almost always overlooked by the beginner, as he is usually concerned with copying one thing at a time. This is unfortunate for one can spend much time on a drawing only to have it come out all wrong for one will have missed the "big thing" of the pose. Drawings *Figs. 14a.b.c. and d.* are just a few examples of some of the different ways these lines, shown with arrows, help obtain the correct drawing and action of the pose. Note how the long curved line in Drawing *c.* helps obtain the position of the rib cage, the back of the buttocks and the bottom of the foot.

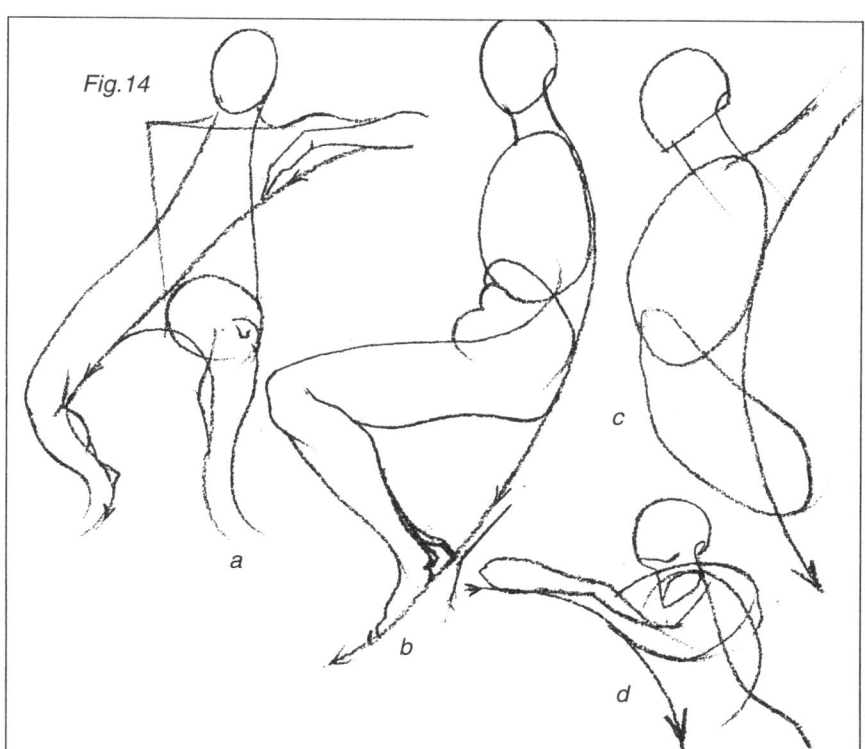

Fig.14

LINES OF ALIGNMENT

Lines of alignment are similar to large sweeping relationship lines. It is surprising how many things you can align if you look for them. This doesn't mean that forms will fall exactly on a line but they can be pretty close to it and thereby be of a great help in solving your drawing problems. Note how in drawing *Fig. 15a.* the curved bottom line aligns the toes of the feet and the fingers of the right hand. The sweeping line in the center aligns the bottom of the buttocks and the bottom of the left hand. The top most line aligns the shoulders. Drawing *Fig. 15b.* is an example of the alignment of two legs, specifically the tops and bottoms of the two knee forms.

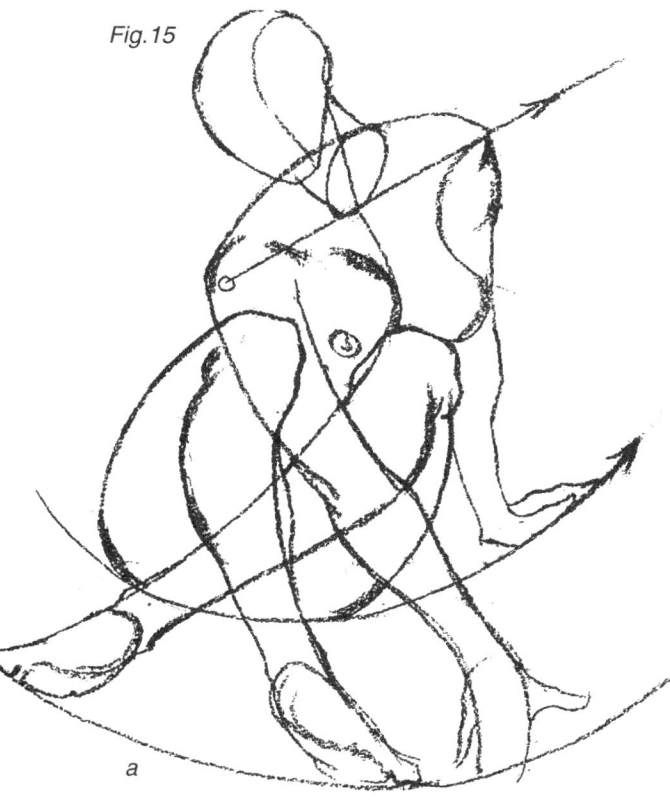

Fig.15

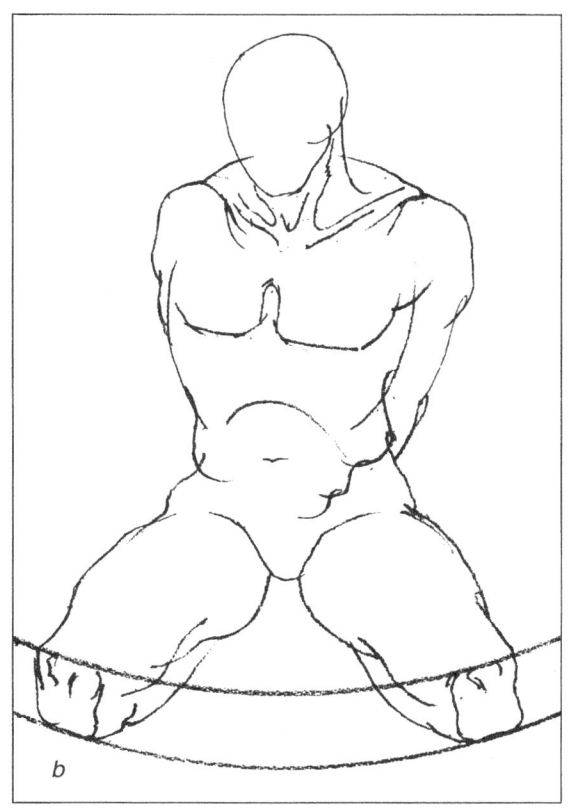

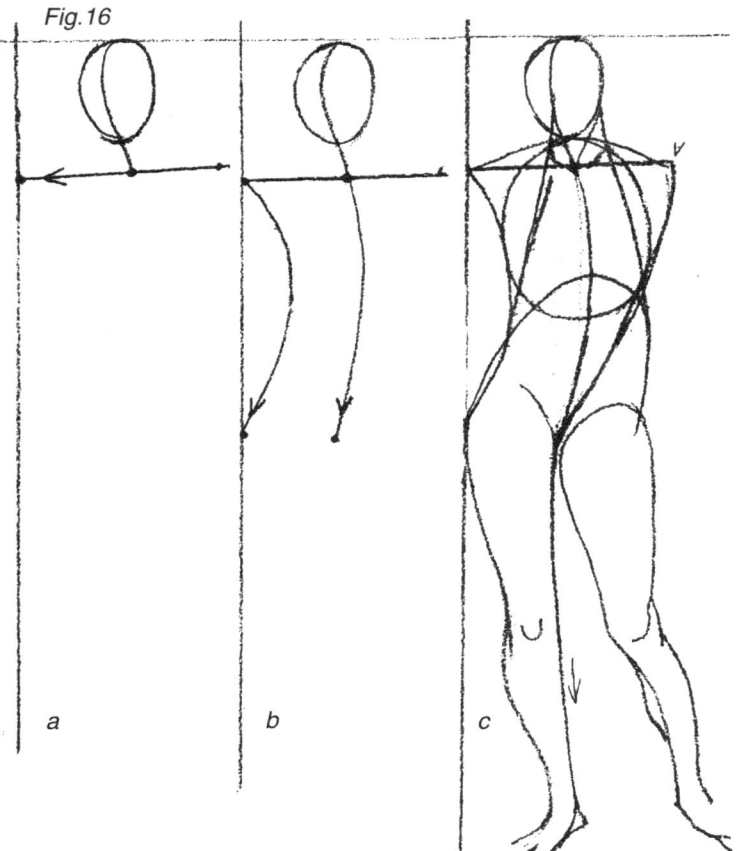

Fig.16

In examples *Figs. 17a.b. and c.* we see how to draw a seated figure in profile. *Fig. a.* shows the head in profile with the neck lines. The rear neck line touches the perpendicular of the wall. *Fig. b.* From this point draw the lines of the back and the buttocks. Again, check the negative space between the wall and the figure. The third example, *Fig. c.,* shows the drawing on its way to completion. The center line is added first, then the structure lines of the rib cage form, the legs, etc. If the figure is on a chair of some sort proceed as follows: before you draw the legs you should drop a perpendicular line from the edge of the seat to the floor. By observing the negative space between the back of the leg and this line and the position of the foot to it, we can determine with fair accuracy where the structure lines should go.

If the buttocks form is a distance from the wall then draw a straight line from the point where the back of the neck touches the wall to the back of the buttocks. Check the approximate distance from the wall to the buttocks and the negative space this creates. Once this is established then proceed in the same manner as described above.

THE USE OF KNOW QUANTITIES

One should not ever neglect using a known quantity – for with a known quantity many of the unknown quantities can be better estimated. A known quantity can be a straight perpendicular line, a horizontal line, a shape such as a circle, triangle or a square to name a few. It is surprising how many of these simple aids are overlooked.

Drawings *Figs. 16a.b. and c.* show how to use a known quantity, in this case a perpendicular line which represents a wall as shown in *Fig. a.* Start with the oval of the head first and draw a center line around it to the pit of the neck. Next draw a shoulder axis line through the pit of the neck to the perpendicular line of the wall. From the point where the shoulder touches the wall draw an arc to a point where the hip touches the wall, *Fig b.* The negative space within this curve should be checked for accuracy and that is fairly easy. The center line to the crotch can now be more accurately placed. The drawing continues as shown in *Fig. c.* by continuing the center line past the crotch down the inside of the leg that the weight is on. Again, check how much distance there is from the foot to the wall. You can proceed with the drawing now with confidence and assurance that it will be fairly correct.

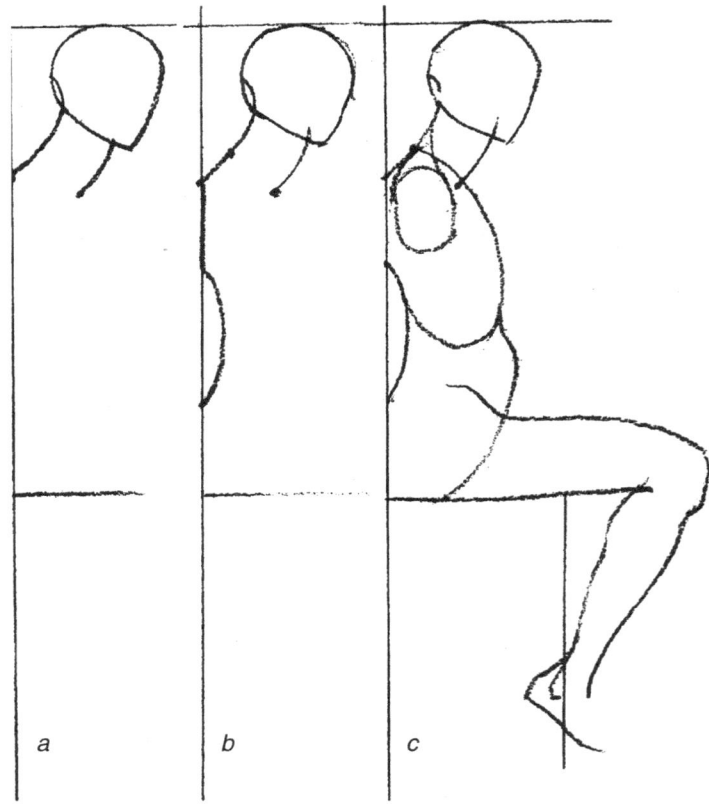

Fig.17

ADDITIONS AND CLARIFICATIONS OF THE STRUCTURE SYSTEM
1. THE HEAD AND SHOULDERS

The drawings shown in *Figs. 18a.b.c.d.e.* explain in greater detail how one uses the structure lines to properly relate the head, neck and shoulders. The shoulder line is an axis line which goes through the pit of the neck to the widest points of the shoulders. Sometimes it follows the clavicles to the widest points, but most times it doesn't as clavicles are seldom horizontal. If one is in doubt as to the width of the shoulders, use the length of the head as a unit of measurement as shown in the diagrams of ideal proportions. There is, in a woman, one head distance from the pit of the neck to the widest point of the shoulder. In a man the distance is one and a third heads distance from the pit of the neck to the widest point of the shoulder. However you will find these proportions vary greatly in real life.

After drawing the head shape one draws a center line down the center of that form to the pit of the neck. Next the axis line to the widest points of the shoulders is drawn through this point. Be careful to get the proper angle of this line. *(Fig. 18a.).*

In our first drawing, *Fig. 18a.*, the length of the head *AB* is equal to *CD*, the distance from the pit of the neck to the widest point of the shoulder. Most times when you reach point *D* you have to go up on an angle to point *E*, *(Fig. b.)*, where the clavicle generally ends. The next step is to go to point *F*, *(Fig. c.)*, which is on the center line on the back of the neck. This gives you the shape of the trapezius muscle. Repeat this on the opposite side and add the clavicles and sterno-mastoid muscles, *(Fig. d.).*

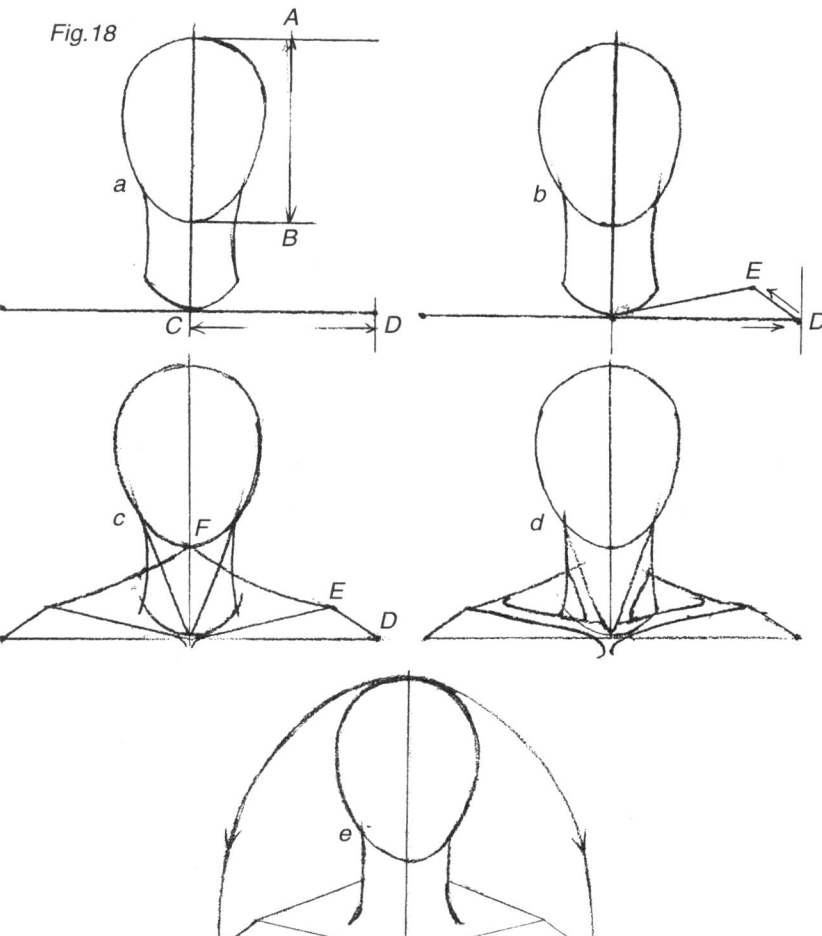

Fig. 18

Fig. 18e., In order to further confirm the width of the shoulders one can draw an arc around the head to the widest points of the shoulders as shown in

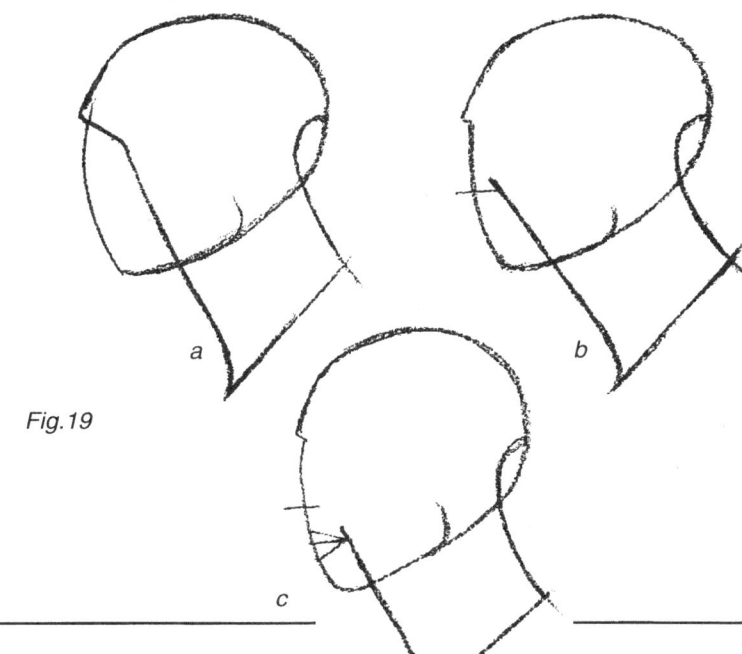

Fig.19

Fig. 19. The most common mistake is to have the neck in the wrong position as it relates to the head. The drawings in *Figs. 20a.b. and c.* show three different ways one may relate the neck to the head. A lot depends on the width of the neck and the position of your viewpoint in relation to the model. In example

Fig. 19a. the line of the neck lines up with the side of the eye socket, in *Fig. b.* with the edge of the nostril and in *Fig. c.* at the corner of the mouth.

2. THE RIB CAGE AND BREAST FORMS

The rib cage form fits within the triangle which is formed by connecting the widest points of the shoulders to the crotch point. This form is a flattened egg shape.

Fig. 21a. shows this egg shape with a horizontal oval, (shown with arrowheads), encircling it.

Keep this in mind when drawing the breasts. The bottom of the breasts have to fall on this line to show the curvature of the underlying form of the rib cage.

Fig. b. The structure lines of the breasts originate from the widest points of the shoulders. At a certain point on the sternum the actual forms become apparent. Notice the symmetry and how the breasts relate to each other. The third drawing, **Fig. c.**, shows overemphasized shading on the forms and planes of the chest and breasts.

Fig. d. The nipples of the breasts are not in the center of the breast forms but rather point outwards. When figuring the angles of the nipples pick a point on the center line and draw lines from this point through the nipples.

Whenever anyone is leaning heavily on one arm, as shown in **Fig. 22.**, then that shoulder will be raised higher than the opposite shoulder and in turn raise the breast on that side. The lines with the arrowheads show the direction of the raising of the left shoulder and left breast. The height of the nipple of the breast can be determined by how much it deviates from a horizontal line.

There are an infinite variety of forms of the breasts. The drawings shown in **Figs. 23a.b.c. and d.** are just some of the few shapes and sizes breasts come in.

The breasts start out small and high in youth and gradually increase in size. Eventually they sag lower and lower and flatten out over the rib cage – and even over the abdominal muscles in some cases.

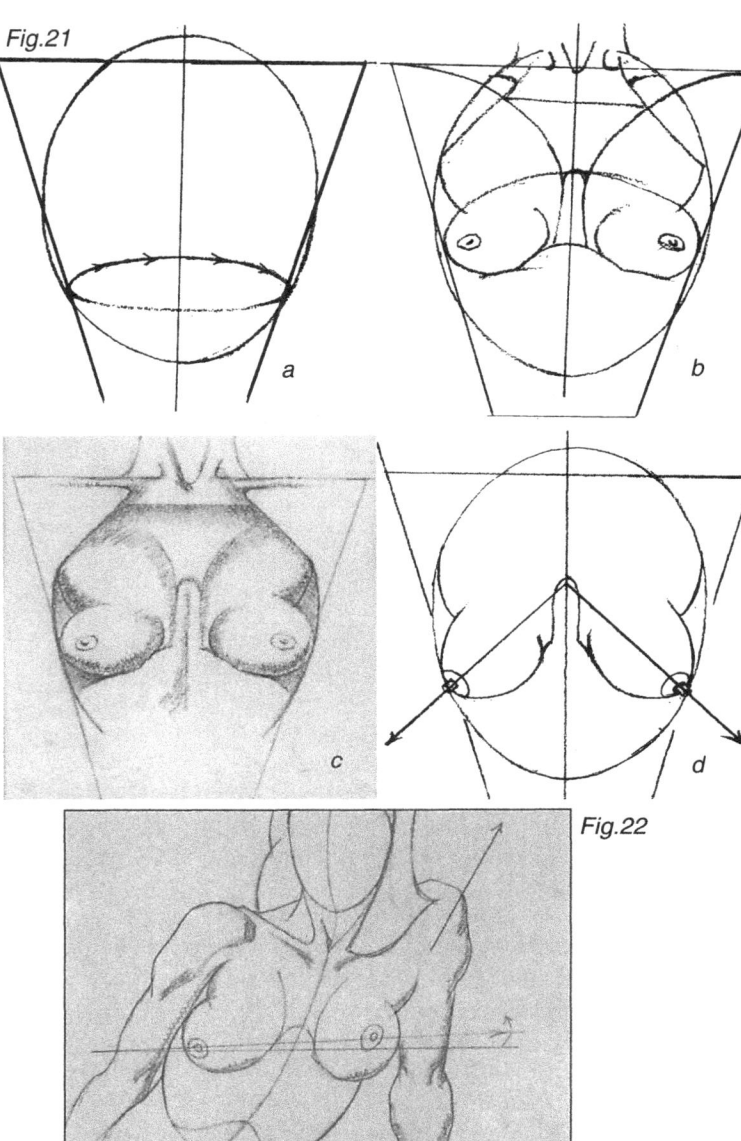

Fig.21

Fig.22

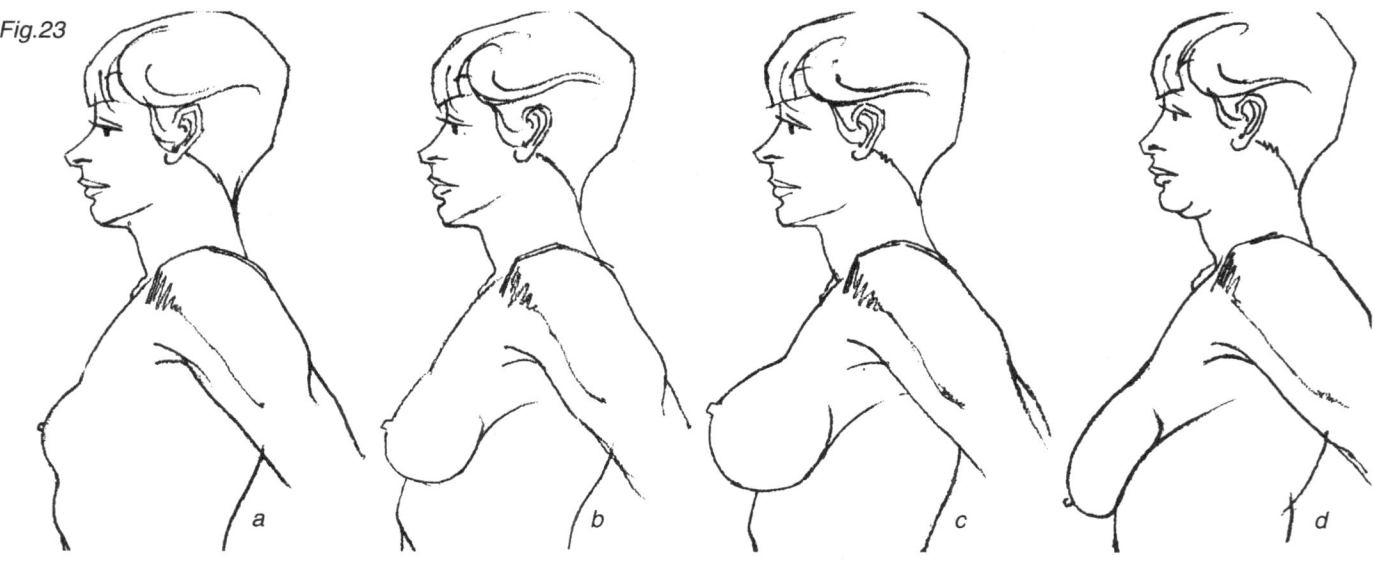

Fig.23

3. THE LYING DOWN POSE

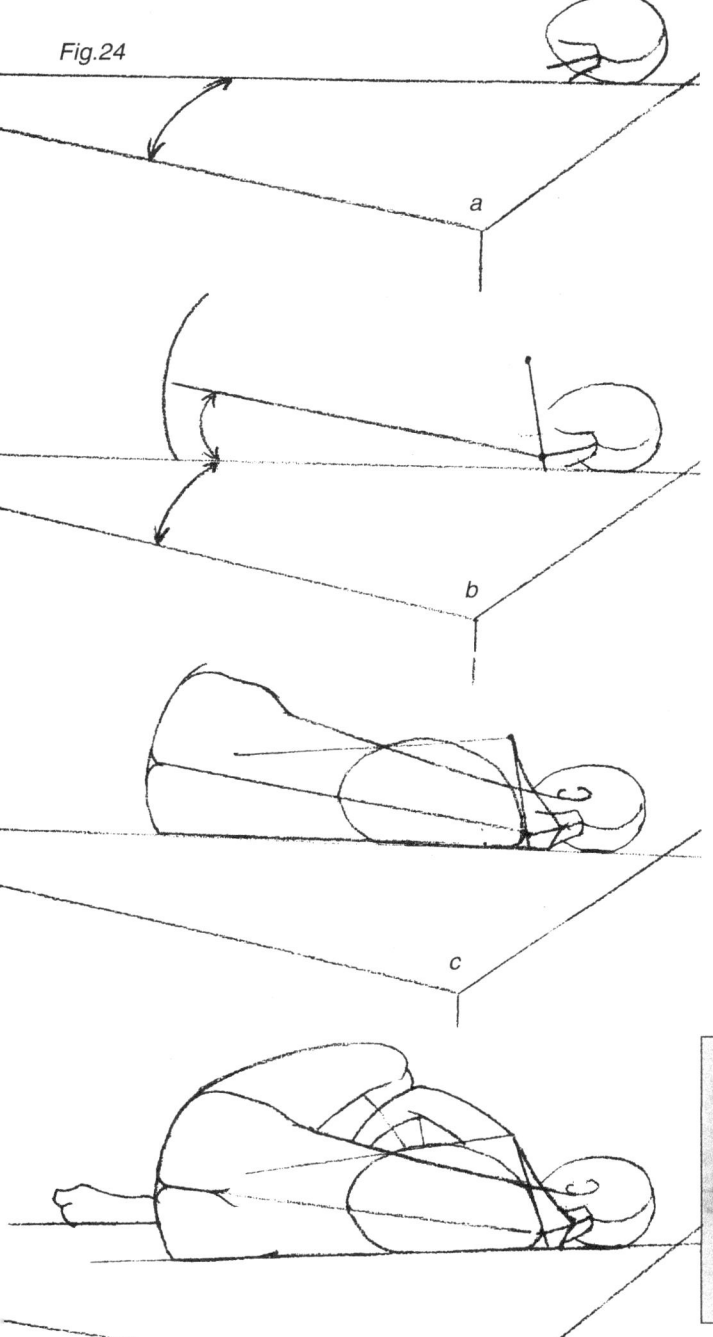

Fig.24

The lying down pose presents many difficulties to students, beginners as well as advanced. In almost all cases the model is drawn without any regard to the solid flat platform. It always seems that the body is not stopped by this flat surface but goes right through it, furthermore the model is never aligned properly in relation to the stand.

Figs. 24a.b.c.d. and e. show a simple and logical way to approach drawing any figure in a lying down position.

Fig. a. Draw at least two sides of the platform trying to get the angles of them from your point of view as accurate as possible. Now draw the head lying on the platform and, where it touches it, extend a base line. Check the angle of the base line to the edge of the platform and complete the neck form with its base line.

Fig. b. Draw a line from the seventh cervical vertebra on the neck to the center of the buttocks and at the end of it make an arc. Add a shoulder axis line going to the widest points of the shoulders.

Fig. c. From the widest point of the shoulder extend a line to the crotch and then draw the rib cage form. Next, extend a line from the ear past a point on the rib cage form and draw the large shape of the buttocks. Divide the buttocks making two forms.

Fig. d. Add the structure lines of the leg and arm and the shape of the form of the foot or whatever else shows in your drawing.

Fig. e. The large forms are subdivided and refined and light and shade added to them. The model is now lying flat on the platform and aligned in the correct direction.

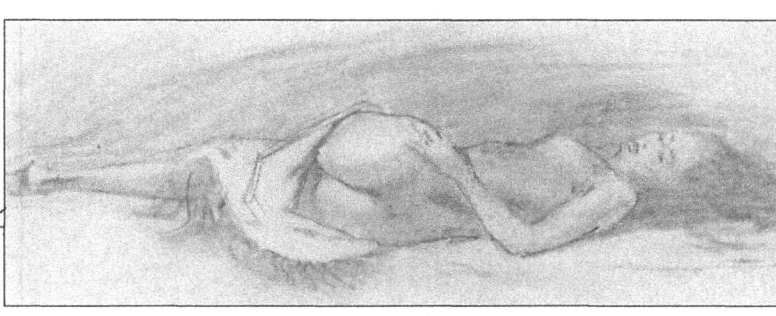

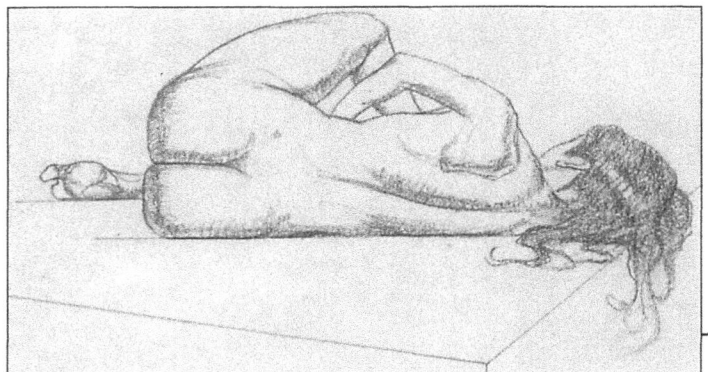

e

Figs. 25a.b. and c. show a sensible approach to drawing the typical lying down pose.

Fig. 25a. Start the lying down pose by drawing at least two sides of the platform. The simple structure lines are added but not until a long base line is established. Note its angle to the edge of the platform. None of the model's forms will go below this base line. Base lines are also drawn at the bottom of the foot and the leg which rests on the box. Check the negative space beneath the lower leg and the box. The lines are best drawn in the direction of the arrows.

Fig. b. The structure is now developed further with smaller forms.

Fig. c. Even further development of the forms with the addition of some shading. The drawing can now be developed to any degree the artist wants to.

Fig. 26. In the lying down pose, unless it is in perfect profile, forms must be aligned and go into perspective. Some of the forms such as the breasts are obvious and are easy to align but there are many other forms that are not so obvious. One must look hard and seize on the slightest indication of forms such as the abdominal muscles or the bottom of the rib cage. By drawing a very light line of the proper angle across the form, perhaps on the bottom of it or perhaps on the top of it, one puts it into perspective. Note also the many base lines at the head, the shoulders and from the edge of the shoulders to the edge of the buttocks.

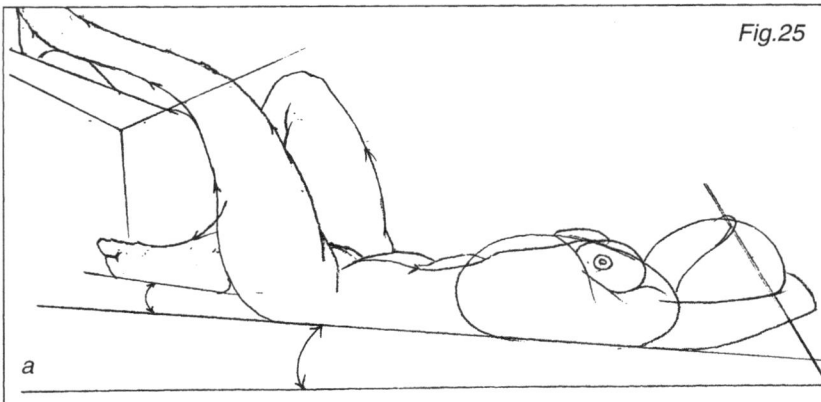
Fig.25

a

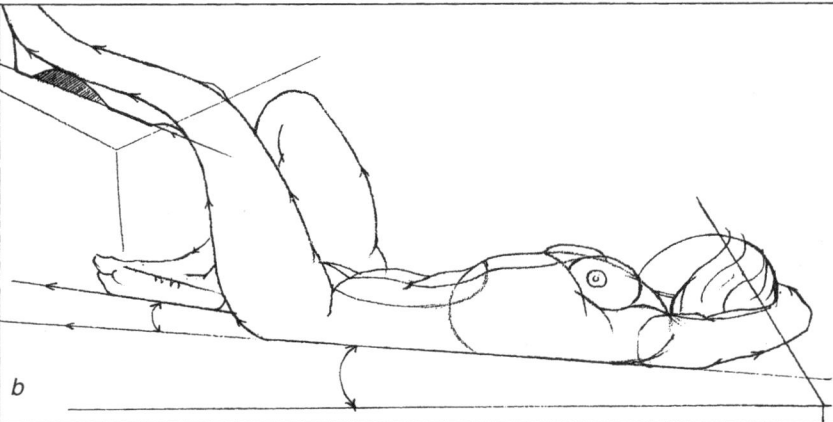

b

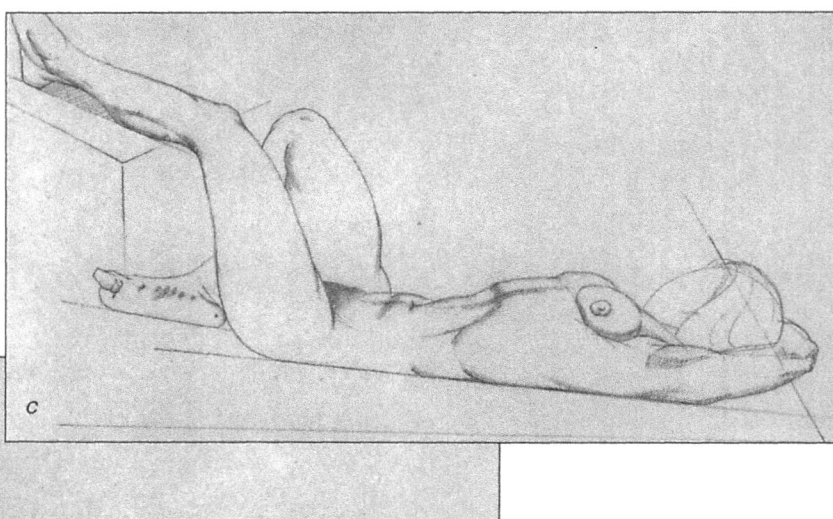

c

Fig.26

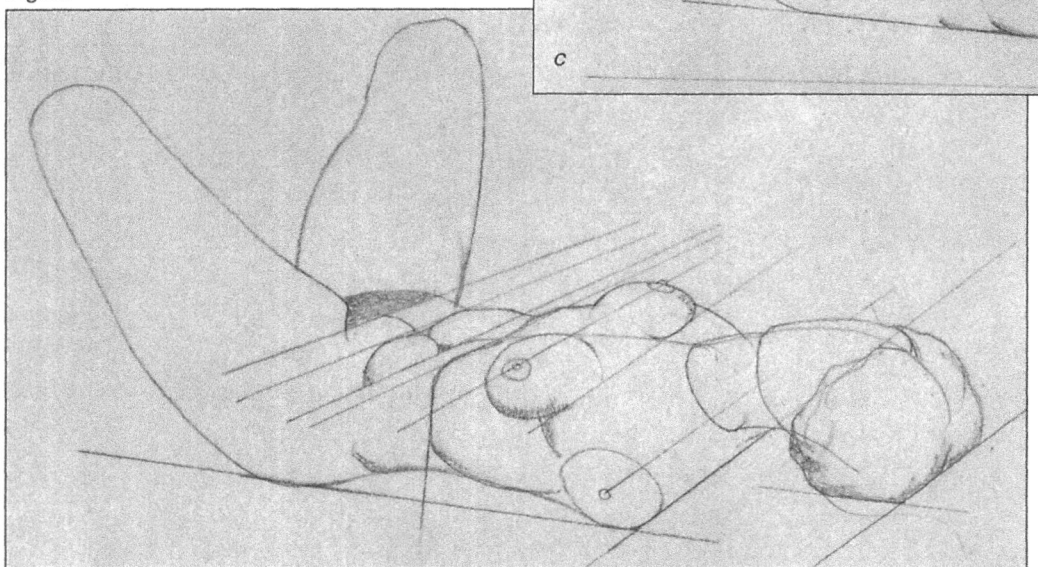

4.THE SEATED POSE

The drawings, *Figs. 27a.b.c.d.e.,* reveal many hidden facts that are overlooked by the student when drawing the seated figure. Whether you draw by the procedure shown or draw your own way, in the end these ideas and principles should be in your drawing if it is to appear correct.

Fig.27

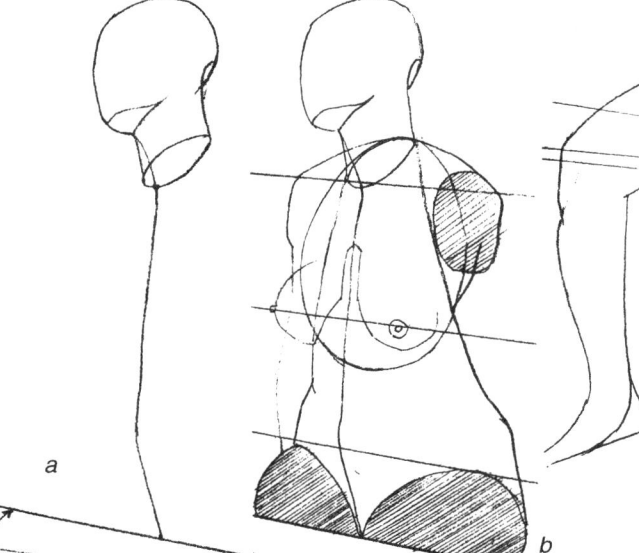

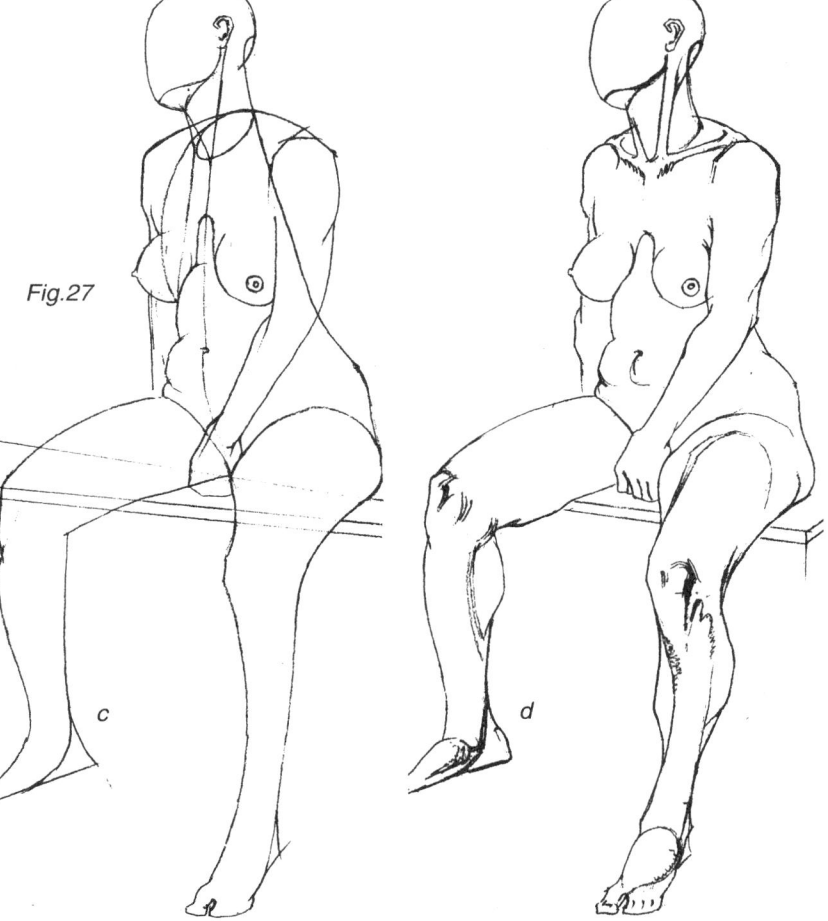

Fig. 27a. Start with the head form as previously shown. Add the neck form with the neck hole and draw a center line from the pit of the neck to where you estimate the crotch touches the flat surface of the chair or seat. Now draw a base line through that point which represents the angle of the figure on the chair. Check the angle of this line against the edge of the chair to get the angle correct.

Fig. b. The basic structure lines and forms are added now. Use line to align the forms in the proper perspective. The shaded areas on the lower torso represent a cross-section of the torso from where the leg forms will originate.

Fig. c. The structure lines of the arms and legs are added. Note that the inside of the legs start at the crotch point. The leg will stay flat as long as it is on the flat surface. Check the position of the kneecaps against the horizontal of the chair. *Most times the top of the knee will be above the chair line.* It is only when the leg is mostly off the seat that the knee is lower than this line.

Fig. d. Large, simple forms are drawn upon the basic structure lines with the assurance that they will be fairly correct. Note how the form of the right leg drops when it leaves the flat surface of the chair.

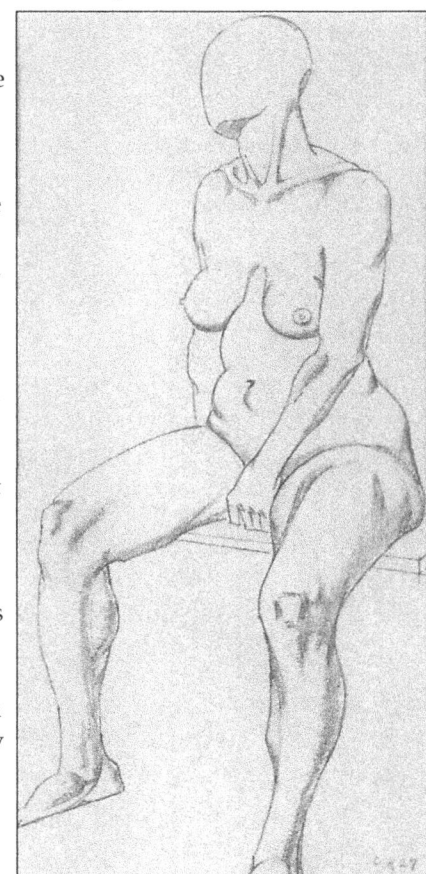

Fig. e. Shading added, mainly on side and bottom planes, to show general form. One can now add features, hair, smaller forms and values to carry the drawing to completion. These drawings have been kept deliberately simple so as to clarify the essential ideas of figure construction.

5.THE ARMS

The series of drawings *Figs. 28a.b. and c.* describe the method of using basic structure lines to draw folded arms. This procedure can be used to great advantage with all complex positions of arms or legs. The main thing to remember is to draw things in the sequence that they occur, that is what is first, what overlaps that and what overlaps that.

Fig. 28a. Draw light structure lines, (follow directions of arrows), to show what the arms are doing. Leave out all forms and details. In the final drawing the right arm crosses over the left arm so the underlying left arm should be drawn first.

Fig. b. The right arm is now drawn over the left arm.

Fig. c. The large basic forms are added to the structure lines. They should always be going in the direction of the action.

Fig. d. Working towards the finish. Smaller forms are added as well as some light and shade. One can continue with smaller and smaller forms and as much light and shade and linear variation as one wishes. The right arm is made to appear on top of the left arm through the use of emphasized lines and shading.

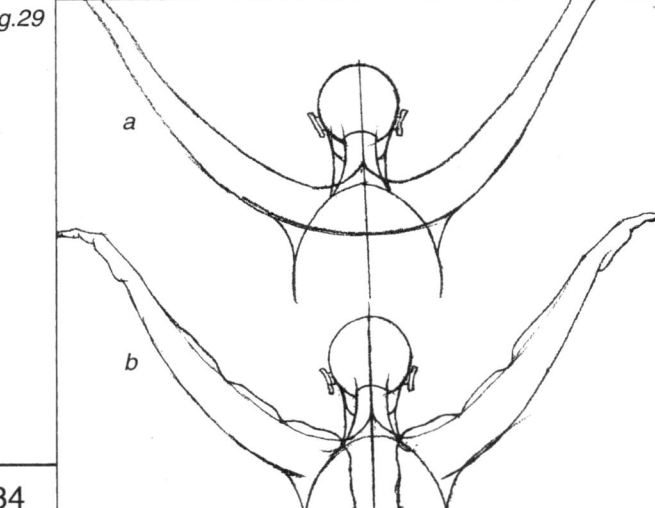

Fig.28

The two drawings, *Fig. 29a. and b.* show how one treats two arms in relation to the other structure lines of the figure. With beginners it frequently seems that one arm starts at one part of the anatomy and the other one starts at another part of the anatomy. This can be avoided by drawing two tapering sweeping lines right through and across the torso.

Fig. 29a. The neck muscles are shown inserting into the base of the skull. A center line is drawn through this form and the skull. On this line pick a point where you start the upper structure line of the arms. The lower sweeping structure line is then added. These lines should terminate at some place on the fingers.

Fig. b. The major forms such as the scapula, deltoid, biceps, etc. are now added. Notice the symmetry of the entire drawing. From here on one draws and refines smaller and smaller forms and adds light and shade if needed.

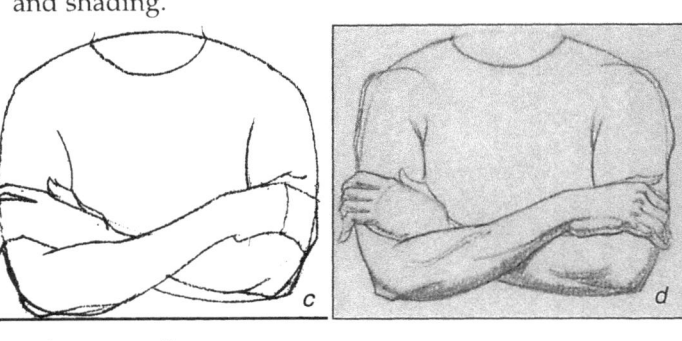

Fig.30

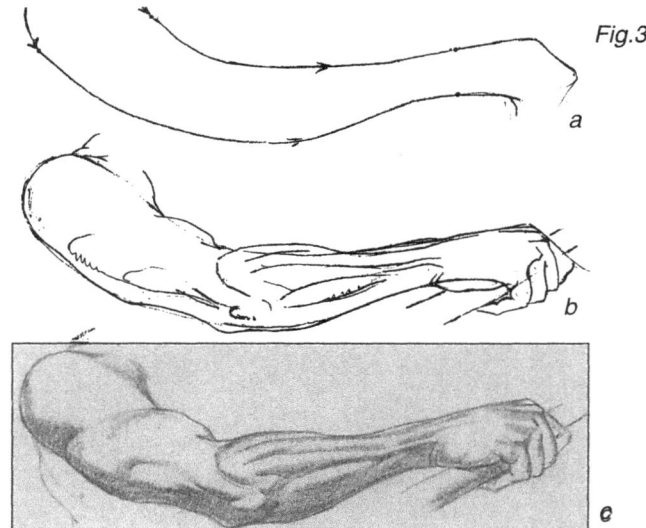

Fig. 30a. The beginner starts by trying to make a drawing as shown in *Fig. 30c.* This almost always results in failure as the underlying unity, movement and direction is not obtained.

The drawing of a very complex anatomical structure can be accomplished more easily by starting with two simple lines as shown in the above drawing. Start at the widest points of the arm, shown with points, and follow the arrows to the narrowest points of the wrist.

Fig. b. The anatomical forms are now added. The size and shape of them is gauged by how much they extend over the two structure lines.

Fig. c. Shading, mainly on the planes, and line emphasis is added – everything drawn going with the action.

Fig.29

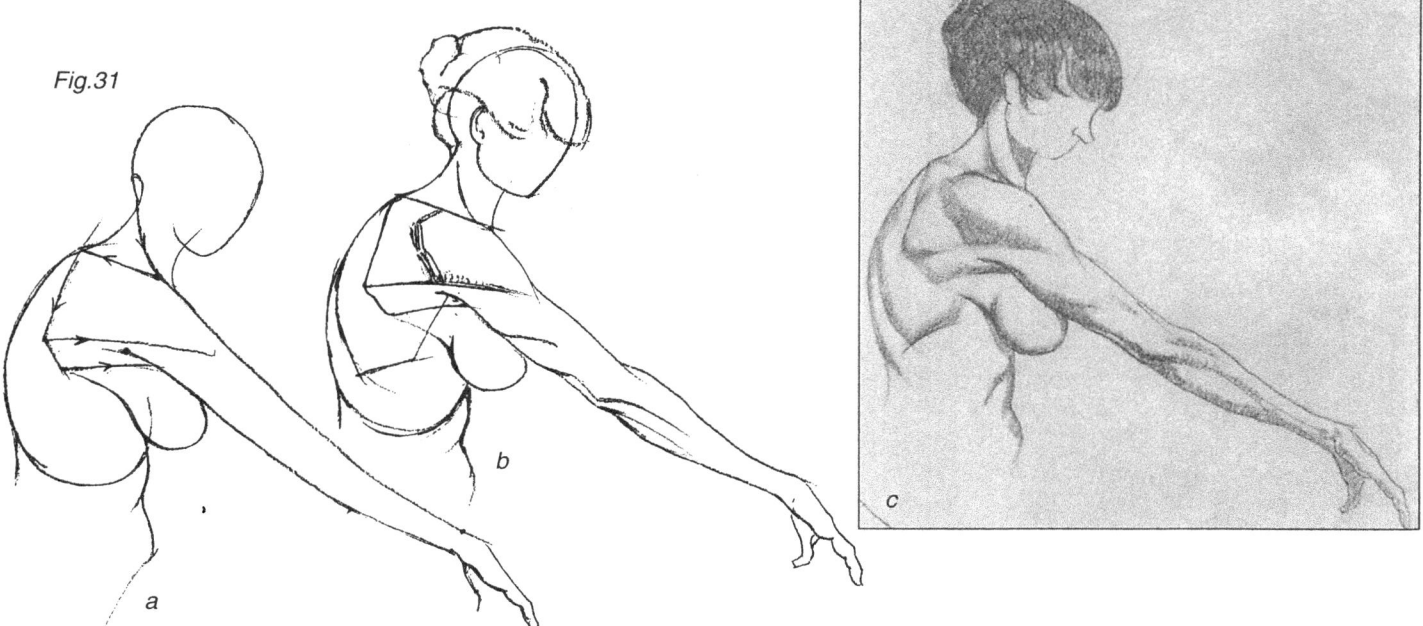

Fig.31

These three simplified schematic drawings, *Figs. 31a.b. and c.* will help explain how to construct the upper half of the torso and its relationship to the arm. The same procedure is used in many, many variations of this position.

Fig. 31a. Start with the form of the head, the neck, the rib cage and breast forms. The next step is to take a line from the back of the center of the neck that carries through the top of the wrist. Estimate the width of the arm and draw the lower structure line to the base of the wrist. The dots will show the widest

and narrowest dimensions of the arm. A line extended from the top of the deltoid will align with the top of the scapula form which in turn sits on the top of the rib cage. Lines with arrows show the direction of the muscles that pull from the scapula to the arm.

Fig. b. Forms are now added to the structure lines.

Fig. c. Shading added to define the forms. Certain lines are emphasized to make forms project. One can further develop this stage to as far as they feel it should be.

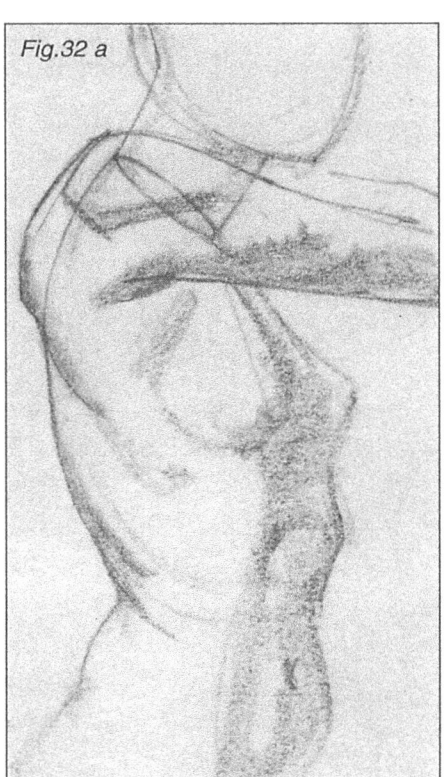

Fig.32 a

Figs. 32a.b. You should always draw as if you could see through the body. In this way things will start and end closer to where they're supposed to be. You should use lines as shown at first. Later you can merely use points and eventually when you are sufficiently advanced you can imagine where these lines or points are.

These two drawings show the position of the head and neck when it is hidden by the shoulder and arm. Start, as usual with the head and neck form. The rib cage form will attach to the base of the neck which in turn will tell you where the scapula sits. Next observe along the neck or face the point that the top of the shoulder starts and from there draw the upper and lower structure lines of the arm. Forms are then added along with as much shading as you feel you need.

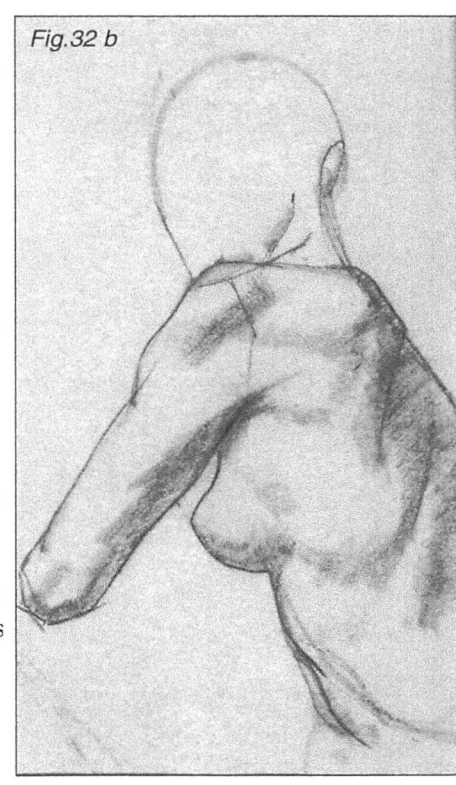

Fig.32 b

6.THE LEGS

The drawings that follow explain the use of the structure lines in the drawing of legs. Many examples are shown and they should cover every position you may encounter or want to invent. In brief you are always using two tapering structure lines starting from the widest points to the narrowest points of the limb. You must always ask yourself, "Where is the limb coming from, where is it going?" The forms are added to these lines and are always related to other lines as discussed in the chapter on Relationships. Light and shade is then added, *however when you are sufficiently advanced you should draw with line and light and shade at the same time.* Refer to Chapter 2 on The Use of Line.

Fig. 33a. Several principles are shown in this drawing. They are most times completely overlooked. Note first the flat, slant line of the wall. This angle gives the proper position of the pose. The major forms will flatten against this line. Check the negative spaces between the forms and the wall. The second principle is a base line that the lower leg flattens on. These forms of the underside of the leg are usually drawn by beginners as going far below the base line. Again, check the negative spaces between the bottom of the leg forms and the base line. The third principle is very important in regards to relating the leg to the torso. You can almost always take the line from the back of the rib cage, making a curved line to the knee and then to the ankle and foot. The bottom structure line is added paying attention to the negative spaces.

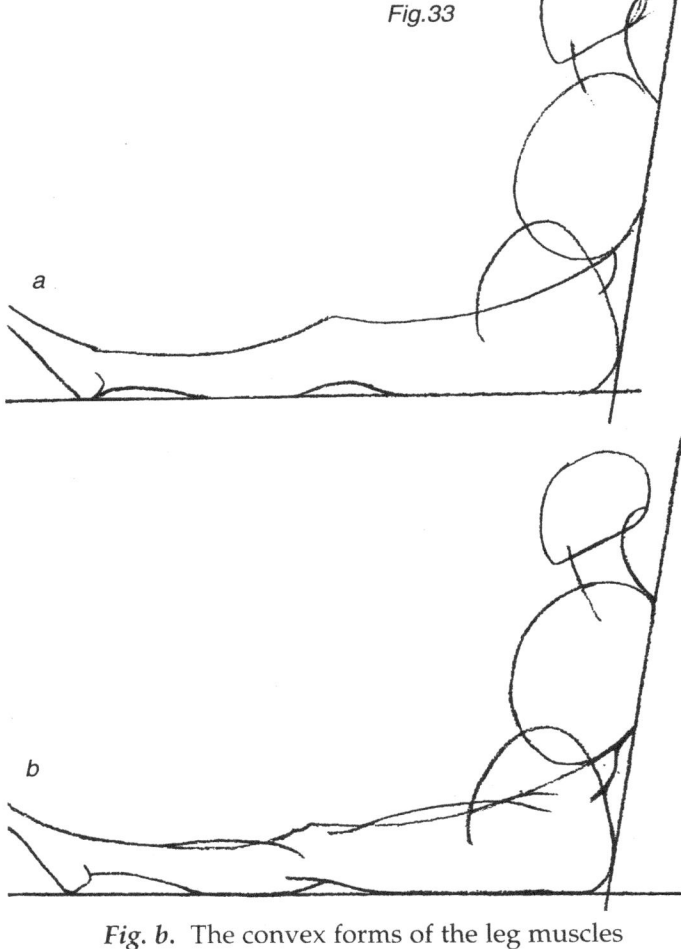

Fig. b. The convex forms of the leg muscles are added. You now have a good basis on which to finish your drawing. Notice the unity and relationships of all the major forms.

Fig. 34a. One of the most common mistakes in the drawing of the upper leg resting on a flat surface is to draw it flat on the bottom. This is wrong for the entire form of the upper part of the leg curves basically upwards. This is due to, in a large measure, to the angle of the femur bone from the trochanter to the knee.

Fig. b. The proper way to draw the structure lines for this position. They should first be drawn curving upwards.

Fig. c. The mostly convex forms are added to the curved structure lines. The leg form now appears more horizontal.

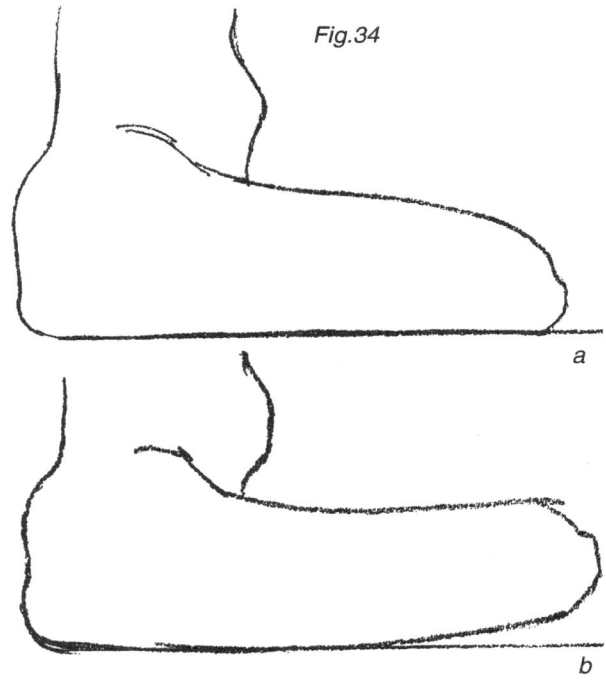

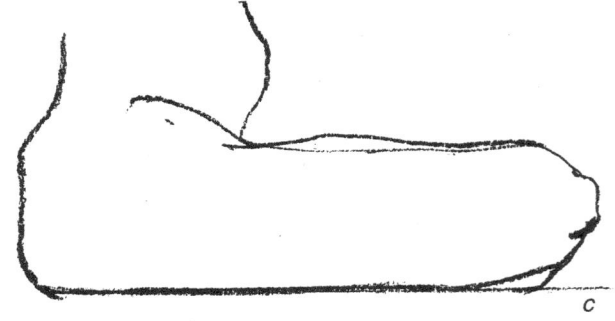

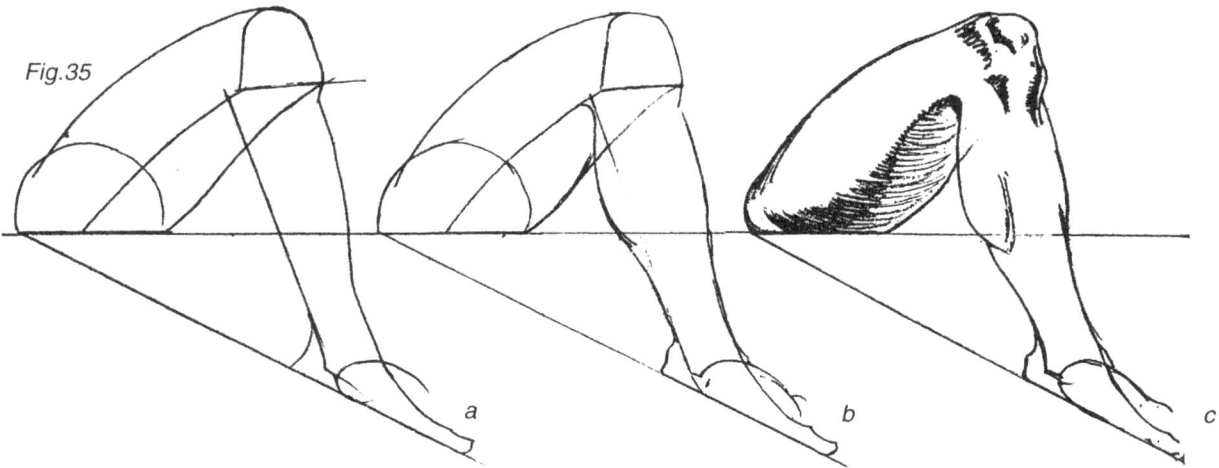

Fig.35

Fig. 35a. Sometimes it is advantageous to construct a leg by using a three dimensional approach especially when it goes into perspective. The mistake most frequently made is positioning the foot in the wrong place. This is because the artist has not used a base line which should have been drawn from the crotch point to the bottom of the foot.

One should start with a semicircle or shape that represents where the leg inserts into the torso. Next draw a shape which is to represent the knee form. Now connect these two shapes with lines which will give you a solid looking geometric shape. Before drawing the lower leg draw a base line of the *correct angle* starting from the crotch point. The structure lines of the lower leg and foot are now added, terminating on the base line.

Fig. b. Large forms are added to the basic structure.

Fig. c. Smaller forms are added. Forms are refined and light and shade is added to show perspective. Hard and soft lines are also used to help forms project or recede.

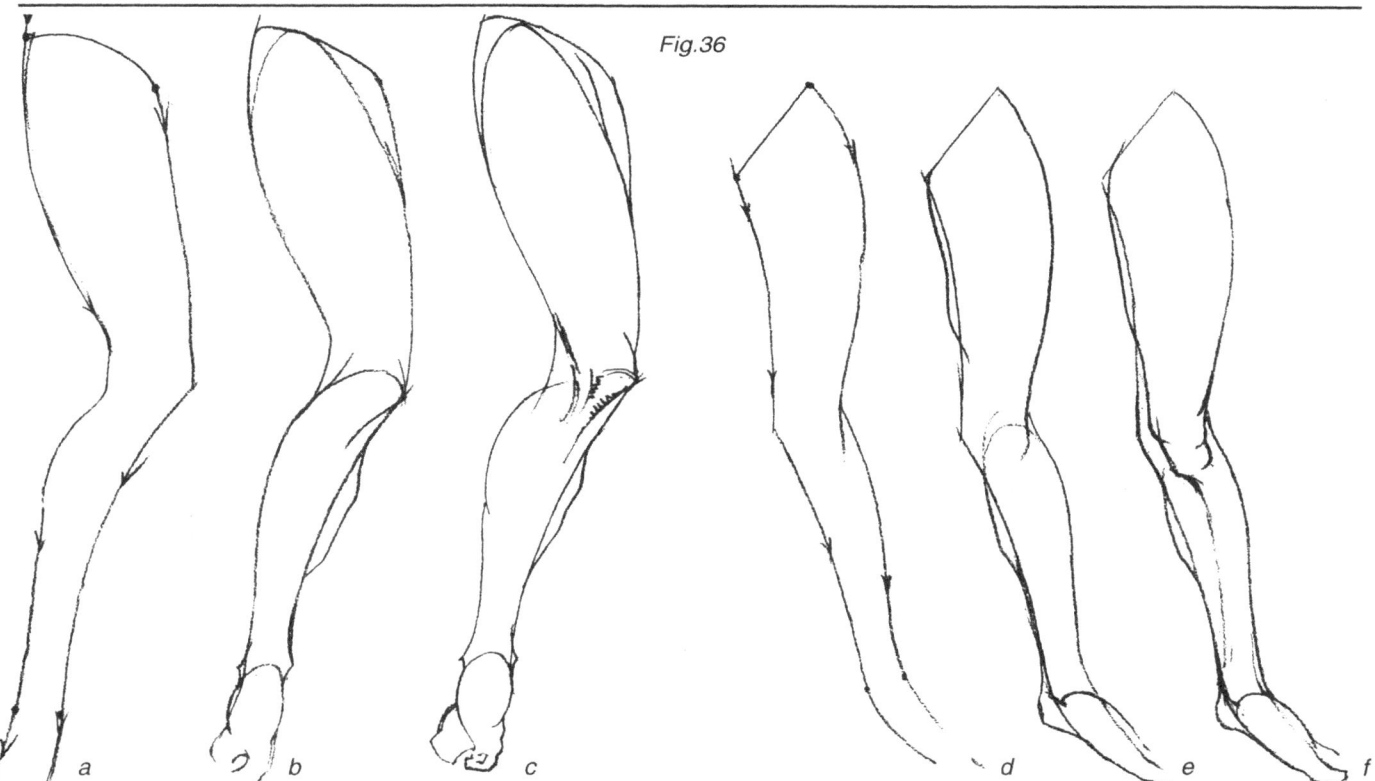

Fig.36

Figs. 36a.b.c.d.e.f. These six drawings show just two of the ways the structure lines of the leg may be drawn. *Figs. 36a.b. and c.* show a right leg and *Figs. 36d.e. and f.* show a left leg. In all cases one starts by drawing lines from the widest points of the form to the narrowest points of the form. The arrows point the direction the lines should be drawn. The second step is to put on the main, large forms and the third stage is to put on smaller forms. From this stage on one works towards the finish by drawing smaller and smaller forms making sure everything relates to everything else.

The drawing of the legs in the front view seated position is not as difficult as it seems if one uses logic. You first need a base line. This line is where you estimate the figure touches the flat surface. You next need to estimate the edge of this surface in relation to the base line. Once these indications are made you are ready to draw the legs. The first step is to draw two semicircle shapes designating where the legs start from the torso. From these semicircles draw the upper and lower structure lines. The two legs are drawn as one by drawing an arched line over both the semicircles to the outsides of the ankles. The bottom lines are drawn from the crotch point to the inside of the ankles. Pay particular attention to the position of the kneecap in relation to the edge of the flat surface. The top of the knee will be at all times on level with or above it unless the major portion of the upper leg is off the surface. Once these lines are established to your satisfaction add the forms to them, always working from the largest ones to the smaller ones. The following instructions give the simplest most logical way to approach this problem as well as many others.

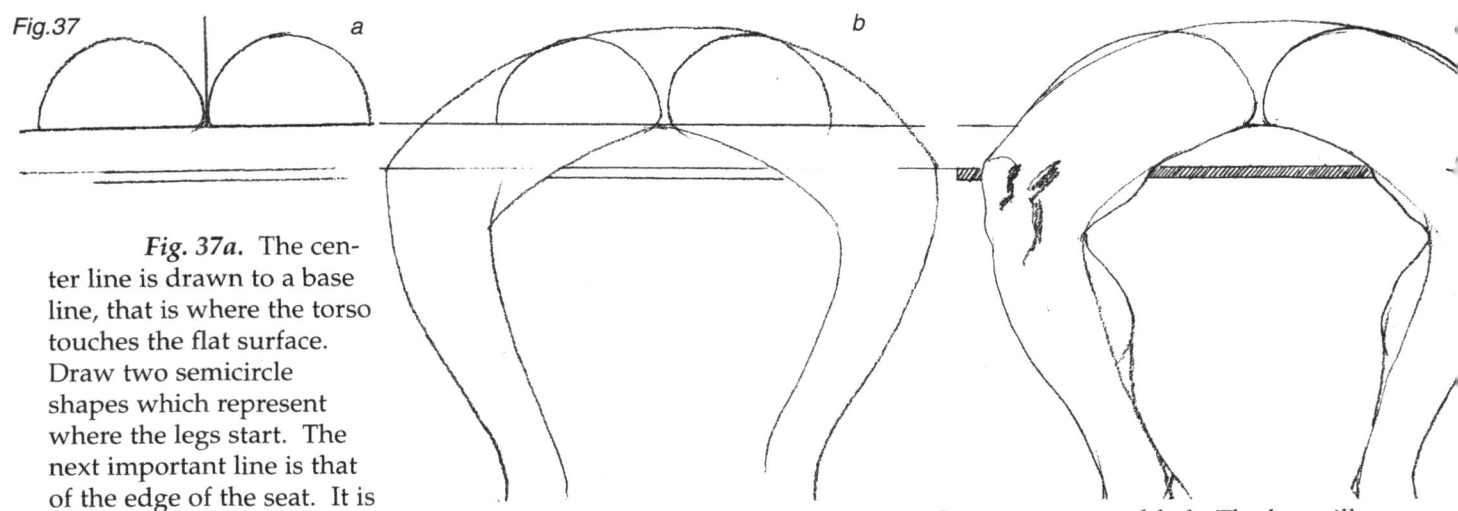

Fig. 37a. The center line is drawn to a base line, that is where the torso touches the flat surface. Draw two semicircle shapes which represent where the legs start. The next important line is that of the edge of the seat. It is estimated from the base line.

Fig. b. The two structure lines of the legs are now drawn. The top line arcs over the semicircles to relate both the legs; it goes to the outside width of the ankles and on to the feet. The bottom lines originate at the crotch point and go to the inside width of the ankles. Note the position of where the kneecaps will be.

Fig. c. Forms are now added. The leg will stay flat as long as it is on the surface. As soon as it leaves this surface the form will bulge downwards. Attention must be paid to the drawing of the kneecap in relation to the edge of the seat or platform.

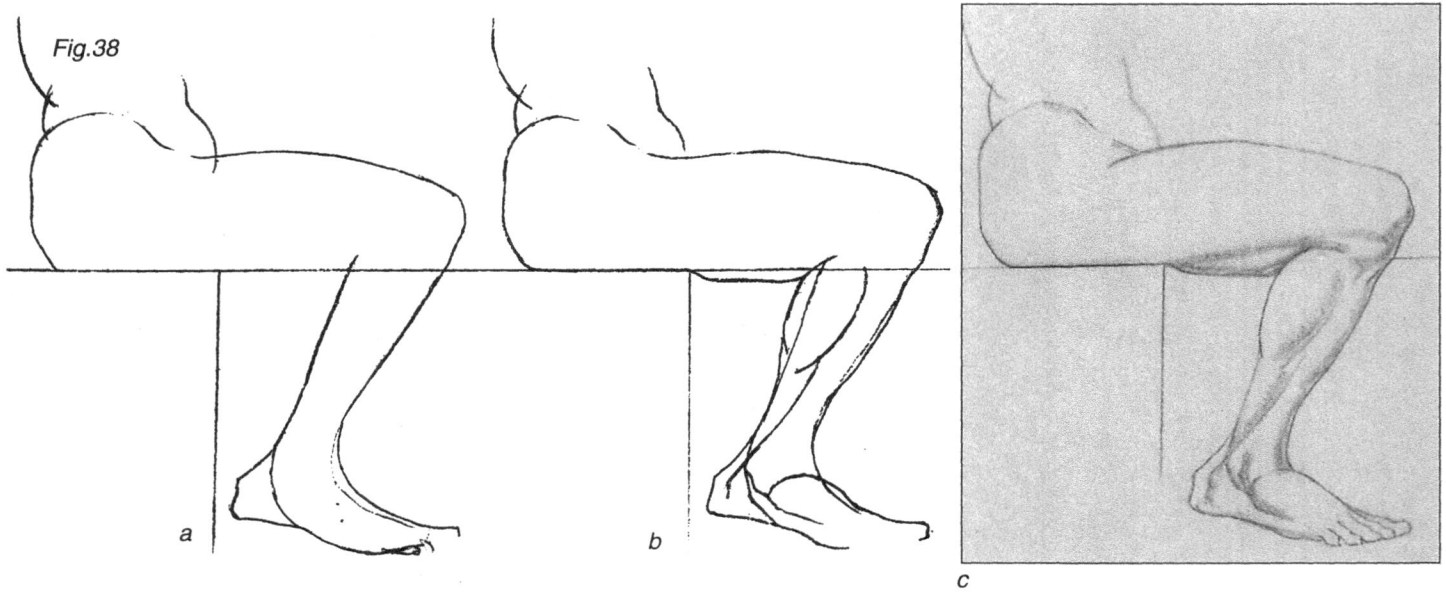

Fig. 38a. To draw the lower half of a seated figure in profile one draws the simple structure lines of the figure to the flat surface of the seat or surface and extends a line from it. This line is used to determine the height and position of the knee. In almost all cases students will draw it below this line, which is wrong unless the leg is almost all off the chair. One also needs a vertical line representing the side of the surface. This line is needed so you may judge the negative space between it and the lower leg.

Fig. b. The basic structure lines are altered by the addition of forms.

Fig. c. The drawing is carried towards completion by the drawing of even smaller forms, shading and variations of line.

Fig. 39a. Three steps showing how to draw the leg in almost front view, (seated). Start as previously discussed with a semicircle shape in the rear – resting on a base line. Next draw the knee shape which is in front of and higher than the semicircle. Be careful at what height you place it then connect both shapes.

Fig. b. Two dots are shown, one on the right side on the top corner of the knee, and one on the left side at the start of the crease of the lower leg. Draw curved structure lines from these points to the dots at the width of the ankle and on to the foot.

Fig. c. Forms and light and shade added. It is necessary to overlap these forms to produce the feeling of recession. Certain lines are shown emphasized to produce projection.

Fig. 40a. Three steps explaining the drawing of the leg from the inside. Start the structure lines

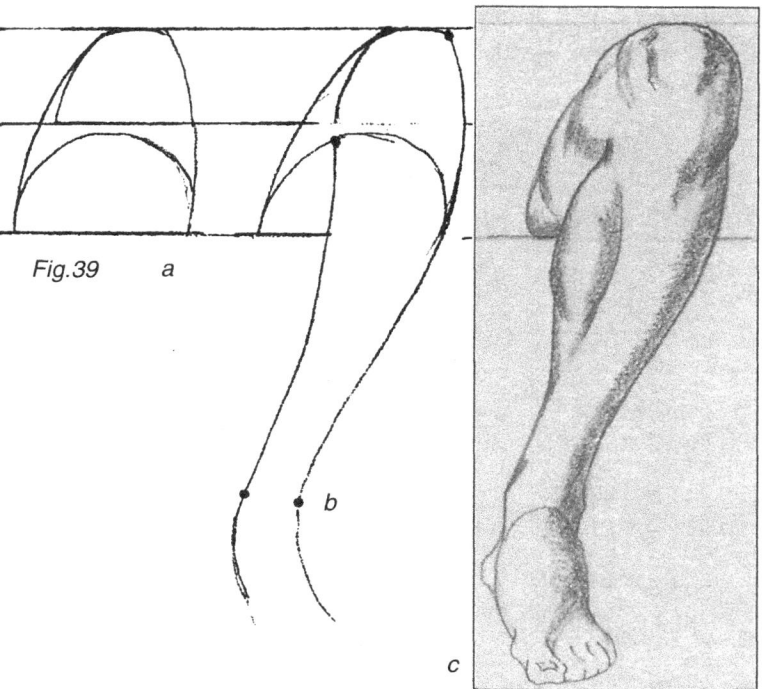

Fig.39 a

c

going from the upper dots to the lower dots following the directions of the arrows.

Fig. b. The forms of the kneecap, gastrocnemius and heel are drawn as well as the indications of the fatty forms. Note how one relates the top of the kneecap to the top of the gastrocnemius muscle. This is a pretty constant relationship and is very helpful.

Fig. c. Forms are further developed. Shading is used to convey the shapes of the forms as well as to convey the overlapping of forms to produce the feeling of the leg receding. Hard thin lines are used on the light side to produce projection and as an accent underneath the leg.

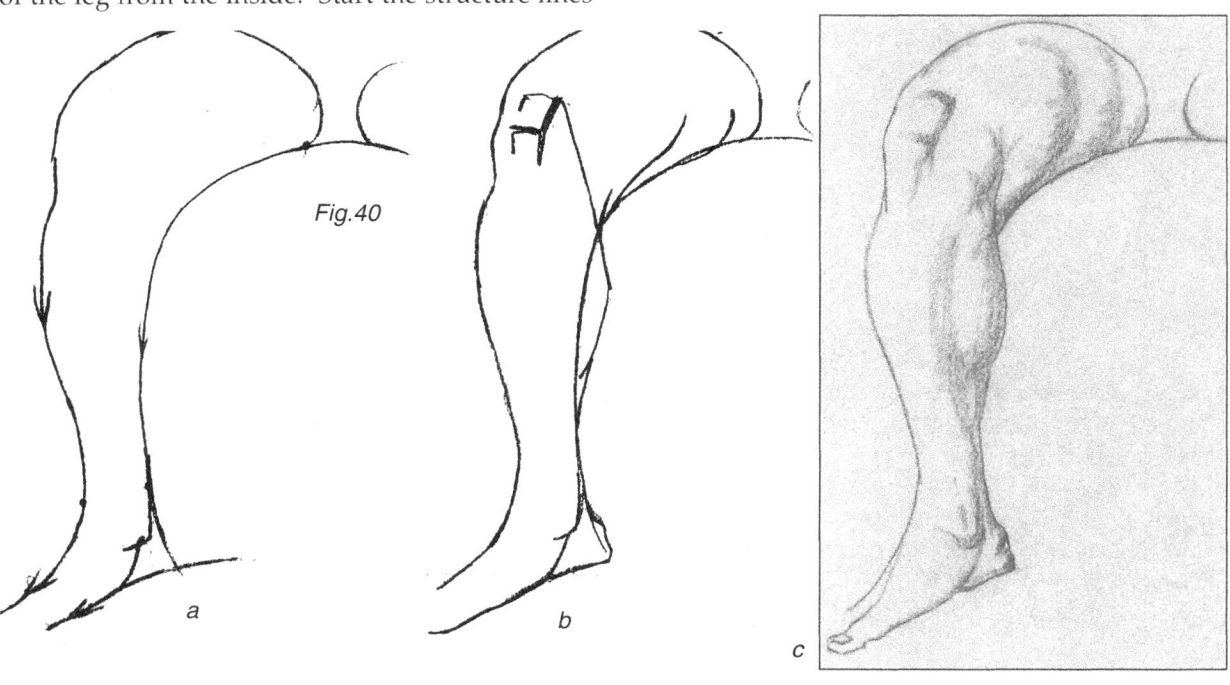

Fig.40

a   b   c

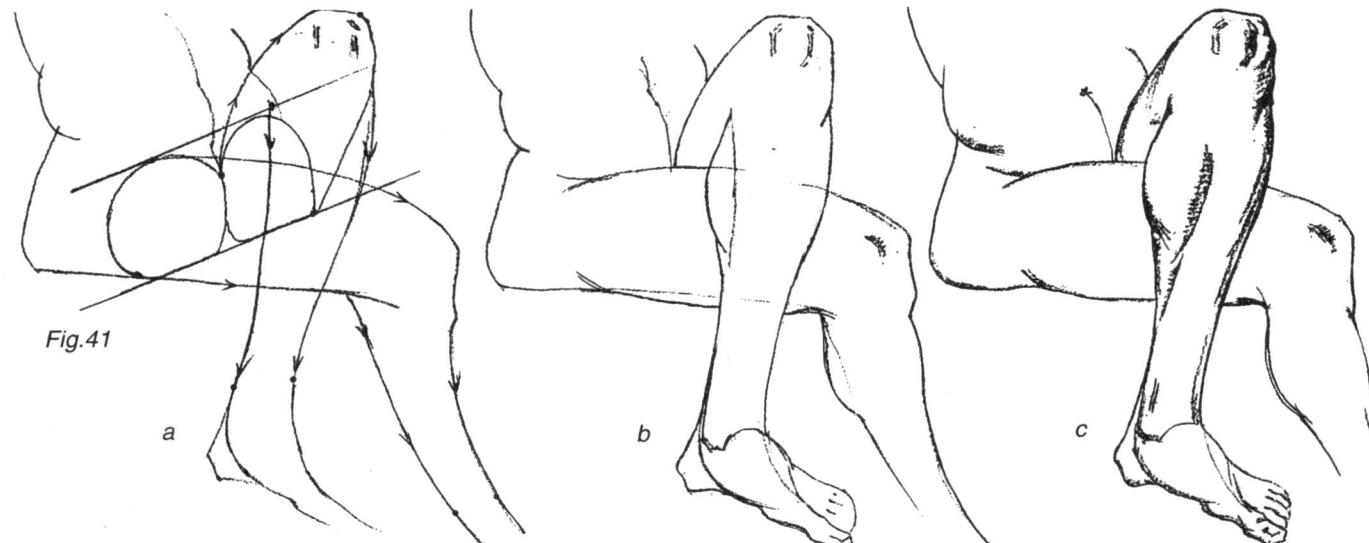

Fig.41

a

b

c

Fig. 41a. Three-quarter seated view with the left leg overlapping the right leg. You needn't draw all these preliminary lines but they would surely help you to get things in the right place and right perspective. Firstly, it is important to get the center line in the correct position. A base line of the proper angle is drawn next as well as shapes designating where the legs insert into the torso. These shapes are aligned with a line on the top of them also. The structure lines of the legs are now drawn. Start with the dots at the top, closest to the torso, follow the arrows and connect with the dots at the ankles.

Fig. b. Large basic forms are added to these structure lines.

Fig. c. Shading added to give a three dimensional aspect to forms. The drawing can continue with smaller and smaller forms with assurance now.

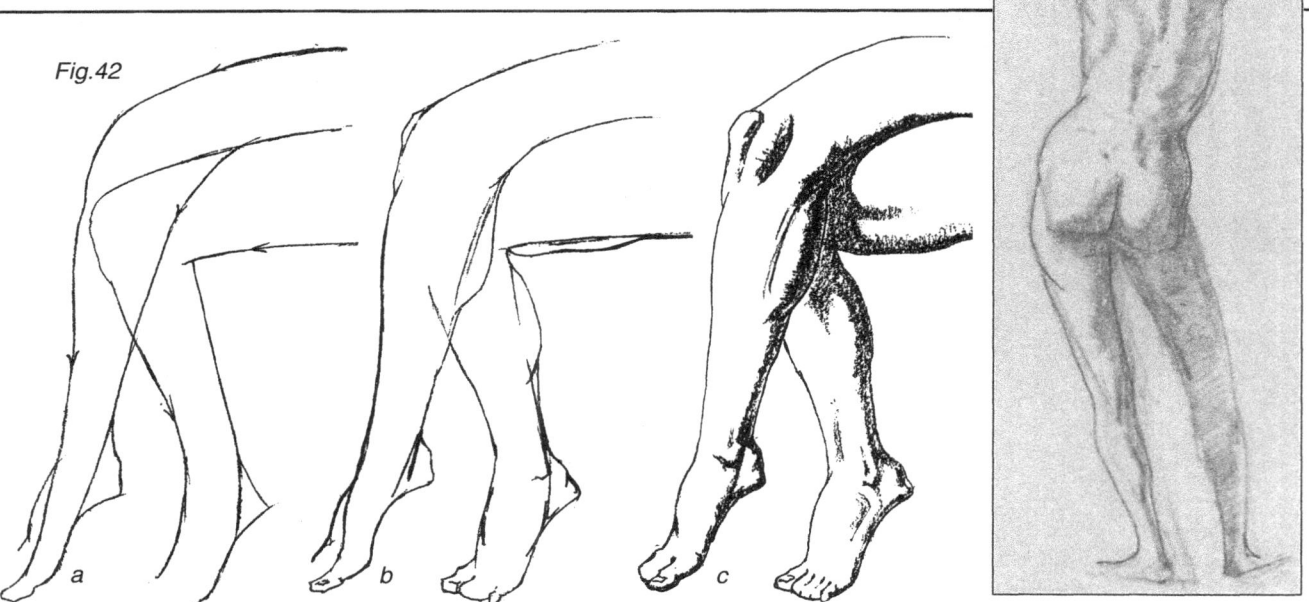

Fig.42

a

b

c

Fig. 42a. Right leg crossing over the left leg. As previously stated draw in the order that things occur. In this case, since the right leg is crossing over the left leg, one starts with the underlying left leg first. Now draw the right leg over the left leg with long sweeping lines that terminate at the end of the foot. Many times these lines will relate directly to the big toe. Please overlook all the anatomical forms at this point.

Fig. b. The large forms are now added. Pay particular attention to their shapes.

Fig. c. Smaller forms and shading added. The use of line is very important here. Notice the emphasis of the line on the back of the gastrocnemius form to make it project in front of the leg behind it. The line on the front of the left leg behind it is deliberately weakened to recede. A strong accent line is used at the bottom of the right overlapping leg. This helps separate the two legs.

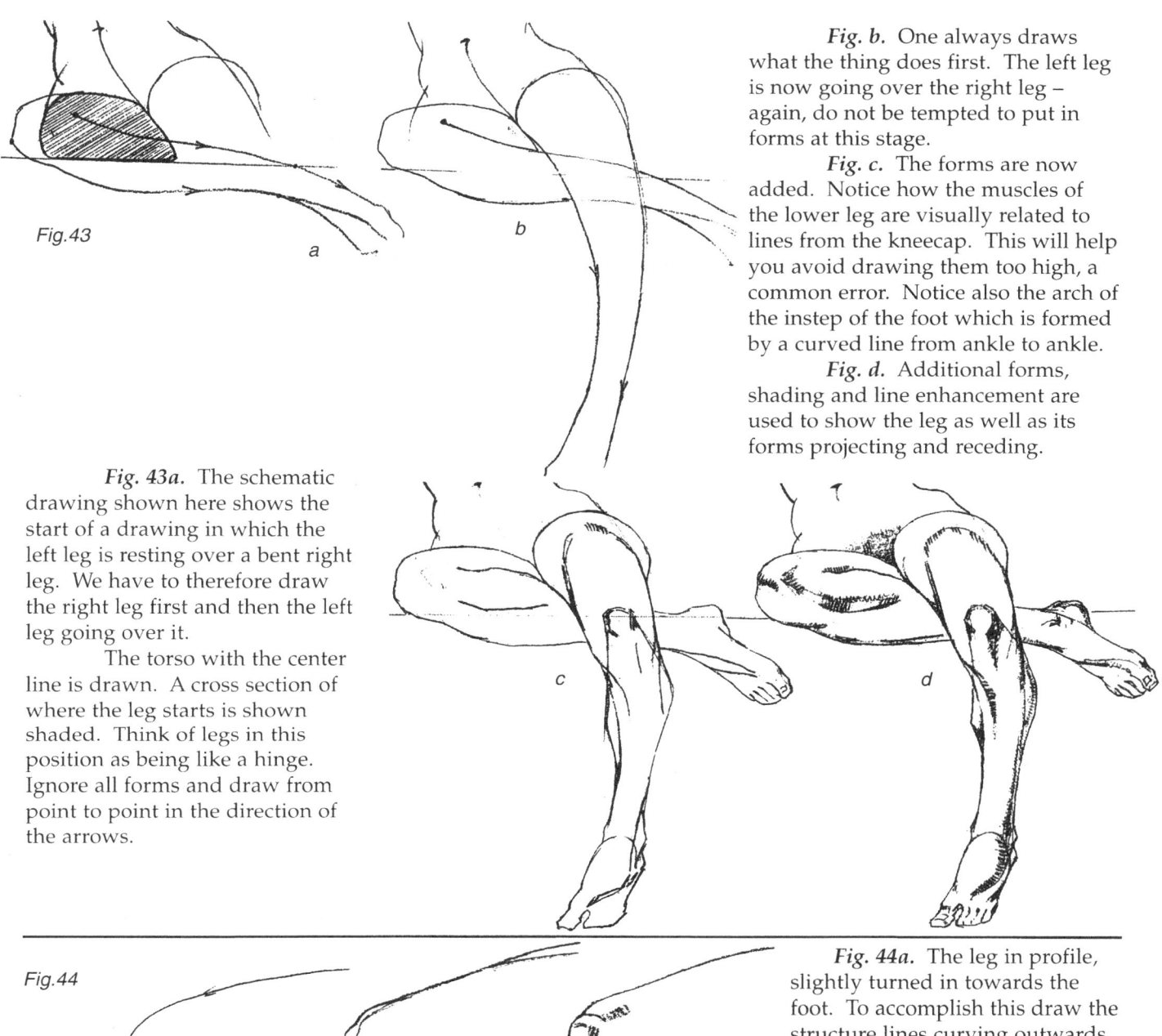

Fig. b. One always draws what the thing does first. The left leg is now going over the right leg – again, do not be tempted to put in forms at this stage.

Fig. c. The forms are now added. Notice how the muscles of the lower leg are visually related to lines from the kneecap. This will help you avoid drawing them too high, a common error. Notice also the arch of the instep of the foot which is formed by a curved line from ankle to ankle.

Fig. d. Additional forms, shading and line enhancement are used to show the leg as well as its forms projecting and receding.

Fig.43

a

Fig. 43a. The schematic drawing shown here shows the start of a drawing in which the left leg is resting over a bent right leg. We have to therefore draw the right leg first and then the left leg going over it.

The torso with the center line is drawn. A cross section of where the leg starts is shown shaded. Think of legs in this position as being like a hinge. Ignore all forms and draw from point to point in the direction of the arrows.

b

c

d

Fig.44

a

b

c

Fig. 44a. The leg in profile, slightly turned in towards the foot. To accomplish this draw the structure lines curving outwards as you approach the ankles. It is important to get the proper curvature of these lines in order to show if one is looking at a leg straight on or if the lower part is further away from your point of sight than the upper part.

Fig. b. Large forms added – always going with the direction of the action. Notice how the original structure line always goes around the ankle to the bottom of the foot.

Fig. c. Smaller forms are now added. Shading and line are used to give the appearance of bulk and volume to these forms.

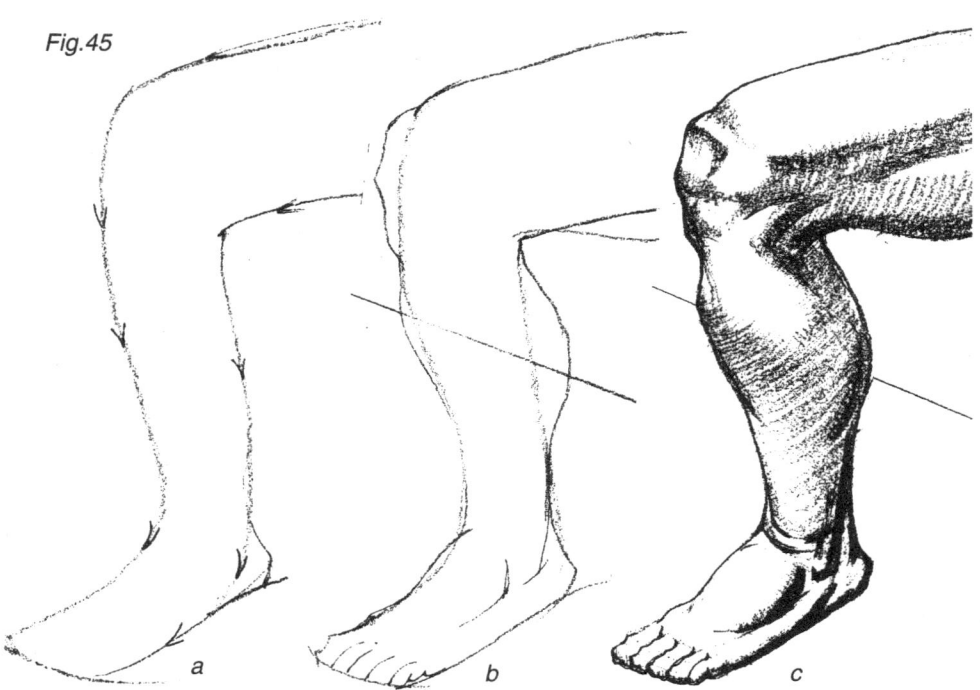

Fig.45

Fig. b. The drawing on its way to completion. Forms and their planes are developed with shading. You must overlap as many forms as you can see by the use of line and value to achieve this effect. The curved strokes of shading suggest the forms going away from you. As you can see almost all of the original lines have vanished but they are responsible for the truthfulness of the drawing.

The following series of drawings, *Figs. 47a.b.c.d. and e.,* show how to use the structure lines in a seemingly complex pose. Actually they're all complex until you learn how to figure them out. I suggest you skip ahead to *Fig. 47e.* first so as to understand what eventually happens to these beginning structure lines.

Figs. 45a.b.c. The same leg as shown in previous *Fig. 44a.b. and c.* only going into more severe perspective. Follow the same procedure with the exception of shading. Here one would have to use curved strokes of shading to represent the form going down and away from you.

Fig. 46a. This schematic reveals the hidden underlying structure lines and relationships of a leg in severe foreshortening. The lines with the arrows on them are the first to be drawn. Notice how all the lines relate to each other.

Fig. 47a. Assume the figure is sitting bending forward with the left leg going over a bottom bent right leg. Start with the oval of the skull and draw a center line through it to the crotch. Since this is basically a three-quarter looking down pose we have to draw a rectangle in perspective representing the width of the top of the shoulders. Now draw lines from the widest points of the shoulders to the crotch forming a triangle. The rib cage form fits

Fig.47

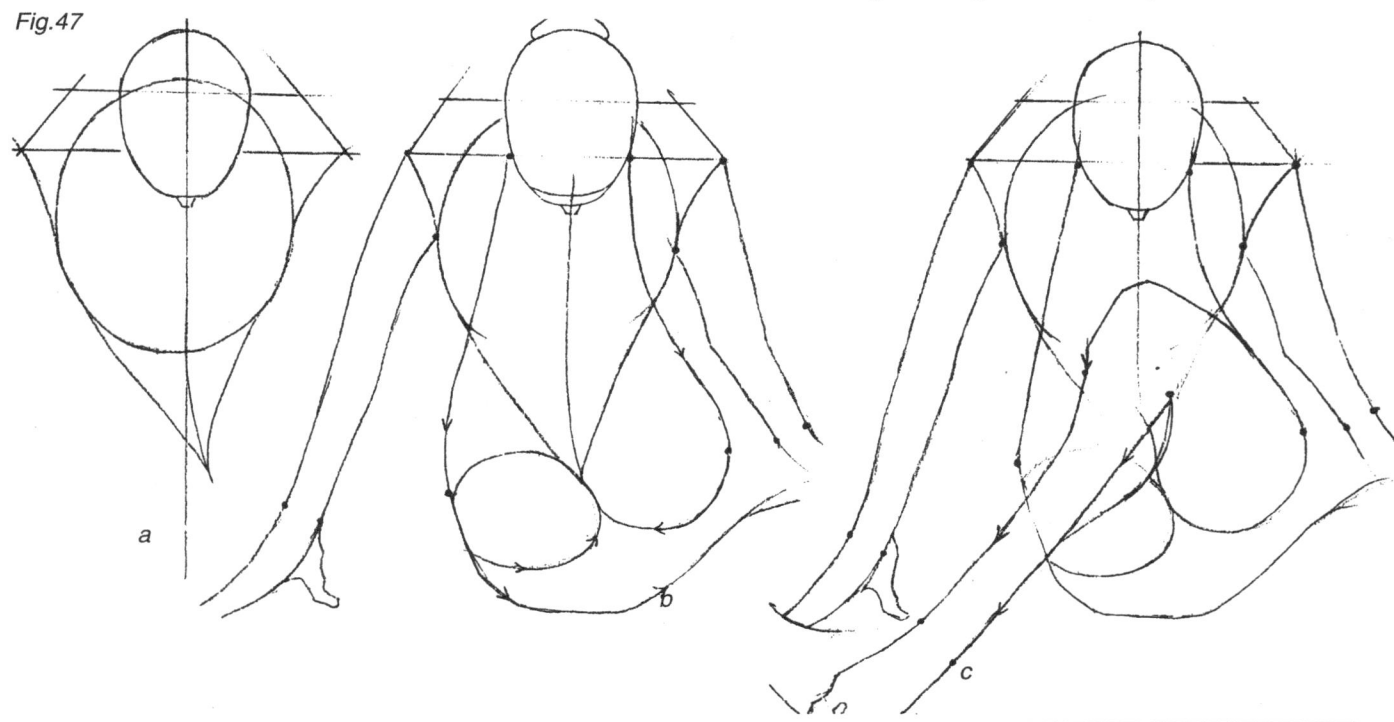

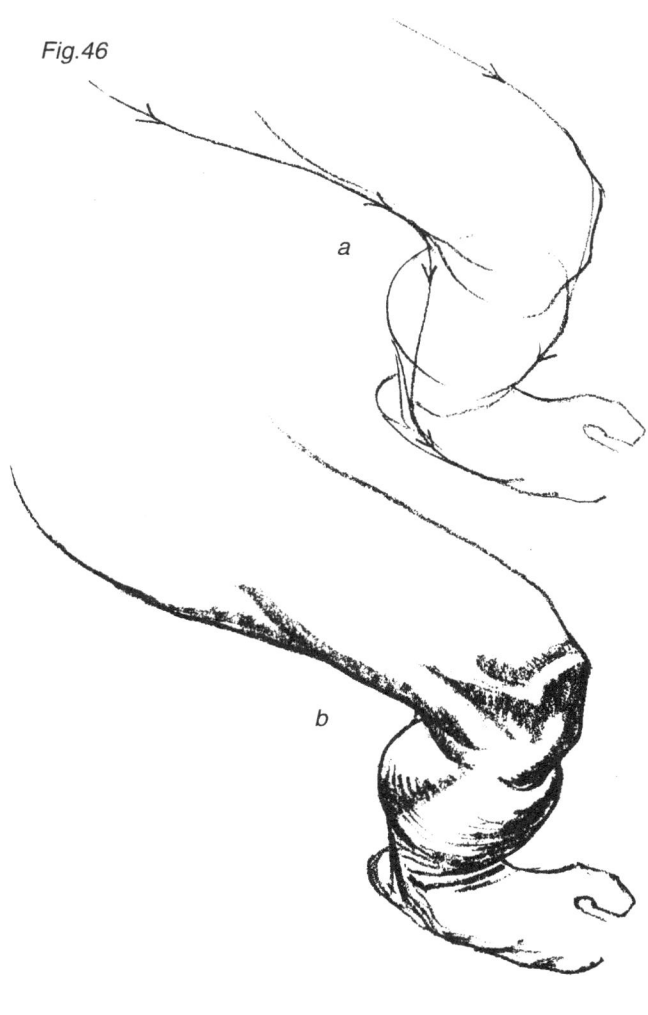

Fig.46

a

b

within this triangle and connects to the back of the neck hole. This stage is basically no different than the previous lessons on figure construction.

Fig. b. Dots represent the points from where you start the rest of the structure lines. The arms come from the two upper points to the two lower points on the wrist and out to the fingers. Two lines also come from near the ear to the widest points on the lower half of the figure. Follow the arrows on these lines to make the cross sections of the leg. The structure line on the model's right side continues to the bottom of the leg.

Fig. c. The basic structure lines of the model's left leg are drawn. Start at the dots and follow the arrows.

Fig. d. The structure lines of the lower leg are completed. Draw from dot to dot. Arrowheads point to breaks in the curvature of the bottom line. It is exceedingly complex here and you have to observe carefully. Forms such as the gastrocnemius and heel of the foot can be added to the left leg.

Fig. e. Forms with their planes and shading are added. Both line and shading have to be used to best explain what the forms are doing. It is essential that one emphasize the knee form on the lower leg to show the difference between the upper and lower part of that leg. Soft curved lines of shading will give the feeling of the bulk of the back leg receding. Hard thin lines are reserved for bony areas and projection. Of course if one was drawing the full figure all the forms of the body would be developed emphasizing certain ones and de-emphasizing others according to one's intent.

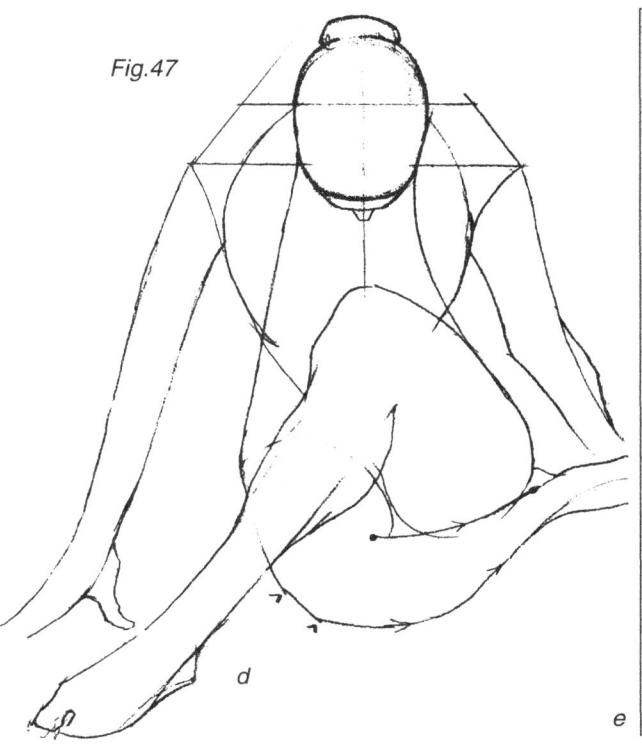

Fig.47

d

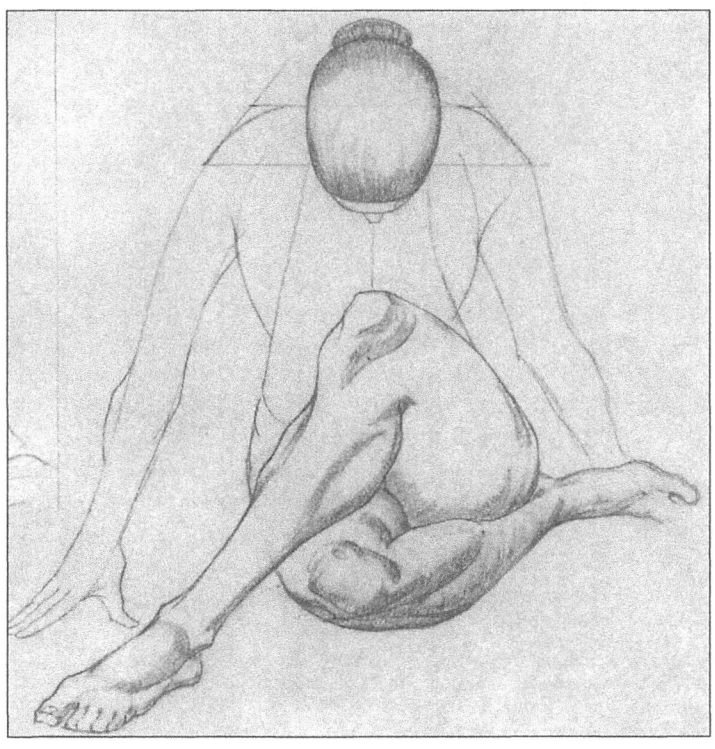

e

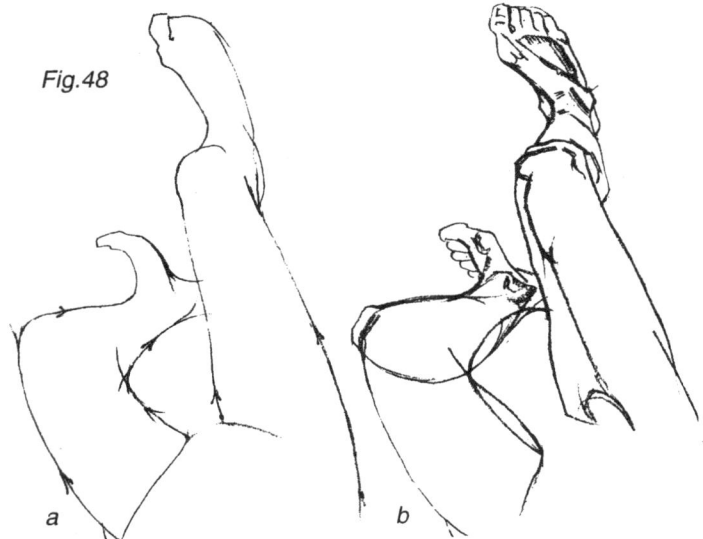

Fig.48

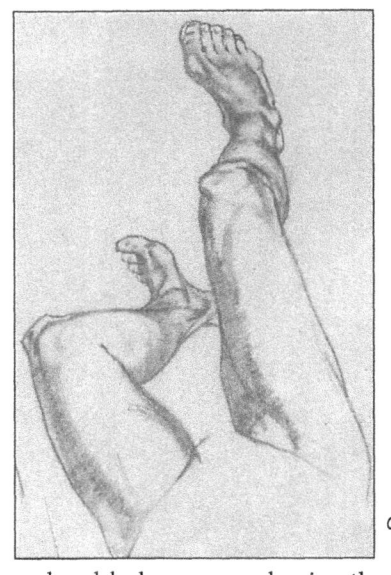

c

Figs. 48a.b.c. These three drawings explain how to use the structure system to draw the legs in foreshortening, in this case, going away from you. Before you start analyze the drawing in *Fig. 48c.* Look past all the anatomical forms and reduce everything to two simple structure lines that run through the entire leg as shown in *Fig. 48a.* The next step is to put on the forms, relating the lines as much as possible as shown on *Fig. 48b.*

One should always emphasize the knee form as shown on the right leg to define separation between the upper and lower leg. *Fig. 48c.* shows shading to define the forms. Show as many overlapping forms as you can. Curve the lines of shading to produce the effect of recession. This drawing is deliberately overdone at the extremities for clarity. To make the lower leg and foot appear to recede more the lines in that area should be lighter and softer.

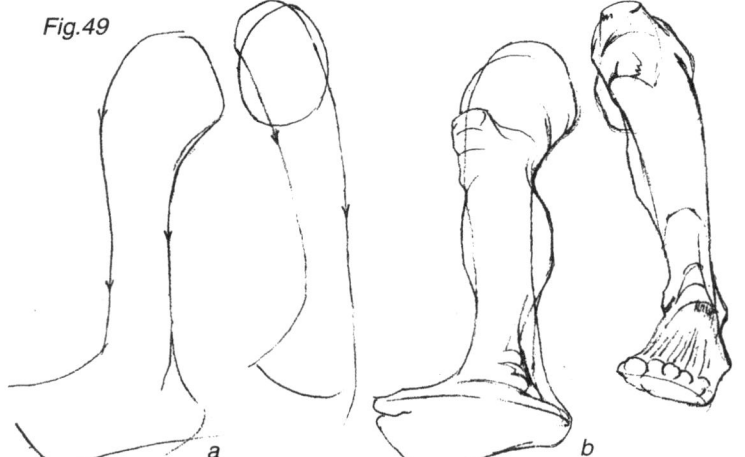

Fig.49

a

b

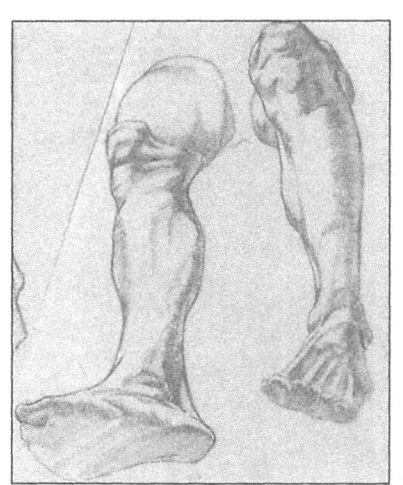

c

Figs. 49a.b.c. Again three drawings showing the legs in foreshortening only this time coming towards you. Follow the same instructions given for *Figs. 48a.b. and c.* The front most parts of the lower leg and feet can be made much larger than they appear to the eye to aid in the perception that they are closest to you. Notice the overlapping of many forms through shading and line. Especially note the thin hard line on top of the kneecap on the right leg and the hard edge of the knee form of the left leg to make them project from the upper rear part of the leg.

The previous examples of drawings made by starting with the use of structure lines should be enough to enable you to figure out how to draw the figure or parts of the figure in any position. As you

can see there is no one way that works for everything but the thinking and procedure is essentially the same, useful and valid.

If you are drawing a limb ask yourself, "Where is it coming from, where is it going?" and draw two simple structure lines to express that idea. Next one adds the forms, the largest ones first paying particular attention to their specific shape. Lastly use shading to designate the overall light and shade, foreshortening and side and bottom planes of the form. In a full value drawing top planes would have to be added by either erasing part of a light undertone or by the use of white chalk. *Once these lessons are learned the skillful artist will make the drawing using line and light and shade all at the same time.*

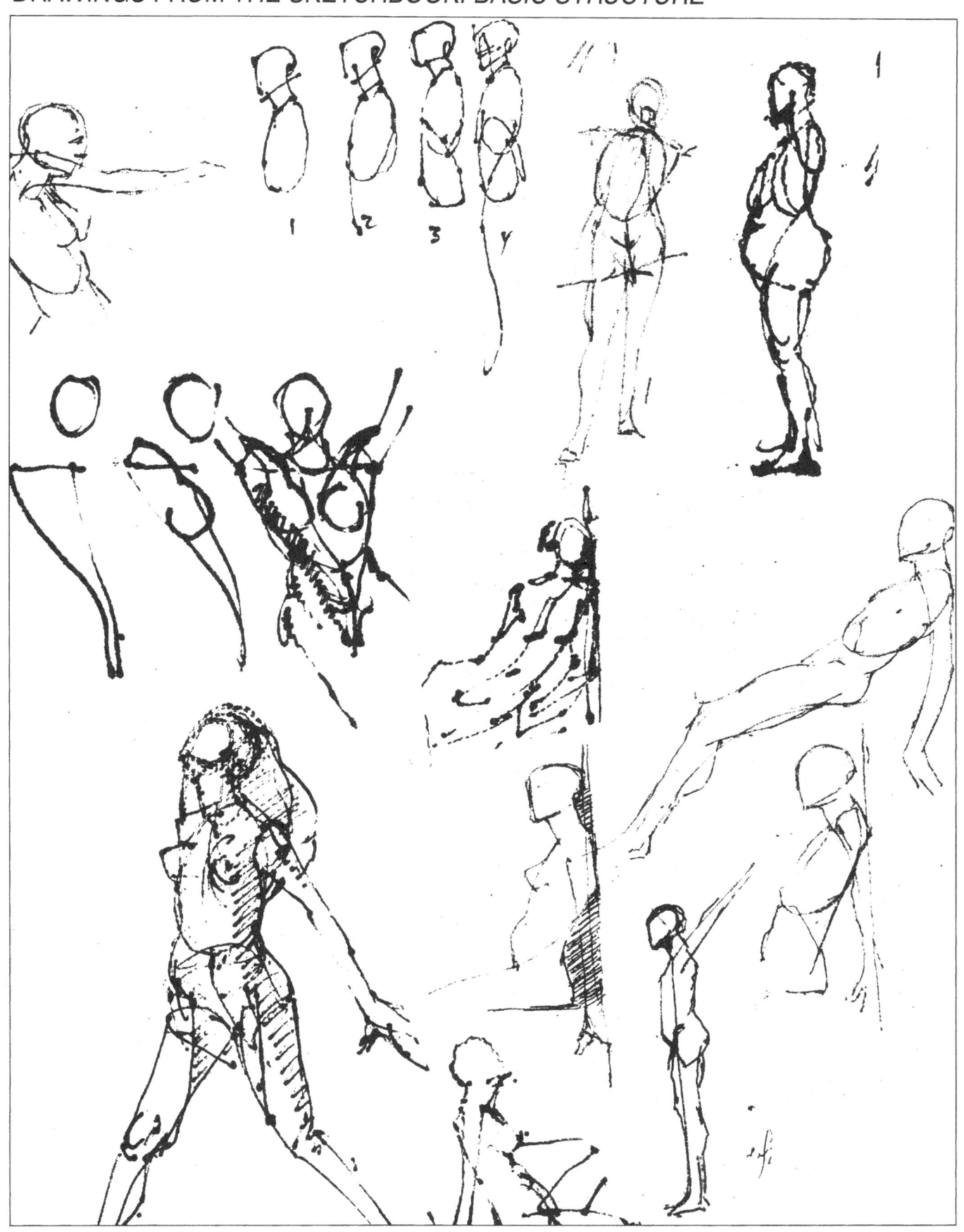

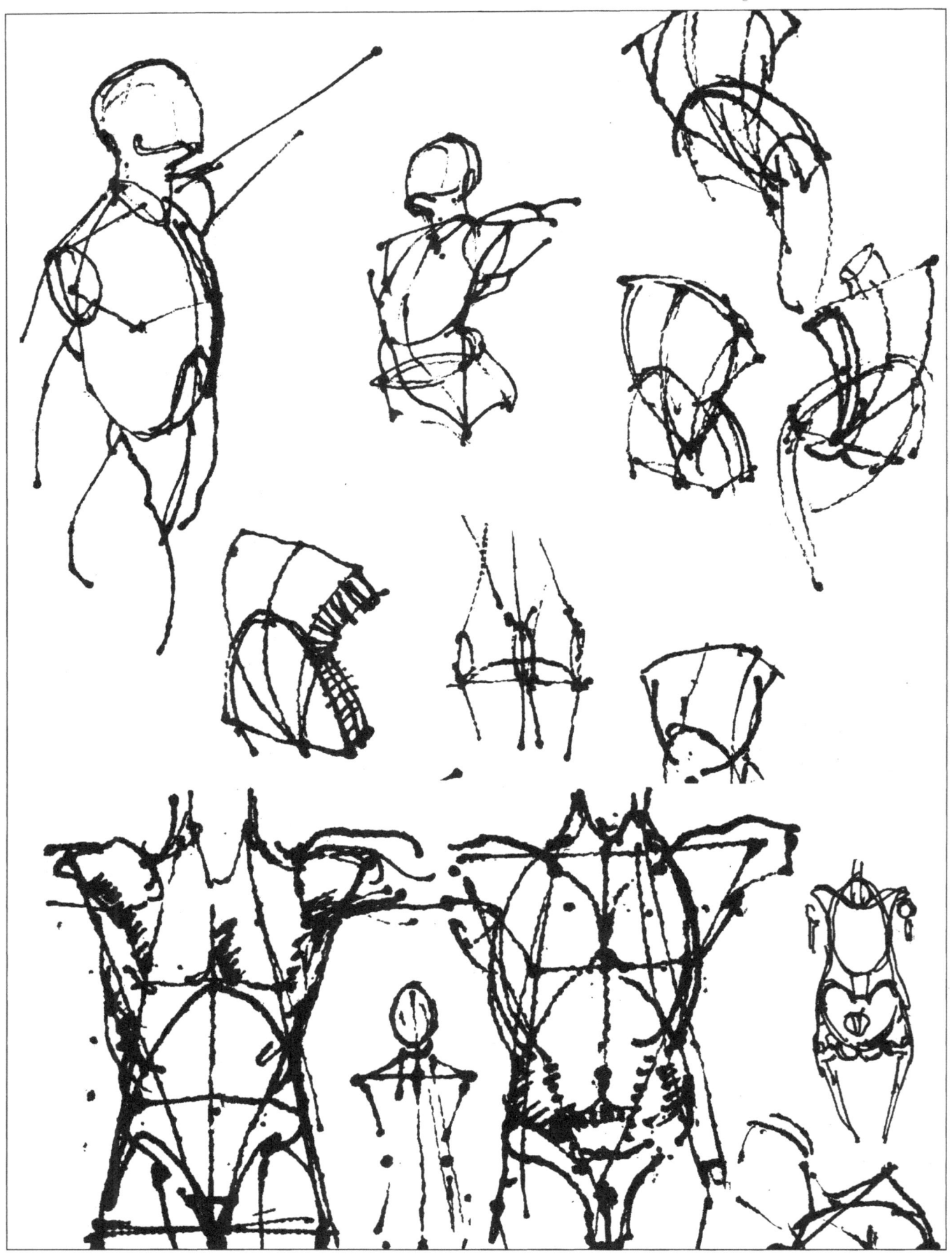

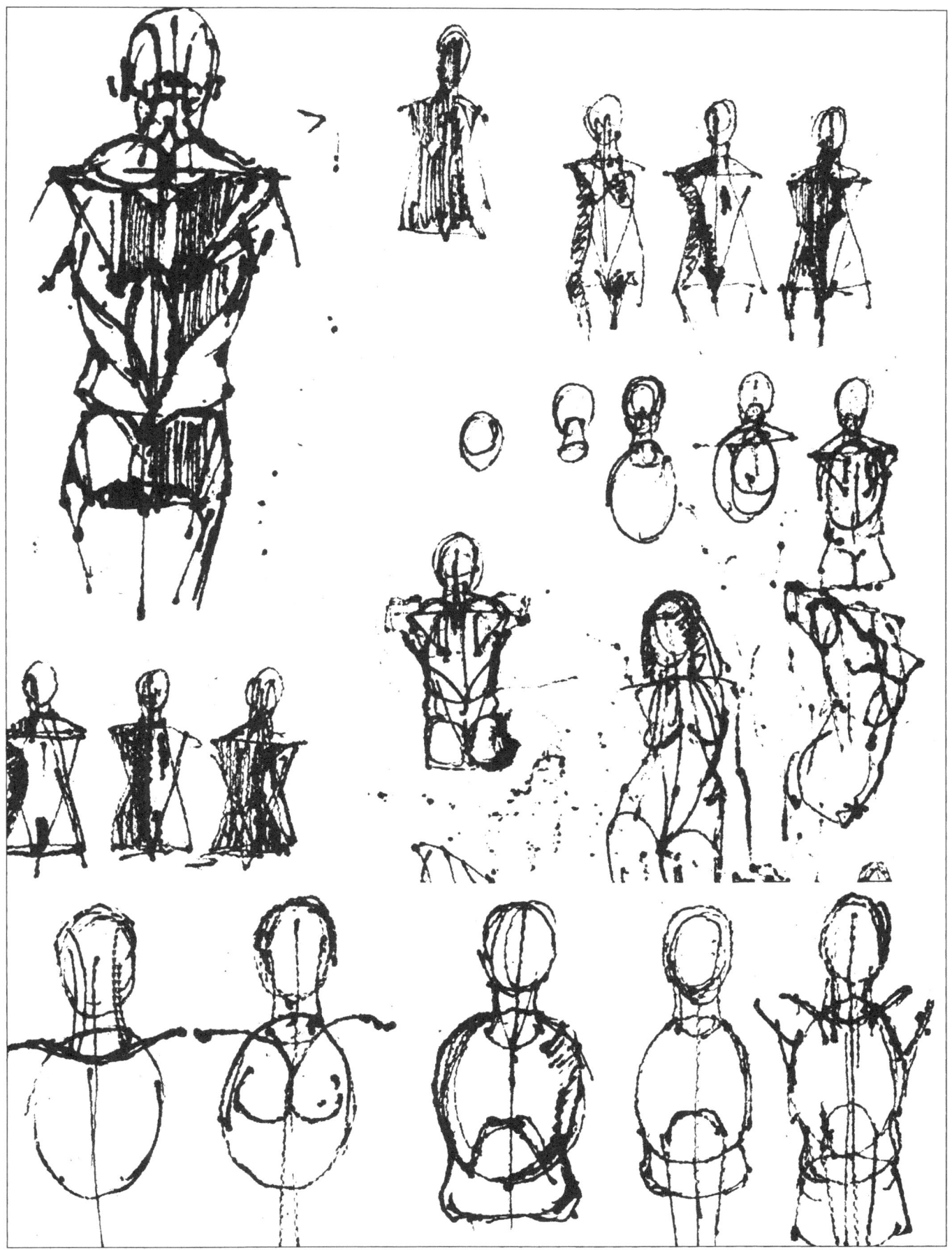

ELEVEN

PLANES OF THE TORSO

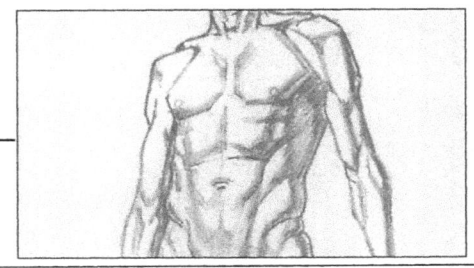

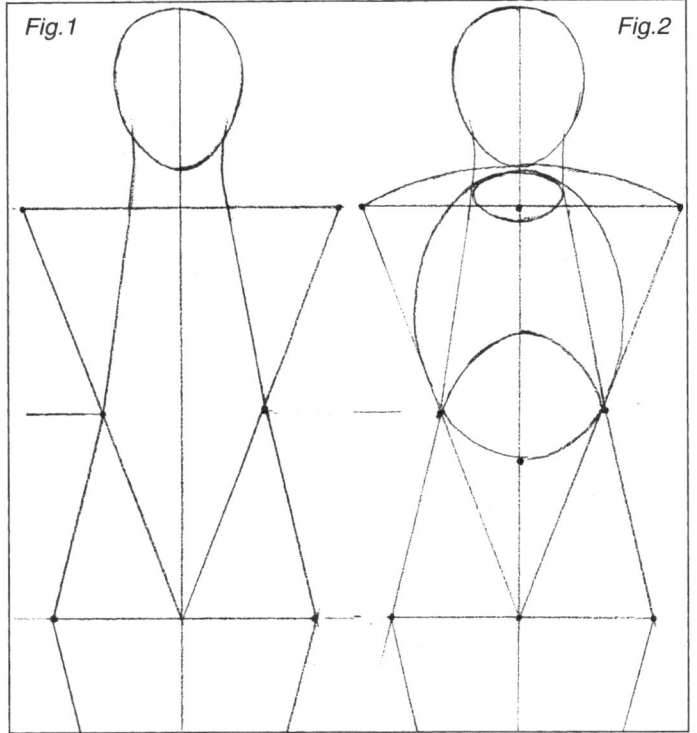

Fig.1

Fig.2

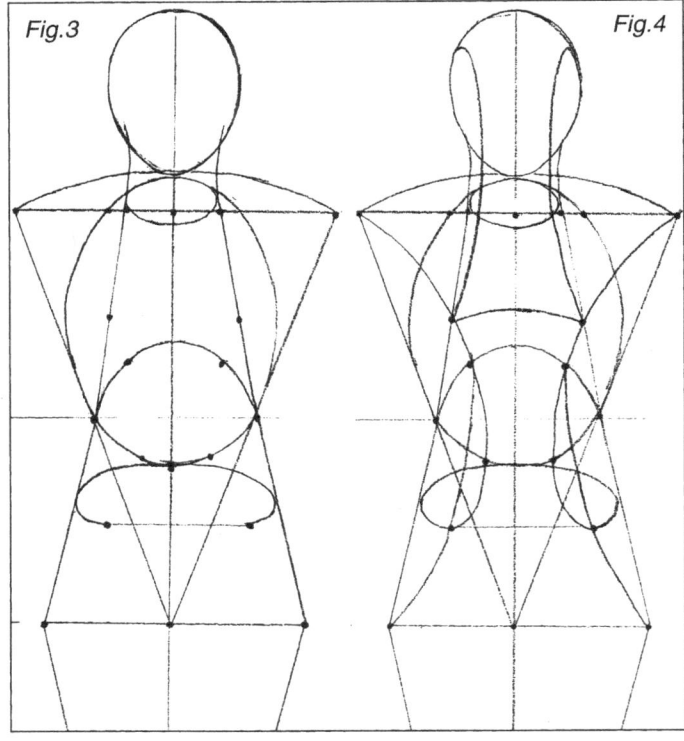

Fig.3

Fig.4

The following chapter on the planes of the torso is of the utmost importance. Before you start these I suggest you reread Chapters 6 and 7 as to what forms and planes really are.

These drawings, or schematics if you will, show how the planes and forms are related to the basic figure drawing which was shown earlier in the book. We now go further.

You will not see all the planes and the forms at the same time for depending on the position of the light some planes will be revealed and others hidden, either by deep shadows or by being bleached out in the bright light; nevertheless they are always present.

Forms and planes will also vary with the individual. The planes of thin, emaciated individuals are more readily apparent than obese, rotund people. Again, certain occupations or activities will develop different muscular shapes thereby making even more planes at a particular area of the body.

These schematics then are a guide for you. They tell you where to look and what to look for; they are essential to creating the illusion of light and shade on form. The human torso will conform generally to what is shown here.

Study these schematics well. Test yourself by drawing them from memory. Put tracing paper over

them, imagine light coming from a certain direction and shade in the planes that go into shadow or halftone. Prepare yourself to draw from the model by drawing the lines of the borders of the planes with a Pentel type pen over good photographic reproductions. Lastly draw from the model searching out the planes, how they interrelate with forms and how it all goes into action.

Not only should the knowledge of the planes and forms help you draw and paint better, but hopefully, by revealing things that you always looked at but never saw, help you appreciate the beauty and design of the human form.

PLANES OF THE TORSO, FRONT

Fig. 1. The basic upper torso figure abstraction. This is divided into thirds. There is one third distance between the top of the head and the top of the shoulders, one third distance between the top of the shoulders to the waist line and one third distance between the waist line and the hip line. There are two dots at the widest points of the shoulders, two dots at the widest points of the waist and two dots at the widest points of the hips. Pay particular attention to these and all the other dots on the diagrams for all the forms and planes connect with them

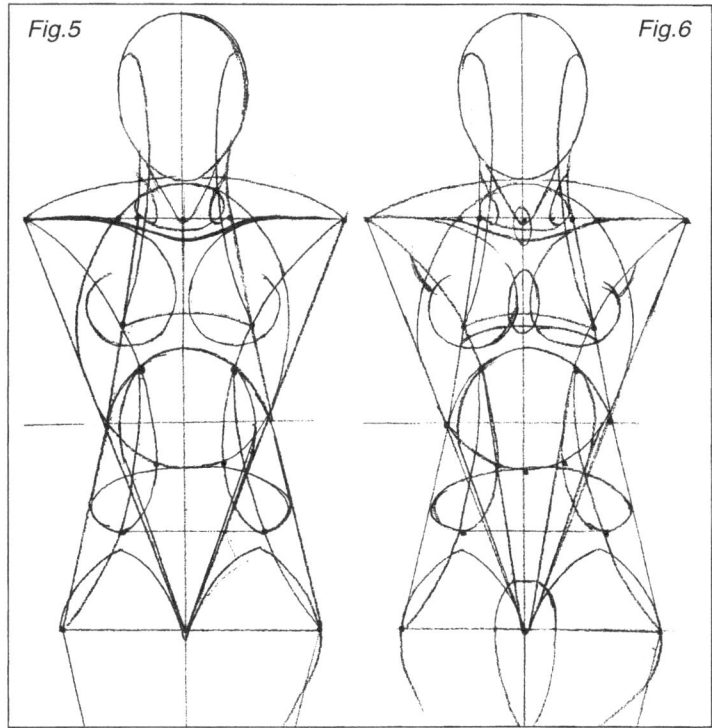

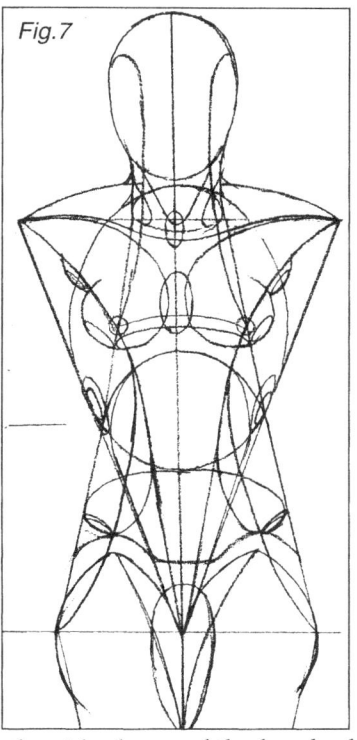

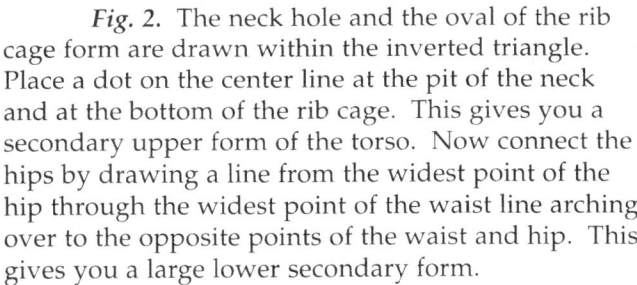

Fig. 2. The neck hole and the oval of the rib cage form are drawn within the inverted triangle. Place a dot on the center line at the pit of the neck and at the bottom of the rib cage. This gives you a secondary upper form of the torso. Now connect the hips by drawing a line from the widest point of the hip through the widest point of the waist line arching over to the opposite points of the waist and hip. This gives you a large lower secondary form.

Fig. 3. Draw a semicircle starting at the point of the navel. This represents the top of the pelvis form. At the ends of this interrupted semicircle are two dots representing the iliac crest. The dots on the lines extending from the neck to the widest points of the hips represent the nipples of the breasts. Place additional dots in the positions they are shown in. To clarify their meaning refer to the final completed diagram.

Fig. 4. The first big sideplanes are made by connecting the dots at the widest points of the torso – that is from the widest point of the shoulder through the nipple of the breast through the point on the top of the pelvis form and on to the widest point of the hip. The line which extends from the point on top of the pelvis form connects with a point which will be the side of the stomach form and goes on to connect with the point of the crest of the iliac. Note also how

the sideplanes of the head relate to the nipples of the breasts forming a squarish shape. This plane seen in profile would appear as a top plane of a 45 degree angle.

Fig. 5. Forms are now added. The sterno-mastoid muscles are drawn within the neck form. The bow shaped line running along the shoulder line is the start of the clavicle. The breast forms are added as well as the form of the combined abdominal muscles. The topmost forms of the legs are shown inserting into the torso.

Fig. 6. Smaller side and bottom planes are added. You will note the oval shapes between the bottom of the sterno-mastoid muscles, the breasts and the insides of the legs. These create some of the sideplanes of the forms. Bottom planes are added to the breasts and pubic area. Lines starting from the wide points of the shoulders through the nipples of the breasts and on to the points on either side of the navel to the crotch form the minor sideplanes of the abdominal region.

Fig. 7. Additional sideplanes added to the breasts and bottom of the rib cage form and the inner leg. Bottom planes added to the external obliques. *All forms can be divided into more and more planes and all planes can be subdivided ad-infinitum.*

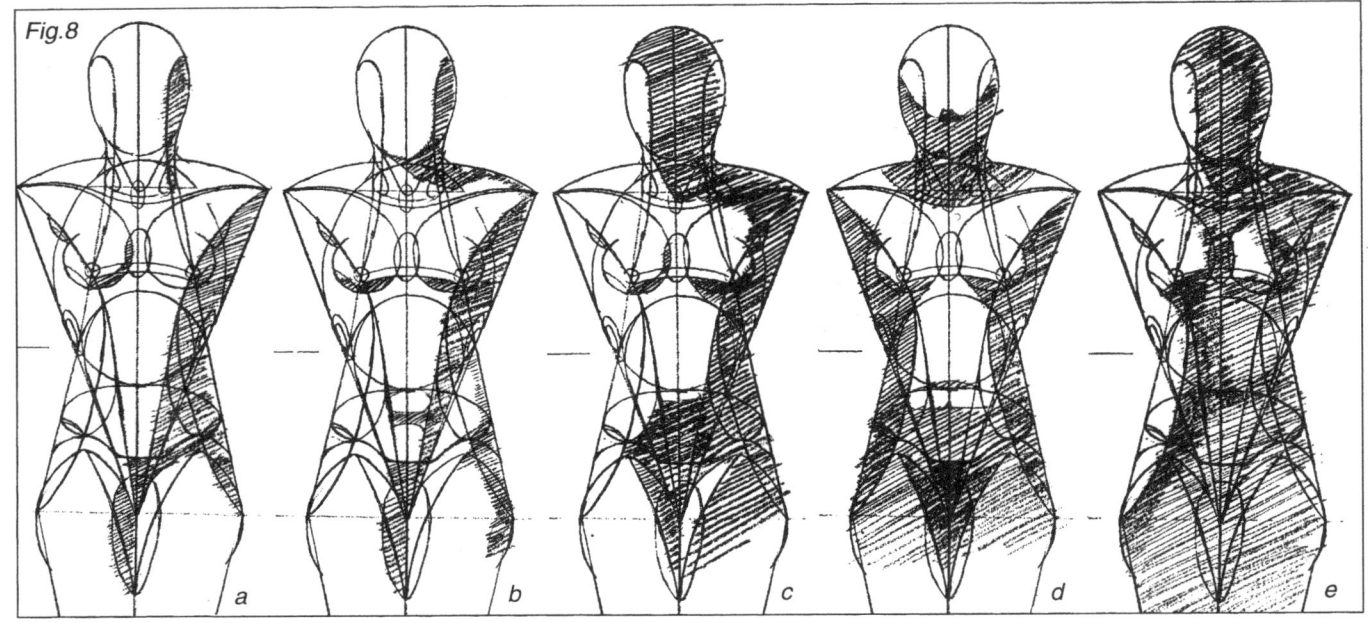

Fig.8

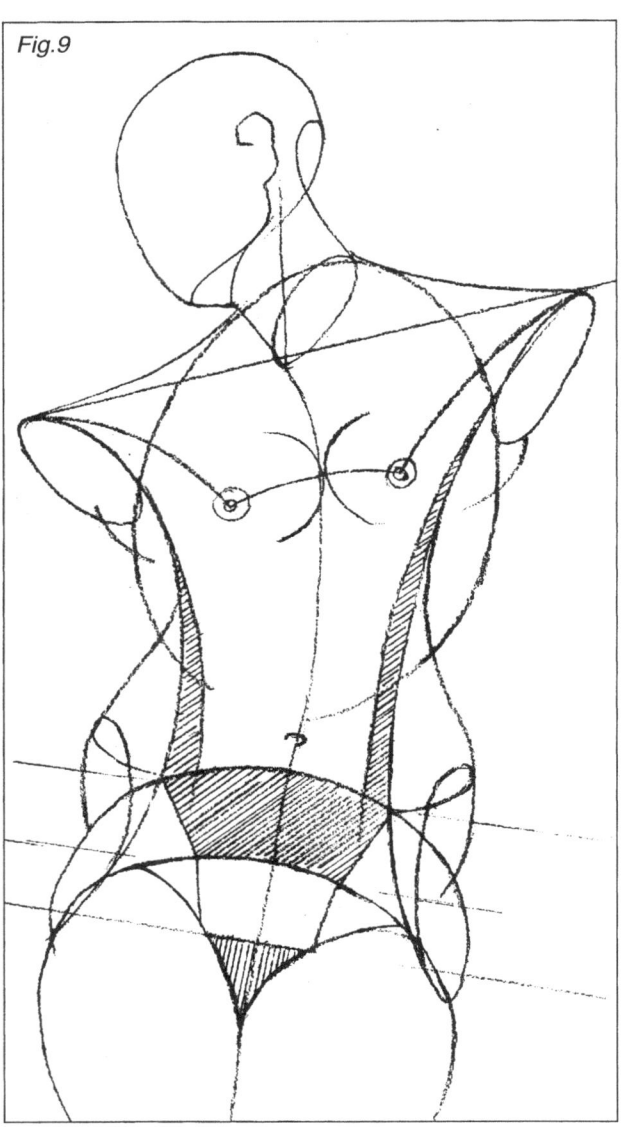

Fig.9

Figs. 8a.b.c.d. and e. This series of schematics show how, depending on the position of the light source, which planes will go into shadow. This series can be carried on indefinitely. Try this exercise. Place tracing paper over ***Fig. 7.*** Imagine the position of a light source and shade on the planes that go into shadow. Rereading the chapter on Light and Shade on Forms and Planes will be helpful to you at this point.

Fig. 9. An example of a more humanized figure in action. The drawing shows in a highly simplified way how the structure lines and the lines of the planes and forms interrelate.

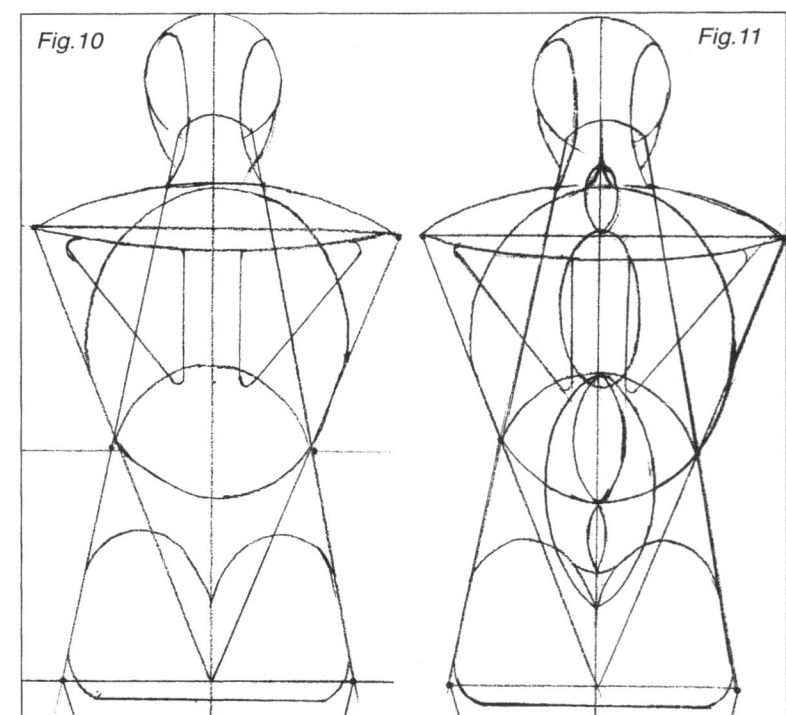

Fig.10

Fig.11

PLANES OF THE TORSO, BACK

Fig. 10. The planes of the back are very complex and of course will vary tremendously depending on which muscles are developed or underdeveloped. Following these schematics step by step will give you the idea or concept you should try to develop.

You will not find many backs with as many forms and planes as shown here but at the same time there are backs that have even more forms and planes. The essential thing is, however, that the big forms and planes are understood; how many other forms and planes there are depends on the individual.

The example, *(Fig. 10.)*, shows the basic figure abstraction with the major forms. Note the spherical shape of the back of the skull, the rib cage form and the buttock forms. Two triangular shapes representing the scapulae rest upon the rib cage form. Notice that the bottom of the buttocks are below the crotch line.

Fig. 11. This schematic shows how the sideplanes of two symmetrical forms are related by drawing ovals. The most obvious ones are seen on the trapezius forms, the scapulae and the buttocks. The ovals represent the small flat planes of the back.

Fig. 12. The first big sideplanes are added in the same manner as in the front view that is by drawing – curved lines from the widest points of the shoulders to the widest points of the hips. As they do this they create the outer sideplanes of the scapula and the buttocks forms. Within these sideplanes of the buttocks are top planes and above them the

forms of the external obliques. A bottom plane runs across the two buttock forms.

Fig. 13. The big sideplanes are now subdivided into narrower planes. They originate from the top of the ovals which are the bottom sideplanes of the rib cage and continue to the widest points of the hips.

Fig. 14. The final stage is the "tying in" of the major forms such as the trapezius and buttocks. The side underplanes of the rib cage are subdivided, as all other planes can be. Smaller side and bottom planes such as on the external obliques are added where needed. Fleshy forms of the leg bulge may have to be added, more or less, depending on the individual.

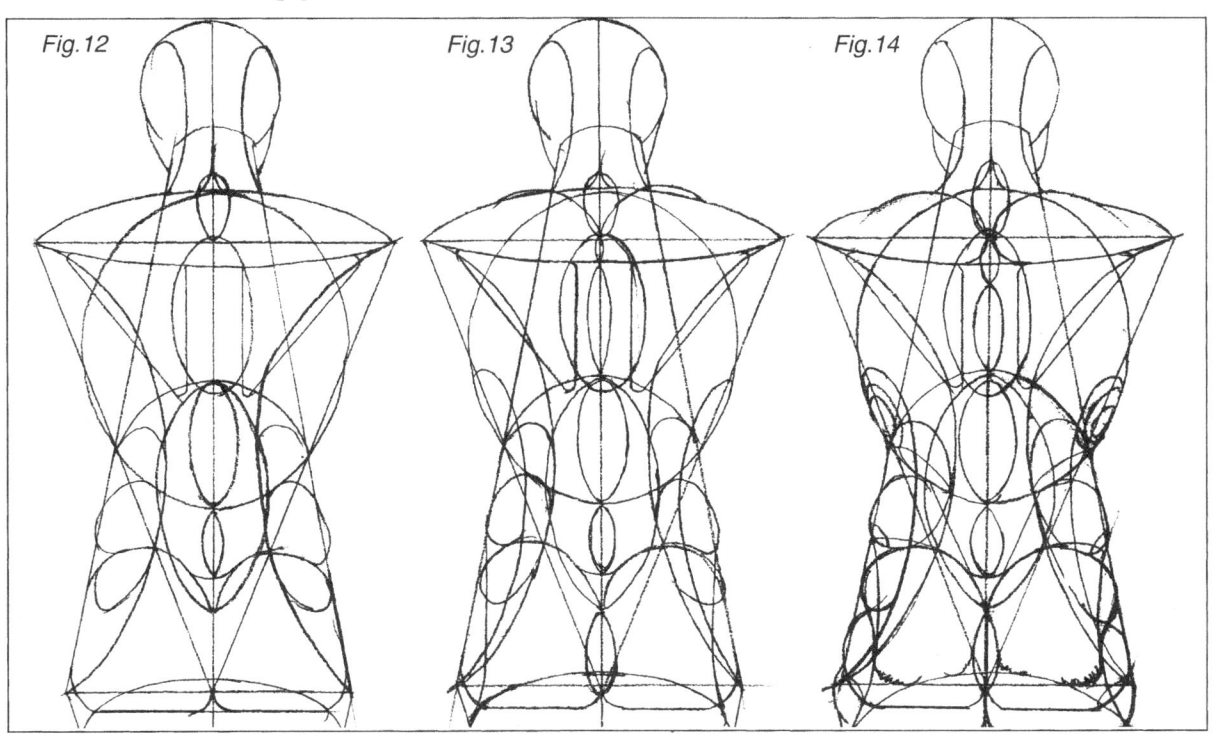

Fig.12 Fig.13 Fig.14

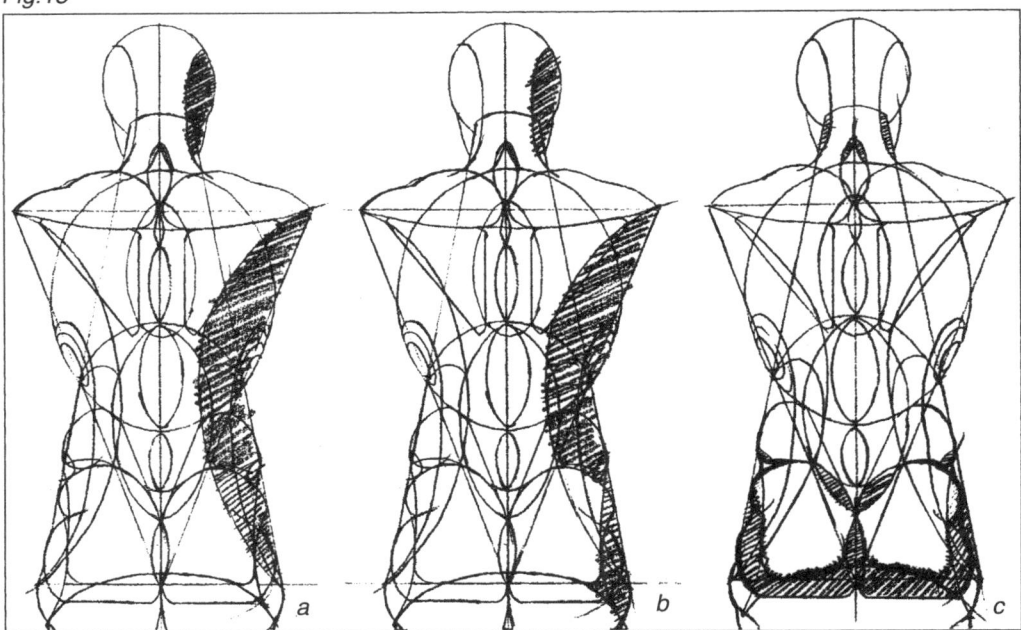

Fig.15

a   b   c

Figs. 15a.b.c.d.e.f. and g.
These partially shaded schematics
should help explain where the
planes and the forms of the back
are and what happens when they
go into light and shade. You can
and should make many more ver-
sions for yourself.

Fig. 16. The planes of the
side view of the figure are sometimes not as obvious as the front
and back view nevertheless they
are present. These planes are
altered due to the shapes of the
forms but will still relate in some
way to the front and back view.
Look carefully for the borders of
value changes and how they relate
to the borders of their values.
Follow the safe procedure of big
forms and big planes first – smaller
forms and smaller planes second,
etc., etc.

Figs. 17a.b.c.d. These
shaded schematics should help
clarify the planes and how they
help create form.

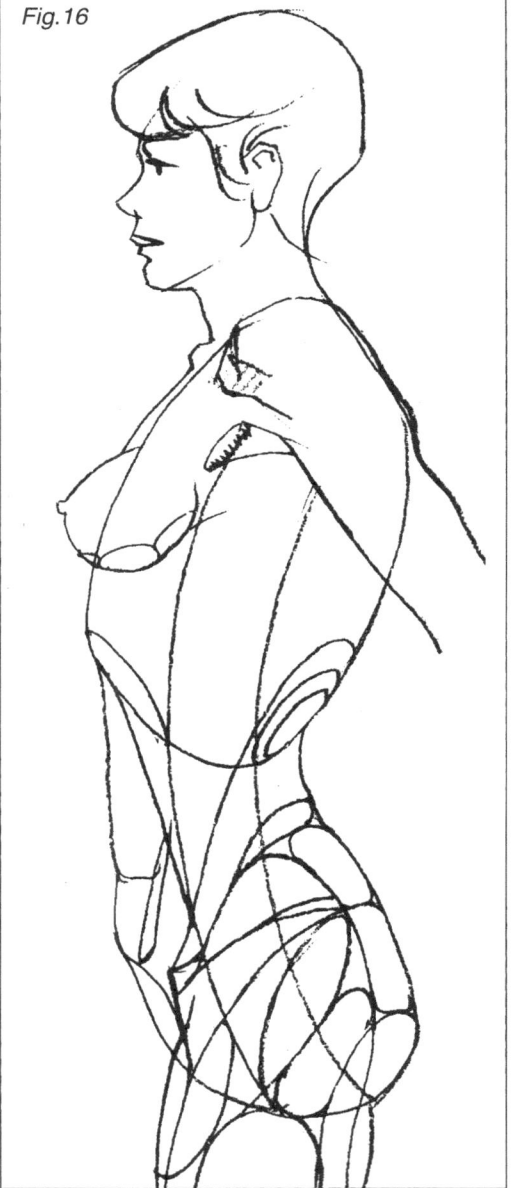

Fig.16

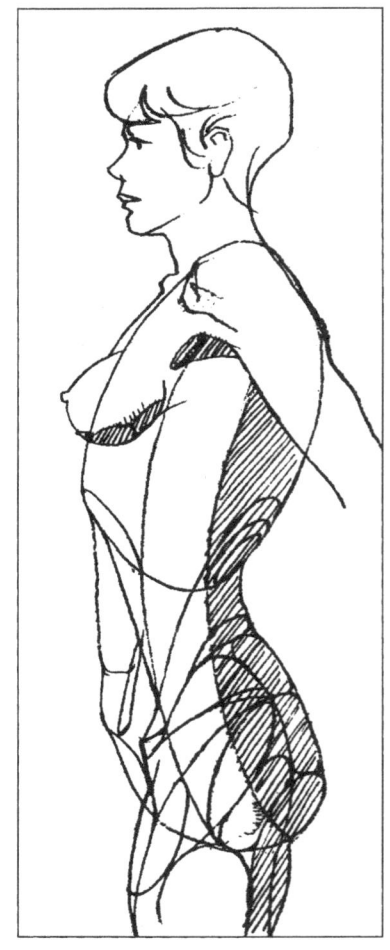

Fig.17a

Fig.15

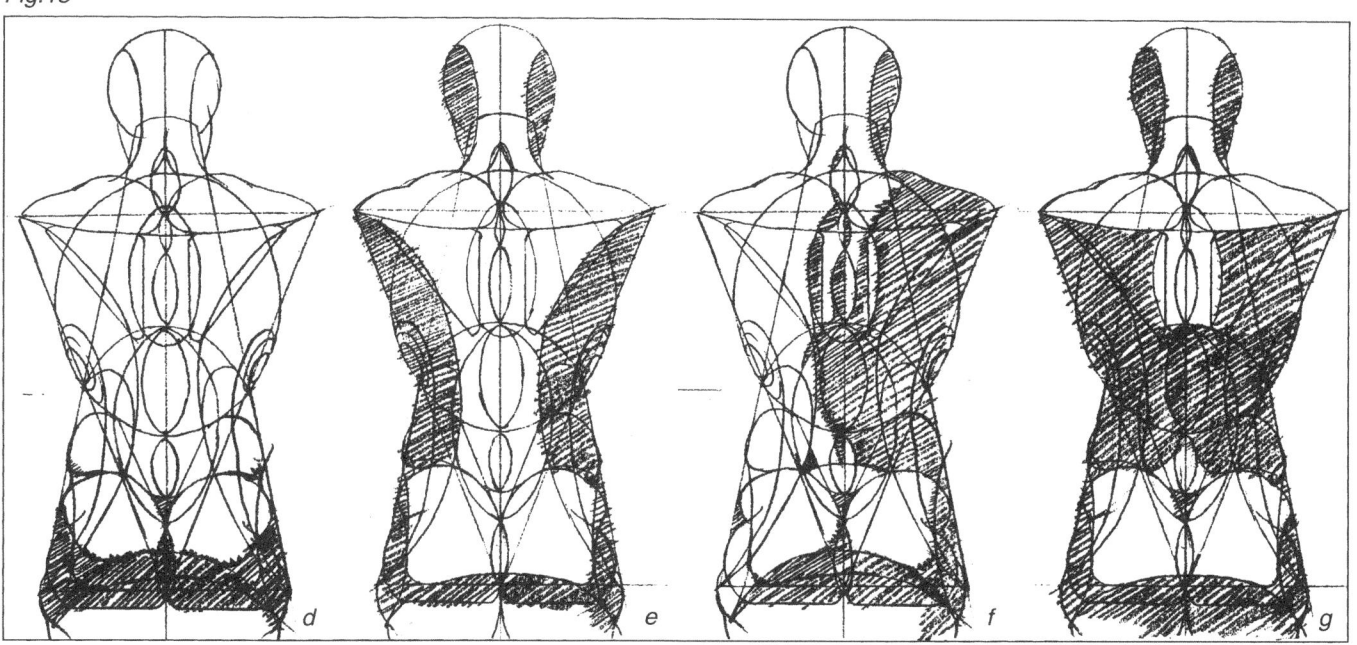

d   e   f   g

Fig.17b   Fig.17c   Fig.17c

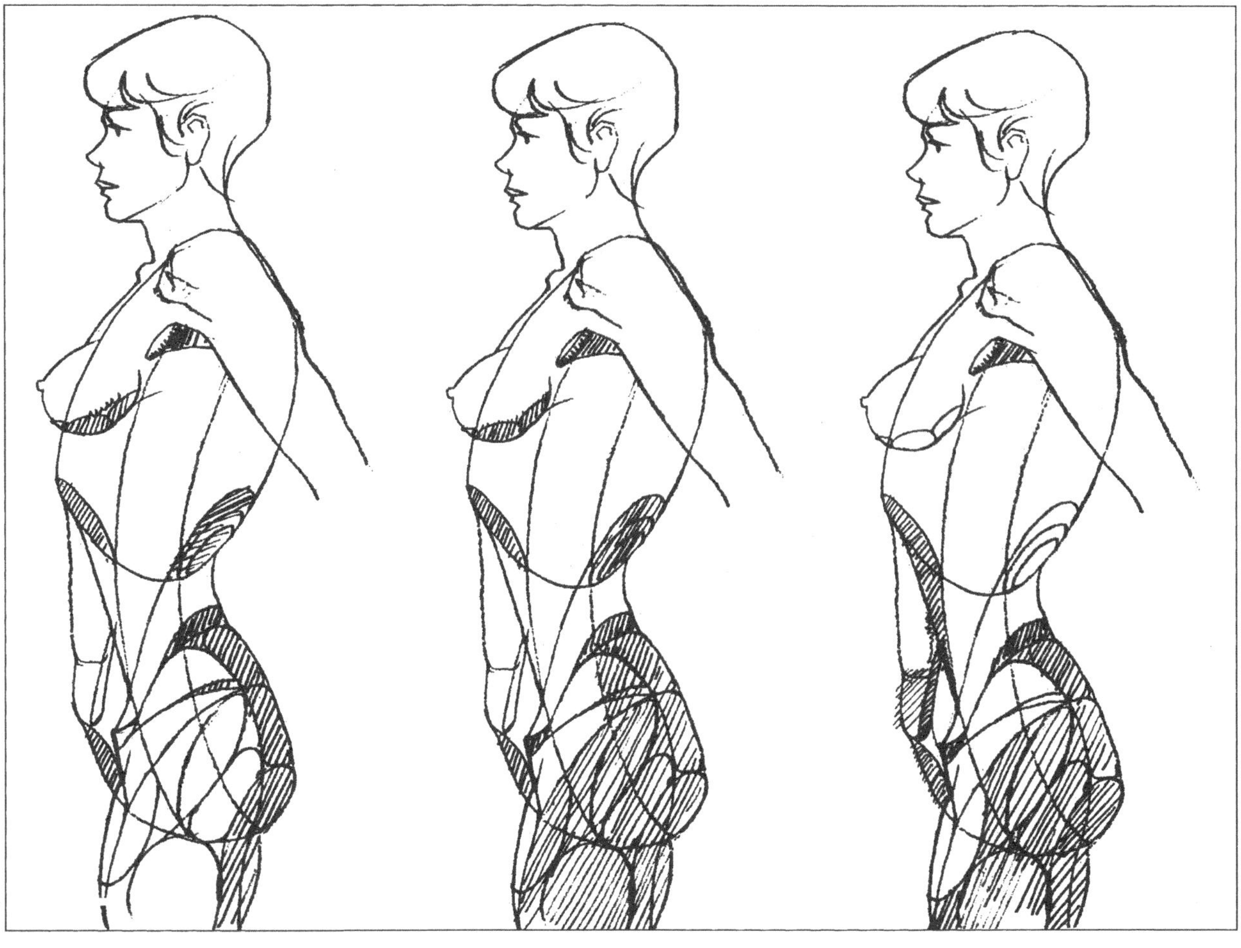

Fig. 18. The basic structure with planes shown in three-quarter view. This schematic drawing shows much more clearly how the planes of the front view coincide and interrelate with the planes of the side view.

Figs. 19a.b.c. Three schematic drawings showing how shading occurs on planes in the three-quarter view. In *Fig. 19a.* the light is coming from the right hand side of the figure. In *Fig. 19b.* the light is directly over the top of the figure. In *Fig. 19c.* the light is also over the top of the head but slightly more to the right hand side of the model.

Figs. 20a.b.c. These little drawings show in a clear simple way how the light and shadow patterns change as the source of the light moves around the model. It is best to first capture the overall shadow pattern and state it in very quickly. You can do this faster and easier if you know where the planes are.

Fig. 20a. shows typical light and shade patterns of the front view, *Fig. 20b.* the side view and *Fig. 20c.* the back view.

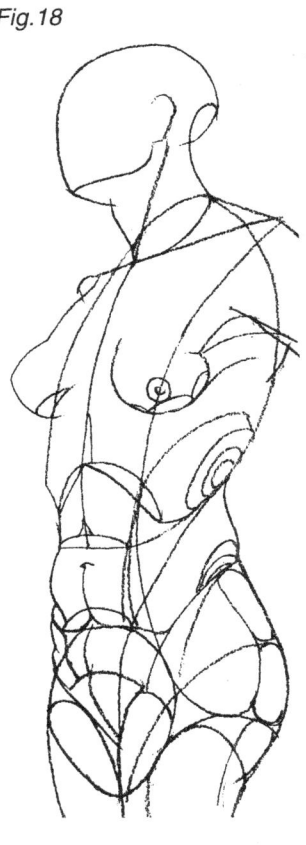
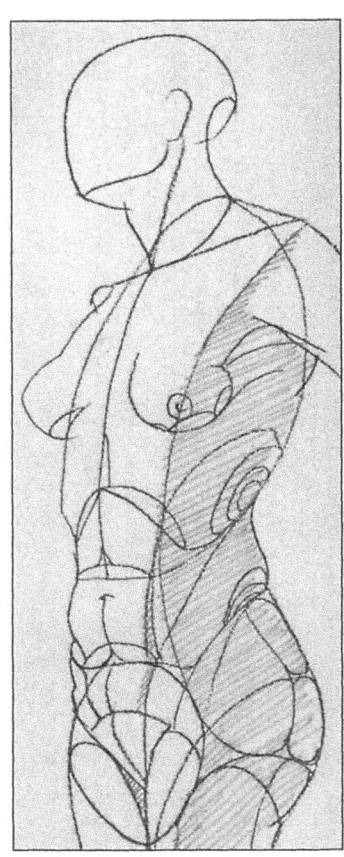

Fig.18

Fig.19 a

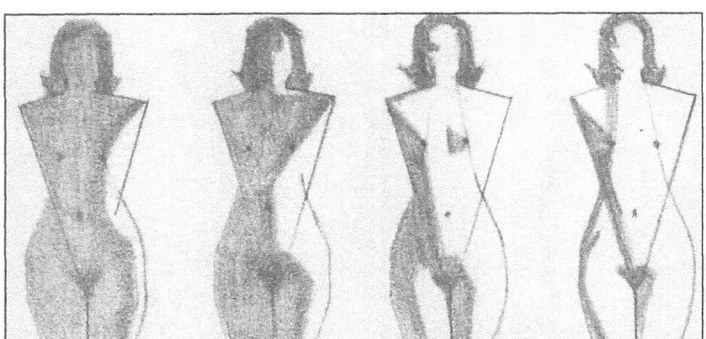

Fig.20 a

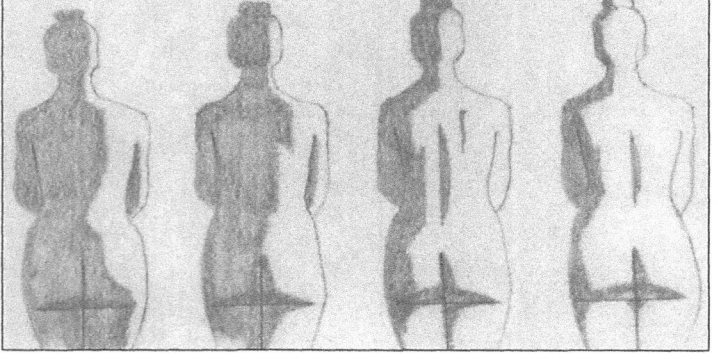

Fig.20 b

Fig.20 c

Fig.22

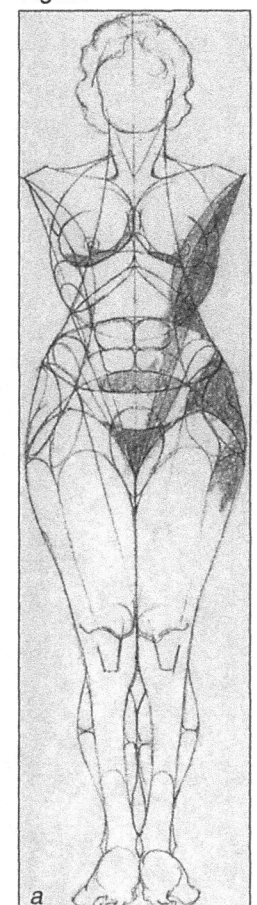
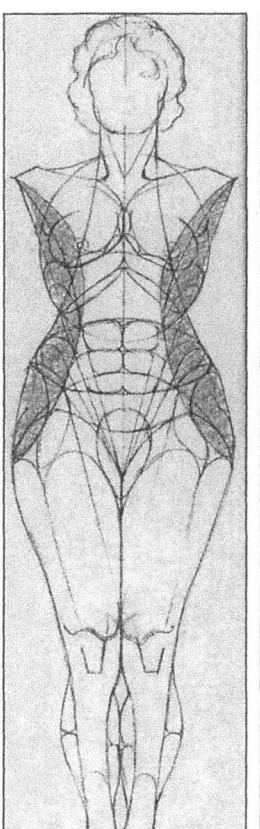
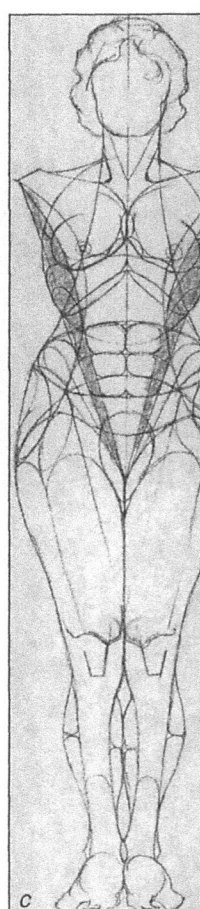

a

b

c

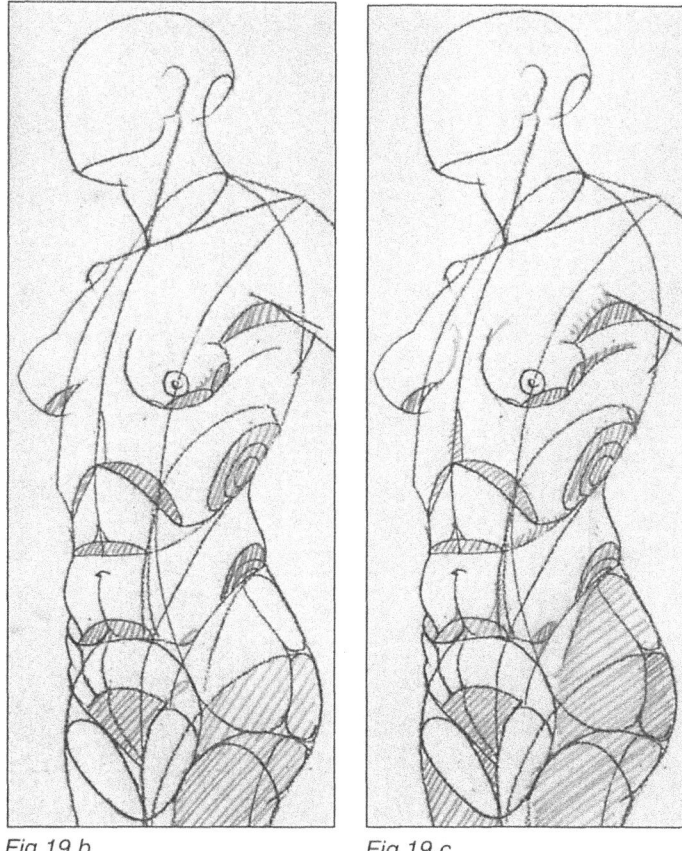

Fig.19 b

Fig.19 c

Fig.22

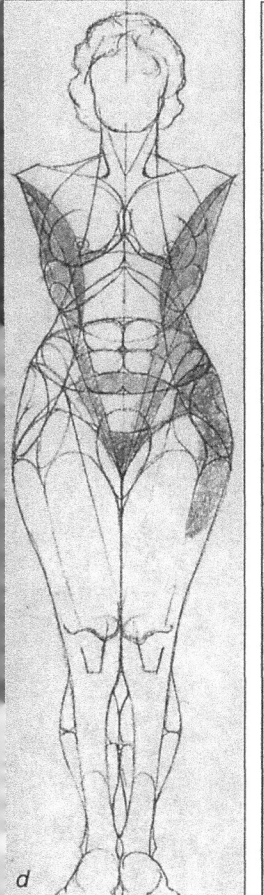

d

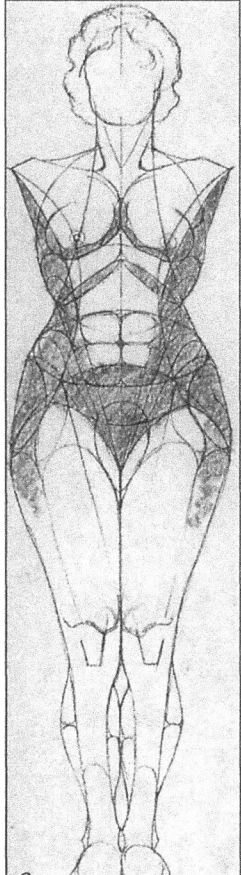

e

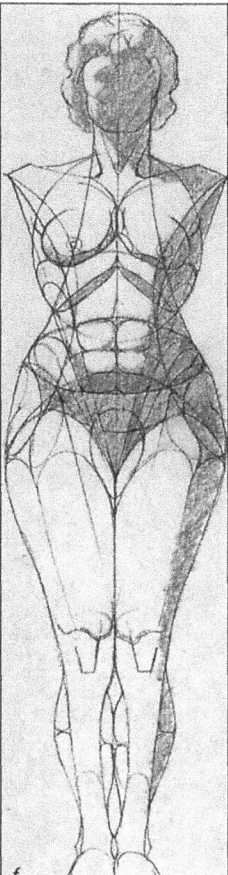

f

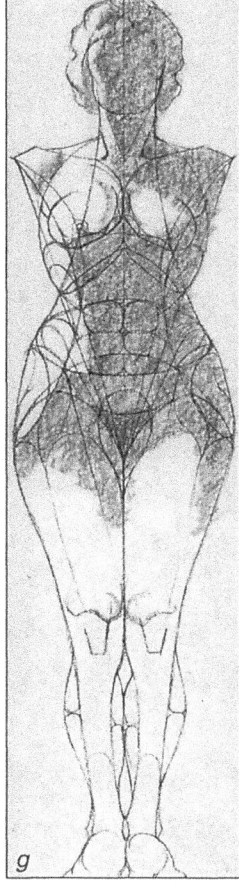

g

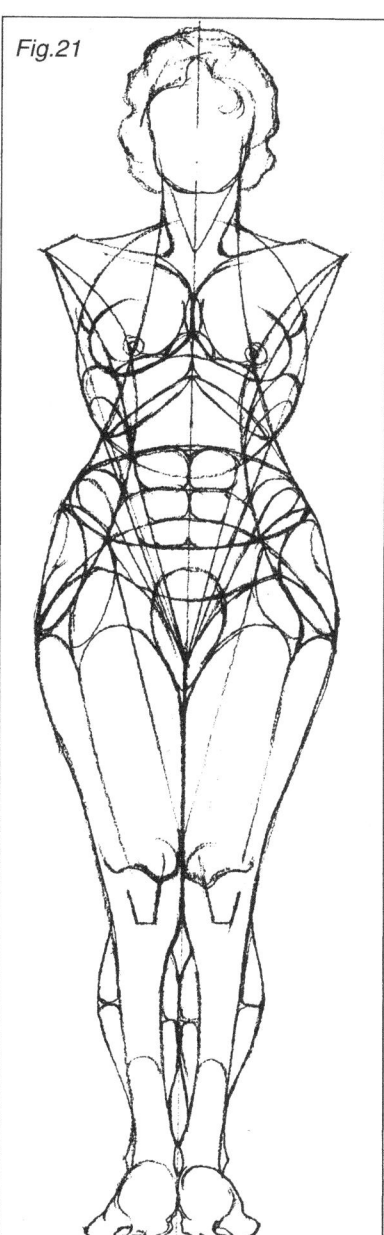

Fig.21

Fig. 21. An example of a more complete version of the forms and planes of the human figure based on an actual individual.

Figs. 22a.b.c.d.e.f. and g. Some examples of shading on the upper torso to clarify and reveal planes. These drawings are made by assuming the source of the light is coming from above or from the right hand side of the model. It takes only a slight shift in the position of the light to cause certain planes and forms to be revealed and others to go into halftone and shadow.

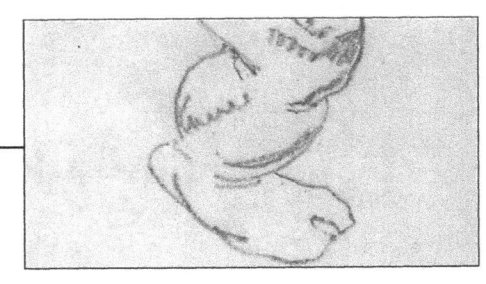

TWELVE

STRUCTURE: THE LEGS

There are many different ways to think of the structure of the legs besides using anatomical forms. In fact you would be better off by not thinking of the muscles until your drawing nears completion. What is important is first to state where the leg starts and where it ends. This is done by drawing two simple lines that taper to the width of the ankle. The second thing is to consider the shapes of the forms, their angles and how they wedge or interlock with each other. In regards to these forms one must always work from the largest forms to the smallest forms. Lastly the proper use of light and shade should define these forms.

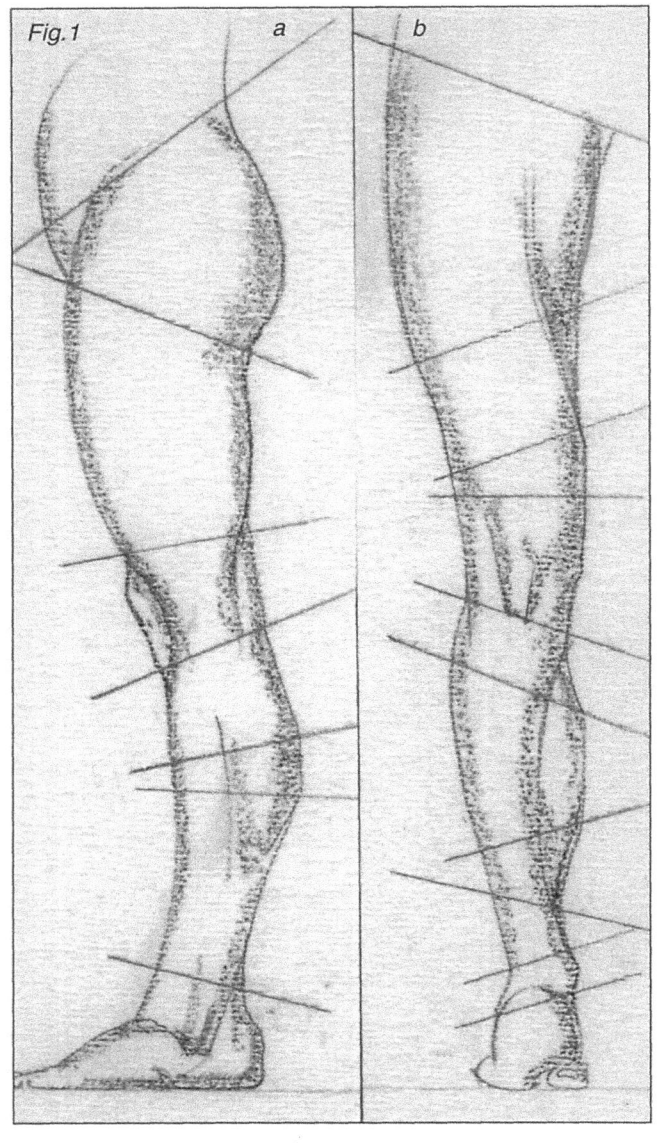

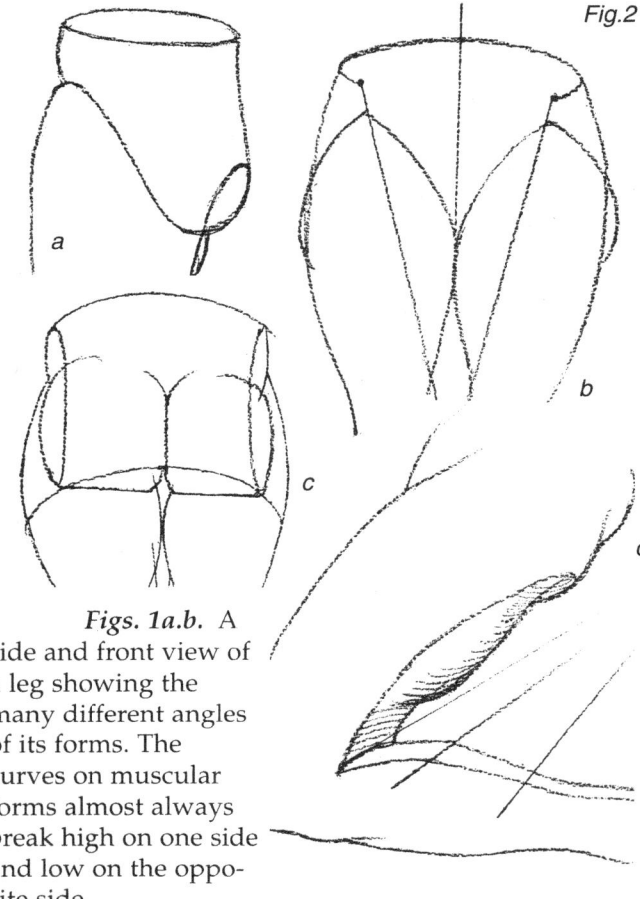

Fig.2

Figs. 1a.b. A side and front view of a leg showing the many different angles of its forms. The curves on muscular forms almost always break high on one side and low on the opposite side.

Figs. 2a.b.c.d. Fig. 2a. shows the leg in profile interlocking into the pelvic form. The structure line for the back of the leg starts with a looping line from the buttocks. This creates at the same time the bottom plane of the buttocks.

Fig. 2b. The forms of the front of the legs wedging into the pelvic area. The lines drawn from the points on the iliac crests represent the sartorius muscle which will wrap around the knee and insert below it. These lines are also the dividing line of the front plane and sideplane of the upper leg.

Fig. 2c. This drawing shows the buttocks forms sitting on top of the leg forms. Note the relationship of the bottom plane of the buttocks to the fleshy bulge of the leg.

Fig. 2d. The leg is very often seen in three-quarter view. Beginners seldom draw it correctly. You have to differentiate between the top planes and sideplanes of the forms, find their corners and draw them in perspective.

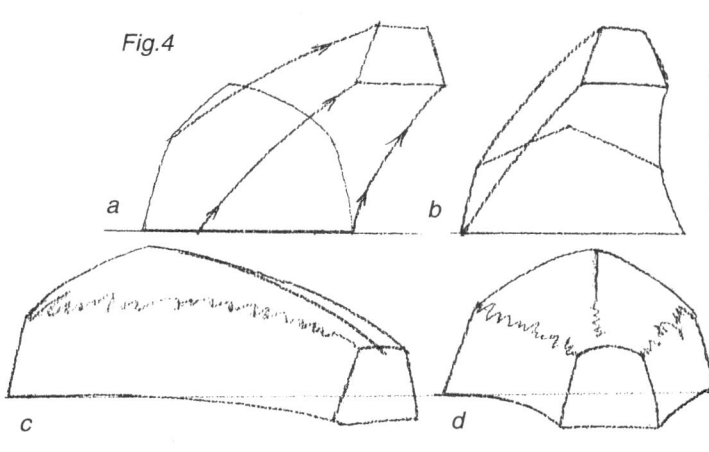

Fig.4

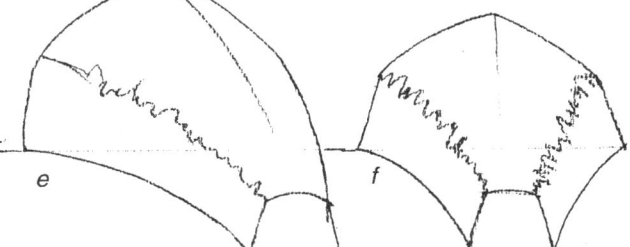

Figs. 4a.b.c.d.e.f. These drawings show how to draw the upper part of the leg in foreshortening by the use of three dimensional geometric forms. When drawing a form in foreshortening start at the back-most part where it begins by drawing a shape of that form there – then draw a shape of the fore-

Figs. 3a.b.c. Fig. 3a. shows a three-quarter view of a standing leg. The forms of the back of the leg are shown overly flattened to get across the idea that the leg is seen from the rear and not in profile.

Fig. b. One can also use cylinders and abstract shapes of the major forms to draw a leg in perspective.

Fig. c. shows the same idea on its way to completion by drawing accurate shapes of the forms. From this point on one adds smaller and smaller forms and light and shade.

most part of the form, being careful where you place it. The next step is to join these front and back shapes. You now have a large geometric shaped form to which you can add any amount of smaller forms with assurance.

If half of the upper leg is on a support then the knee cannot, as stated previously, go below the line of the support. Students and even advanced draughtsmen will almost always draw the knee far lower than it really is. The way to avoid this error is to draw the edge of the support, (chair, stool, etc.), and measure how far below that line is the knee cap or knee form.

Figs. 5a.b. These two drawings show how to think of and draw the forms of the legs coming forward towards you or going back away from you. In *Fig. 5a.* line as well as shading is used to portray this. The hard thin line on the left knee form brings it forward, in front of the right leg. The shading is curved to show forms going upwards or downwards and away.

Fig. b. shows graphically how the direction of the shading should be rendered to express the coming forwards or going away from you.

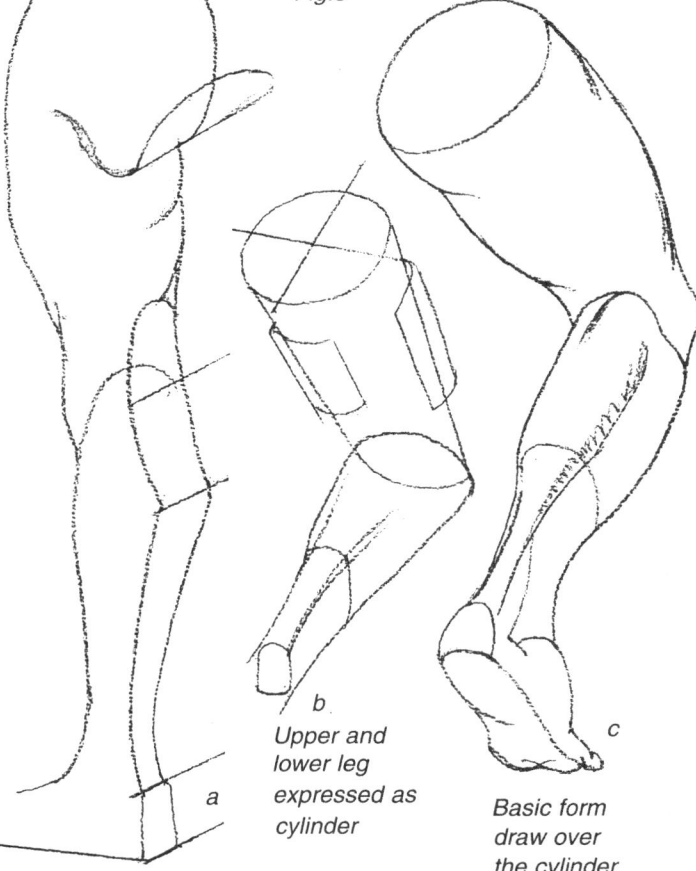

Fig.3

b

Upper and lower leg expressed as cylinder

c

Basic form draw over the cylinder

a

Leg and buttock form in three-quarter view and perspective

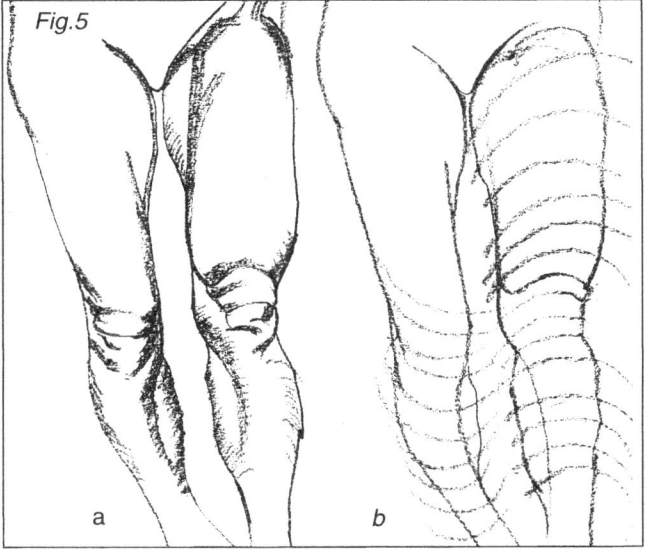

Fig.5

a

b

CHAPTER THIRTEEN

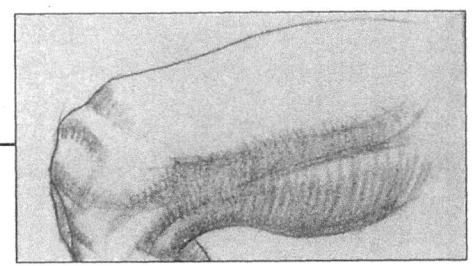

PLANES OF THE LEGS

The purpose of these schematic drawings is to instill in you an idea, a concept, a way of looking and thinking about the forms and planes of the leg, as well as, of course the rest of the body.

Although it would be a good idea for you to make copies of them to familiarize yourself with these forms and planes you must not expect to find them exactly as such on every human being. What is shown here is general and that is how you must see, think and draw – from the large shapes, forms and planes to the smaller forms and planes. You should also consider how they relate to one another, how they overlap or wedge into one another. As I've mentioned before, each person will be different depending on their genetic make-up, environment and activities. These schematics then will serve as a guide for you, a point to start from and a point to depart from. By shading in different planes you can see how form is built up thereby lending credence to the concept.

Figs. 1a.b.c. It will be easier to comprehend the planes of the legs if we start with the simple outside shapes of them. Shown here are the big outside shapes of the front, side and back views of the legs.

Fig. 1a. shows the first large form of the upper leg starting above the knee and wedging into the torso. The side view, *Fig. b.*, shows how this upper form is divided into two forms. The upper part is on an angle which catches more light than the upright plane and therefore is always lighter than the upright plane, assuming of course the light comes from above. In *Fig. c.* note how the form of the gastrocnemius muscles wedge into the upper leg. Note also how the forms of the buttocks are below the crotch line and overlap the leg forms.

The big outside shapes and largest forms of the legs, Front, Side and Back.

Fig.1

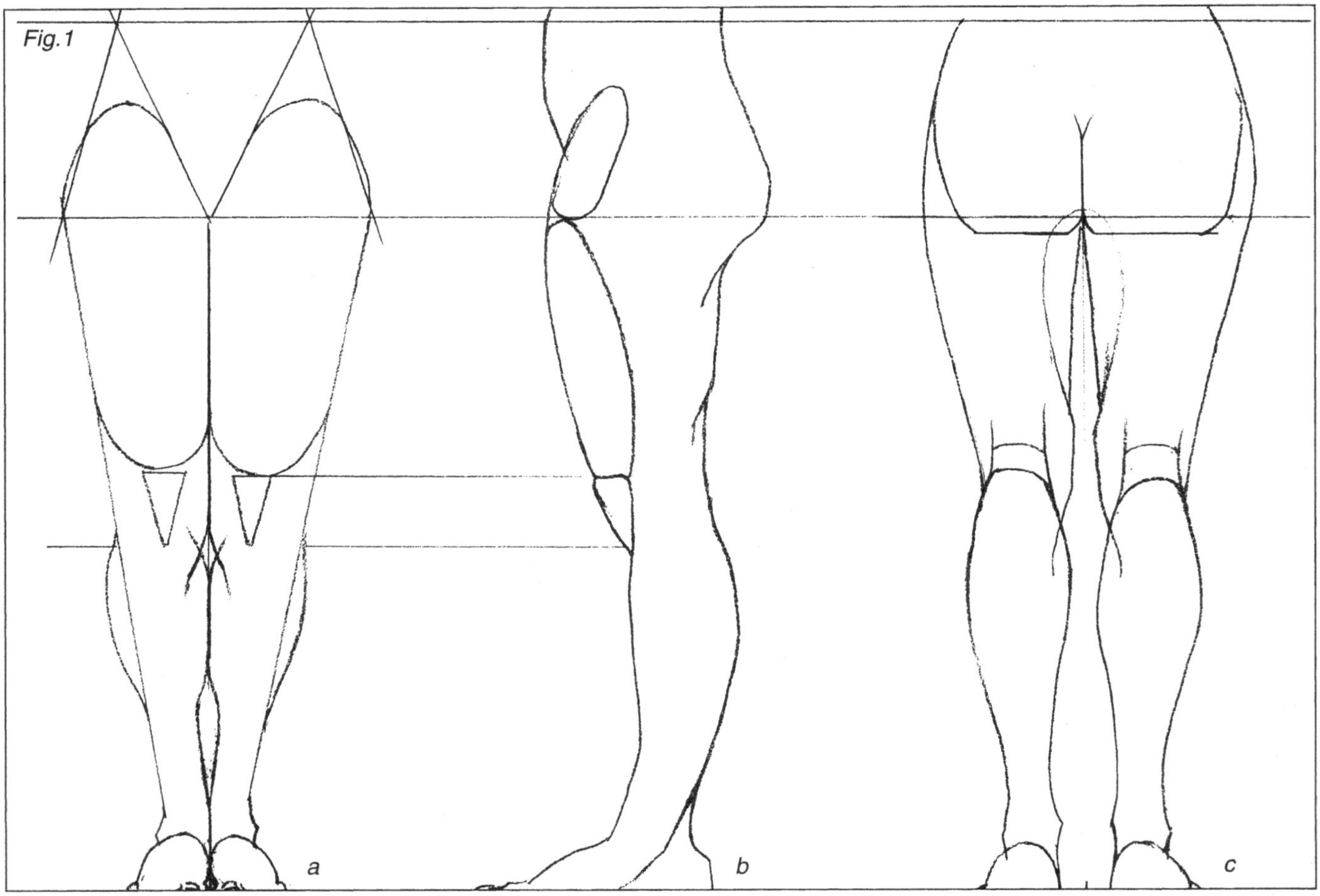

a

b

c

Fig. 2a. The large form of the upper leg is divided lengthwise into a narrower form and this in turn is then divided into an upper and lower form. A center plane, which is really a front plane, runs the whole length of the leg and ends at the width of the ankle. This center plane starts at the dots, one of which at the crest of the iliac, runs the whole length of the leg and ends at the inner side of the ankle, (follow the arrowheads). The other line terminates at the outer side of the ankle. By making this front plane you automatically create sideplanes.

Fig. 2b. Side view. Again start with its center plane. This starts at below the circle of the hip which represents the great trochanter. Follow the arrowheads on the two lines. This center plane is subdivided into three planes, an upper one, a middle one and a lower one. The back side of the leg has a top and bottom plane at the top and the bottom of the gastrocnemius form. There is a flat plane shown on the side of the hip. It runs through the circle representing the head of the trochanter bone. This leaves the sideplanes of various angles of the buttocks.

Fig. 2c. Start with the center plane first as usual. You can start at the dot on the outside of the buttocks and at the crotch point. Follow the arrowheads on the lines which will run the full length of the leg and terminate at the heel form. You are now left with the side planes which are subdivided into upper and lower planes.

The large front planes are added which in turn create side planes, within these planes are top planes and bottom planes.

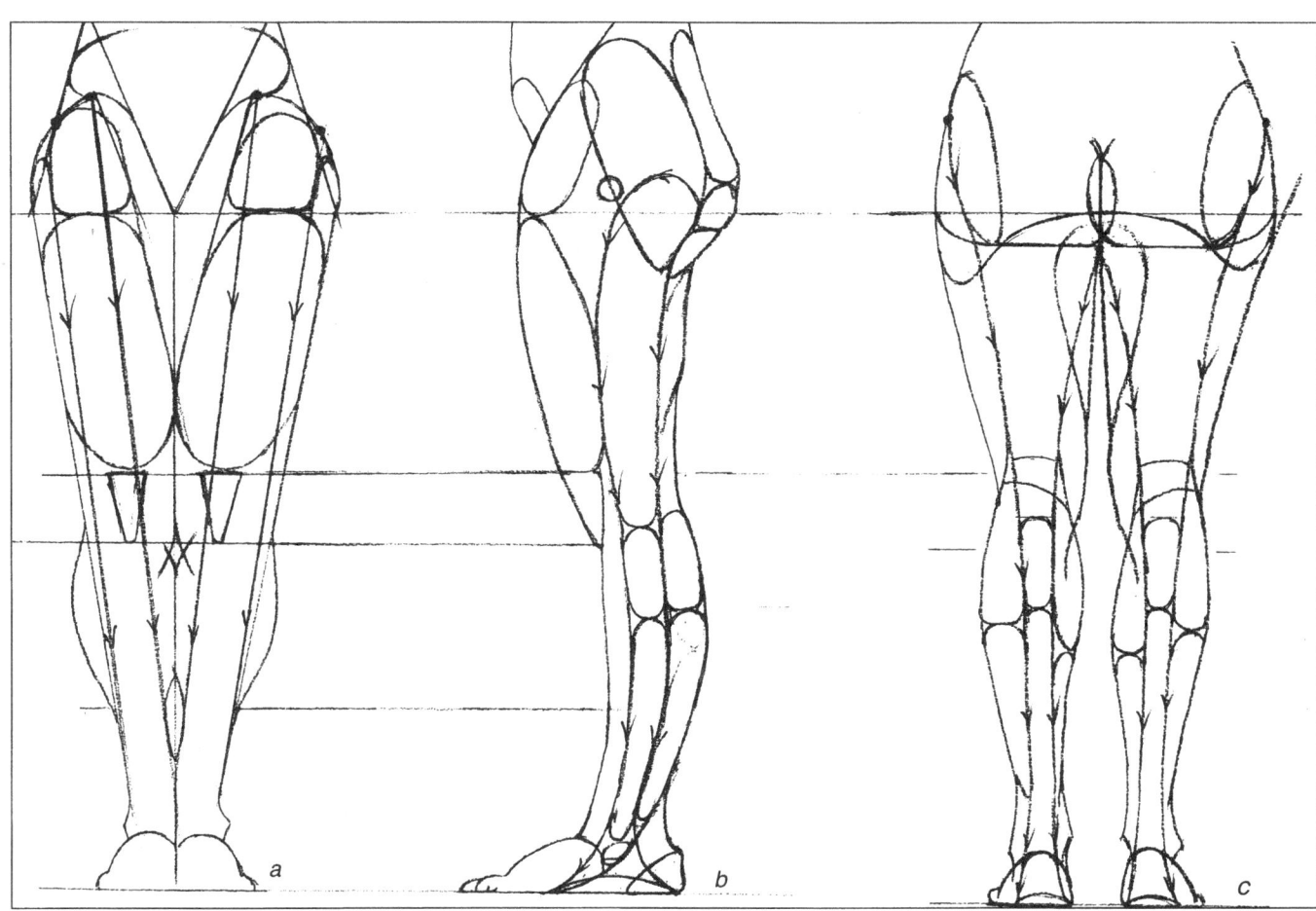

Fig.2

a

b

c

Figs. 3a.b.c. Completion of the major planes. Remember all planes can be subdivided ad-infinitum. Note how the plane of the lower leg turns outwards. Because of this it catches more light and is usually lighter than the upright plane.

Fig. 3c. shows the fatty, fleshy parts of the back of the leg. These areas of course vary tremendously and planes are subject to great variation.

Figs. 4a.b.c.d.e.f.g.h.i. Examples of shading to clarify certain planes and forms.

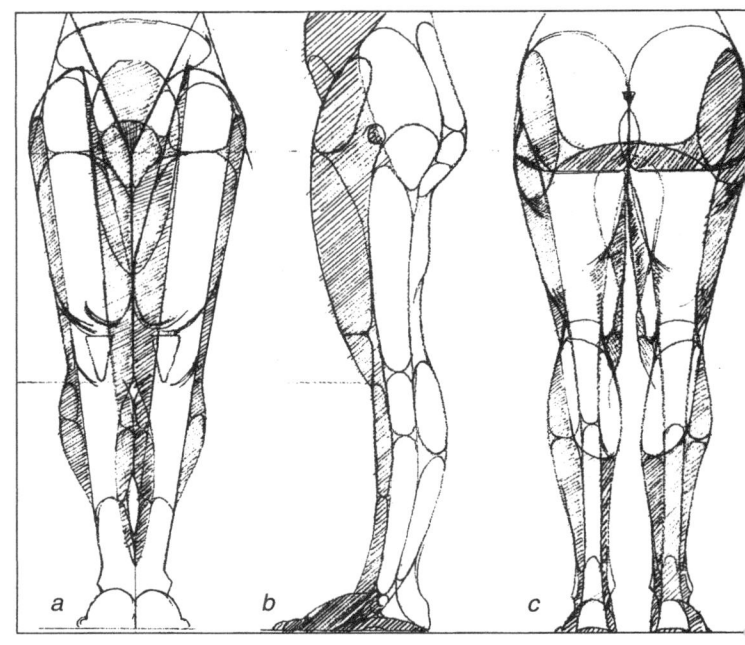

Fig.4

Towards completion by adding smaller forms and planes. Fleshy parts of the buttocks and legs shown in fig.c.

Fig.3

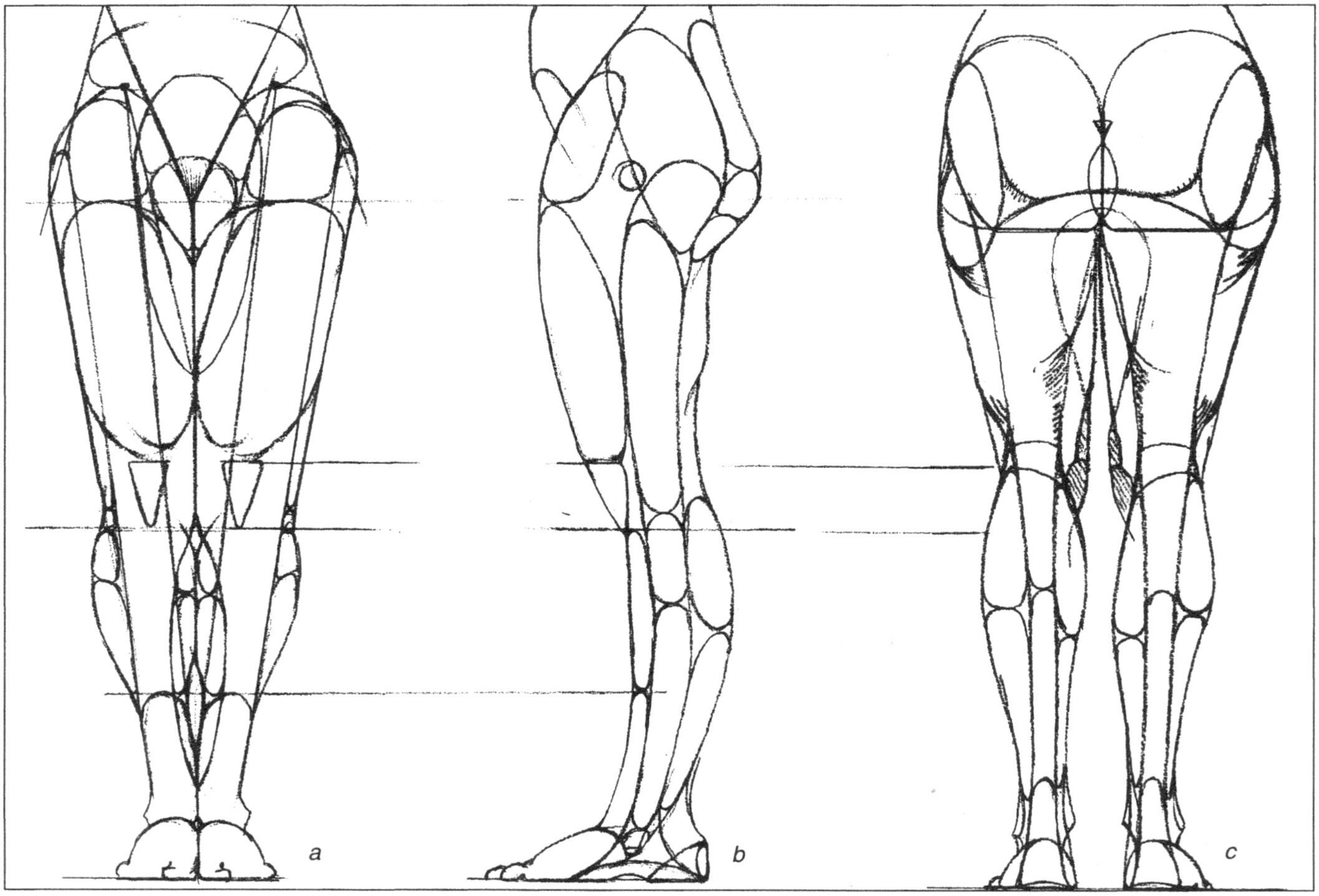

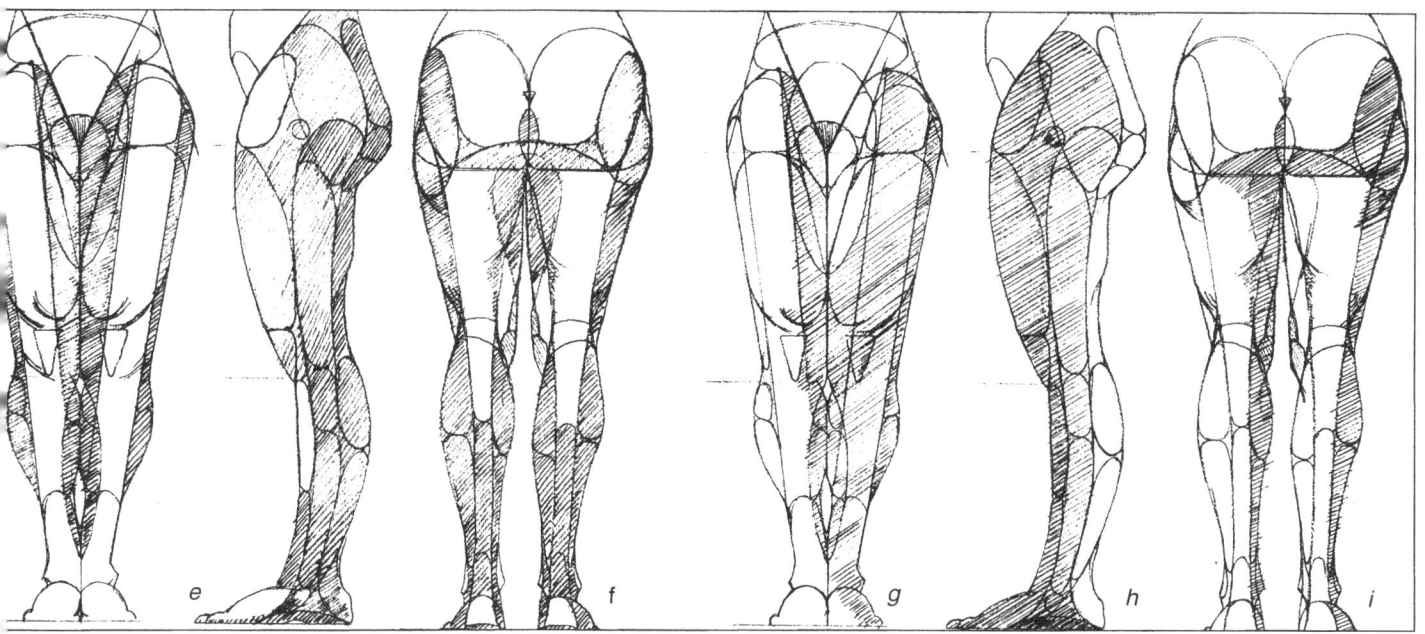

Figs. 5a.b.c. There are many individuals who have highly developed muscles either through birth or exercise or both. With these individuals it will be difficult to see the major planes for there are many small planes and forms which tend to obscure them.

However, the procedure of drawing them is always the same. Always look for the largest forms first, then the largest planes. Next search out the smaller forms and smaller planes and so on. Always work from large to small. These three drawings are only some ways that complex highly developed forms can be broken down to simple forms and planes. As you can see they produce many different very solid shapes as contrasted to smooth rounded surfaces. Refer to the chapter on Light and Shade on Form and Planes for further clarification.

Example of forms broken up into many small planes

Fig.5

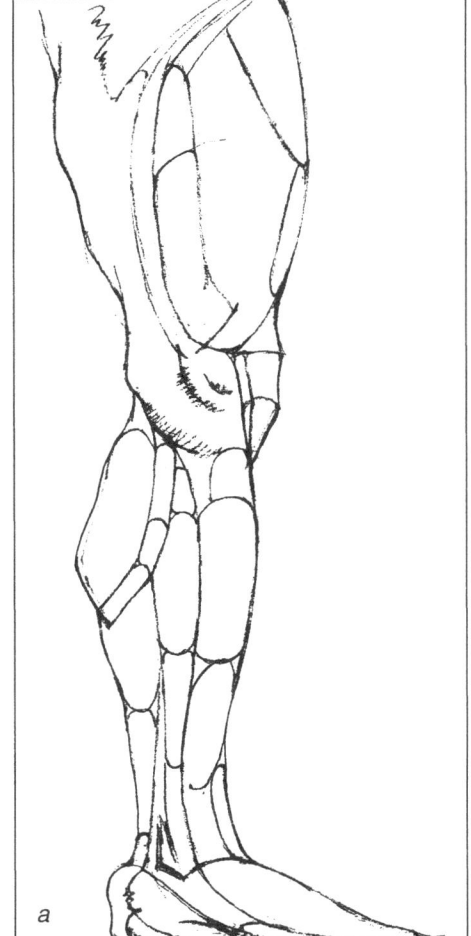

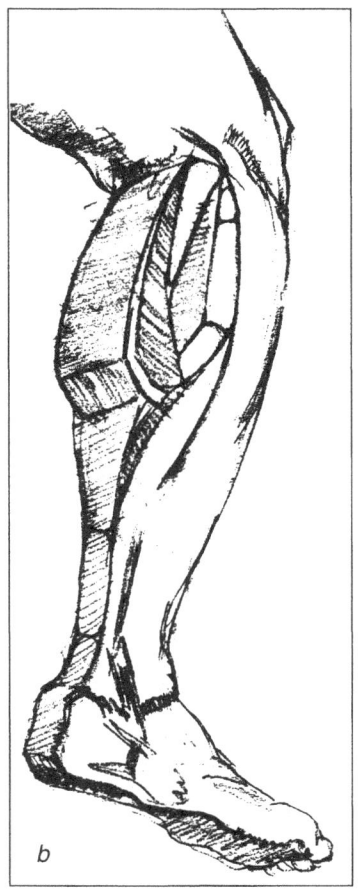

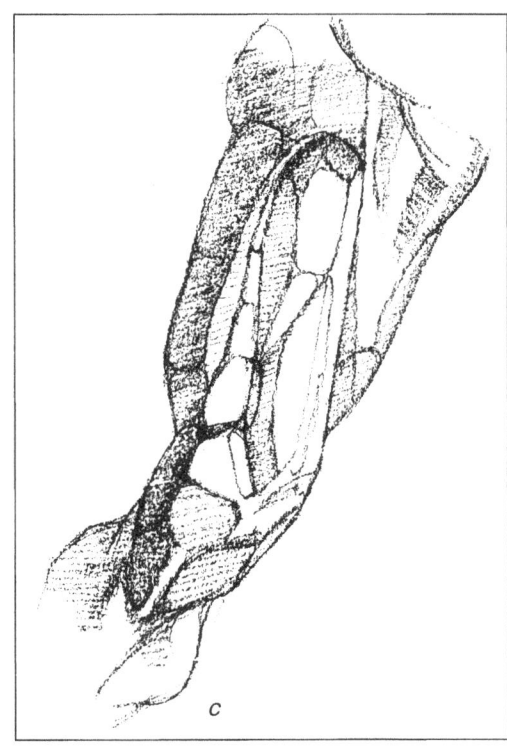

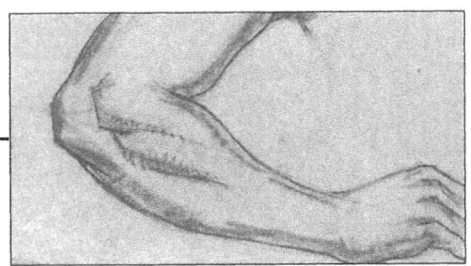

CHAPTER FOURTEEN

STRUCTURE AND PLANES OF THE ARMS

Much has been explained about the use of structure in the drawing of the arms in the previous chapter on Basic Structure. I would like, however, to cover a few points before going into explaining the planes of the arm.

Fig. 1. shows how the arm is constructed on the structure lines. These lines go from the two points shown at the top of the deltoid form to the width

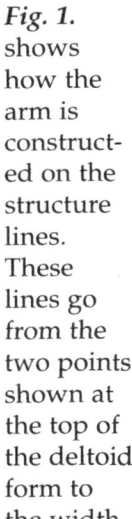

Construction of the arm based on the simple structure lines.

Fig.1

of the wrist. Draw two gently curving lines from these points following the directions of the arrowheads. This curve must not appear as a right angle pipe or an elbow macaroni as shown to the right of the drawing. The forms are then added on these two lines, always the largest ones first. Note how the elbow bone juts out of the curve and how its bottom line continues into the arm to the point at the bottom of the wrist. This is a fairly constant relationship which you can use all the time.

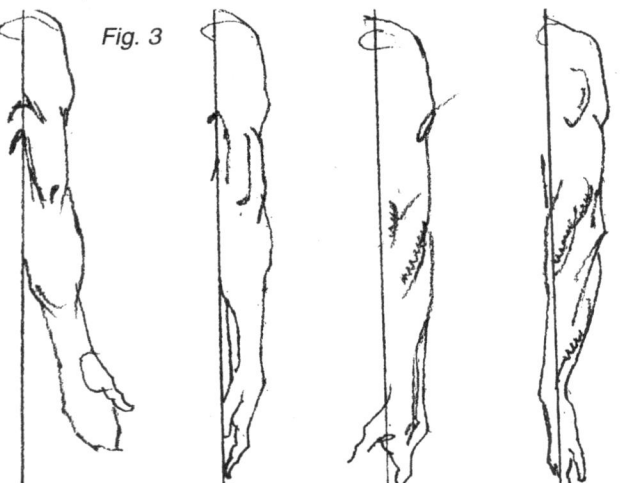

Fig. 3

Showing the change of the shapes of the four forms as the arm twists.

Fig. 2. The arm consists of basically four large forms, the deltoid form, the biceps form, the combined flexor and supinator forms and the form of the lower arm. Contour lines show the general shape of these forms.

Figs. 3a.b.c.d. show how these forms change shape as the arm twists from a frontal position to a side position. The planes must change accordingly.

Figs. 4a.b.c.d. Think of the drawing of the planes of the arm in the same way as described in the drawing of the planes of the leg. The drawing of the planes of the arm are shown in four stages.

Fig. 4a. shows the big outside shape of the arm.

Fig. 4b. shows the four major forms built on these two lines. Notice their shapes and the angles of the high points and low points of the forms.

Fig. 4c. is the same drawing with the center plane added – running down the length of the arm. Start at the dots on the top of the drawing and follow the arrowheads on the lines.

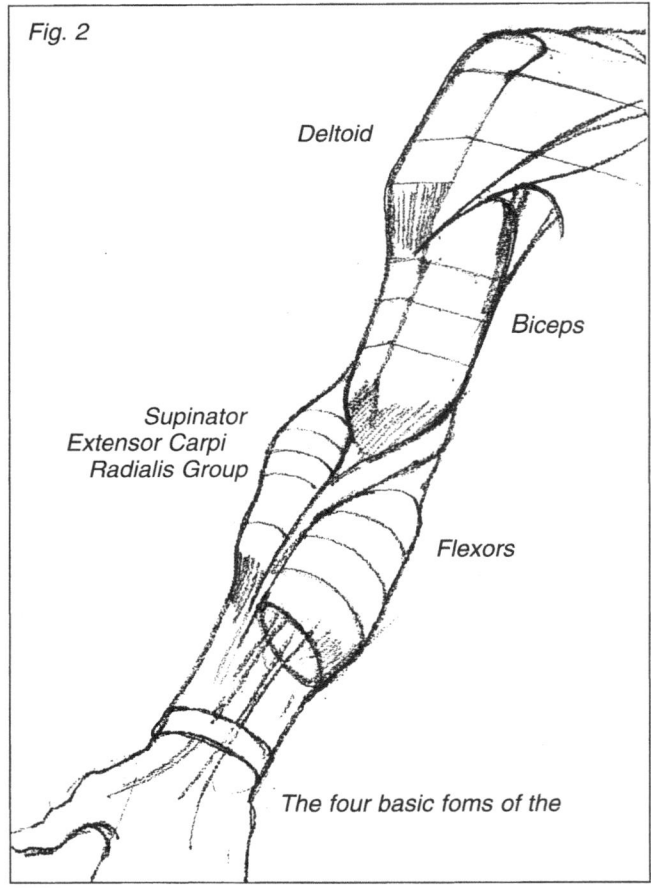

Fig. 2

Deltoid

Biceps

Supinator
Extensor Carpi
Radialis Group

Flexors

The four basic foms of the

Fig.4

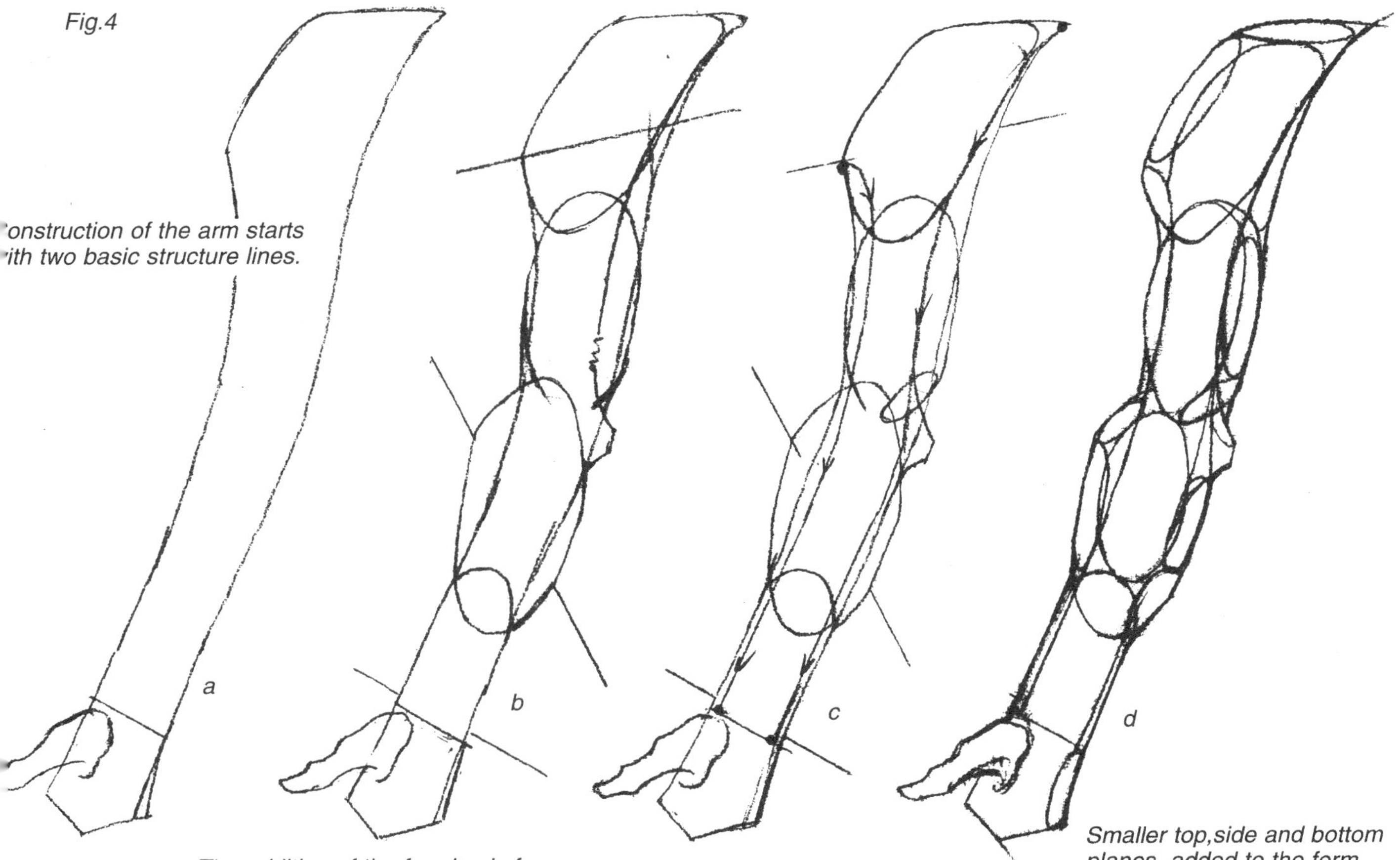

Construction of the arm starts with two basic structure lines.

a

b

c

d

The addition of the four basic forms. notice the angles of these forms.

The large center plane is added.

Smaller top, side and bottom planes added to the form.

Fig. 4d. The forms are shown broken up with planes. Basically you have sideplanes, top sideplanes and bottom sideplanes. This approach will give you the three dimensional effect of the largest forms. Many other minor planes can be added. The more muscular the arm the more one must add smaller and smaller forms within the larger forms and, of course, add their planes.

Figs. 5a.b.c.d.e. The shaded areas of these five examples will help you recognize the major forms and planes of the arm.

Fig. 5a. The front plane.

Fig. 5b. The sideplanes.

Fig. 5c. Front and sideplanes of the left shown. The light is coming from the right hand side putting those planes in the light.

Fig. 5d. Light coming from the left hand side putting the planes on the left hand side in the light and the center

plane and sideplanes of the right hand side in shadow. Also shown are darker underplanes in the center plane.

Fig. 5e. Light coming from the right hand side lighting the sideplanes of the right hand side. The center plane and sideplanes of the left hand side are in shadow. The underplanes of the sideplanes on the left side are also emphasized.

Fig.5

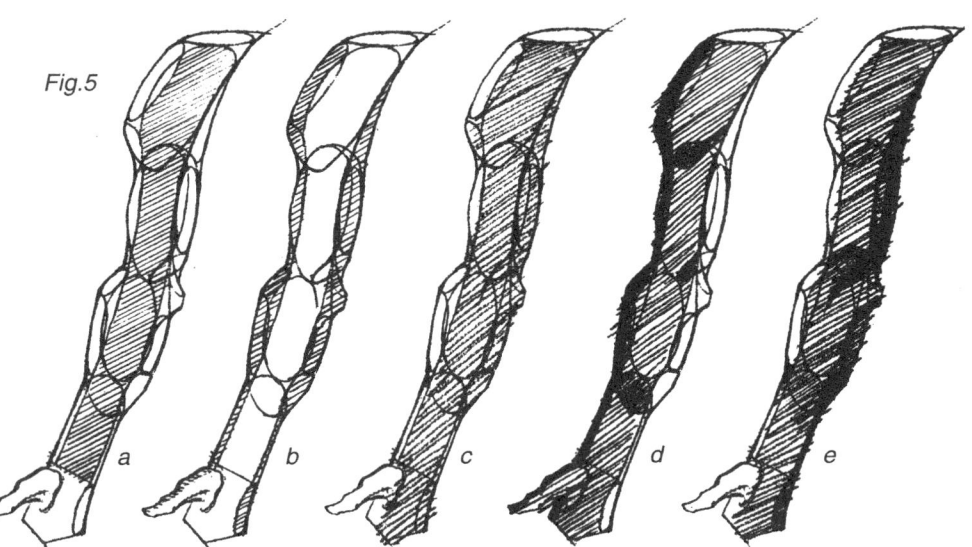

a   b   c   d   e

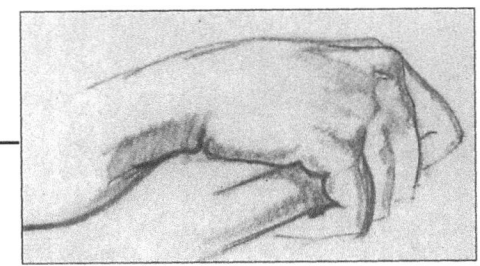

CHAPTER FIFTEEN

STRUCTURE: HANDS AND FEET

Anatomy is not stressed in these instructions on how to draw the hands and feet. The reason for this is that, in the first place, there are many excellent books that present human anatomy in many different ways. One can obtain a wealth of information from these books and buy as many as he thinks will help him. In the second place we are learning here how to draw from the standpoint of structure not anatomy. The approach presented here, drawing with structure steers you, I feel, in a more correct direction by making you draw all the forms and planes related to each other in action and unified by light and shade. One is always working from the large to the small, small to smaller so the larger truth is always expressed and maintained.

Knowledge of anatomy may help you perceive certain forms but if you train your eye to see values correctly and relate all your lines, forms and planes you will do well. Stressing anatomical forms may cause you to "bump" them up too much and lose the unity of the whole. Da Vinci warned against this saying that some artists drew figures that looked like a "sack of walnuts." As for inventing poses of figures based on anatomical knowledge alone I do not believe it works. I have known artists who drew and painted this way the result being every face and torso looked alike. The poses were also limited in their variety. One should work from the living model and memory and imagination (which incidentally eliminates more detail than it reveals). No two people can take the exact same pose. Every model will give you poses and inspiration different from any other model and that is the beauty of it all. Again da Vinci gives wise advice, "Go to nature."

STRUCTURE: THE HAND

Fig. 1a. The two structure lines of the arm continue to the width of the wrist, located at the dots, and go on to the outsides of the forefinger and little finger.

Fig. 1b. A spade shaped palm is drawn within these two lines. The corner of the spade should be at the center of the middle finger. A triangular shape is then added to the side of this spade shape.

Fig. 1c. The thumb is now drawn originating from this triangular shape. Ovals representing the knuckles are added. They will be at the center of the fingers. The overall shape of the wrist bones and the radius and ulna bones are shown for placement within this schematic.

Figs. 2a.b.c. and d. These show how the same idea is applied to draw the hand going in a different direction and of course any other direction you wish. We start with *Fig. 2a.* using the same two structure lines only this time swerving to the right hand side. Next add the spade and triangular shapes. *Fig 2b.* Draw the middle finger first. Let it follow the gesture of the hand. *Fig. 2c.* The rest of the fingers and thumb added.

Fig. 2d. The start of shading on the forms of the fingers. One carries the drawing as far as he needs from this point.

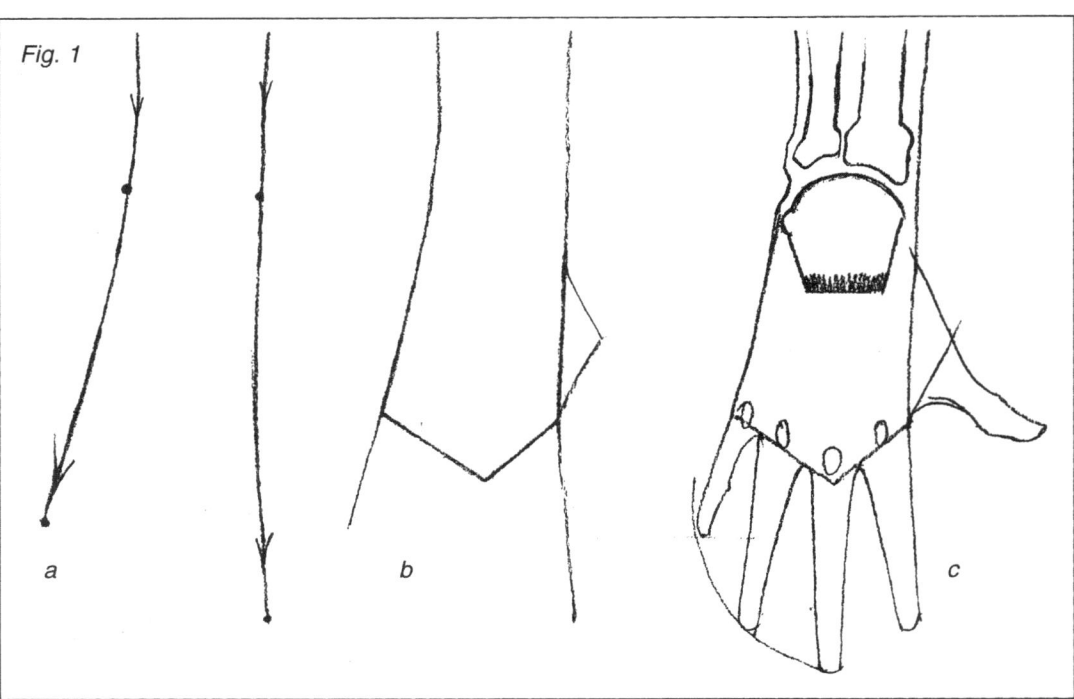

Fig. 1

a

b

c

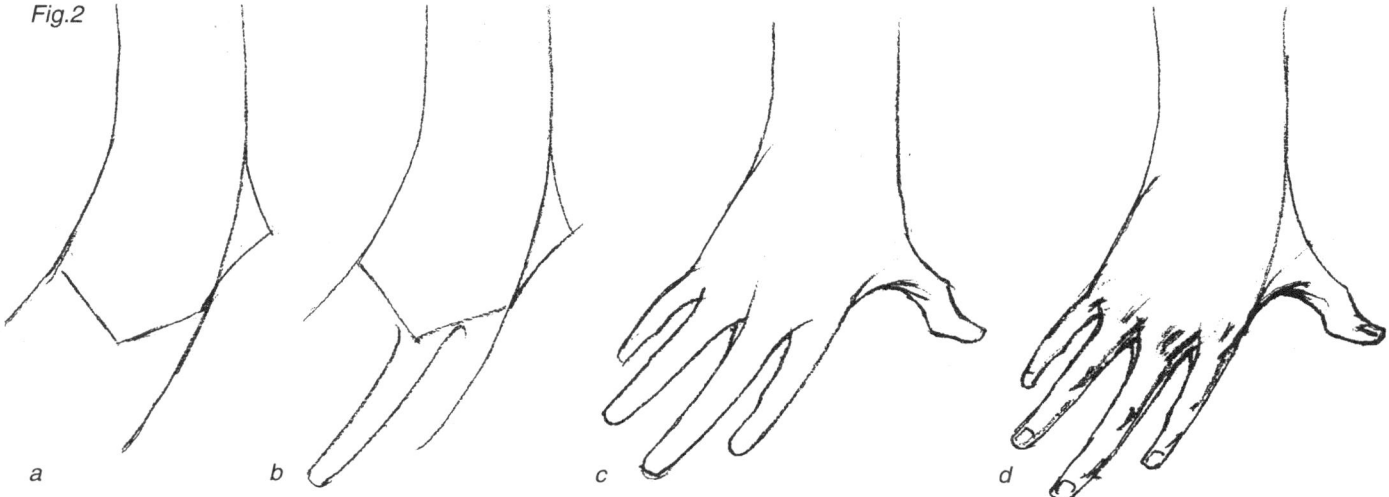

Fig.2

a   *b*   *c*   *d*

Figs. 3a.b.c.d. The side view of the hand is to be thought of as a shape consisting of two sections, one a wedge shape representing the palm and the other representing the finger or fingers. *Fig. 3a.* shows the basic wedge shape of the hand on the little finger side. Note the slant of the shape where the fingers start. Continue the lines of this wedge, tapering them to the fingertips.

Fig. 3b. The large forms of the palm and little finger are added.

Fig. 3c. The thumb side. Start again with a wedge shape. Its lines continue on to the width of the finger. Again note the slant at the end of the wedge and the beginning of the fingers.

Fig. 3d. A bulge representing the wrist form is added on top of the wedge shape. The thumb and its forms come off the structure line of the bottom of the wrist. The line leads away from the thumb and relates to the forms of the fingers. The knuckles and smaller forms are added to this beginning.

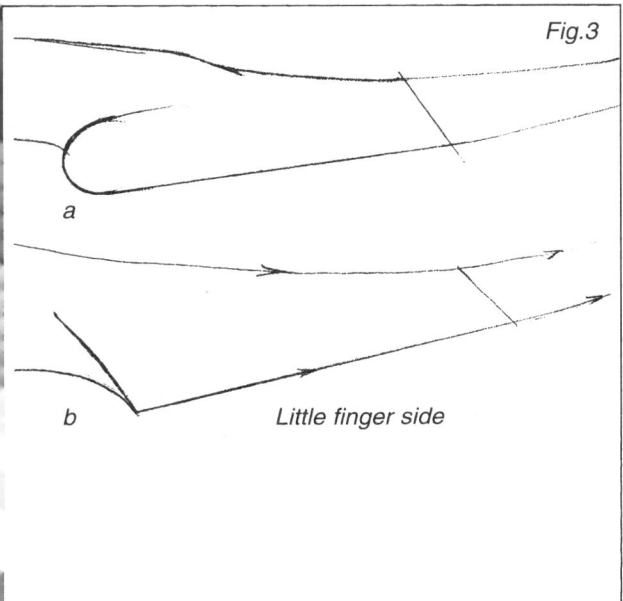

Fig.3

a

b   *Little finger side*

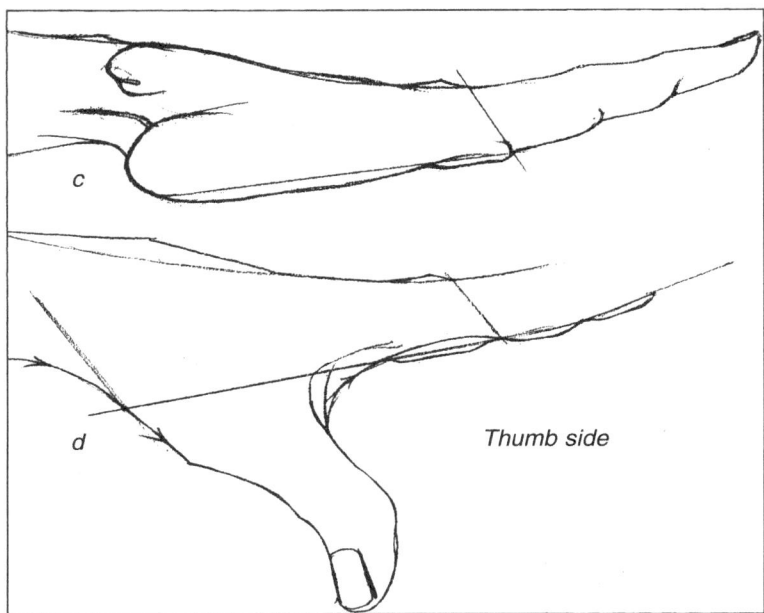

c

d   *Thumb side*

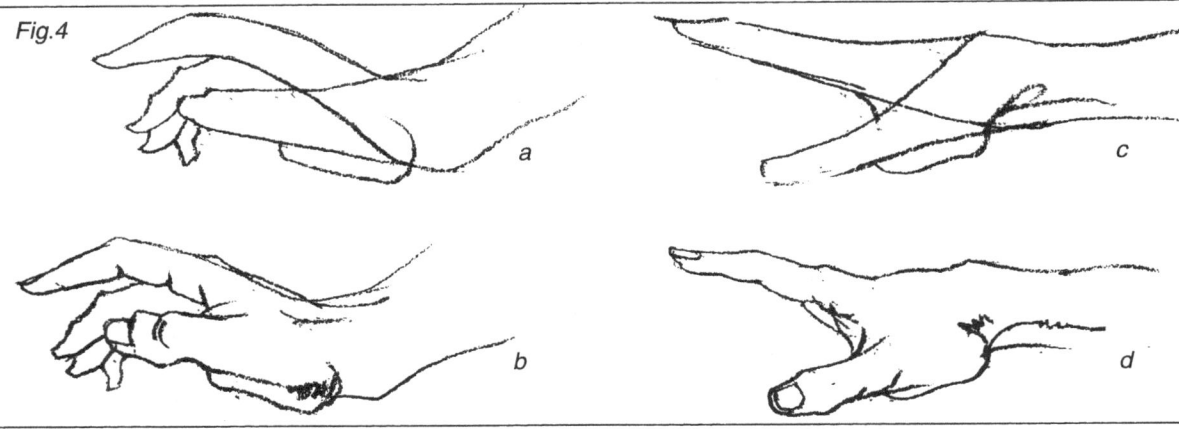

Figs. 4a.b.c.d. These drawings demonstrate in a simplified way just two variations of the ideas previously described.

Fig. 4a. The basic structure lines.

Fig. 4b. shows the same lines with forms added to them.

Fig. 4c. Again the underlying structure lines.

Fig. 4d. The idea lines with forms added.

Fig. 5a. A schematic drawing showing the development and relationships of forms. Note the three different angles of the creases at the finger joints.

Figs. 5b.c. These two drawings show an emphasis on major planes and forms to give dimension and bulk to them. You should apply this same idea and thinking to all of the hands that you draw as the positions can be infinite.

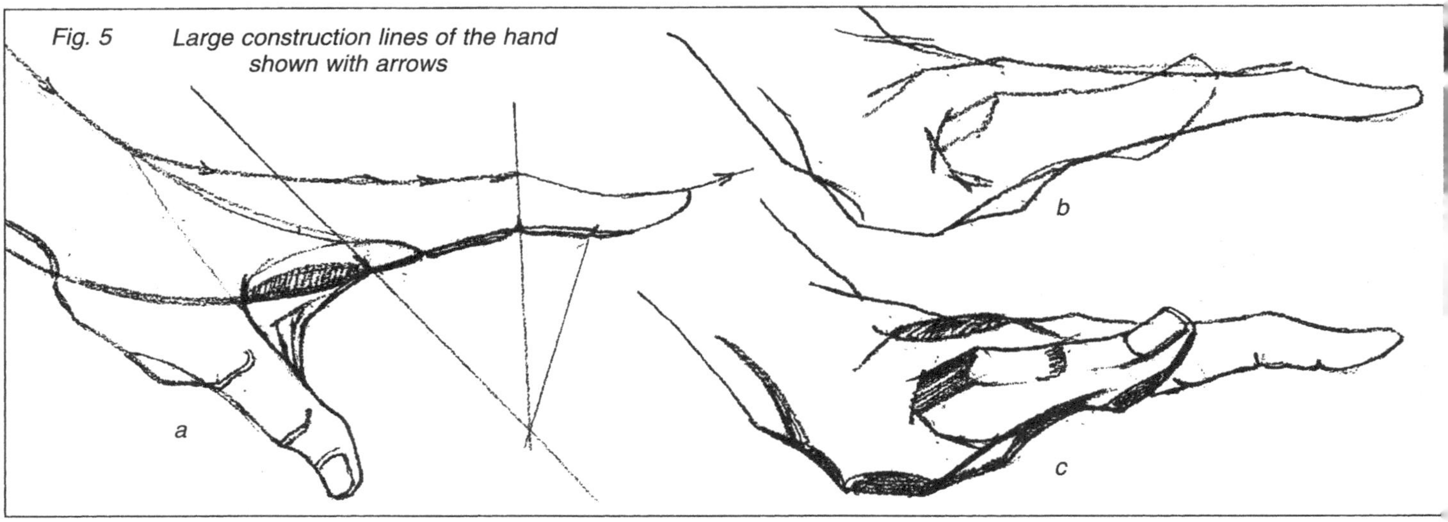

Fig. 5   Large construction lines of the hand
shown with arrows

a

b

c

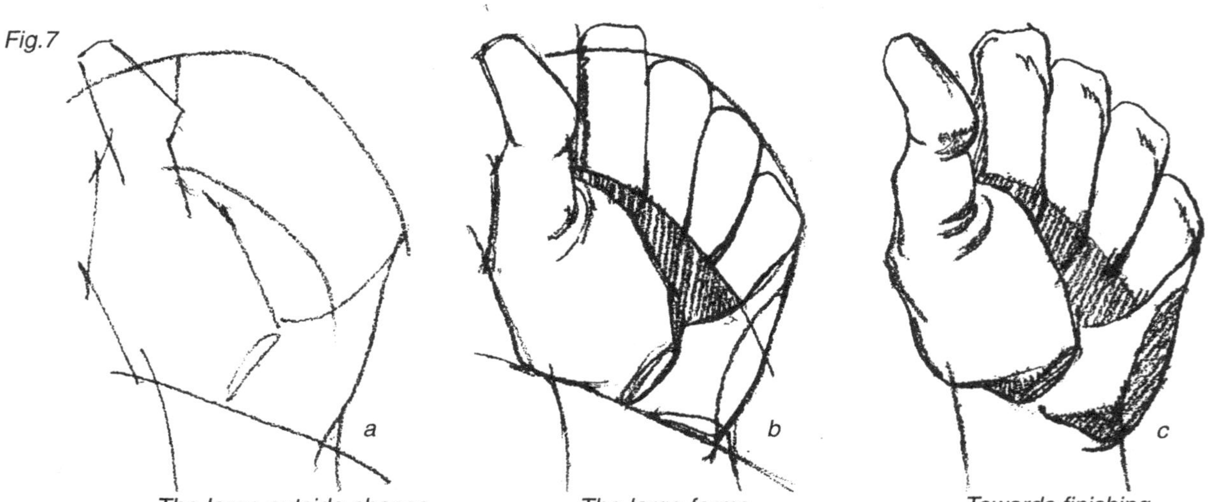

Fig.7

a

b

c

The large outside shapes   The large forms   Towards finishing

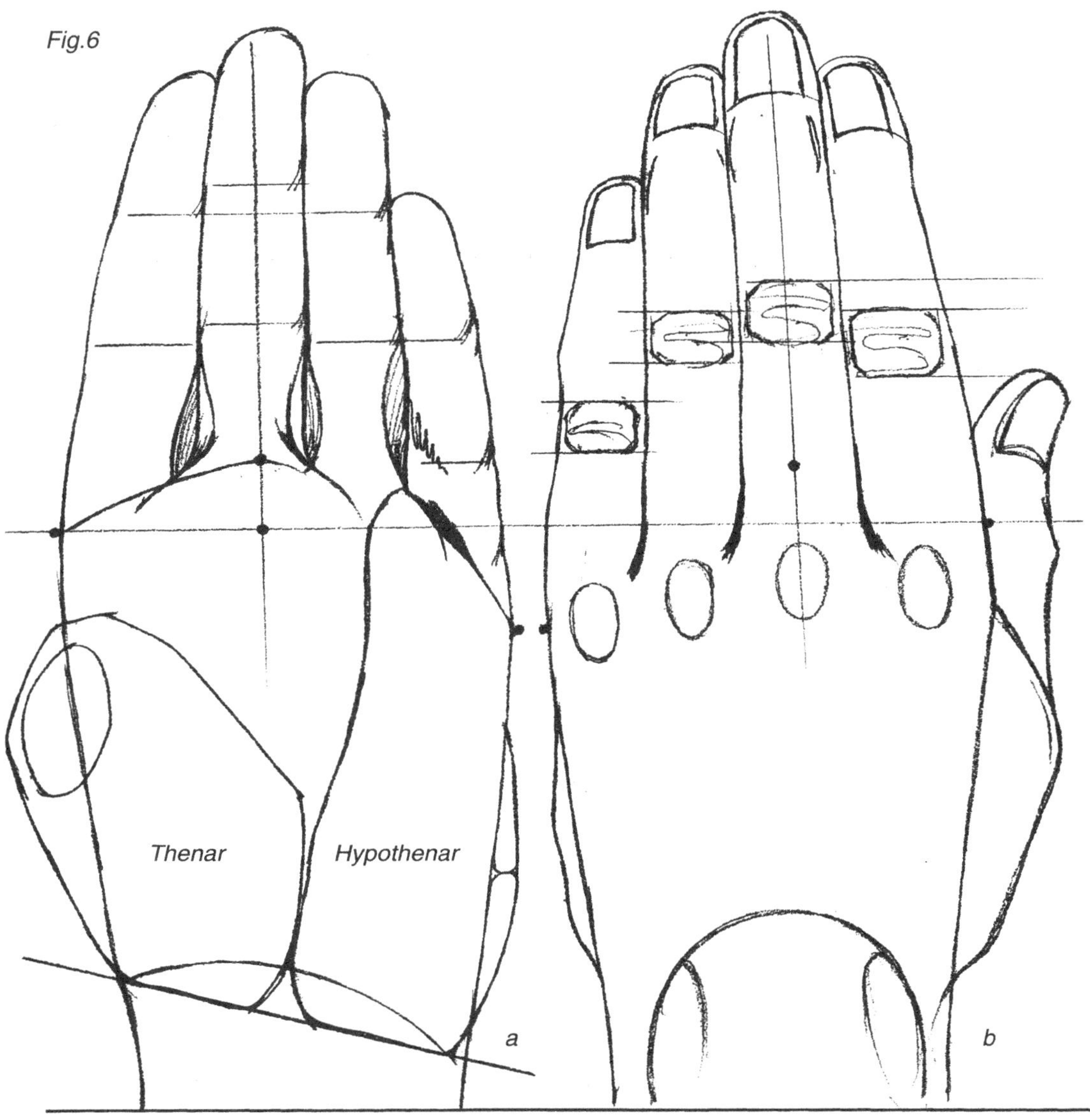

Fig.6

Thenar *Hypothenar*

a

b

Figs. 6a.b. These two drawings show the relationship of the palm side to the top surface side of the hand. Dots in the center of the mid finger are on a center line of the first finger you draw to. The two basic structure lines of the hand go past the dots at the outer edges of the palm.

Fig. 6a. The two large forms of the palm of the hand with some simple planes. The form of the thumb side is called the *thenar pad* and the form of the little finger side is called the *hypothenar pad*. Note the slant angle at the base of these two forms.

Figs. 7a.b.c.d.e.f. These drawings show a simple way to draw seemingly complex arrangements of fingers and forms of the hand.

Fig. 7a. Using simple straight and curved lines block in the major shapes of the forms.

Fig. 7b. Divide the large forms up with smaller forms such as the fingers and thumb, the thenar and hypothenar. Emphasize large planes such as are created where the fingers bend under.

Fig. 7c. Add as much detail and shading as needed to complete your drawing.

Figs. 7d.e.f. Follow the same instructions as given above.

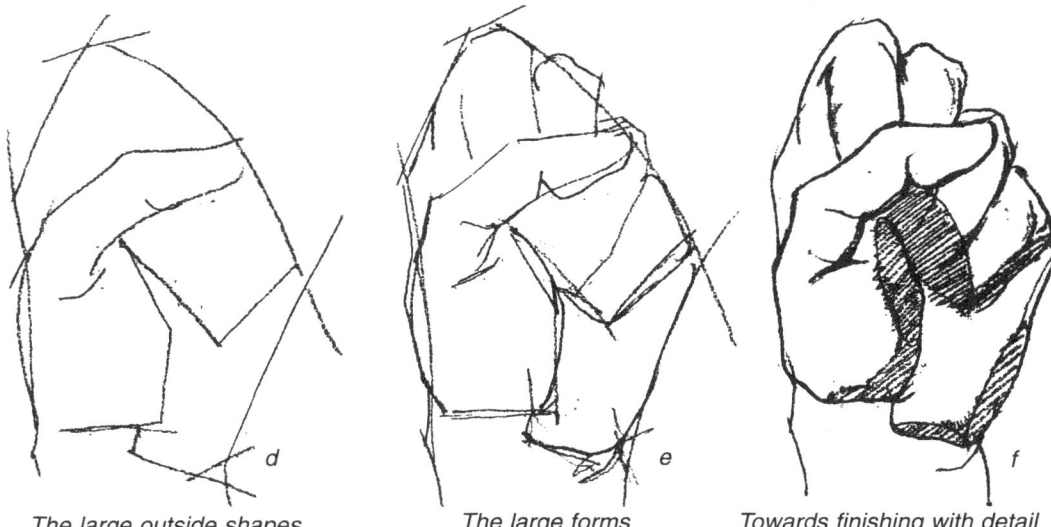

d

e

f

The large outside shapes *The large forms* *Towards finishing with detail*

STRUCTURE: FEET

Many students either leave the feet off in their drawings or draw them so they bear no relationship to the leg. The following examples show not only how to draw the structure of the foot but also how to have it properly related to the leg.

Fig. 1a. Front view. The two structure lines of the leg go to the width of the ankle shown at the dots to any place they lead you to at the extremity of the foot. In this case one line ends at the outside of the little toe and the other line ends at the outside of the joint of the big toe. Depending on the model and the pose these two lines can end at other points on the foot. For instance one line, instead of ending on the outside joint of the big toe, can end on the inside of the big toe.

Fig. 1b. One now adds the form of the instep bones with the ankles resting on top of them. Notice how the curvature of the instep relates directly to the inside of the big toe. The form of the instep can slightly overlap the two basic structure lines.

Fig. 1c. The arrowheads are on a line which forms a sideplane on the leg and instep form and relates to the rear bone form of the toe.

Fig. 1d. Bottom planes are put on the ankles. Details are added such as the step down of the toes.

Fig. 1e. Shading, which shows the flatness of the planes and roundness of forms, produces a basic simple drawing of a foot. Further details of tendons, bones, muscles, veins, etc. can be added as needed but must not interfere with the large forms.

Fig. 2a. Back view. Two structure lines going to the width of the ankle to the outer edges of the foot they relate to.

Fig. 2b. Draw a large arched form which the ankles rest upon.

Fig. 2c. The shape of the heel is added within the large arched form. The arrows now show two more lines which relate to the Achilles tendon. Continue these lines to make the sideplanes of the heel form, loop around the bottom and connect them

to the shape of this form. Bottom planes may be added on the ankles.

Fig. 2d. This drawing shows how the form of the little toe is added and related to the mass of the foot. A top plane is added to the heel form. The shading represents the Achilles tendon attaching to the heel form.

Fig. 3a. Bottom view. The foot is often seen from the bottom or partially from the bottom. Shown are three steps to use to solve this seemingly complex problem. Start first with a base line where the foot rests on a surface. Make sure this angle is correct. Next draw a triangular shape which is the general shape of the foot and draw the two structure lines of the leg connecting to it.

Fig. 3b. The forms of the toes are added to the basic shape.

Fig. 3c. One now has to find as many overlapping forms as he can that show which forms are in front of others in order to give the illusion of projection and recession. Even though they may be barely visible one must emphasize them in order to achieve the effect. Underplay forms and planes that do not help. The correct use of line is also important of course.

Fig.3

a

b

c

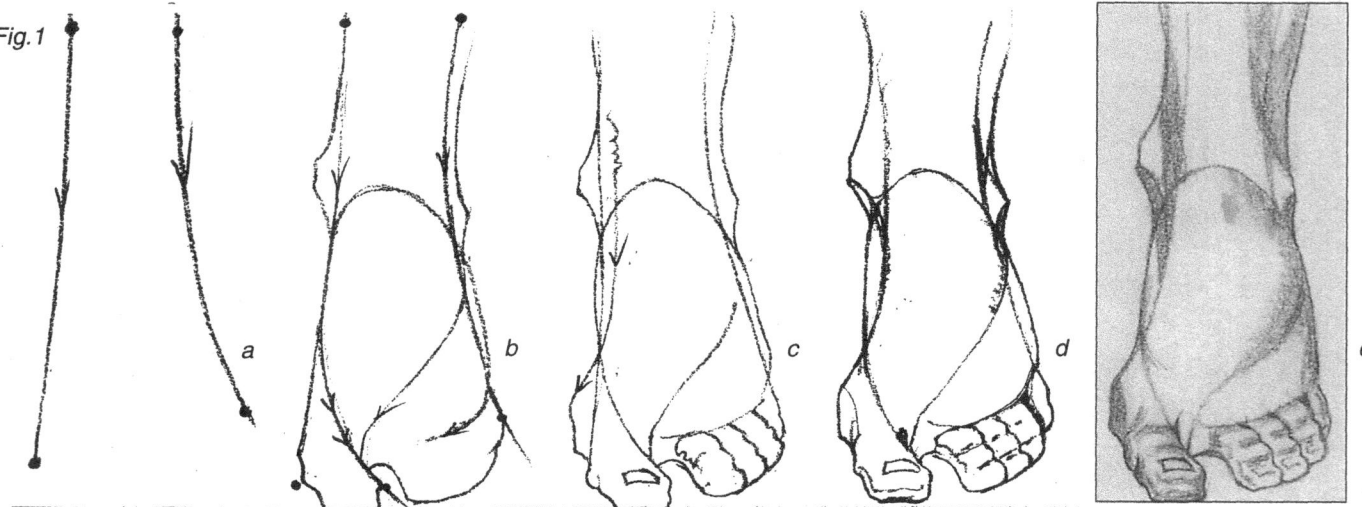

Fig.1   *a*   *b*   *c*   *d*   *e*

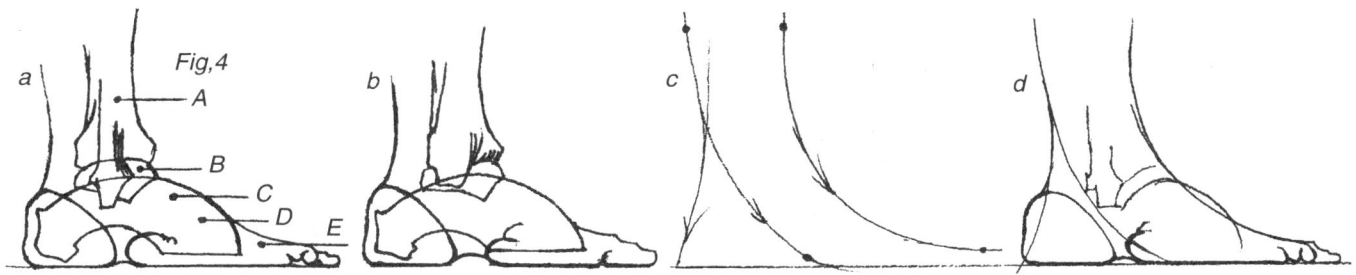

Fig. 4a. Little toe side. Anatomical forms shown in simplified shapes to explain how the structure lines of the foot in the side view are arrived at. A. The combined tibia and fibula form. B. The astralagus bone. C. Cuneiform bones. D. Metarsus (5 separate bones). E. Phalanges (5 sets of 3 bones).

Fig. 4b. A view of the big toe side.

Fig. 4c. Starting the drawing of the foot in profile. Two structure lines going from the width of the ankle, at the two upper dots, to the two lower dots. An additional line comes off the back structure line to the back of the heel.

Fig. 4d. The major forms built upon the structure lines.

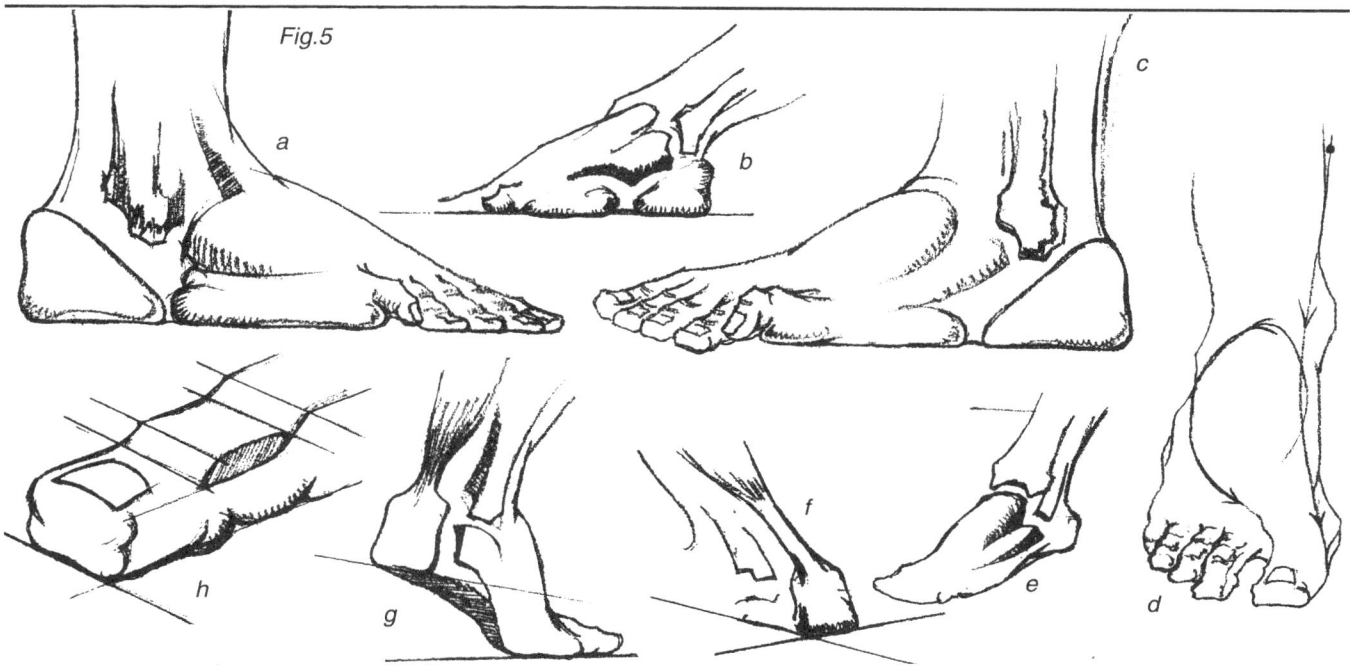

Figs. 5a.b.c.d.e.f.g.h. A series of drawings showing stylized forms of the foot in various positions. **Fig. 5d.** shows the forms of a right foot built on the basic structure lines. Note the constant relationship of the line of the form of the instep to the inside of the big toe.

Figs. 5f. and g. show lines which put the forms in perspective. Both the bottom of the heel and the foot should have the correct angle. This is frequently overlooked.

Fig. 5h. Showing the step downs of the big toe in perspective

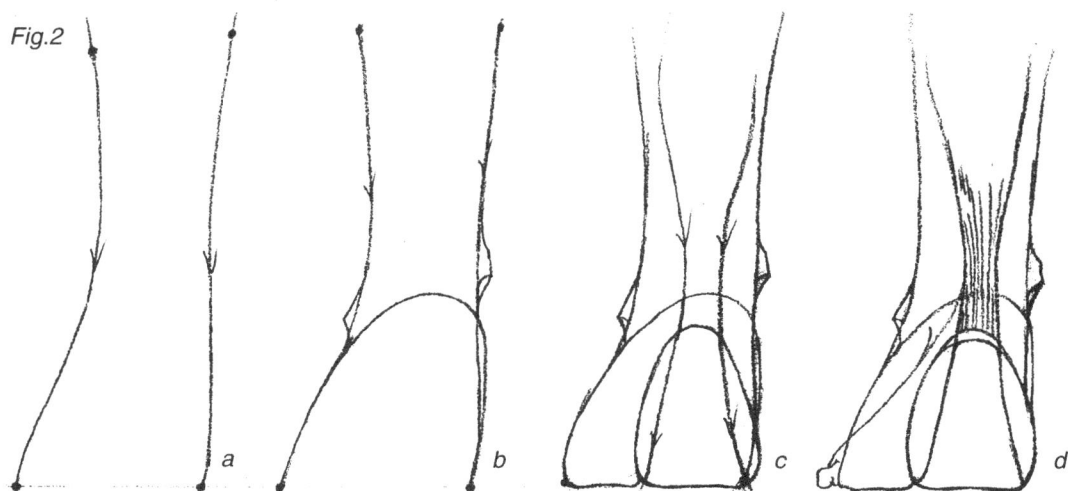

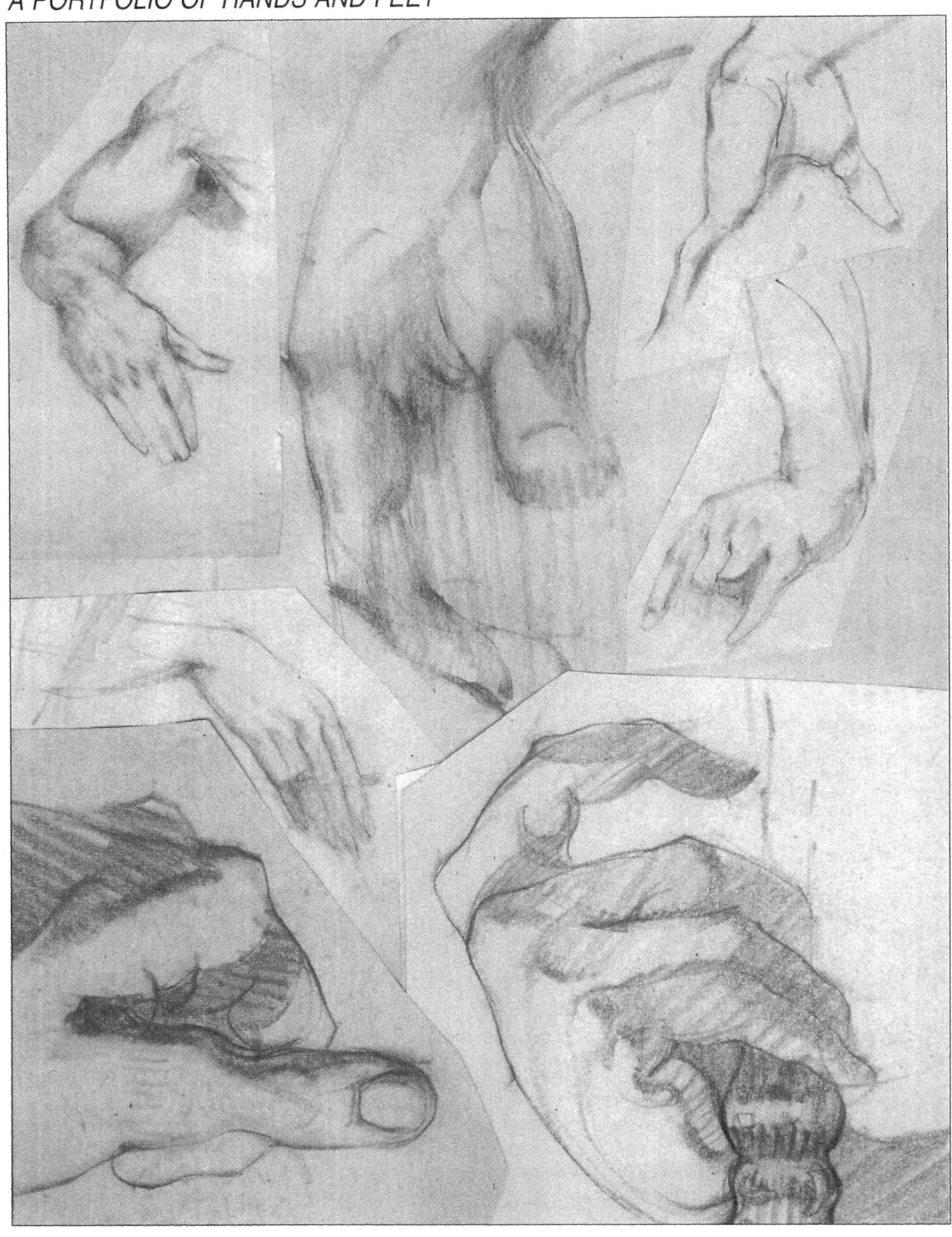

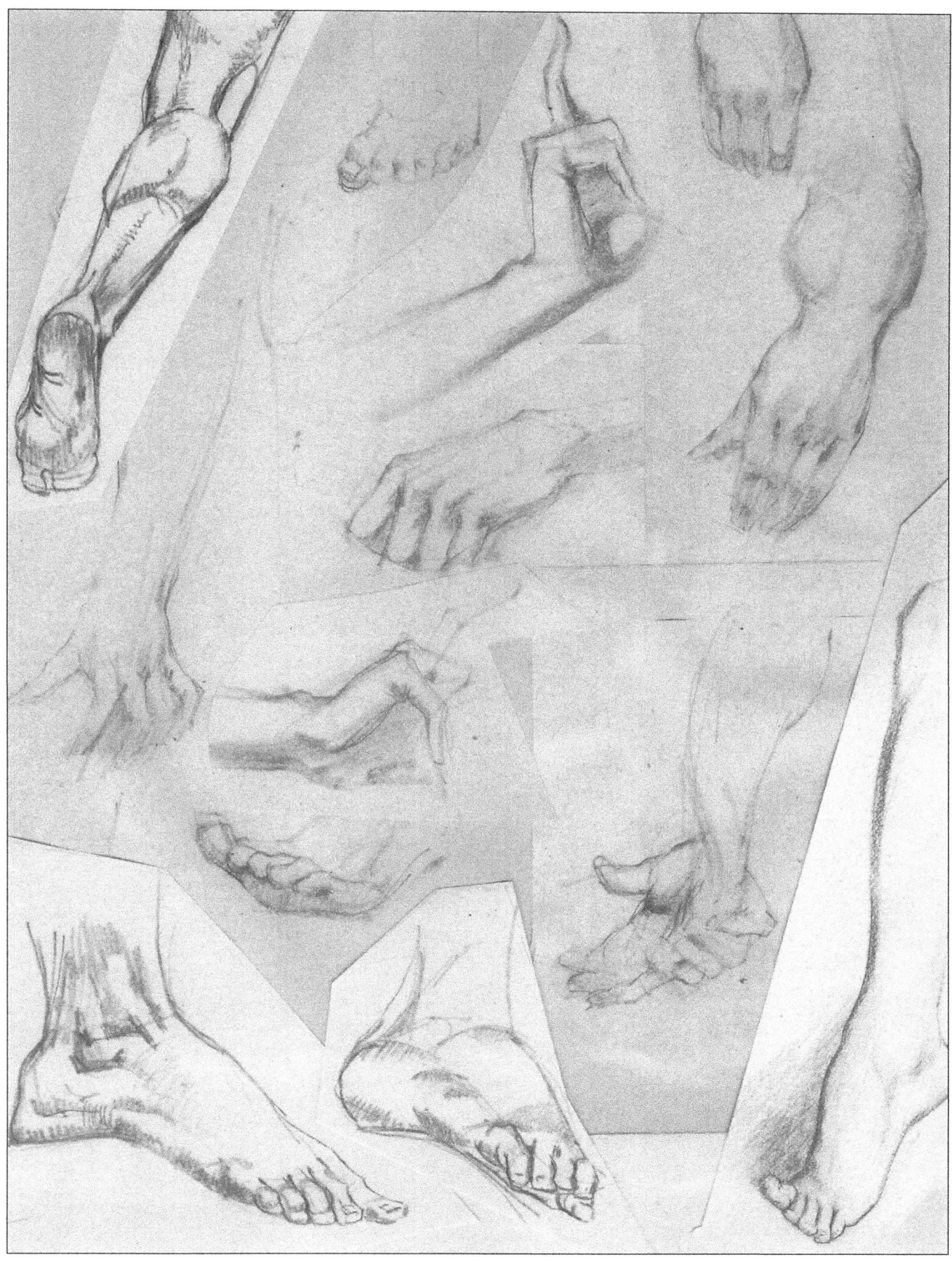

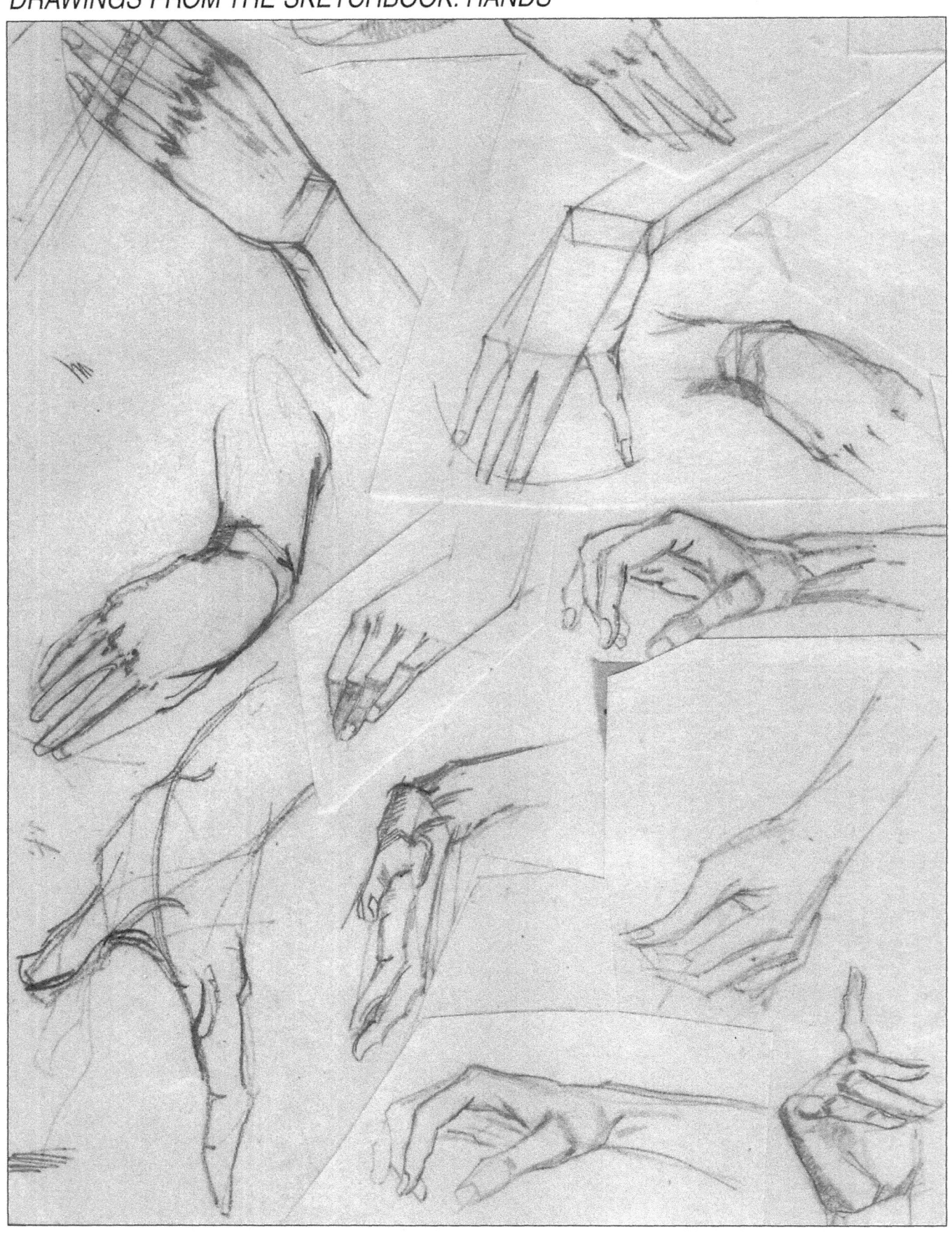

PORTFOLIO OF DRAWINGS:
NUDE STUDIES

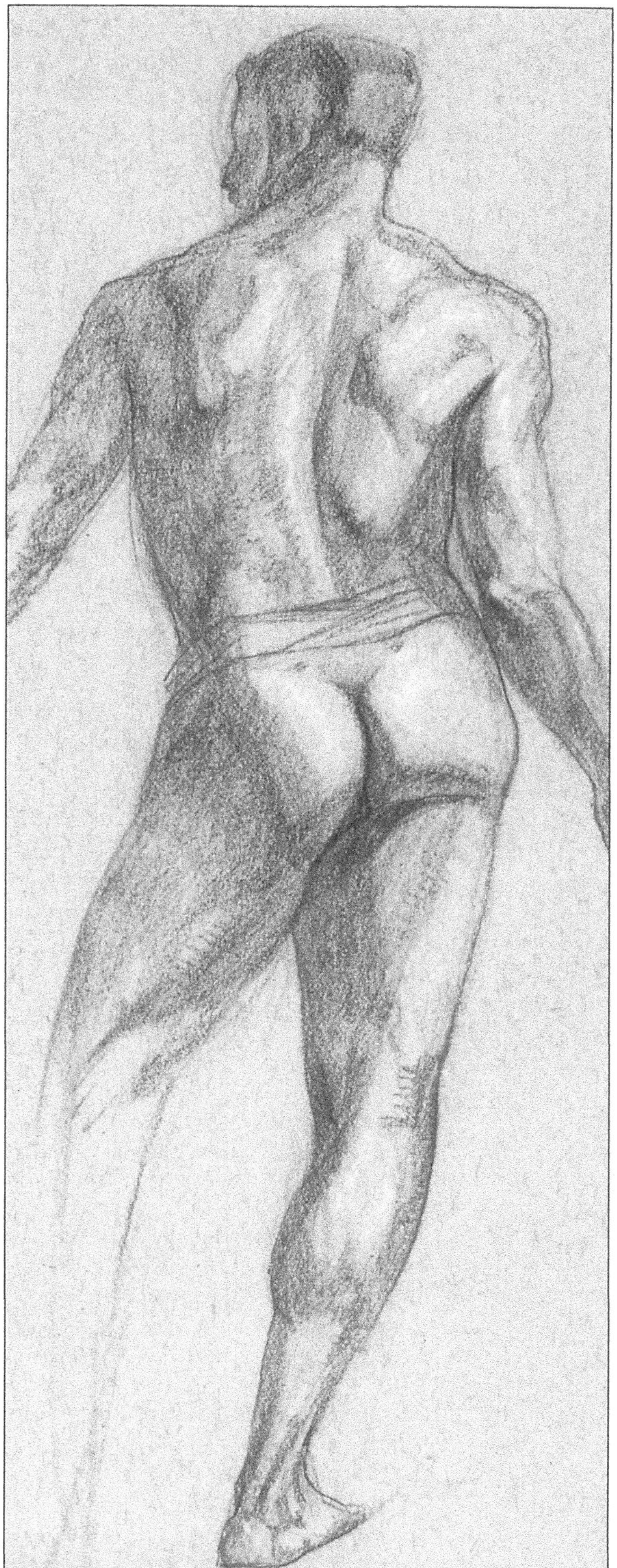

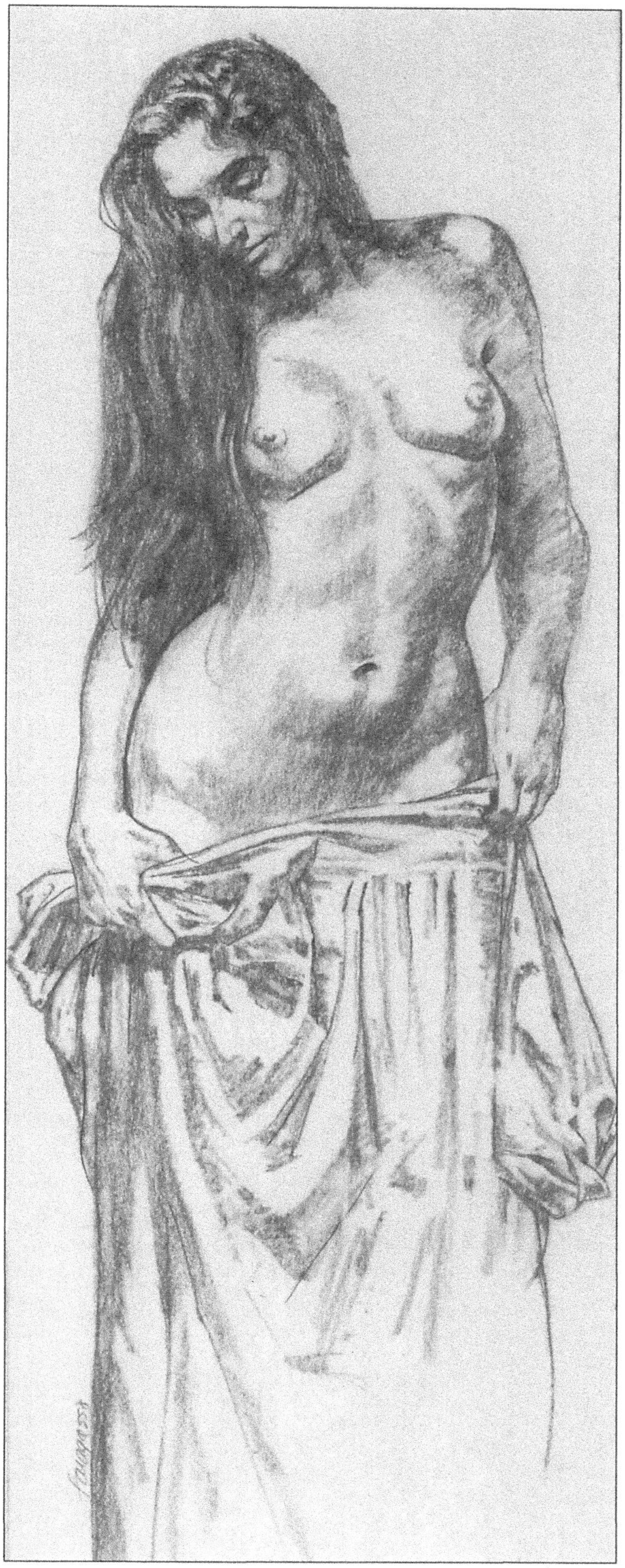

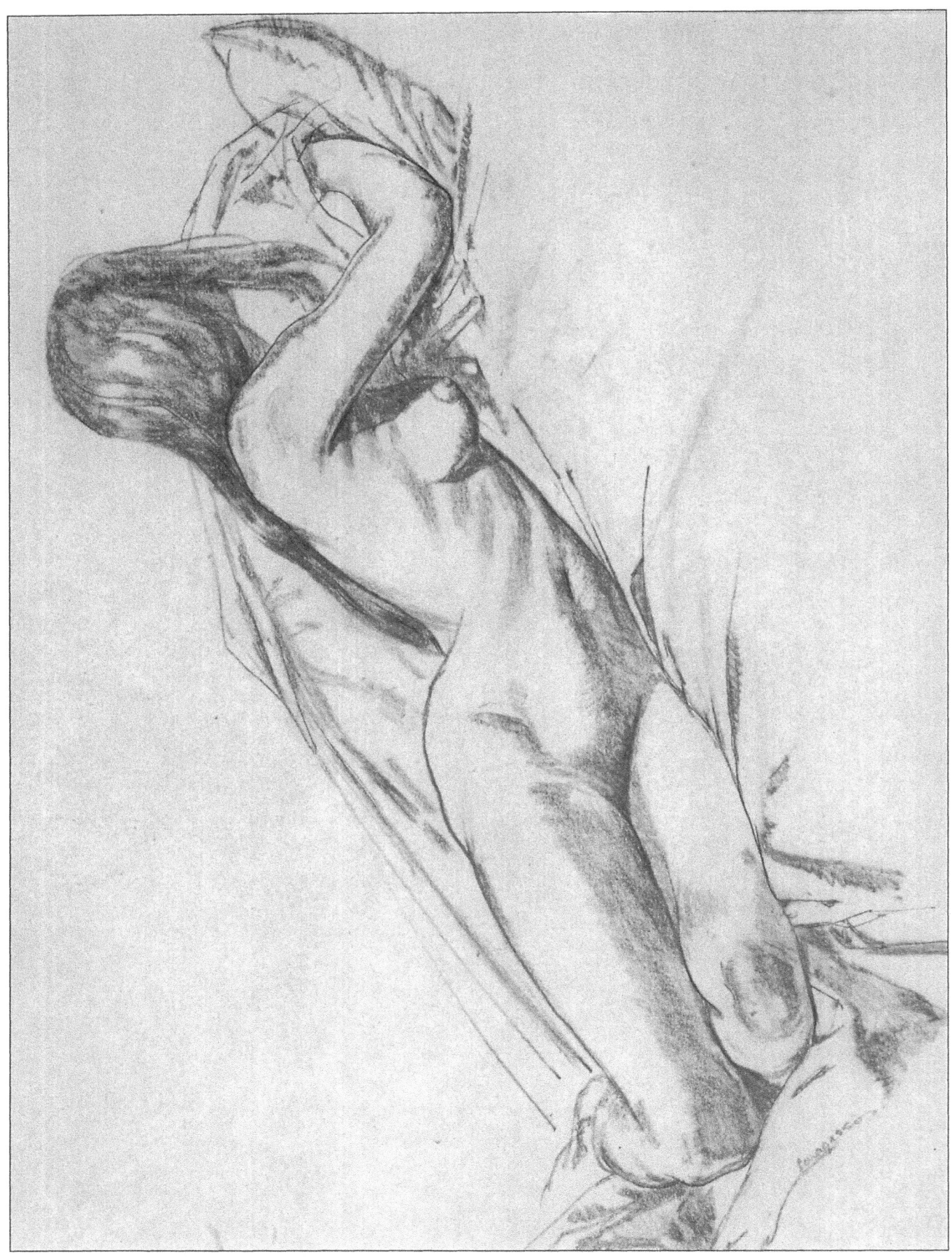

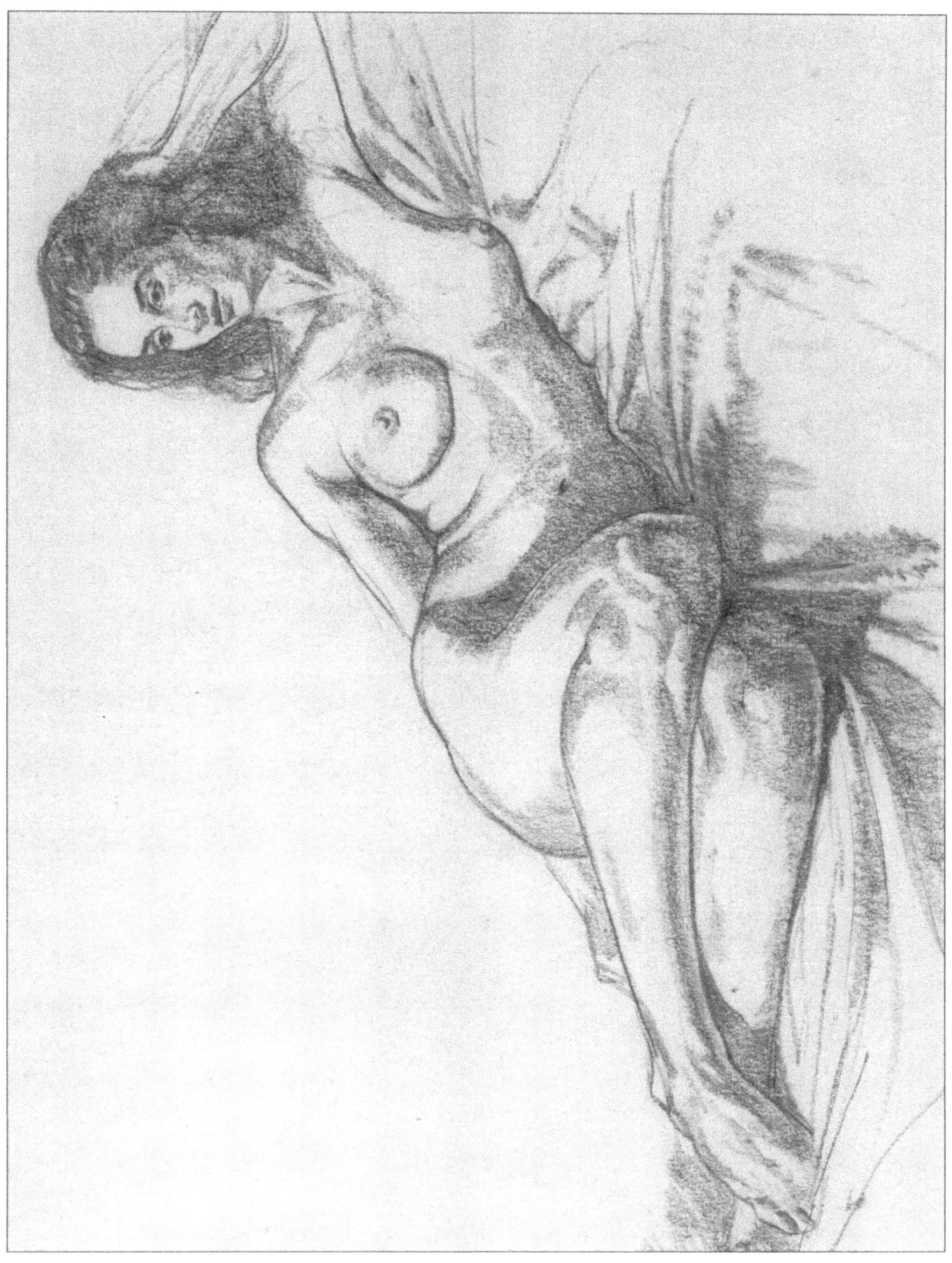

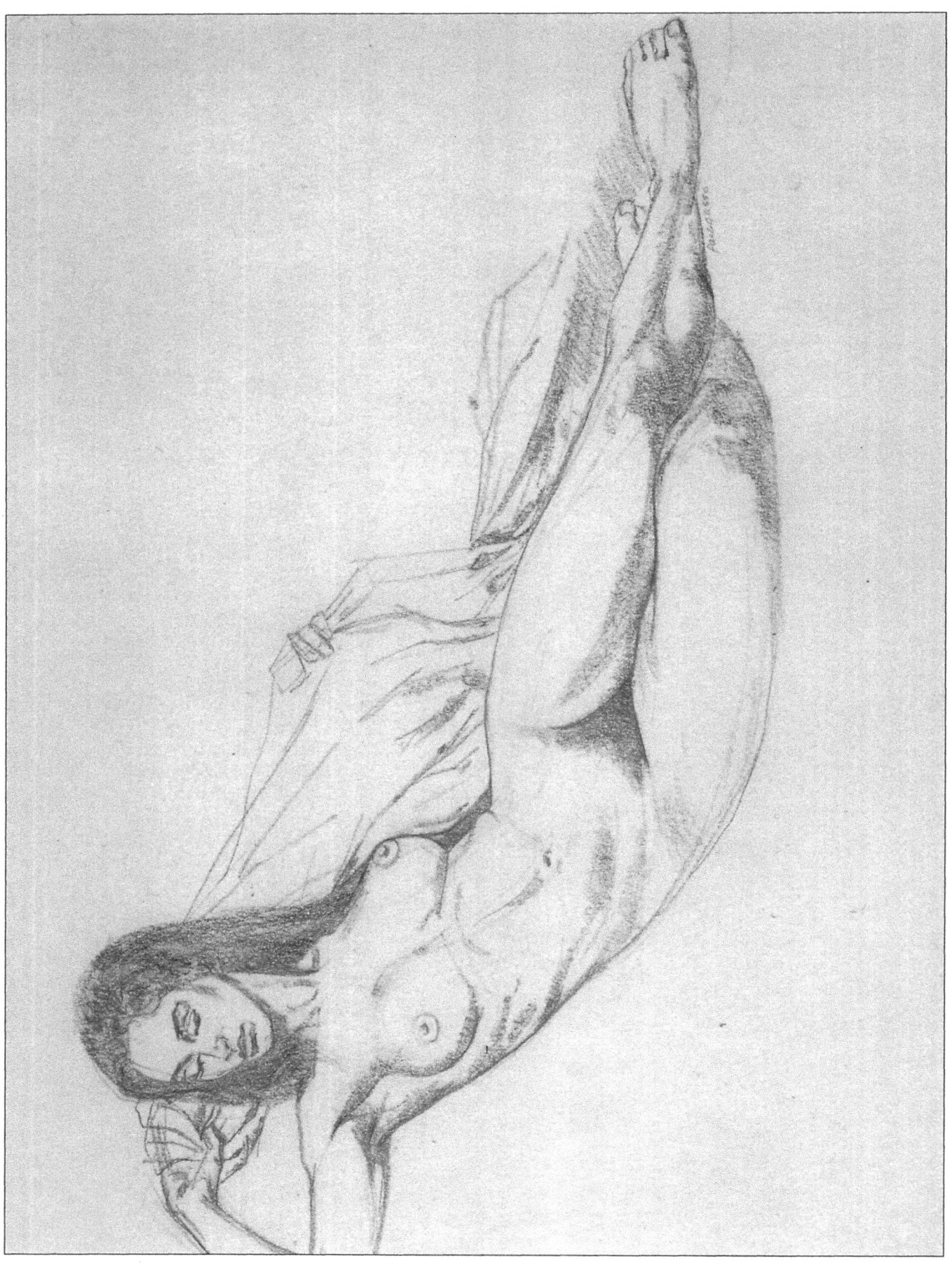

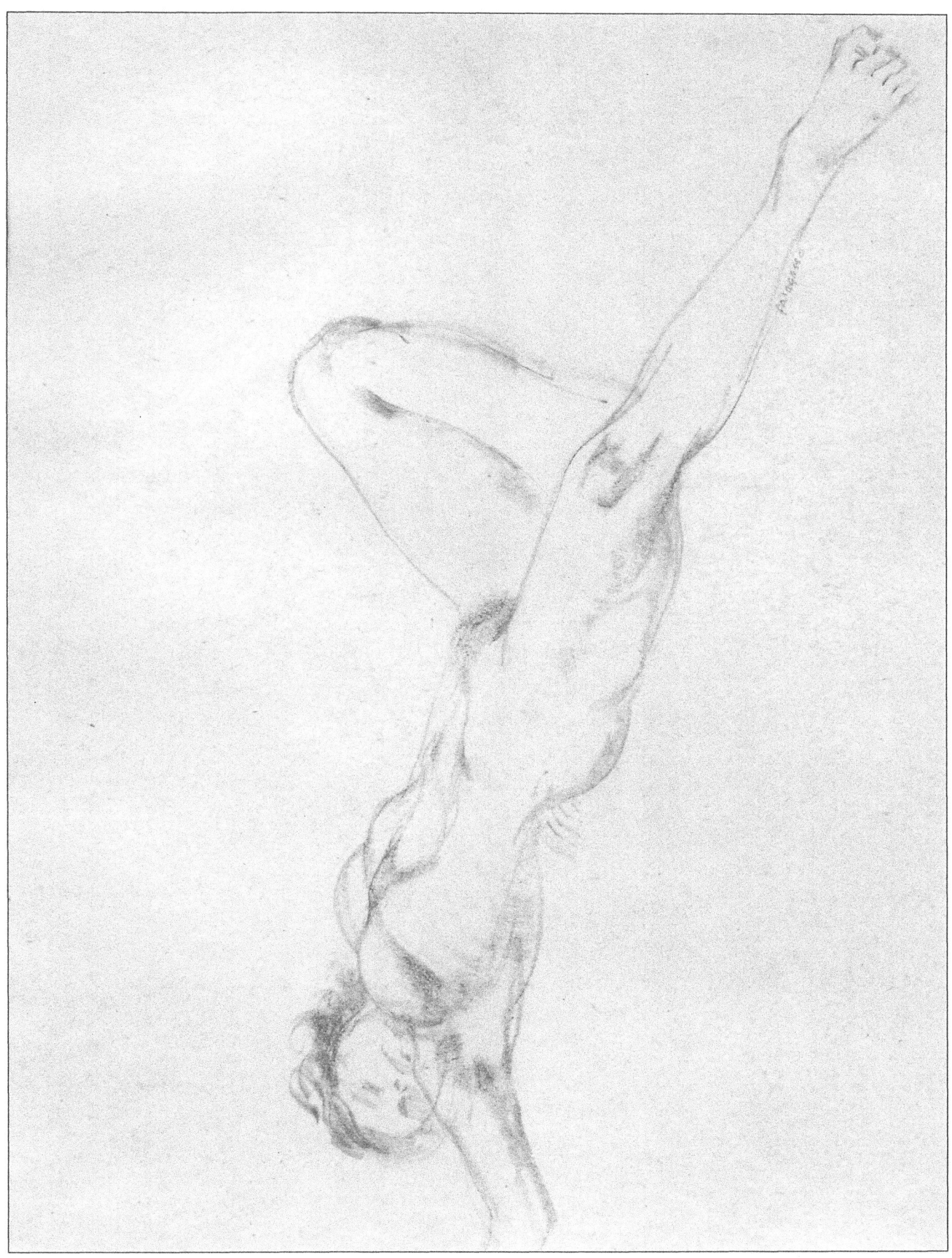

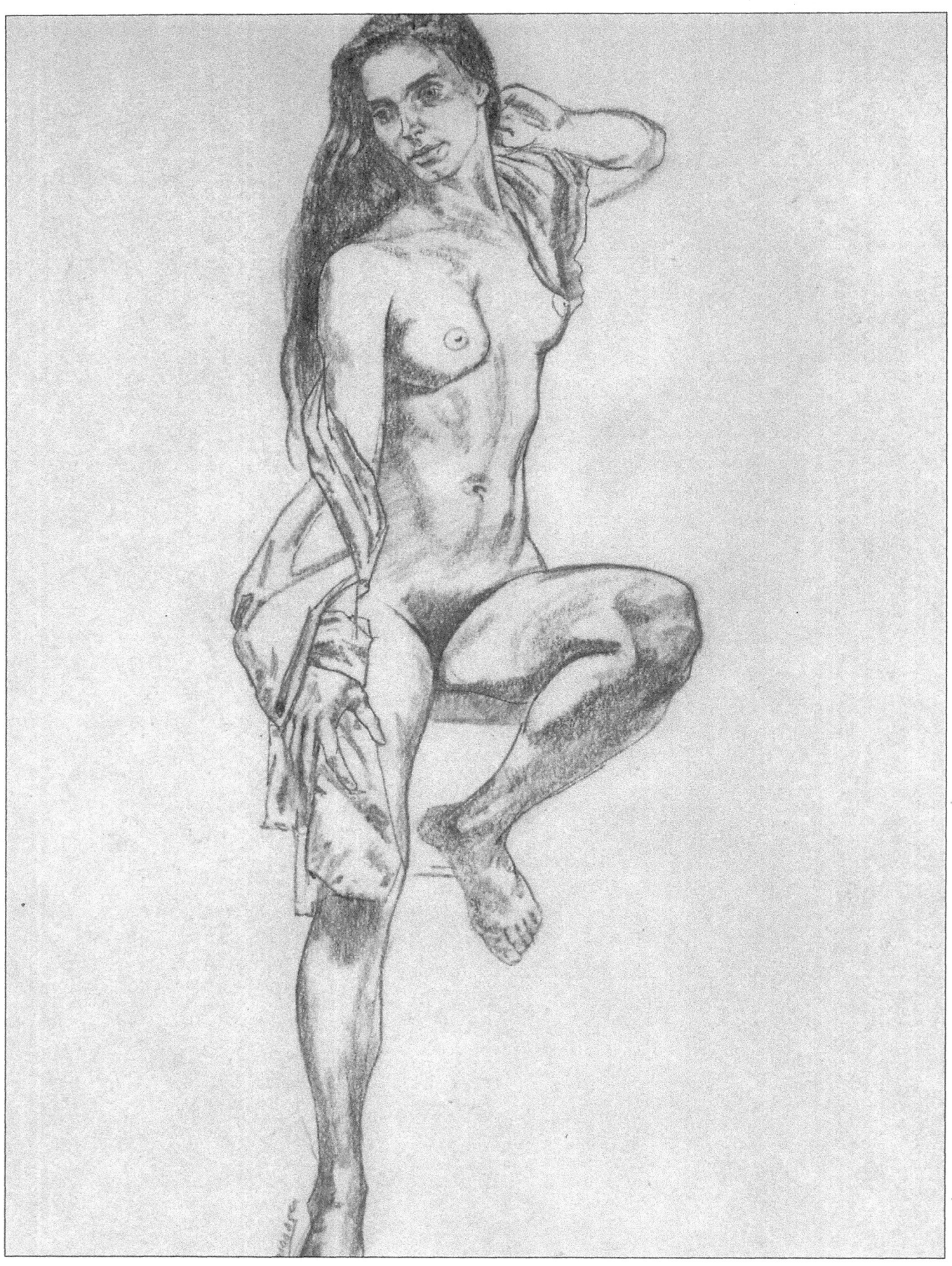

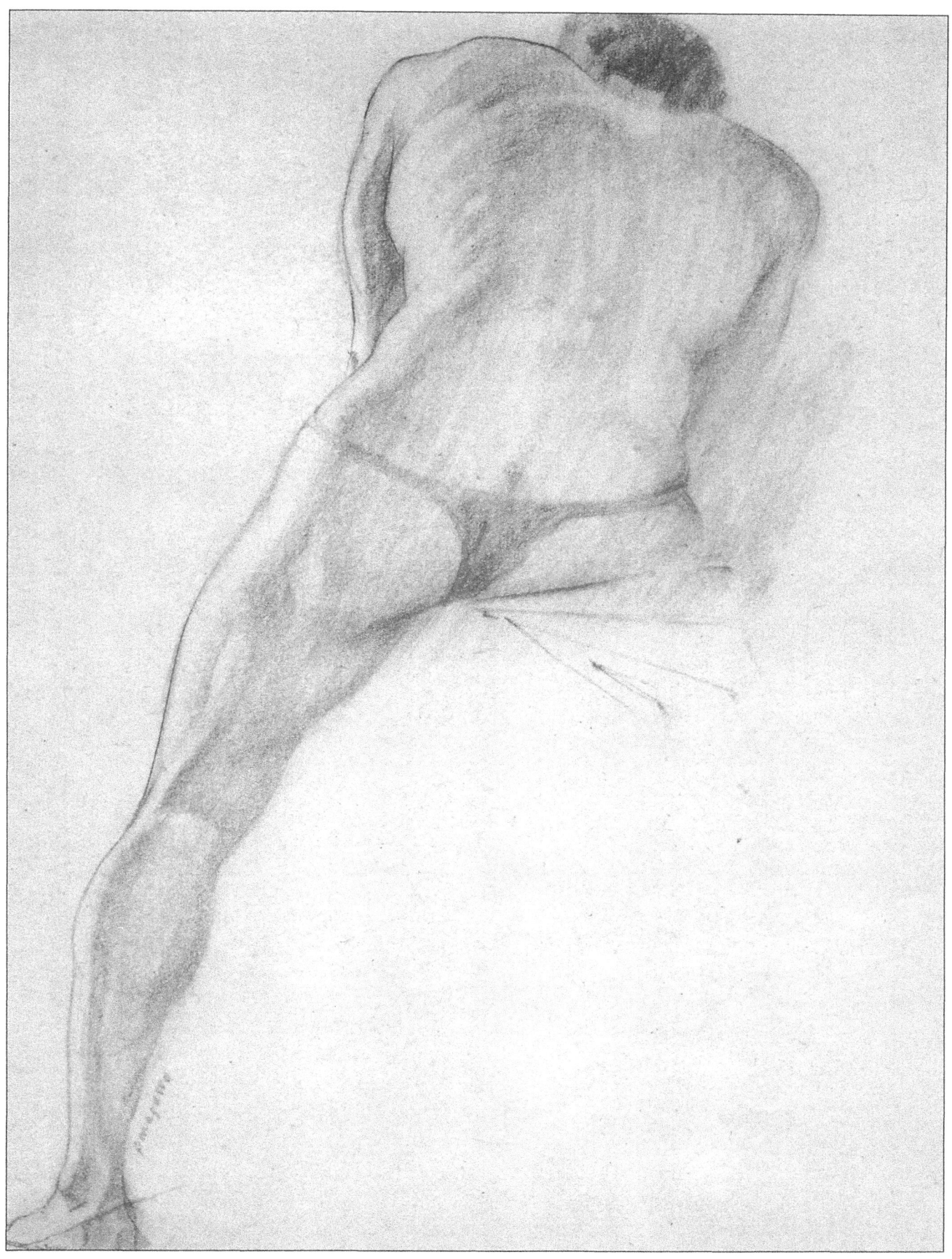

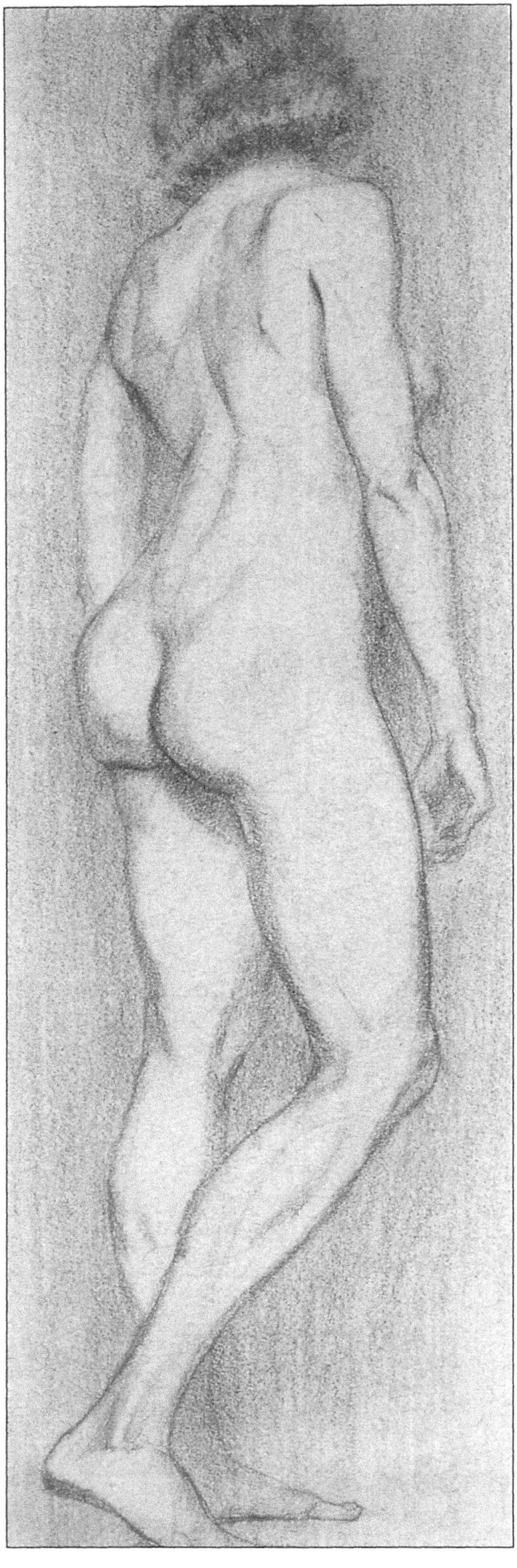

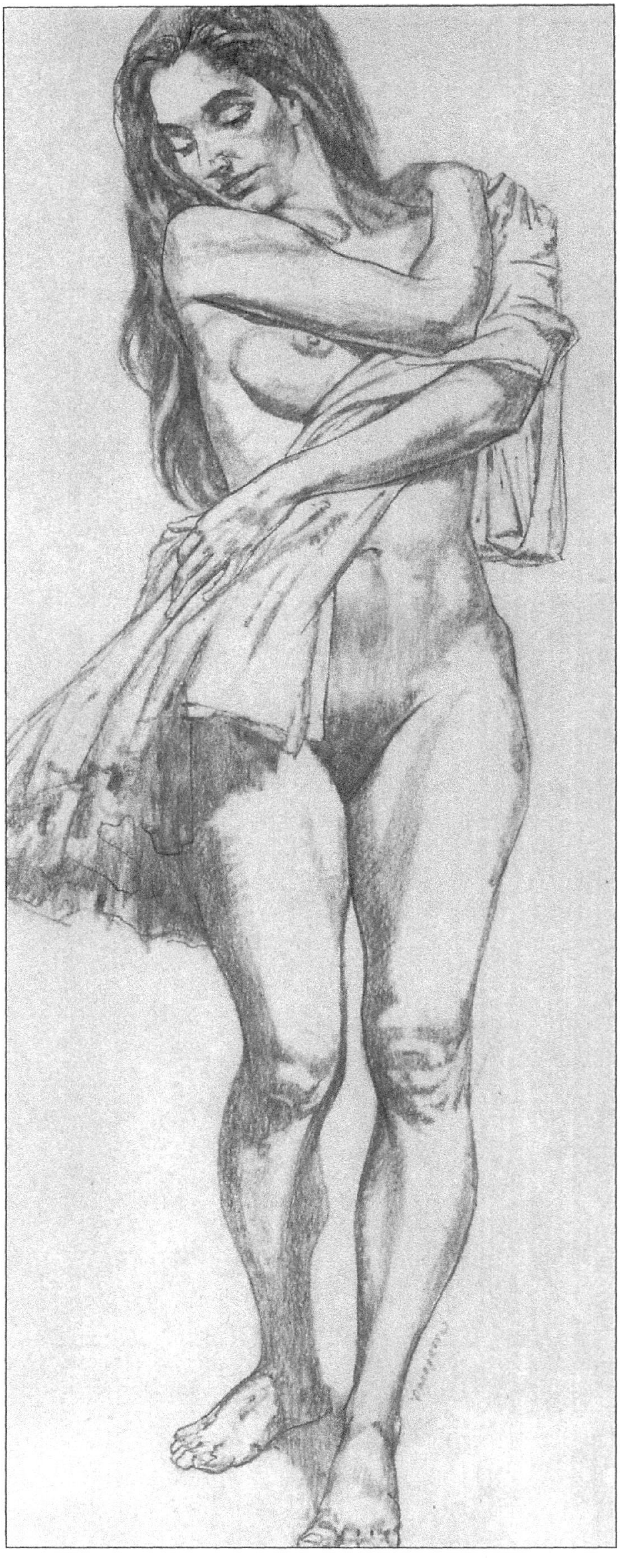

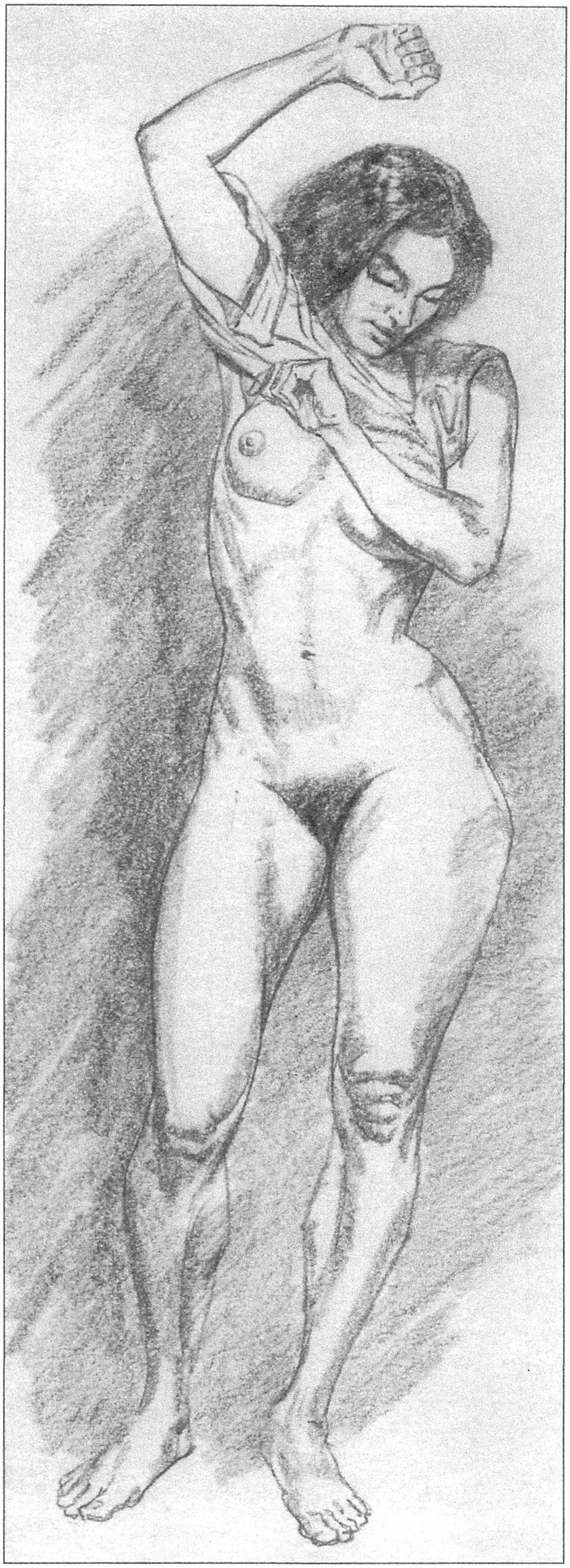

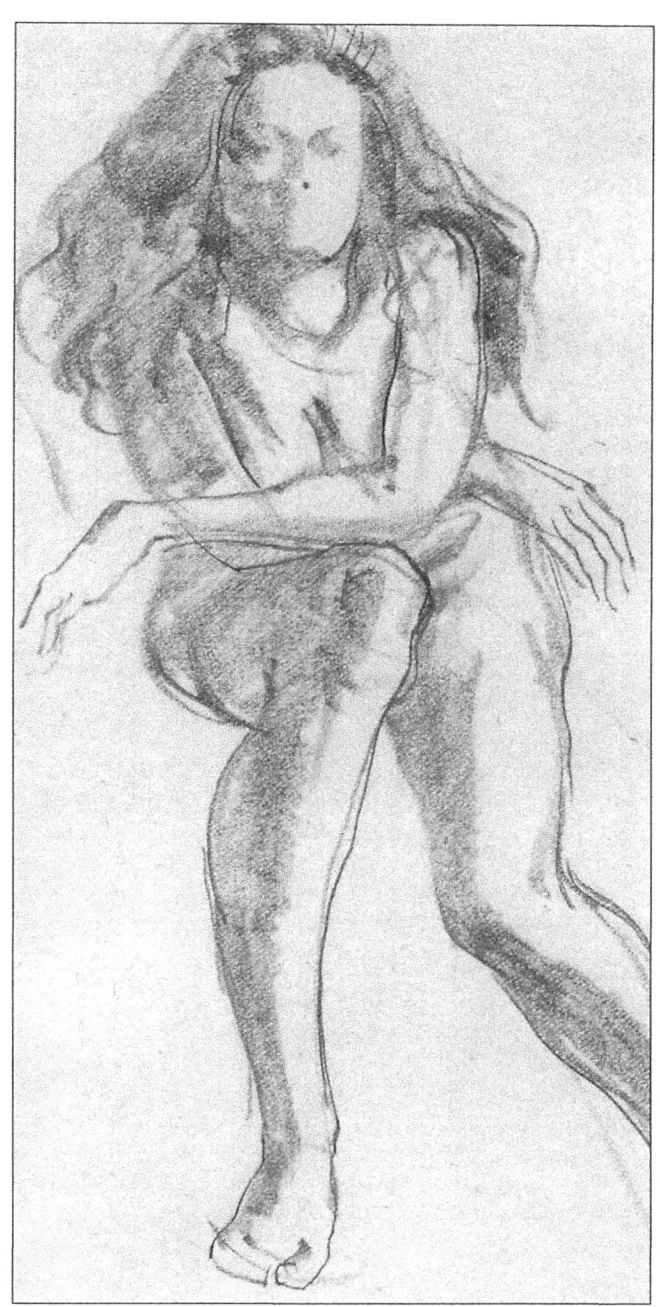

SIXTEEN

THE SKULL AND ITS CONSTRUCTION

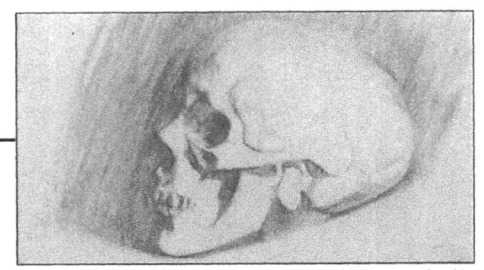

Of all the concerns of the artist the drawing of the human head is and has been of the greatest importance. Much has been written on this subject throughout the ages from every conceivable standpoint. The subject has been approached from the standpoint of the study of anatomy and evolution, through ideal proportions, through meditation, memory and through just plain copying. Much has been written also on the expressions of the face and how to achieve them as well as how to determine and read the physiognomy of the face.

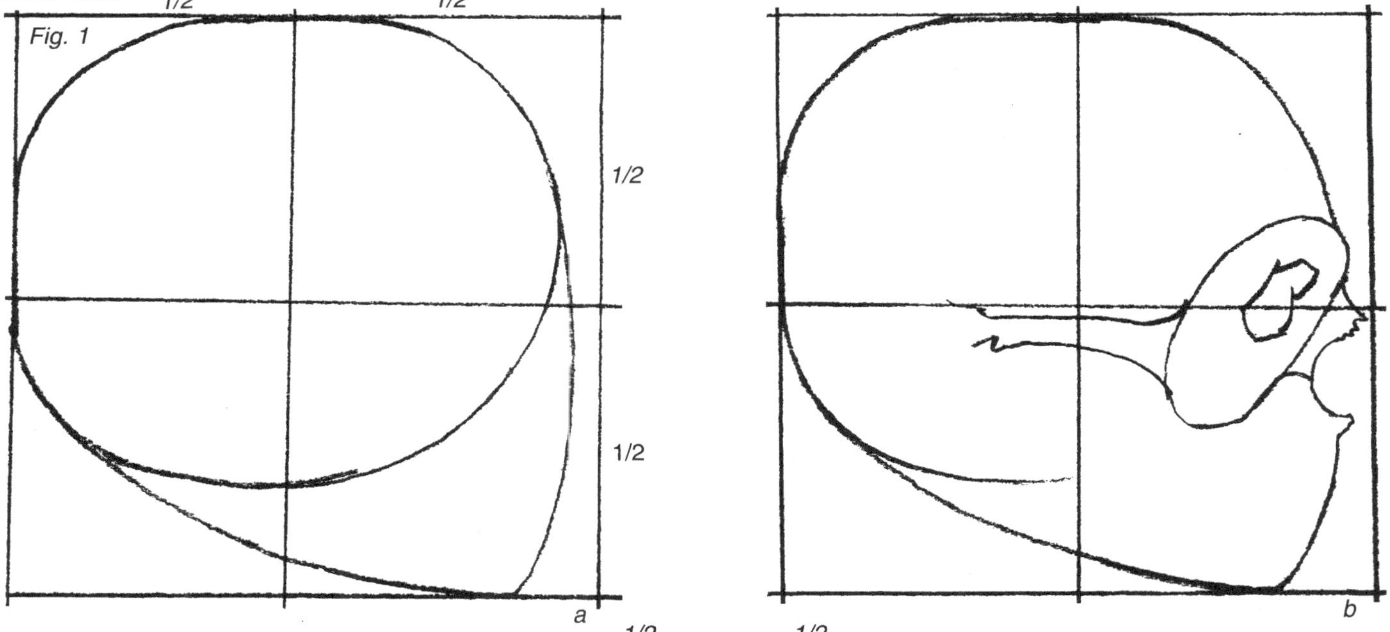

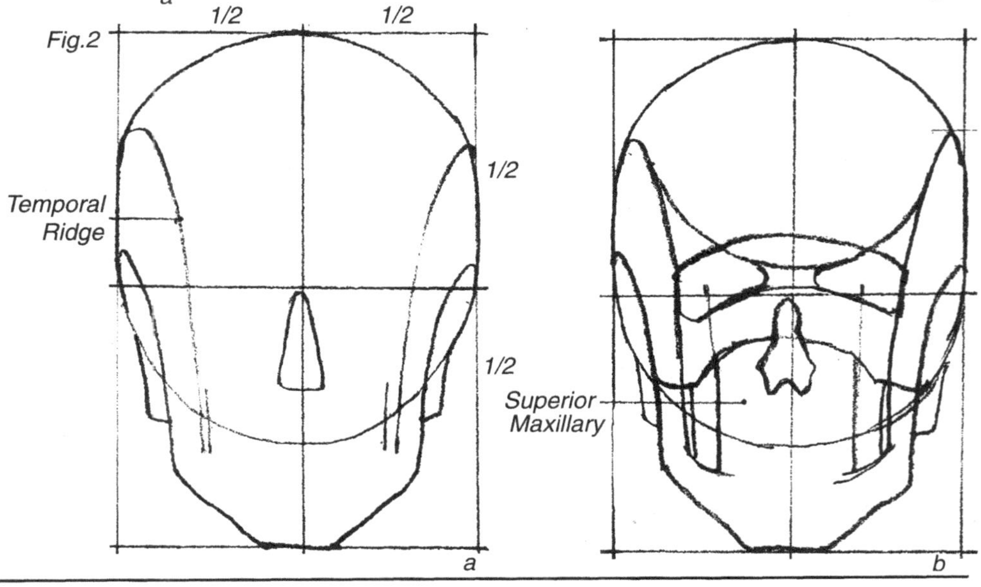

muscles, or cartilage or fat but on combinations of all of them.

These then create forms and planes which are interrelated into one cohesive whole

Forms and planes are present on everyone but are more obvious on some people than others. Planes are more apparent on thin bony people than on those with fatty, fleshy areas. Therefore a little knowledge of the underlying bone structure of the head is necessary to help in the understanding of the

SIDE VIEW   1/2   1/2

Fig. 1

1/2

1/2

1/2

a

b

All of these approaches are valid to some degree and you should read and study everything you can on the subject. However this book is concerned about drawing from the standpoint of structure, an unknown approach to many if not most people who study art. Although it may seem complicated it really isn't and will be presented in a simple orderly manner.

It has to be stressed that the forms and planes are not based solely on bones or

Fig.2   1/2   1/2

1/2

Temporal
Ridge

1/2

Superior
Maxillary

a

b

surface. It is also helpful to understand the relationships of the various bony sections of the skull to obtain a cohesive mental picture of the skull. We shall start this study, therefore, with simplified drawings of the large shapes of the skull to which we will add smaller and smaller forms.

CONSTRUCTION OF THE SKULL – SIDE VIEW

Fig. 1a. The overall shape of the skull. The cranium is a flattened circle to which is added the facial angle and the jaw shape.

Fig. 1b. A unified section of the zygomatic arch, malar bone and frontal ridge is added. The position of the eye socket within this form is indicated. The nasal bone, nasal spine and curvature of the tooth cylinder projects from the basic shape.

Fig. 1c. Starting near the top of the skull add the temporal ridge. Follow its line downwards to the jaw and add the back of the jaw. Behind the back of

the jaw shape is the mastoid process and styloid bone. Lastly add the chin form and shape out the jaw.

Fig. 1d. The zigzag lines show the position of the sutures. The teeth are added, the jaw completed and the bones angled out.

CONSTRUCTION OF THE SKULL – FRONT VIEW

Fig. 2a. The basic shape of the skull which consists of the circular cranium and jaw shape. Sideplanes originating at the temporal bone relate to the jaw. Note the positions of the center lines in relation to these forms.

Fig. 2b. The combined form of the zygomatic arch, malar bone and superior maxillary bones is added. The shape of the lower jaw is completed. Orifices of the eye socket and nose are added. Notice the line sweeping from the left to right temporal bones. It forms the deep underplanes of the eye sockets.

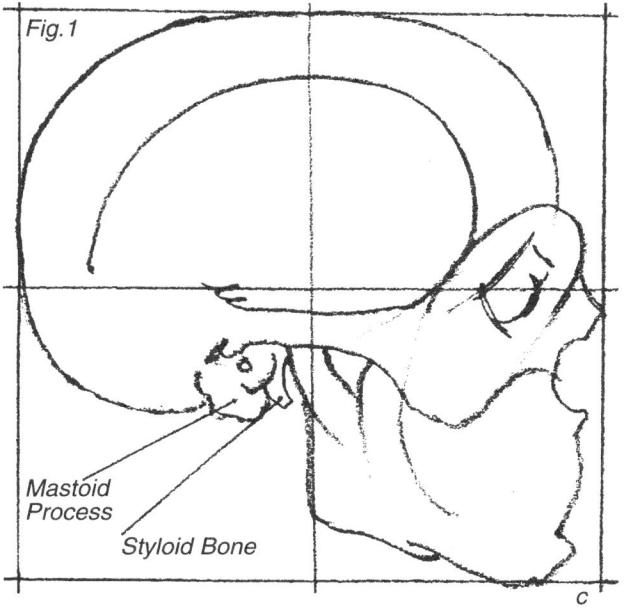

Fig.1

Mastoid Process

Styloid Bone

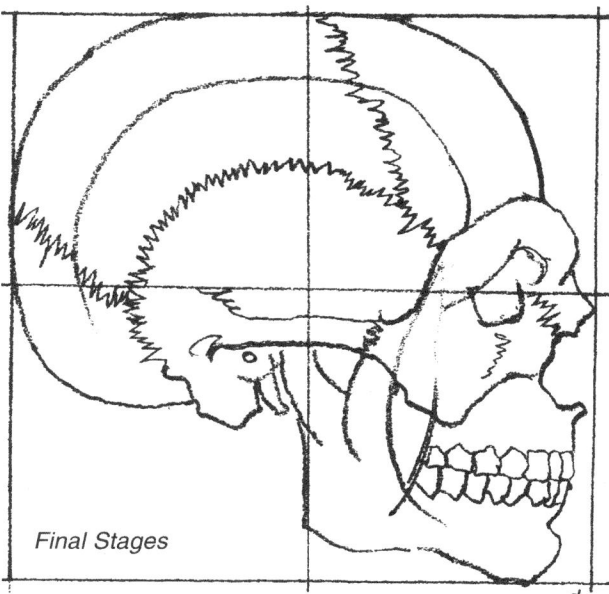

Final Stages

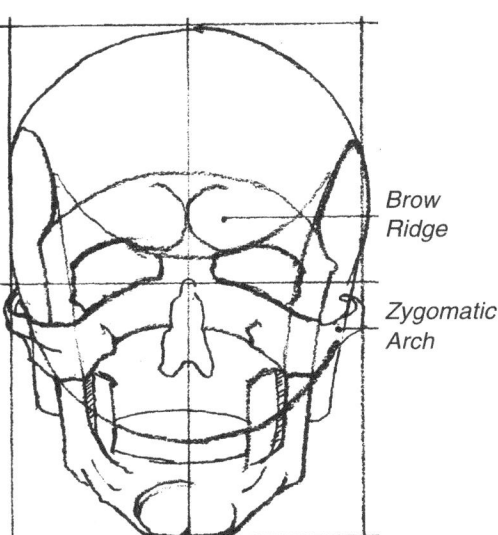

Brow Ridge

Zygomatic Arch

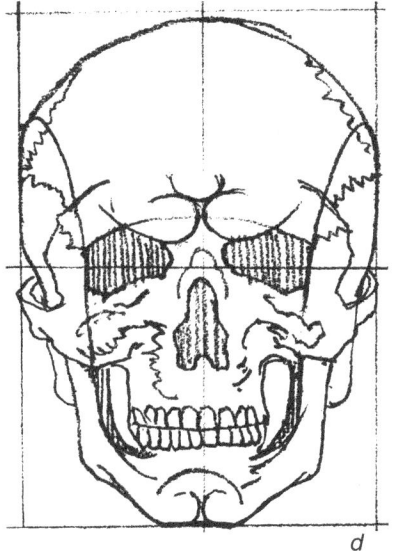

Fig. 2c. Add the brow and divide it into three forms. Finish the drawing of the zygomatic arch. Add the chin and designate a rectangular area for the teeth.

Fig. 2d. Sutures are added as well as the nasal ridge and teeth. The chin form is divided. The malar bone and zygomatic arch are refined in drawing as well as the shape of the superior and inferior maxillary.

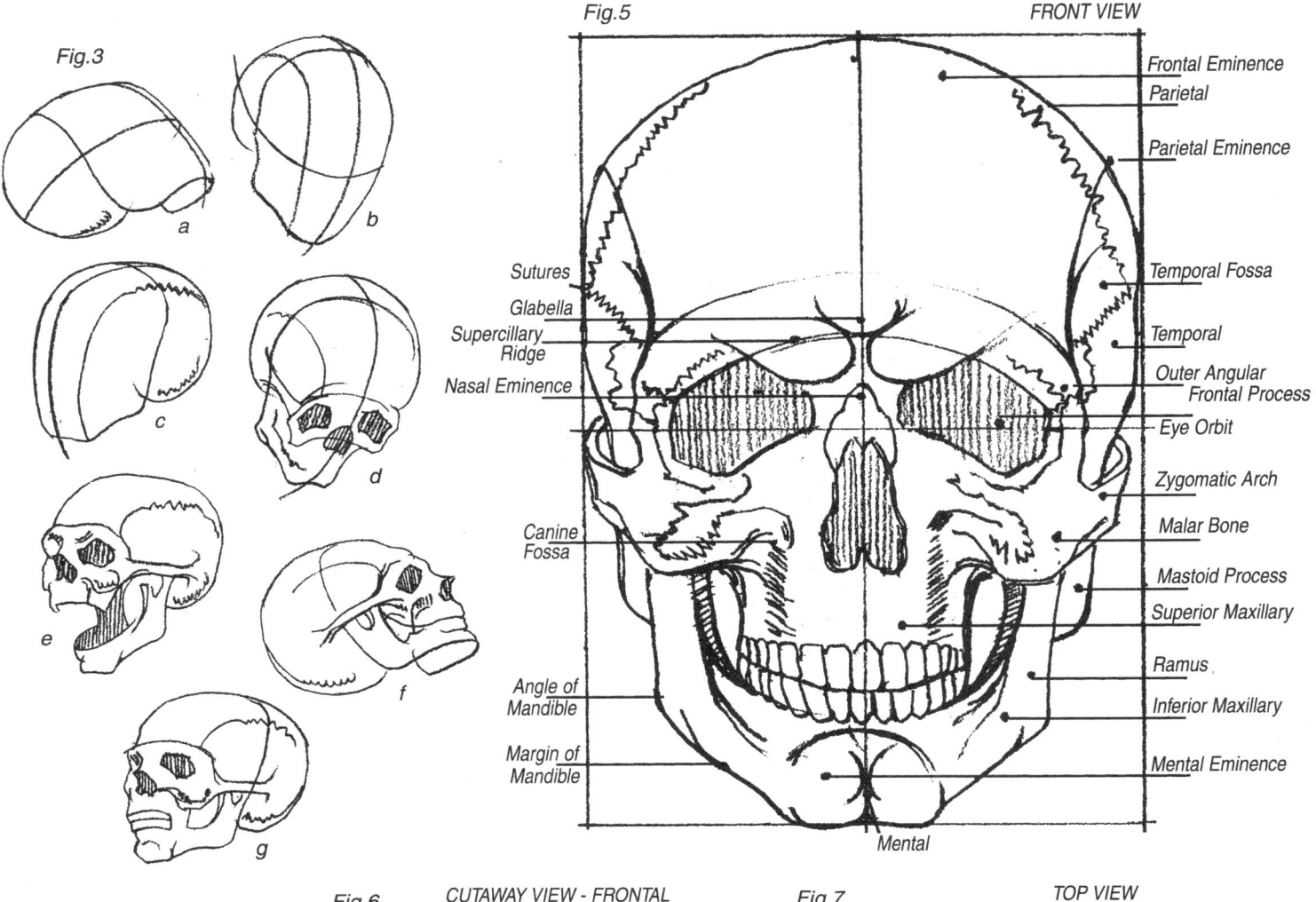

Fig.3

a   *b*

c   *d*

e   *f*

g

Fig.5   FRONT VIEW

Frontal Eminence
Parietal
Parietal Eminence

Temporal Fossa

Temporal

Outer Angular
Frontal Process
Eye Orbit
Zygomatic Arch
Malar Bone
Mastoid Process
Superior Maxillary
Ramus
Inferior Maxillary
Mental Eminence

Sutures
Glabella
Supercillary
Ridge
Nasal Eminence

Canine
Fossa

Angle of
Mandible

Margin of
Mandible

Mental

Fig.6   CUTAWAY VIEW - FRONTAL

Parietal
Sutures
Temporal
Ridge
Parietal
Eminence
Temporal
Occipital
Bone
Protuberance
Nuchal line
Mastoid
Procces
Ramus
Jaw Angle

Fig. 7   TOP VIEW

Frontal Eminence
Frontal

Zygomatic Arch
Temporal Ridge
Parietal Eminence
Parietal
Sutures

Occipital

Figs.3a.b.c.d.e.f.g.
Combinations of the
previous front and
side views of skull
are shown in differ-
ent positions. One
can easily start one's
drawing with the
shapes shown in
Figs. 3a.b. and c.

    Fig. 4. Side
view of the skull
showing the major
bones and their
names. The slanted
line running
through the whole
skull is called the skull line, it is the area of the brain
case.

    Fig. 5. Front view of the skull showing
major bones and their names.

    Fig. 6. A partially cut away frontal view of

the skull. In this drawing you are looking through
the upper half of the skull into its rear and sides.
The bottom part is the outside frontal view.

    Fig. 7. Top view of the skull showing the
position of the sutures and temporal ridges.

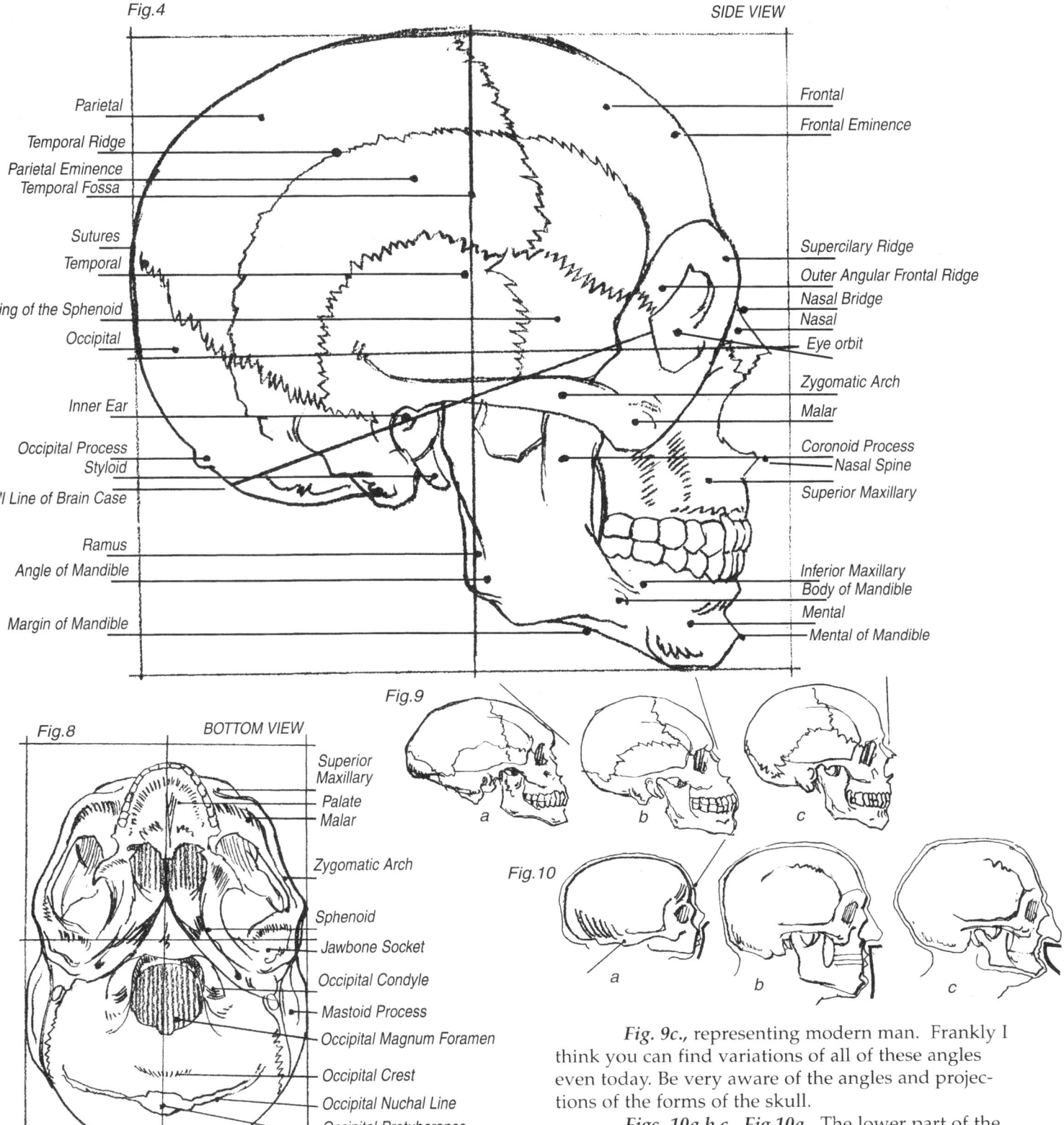

Fig.4 — SIDE VIEW

Parietal
Temporal Ridge
Parietal Eminence
Temporal Fossa
Sutures
Temporal
ing of the Sphenoid
Occipital
Inner Ear
Occipital Process
Styloid
l Line of Brain Case
Ramus
Angle of Mandible
Margin of Mandible

Frontal
Frontal Eminence
Supercilary Ridge
Outer Angular Frontal Ridge
Nasal Bridge
Nasal
Eye orbit
Zygomatic Arch
Malar
Coronoid Process
Nasal Spine
Superior Maxillary
Inferior Maxillary
Body of Mandible
Mental
Mental of Mandible

Fig.8 — BOTTOM VIEW

Superior Maxillary
Palate
Malar
Zygomatic Arch
Sphenoid
Jawbone Socket
Occipital Condyle
Mastoid Process
Occipital Magnum Foramen
Occipital Crest
Occipital Nuchal Line
Occipital Protuberance

Fig.9

a   b   c

Fig.10

a   b   c

Fig. 8. Bottom view of the skull with the lower jaw removed.

Figs. 9a.b.c. Three drawings showing the "progressive" development of the skull according to evolutionary theory. Notice how the line of the angle of the forehead shown in **Fig. 9a.** changes from very slanted towards a more upright angle as shown in **Fig. 9c.**, representing modern man. Frankly I think you can find variations of all of these angles even today. Be very aware of the angles and projections of the forms of the skull.

Figs. 10a.b.c. Fig.10a. The lower part of the child's skull is slightly convex. There is no brow ridge or mastoid bone at this age.

Fig. 10b. shows the fully developed adult. Notice the angle of the lower part of the skull below the nose. As the person ages this bottom part shrinks and becomes concave. Gravity keeps asserting itself causing the nose as well as the flesh below the chin to droop downwards.

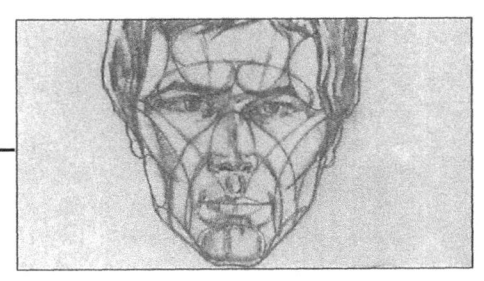

CHAPTER SEVENTEEN

THE PLANES AND FORMS OF THE HEAD

A prerequisite to the proper rendering of forms and planes is first that one must be able to perceive values, (degrees of light and dark), and secondly to know where the forms and planes are. A third thing to consider is that the smaller planes and forms have to be subordinated to the larger planes and forms.

The following series of drawings will explain what and where the planes and forms of the head are. I have spent considerable time trying over and over again how to best to present this seemingly complex subject in the simplest understandable manner.

The lines shown in the drawings either describe the shape of a form or the edge and shape of a plane. When the plane changes the value changes, sometimes to a great degree sometimes to an infinitesimal degree depending on the anatomical construction and the lighting.

At this point I would like to give a word of advice based on previous experience with some students. I do not approve of drawing the head by making it look like a roadmap and then filling it in with shading.

One should start with the large outside shape of the head first, generally some kind of oval shape, and alter it, mostly with straight lines, to obtain its character. Some examples of overall head shapes are shown in the section of sketchbook drawings. This shape should have a center line and be marked off for basic proportions. The most obvious divisions should be used such as from the forehead to the top of the eyebrows, from the top of the brows to the bottom of the nose and from the bottom of the nose to the bottom of the chin. Slight indications of eyes, nose and lips should be stated. If there is a large shadow shape it should be blocked in rapidly *using the following diagrams as a guide but conforming to the individual.* Continue the drawing by developing the features making good use of the planes which you will soon learn. Aim for accuracy and character.

It might be of help to you before you delve into this study to look at the series of photographs following this chapter. These are photographs I've taken of a cast made from the deceased professor of sculpture Don Miller. Professor Miller made the cast under Mr. Reilly's supervision when he was at his class at the Art Students League of New York. The cast is of a generic male head with as many forms and planes that could be represented on a solid form. By changing the position of a spot source of light by even the slightest degree one way or another different planes are revealed while others disappear into lights, halftones or shadows. You are bound to benefit from the study of this chapter if it only opens your eyes to things you never knew existed.

A small version of the final drawing of the planes of the head is placed at the bottom of the page so you understand where and to what the lines lead to. To the side of it is another small version of the particular stage shown with shading on the planes and forms discussed.

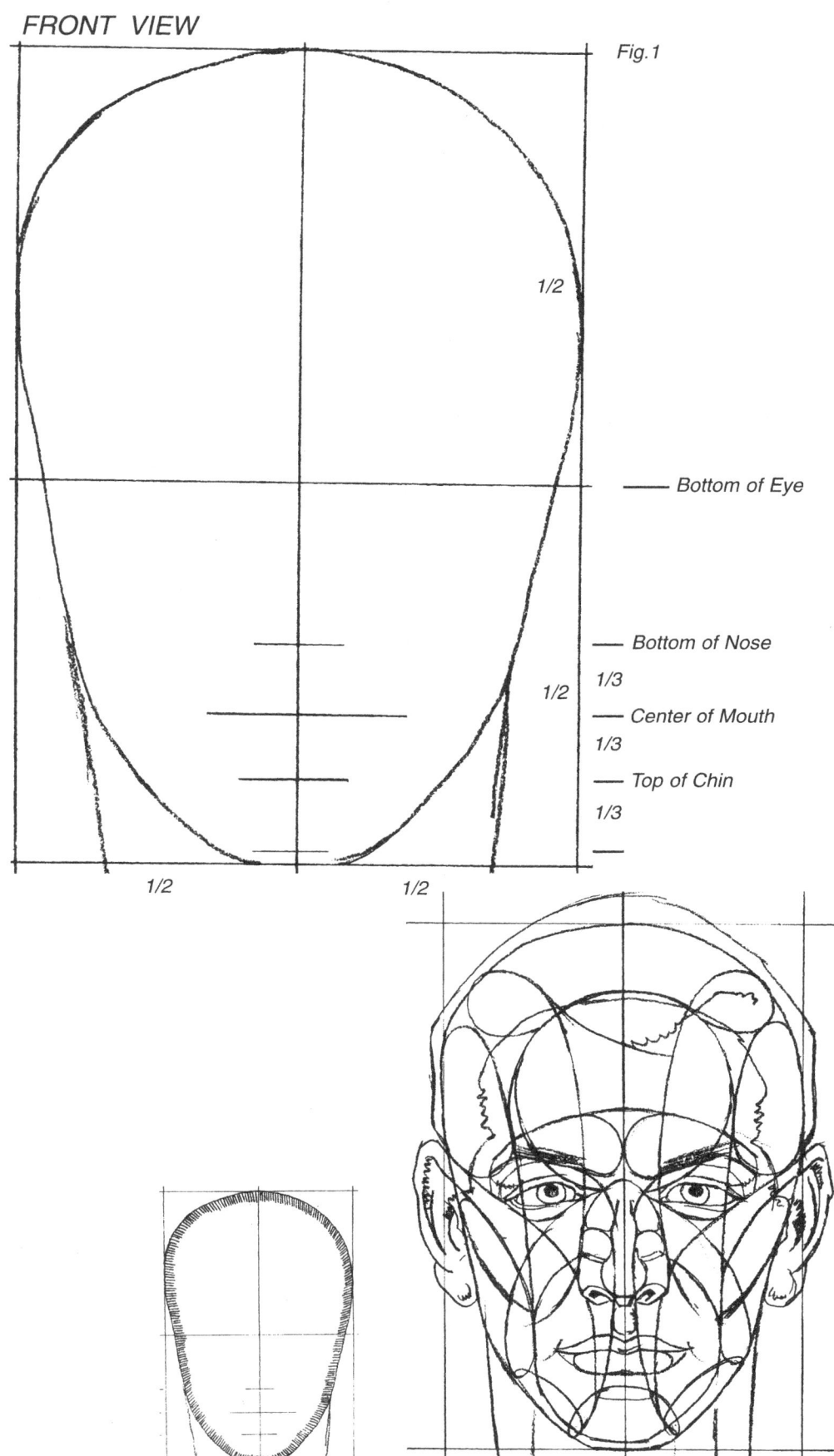

FRONT VIEW

Fig. 1

1/2

—— Bottom of Eye

Bottom of Nose
1/3

1/2

Center of Mouth
1/3

Top of Chin
1/3

1/2   1/2

Fig. 1. Front view of the first large form of the head. Notice the center line which divides the form in halves. The horizontal center line runs somewhere along the bottom of the eye. Ideally the head would be five eyes wide with a one eye distance between the two eyes. The space between the bottom of the nose and the bottom of the chin is divided roughly into thirds.
Fig. 1a. The shading shows the overall large shape of the head.

a

FINAL VERSION

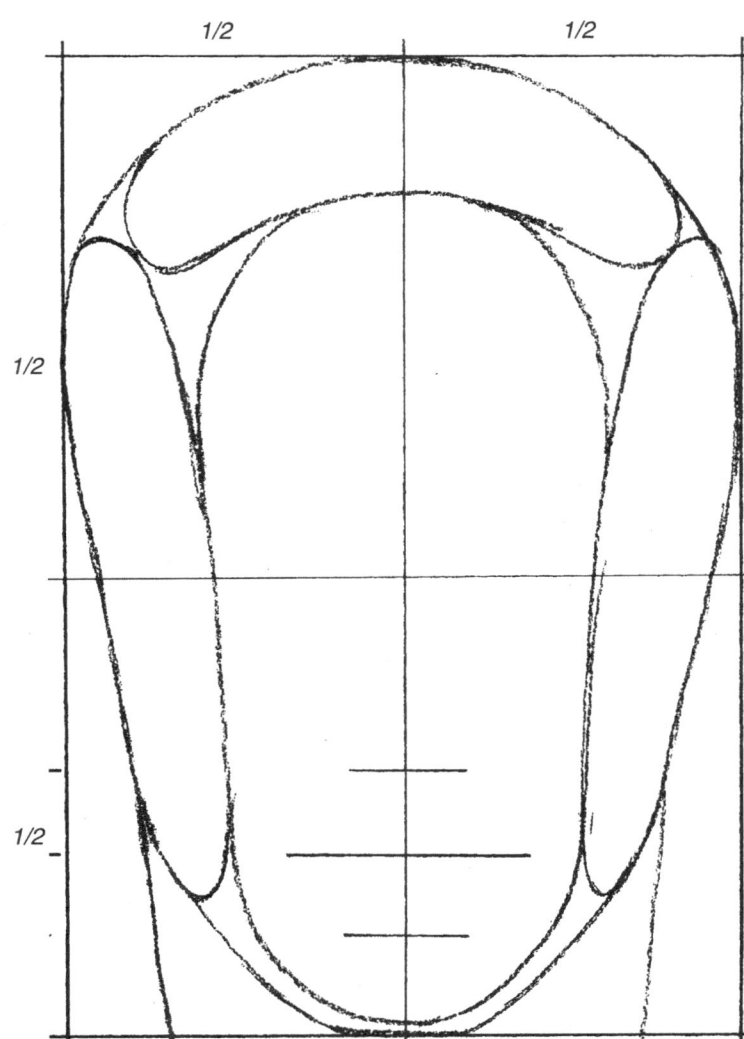

1/2 1/2

1/2

1/2

Fig.2. The first large planes of the form. Shown are the top, front and the first sideplanes which line up with the *outer edge* of the eyes.

Fig. 2a. Sideplanes. In all cases the planes discussed will be the shaded areas so I do not need to repeat this.

Fig. 2b. The top plane.

Fig. 2c. Top and side planes.

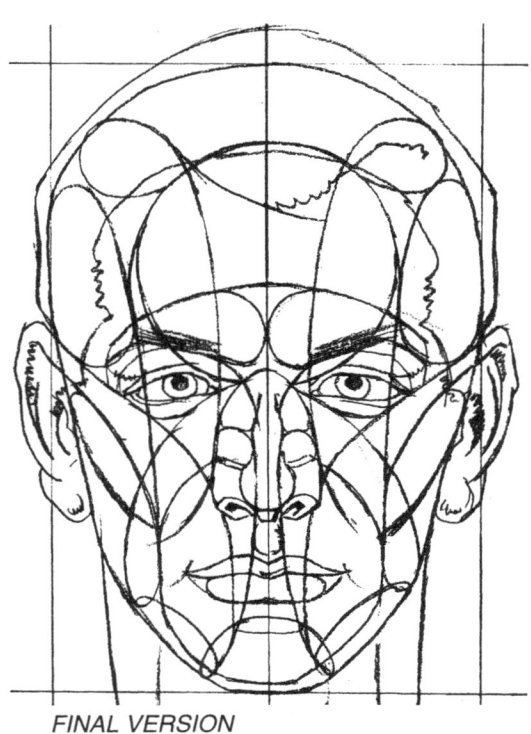

FINAL VERSION

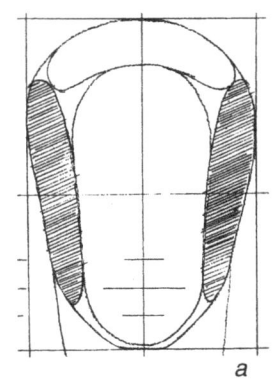

a

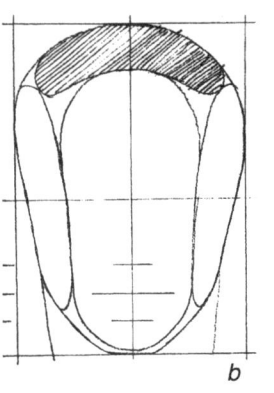

b

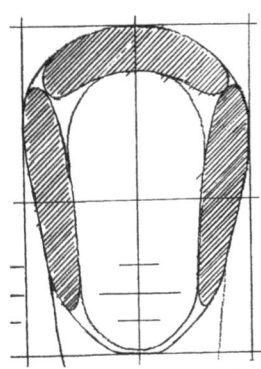

c

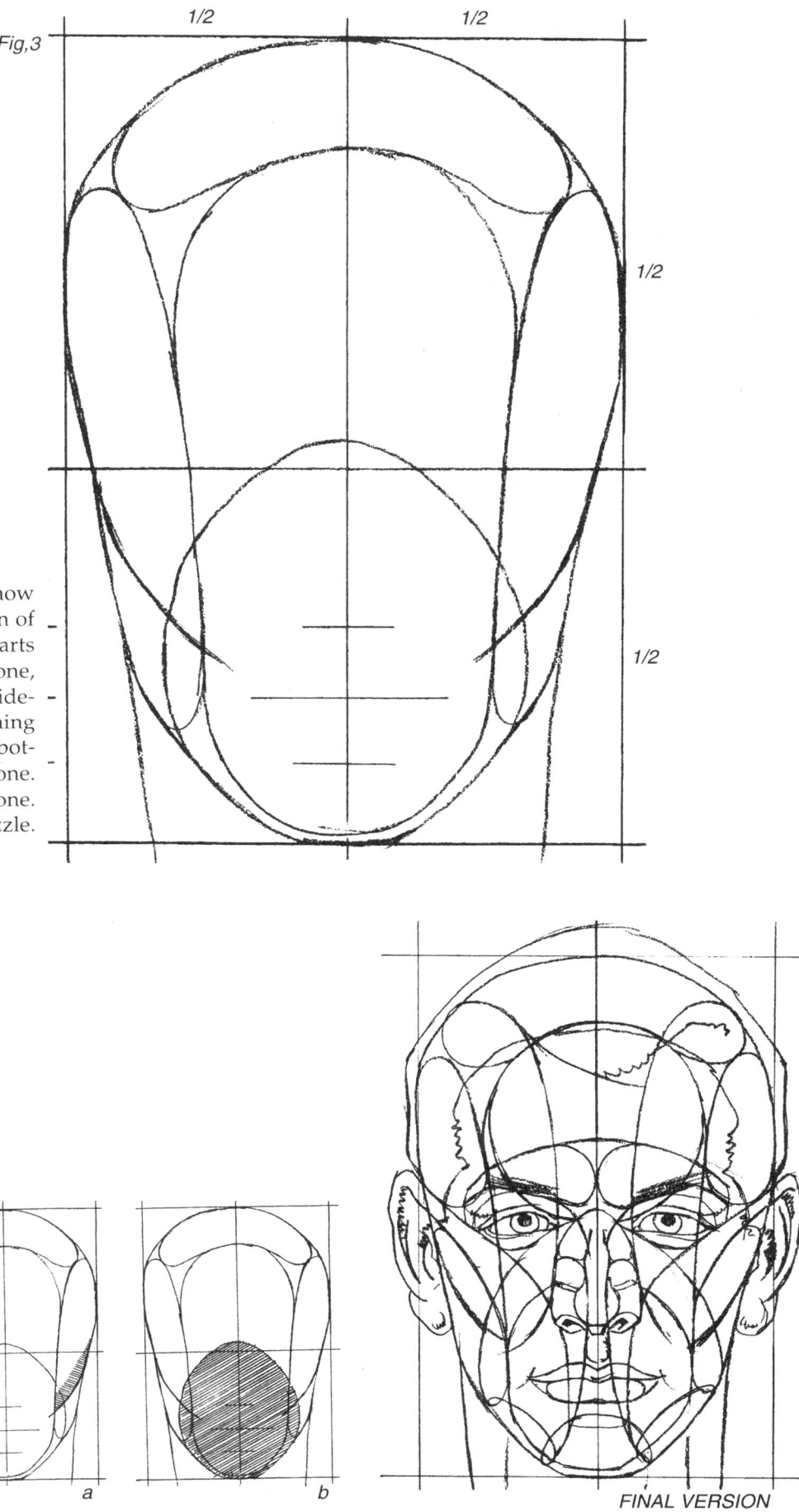

Fig. 3. Secondary forms are now added. Notice the position of the "muzzle" form which starts at the top of the nasal bone, overlaps and ties into the sideplane. The curved lines coming off the skull will become the bottom of the malar bone.
Fig. 3a. The malar bone.
Fig. 3b. The muzzle.

1/2   1/2

1/2

1/2

Fig,3

a   b

FINAL VERSION

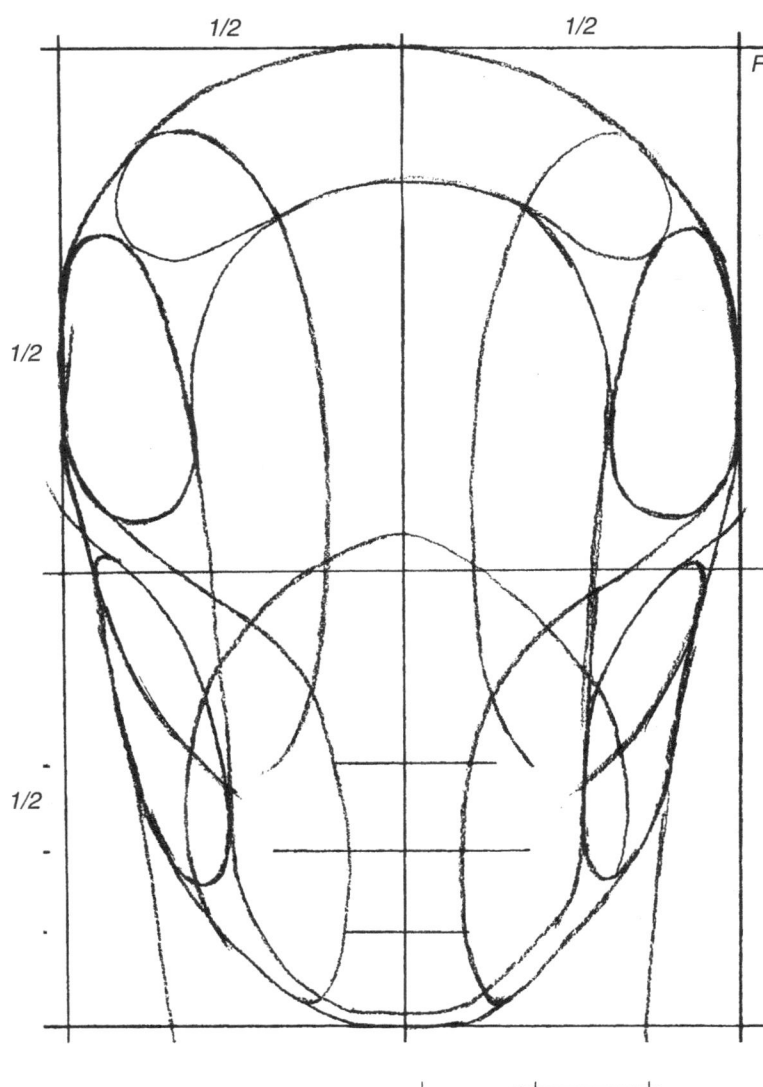

1/2 *1/2*

1/2

1/2

Fig.4

Fig. 4. The secondary planes. The secondary sideplane relates to and comes off the top plane. It makes tangent with the inner corner of the eye. The bottom of this line curves to form the bottom of the cheek and continues to relate to the bottom of the malar bone. The zygomatic arch is formed by these planes.

Fig. 4a. The secondary sideplanes.

Fig. 4b. Upper and lower divisions of the first sideplane.

Fig. 4c. The relationship between the lower part of the secondary sideplane to the zygomatic arch.

Fig. 4d. The malar bone, bottom of the zygomatic arch.

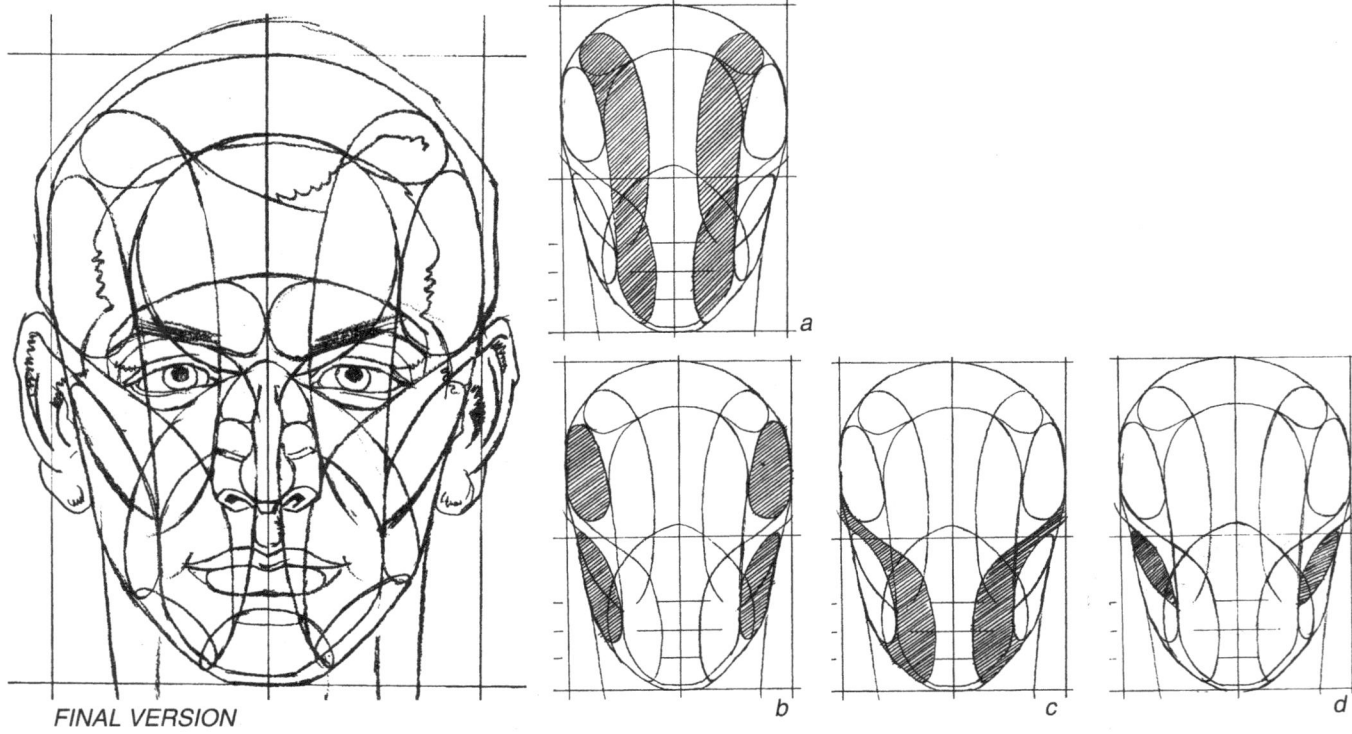

FINAL VERSION

a

b

c

d

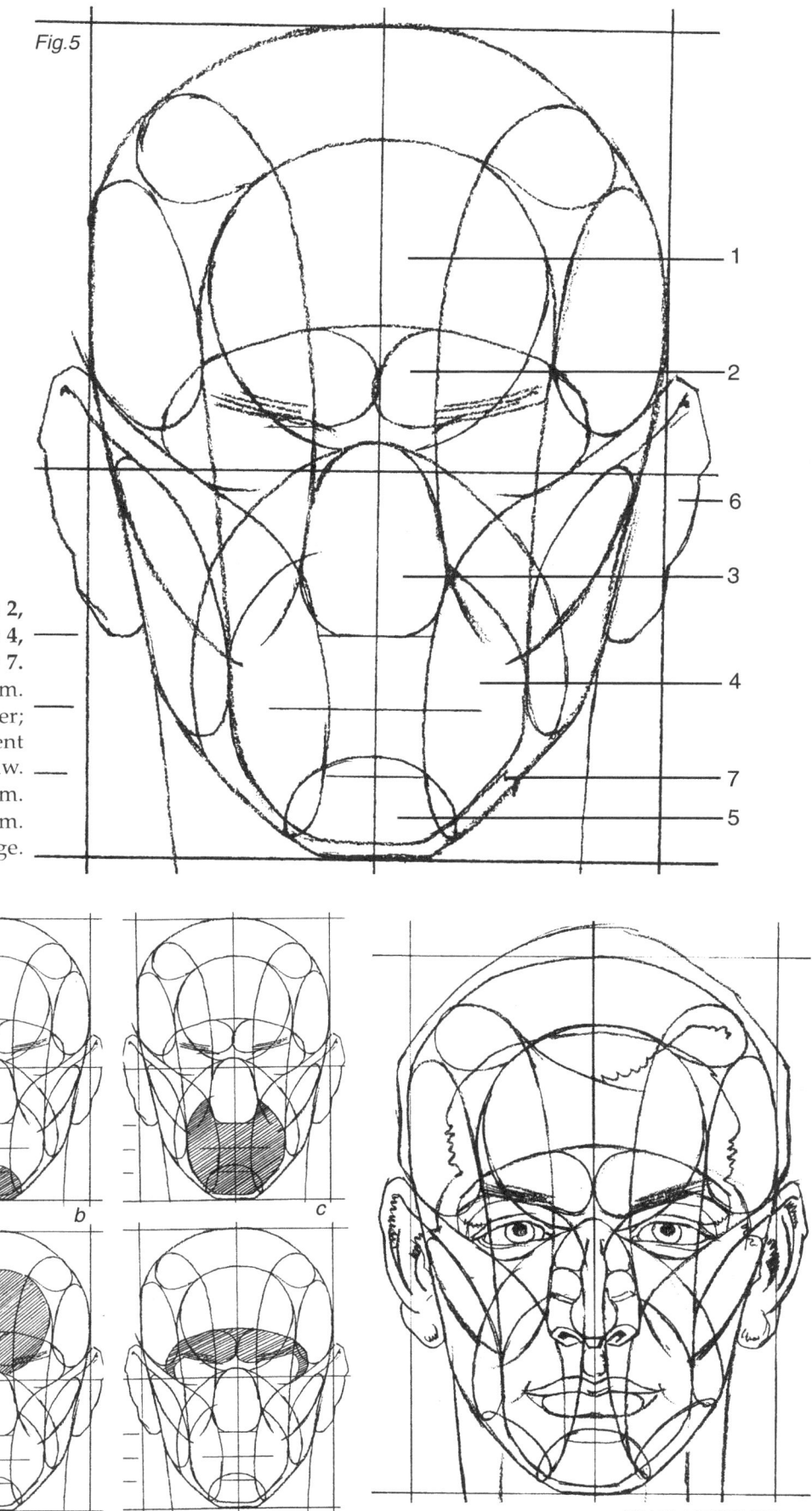

Figs. 5 and 5a. Shown are the forehead **1**, the brow ridge **2**, the nose form **3**, the teeth cylinder **4**, the chin **5**, the ears **6**, and the jaw **7**.
Fig. 5b. The chin form.
Fig. 5c. The teeth cylinder; note that it does not make tangent with the bottom of the jaw.
Fig. 5d. The nose form.
Fig. 5e. The forehead form.
Fig. 5f. The brow ridge.

FINAL VERSION

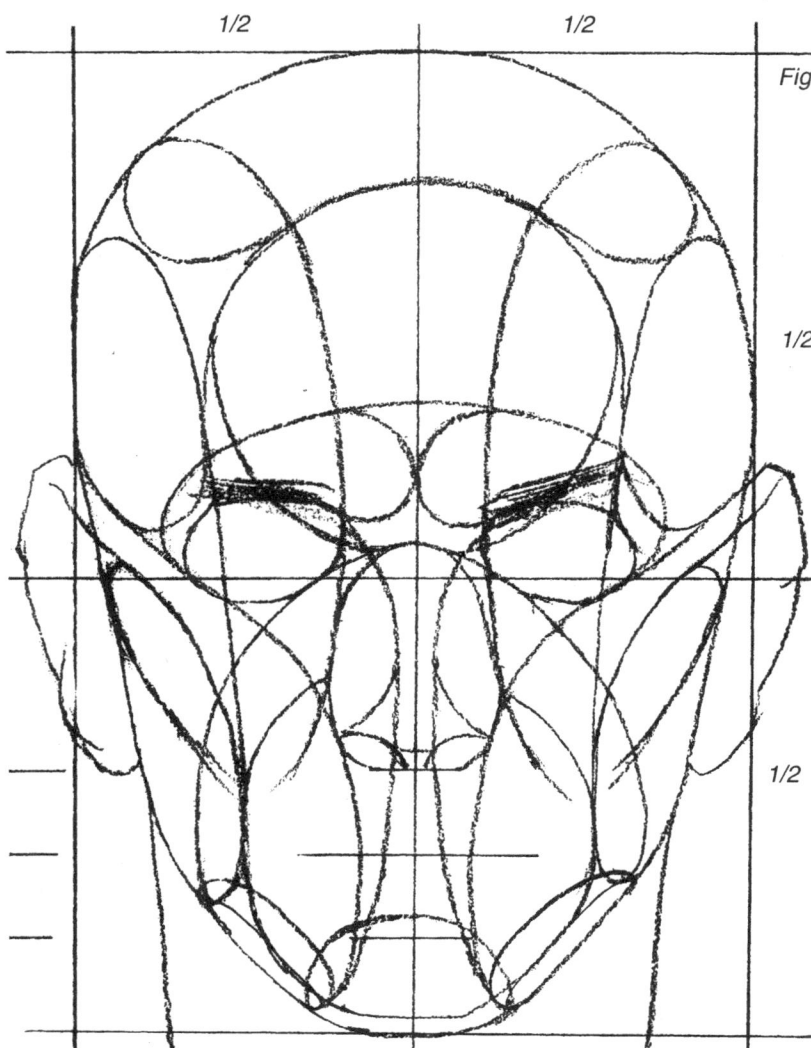

Fig. 6. The eye orbit and third planes. Draw in the eye orbit then take a line from the top of it down to the nasal bone to the bottom of the jaw. Here it will loop round the chin form making a sideplane of the chin. Add bottom planes to the nose and the jaw.

Fig. 6a. Sideplanes of the nose.

Fig. 6b. The eye orbit, bottom planes of the nose, chin and jaw.

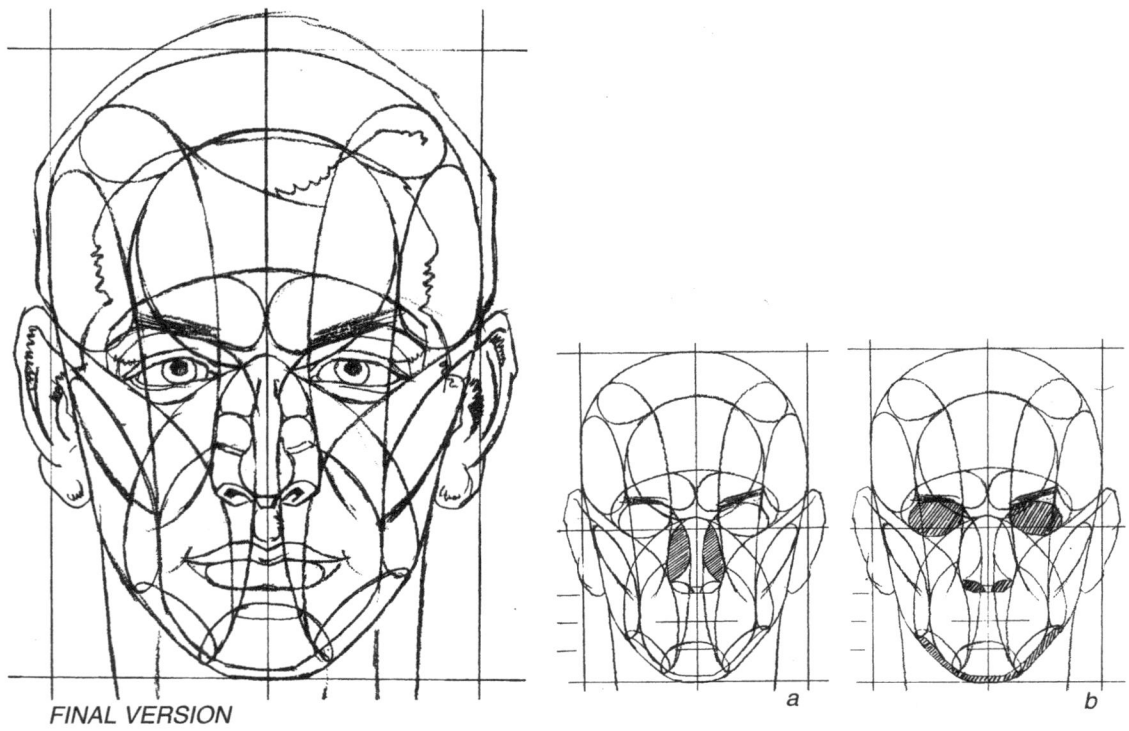

FINAL VERSION

Fig.7

Fig. 7. Finishing the basic forms and planes with the addition of features. Shown are, **1** the eyebrows, **2** the eyes and eyelids, **3** the ball of the nose and nostrils. Add also the top and bottom planes of the nostrils. The nose form is divided into an upper and lower form. Since the upper one usually catches the most light it is lighter in value than the lower part. **4** the mouth and lips, **5** the septum, **6** the detail of the ears, **7** the jaw, **8** the hairline.

8

1

2

6

3

5

4

7

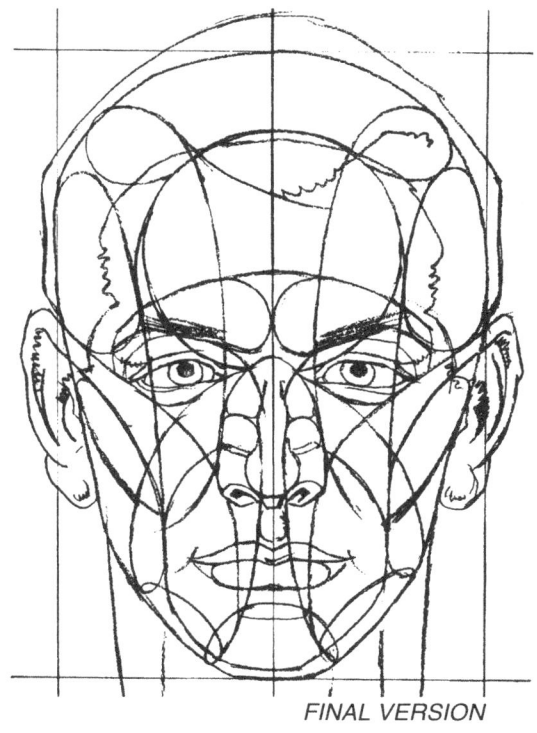

FINAL VERSION

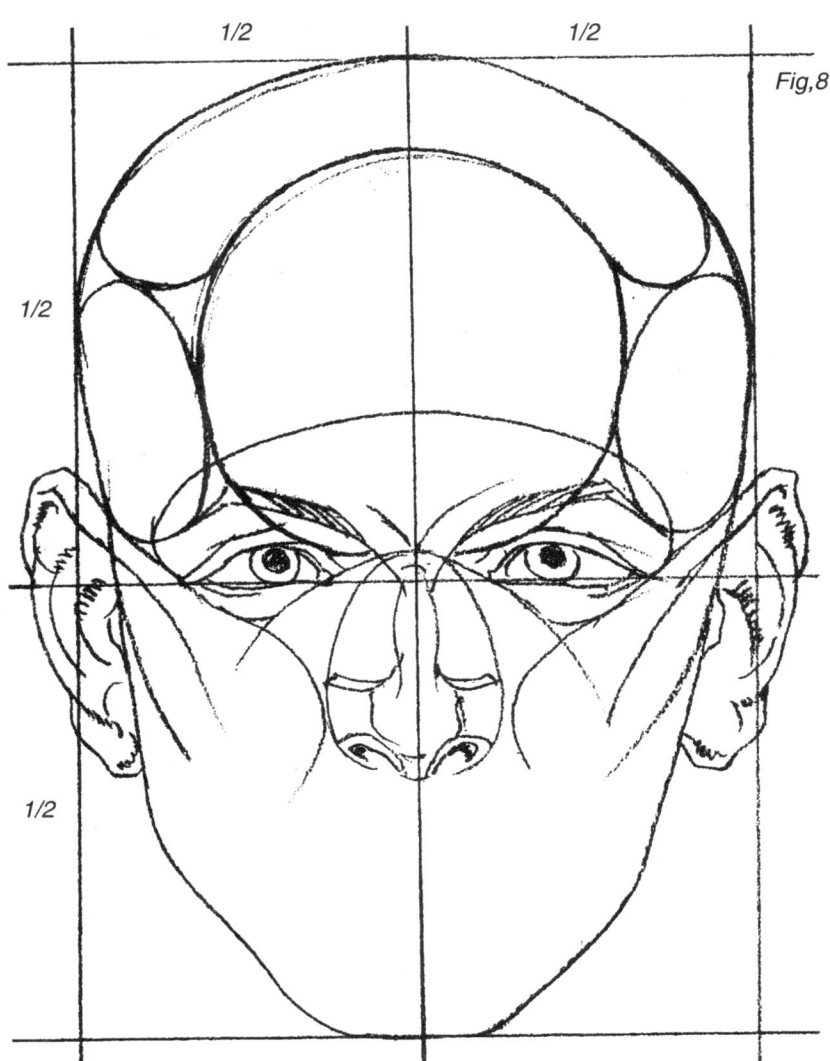

Fig. 8. This series will show the planes and forms on a forehead which has more prominently developed bones. It is a variation on the previous theme to make you conscious of the great differences there can be in skull structure. Since we are dealing only with the upper part of the skull it is unnecessary to show the lower half. In this *Fig. 8.* the forehead form is the same as the one shown in *Fig. 5.*

    Fig.8a. The forehead form.

    Fig. 8b The brow form.

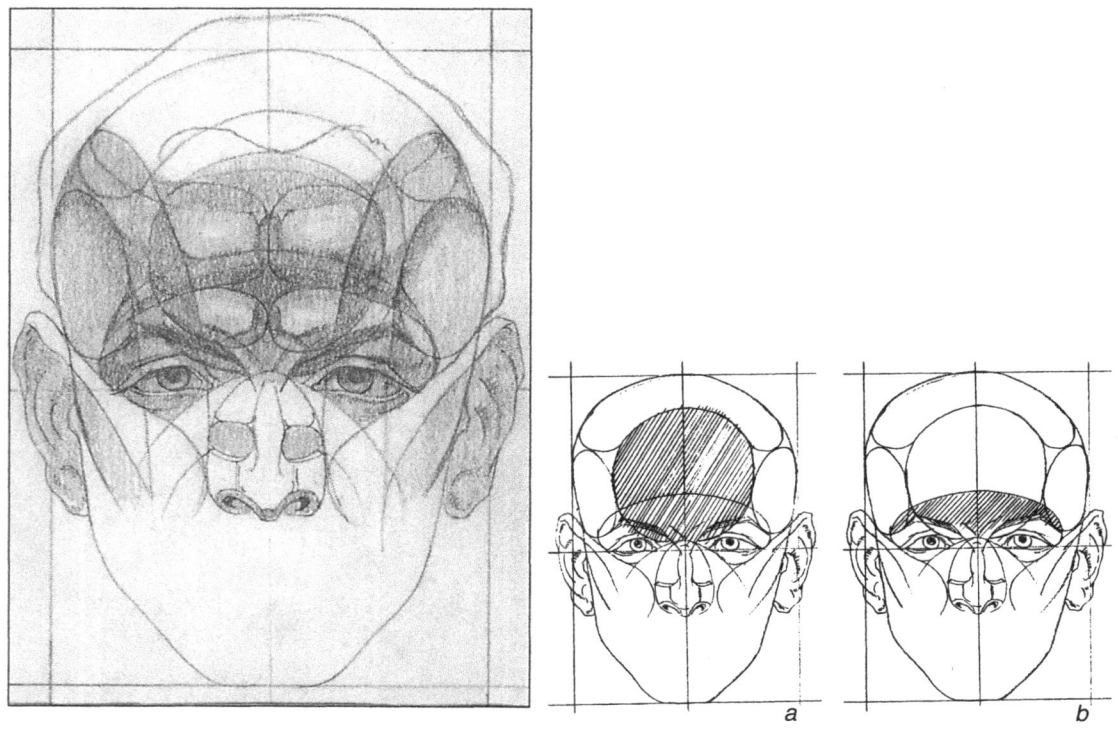

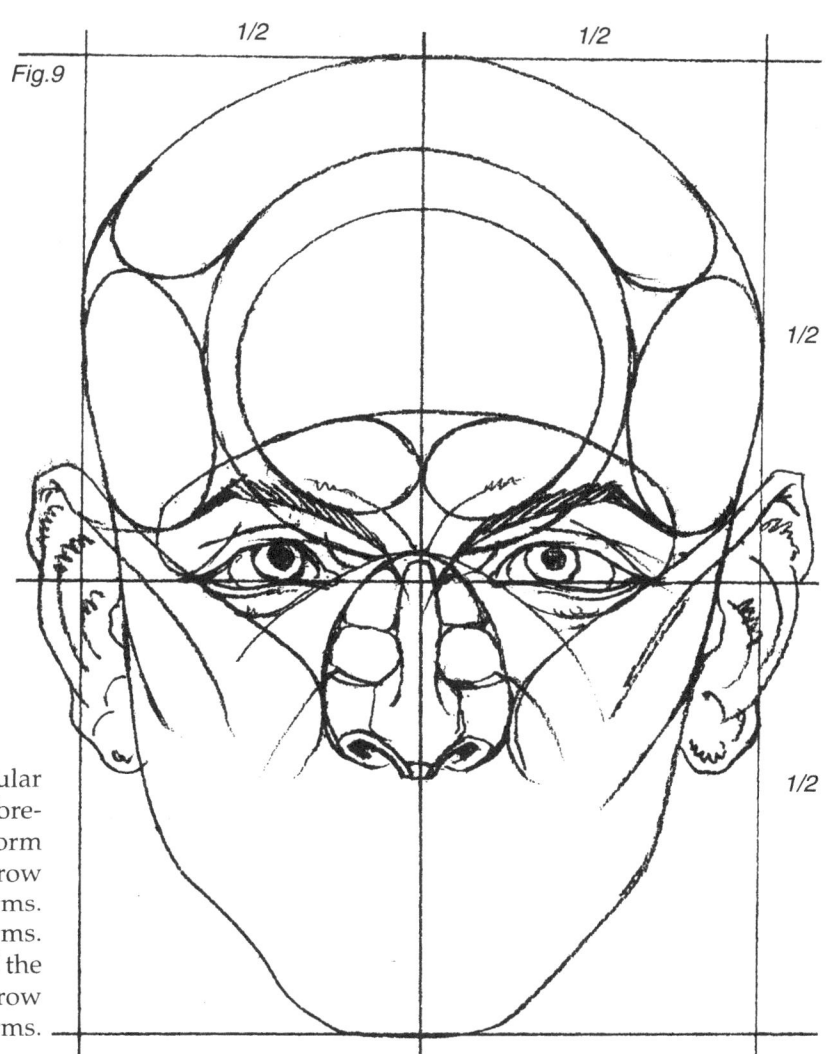

Fig. 9. A smaller circular form on top of the first large forehead form. The circle of this form relates directly to the two brow forms.
Fig. 9a. The brow forms.
Fig. 9b. The position of the secondary form relating to the brow and its forms.

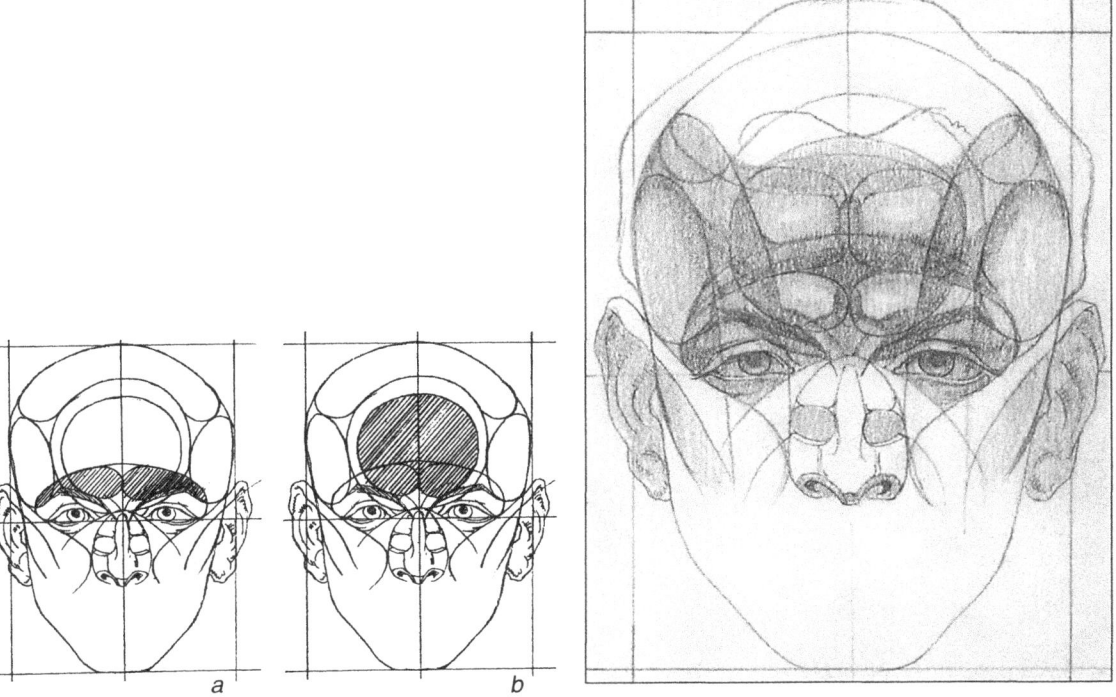

a

b

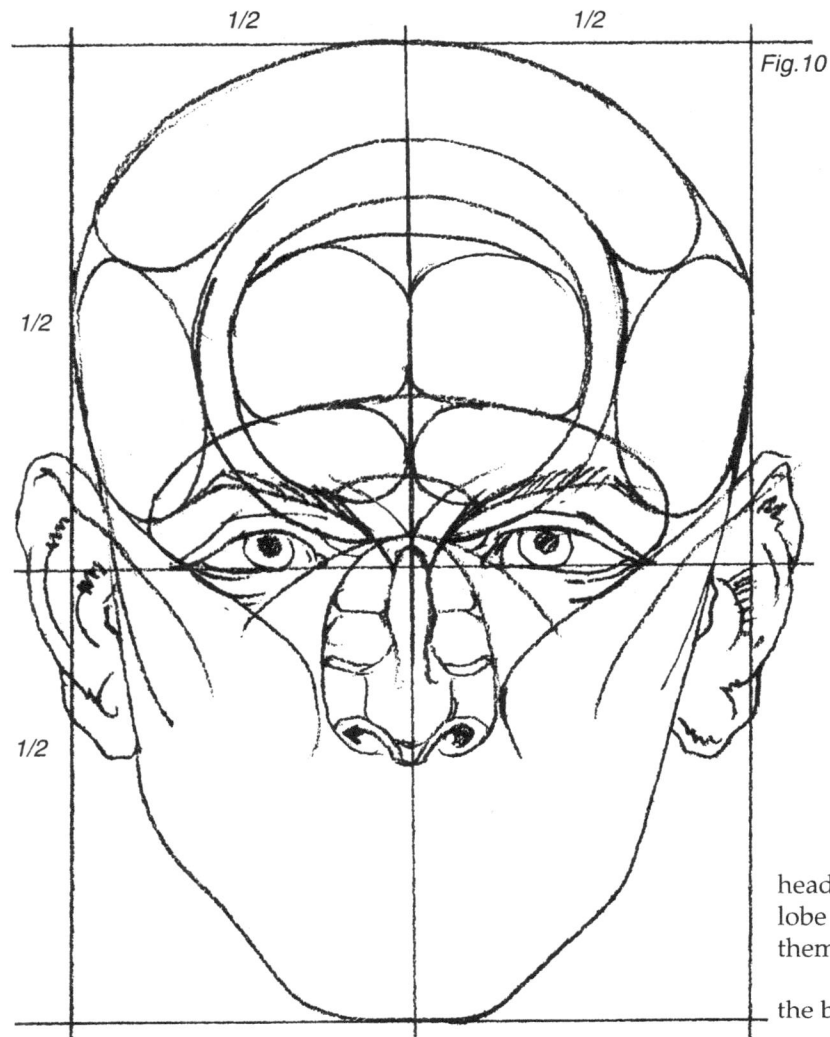

Fig. 10. The smaller forehead form divided into two frontal lobe forms. Immediately above them is a narrow, slant top plane.

Fig. 10a. Two new forms on the basic form.

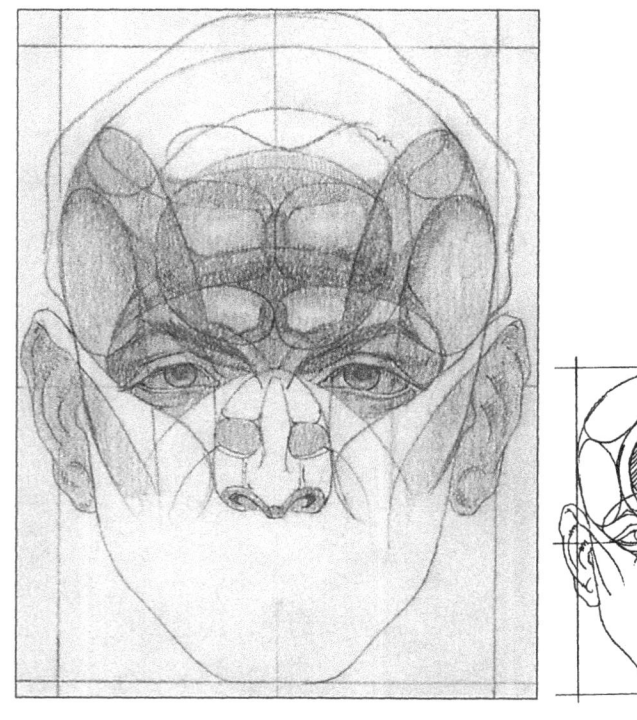

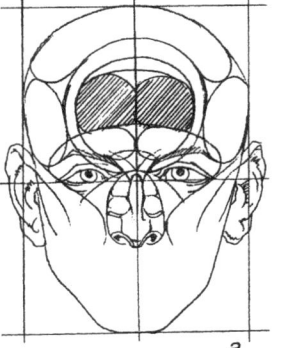

a

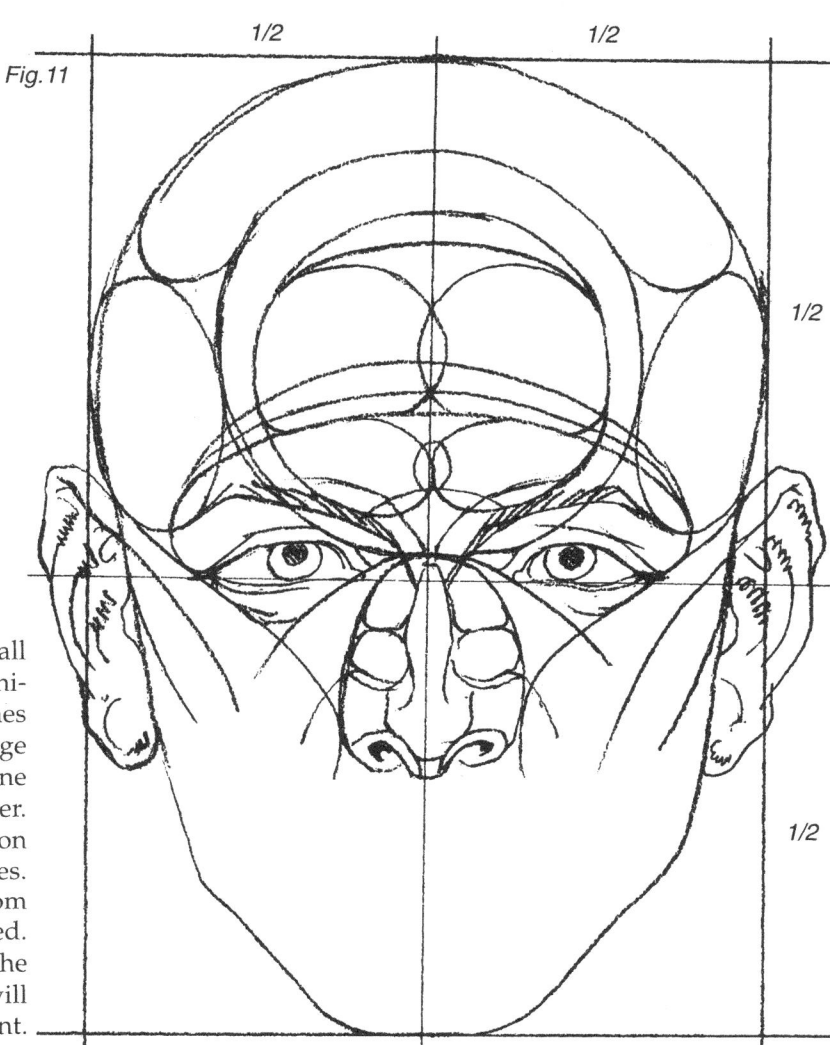

1/2 **1/2** **1/2** **1/2**

Fig. 11

Fig. 11. As stated before all planes can be subdivided ad-infinitum. In this drawing bottom planes immediately above the brow ridge are made by drawing arcs from one side of the brow to the other. Sideplanes are also added here on the brow forms and frontal lobes.
Fig. 11a. The first bottom and sideplanes are shown shaded.
Fig. 11b. Depending on the lighting position other planes will become apparent.

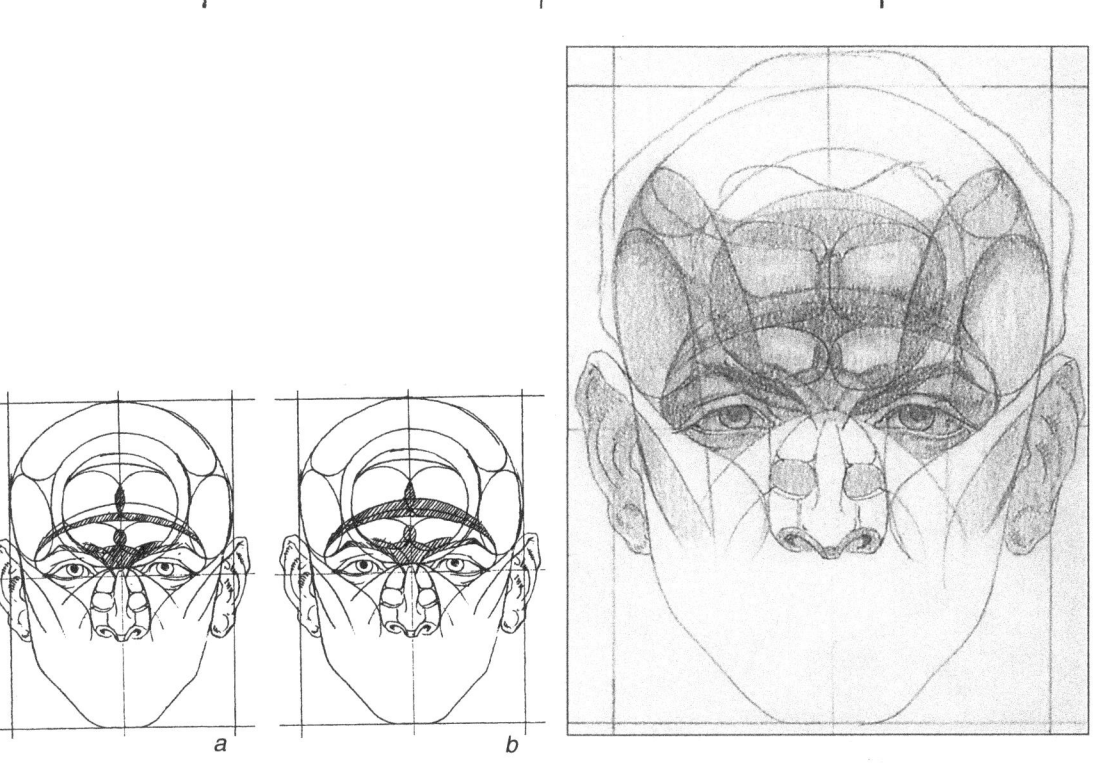

a   *b*

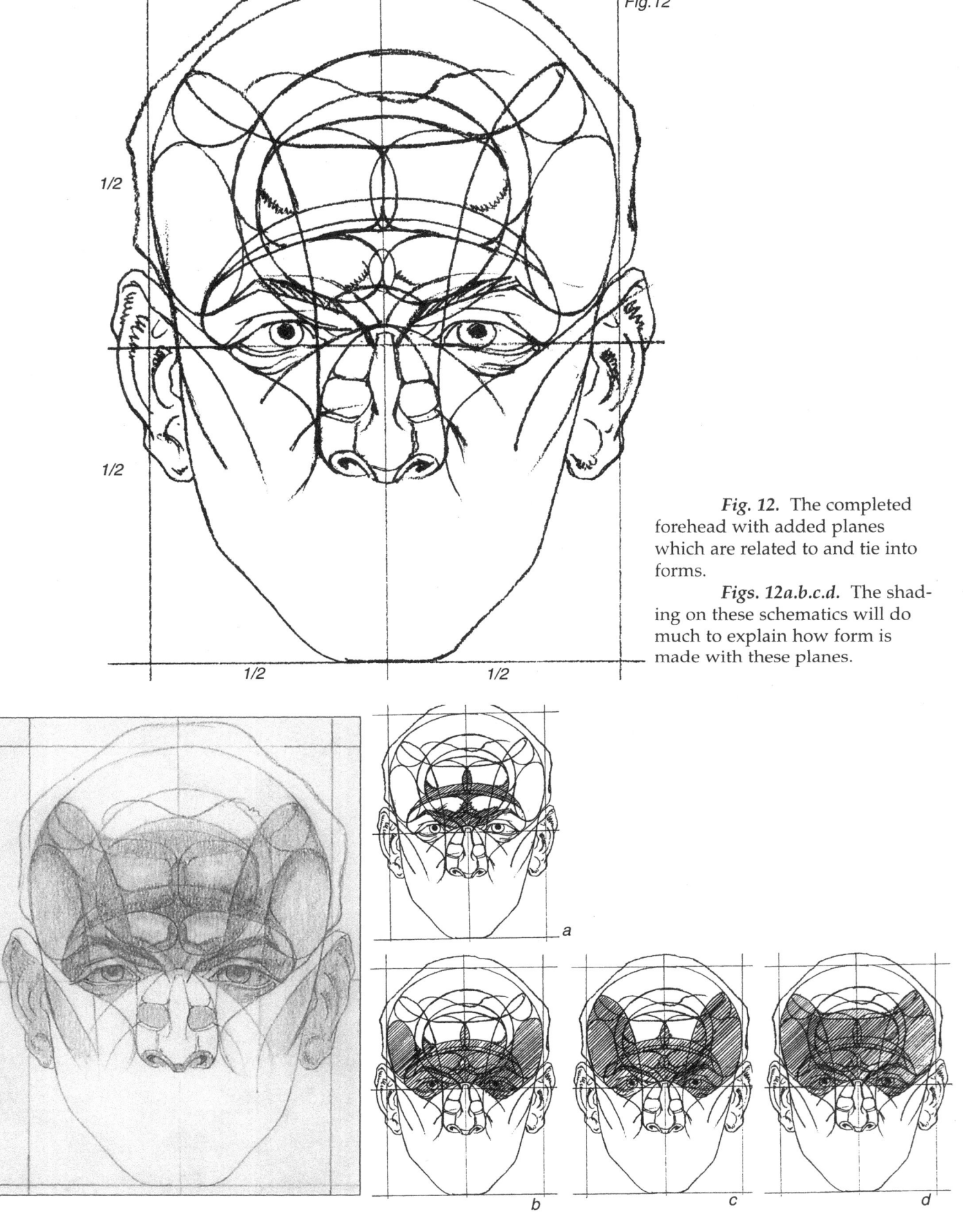

Fig. 12. The completed forehead with added planes which are related to and tie into forms.

Figs. 12a.b.c.d. The shading on these schematics will do much to explain how form is made with these planes.

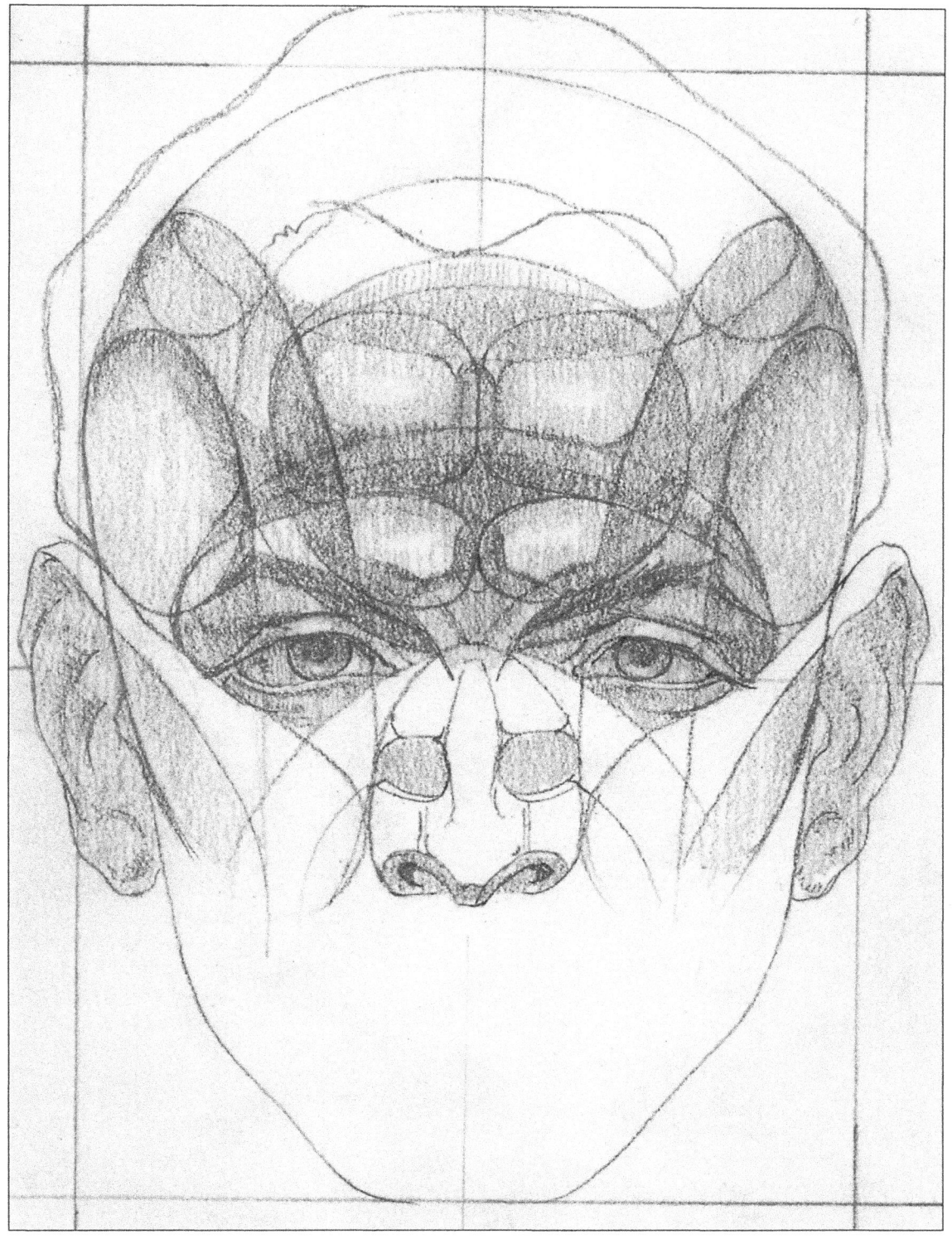

Fig. 13. A value drawing to help clarify and
explain the planes and forms of the upper skull.

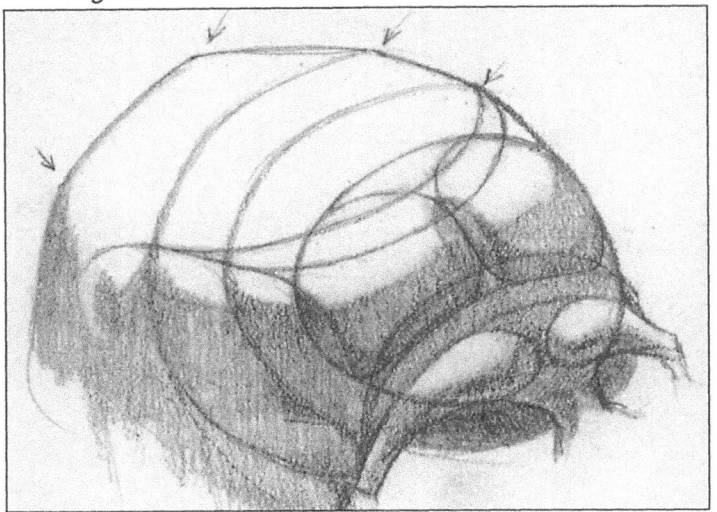

Fig.15

Fig. 15. An example of any upper half of a particular skull. The arrows point to corners where the planes break. The curvature is seemingly even and smooth but really isn't. *Shadows will always begin and end at the corners of the planes.*

Figs. 16a.b.c.d.e.f. The major forms of the front of the head presented in a simplified dimensional manner for greater understanding. **Fig. 16a.**, the muzzle. **Fig. 16b.**, the teeth cylinder. **Fig. 16c.**, the teeth cylinder on top of the muzzle. **Fig. 16d.**, the nose form. **Fig. 16e.**, the muzzle, the teeth cylinder and the nose form. **Fig. 16f.**, the muzzle, the teeth cylinder, nose form and chin form. These forms can individually or in combination protrude in various degrees from the basic skull shape, determining the character of the individual. Sometimes they are barely perceptible and other times they can be very apparent. The forms which usually protrude the most are the nose form, the teeth cylinder and the chin form. We tend to form an unconscious opinion of a person by the shape and size of these forms even without taking the features into consideration.

Fig. 17. This drawing represents my conception of a "life force" pushing from the inside to the outside creating definite forms and planes out of an indefinite amorphous mass. The tendency of nature seems to be towards evolving finer and finer planes.

Fig. 18a. The forms of the chin, teeth cylinder, nose and muzzle shown in an exploded view to further explain their relationship to each other.

Fig. 18b. Another way of showing the basic forms, this time fitted together in a three quarter view. Depending on the individual certain forms may be more dominant than others. For instance one may have a highly developed muzzle form and weak teeth cylinder form. Another might have a very prominent teeth cylinder form and a weak muzzle and chin form. The combinations, of course, are endless – you must seek these characteristics out and emphasize or de-emphasize them as the case may be.

Fig.16

a Muzzle	*b* Teeth Cylinder	*c* Teeth Cylinder on Top of Muzzle
d Nose Form	*e* Nose Form on Top of Teeth Cylinder & Muzzle	*f* and Chin Form

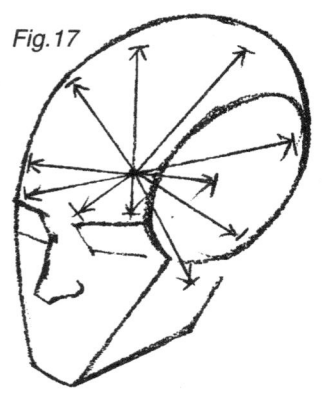

Fig.17

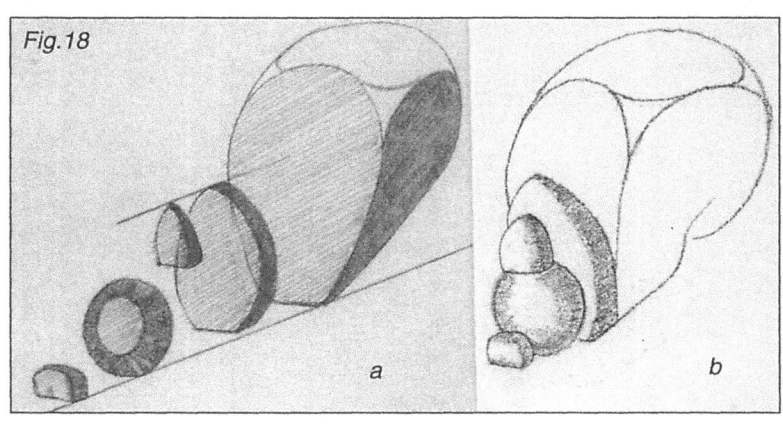

Fig.18

a   *b*

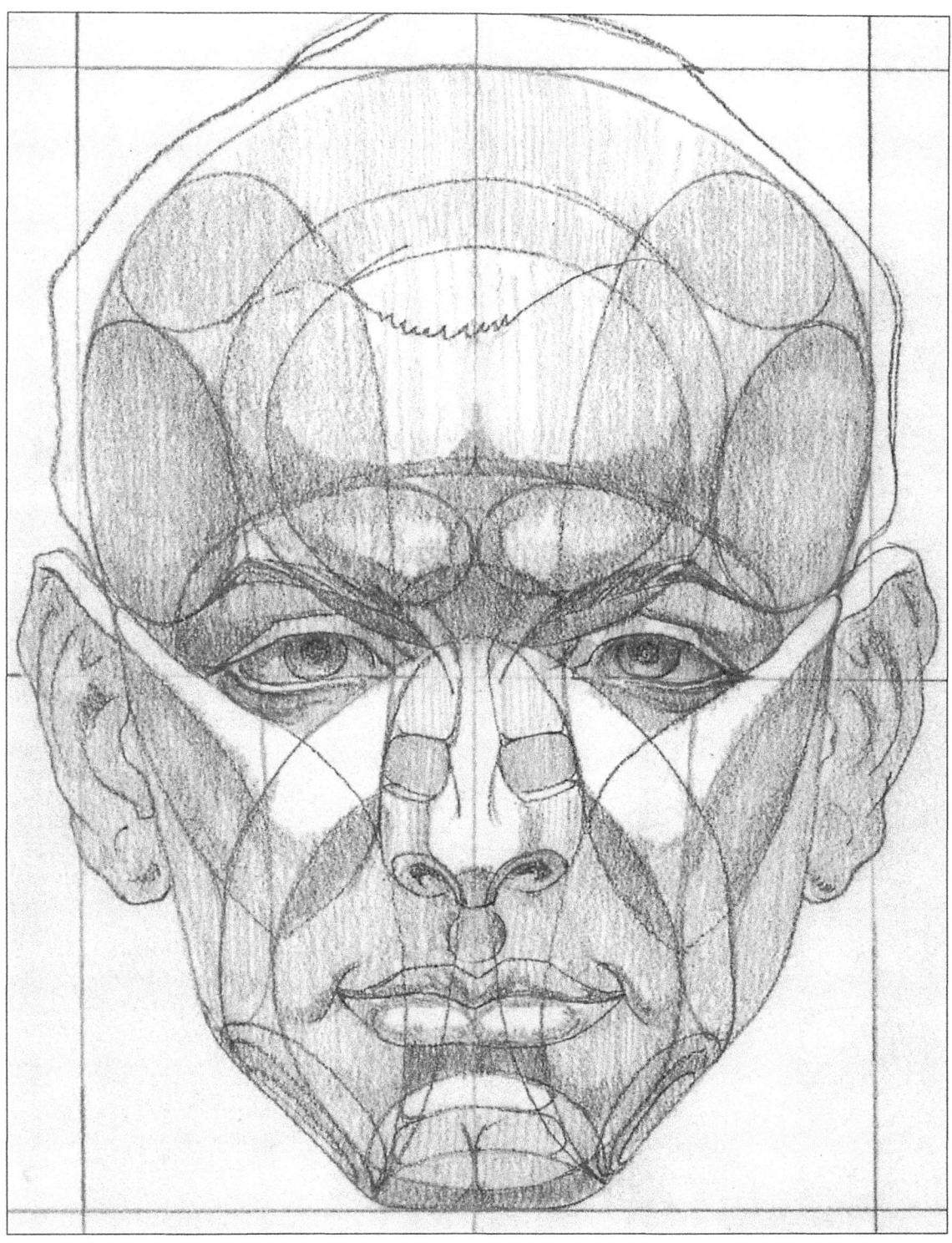

Fig. 14. Values as well as lines are used here to show how planes do produce a strong impression or illusion of solid form.

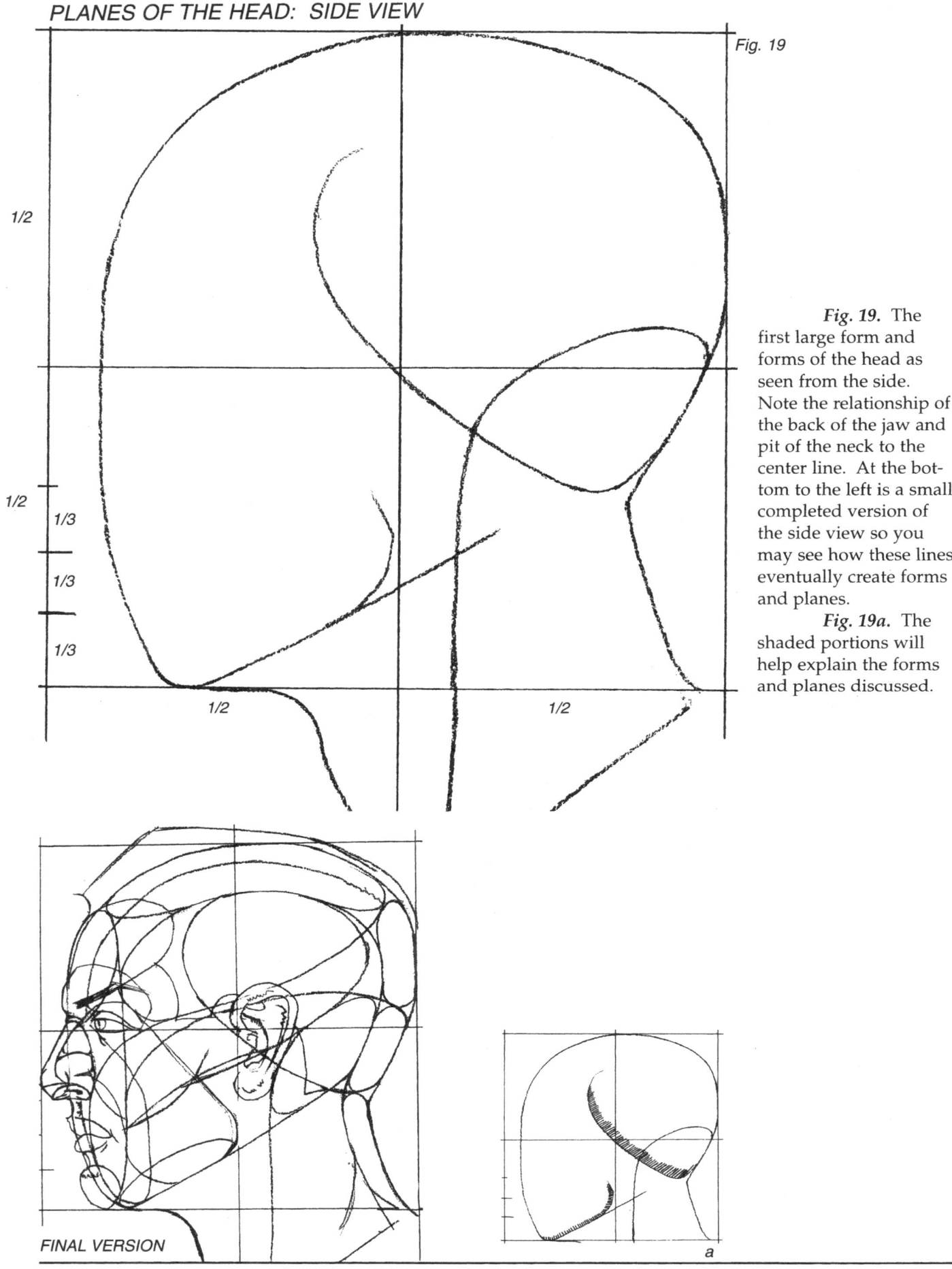

Fig. 19

1/2

1/2

1/3

1/3

1/3

1/2

1/2

Fig. 19. The first large form and forms of the head as seen from the side. Note the relationship of the back of the jaw and pit of the neck to the center line. At the bottom to the left is a small completed version of the side view so you may see how these lines eventually create forms and planes.

Fig. 19a. The shaded portions will help explain the forms and planes discussed.

FINAL VERSION

a

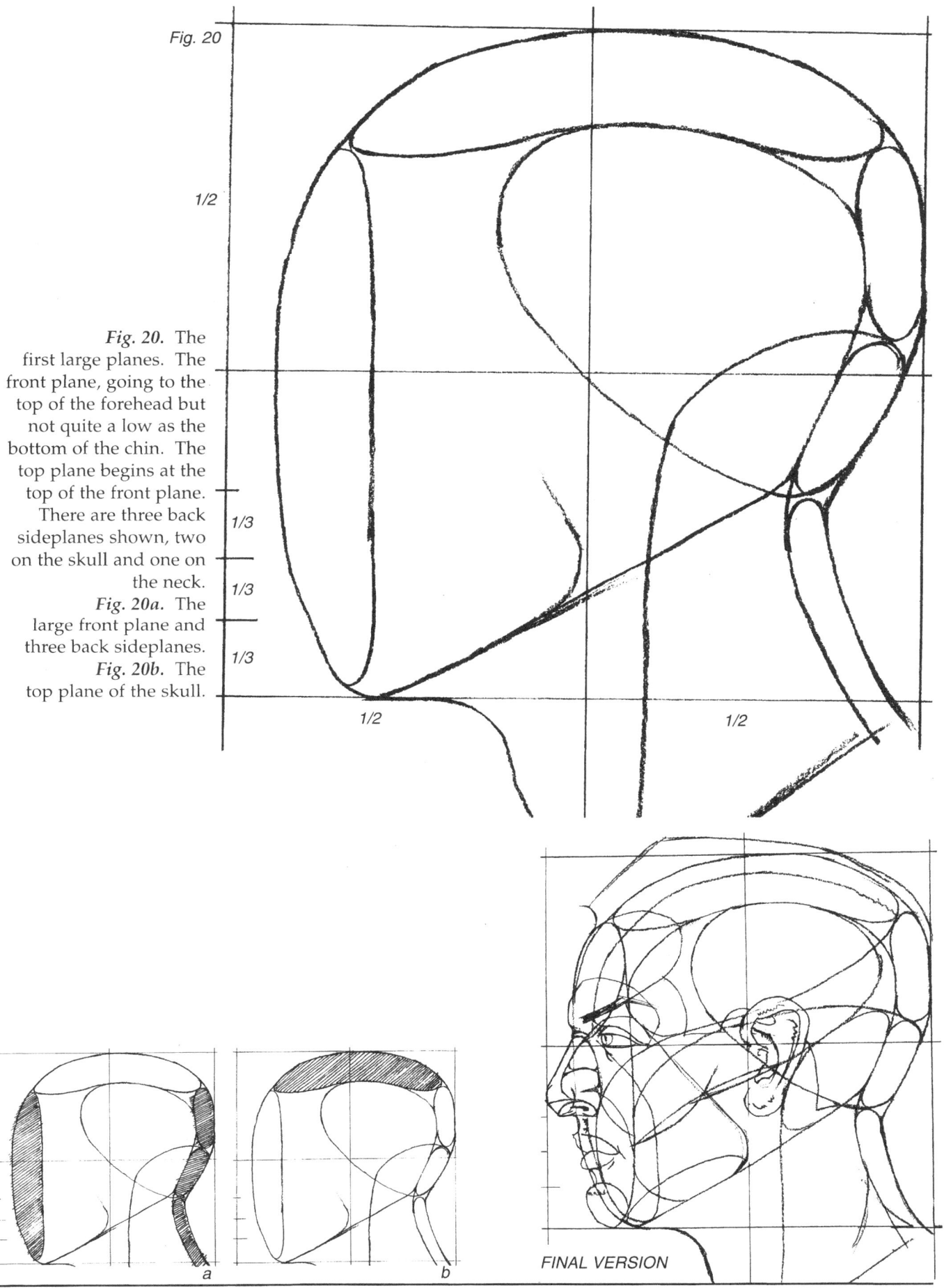

Fig. 20

1/2

Fig. 20. The first large planes. The front plane, going to the top of the forehead but not quite a low as the bottom of the chin. The top plane begins at the top of the front plane. There are three back sideplanes shown, two on the skull and one on the neck.
Fig. 20a. The large front plane and three back sideplanes.
Fig. 20b. The top plane of the skull.

1/3

1/3

1/3

1/2

1/2

a

b

FINAL VERSION

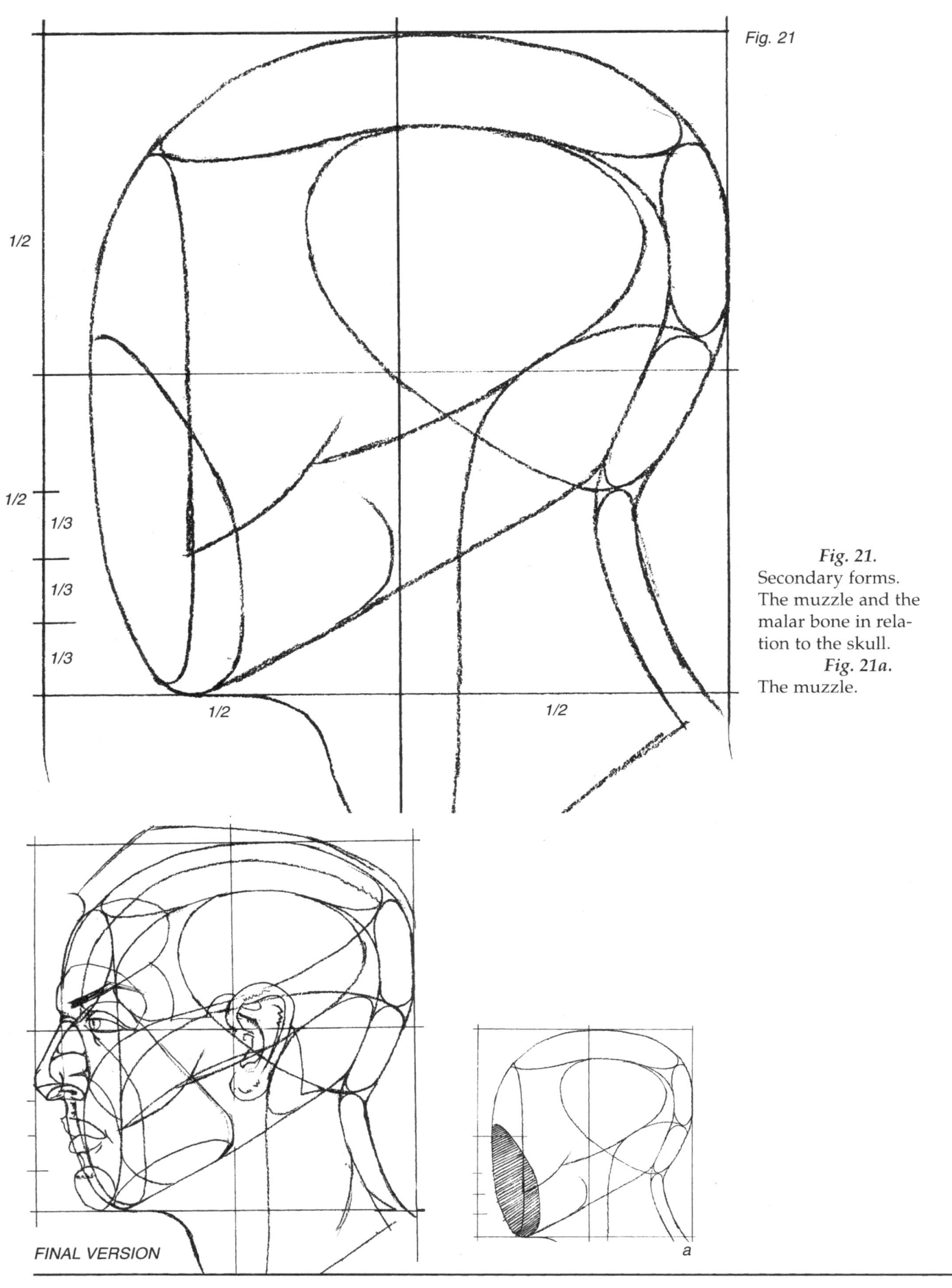

1/2

1/2
1/3
1/3
1/3

1/2   1/2

Fig. 21.
Secondary forms.
The muzzle and the
malar bone in rela-
tion to the skull.
Fig. 21a.
The muzzle.

Fig. 21

FINAL VERSION

a

154

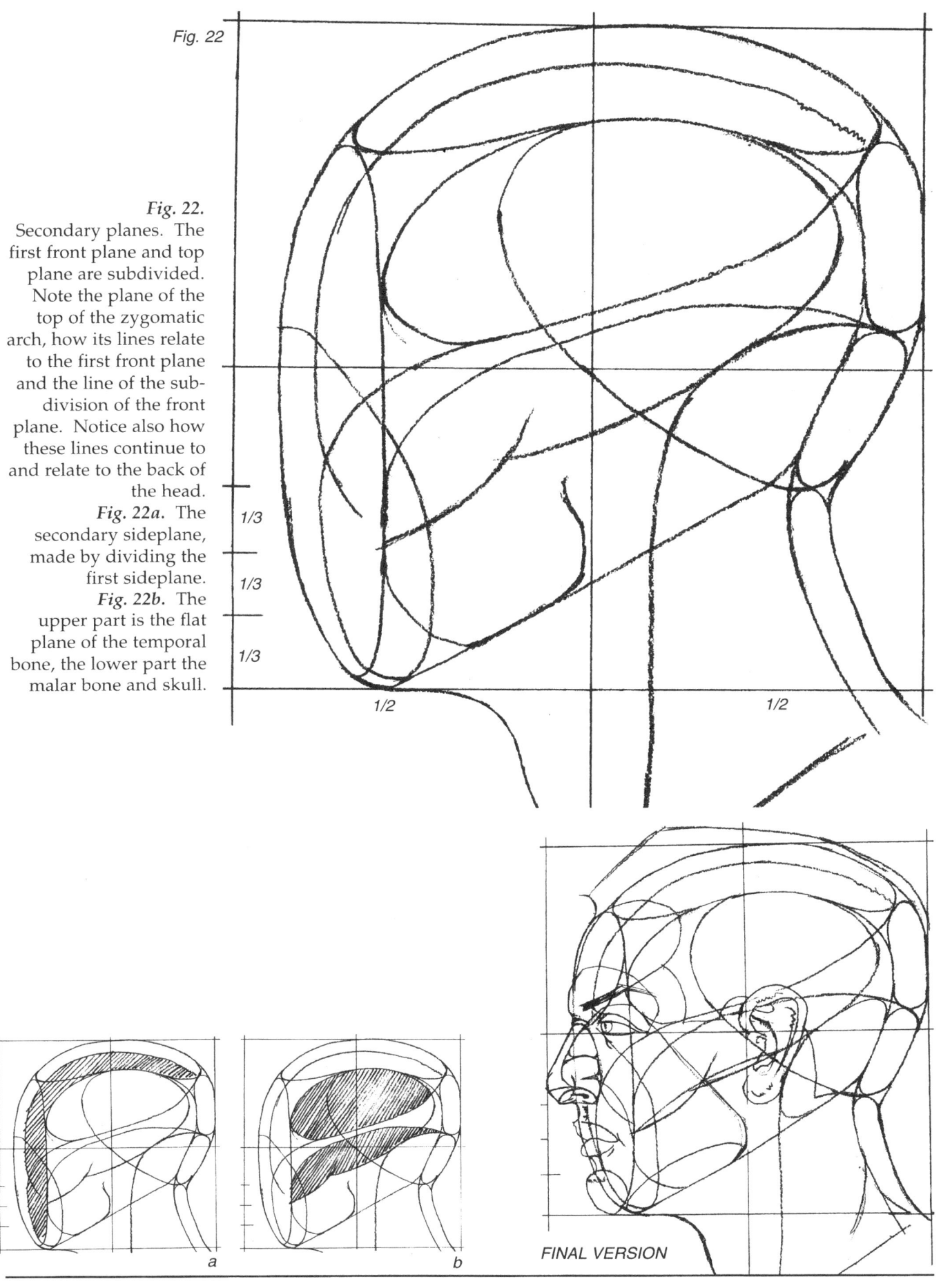

Fig. 22

Fig. 22. Secondary planes. The first front plane and top plane are subdivided. Note the plane of the top of the zygomatic arch, how its lines relate to the first front plane and the line of the subdivision of the front plane. Notice also how these lines continue to and relate to the back of the head.

Fig. 22a. The secondary sideplane, made by dividing the first sideplane.

Fig. 22b. The upper part is the flat plane of the temporal bone, the lower part the malar bone and skull.

1/3

1/3

1/3

1/2

1/2

a

b

FINAL VERSION

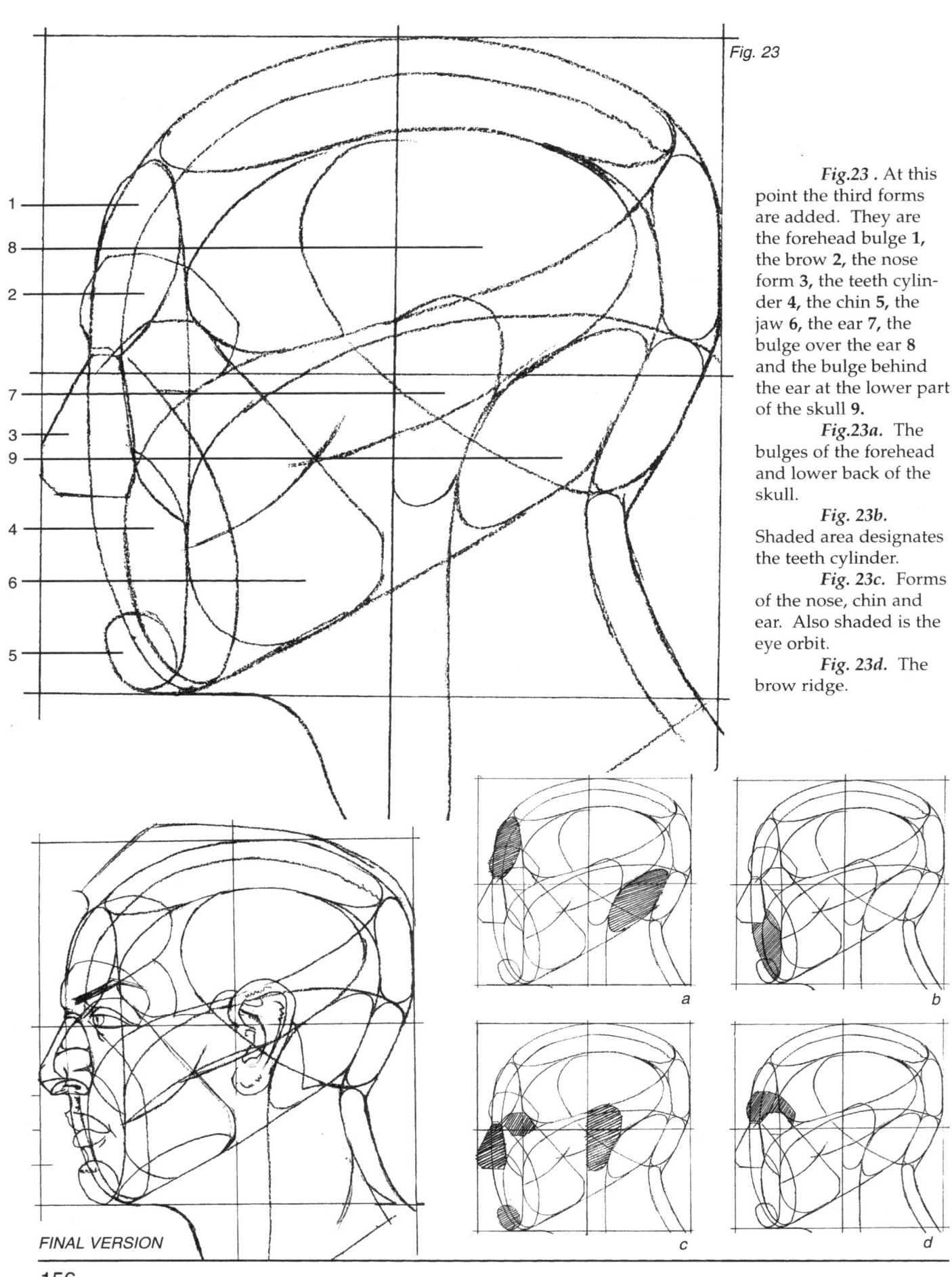

Fig. 23

1
8
2
7
3
9
4
6
5

Fig.23 . At this point the third forms are added. They are the forehead bulge **1**, the brow **2**, the nose form **3**, the teeth cylinder **4**, the chin **5**, the jaw **6**, the ear **7**, the bulge over the ear **8** and the bulge behind the ear at the lower part of the skull **9**.

Fig.23a. The bulges of the forehead and lower back of the skull.

Fig. 23b. Shaded area designates the teeth cylinder.

Fig. 23c. Forms of the nose, chin and ear. Also shaded is the eye orbit.

Fig. 23d. The brow ridge.

FINAL VERSION

a

b

c

d

156

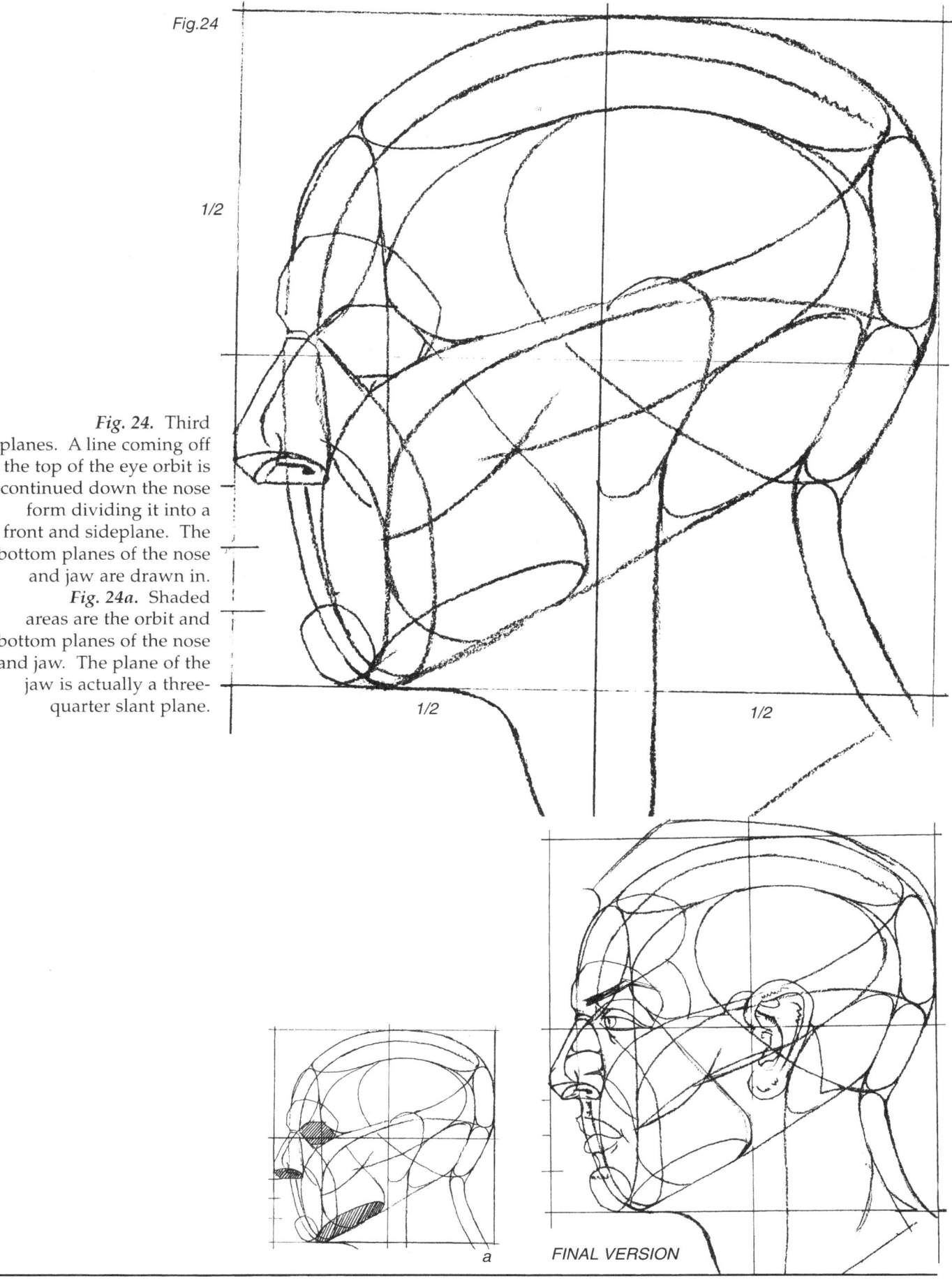

Fig.24

1/2

1/2

1/2

Fig. 24. Third planes. A line coming off the top of the eye orbit is continued down the nose form dividing it into a front and sideplane. The bottom planes of the nose and jaw are drawn in.
Fig. 24a. Shaded areas are the orbit and bottom planes of the nose and jaw. The plane of the jaw is actually a three-quarter slant plane.

a

FINAL VERSION

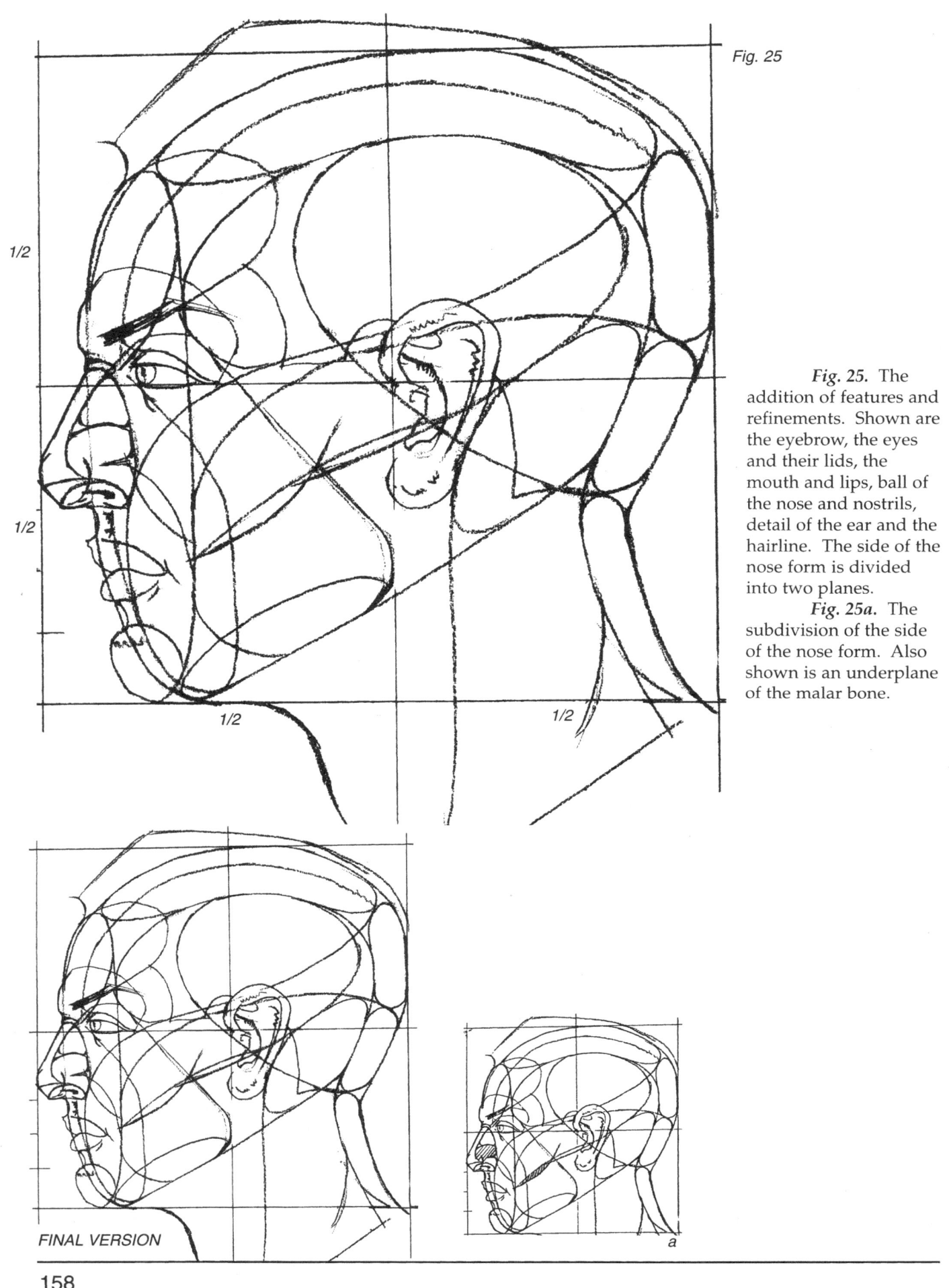

Fig. 25. The addition of features and refinements. Shown are the eyebrow, the eyes and their lids, the mouth and lips, ball of the nose and nostrils, detail of the ear and the hairline. The side of the nose form is divided into two planes.

Fig. 25a. The subdivision of the side of the nose form. Also shown is an underplane of the malar bone.

FINAL VERSION

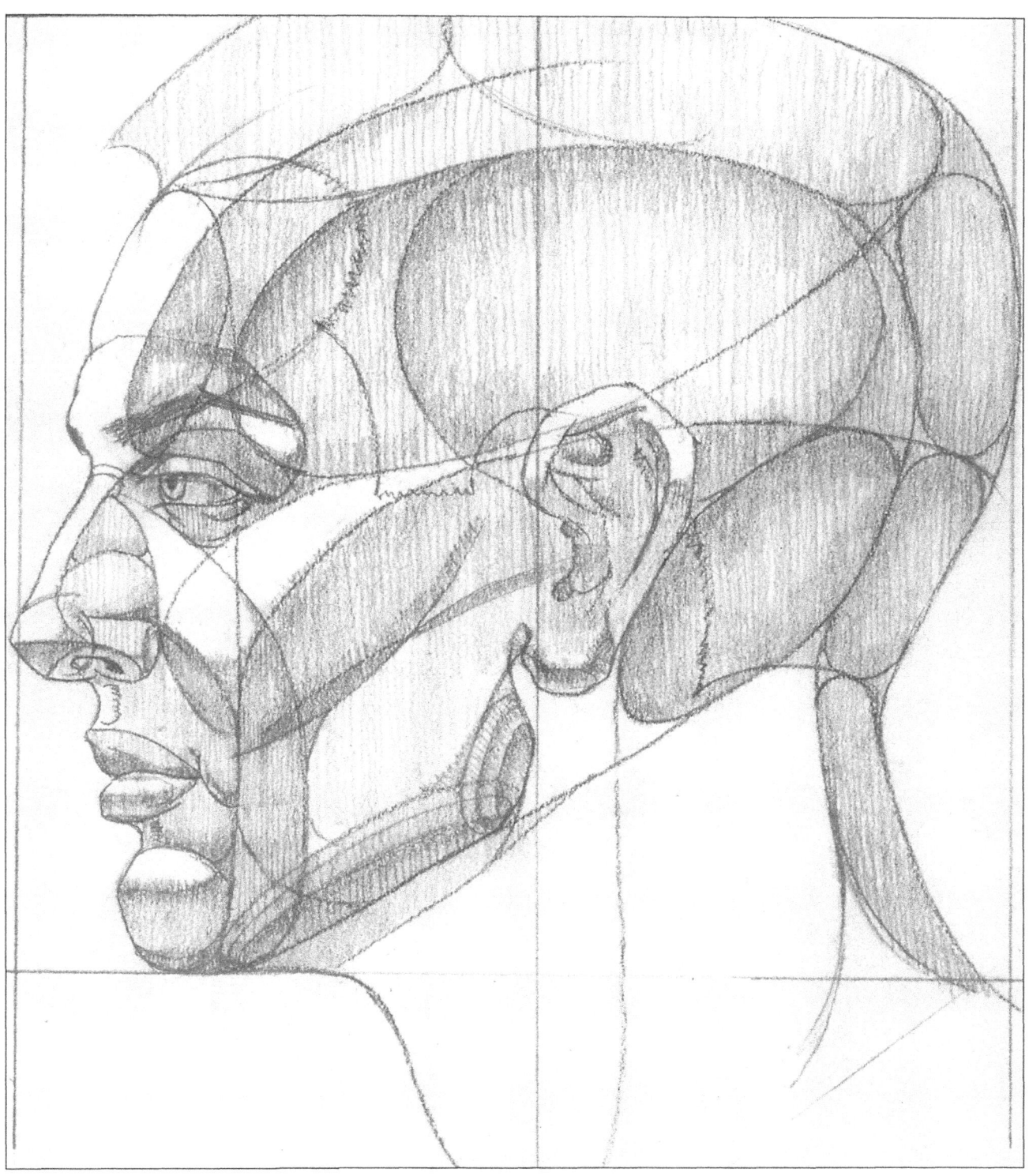

Fig. 26. A simplified modeled version of the planes and forms of the side view for further understanding. Keep in mind that all planes can be subdivided as much as needed or depending on the individual's character.

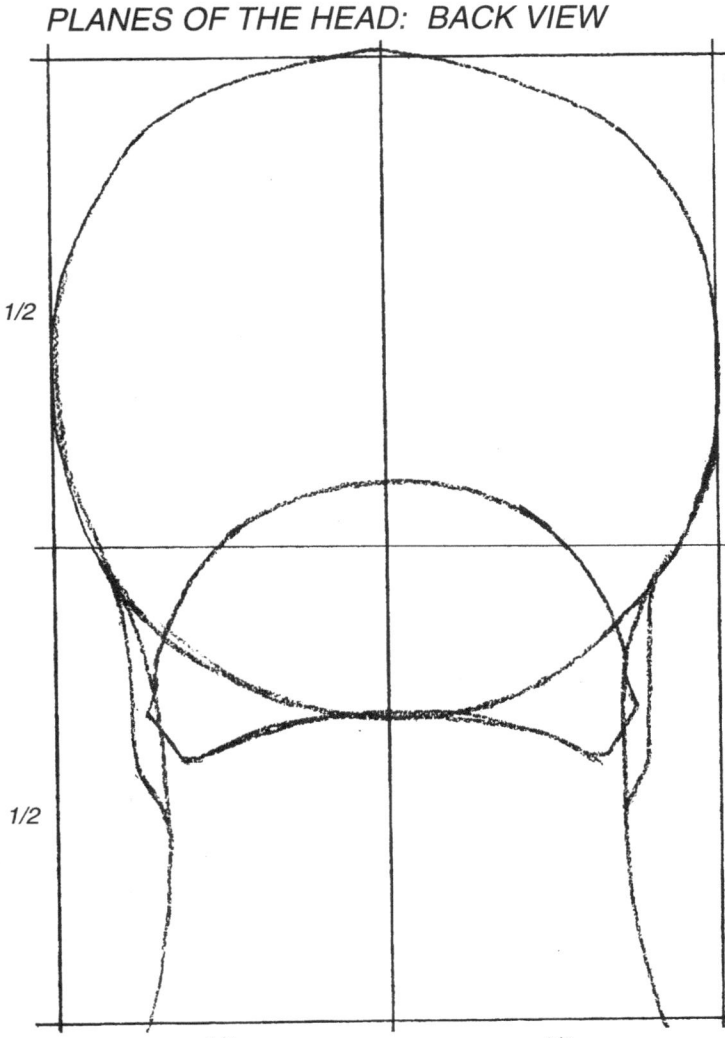

Fig.27

1/2

1/2

1/2   1/2

Fig. 27. The first large forms of the rear of the skull. The cranium is spherical and sits on a cylindrical neck form. The edge of the jaw is shown on both sides of the neck.

Fig. 27a. The shaded portion shows the slant bottom plane of the skull.

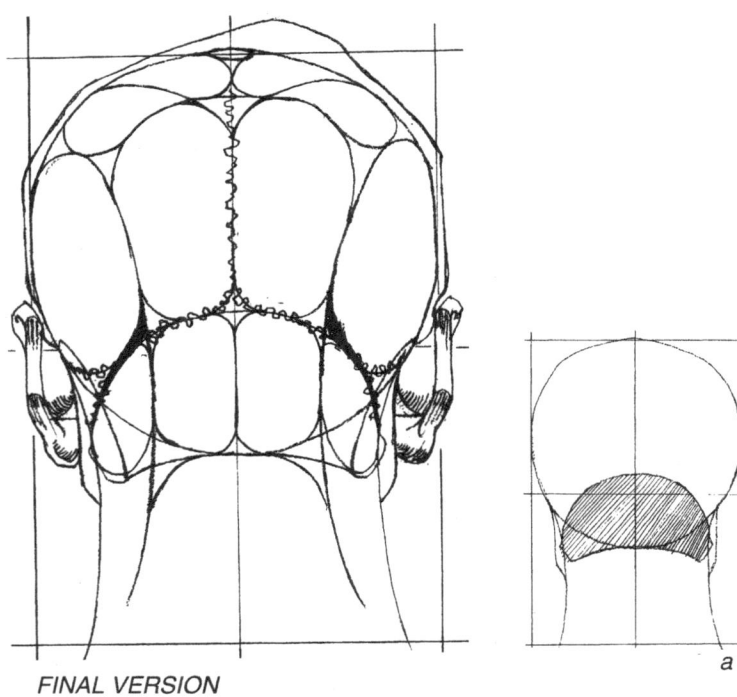

FINAL VERSION

a

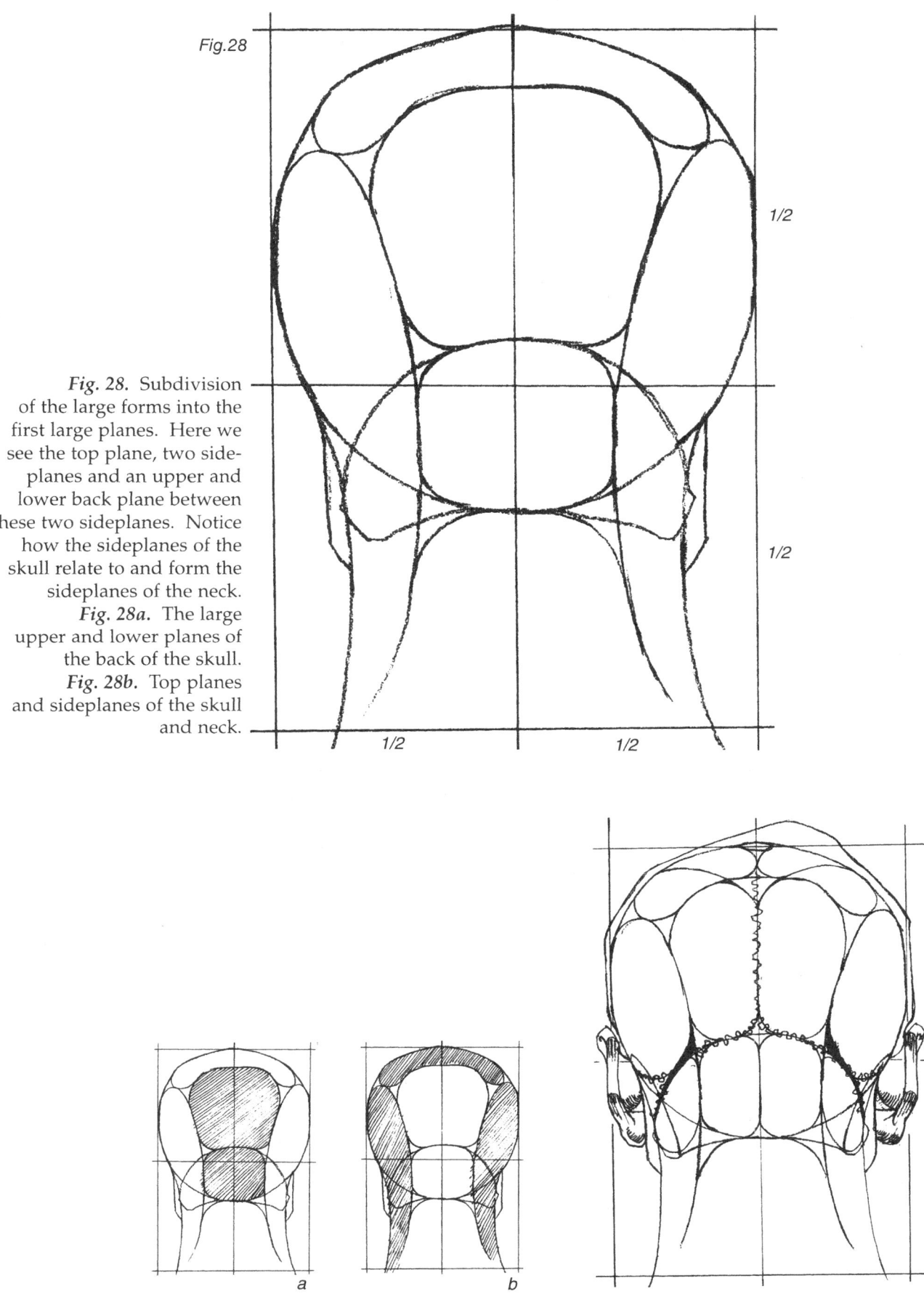

Fig. 28. Subdivision of the large forms into the first large planes. Here we see the top plane, two sideplanes and an upper and lower back plane between these two sideplanes. Notice how the sideplanes of the skull relate to and form the sideplanes of the neck.
Fig. 28a. The large upper and lower planes of the back of the skull.
Fig. 28b. Top planes and sideplanes of the skull and neck.

Fig.28

1/2

1/2

1/2

1/2

a

b

FINAL VERSION

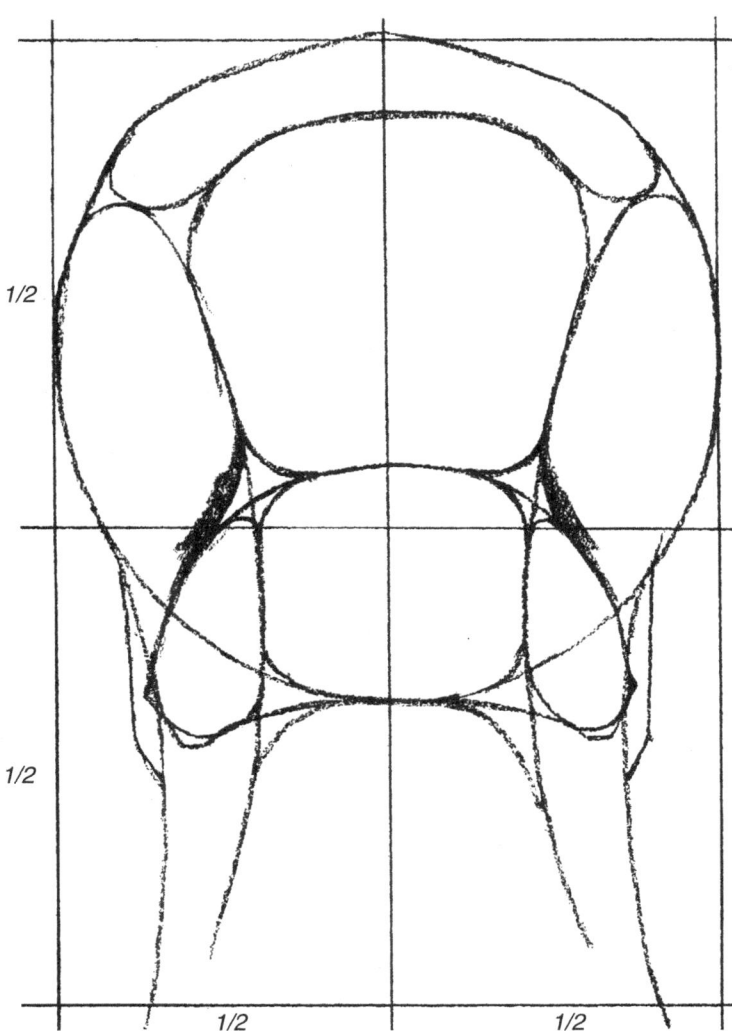

Fig. 29

1/2

1/2

1/2

1/2   1/2

Fig. 29. The secondary large form of the skull shape is developed. This is shown by the emphasized lines. The forms of the lower back of the skull are also added.

Fig. 29a. Shaded areas are of the lower back bulges of the skull.

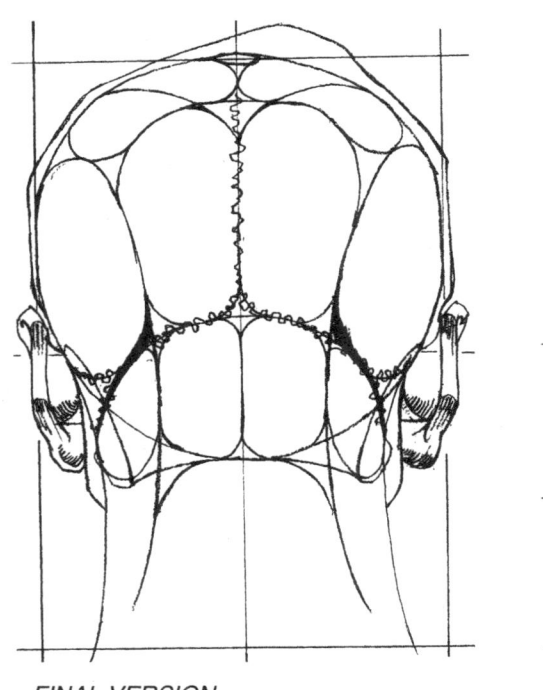

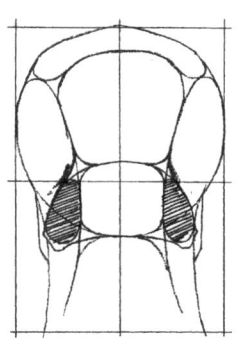

a

FINAL VERSION

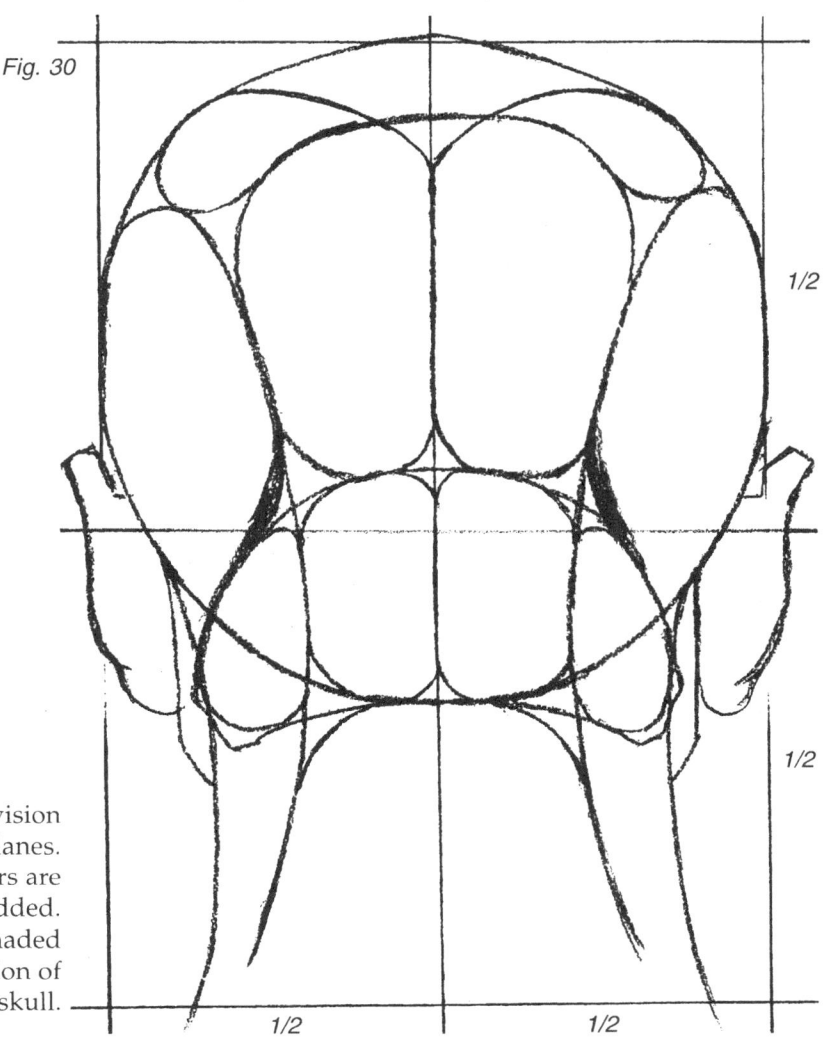

Fig. 30. Subdivision of the top and back planes. The forms of the ears are added.
Fig. 30a. Shaded areas showing the division of the back planes of the skull.

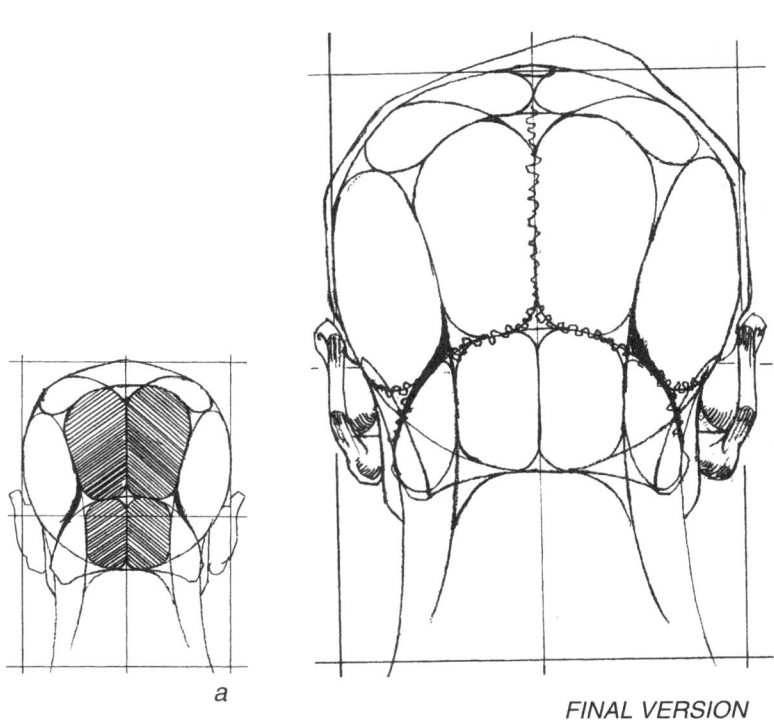

a

FINAL VERSION

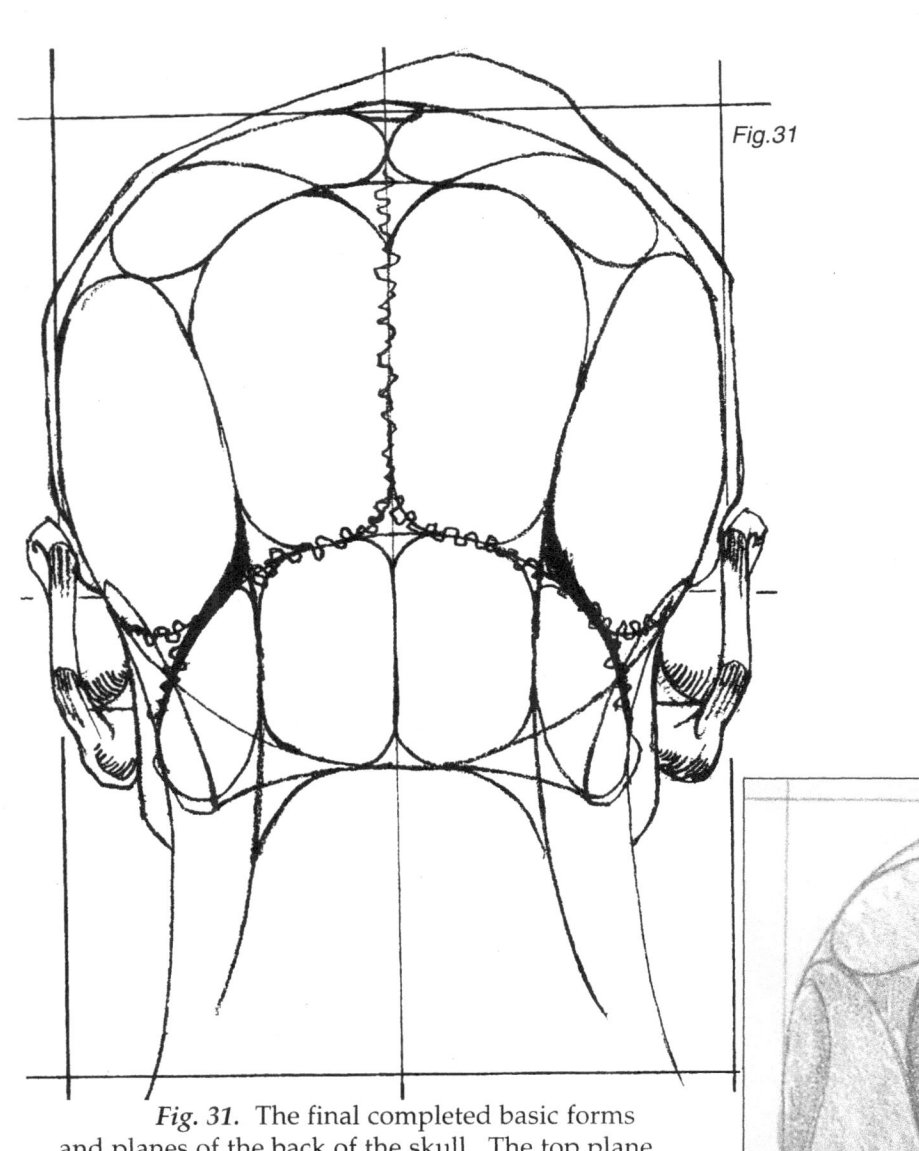

Fig.31

Fig. 31. The final completed basic forms and planes of the back of the skull. The top plane is divided again. Forms of the ears are developed and sutures and hairline are designated.

Fig.32

Fig. 32. Another version of the back of the skull. This one is of a bald headed male taken from life. It shows the large sideplanes further divided and a large occipital protuberance near the base of a short cranium case. Below it starting at the superior nuchal line is a large form of fatty muscular tissue that wraps around the neck muscles and attaches at the mastoid temporal process.

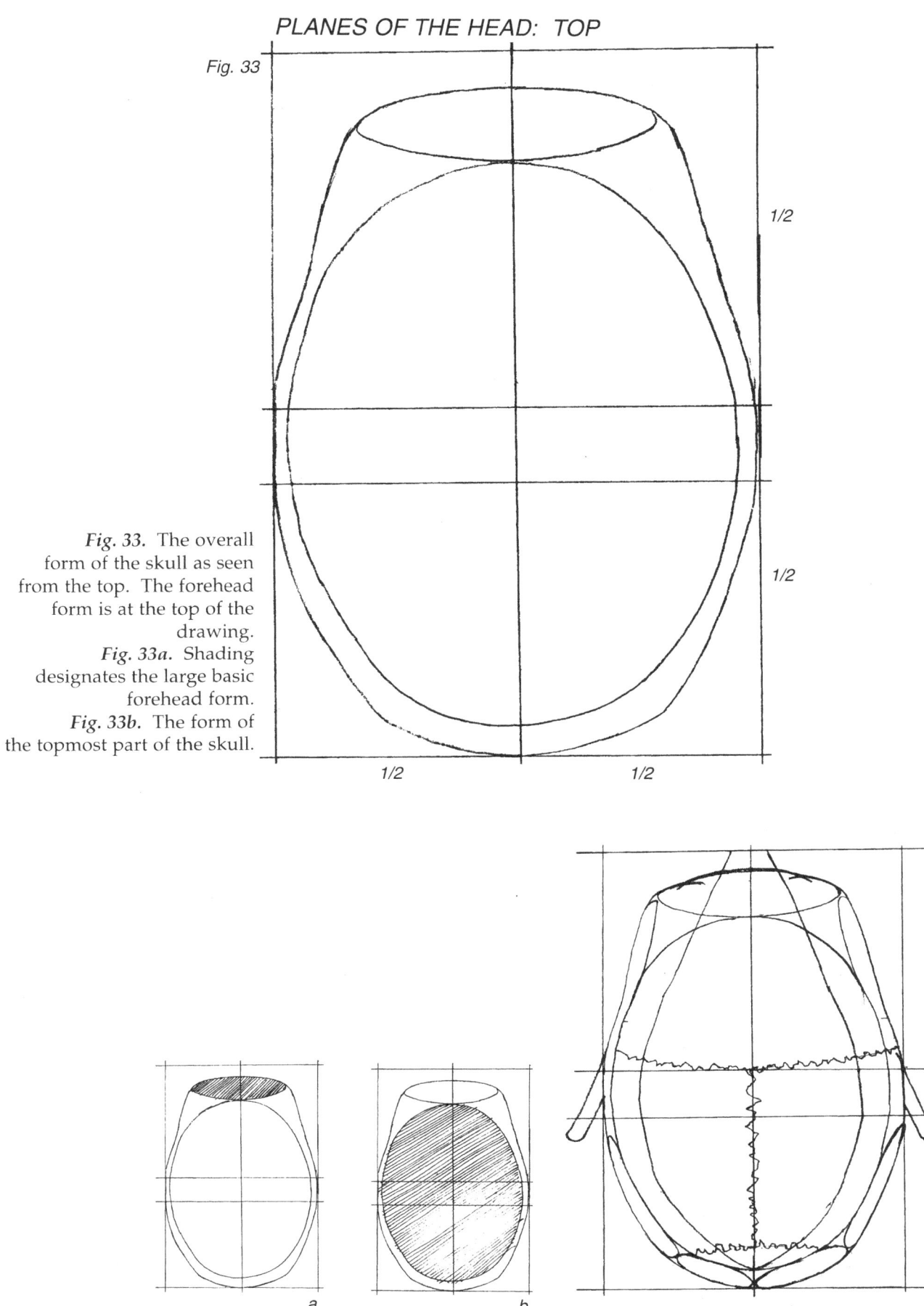

Fig. 33

Fig. 33. The overall form of the skull as seen from the top. The forehead form is at the top of the drawing.
Fig. 33a. Shading designates the large basic forehead form.
Fig. 33b. The form of the topmost part of the skull.

1/2

1/2

1/2

1/2

a

b

FINAL VERSION

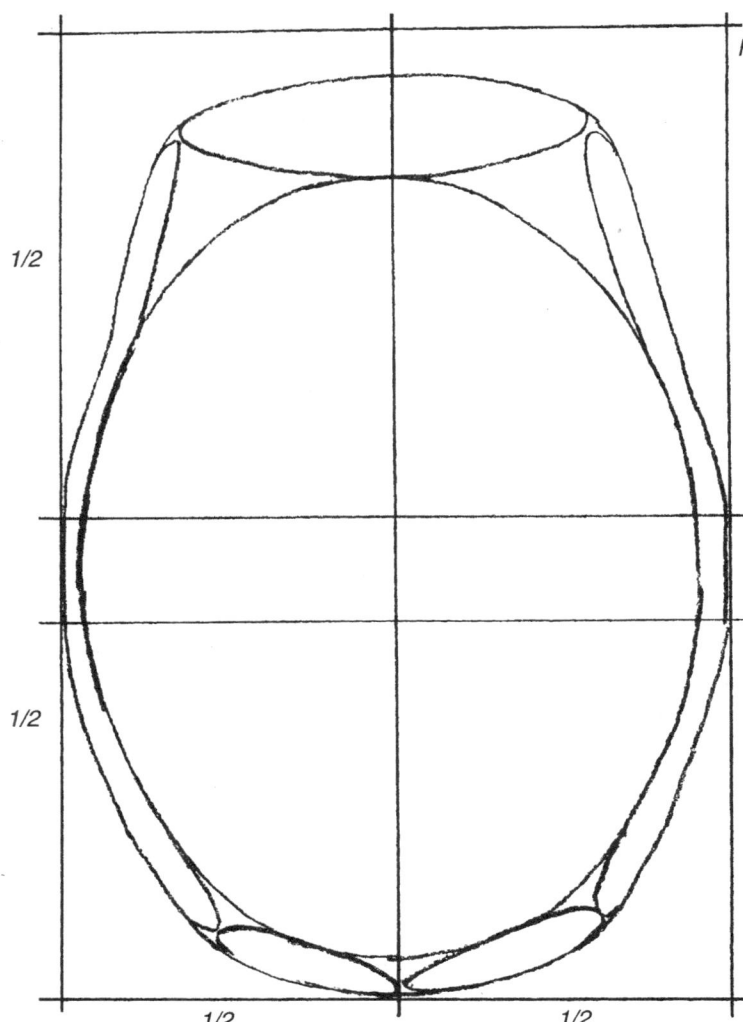

1/2

1/2

1/2

1/2   1/2

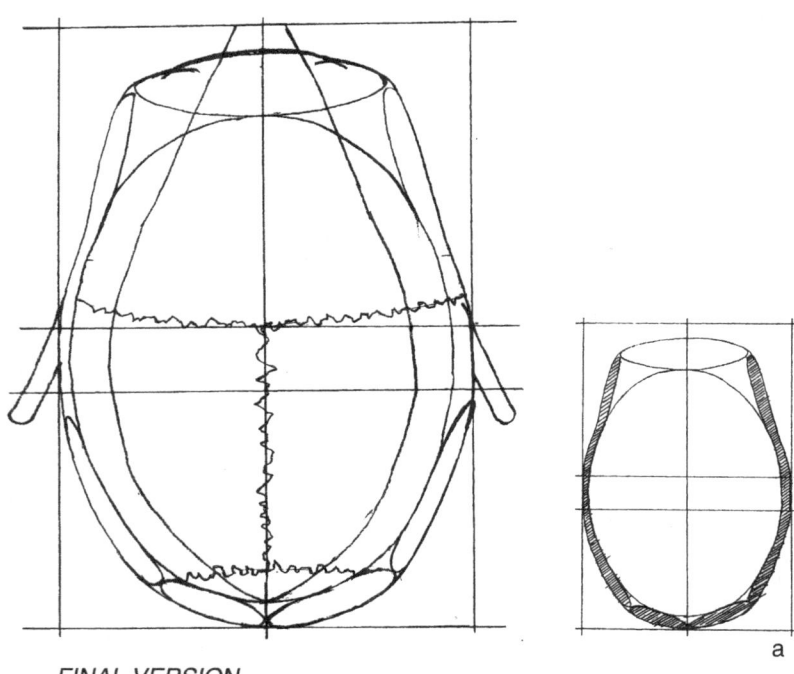

FINAL VERSION

a

Fig. 34. First sideplanes of the skull.
Fig. 34a. Sideplanes shown shaded.

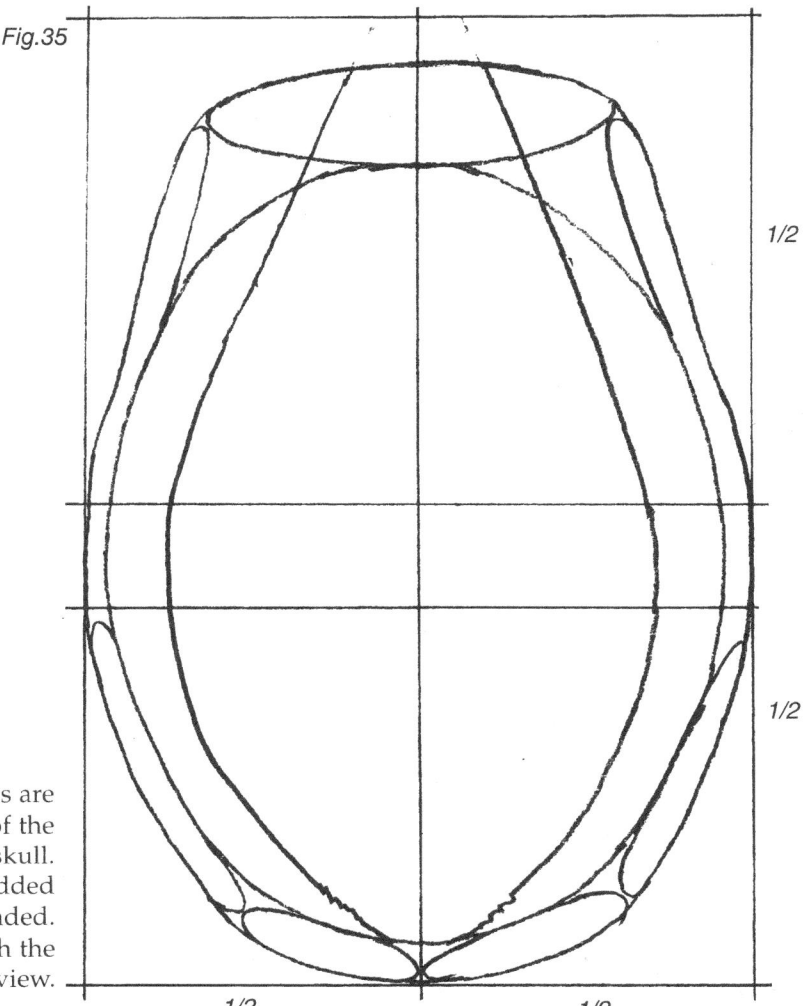

Fig.35

1/2

1/2

Fig. 35. Planes are added to the top form of the skull.
Fig. 35a. The added top planes are shown shaded. Coordinate these with the front view.

1/2   1/2

a

FINAL VERSION

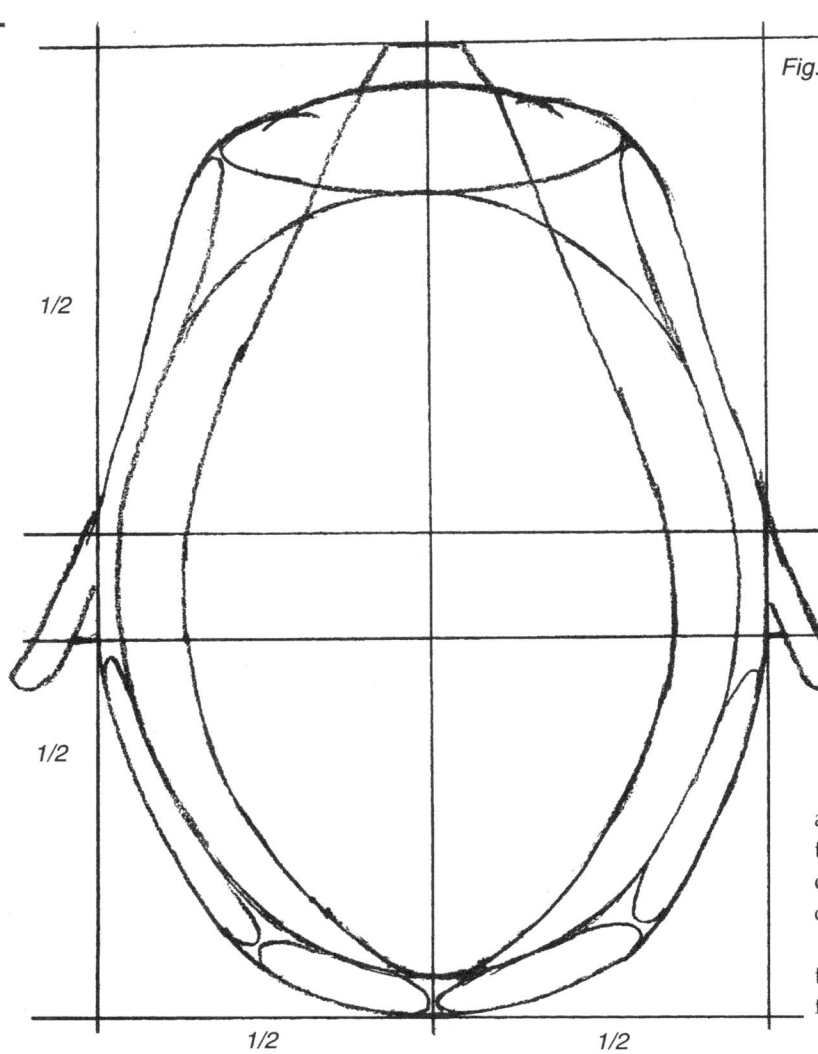

1/2

1/2

1/2

1/2   1/2

Fig. 36. The nose form and ears are added. Notice how the nose form relates to the lines of the top planes. The brow is developed further.

Fig. 36a. Shading shows the forms of the ears, nose and forehead.

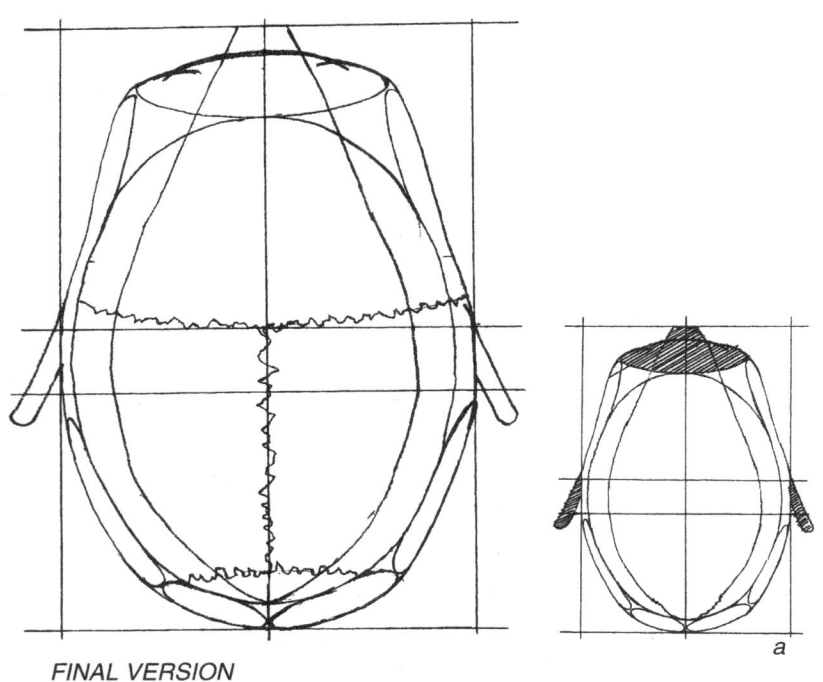

FINAL VERSION

a

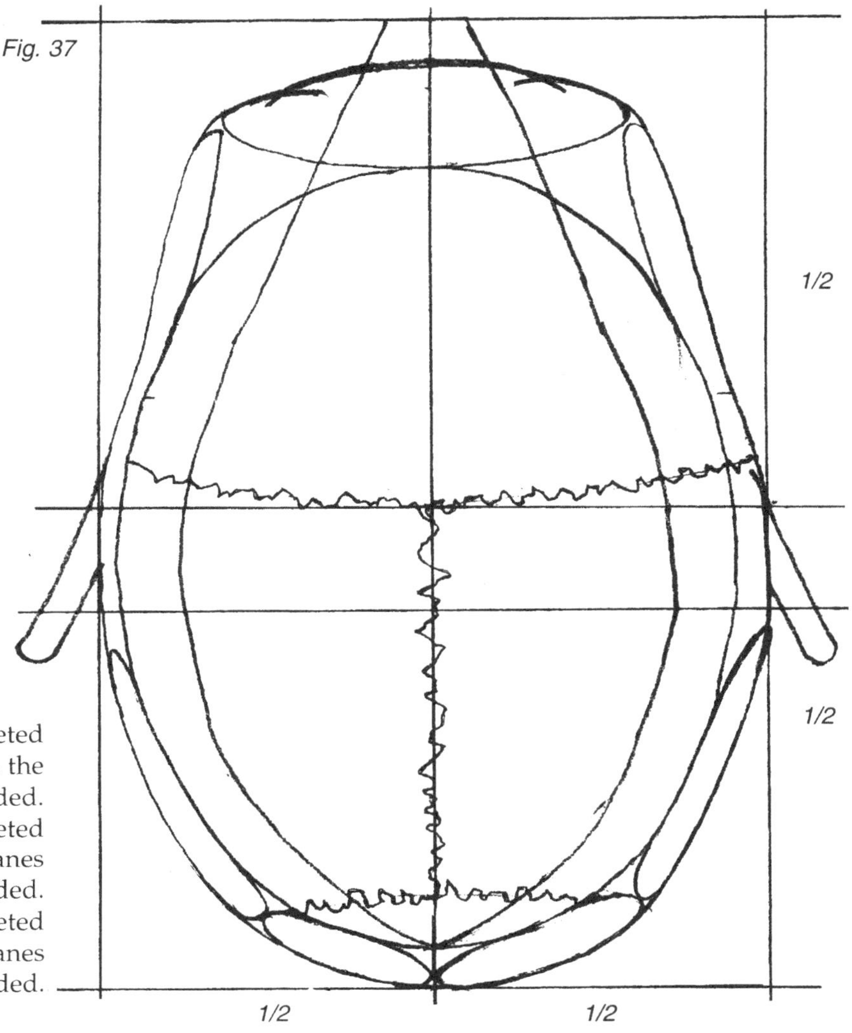

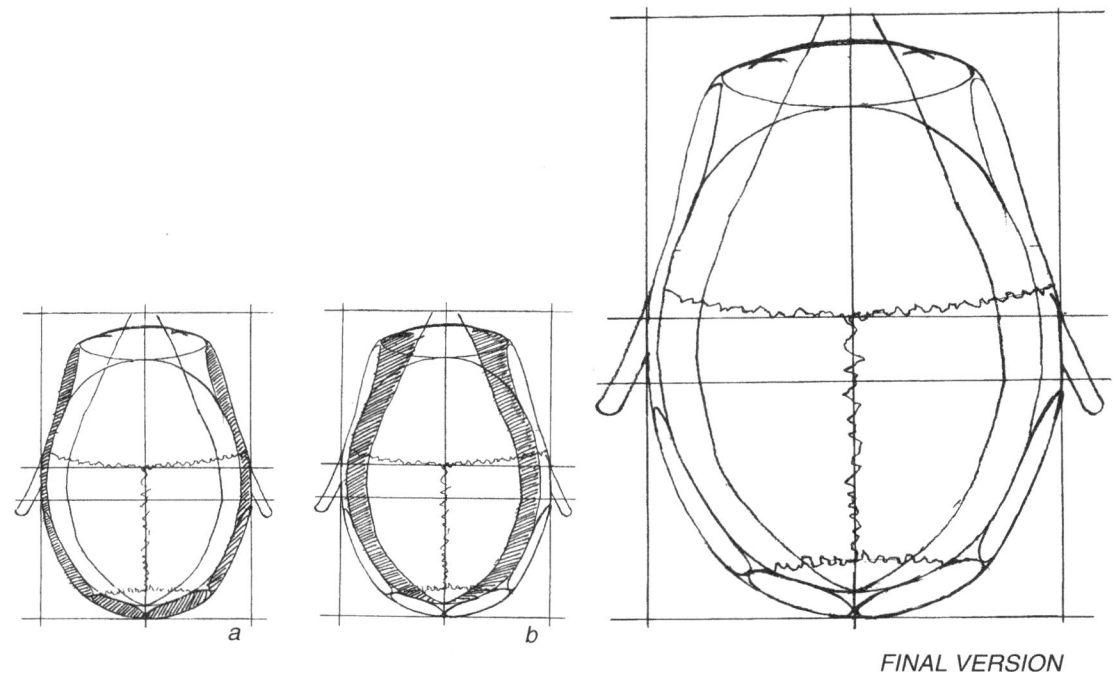

Fig. 37

1/2

1/2

1/2

Fig. 37. The completed top view of the skull with the sutures added.
Fig. 37a. Completed version with first sideplanes added.
Fig. 37b. Completed version with secondary planes shaded.

1/2   1/2

a   *b*

FINAL VERSION

169

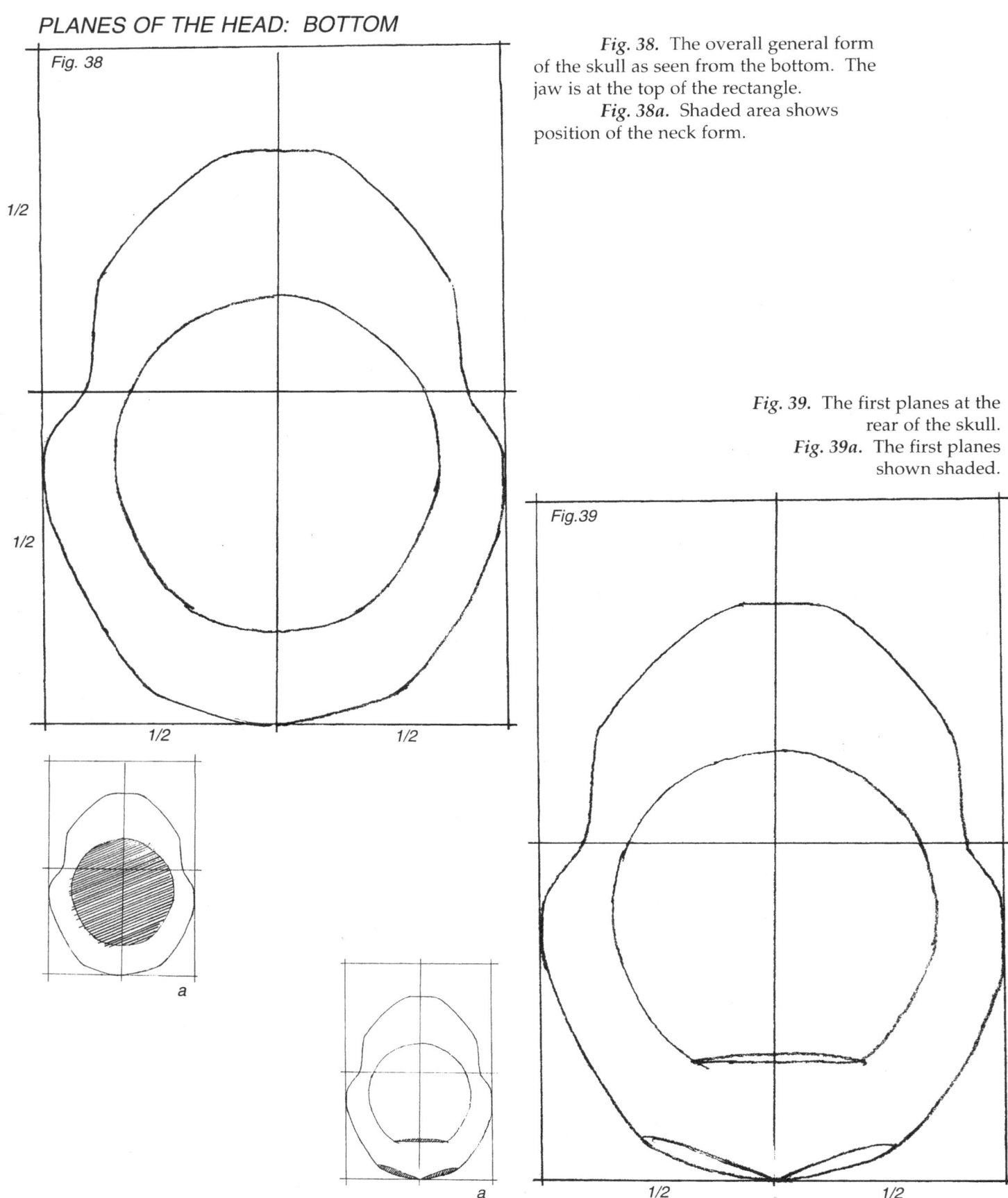

Fig. 38. The overall general form of the skull as seen from the bottom. The jaw is at the top of the rectangle.

Fig. 38a. Shaded area shows position of the neck form.

Fig. 39. The first planes at the rear of the skull.

Fig. 39a. The first planes shown shaded.

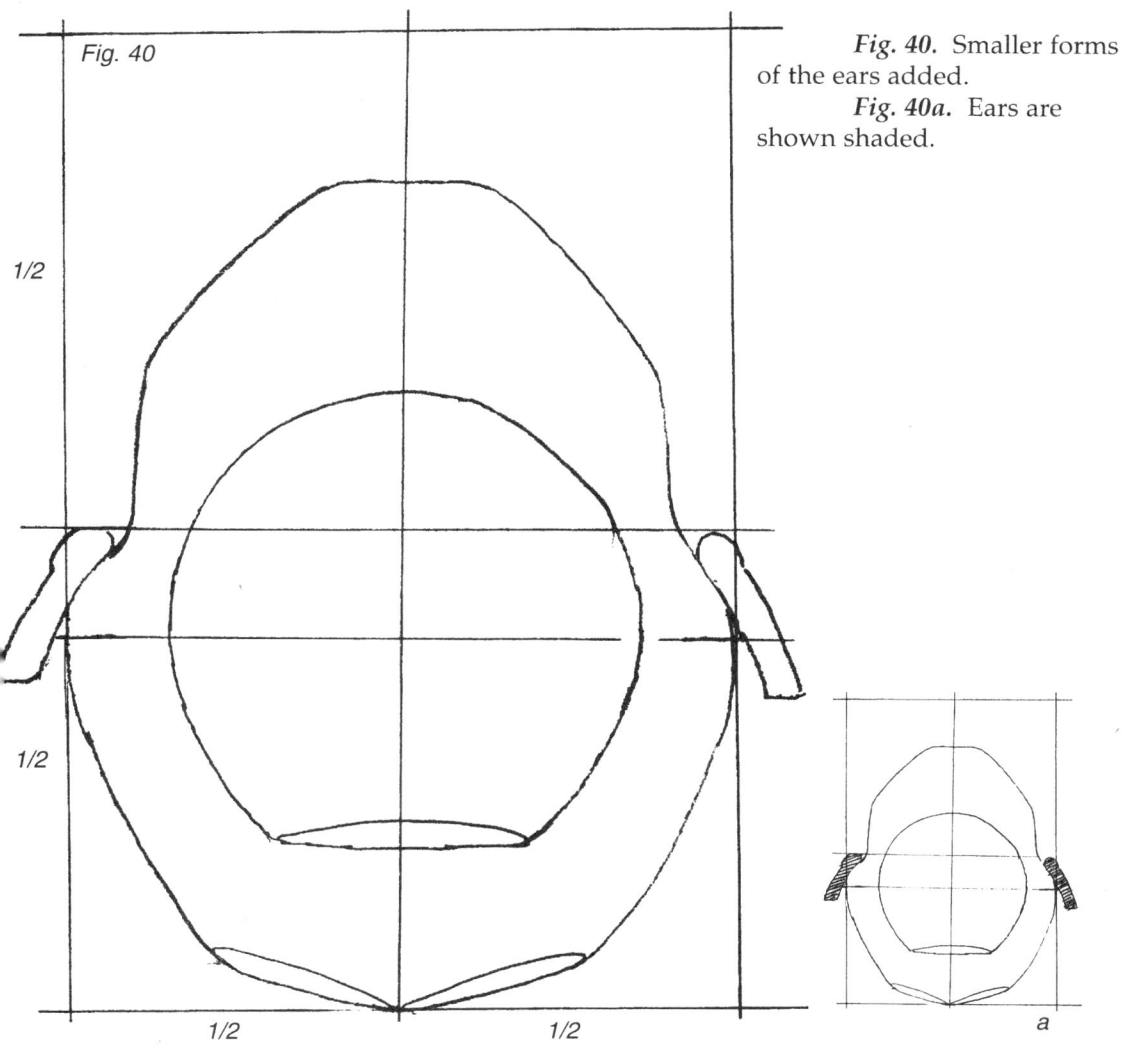

Fig. 40 *Fig. 40.* Smaller forms of the ears added.

Fig. 40a. Ears are shown shaded.

This completes the study of the basic planes of the front, side, top and bottom of the skull. These drawings are by no means complete and will vary with individuals. Nature makes no two things alike. Generally, however, they will be of great help in increasing your perception and understanding of form whether you apply them to drawing, painting or sculpture. If nothing else, after you have studied this chapter you will never look at people the same way again and hopefully you will have a greater appreciation of the harmony, beauty and design of the human form.

PHOTO SERIES OF A CAST SHOWING PLANES OF THE HEAD

This series of photographs should do much to clarify the drawings of the planes and forms of the head as presented in the previous pages. You can clearly see how the light and shade breaks on the lines of these forms and planes thereby producing a three dimensional effect. Hopefully you will see similar effects on everyone you look at and be able to draw or paint them correctly.

Every time you change the position of the light new planes will be revealed while others will seem to disappear.

Taking photographs of the cast as well as reproducing the photographs accurately is difficult as the lights tend to bleach out and darks pull together and appear denser. However they are not meant for you to copy exactly but to learn from as well as to increase your perception of form.

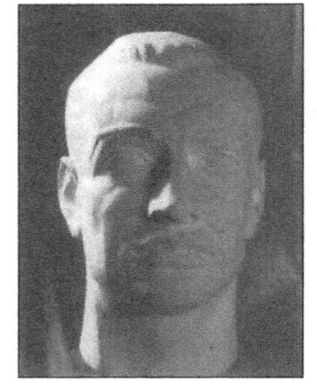

1

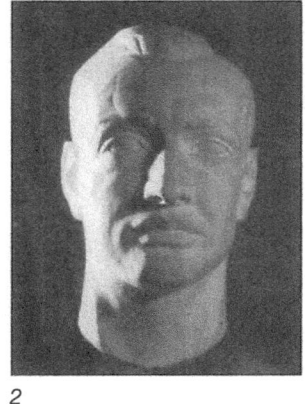

2

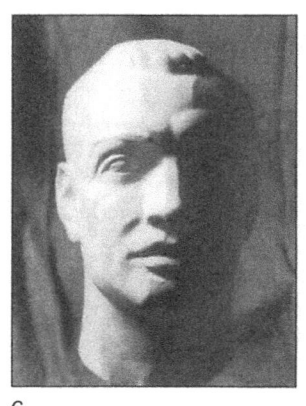

6

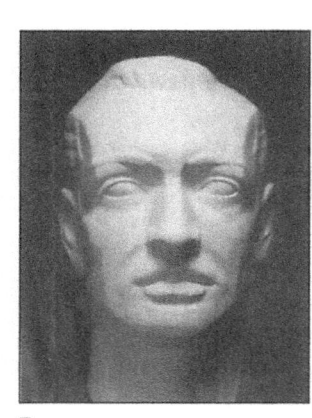

7

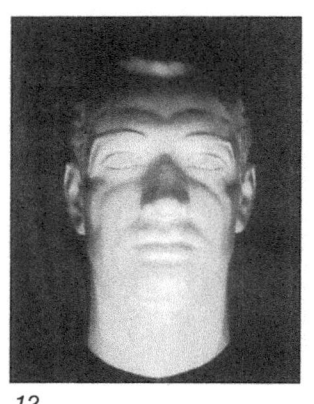

12

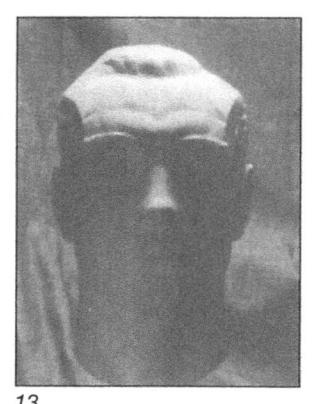

13

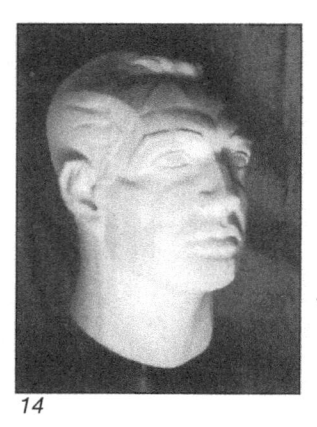

14

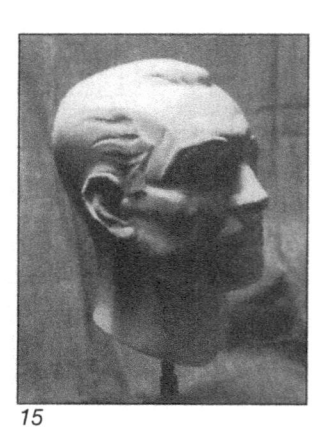

15

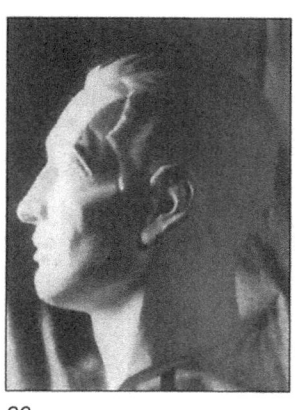

20

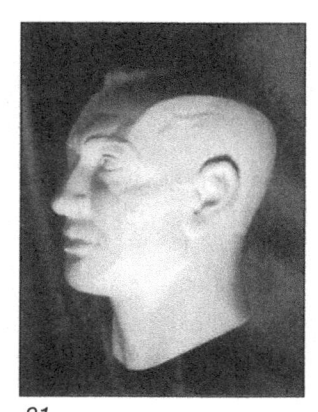

21

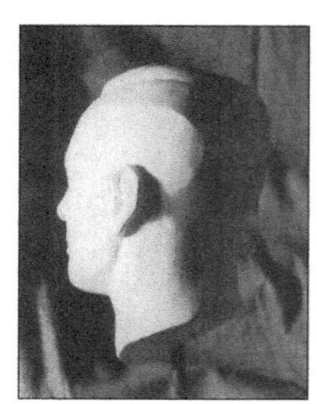

22

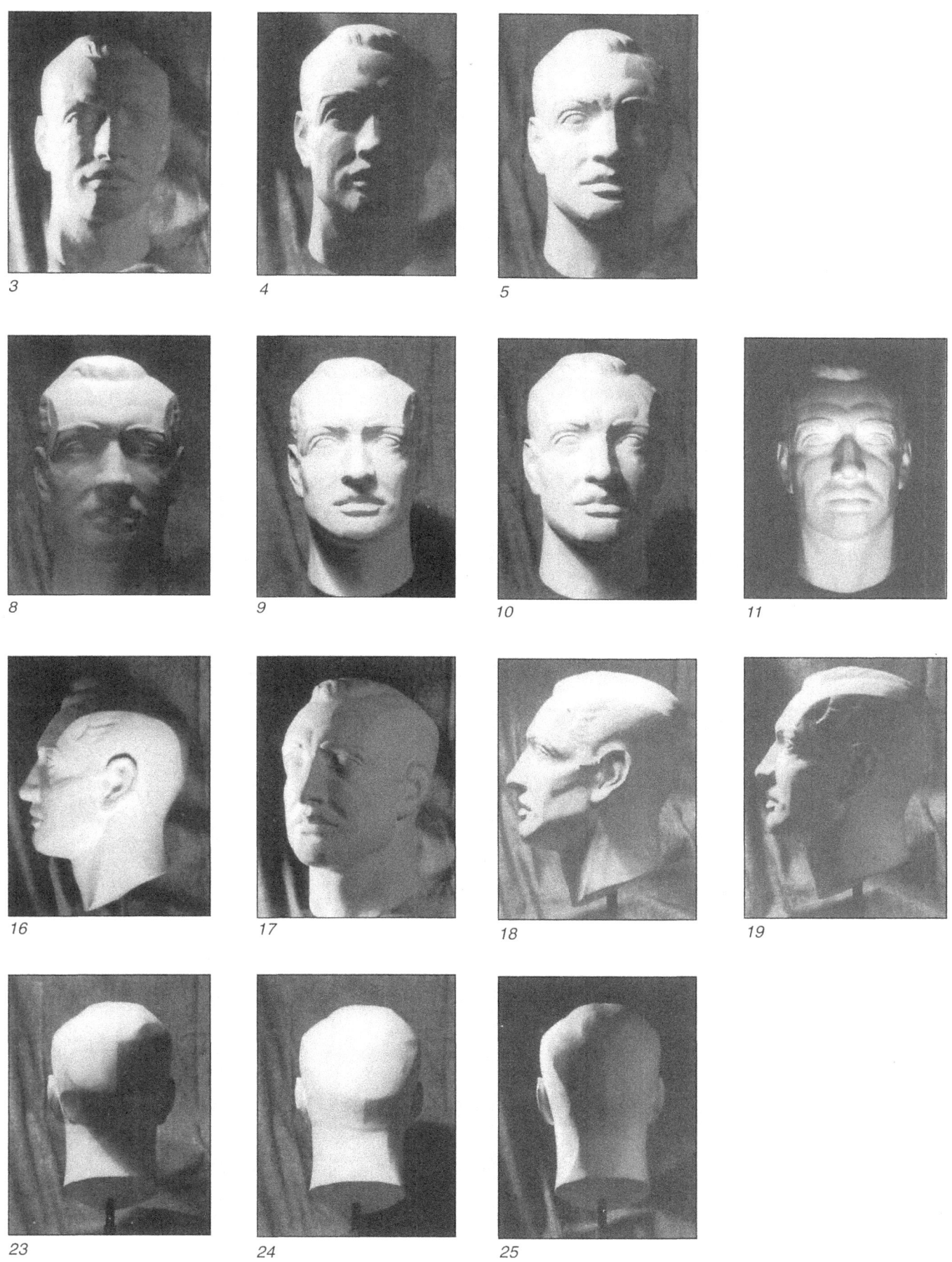

3

4

5

8

9

10

11

16

17

18

19

23

24

25

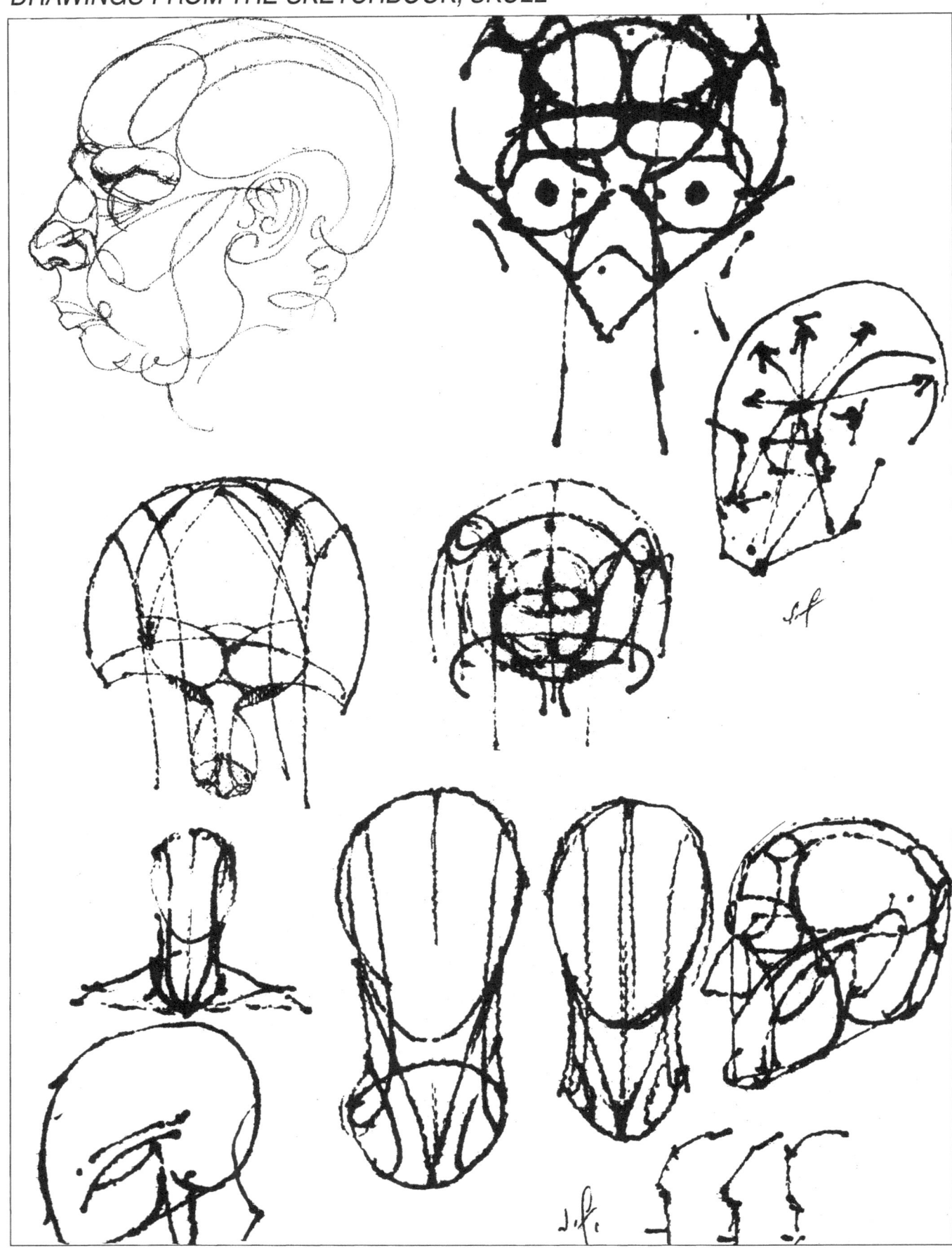

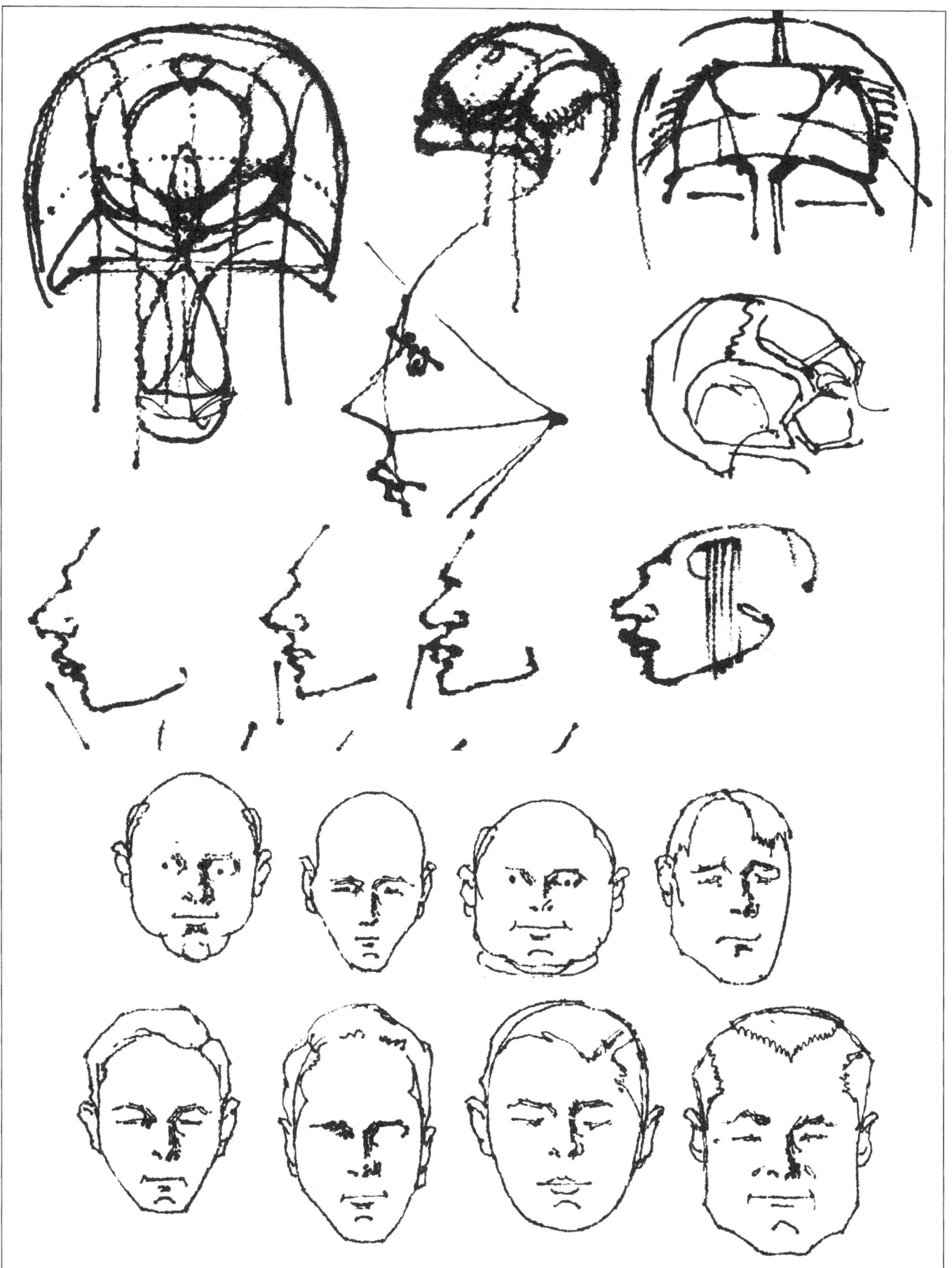

EIGHTEEN

THE CONSTRUCTION AND PLANES OF THE FEATURES OF THE HEAD

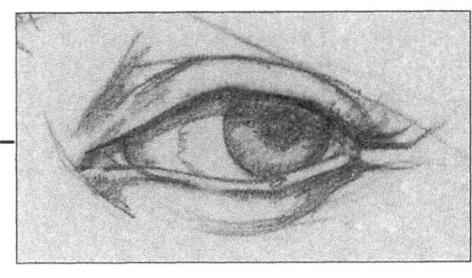

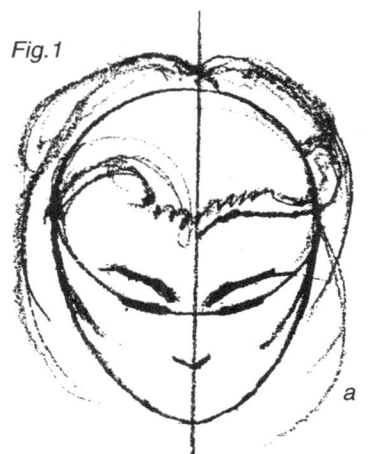
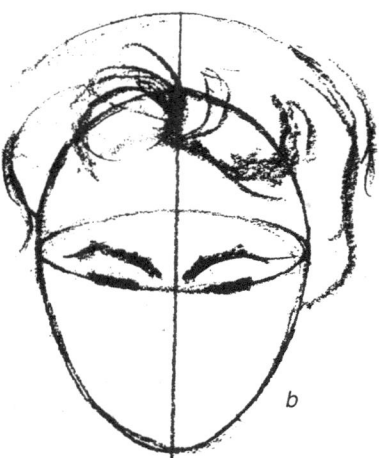
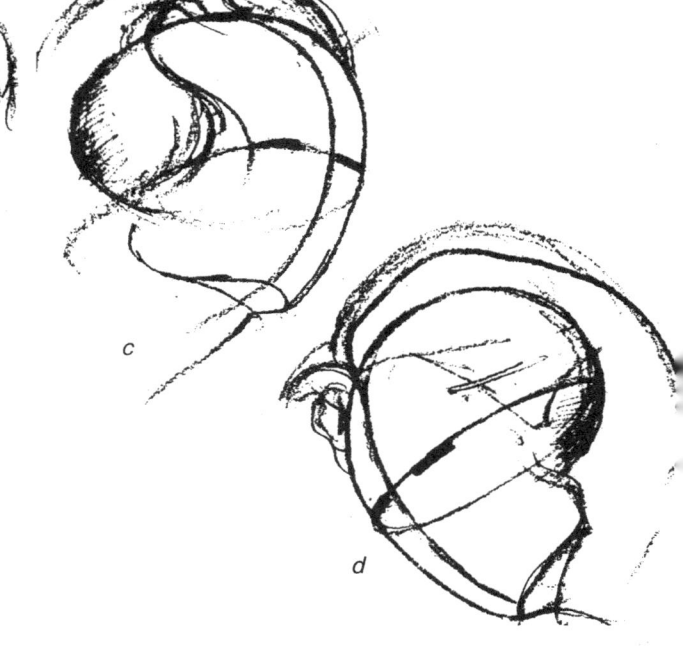

Fig.1

a　　*b*　　*c*　　*d*

THE EYES

Of all the features of the head the eyes and mouth receive the most attention – both by artists and writers as well as ordinary people. Of the two features the eyes are of the utmost importance and the artist should know as much as possible about them both from the standpoint of structure and rendering as well as expression.

The details of the eye structure are subtle and elusive and are therefore missed by all but the most discerning individuals. A sharply observant artist such as John Singer Sargeant could capture the character of an individual so well because he accurately recorded the subtle change of angles of the eye structure as well as the other features.

I have noticed in my many years of teaching that the drawings and paintings that students work on look more like themselves than the model. It is as if they are projecting themselves onto the drawing or painting. Artists, therefore, have to beware of infusing their own characteristics into the features of those they are recording. For example, those who have rounded features paint or draw all others with round features. Those with long noses give everyone a long nose, and on and on. The first step of a student is to be an accurate observer. He should analyze and learn everything he can about what he draws. He has to make an effort and to be aware of how much he is altering what he sees. Hopefully these drawings and information will correctly guide you and help you avoid errors of perception and judgement.

Concerning the eyes the first thing to consider is that they, like the nose and mouth, must give the feeling that they are going around the head. This can

be accomplished by first drawing the shape of the skull and then drawing an oval around this skull shape. The eyes should follow the curvature of this oval line as shown in Figs. 1a.b.c. and d.

Fig. 1a. Looking down.
Fig. b. Almost straight on.
Fig. c. Three-quarters looking up.
Fig. d. Three-quarters looking down.

Fig. 2. This schematic shows the basic structure of the eyes. Too often one eye is drawn higher than the other – even with the best of artists. You can avoid this by always drawing the two eyes at the same time, constantly relating one side to the other. The "normal" head is five eyes wide seen in the frontal view. Draw a horizontal line and mark off five equal spaces. There is usually one eye space between the left and right eyes, sometimes less, sometimes more. I have seen many instances of less than one eye space distance but seldom have seen a greater than one eye distance between the eyes.

Notice the overall shape of the eye sockets and their relationship to the eyebrows and brows. The top of the nose form sits between the eyes – this alone should prevent you from drawing the eyes too close. Lines originating at the eyebrows continue

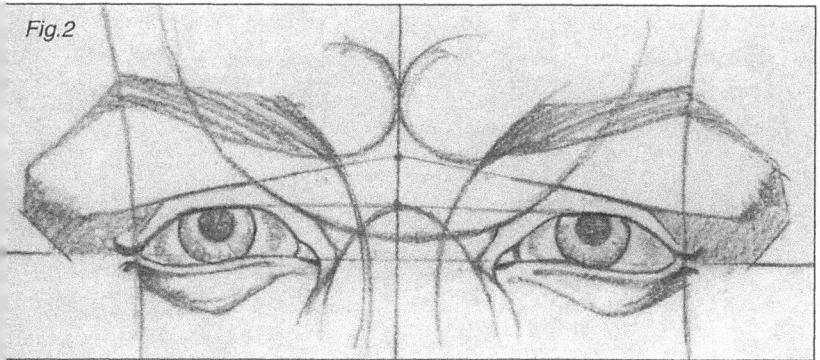

Fig.2

Fig. 4. This three-quarter view drawing shows how a shadow, cast from the upper lid follows the curvature of the eyeball. Note also how the lower lid conforms to the shape of the eyeball.

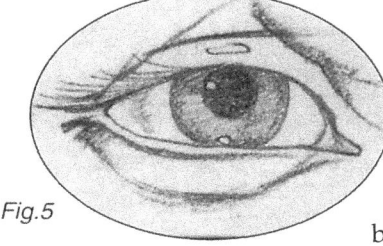

Fig.4

Fig. 5. The position of the highlights are shown on the upper lid, the pupil and at the bottom of the iris.

Fig.5

The position of the light is directly above the eye. The highlight at the bottom of the iris and on the lid is frequently overlooked. It is actually caused by a reflection of light off tears.

downwards along the nasal bone. The very important underplanes of the eye sockets are formed by a semicircle which relates to the forehead form. These underplanes press in on the eyelids interrupting their curvature. The two eyes are related by drawing lines from the eyelids to points shown on the center line. These points can vary in position. Be aware however that the eyelids do not necessarily have to be exactly the same. It is not too uncommon for the left eyelid to droop lower than the right eyelid as shown in Fig. 8. Most times this is found in the male. It should be looked for in expressions and for psychological insight.

The position of the iris and pupil in relation to the eyelids is important. There actually is a "normal" resting position for the iris. In the normal resting position the bottom of the iris makes tangent with the lower lid and the top of the pupil makes tangent with the bottom of the top eyelid. Changes in these positions will convey different expressions.

Fig.3

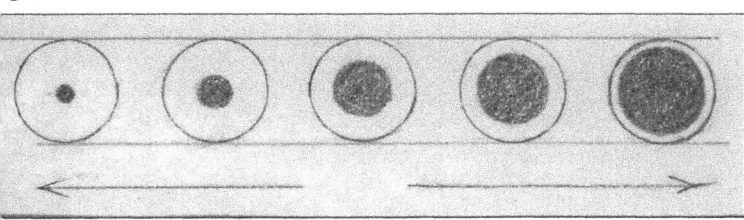

Fig. 6. The eye shown in its socket in profile. The line with the arrowhead shows the tilted angle of the eyeball within the eye socket. Notice the shape of the iris and the curvatures of the upper and lower eyelids which follow the curvature of the eyeball. As regards the iris and pupil close observation reveals that there is less space between the pupil and the edge of the iris on the left side rather than on the right side

Fig.6

Fig. 3. This series of drawings shows the variation of the size of the pupil due to the increase or decrease in the quantity of light. As the light increases the pupil becomes smaller and smaller in size as shown towards the left. As the light decreases the pupil enlarges as shown going towards the right. It is little known that the pupil will also enlarge in *normal or bright light* if a person expresses interest in something or someone. Be advised, therefore, that if you are with someone and you want to know if they're interested in you or what you are saying try to observe the change in the size of their pupils.

Many artists and illustrators deliberately make the pupils larger when drawing or painting women as it makes them appear more attractive. The madonnas you see in Renaissance paintings always have larger than normal size pupils.

Fig. 7. The eyeball turned upwards. The spherical shape of the eye has to be pronounced by modeling. More white space will be seen between the iris and the lower lid. The iris should not be drawn perfectly round but angled off especially at the lower part.

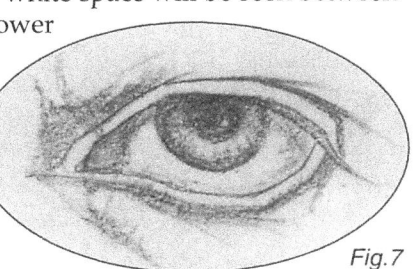

Fig. 7

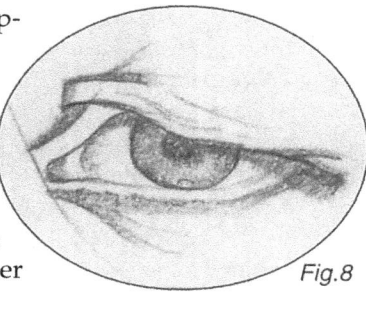

Fig. 8. A drooping lid. Some people are born with this condition and with others it develops as they get older. It is usually on the left eye and on a male of a young age and on either sex in old age.

Fig.8

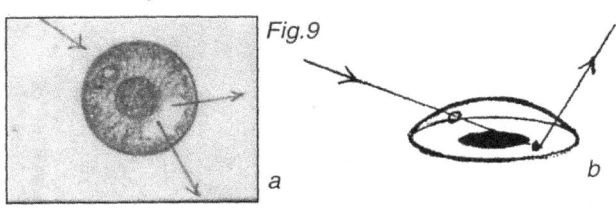

Fig.9

a

b

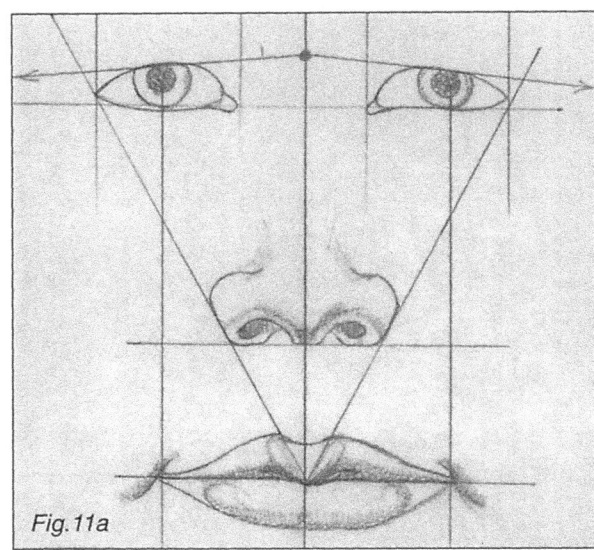

Fig.11a

Fig. 9a.b. Light entering the iris will go through it and be refracted out of the iris on the opposite side. The highlight on the iris will be on the side of the light source, whereas the lightest part of the iris will be opposite the highlight. Fig. 9b. shows this diagrammatically.

An eye has an axis line that goes from the inner corner of the tear duct to the outer corner of the eye. This should be looked for first. This line is seldom absolutely horizontal. The outer corner of the axis of the eye tilts up to angles of various degrees from a horizontal line drawn across the bottom of the two eyes. The greatest angle is to be found in oriental peoples. In general women will look prettier and more beautiful in illustrations and paintings if this axis line of the eye is slightly higher than average at the outer edge. This is not an ironclad rule, however. There are rare cases, too, where the axis line from the outer edge of the eye is lower than the inner edge of the tear duct.

Figs. 10a.b.c. Three examples of the axis of the eye shown compared to a horizontal line.

Fig. 10a. An average angle of the axis of the eye.

Fig. 10b. A greater than average angle of the axis.

Fig. 10c. An example of an axis line going below the horizontal.

Fig. 11a. It is very helpful in the drawing of heads to align the eyes with the mouth. One thing can be used to determine the other. A good place to start is to align the centers of the pupils with the corners of the mouth. This works most of the time. If not, you can easily ascertain if the mouth is wider or narrower. Another relationship that can be used is to draw a line from the center of the lips past the corner of the nostril to the corner of the eye.

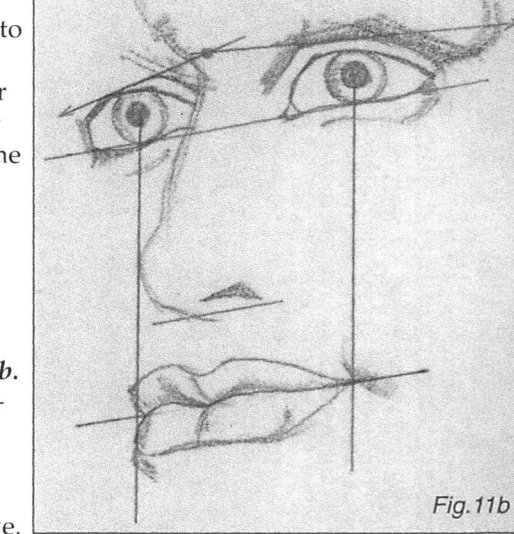

Fig. 11b. The same principles apply when the head turns or goes into perspective.

Fig.11b

Lines dropped from the pupils should align with the corners of the mouth.

Fig.10

a   b   c

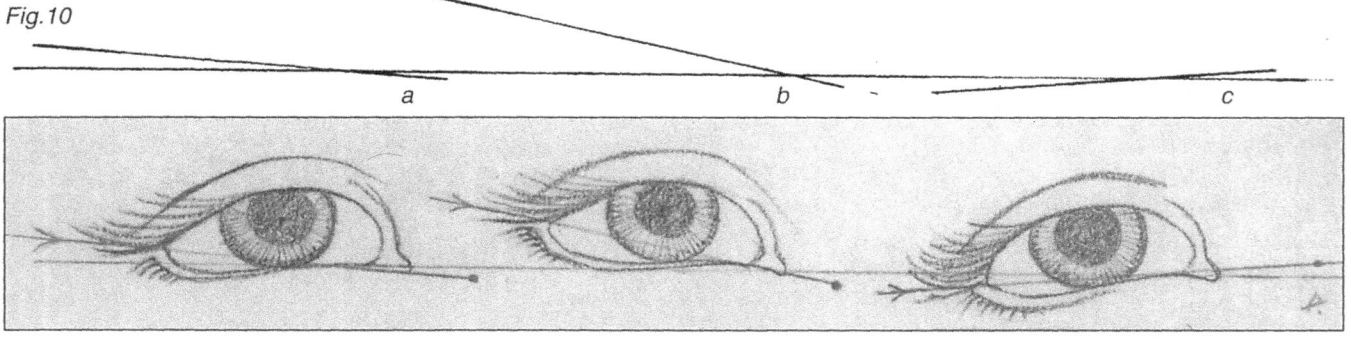

Fig. 12. This series of twelve drawings of eyes are meant to impress upon you the many subtle straight and curved lines of their construction. A beginner is never even remotely aware of the complexity of these lines much less able to draw them. To be regarded as a truly skilled draughtsman *the line should have an accuracy and sureness about it.* Before you draw a line ask yourself, "Where does it come from and where is it going?" Then draw the line confidently and rapidly.

What appears as a continuous line is really made up of a series of lines of different angles made by sweeping lines. I have placed small arrowheads on most of these lines to show you how the stroke is made. This stroke can then be slightly modified and heavied up for emphasis. The direction you start the line from depends on whether you are left handed or right handed or which ever way seems easiest for you.

Much has been written about the expressions of the eye. The eye has been referred to as "the mirror of the soul," and we read of the "love light" or the hatred expressed by the eye. But it is a mistake to think that expressions are solely conveyed by the eyes. Although the eyes are indeed an important element in expression it is more likely that all the features and muscles of the face are involved to a degree. It has even been shown that time plays a part in our perception of an expression. For instance a smile of a very short duration is perceived as friendly but if it goes past a certain amount of milliseconds it is regarded as unfriendly and a threat.

There are certain positions of the anatomy of the eye which convey definite expressions but I maintain that it is quite impossible to draw or paint every expression the human being is capable of solely through the drawing of the eyes. If you doubt this I have listed below about one hundred basic human emotions which produce like expressions. They are divided into positive and negative or light and dark aspects. Can you draw facial expressions to convey all of these?

Positive: Love – respect, fancy, goodness, mirth, joy, flattery, ecstasy, affection, animal passion.
Negative: Hate – defiance, disdain, contempt, scorn, jealousy, anger, treachery, revenge, rage.

Positive: Hope – peace, mercy, reverence, ambition, prayer, longing, wishing, trusting, faith.
Negative: Grief – disappointment, regret, sadness, sympathy, melancholy, disconsolation, desolation, despair, frenzy.
Positive: Pride – sacrifice, dignity, triumph, nobility, patriotism, eloquence, solemnity, sublimity, grandeur.
Negative: Shame – anxiety, petulance, humility, repentance.   Guilt – remorse, agony, desperation, intent to murder.
Positive: Resolution – resentment, warning, threatening, challenge, courage, daring, intensity.

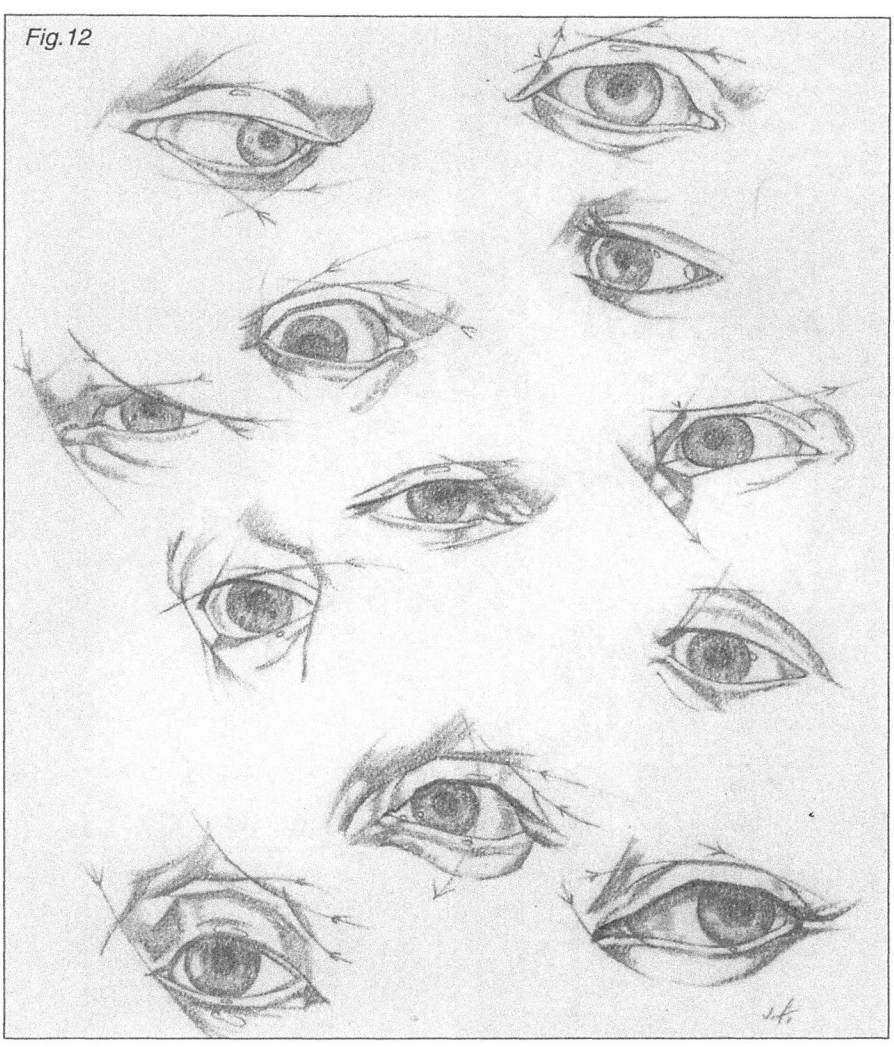

Fig. 12

Negative: Fear – superstition, stealth, apprehension, alarm, fright, awe, terror, horror, frantic fear.
Positive: Excitement – doubt, wonder, perturbation, surprise, bewilderment, amazement, embarrassment.
Negative: Depression – decrepitude of age, willingness of resignation, falling to sleep, dizziness, fainting, pain affecting the nerves, cataleptic trance, purpose of suicide, insanity, madness.

Fig. 13. I have already alluded to the change in the size of the pupil due to the change in the intensity of the light or shift in interest or emotions.

The size of the pupil combined with the position of the eyelids conveys expression to a certain degree but they have to be consistent with the rest of the features. Emotions also stimulate an increase in tears which will give a softer look as well as a degree of translucency to the entire eye – the iris, pupil, cornea and even the highlights.

Shown are some drawings of eyes which convey expression to a greater or lesser degree. This is a difficult thing to do as the eye is isolated and not shown in conjunction with the other features. Nevertheless there are certain positions of the lids in different expressions that you should be aware of.

Fig. 13a. Intense concentration, determination. The emphasis is on the strong line of the upper lid.

Fig. b. Horror, fear, looking downwards. The upper lid is raised revealing the white of the eye.

Figs. c.d. Scrutiny, suspicion. The upper lid lowers and the lower lid raises. The more one scrutinizes someone or something the more the lower lid will rise.

Fig. e. Devious. The upper and lower lids are very close. The eye shifts, never directly looking at you.

Fig. f. Concern. Upper lid slightly below top of pupil.

Fig. g. Amazement. The upper lid rises above the top of the pupil.

Fig. h. In this drawing the white of the eye is shown on three sides of the iris. This is a congenital condition and does not convey any definite expression. Some very famous people in history have had this condition.

Fig. i. Intense excitement. As excitement increases the upper lid rises showing more and more of the white of the eye. A step past this stage would show the white of the eye showing below the iris as well as above it.

Fig. j. A drooping upper lid signifying sorrow and despair.

Fig. k. The eyeball turned upwards. An expression of one devoid of rationality.

Fig. l. Intense concentration. The upper lid rests on the top of the pupil, the lower lid is slightly raised.

Fig. m. An increase of interest is shown by the eyelid rising above the pupil instead of resting on the top of it.

Fig. n. Profile view signifying a contemplative mood.

Fig. o. Cheerfulness. Lids slightly pinched at outer corner.

Fig. p. Concern. The upper lid tangents with the top of the iris. When concern turns to fear the eyelid will go higher as in *Fig. 13i.*

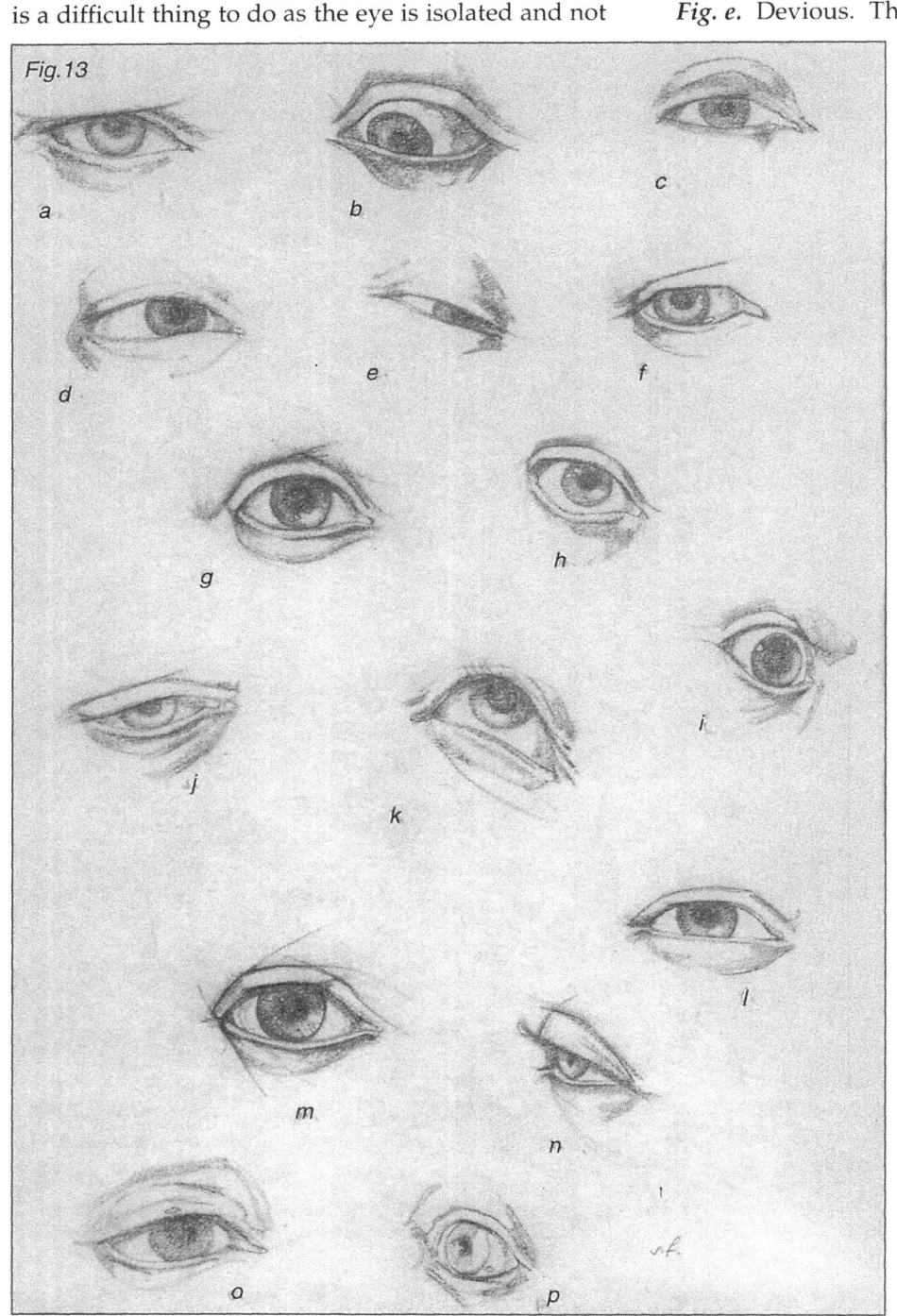

Fig. 13

a b c d e f g h i j k l m n o p

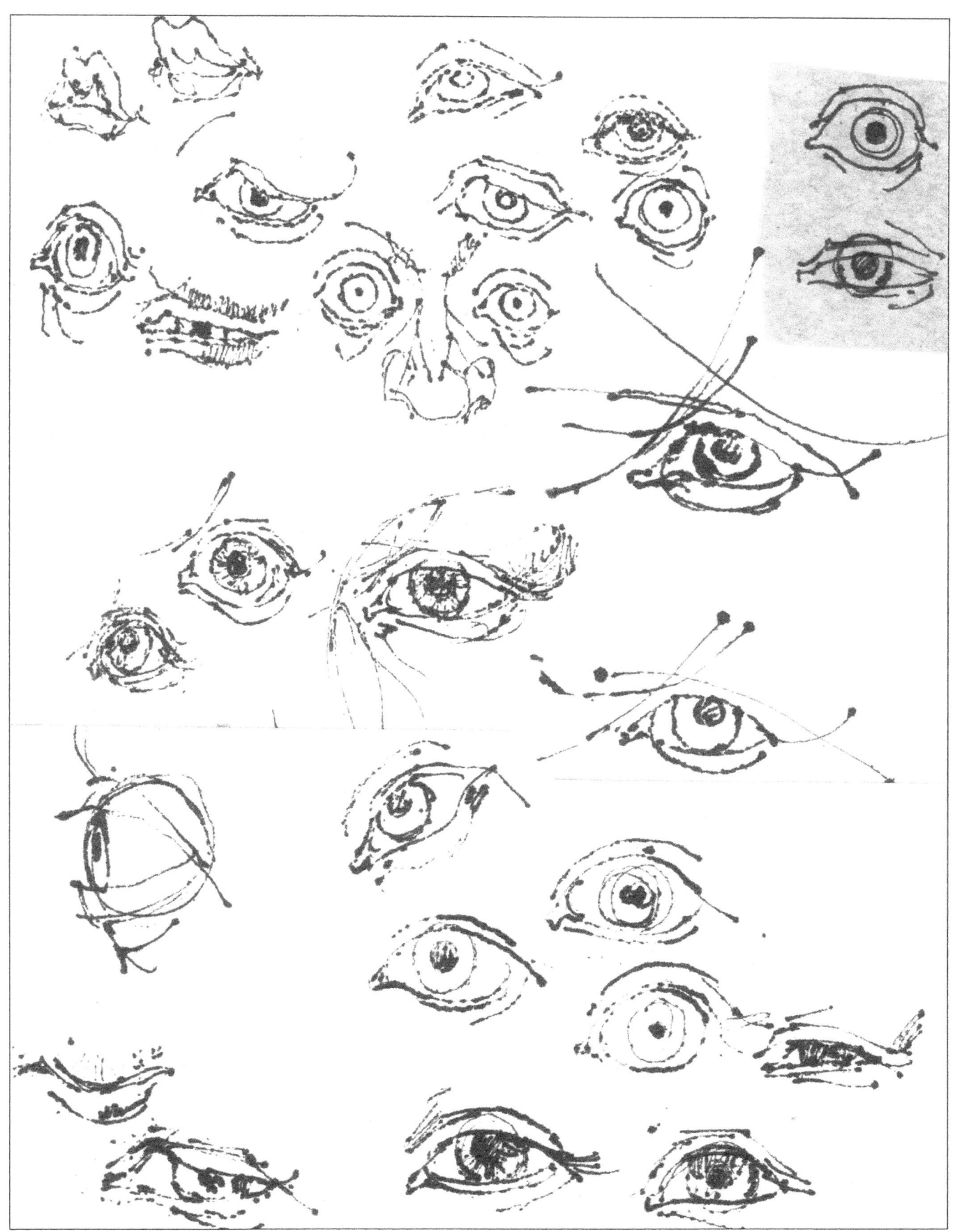

CONSTRUCTION AND PLANES OF THE LIPS AND MOUTH

There is an oft-quoted saying by a famous artist who said that a portrait is a painting that has something wrong with the mouth. This is quite true as the mouth and lips are more complex and difficult to draw and paint than it seems and the slightest line or value in the wrong place is immediately apparent, especially to relatives and other art critics. The use of lipstick also complicates the shape and form of the lips as it masks the basic forms. However if the lips are overdone or over-modeled they will also look wrong.

These drawings and diagrams are meant to familiarize you with the lines, forms, planes and the many variations of the size and shapes of the lips. Following are four steps showing how to construct the forms and planes of the lips.

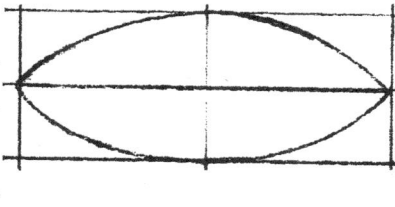

Fig. 1a. Draw a rectangle and divide it into halves for simplicity. Next draw an oval shape going from corner to corner of th

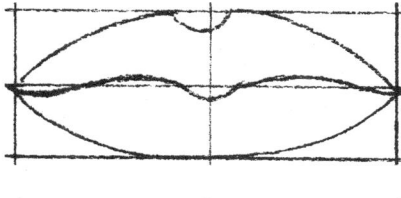

Fig. b. Draw the outlines of the upper and lower lip. In this case both are equal in width.

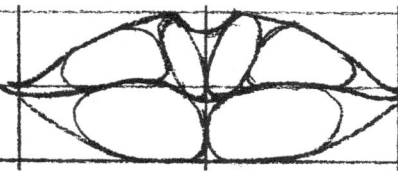

Fig. c. The basic forms of the lips are added.

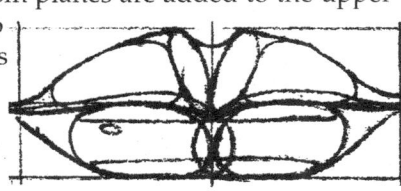

Fig. d. Bottom planes are added to the upper and lower lip. A top plane and sideplanes are also added on the lower lip.

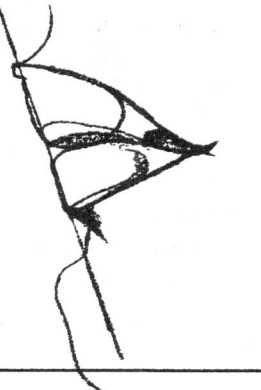

Fig. e. The same planes and forms shown in profile. Note the angle of the lips.

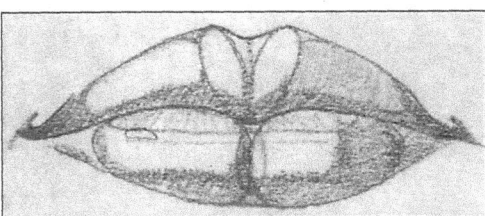

Fig. f. Light and shade added to the forms and planes.

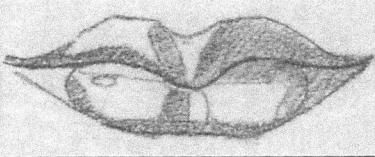

Fig. g. The planes and forms are the same but the position of the light is changed resulting in a different arrangement of light and shade.

It is easier to get the proper curvature of the mouth by drawing or visualizing a straight line from corner to corner of the lips rather than drawing a curved line right off hoping it ends in the right place.

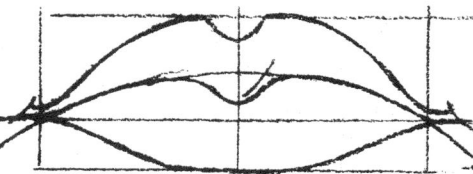

Fig. 2a. Even though the lower lip is thicker than the upper lip the upper part of the rectangle is wider than the lower part of the rectangle. A sweeping curved line, shown with arrowheads, goes from one corner of the mouth to the other corner. The upper and lower lips are then drawn.

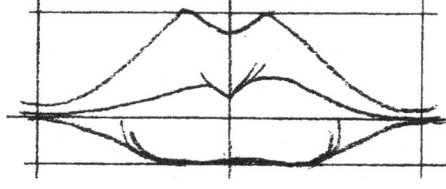

Fig. b. Lips are by no means always absolutely symmetrical. The right hand side of the lower lip is fatter than the left hand side. This is judged from the deviation from the horizontal line.

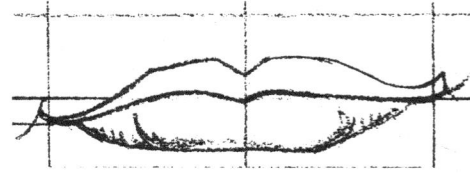

Fig. c. It happens occasionally that one side of the mouth will be lower than the other side. Here we see the mouth starting lower on the left hand side of the drawing. It could just as well be the reverse.

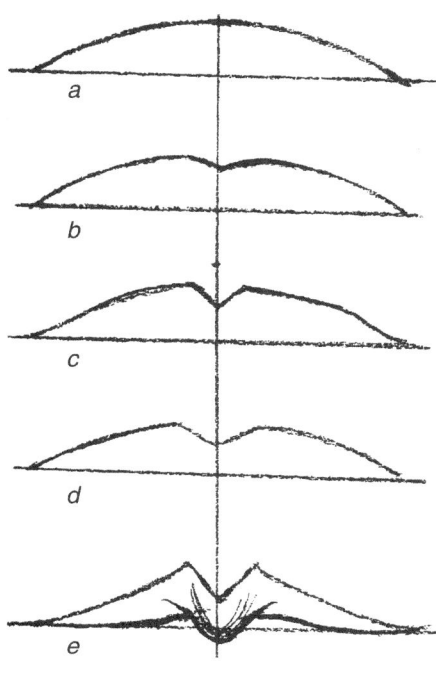

Figs. 3a.b.c.d.e. There is a tremendous variety of the shape of the dip in the center of the upper lip. Here are just five examples that go from a perfect curvature across the top to a slight dip to a very severe dip. One of the most important things to look for in lips is the ratio of the upper one to the lower one. This is frequently overlooked and should be one of the first things to be considered.

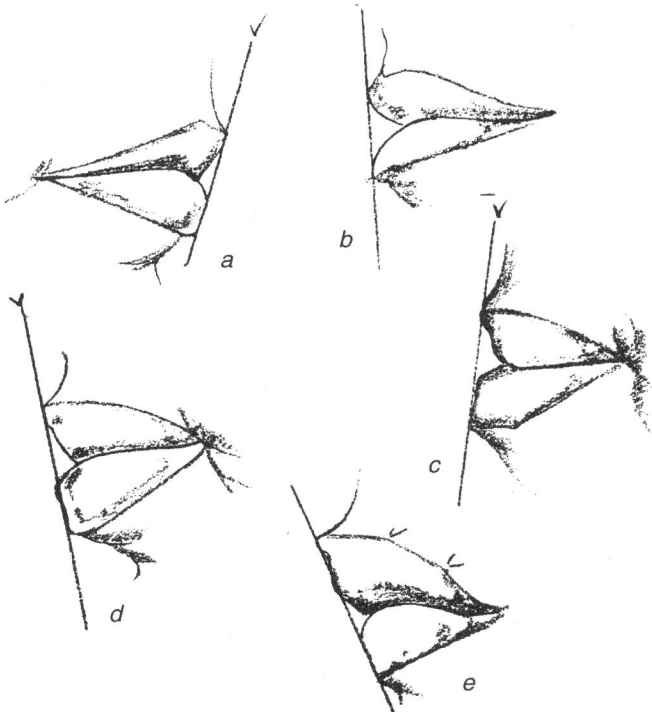

Figs. 5a.b.c.d.e. A series of drawings showing the different angles of the lips in profile.

Fig. 4a. The lower lip is wider than the upper lip.

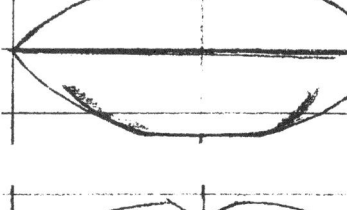

Fig. b. Upper and lower lips are of equal width.

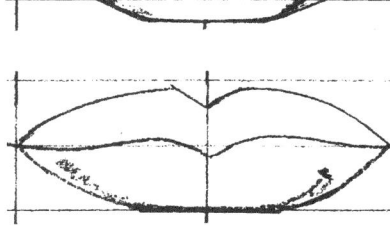

Fig. c. Upper lip wider than lower lip.

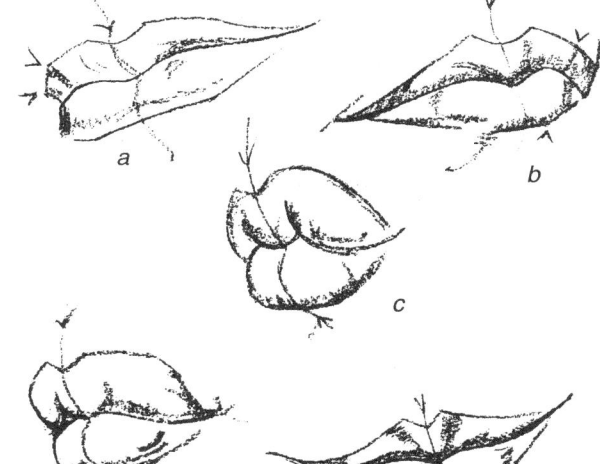

Fig. d. Both upper and lower lips shown narrower than average.

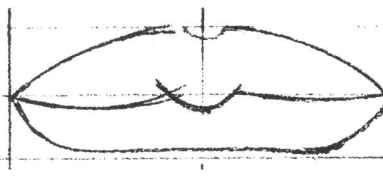

Figs. 6a.b.c.d.e. Center lines will aid you to draw correctly as well as to define the contours of the lips. Arrowheads point to important corners or turning points on the lips. In **Fig. 6e.** we are looking down on lips which curve to conform to the skull. Here we see more of the top of the lower lid.

Fig. e. Both upper and lower lips shown wider than average.

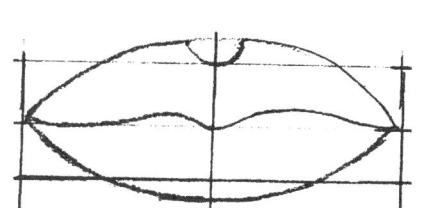

Fig. 7. Contour lines showing the basic form of the upper and lower lip. Keep this in mind when you are modeling

Fig.8

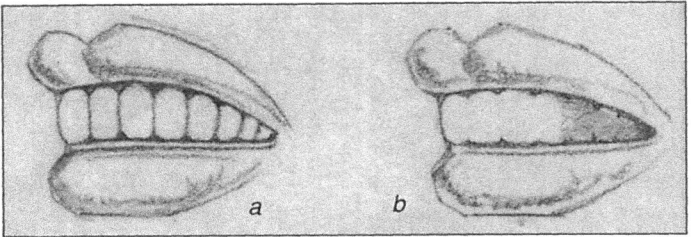

a *b*

Figs. 8a.b. There is a right way and a wrong way to draw the teeth when the lips are parted. *Fig. 8a.* is the *wrong way*. The individual will look like a skeleton or a carved pumpkin if drawn as shown.

Fig. b. is the more sensible way to draw the teeth. The teeth are suggested by slight indications of their dimensions at top and bottom. All of the teeth should be considered one curved form and modeled with value or color or both.

Fig. 9. Stylized shading on the forms of the lips to more clearly define the beginning and the end of the tones. It is frequently over-looked that immediately below the lower lip is a thin band of light followed by a darker underplane.

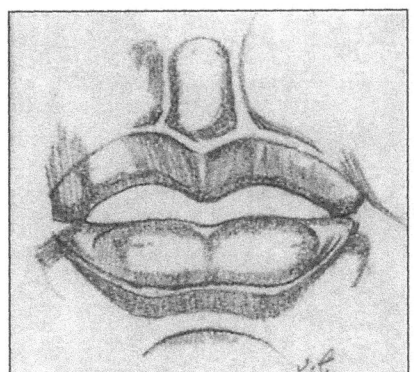

Fig.10

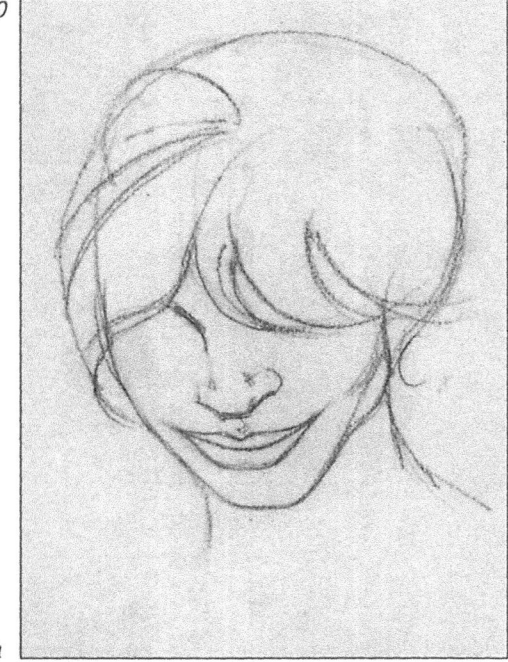

a

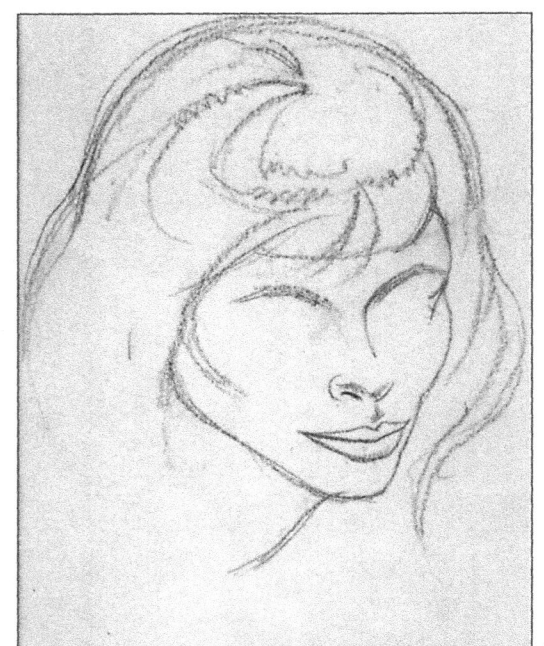

b

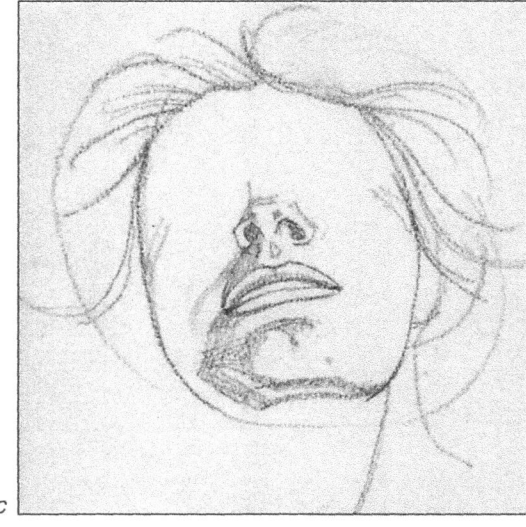

c

Fig. 10a. The lips must always appear as going around the skull. When the head is tilted down the upper lip will appear narrower than the lower lip. Since we are seeing the top of the lower lip it will appear fuller.

Fig. b. Three-quarter view, head slightly looking down.

Fig. c. Looking up. Here we are seeing more of the bottom of the upper lip so it appears wider than the thinner lower lip. Note the arcs of lines curving upwards on the chin, lips and nose.

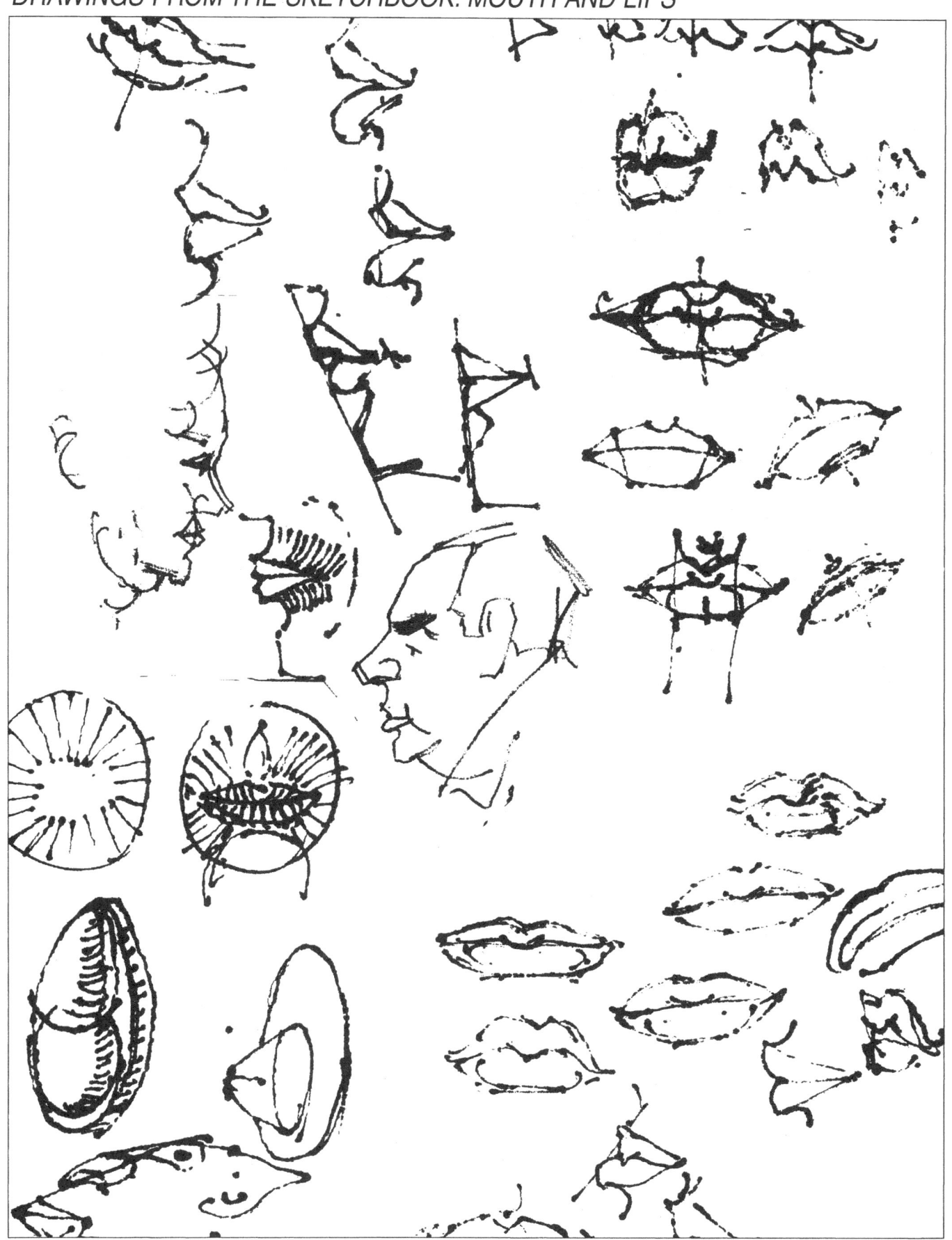

PLANES AND FORMS OF THE NOSE

With some people the nose is very prominent and therefore it is important to the representation of their character. With others it is hardly noticeable. In some instances you may want to emphasize the nose and in other instances such as portraits you may want to underplay the nose – usually because you want to feature the eyes and mouth.

Now you can learn much about the nose by observation and practice but you may overlook some very obvious important things. The purpose of these drawings then is to make you aware of the forms and planes and other fine points of the drawing of the nose. They will help speed up your learning and to observe things more accurately.

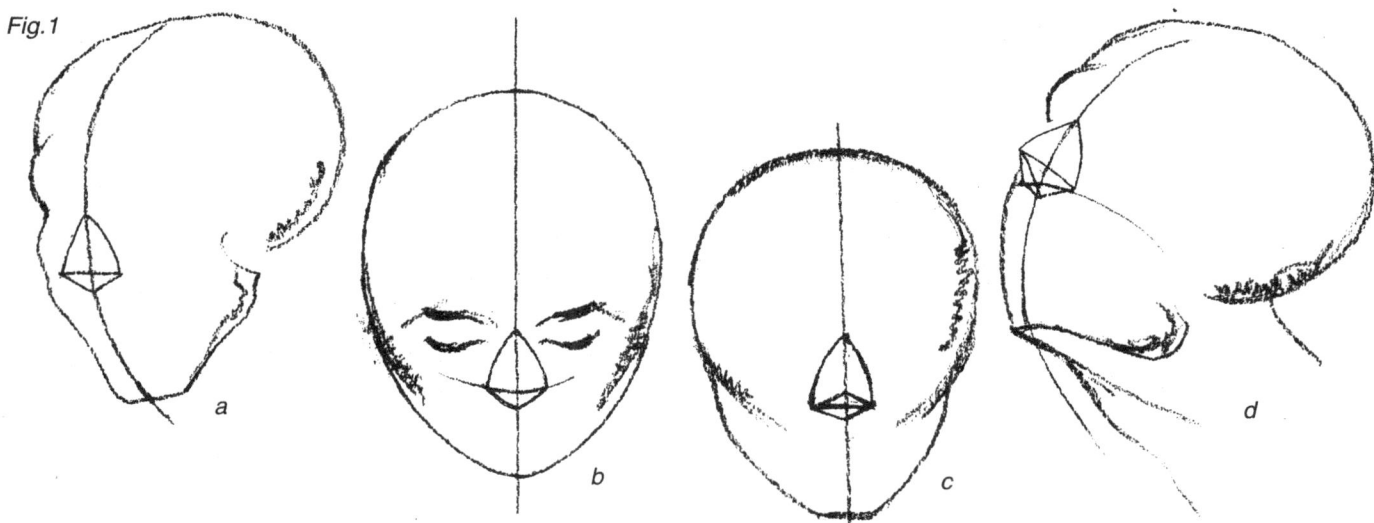

Fig. 1

Fig. 1a. Before any details of the nose are drawn it should be considered as a triangular form that is divided with a bottom plane. The center line of this form is on the same center line of the skull. Here we see the nose form in three-quarter view

Fig. b. Looking down. Note the curve of the bottom plane.

Fig. c. Level, straight on.

Fig. d. Three-quarter view looking up. Again watch the curvature of the bottom plane that follows the curvature of the skull.

PLANES OF THE NOSE, PROFILE

Fig. 2a. The nose in profile is a triangular shaped form that has a bottom plane, (shown shaded). This bottom plane is designated by a line which goes from a point on the ball of the nose to a point on the lower corner of the nostril.

Fig. b. The basic lines and shape of the nose.

Fig. c. The addition of the basic forms and planes. Start with the ball of the nose and then add the wing of the nostril. The shape of the nasal bone is estimated by how much it deviates from the straight line. The large lower plane is subdivided into a small plane which contains the nostril. Reflected light is frequently seen on this plane. Smaller top and side planes are added.

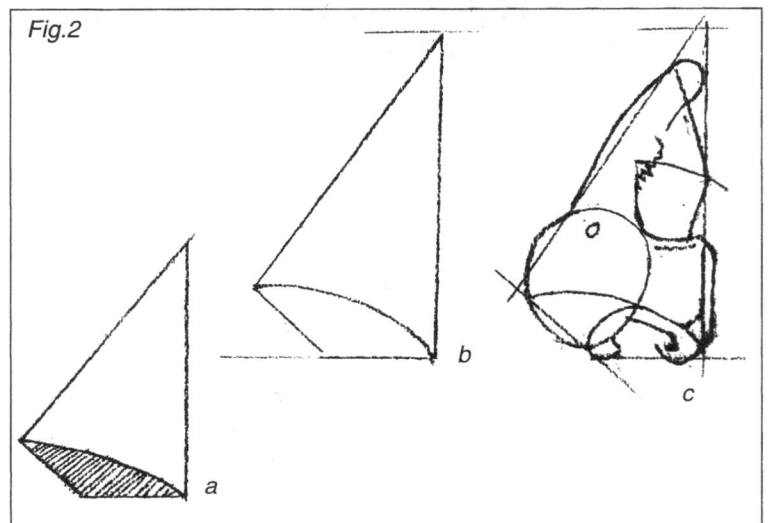

Fig. 2

PLANES OF THE NOSE, FRONT VIEW

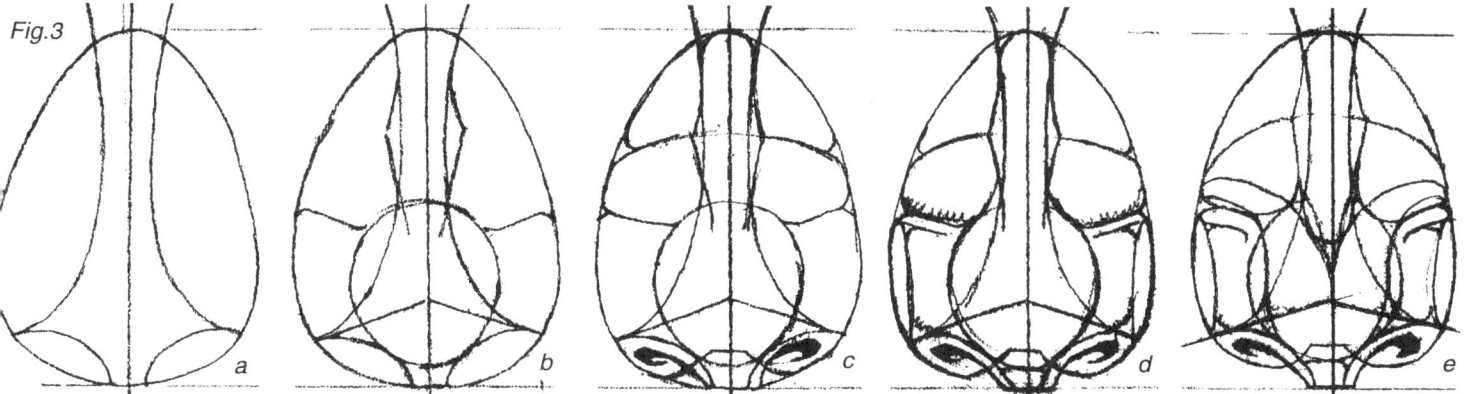

Fig.3

Fig. 3a. Start with the basic oval nose form. Shown are two lines that originate from below the eyebrows and that are the approximate width of the nasal bone. These lines terminate at the corners of the top of the bottom plane.

Fig. b. The ball of the nose, the wings of the nostrils and the shape of the nasal bone are added. There is a point on the ball of the nose from which one draws to the tops of the bottom plane. Refer to profile view **Fig. 2a.** to clarify this plane.

Fig. c. The section of the nose form above the nostrils is divided into upper and lower planes. Nostrils are added and related forming another bottom plane.

Fig. d. Sideplanes and top planes are added to the wings of the nostrils.

Fig. e. Finishing with the addition of smaller planes and forms. Whatever you add should be related in some manner.

PLANES OF THE NOSE IN LIGHT AND SHADE

Fig. 4a. Side view. The shaded area shows the large bottom plane of the nose.

Fig. b. Shading on the sideplane of the wing of the nostril and on the lower half of the cartilage of the nose form.

Figs. 5a.b.c.d.e. Front view. Shaded areas show planes of the nose and how they are arrived at. Depending on the position of the light different planes will go into shadow while others will become top planes. The change of value will be at the lines shown.

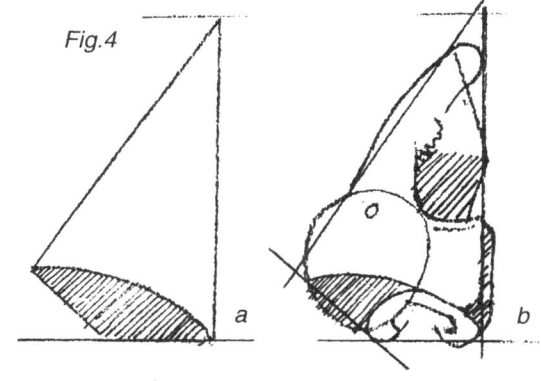

Fig.4

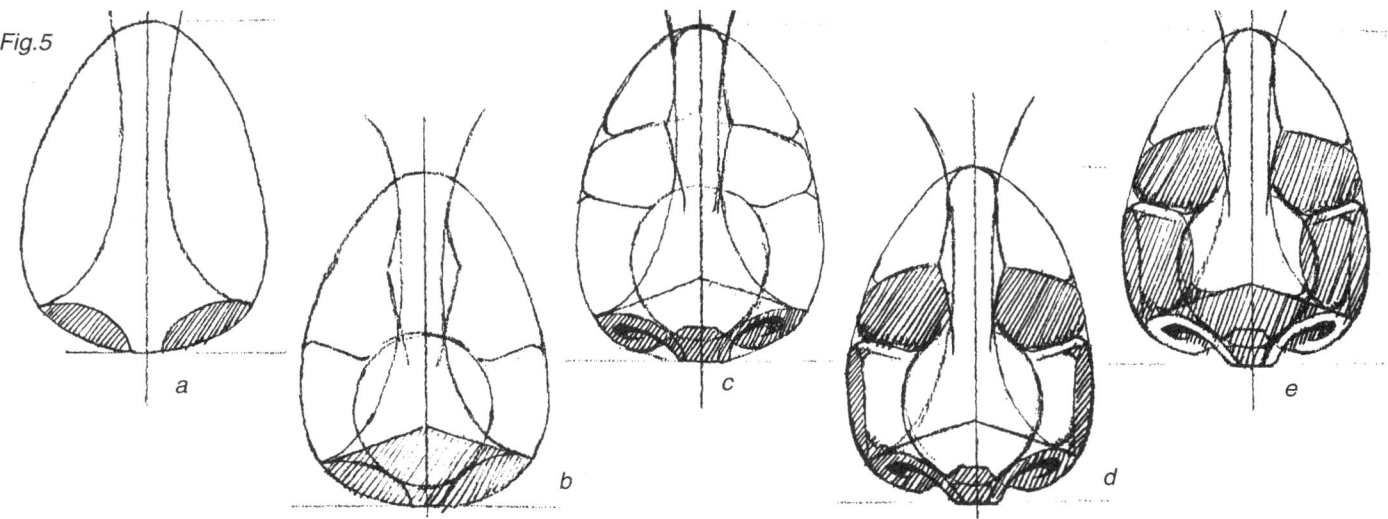

Fig.5

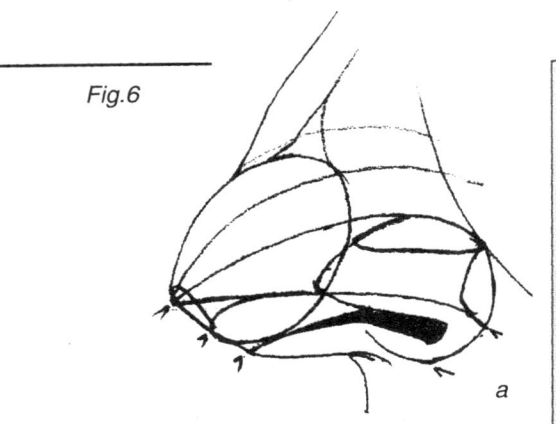

Fig.6

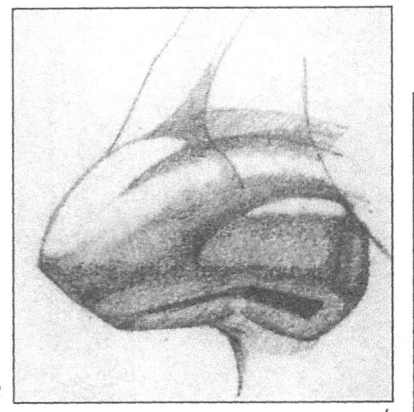

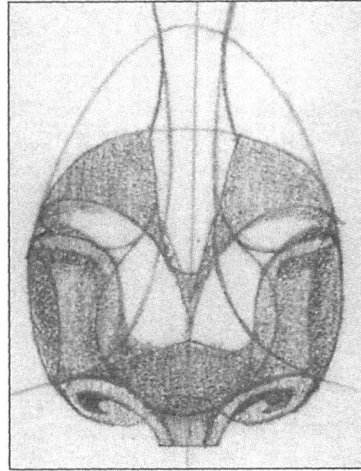

Figs. 6a.b.c. The fatty tissues of alar and the greater alar cartilage form a greater pronounced "ball" of the nose. These schematic drawings show the profile and front view of their planes. Small arrowheads designate the points where the lines of the planes start. **Fig. b.** shows shading along these lines and **Fig. c.** shows the planes of the same nose in front view.

Figs. 7a.b.c. These three drawings show how the commonly perceived individual forms of the nose are intricately related to and conform to the basic nose form. **Fig. c.** shows the accurate positioning of the highlights on the nasal bone and on the ball of the nose.

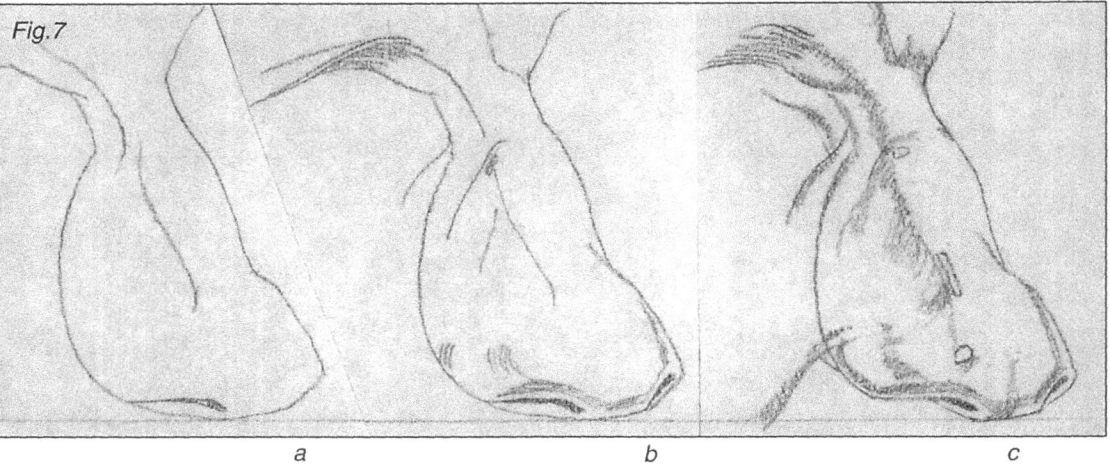

Fig.7

Figs. 8a.b.c.d.e.f.g.h. Too little attention is paid to the shape of the nostrils. Perhaps it is because they are usually hidden in shadow. There are more varieties of nostrils than you can imagine. Eight different types are shown here. Since nostrils conform to the shapes of the fat and cartilage of the nose forms they have to be perceived and drawn correctly.

You should be aware of two things. One of them is the angle of the nostril as shown in **Figs. 8a.**

and b. Notice how the lines go from the front corner to the back corner of the nostril. The next thing to decide is the shape or angularity of the nostril. There is a short side and long side to this angle. Sometimes the short side is towards the front of the nose with the long side going towards the back of the nose and sometimes the long side goes towards the front of the nose with the short side towards the rear of the nose.

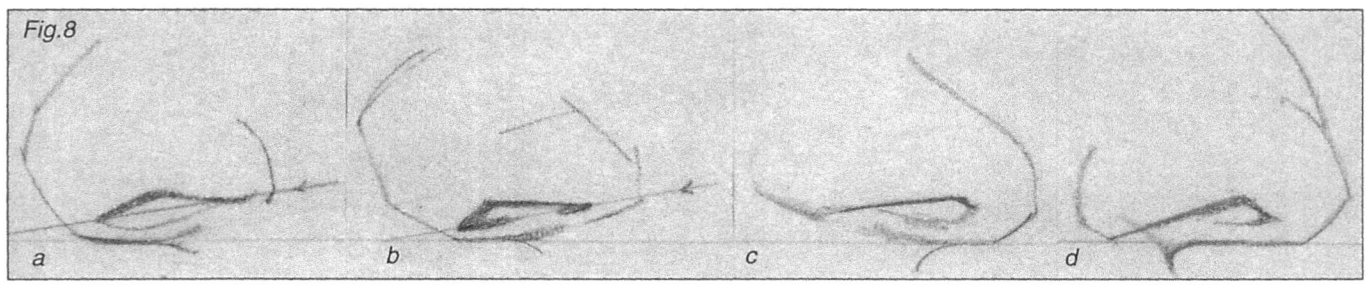

Fig.8

Figs. 9a.b.c.d.e.f.g.h.i.j.k.l. A series of different sizes and shapes of noses. The arrowheads point to where the line changes angle in most examples. In other examples the arrowheads show sweeping lines of alignment which put forms in perspective, *(Figs.9h. j.),* or relate form to form, *(Figs. 9a.b.c.d.h. and i.).*

The small ovals or circles represent highlights. Notice how they fall on lines that connect corners of forms such as in *Figs. 9f.h.j. and l.*

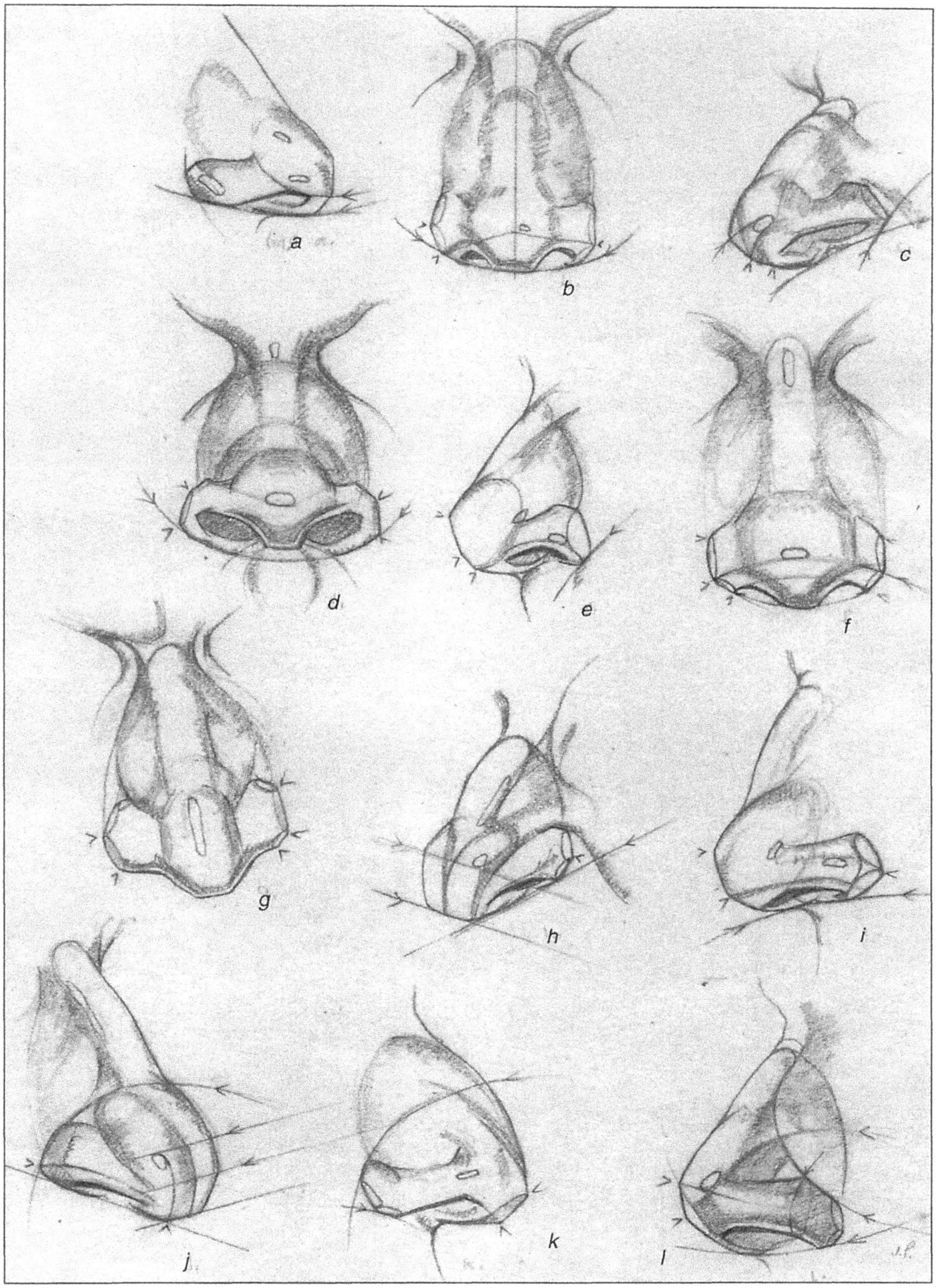

Fig.8

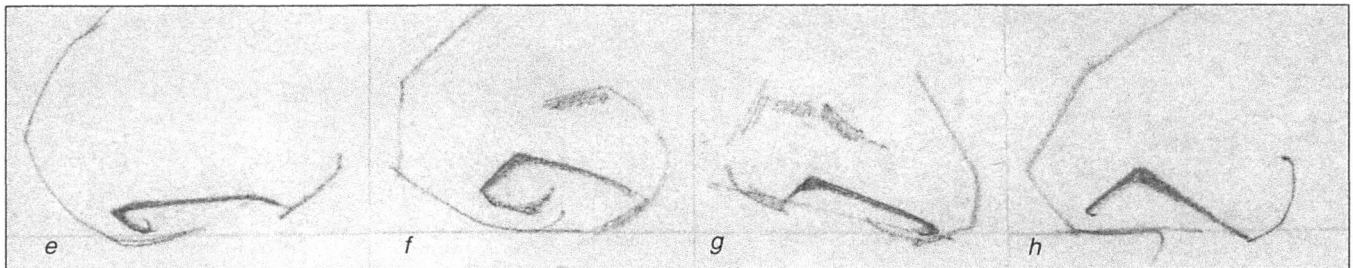

Fig.10

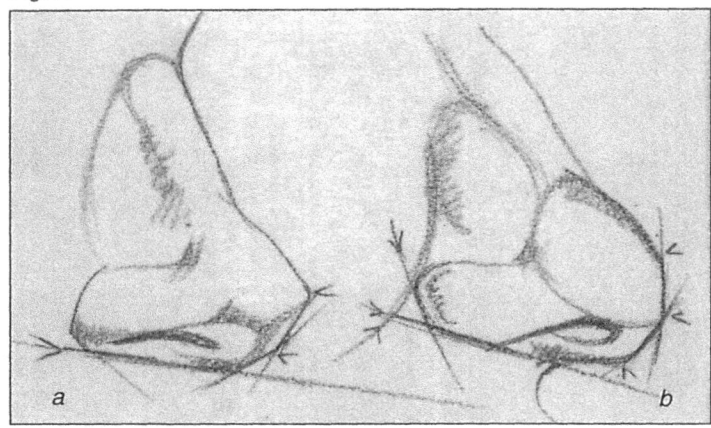

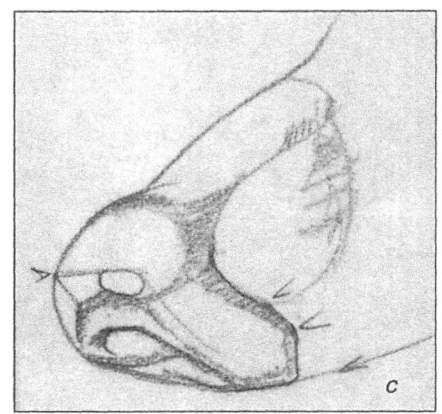

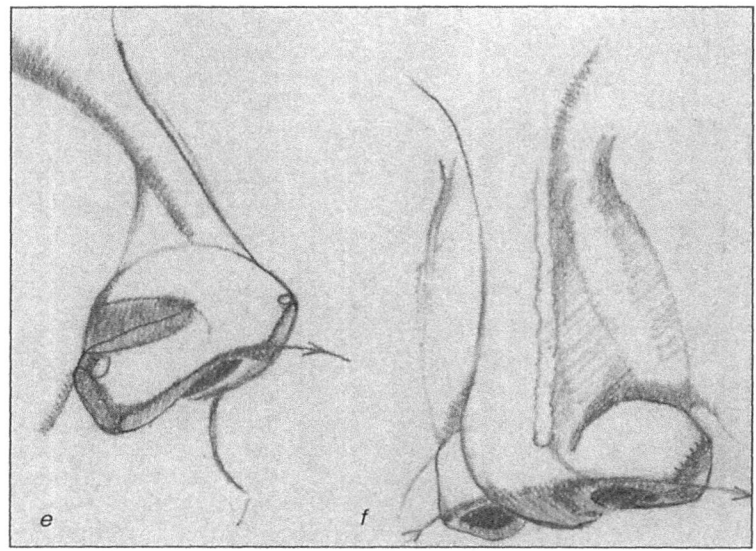

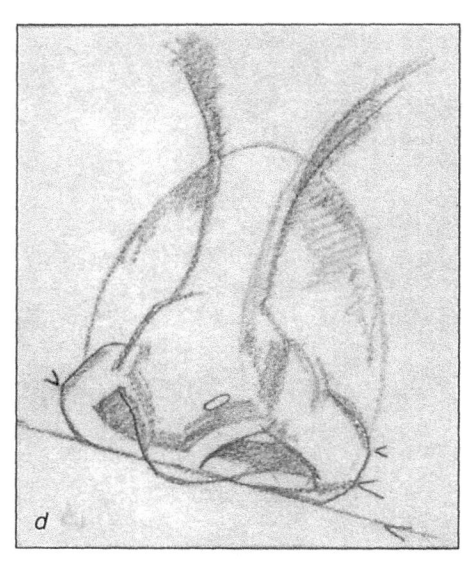

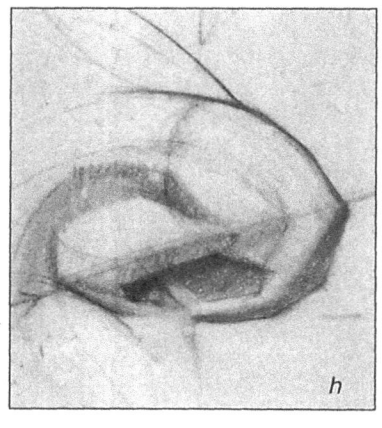

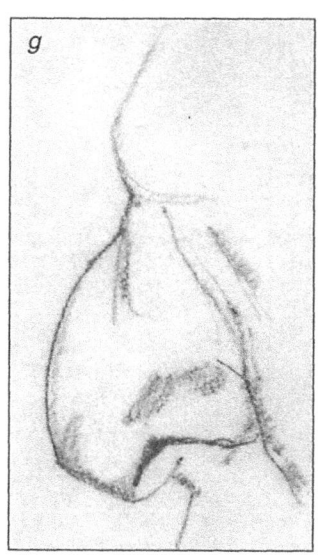

Figs. 10a.b.c.d.e.f.g.h. Further drawings of different types of noses pointing out the very subtle angles of the forms and the positioning of the highlights. **Figs. 10e. and f.** are examples of a flattish Mongolian type of nose, profile and three-quarter view. **Fig. g.** is an example of the nasal bone going in the opposite direction. There are dozens of variations of this kind of nose. **Fig. h.** shows well defined forms and planes of the lower nose.

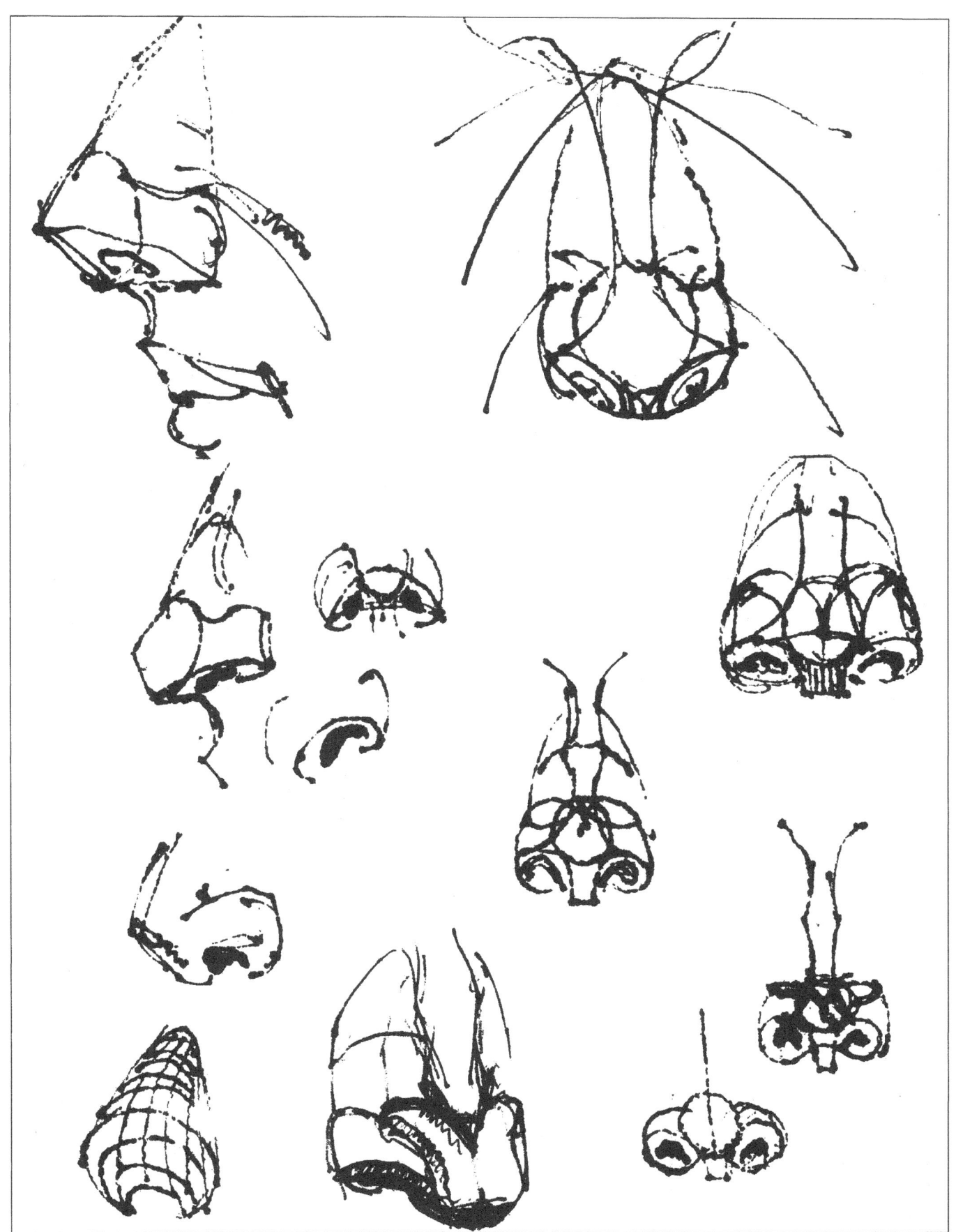

FORMS AND PLANES OF THE EAR

The ear is often neglected by artists as it plays no part in expression and is often hidden by the hair of the head. It is also not readily admitted that the ear is a very complex structure which is really difficult to draw and paint. Personally I find ears interesting – filled with many subtle forms and planes and quite a challenge to do correctly.

There is just too much variation in the design and structure of ears to make a sort of standardized version of them or some gimmicky symbol that all ears could conform to. However there are a few important things to remember which will aid you when drawing them. One is the angle of the ear on the head. Generally this angle is parallel to the angle of the nose although I have seen it on occasions tilting forwards while the angle of the nose was tilting backwards. The other thing to remember is that the top of the ear aligns with the top of the eyebrows and the bottom of it aligns with the bottom of the nose.

Once the angle of the ear is determined the big outside shape is drawn. It consists of two bowl like shapes, a large one, and a small one representing the ear lobe. The next step is to draw the outer rim and the shape of the ear lobe. Once established the inner forms are then drawn to which planes with their values are added. The same rules about forms and planes concerning the other features also apply to the ear. They are small and very refined but are there nevertheless.

Fig. 1a. The start. A straight line or an angle to which is added two rounded, general outside shapes.

Fig. b. The shape of the ear lobe is defined. The outer rim, called the helix, is drawn. The rounded lines now are angled off a bit.

Fig. c. The inner forms of the ear, the antihelix, are added. The hollow of the ear is called the concha. This is protected by a little flap of cartilage called the tragus. All the lines are now angled with greater accuracy.

Fig. d. Small precise planes are added and properly shaded. Notice how they start at the corners of the form. These are also subtle, delicate forms that are modeled. This drawing shows wedge like shapes and rounded shapes that are related in a harmonious whole.

Fig.1

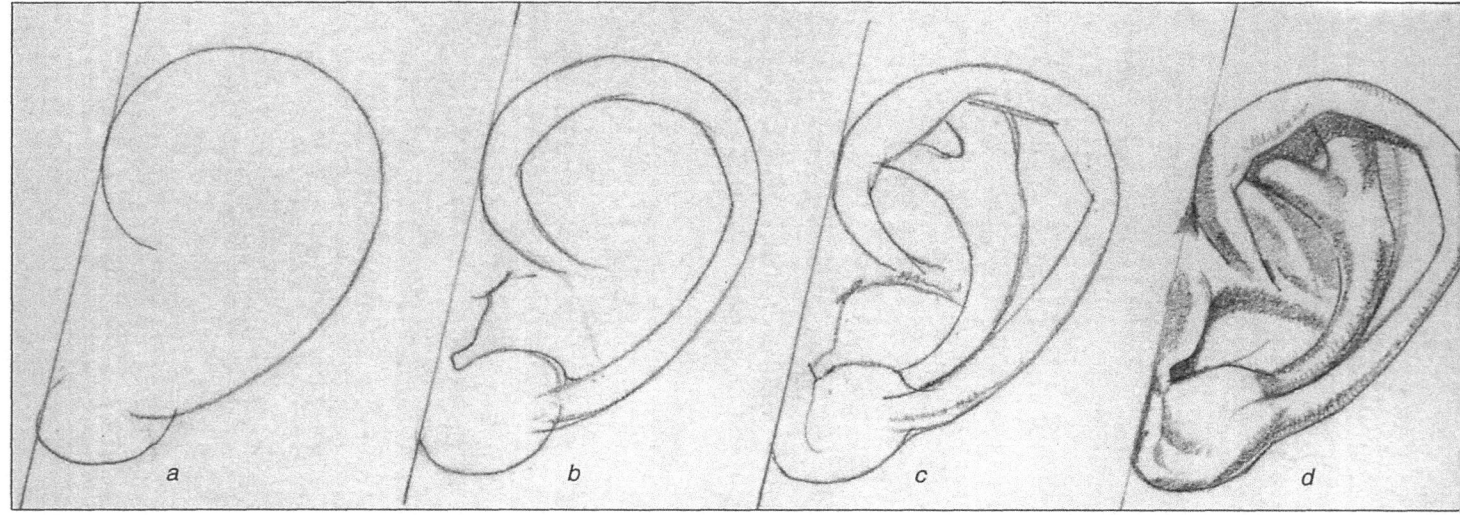

a   b   c   d

Fig.2

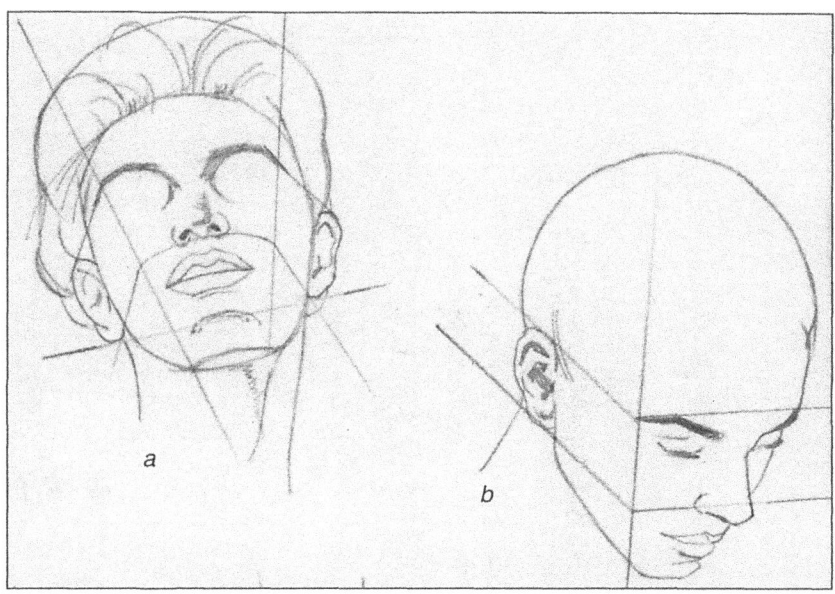

a

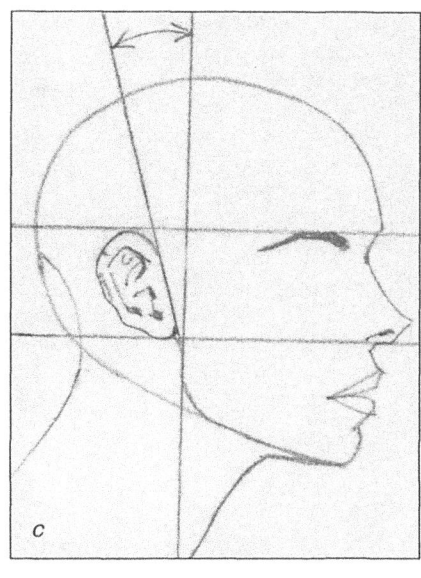

b

c

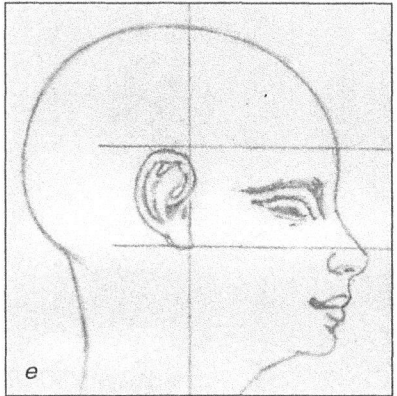

e

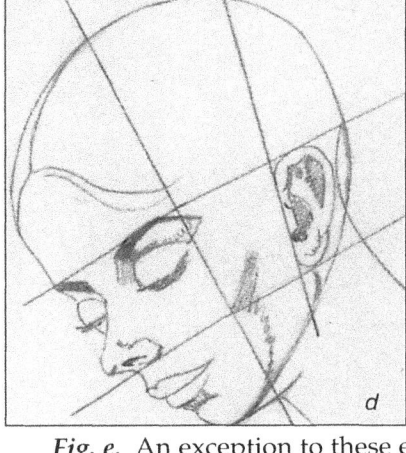

d

The drawings, **Figs. 2a.b.c. and d.** show how one uses lines to properly position the ears on the head in various positions.

Fig. 2a. Looking up. Note alignment of the lower ear with a horizontal line that goes through the top of the chin and lines that angle downwards from the sideplanes.

Fig. b. Looking down.

Fig. c. Straight profile, the angle of the ear is determined by its deviation from a perpendicular.

Fig. d. Three-quarter view, looking down.

Fig. e. An exception to these examples is found in many of the ancient Egyptian sculptures. For some unknown reason, to me at least, they placed the ear very high on the head. Generally the bottom of the ear lines up somewhere with the top of the ball of the nose and the top of the ear on a line far above the eyebrow.

Figs. 3a.b.c.d.e.f.g. These drawings show some of the many varieties of ear shapes. There are more straight lines in the drawing of ears than you generally imagine. Some of these lines are shown with arrowheads on them.

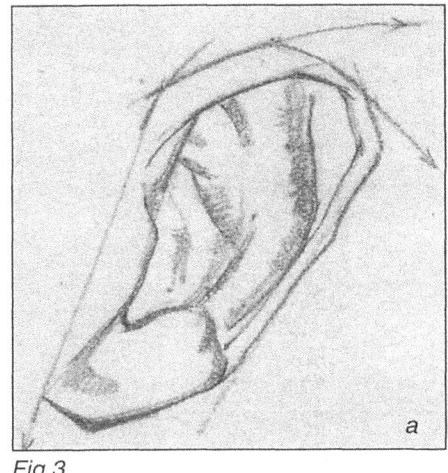

Fig.3

a

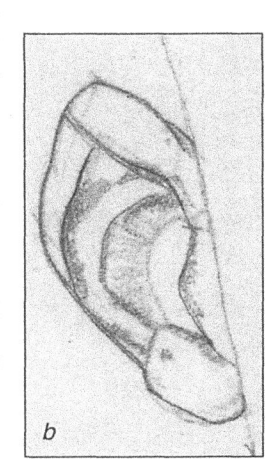

b

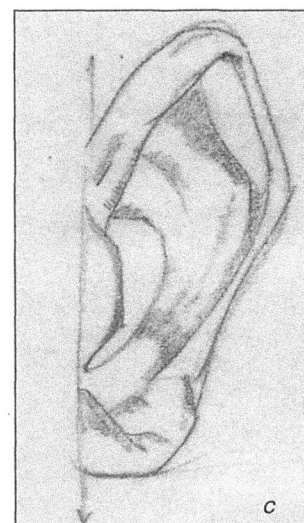

c

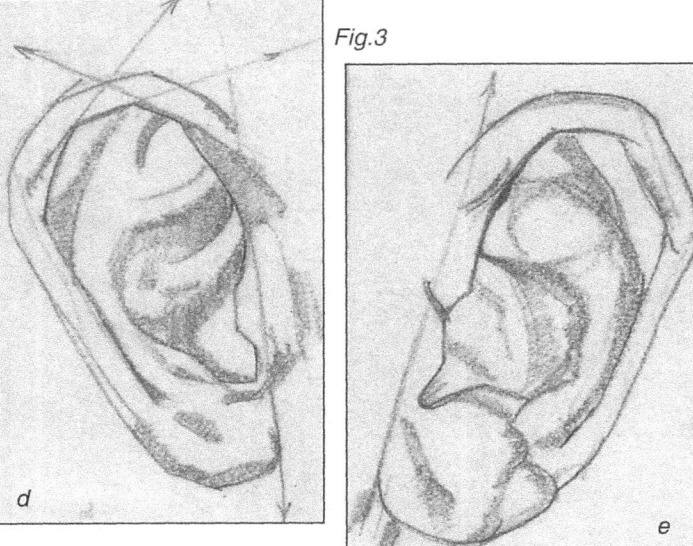

Fig.3

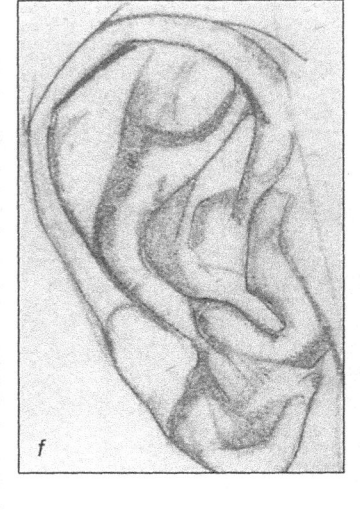

e

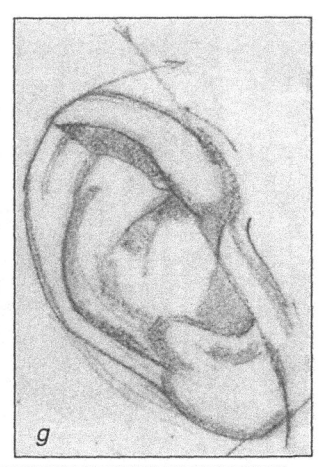

f

g

d

Figs. 4a.b.c.d.e.f. Ear lobes can vary tremendously, from almost nonexistent to huge hanging ones. They can also be very smooth or have many little forms and wrinkles on them. It seems to me that ears are more complex and varied than the eyes, nose or mouth. Here we see only six examples of the infinitely varied ear lobes

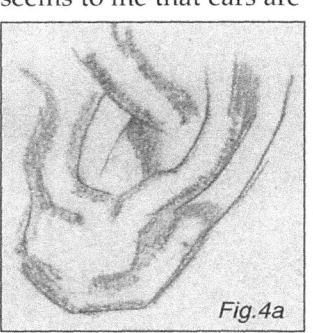

Fig.4a

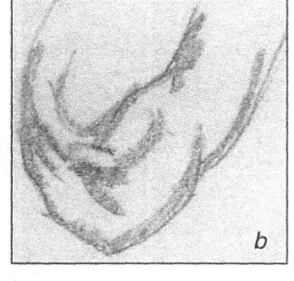

b

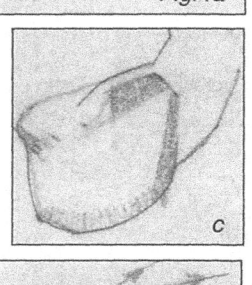

c

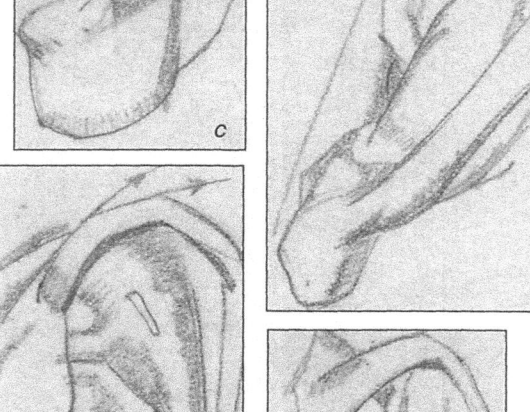

d

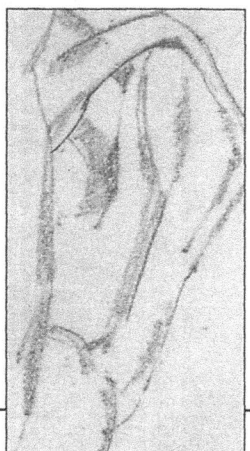

e

f

CHARACTER

At this point I feel I must say something about getting the "character" of the individual. One may obtain a likeness of a person by carefully observing the distance between all parts of the face and the straightness or curvature of its lines. However this likeness may not be satisfactory to the artist, something will be missing and there will be an inherent weakness. What is missing is the essential meaning and character of the particular person. The reason for this is that all parts of the head are treated equally without any emphasis on particular musculature, forms, planes and the directions they take.

One must have an empathy with the forms and planes of the face, how they merge and mass with each other and in what direction they're going. One must sense the lines of force,(growth), and decide which are the strongest. *Observe the order in which these forms and planes impress you and emphasize them in that order.* Keep going back to the major masses and follow them to where they are going. Once these major masses of forms and planes are stated the lesser ones will fall into place.

The artist should study the face he wants to portray for a long time before committing a stroke. As I have said he should have an empathy with the face and let the dominant forms, planes, features or lines of action impress him. You will find that there are certain qualities which should be exaggerated, their uniqueness emphasized simply because these things impress you first and therefore should impress the viewer first. Things that are less impressive are drawn or painted subordinated to the major "idea" of the head.

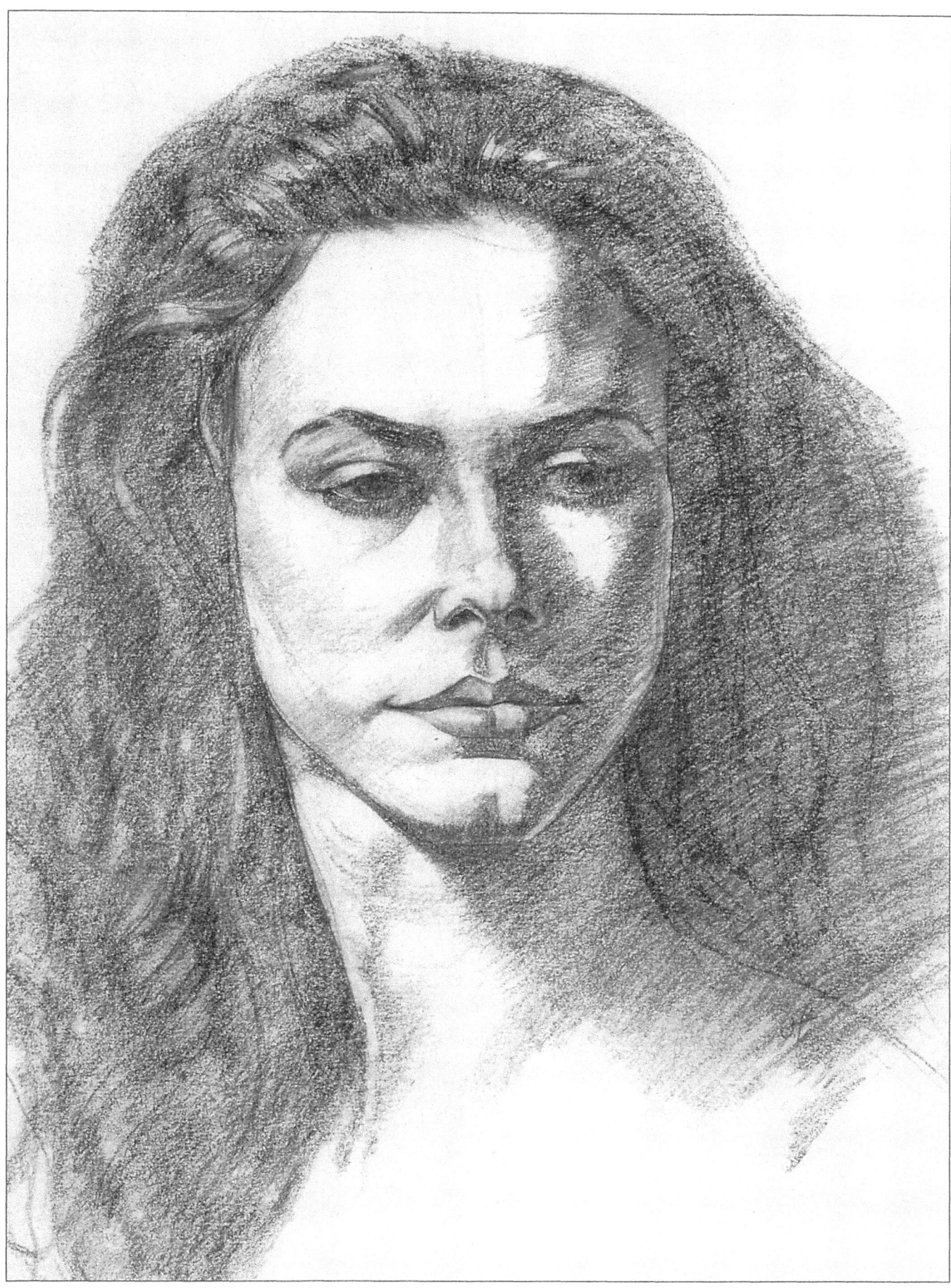

NINETEEN

THE CONSTRUCTION, DRAWING AND RENDERING OF HAIR AND BEARDS

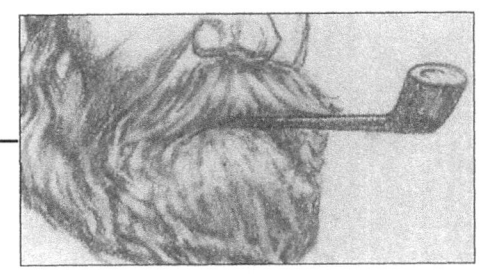

In almost all cases a student, when drawing a face, will spend all of his time on trying to get the features accurate. He pays little or no attention to the hair or hairline. This usually results in a drawing or painting in which there is a perception that there is no skull under the hair or it is perceived subliminally to be the wrong size or shape. To avoid this it is obvious that the proper size and shape of the entire skull must be correctly established first and then the masses of hair drawn upon it. When it is pointed out you will see that the hairline breaks very definitely on the planes of the head. *The planes will show you the point where the hairline changes direction and that point will show you where the plane is.* Thus the two confirm each other and will give you greater accuracy and unity of the whole. Refresh your memory of the planes and forms of the head described in the previous chapters

Fig. 1a. In this drawing the "widow's peak" is on the center line. The hairline is shown breaking on the first and second sideplanes.

Fig. b. Hair parted in the middle and brushed to both sides.

Fig. c. Hair parted on the individual's left side on the secondary sideplane and breaking on the first sideplane.

Fig. d. An almost bald head. The hair keeps retreating to the rear of the skull holding out on the first sideplanes.

Fig. e. The hair is parted on the first sideplane of the individual's left side.

Fig. f. When baldness starts the hair will recede between the first and secondary sideplanes. The center part of the hair will eventually start receding towards the rear of the skull.

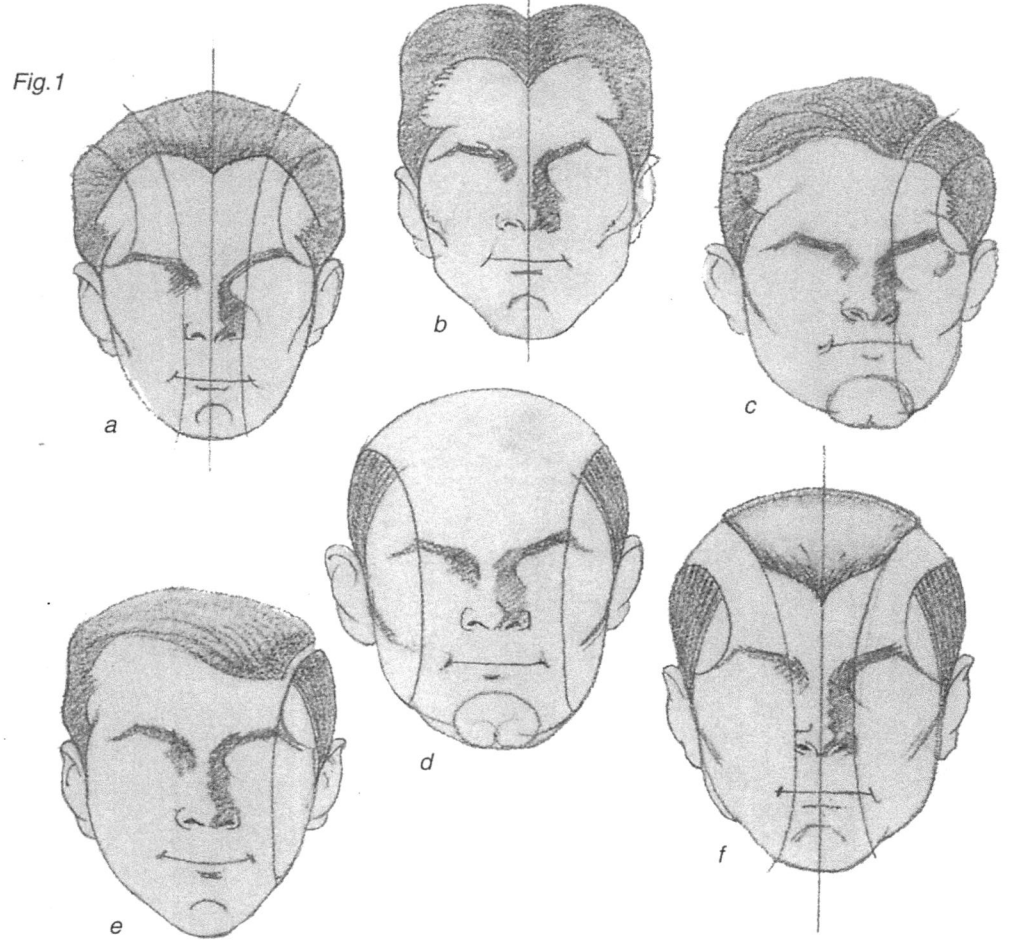

Fig. 1

a

b

c

d

e

f

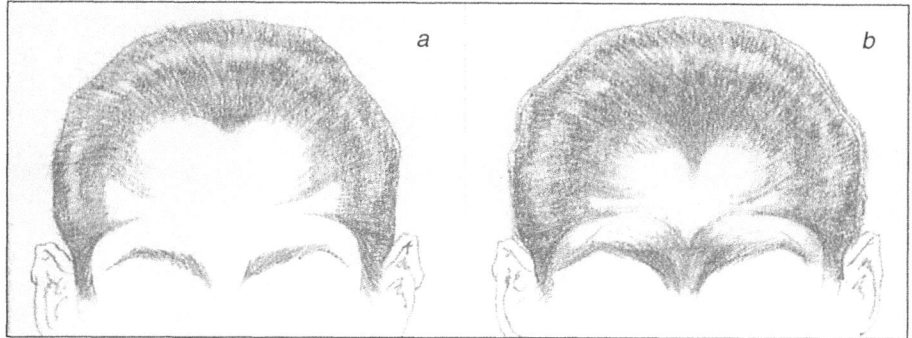
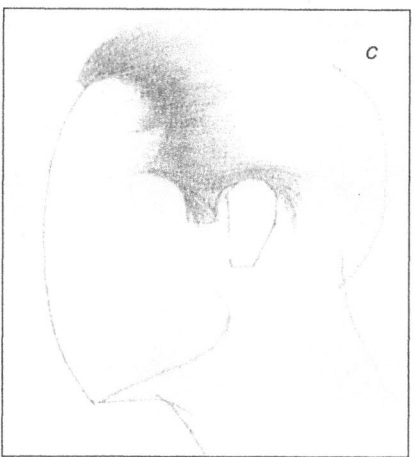

Figs. 2a.c. One can see in some individuals hair which seems to march onto the frontal lobes as shown in the front and profile view.

Fig. 2b. This is my imaginary, hypothetical version of how the hair may have covered the forehead of humanoids many thousands of years ago. The hair of the eyebrows would connect and grow upwards onto and along the brow ridge while other hair would converge on the frontal lobes leaving only a small area of skin uncovered. I conjecture that as time went on the hair retreated outwards and upwards to the present positions. Probably the forehead sloped back at a steep angle and the brow ridge was more prominent. Even today one can observe indications of this hair growth on some individuals.

FACIAL HAIR

Facial hair, that of beards, moustaches and sideburns also conform and relate to the forms and planes of the head. The following seven drawings show some examples which should increase your perception of where facial hair begins and ends. Design the shapes and treat them as any other solid form as regards light and shade.

Fig. 3a. Showing a moustache following the curvature of the form of the teeth cylinder.

Fig. b. Hair below the lower lip and top of the chin falls between the secondary sideplanes.

Fig. c. Here we see the chin whiskers starting at the middle of the chin form.

Fig. d. Sideburns and whiskers follow the zygomatic arch and terminate at the rim of the teeth cylinder and chin form.

Fig. e. A similar arrangement with the addition of a moustache and chin whiskers.

Fig. f. This drawing shows the relationship of the facial hair to the first sideplane.

Fig. g. A neatly trimmed beard terminating on the boundaries of the first sideplanes. Chin whiskers start immediately below the lower lip and grow over the chin form.

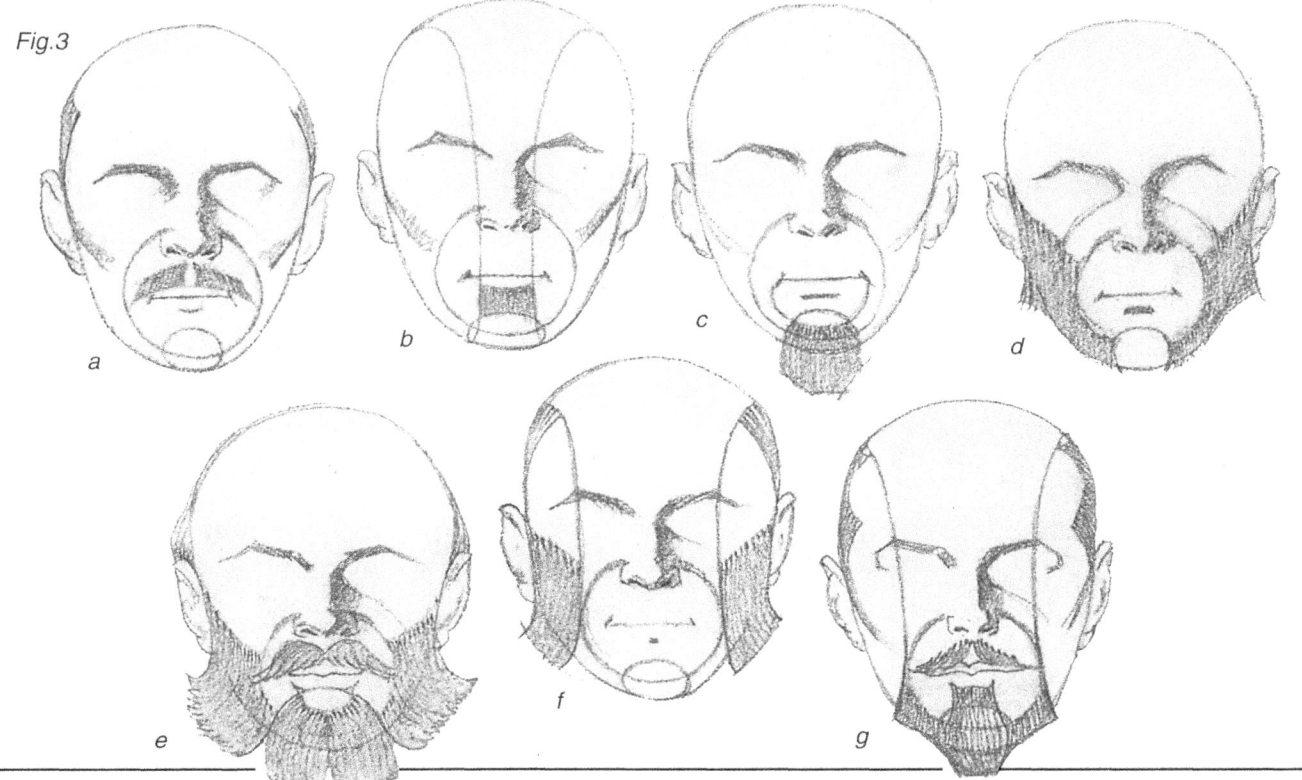

197

A series of fully rendered facial hair examples drawn with the previous instructions. Notice the emphasis on the bottom planes to produce a solid looking form. The individual locks of hair should not be allowed to detract from the large form in light and shade.

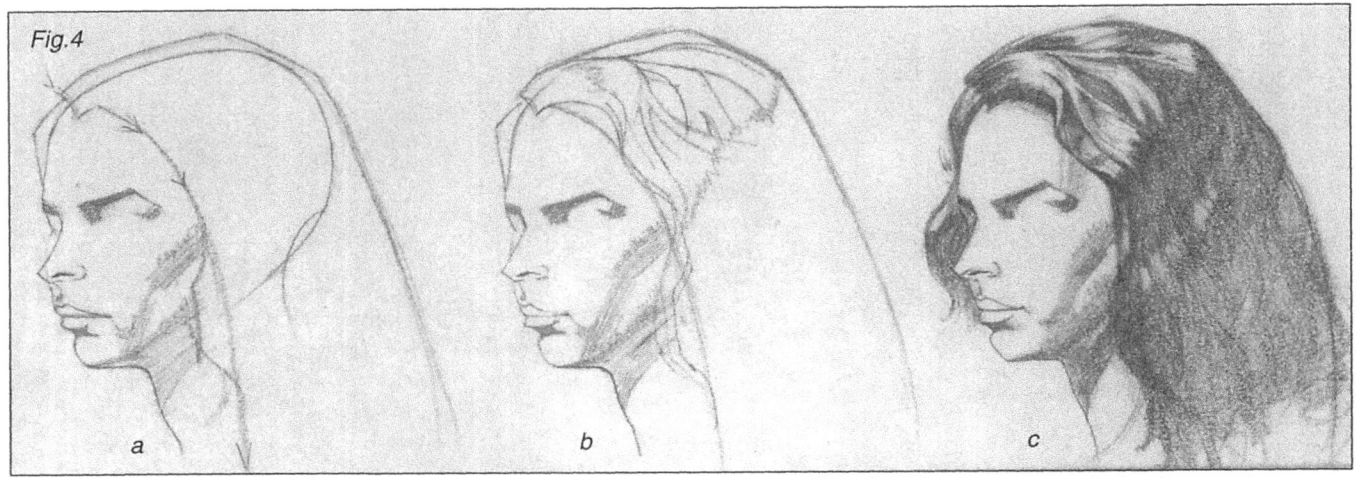

Figs. 4a.b.c. Starting the drawing of the hair. The large skull shape and outline of the major hair mass is drawn first. Notice how the outline of the hair conforms to the shape of the skull.

Fig. b. The large mass is broken up into smaller masses or locks of hair. Notice how the shadow plane of the face extends onto the hair form.

Fig. c. The hair fully rendered in light and shade.

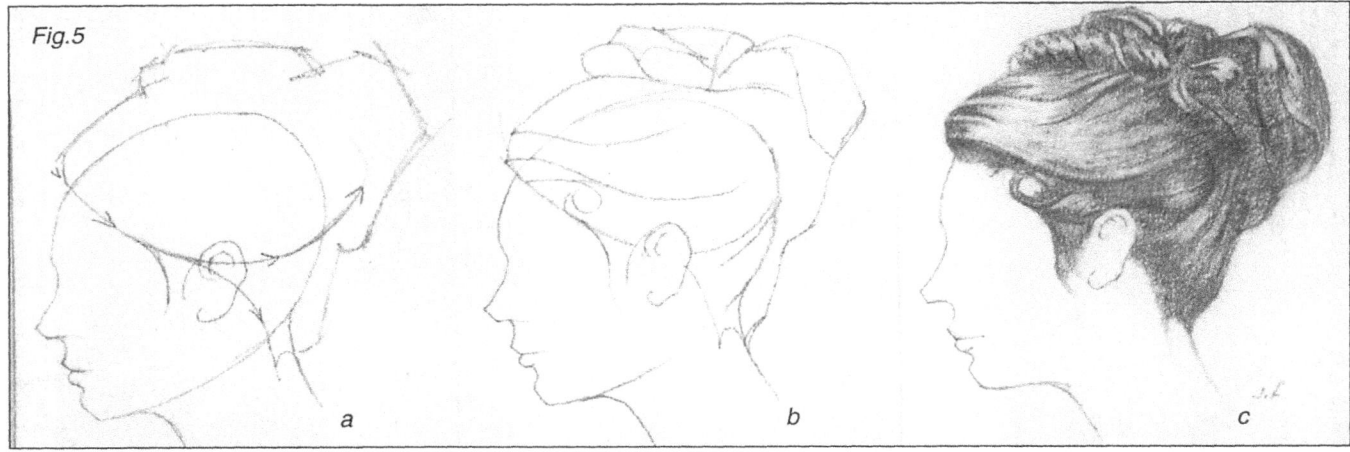

Figs. 5a.b.c. Another example. Another entirely different hair style. The procedure is the same as in the previous drawings.

Figs. 6a.b. Back view showing the hair pulled back and made into a bun. Start with the sphere of the skull and show the neck muscles inserting into the base of the skull. Draw the overall shape of the hair and the bun and divide it up with the individual locks. Add light and shade to show the form. Notice how the hair grows downwards on the muscles of the neck and directly down the center of these forms

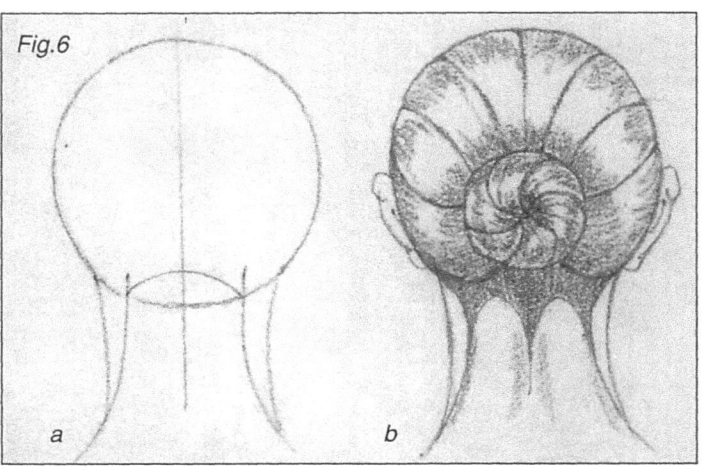

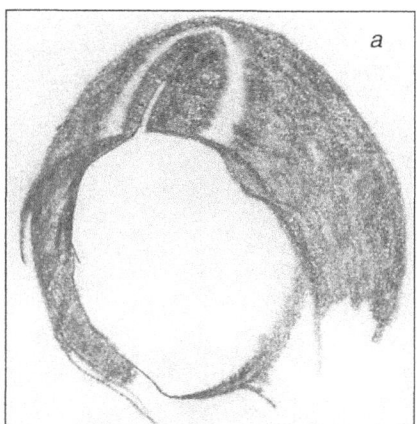

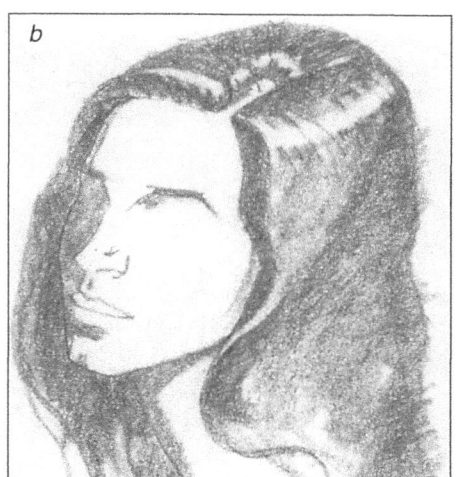

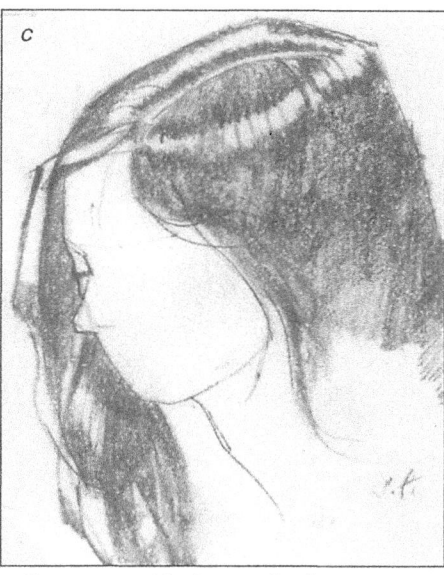

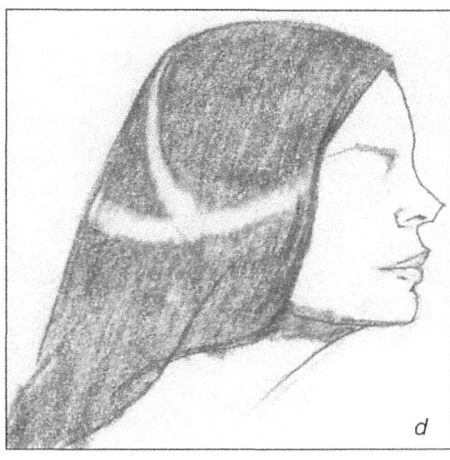

Fig.7

Figs. 7a.b.c.d. There is usually a rim of light on the hair which follows the shape of the skull or the shapes of major locks. This is not necessarily a highlight but a highlight will usually be in the center of it. This light is most obvious on fine shiny textured hair and the simpler the hairstyle the more obvious it will be. Too many curls, waves and strands of hair will seem to negate this band of light but they only interrupt it as it continues on its course

The following pages show finished drawings of many different hairstyles drawn according to the preceding instructions.

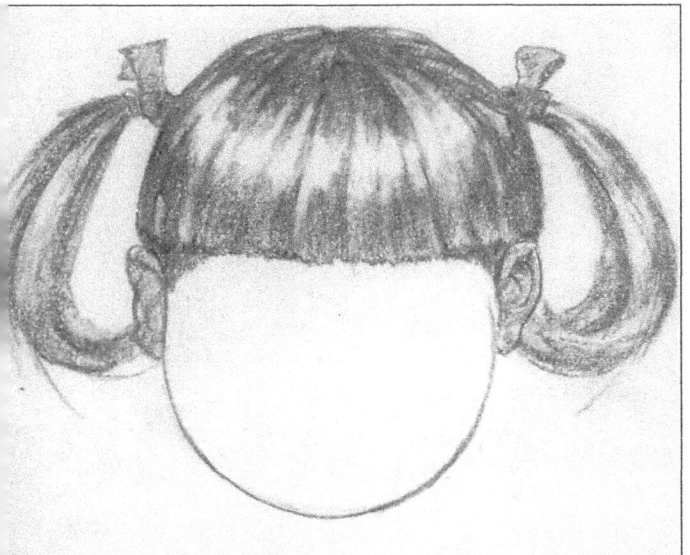

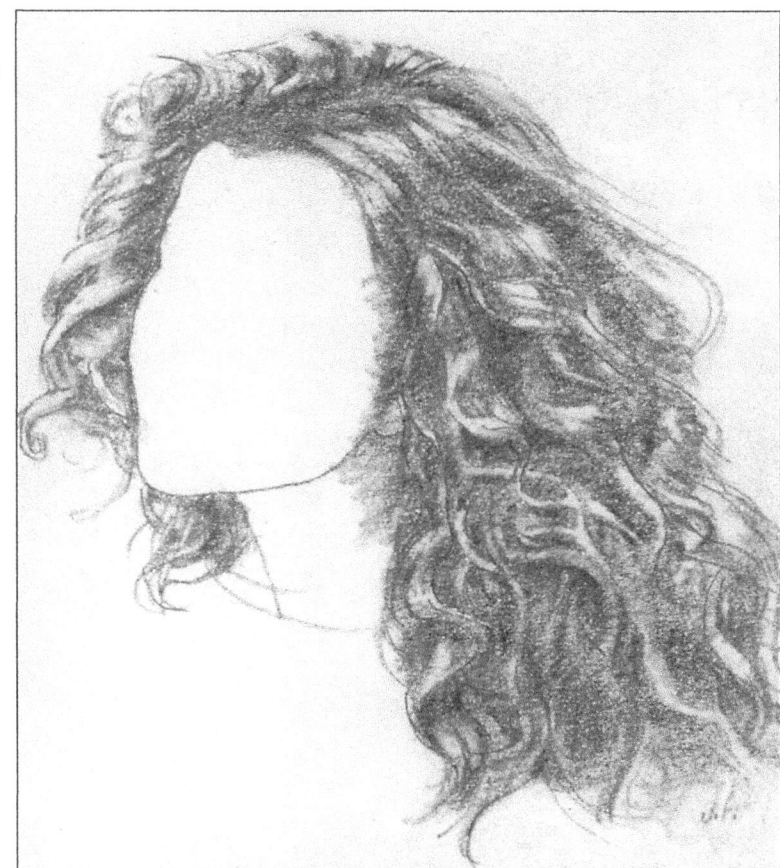

A SELECTION OF FINISHED DRAWINGS OF DIFFERENT HAIRSTYLES AND BEARDS

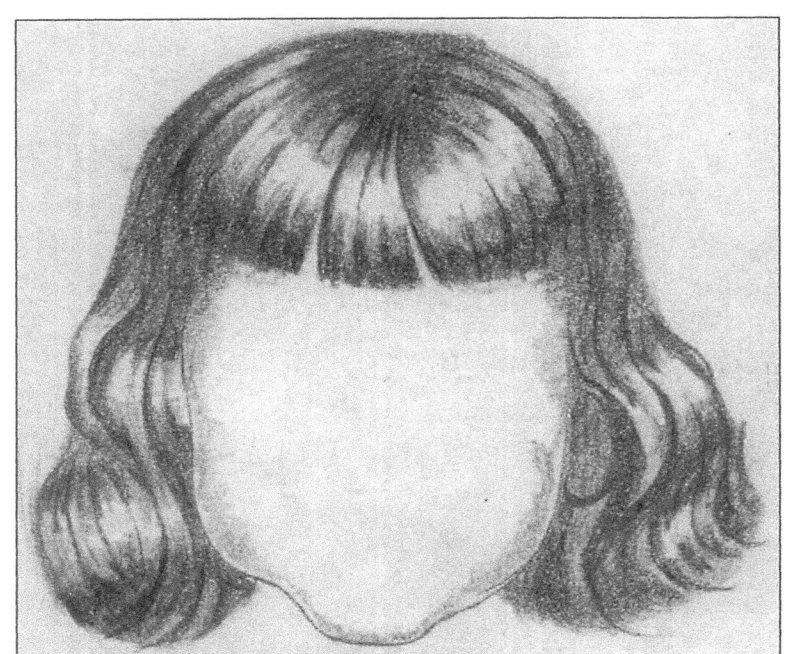

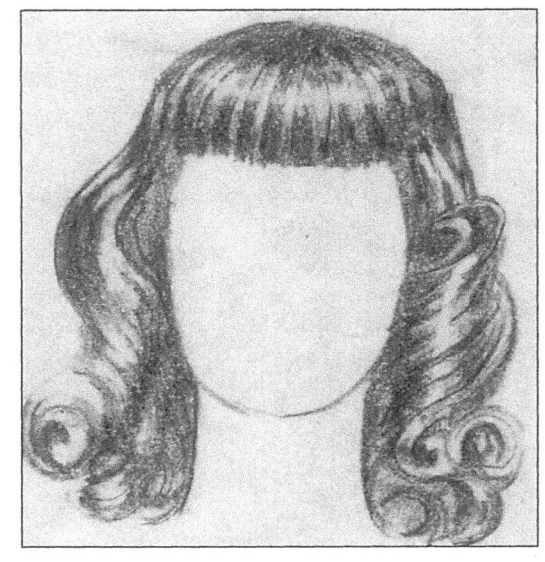

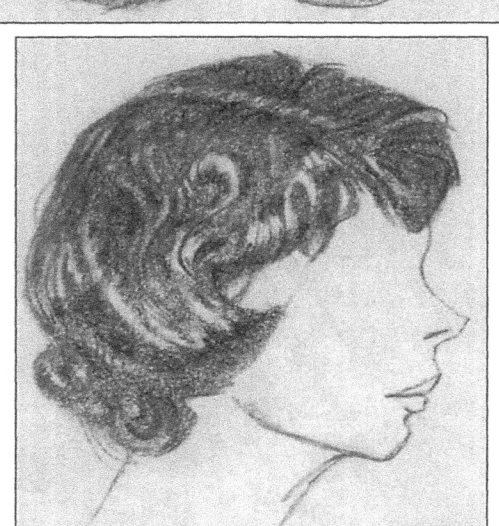

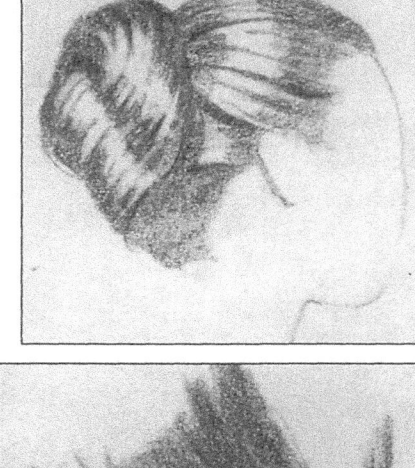

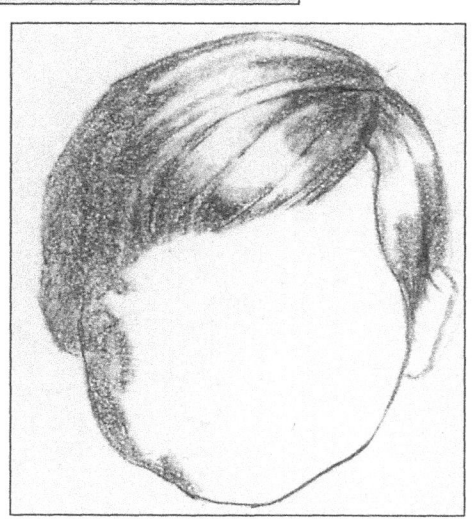

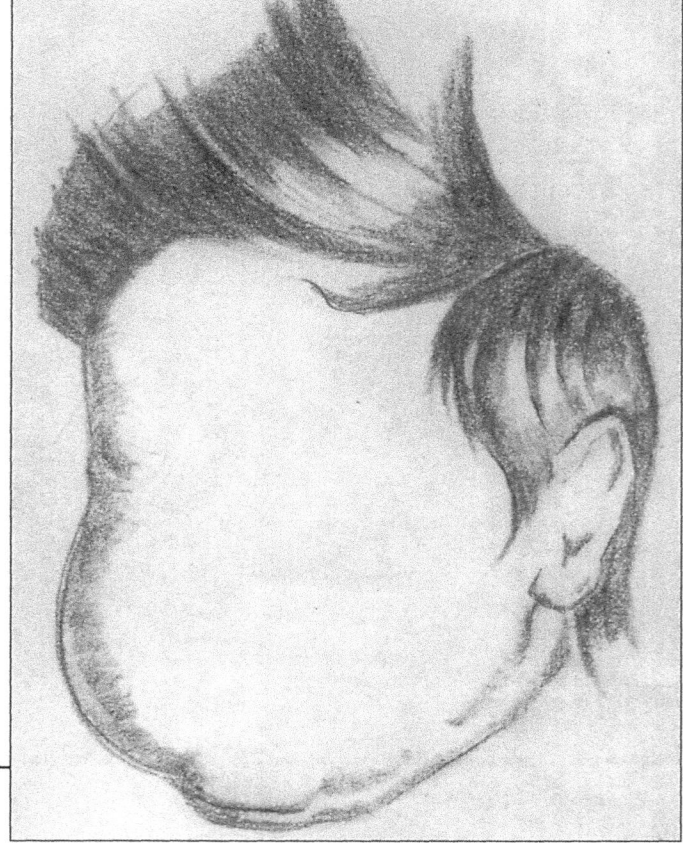

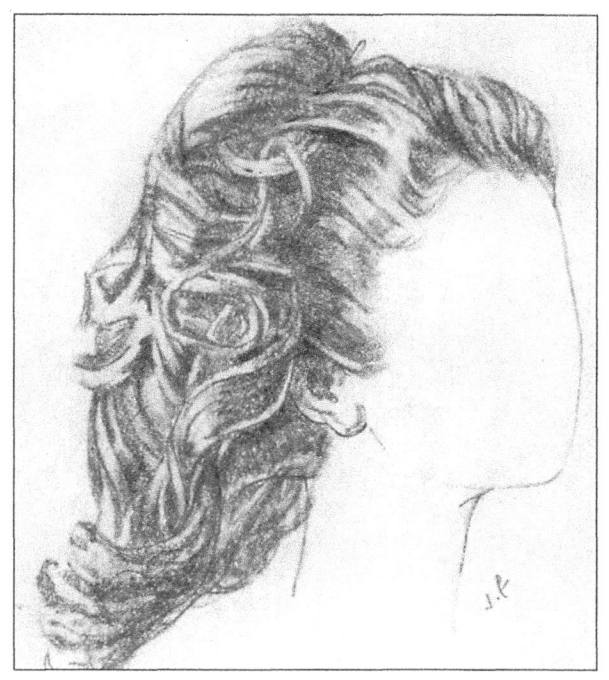
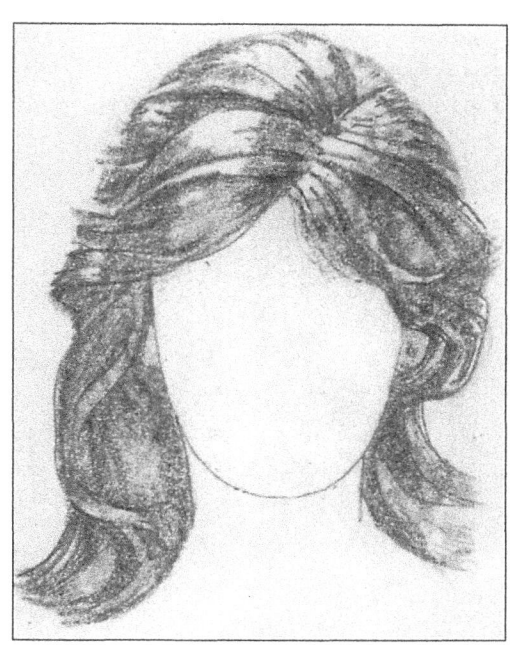
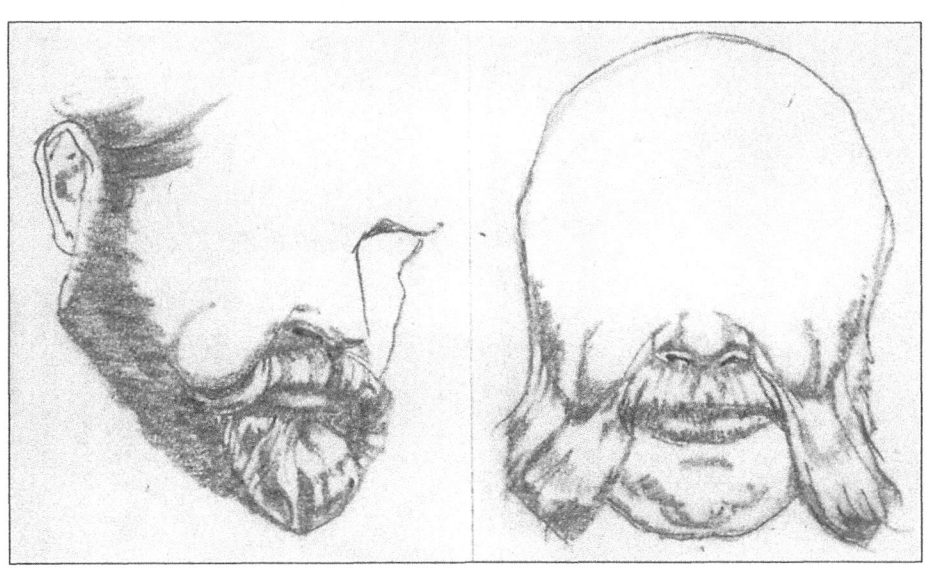
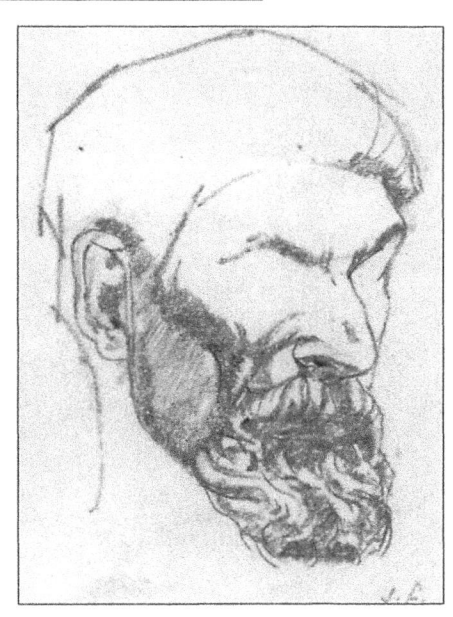
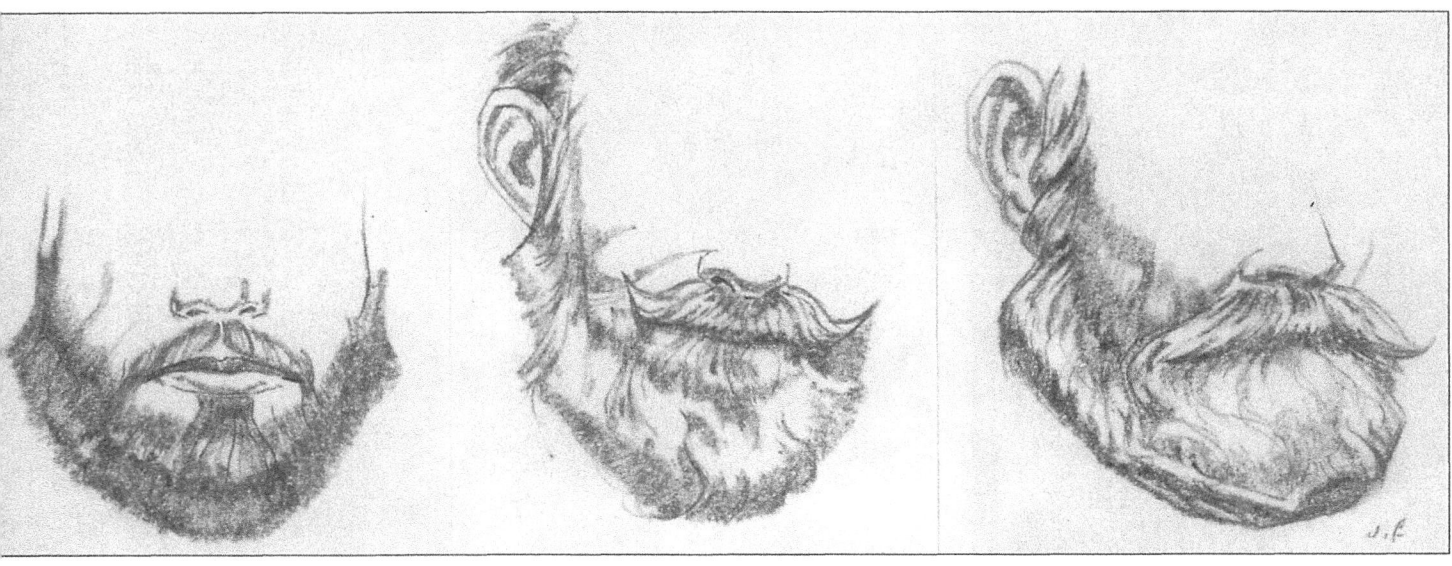

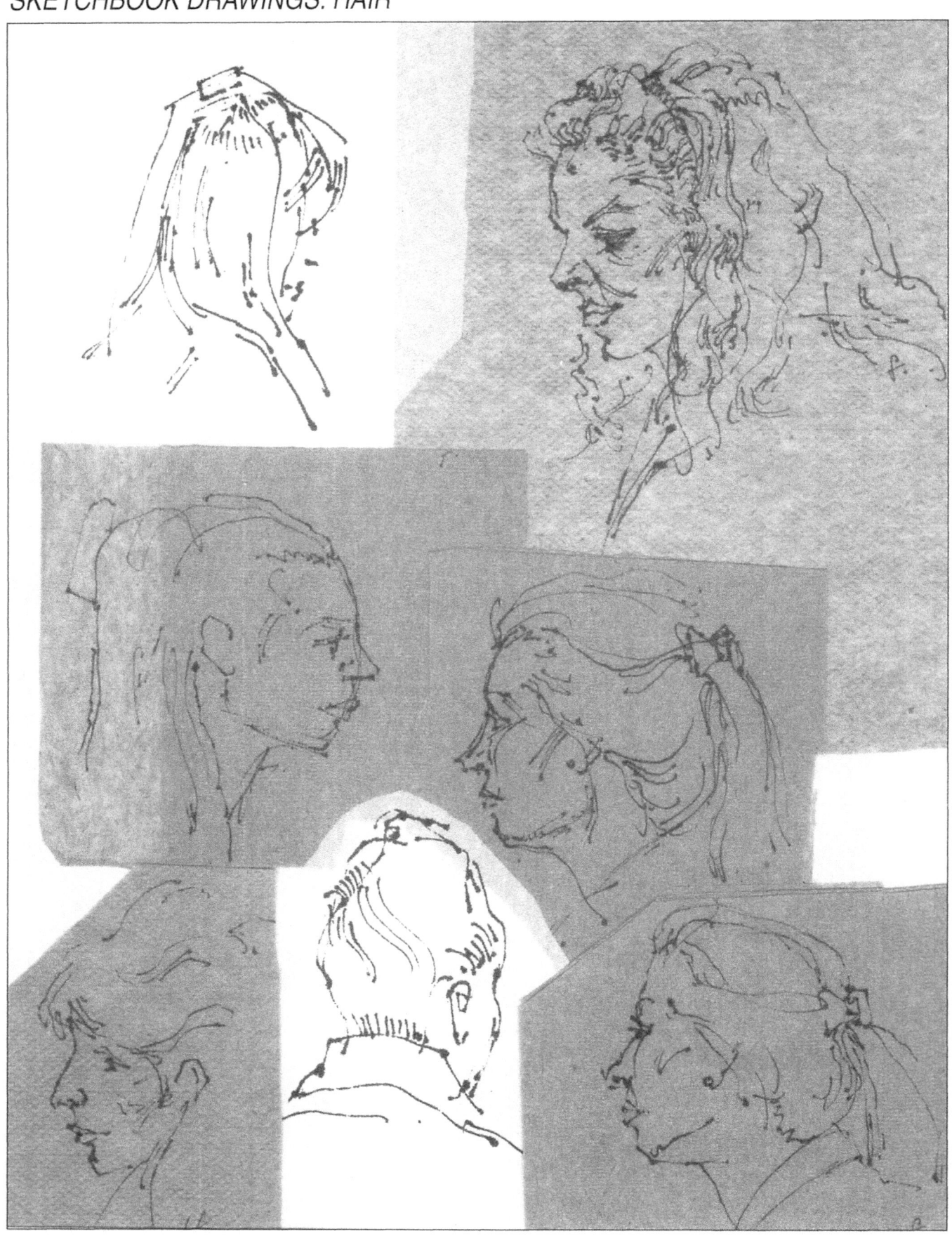

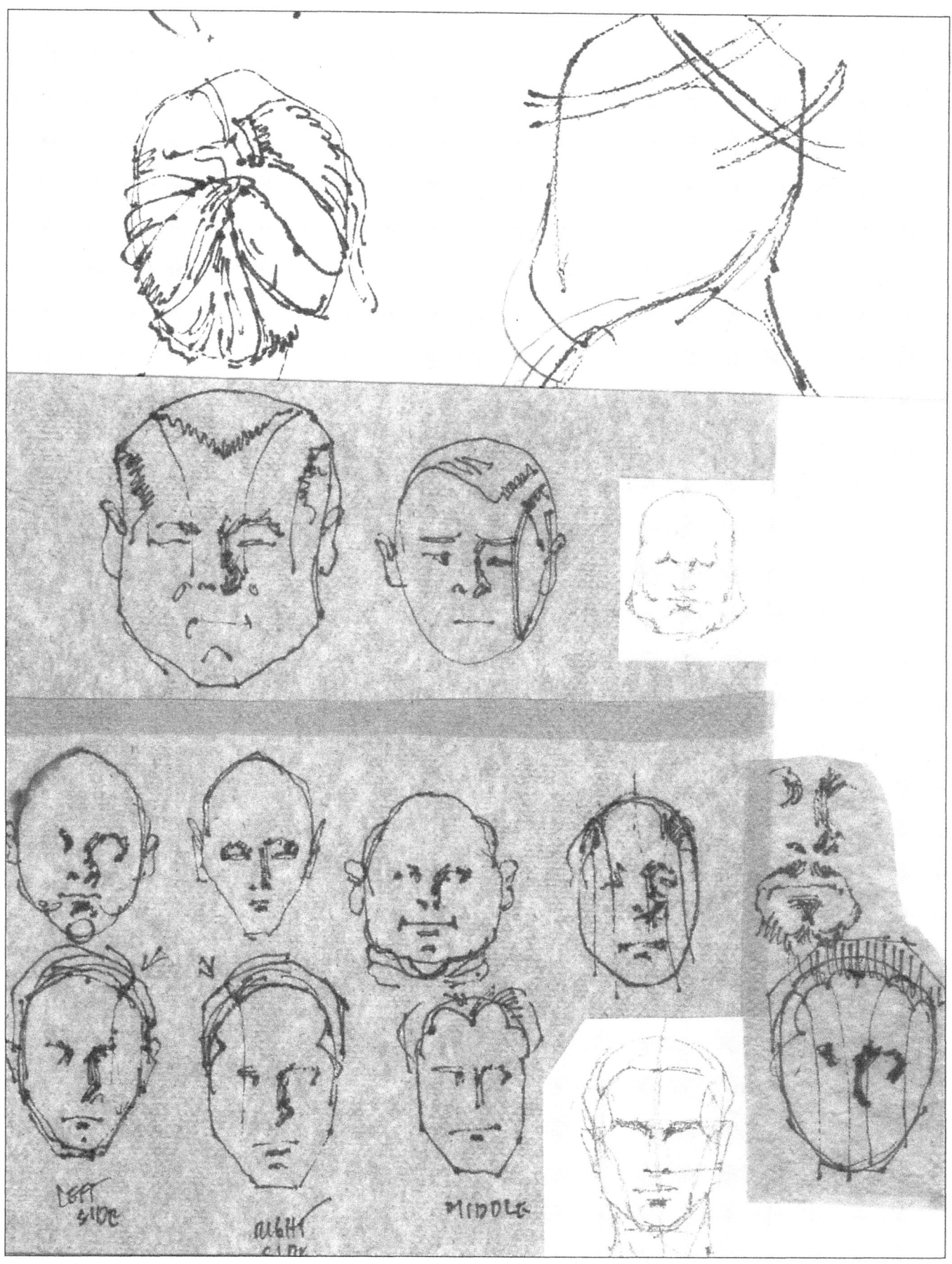

LEFT SIDE

RIGHT SIDE

MIDDLE

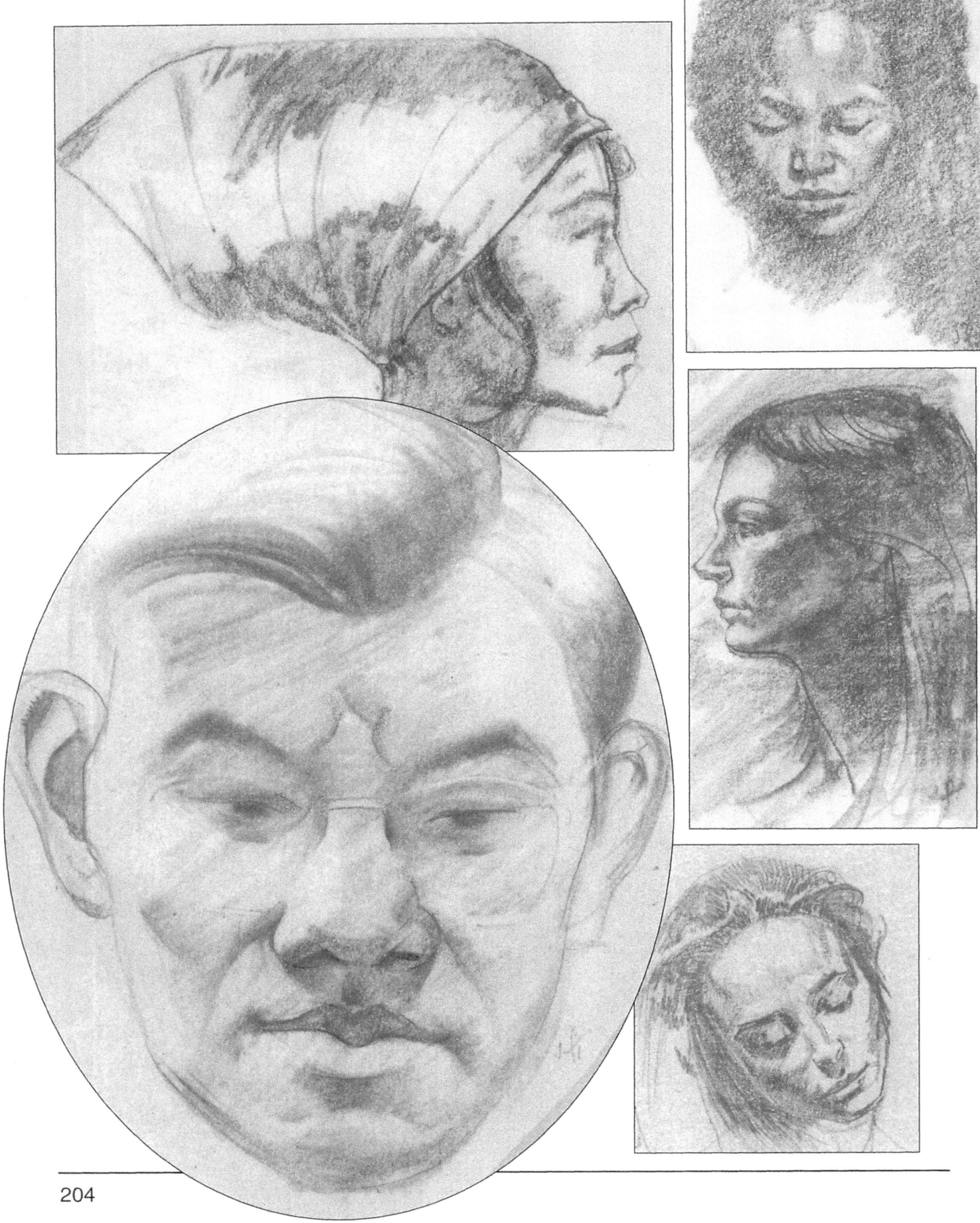

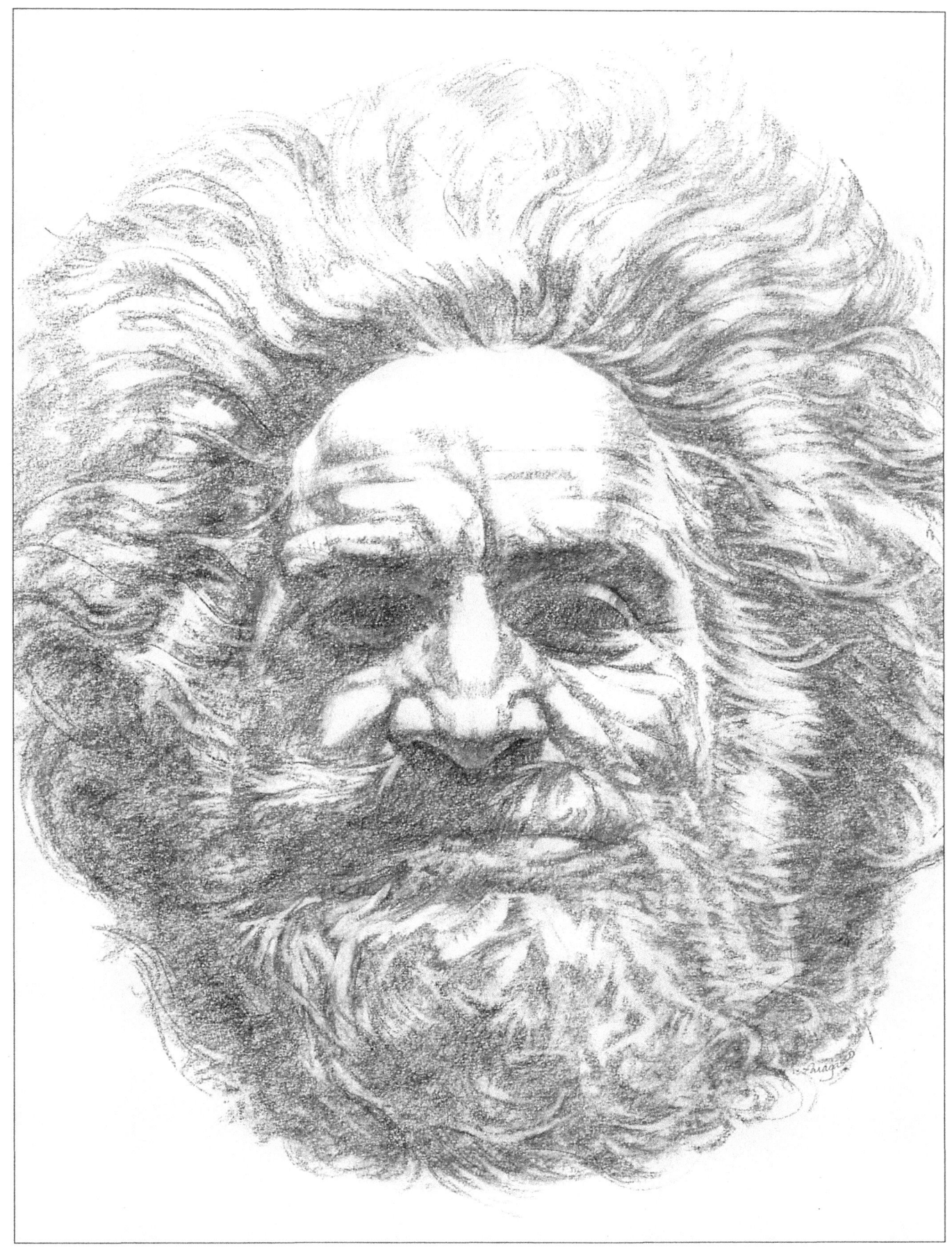

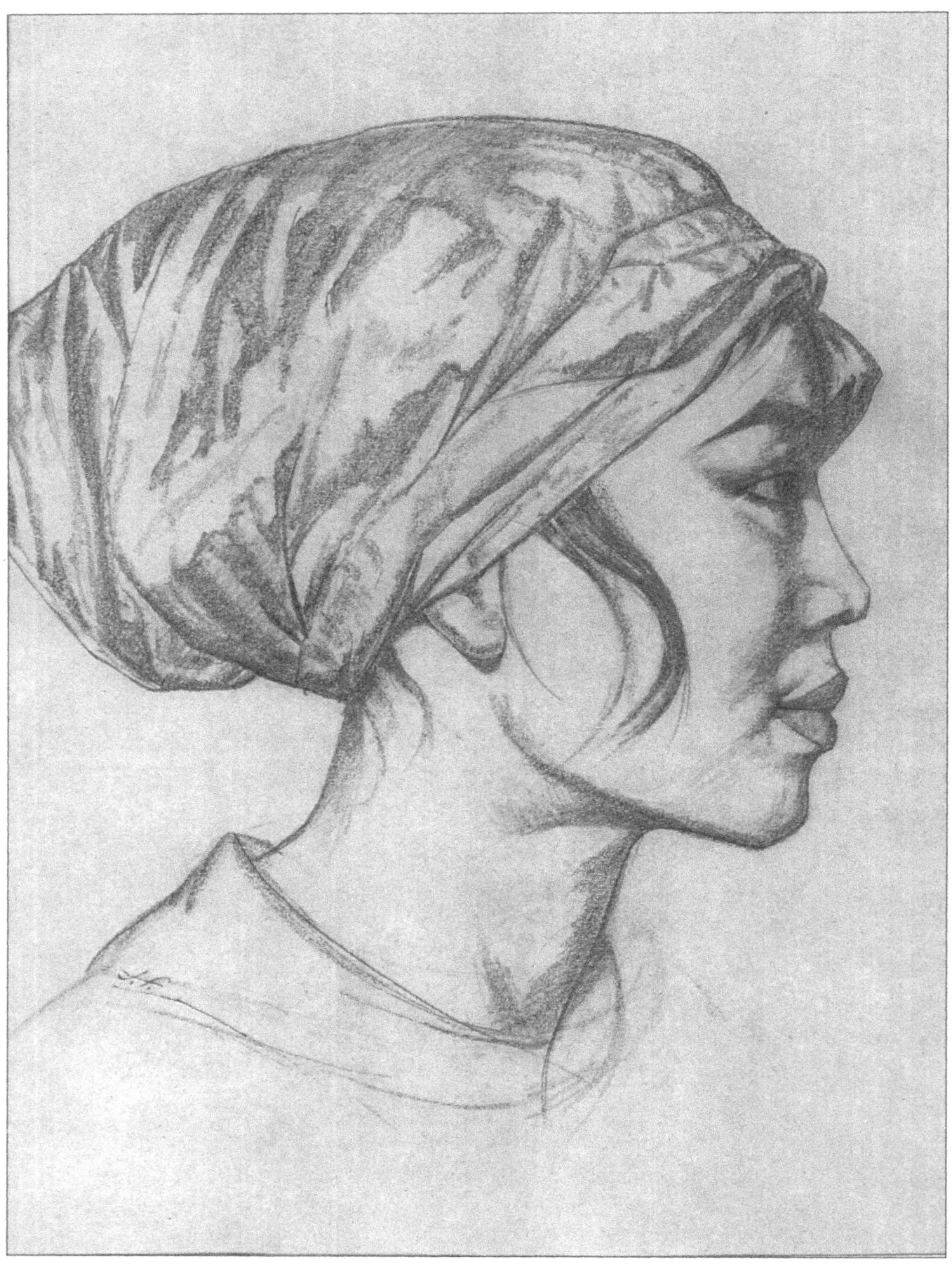

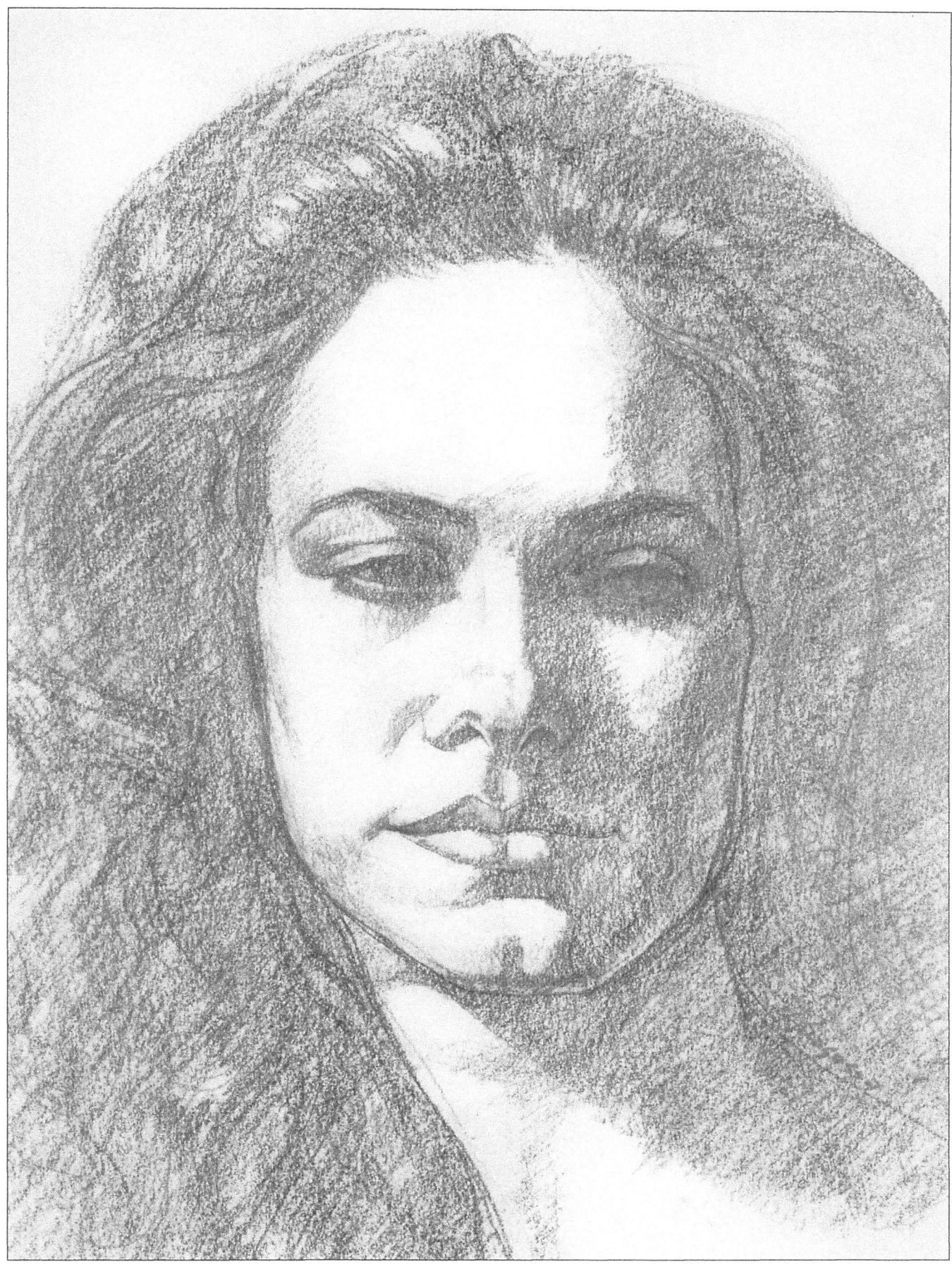

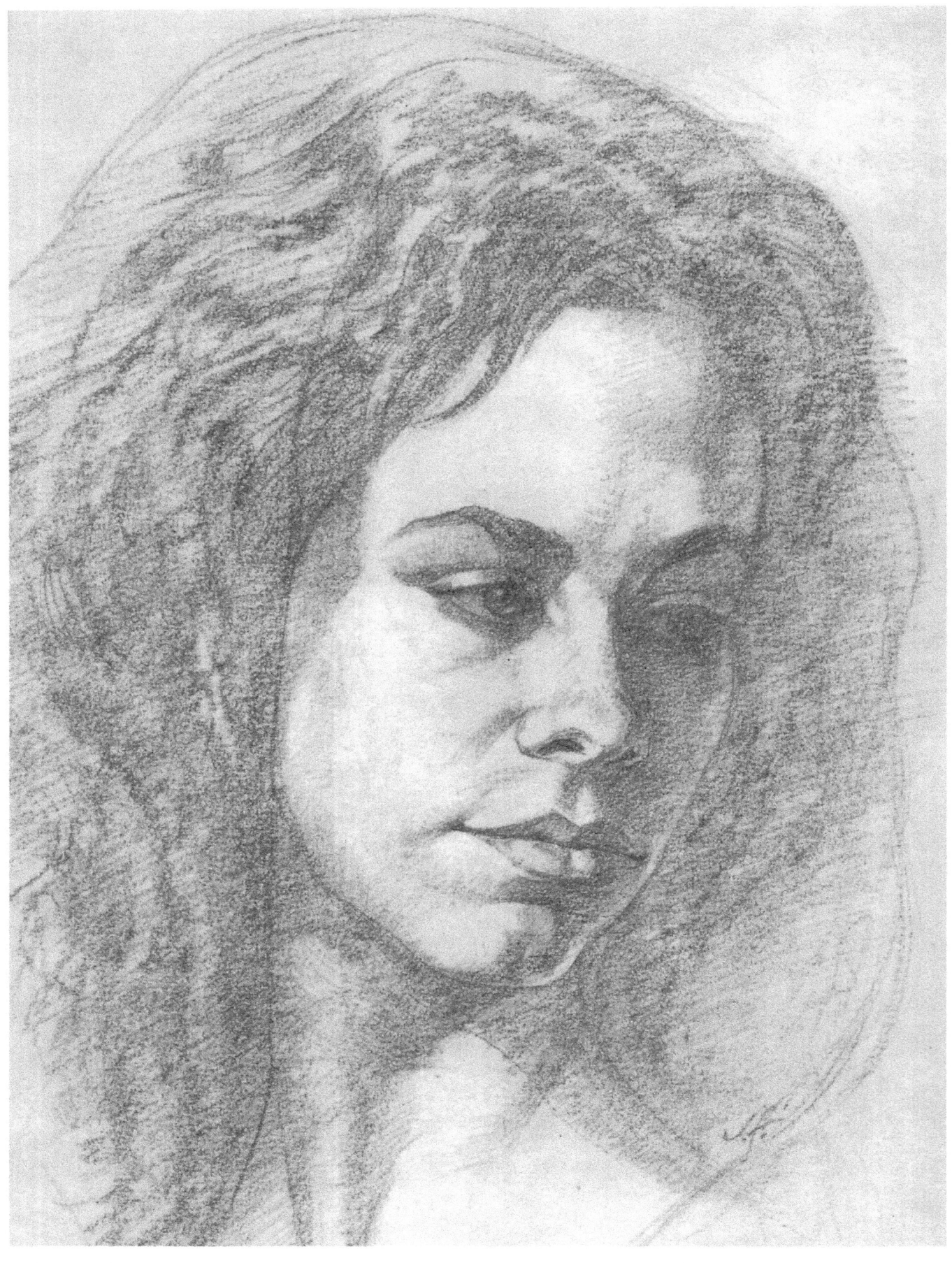

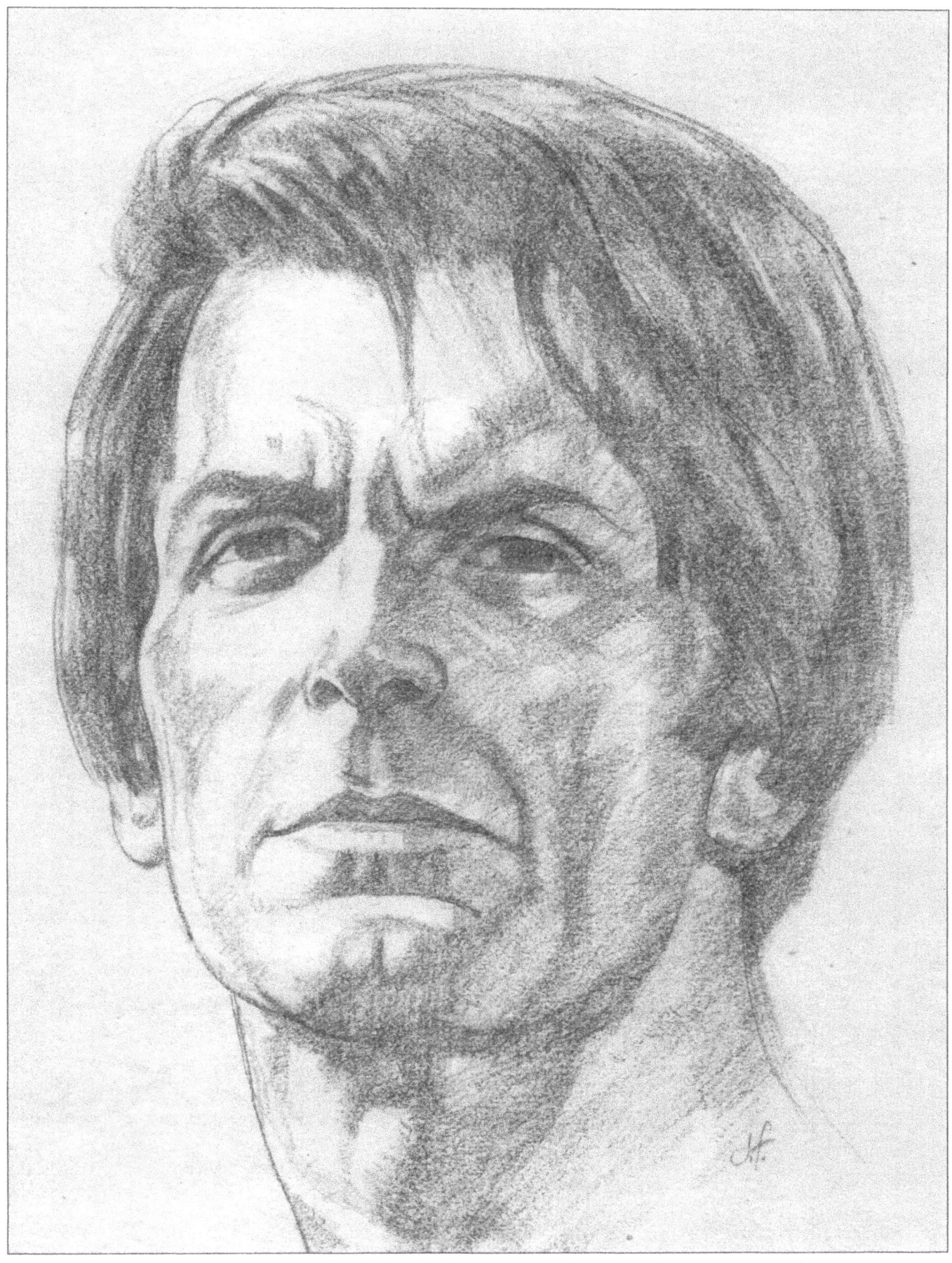

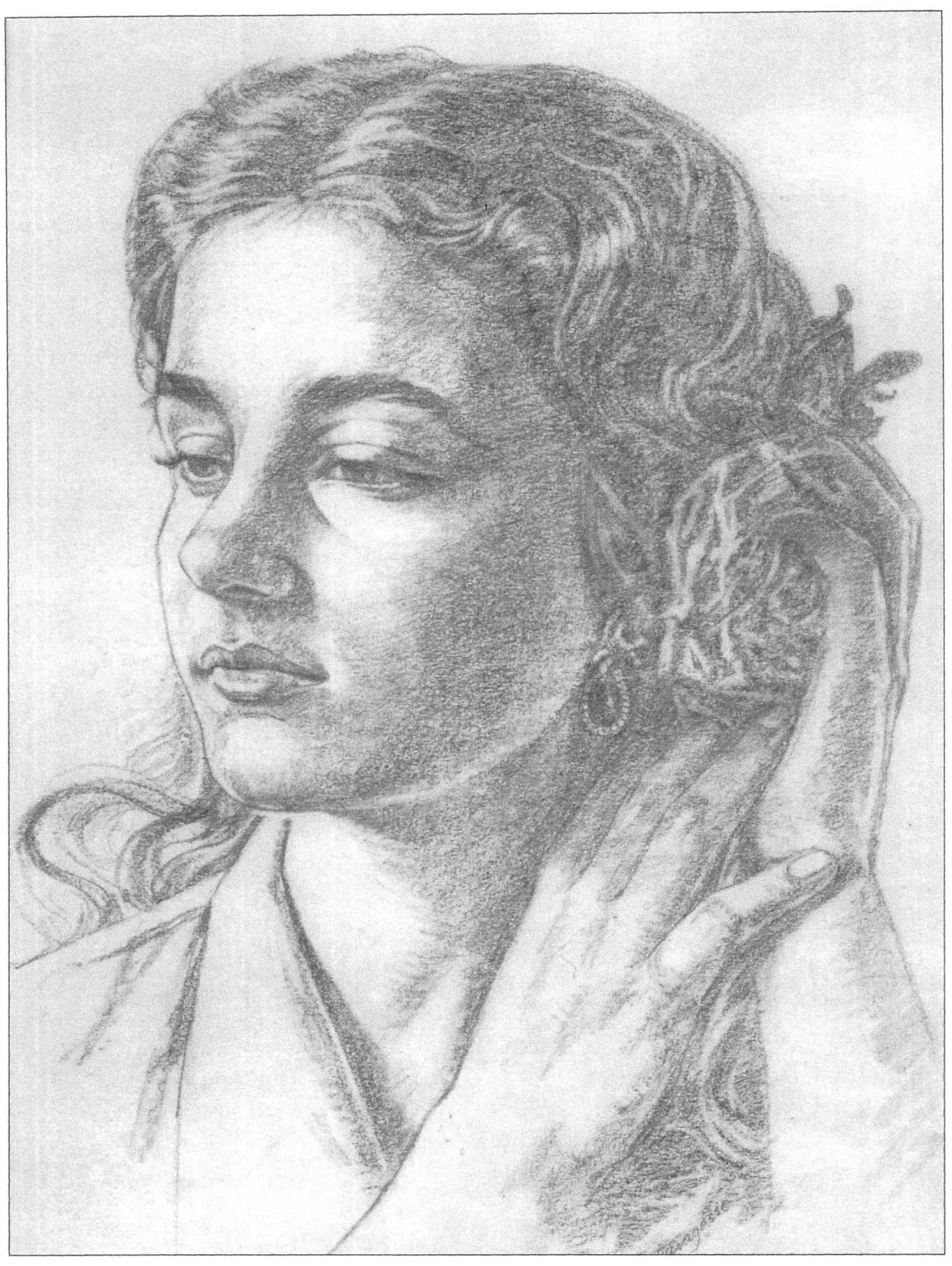

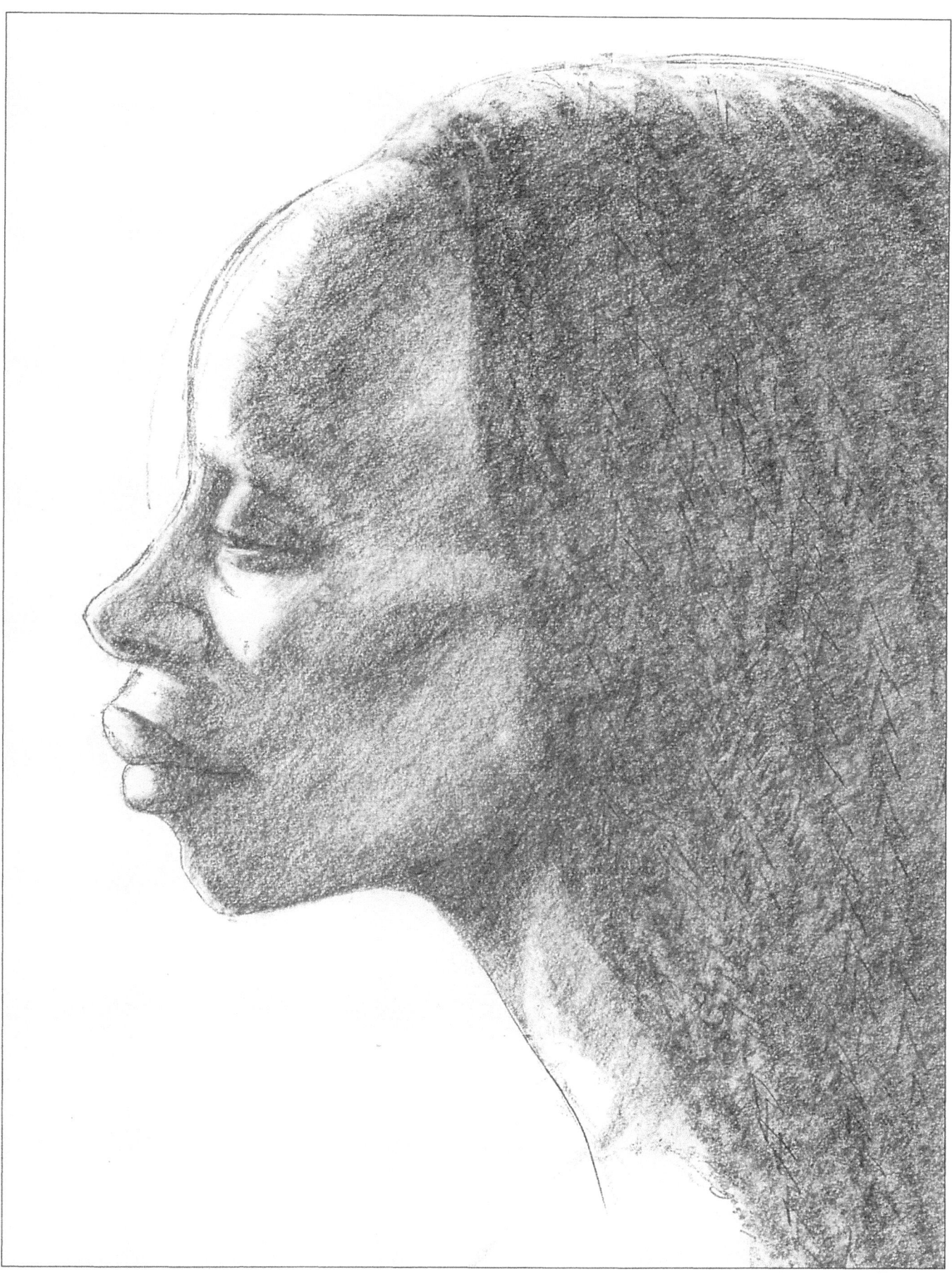

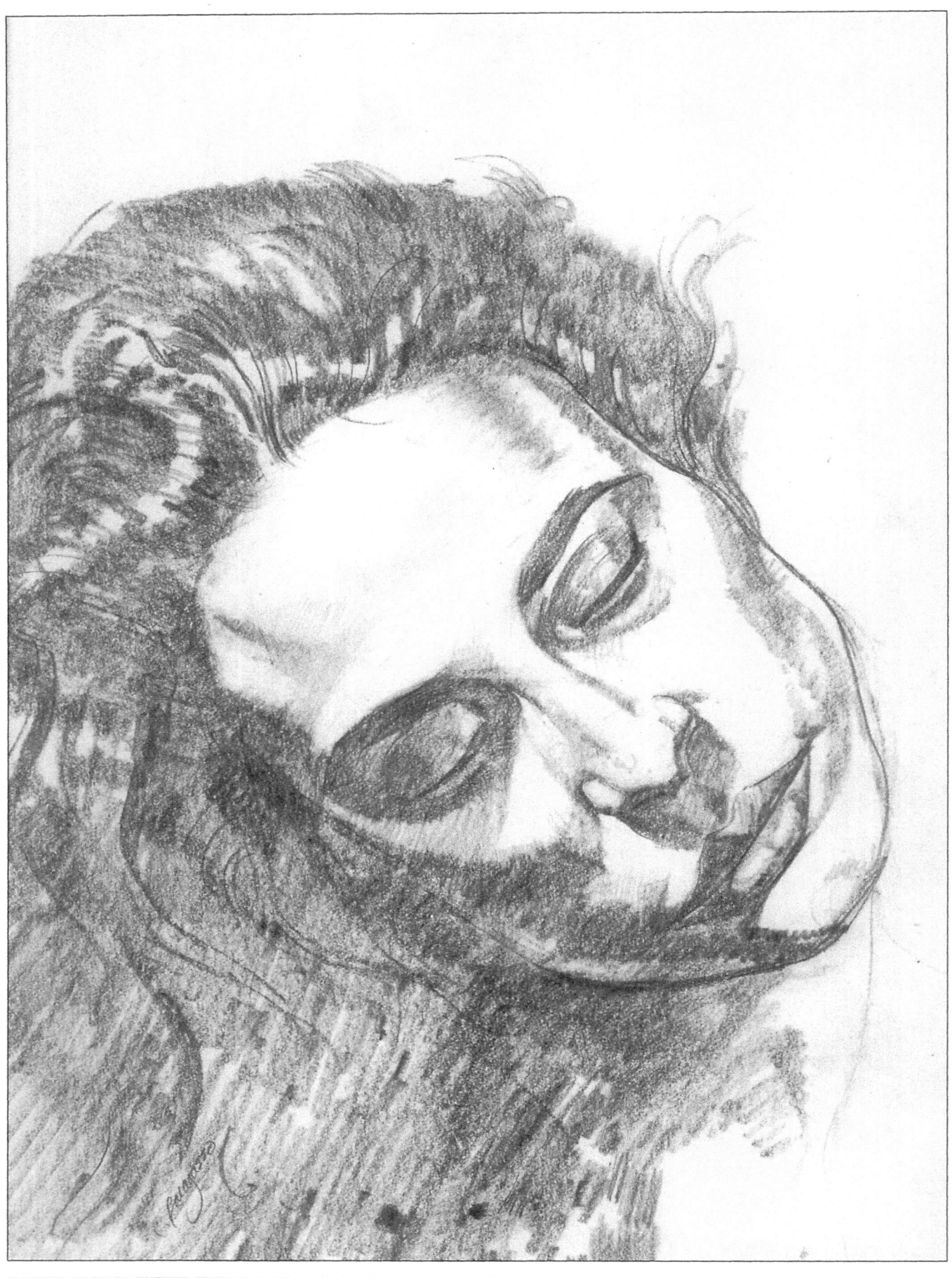

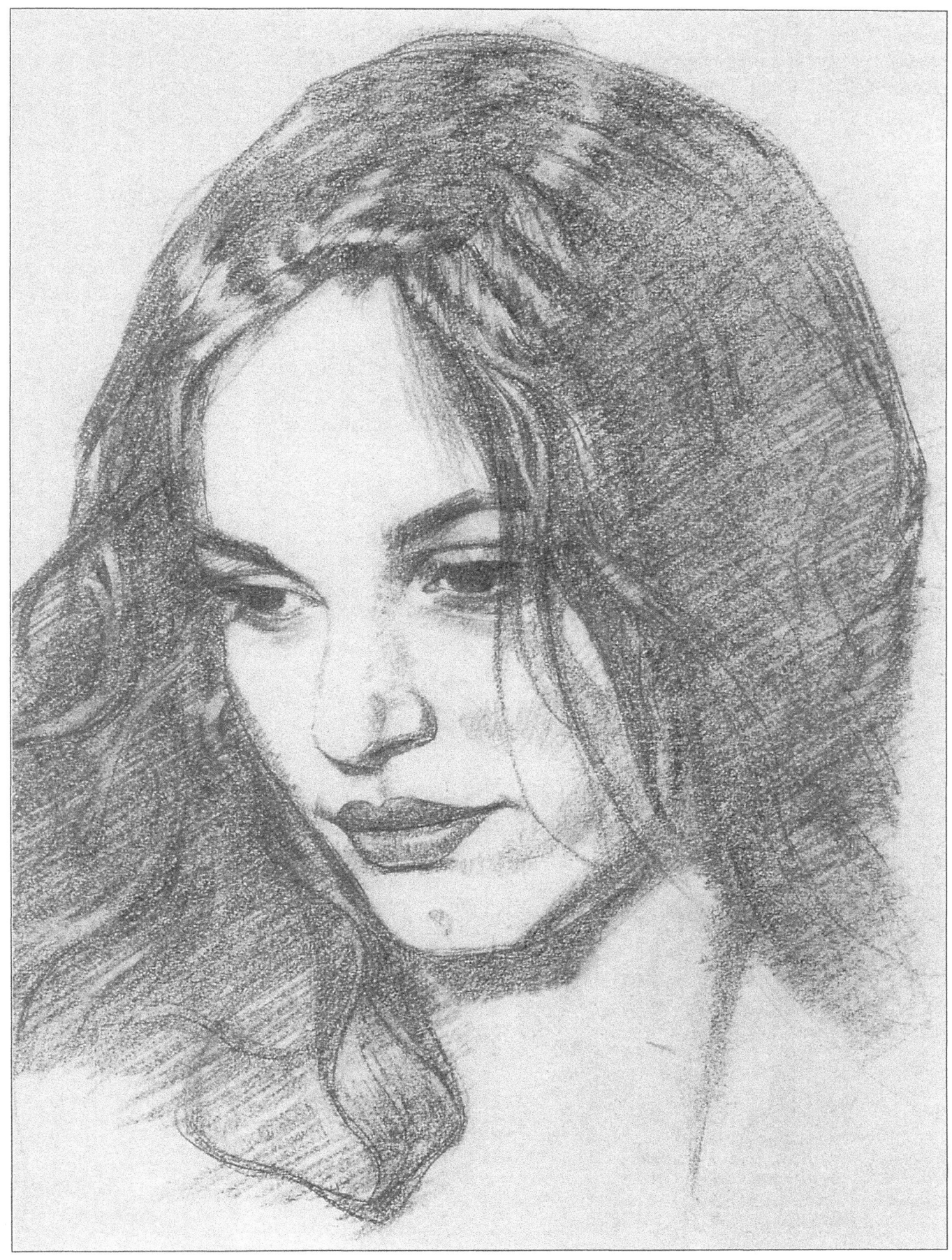

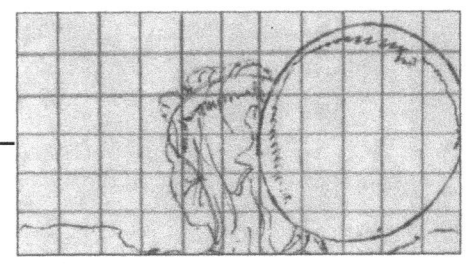

CHAPTER TWENTY

THE WORKING DRAWING

When you have a large mural to do, or a portrait or a large complex work of art, you may want to make what is called a "working drawing." The working drawing is strictly linear – that is there are no value gradations on it. The lines, especially the outlines, are hard and well defined and suggest where the forms, shadows and halftones are.

The reason why the working drawing is all linear is because it usually is squared up or projected up onto a larger dimension. For this reason you need strong well defined lines that you can trace.

SQUARING UP

Say you want to make a large painting of a figure. First make an accurate drawing of any convenient size. Next mark off as many one inch units on the height of your drawing and draw horizontal lines. Now mark off one inch units at the bottom of your drawing and draw vertical lines. You now have a grid over your drawing. These little squares of the grid can be divided by using diagonals wherever you wish. You can mark your units as *a, b, c*, etc. or *1, 2, 3, 4*, etc. *Fig. 1.* shows a working drawing that is squared off.

Repeat this process on the surface you want to work on except make an equal amount of one foot units on the height and an equal amount of one foot units on the width. Now draw your grid. The drawing is transposed by observing where the lines of your drawing cross the lines of your grid and where they coincide with the larger grid. One square inch of your drawing will, therefore, become one square foot of the enlarged squared off drawing. Many of the great works by the Old Masters were started this way.

PROJECTING UP

You can save a lot of time by instead of drawing up everything manually by merely projecting your drawing onto your squared off surface making sure the grid of your drawing exactly matches the enlarged grid. Trace the lines with hard charcoal or pencil. This can be gone over with a diluted india ink and a round sable brush – or merely sprayed with matte fixative.

If your original drawing is too large you can have it xeroxed down to a smaller size and then project it up. If the work is, say a large mural, with dozens of figures and architectural details then the squared off drawing could be photographed in sections onto glass slides. These can then be projected up to the squared off surface and traced.

A second type of working drawing which has been traditionally used for portraits is one that is exactly the same as the one described above but executed on grey paper. The grey paper represents the value of the skin tone average while hatching designates the halftone and shadow areas. White chalk is used sparingly for the lights. Grids are drawn and the drawing is squared up in the usual manner. The knowledgeable and skillful artist can easily make a finished painting from this drawing and a color sketch.

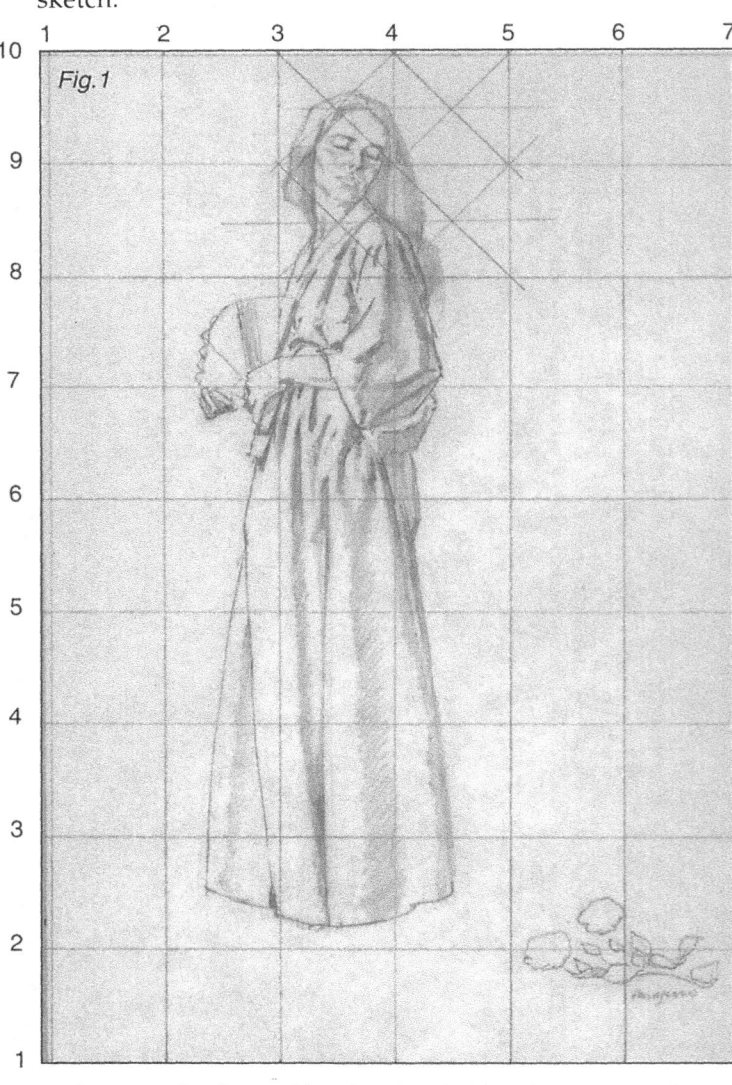

An example of a working drawing that has been squared off. The working drawing is basically linear with hatching to represent halftone and shadow.

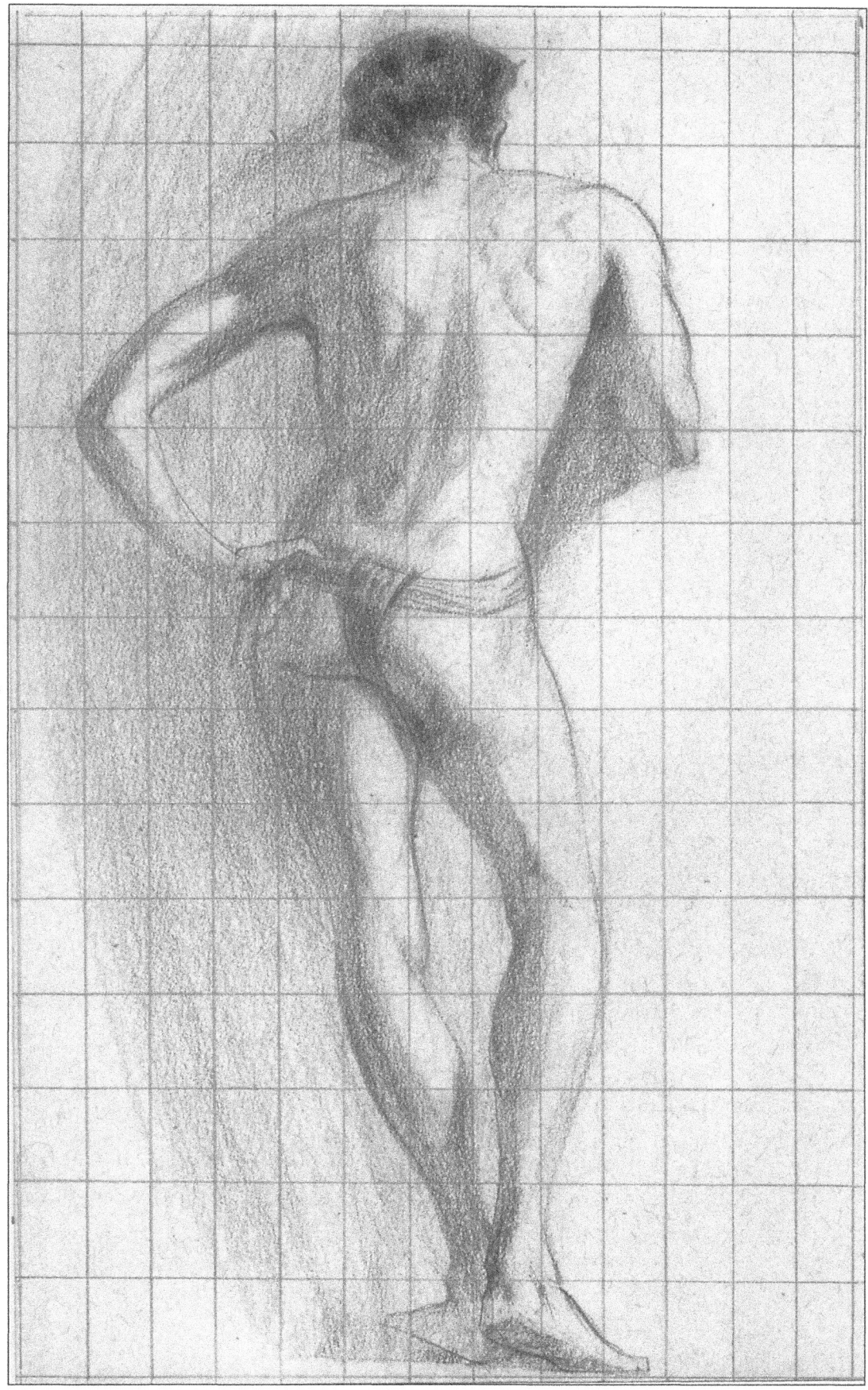

Fig.2

An example of a working drawing on Grey Paper, White chalk is used sparingly.

CHAPTER TWENTY-ONE

DRAWING FROM MEMORY AND IMAGINATION

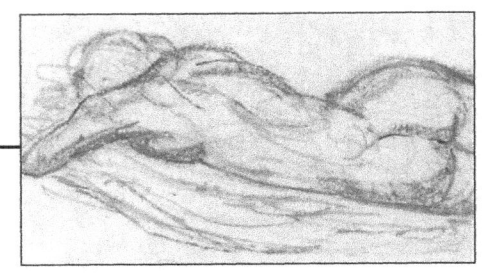

Memory and imagination are oft times confused. Dictionaries will say imagination is the picturing process of the mind, but so is memory. I prefer to think of memory as the *deliberate recalling* of a previously seen object or scene whereas imagination comes into play by its own volition and gives a new previously unthought-of image.

A great benefit that comes from drawing from memory is that it seems to drop out unessential details leaving only the vital essential aspects of the object or scene no matter what it may be. For this reason I believe the ancient Egyptian sculptures of animals, birds and humans were for the most part made from memory. *Imagination does this also but goes further by greatly exaggerating effects beyond what is ordinary reality and adds new and unusual beauty which is beyond the mere photographic image.* Van Gogh's "Starry Night" could have only been produced from imagination and feeling – not memory alone. There are many other paintings like this and for the most part they are universally liked and remembered.

The reason why memory and imagination are confused is that the imaginative state is fleeting, does not last long and is constantly interrupted – interrupted many times by input from the five senses and memory which seeks to fill out images. It is quite possible that nothing, in this waking life anyhow, could be produced while the mind is occupied with a constant flow of imaginative images. Memory and imagination seem to be faculties of two separate minds, a rational mind and a subconscious mind and it seems only one of them can be operating at any given time.

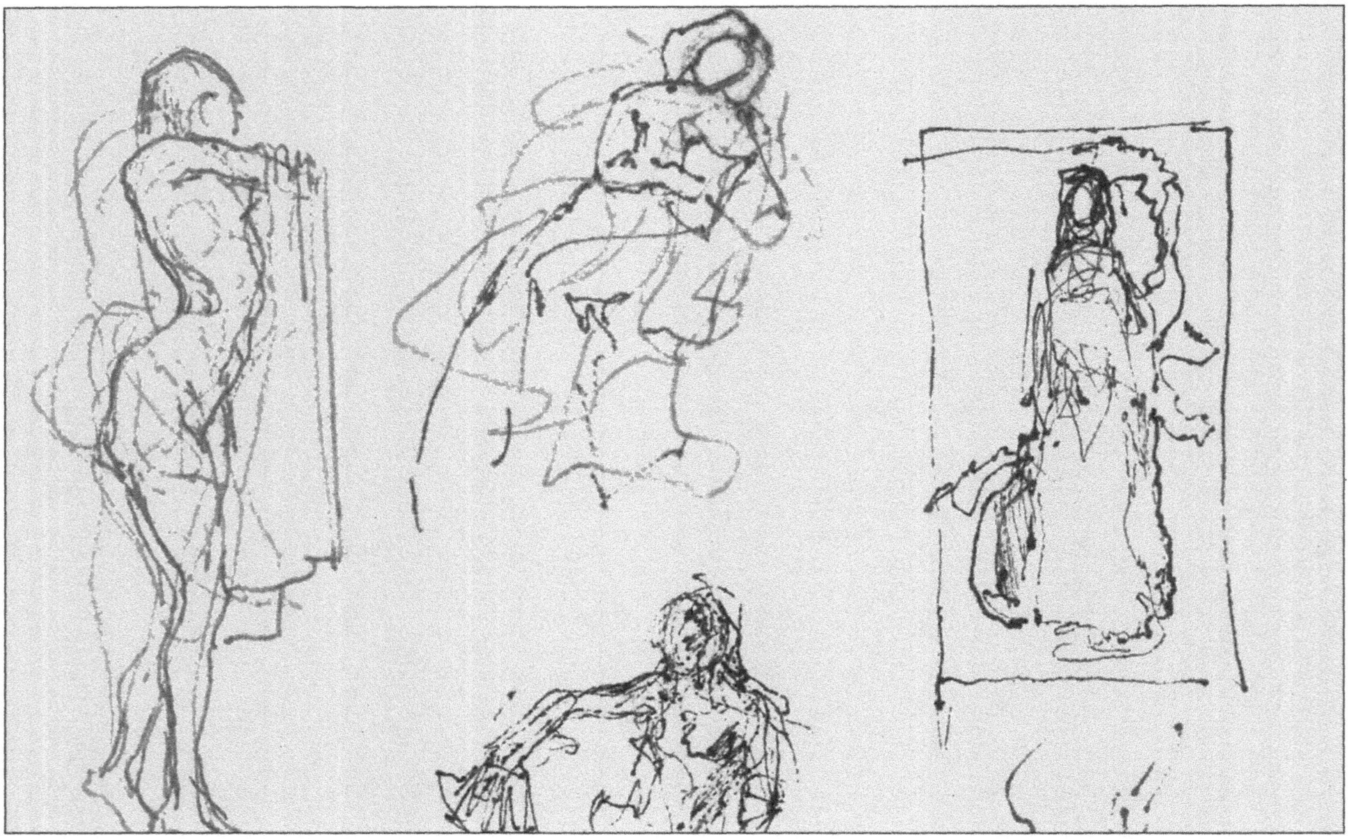

There is quite a range of memory in human beings – from those who can barely remember their name to those who have almost total recall of an entire lifetime. Many times this facility is in one sphere only, say in music or mathematics, however, it seems to come at the expense of other faculties. Why this is so is still a mystery despite an enormous amount of work that has been going on in this realm. Undoubtedly a healthy nervous system, or in some cases an unhealthy nervous system, early training habits and proper nutrition have a lot to do with

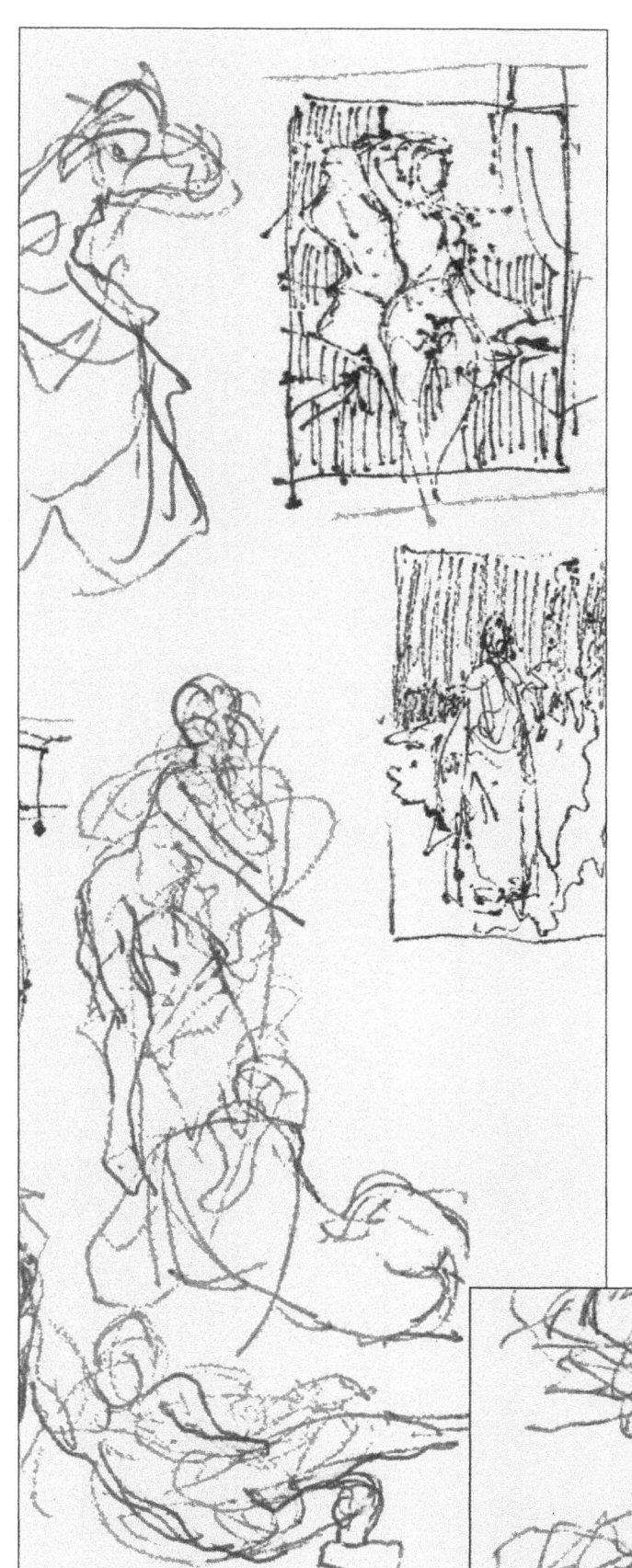

memory, although this is not the whole story. *Having enthusiasm, a keen interest in and love of what you want to draw and paint is essential to a good memory of the artist.*

There are those who claim that too many facts and too much thinking will prevent the memory from functioning properly. Let us examine this statement. There is both passive memory and active memory. All day long you are passively receiving sounds, smells and images which are recorded in your memory banks. Thinking is not involved here as that may interfere with or overly burden and clutter your mind, however the impressions will be strong enough to give you a subconscious feeling of rightness and wrongness. No effort is required to recall these impressions as they went into your mind passively and will come out of your mind easily provided you don't try to interfere with them.

Active thinking is when you make a deliberate effort to remember something. Here you will have to use all kinds of mental gymnastics to remember what you are observing. For instance you may find a distinctive shape of what you're looking at that when you bring it to mind will bring the image along with it. Association can be used very effectively. The more things you can associate with something the easier it will be to recall it and there are endless ways. Indeed you can associate textures, colors, sounds, almost anything with an object to help retrieve its image.

As to the head and the figure there are all the drawings, diagrams and schemas that are presented in this book to use. If you remember them and the principles outlined in the text it will take you a long way towards helping you to draw from memory.

Da Vinci and other researchers of the mind have recommended a process of "retracing" wherein upon retiring at night one visualizes a blackboard and mentally draws images with a white chalk upon it. In this way the images are engraved onto the deeper layers of the mind. Others have observed a scene, turned their backs on it and either drew it or described it to a companion.

Leonardo da Vinci, Durer and many of the masters took many measurements of people, animals and architectural structures. They also made hundreds of notations of their observations of nature. Would they have done all of this if they had a superior memory? I think not. The drawings and notations were needed to revive and hold the memory of the observation. The artist should accumulate as many facts as he can concerning his subject if he is going to work well from memory. Don't forget, there were no cameras in the past. The artist had to invent most of what he did. The only way to succeed was through training, memory, imagination, feeling and of course inspiration.

It is my opinion that with the advent of photography, motion pictures, television and now computer graphics we have lost and are rapidly losing the use of these faculties of memory and imagination. What you don't use you lose and that goes for everything concerning the human organism. The artist of today can be extraordinarily proficient technically but he will never approach the greatness of the artist of the past in regards to what we refer to as "art" if he continues on the present path.

The drawing from memory is very much like the drawing from imagination. The difference is when you draw from memory you have, or should have, an image in your mind. You are going to recreate it on paper or canvas by letting brush or pencil recreate your mental image. When you work from imagination however, you have no preconceived image. You try to coax something out of the imaginative faculty. When it comes you embellish it with your knowledge and skill utilizing your memory. It will then be a new thing.

When looking at a page of drawings from memory and a page of drawings from imagination one will detect little or no difference although the ones drawn from memory will be perhaps a little stiffer and repetitious.

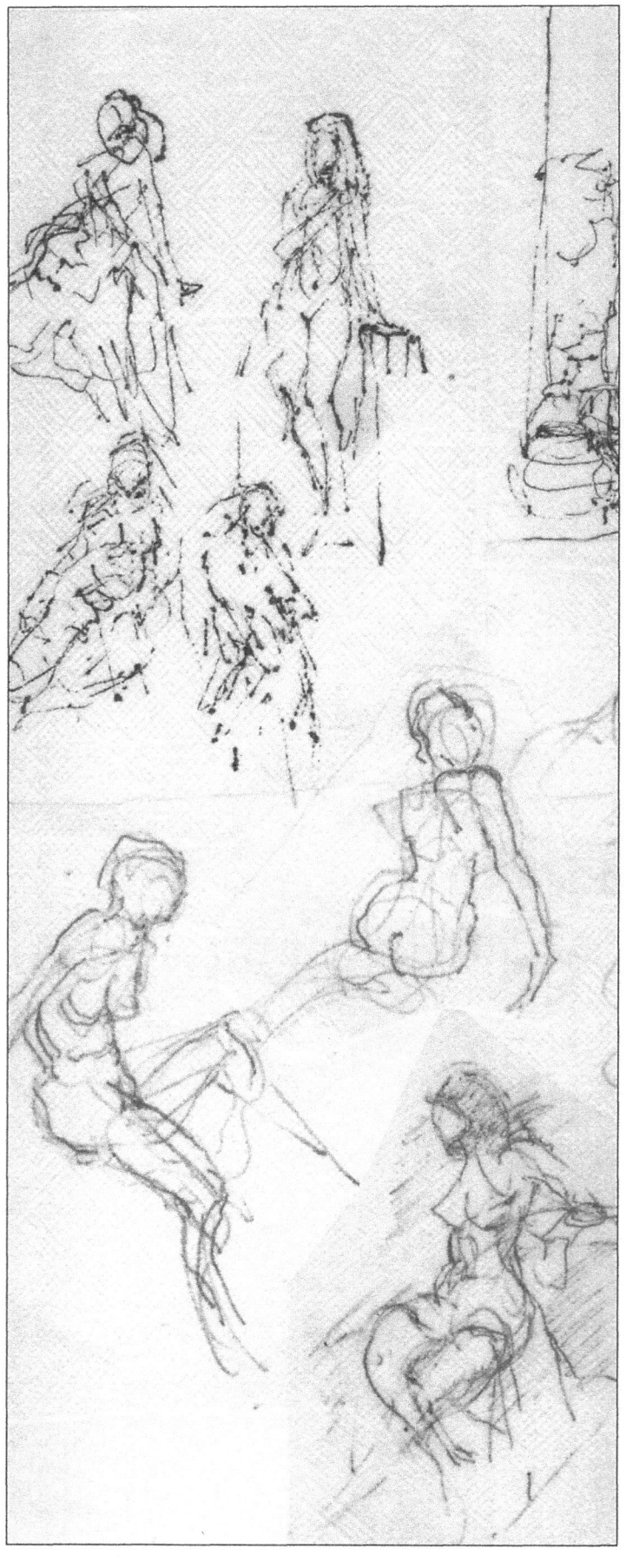

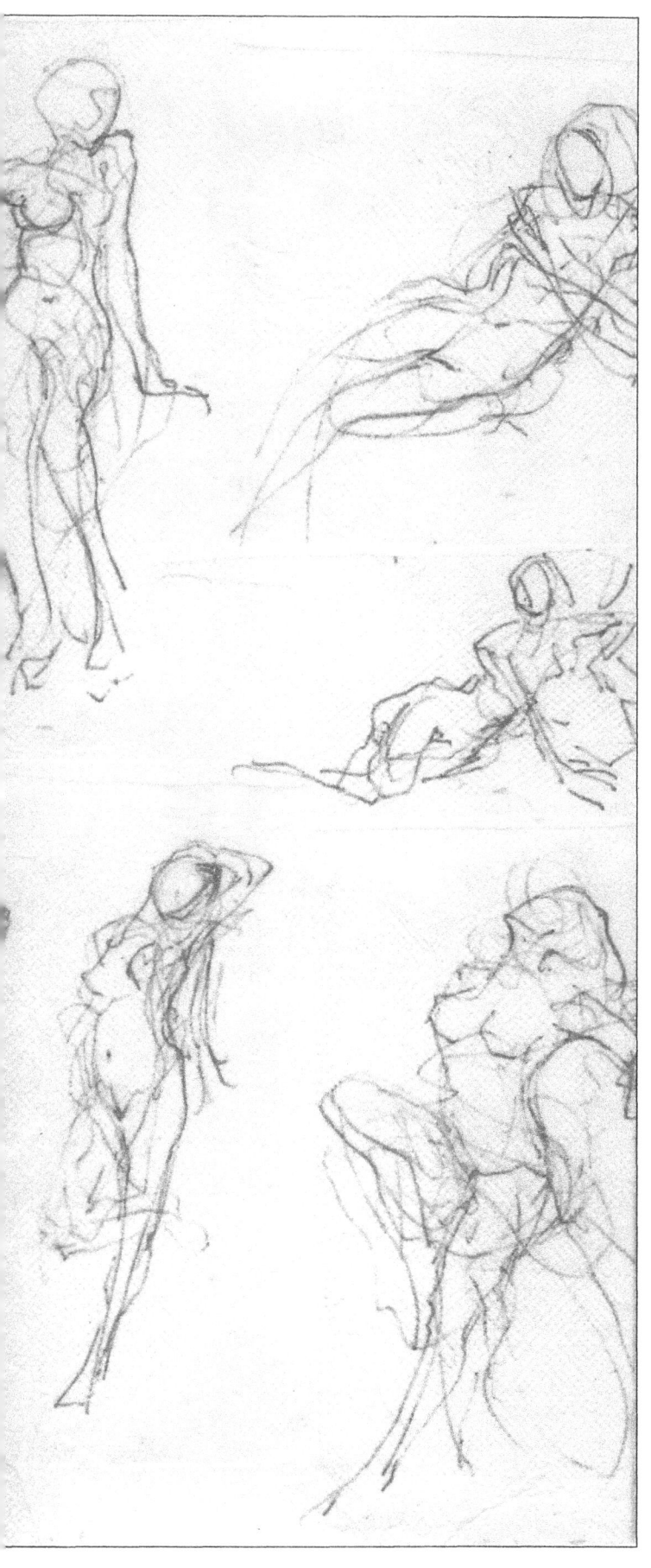

As far as I'm concerned I start both these types of drawings in a similar way. For memory drawings of the figure I prefer to start with an oval which represents the head and use loose, scribbly lines to search out the replication of the form that is in my mind. I am mentally projecting the image on paper or canvas. Everything at first is general. When the image starts to emerge then I true things up. Here the rational, thinking mind comes into play working hand in hand with the memory and its storehouse of information and images. Once this is achieved you can square up the drawing to whatever size you want and further perfect it. It may be necessary to hire a model at this stage to pose in a position similar to your drawing for even further completion especially in regards to light and shade. Working this way one avoids the stiff, dull type of drawing that looks like a marble statue when one copies the model, or a photograph of the model in every detail. By working from memory and imagination one achieves a drawing or painting of a life-like animated human being existing in space, time and action.

It should be apparent to anyone who has tried that the creative process, the imagination, cannot be turned on or off by will. The creative process has its own hidden mechanism that seems to work independently of the rational conscious mind. It seems to come and go of its own volition and cannot be forced. It picks its own time and place for revelation. You must accept these facts.

Much of this subject has been written about over the centuries and I have tried to find and read everything I could on the subject. I have also kept notes of my own observations and ideas. From all of these I have drawn some conclusions. Essentially every writer, poet or artist draws strikingly similar conclusions concerning the imagination.

The consensus of opinion is that there must be first an intensive study of the subject. One must study, study hard and intensely until one is exhausted with the subject. This should be followed by a period of rest, relaxation and forgetfulness. Forgetfulness? Yes. Put the subject out of your mind and indulge in thinking of and doing anything else which will get you away from the problem. Odd as it may seem the more you can eliminate the problem from your mind the better off you will be in the end.

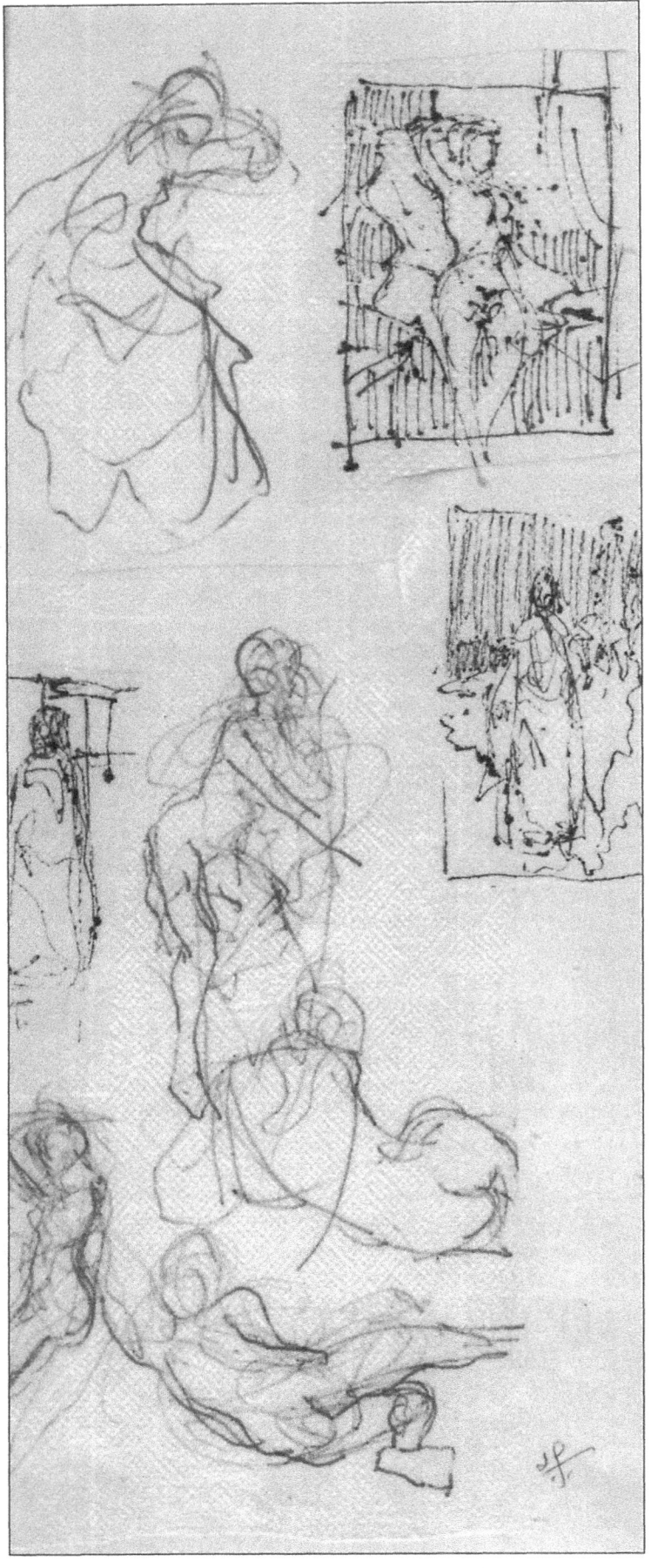

Your subconscious mind will be working out a solution unbeknown to you. Then when you are in a relaxed state and least expect it the answer will pop spontaneously into your conscious mind. *At this point you must record the impression by writing, drawing or recording it.* It is a grave mistake to think you will remember it at a later time for it will vanish as quickly as melting snow in the sun and will not appear the same way again, if indeed ever again.

Throughout the ages great men in all fields of endeavors were prodigious note takers, many of them having pocketfuls of notes accumulated during the day. They constantly jotted down their ideas wherever and whenever they occurred. This encouraged the creative faculty to come to the surface more easily and freely than if no notations were made and is therefore a good practice to adopt.

I have discovered that the creative process of the mind, in relation to the artist at least, can be coaxed, or drawn out or stimulated as it may be. Some of these ideas are not new and go back centuries. Da Vinci, for instance recommended looking at stains or variations of colors and textures on walls to bring the imagination into play wherein one may see imaginary landscapes, battle scenes, faces, etc., etc. Even the ancient Chinese master painters were aware of this and recommended the practice of staring at a weathered piece of material until the imagination created images of mountains, rivers, lakes – indeed an entire world. The imagination can also be stimulated by natural phenomena such as cloud formations, sunsets and unusual atmospheric effects, whirlpools and other water formations. Sounds, music and smells also stimulate the imagination.

One could, however, carry the process a bit further by making their own stimuli. There are unlimited ways of doing this and each must find his own way.

The artist Alexander Cozzens published a book titled, *A New Method of Assisting the Invention in Drawing Original Compositions of Landscape,* which contained a series of accidental inkblots. From these one could evolve a landscape that was much more personal and interesting than one that was copied from nature. The random accidental blots suggest things and draw out the imagination. Of course depending on who is looking at them, the blots will suggest different objects or subject matters.

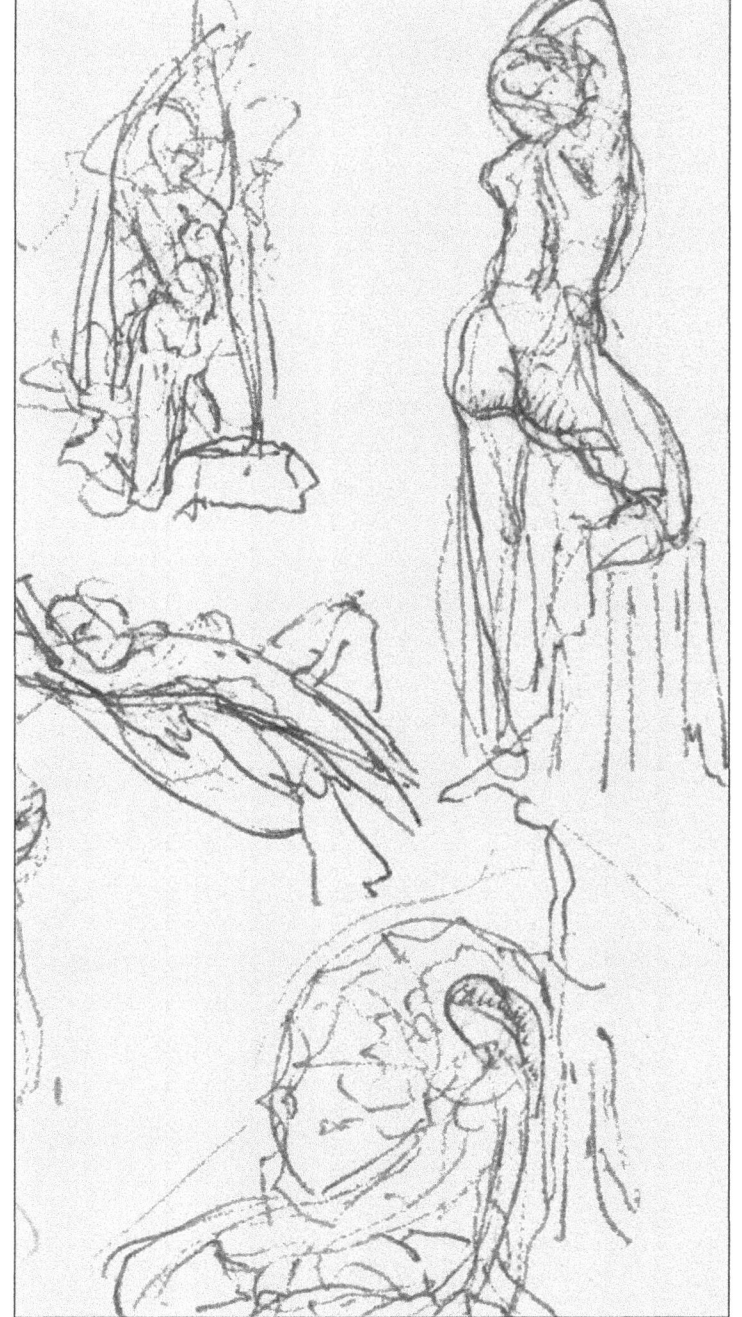

When it comes to drawing the figure one can draw from life, from memory, from imagination or all three at the same time. Although memory and imagination are closely related I prefer to treat them separately. When you draw from memory it is a mental image of something you have seen and retained in your memory banks. However when you draw from imagination you are creating a new image, one not in your memory – something you are not looking at.

For this reason compositions are best started from imagination for we are all always seeking something new, original and individual.

Once the idea is fairly well formed by the imagination then one relies on memory as well as knowledge to perfect the drawing and modeling and later from the model for further precision and accuracy if desired.

It is obvious then that the more the work is carried to a "finish" the further away it gets from the original imaginative impulse thereby losing much of the greater appeal of the original conception. Throughout the ages it has been said in the artistic communities of great civilizations that a beautiful paint sketch is a far greater work of art than its highly finished version. It is difficult however to impress this idea on the mentality of the average mind that prefers to see works of art looking as photographic as possible.

I have evolved a technique for drawing the figure from imagination which conforms to much of what has been stated above. The idea came to me while I was in a *relaxed state* having a cup of coffee and aimlessly scribbling on a paper napkin with a ballpoint pen. I soon found out that I started seeing figures or landscapes in the scribbles. These I then emphasized with a more concise line. I found, in my case anyhow, that I have to start with a few scribbles and then draw an oval shape which represents the head. I then let the pen wander freely over the paper any and every which way – having no conception at all. It helps to look away occasionally as one may start getting an image too early. This would be more like memory drawing where you draw an image that is clear in your mind. Every once in a while throw in a straight line that is unrelated to anything. *Try as long as you can to avoid getting an image.* Soon, though, an image will appear in the scribbles that you have not thought of. At this point you should emphasize the lines that form that image. You will be delighted by the new drawing you have created.

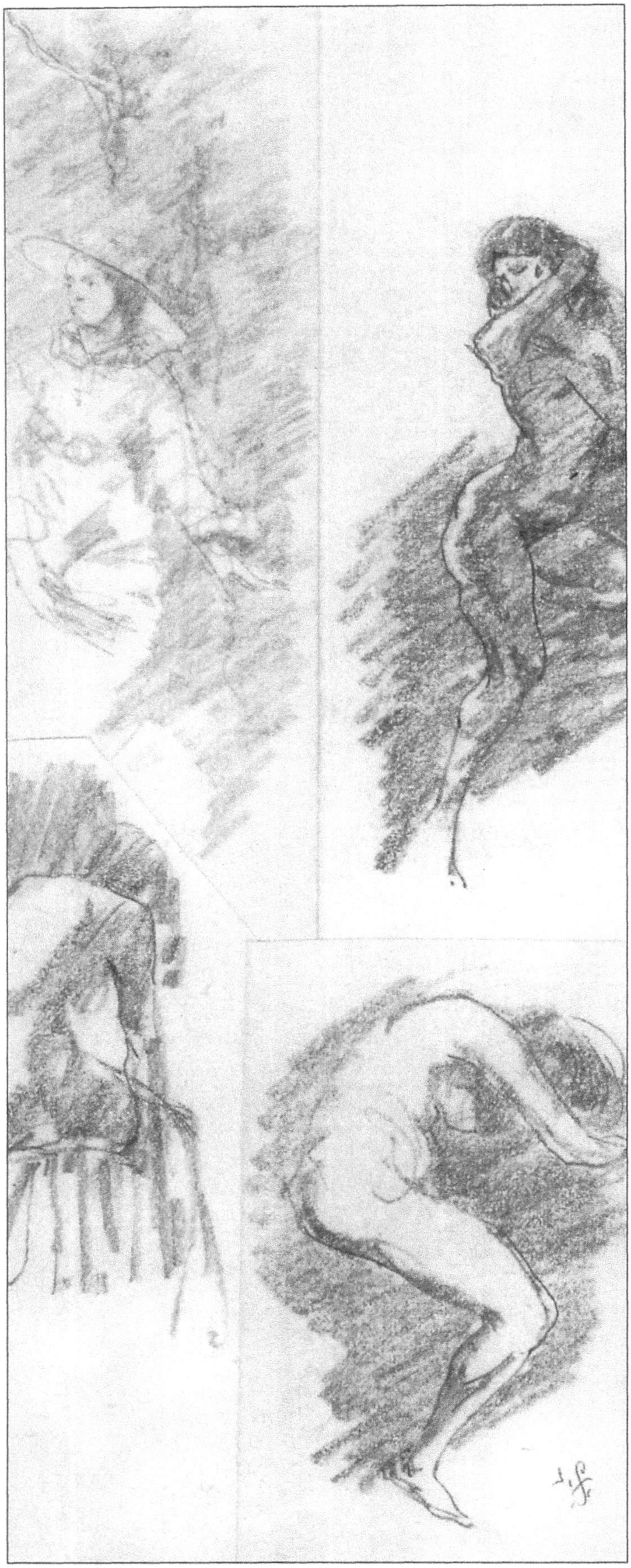

To repeat, when in a relaxed mood start scribbling anything; let the pen or pencil wander. Soon you will feel you're ready to draw the oval head shape then continue to let your drawing instrument roam freely all over the paper. *Avoid at all costs at this stage to try to draw something.* The drawing you are looking for will come of itself as the imagination will supply a new unthought-of image within the lines.

I find it best to use a very light line in the beginning, so light that sometimes the pen seems it doesn't even touch the page – the more indistinct the better. Go with the flow. Follow your impulses with the line without trying to visualize anything – eventually an image comes. The image can then be squared up and brought to a finish. This seems to me to be the process of the Old Masters. We can see the first nervous imaginative scribbles searching out poses and compositions. From these we see more finished drawings made from these scribbles that are squared off ready to be transferred to a larger surface. Works originating from the imagination will always be regarded superior to works which have been mechanically planned.

This only one method. There are countless others. Each one of you will have to invent your own method to get your imagination to work for you.

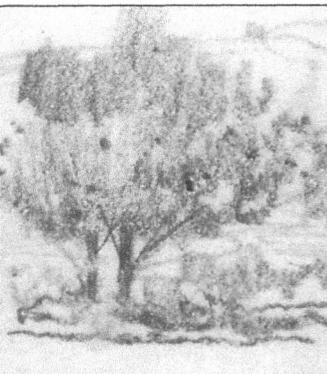

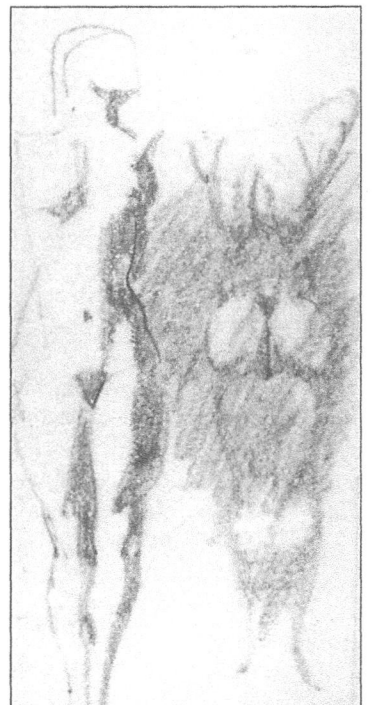

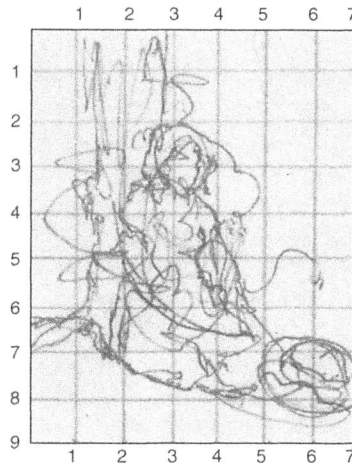

EVOLVING A DRAWING
FROM IMAGINATION OR MEMORY

Step 1. Choose a drawing done from your imagination or memory and draw a grid over it. In the example shown the grid above is made up of 1/4" inch squares although one can use any measurement one wants as long as the intervals are equal.

Step 2. Enlarge the grid to whatever size you feel comfortable working with. The intervals must be in proportion to the original grid, that is, twice the size, two and a half times, three times, etc. The grid shown here has been made up of 1/2" inch intervals. Start drawing on this grid by placing your lines at approximately the same position as on the smaller grid. You can, many times, find intersections where lines of the drawing cross lines of the grid. Seize these to help you work up the outline of the drawing. Continue to complete the drawing as much as possible from memory as you alter and correct the forms and contours.

Step 3. In many cases this cartoon-like drawing can be used for paintings or murals by more advanced artists, such as was common during the Renaissance. However, if you wish to develop the drawing further trace this cartoon onto a fresh, clean sheet of paper. Try to finish the drawing with line and light and shade as much as you can from memory. If you can't develop it enough you can use a live model for reference or drape a manikin for the drapery folds.

Once the drawing is completed to your satisfaction, you can place tracing paper over it and draw different backgrounds or work out a black and white composition. One can also place a heavy sheet of acetate over the drawing and paint with oil paints in full color.

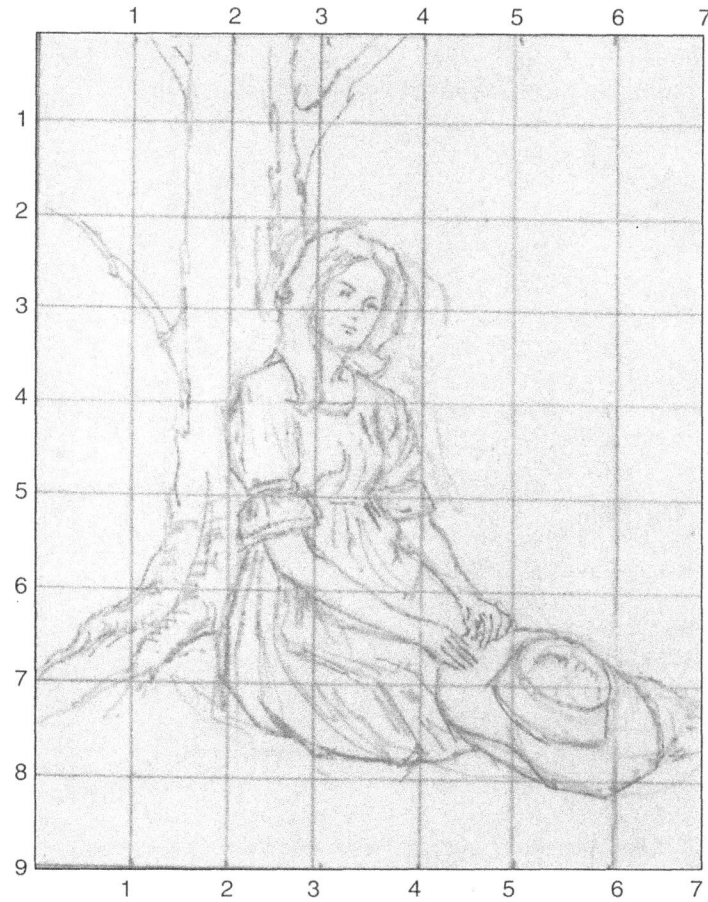

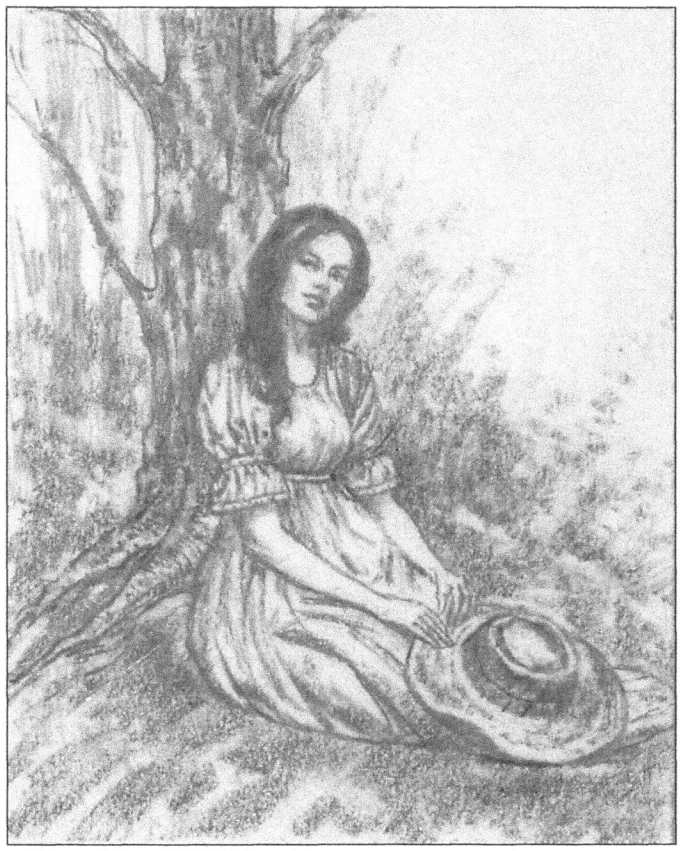

IMAGINATION, DRAWING AND MUSIC

I have mentioned before that music can stimulate the imaginative process. I'm sure everyone knows this or is at least aware of it at times. In many cases this is the intent of the composer. He wants, by the use of his musical composition for your mind to conjure up a scene or a feeling that he wishes to convey. Or perhaps he only aspires that his music will stimulate your imagination to enchanted realms.

If you are aware or have been made aware of the composer's intent then your rational mind will try to evoke images along those lines, but if you are not aware of his intent then your imagination may supply images of almost anything depending on you and the mood you're in.

The drawings on the following pages 226 and 227 are imaginary drawings that flowed out of my pencil while listening to a symphonic piece many years ago. As far as I can remember there was no thinking involved, just furiously putting down lines, dots and dashes as I was carried along with the music. I must have done thirty of them within a very short space of time. I feel, fortunately or unfortunately, that my best ones were sold and these few are the only examples I have left of the series.

One doesn't start drawing furiously right off. The process is akin to a locomotive starting very slowly and gradually building up to top speed. You have to be in a relaxed state and be prepared with a sufficient amount of materials you intend to use for when you get going you can tolerate no interruptions. Start drawing anything slowly and leisurely with a few lines and begin merging yourself with the music. Soon you will find that you are one with the music and your lines also will become one with it. Your rational thinking vanishes as you, the music and your lines will become as one. Go as far as you can with the feeling and when you see some kind of image emerge rapidly change the paper and continue on to another sheet. Keep drawing as long as you can sustain this state for at one point the inspiration will fade away and no more images will come. By constant practice, however, this faculty will increase in power and duration and bring great satisfaction, for you will produce new and exciting things.

The drawings shown must have been made in the winter around Christmas time for what came as a result of the music were winter landscapes and angels. It's quite likely that if the same procedure was followed in the summer a whole different set of images could or would have appeared. I find this is a very pleasurable and rewarding exercise.

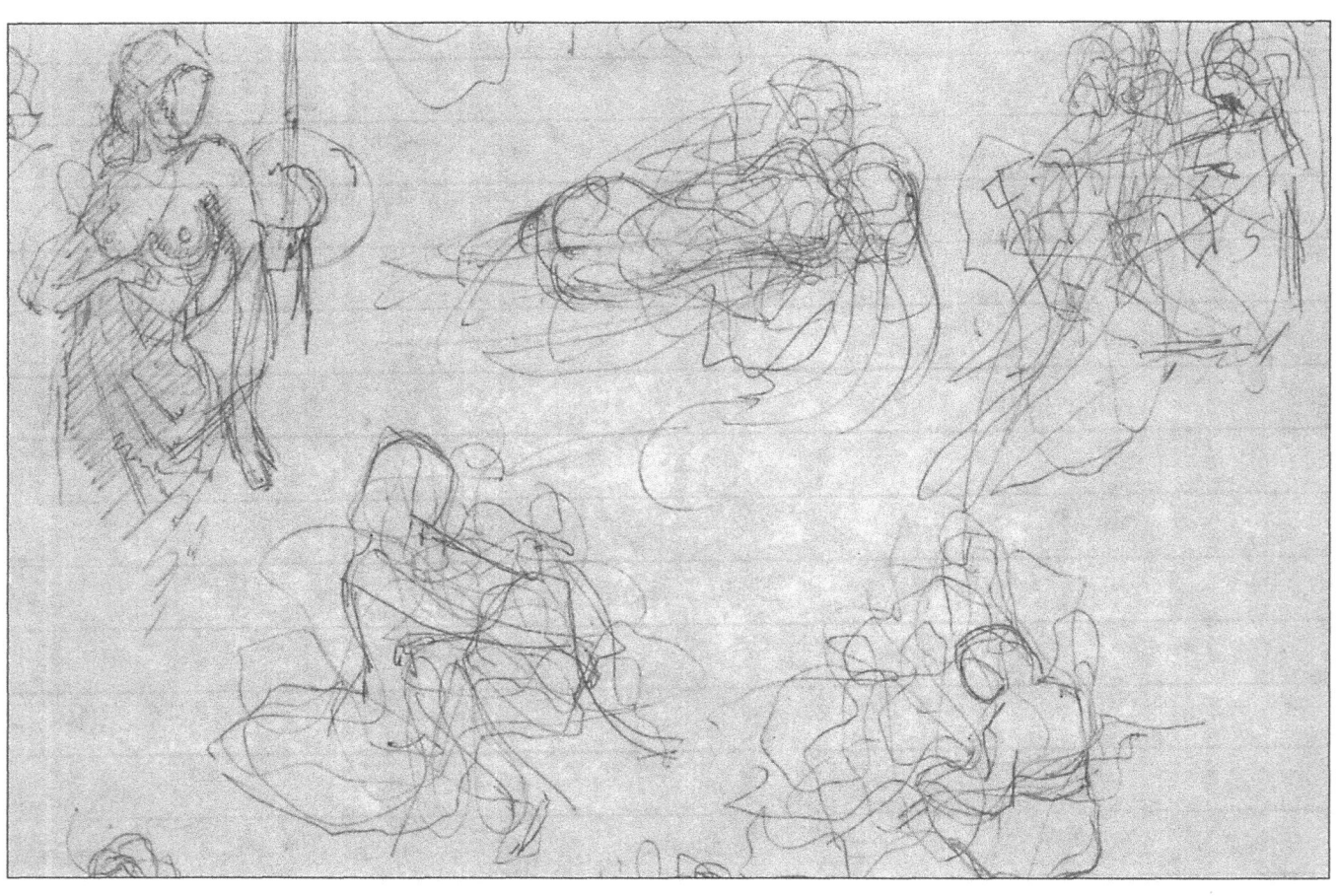

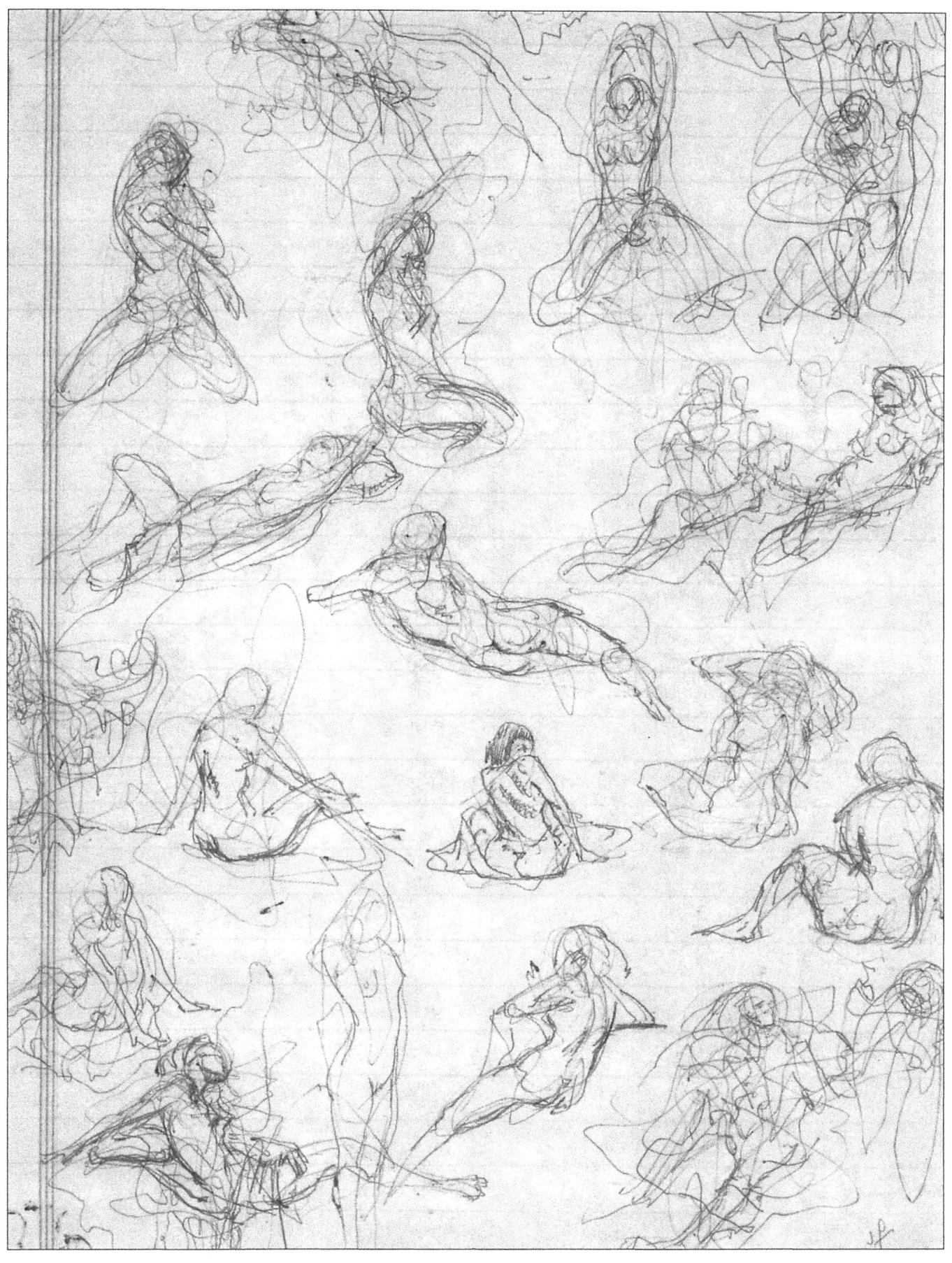

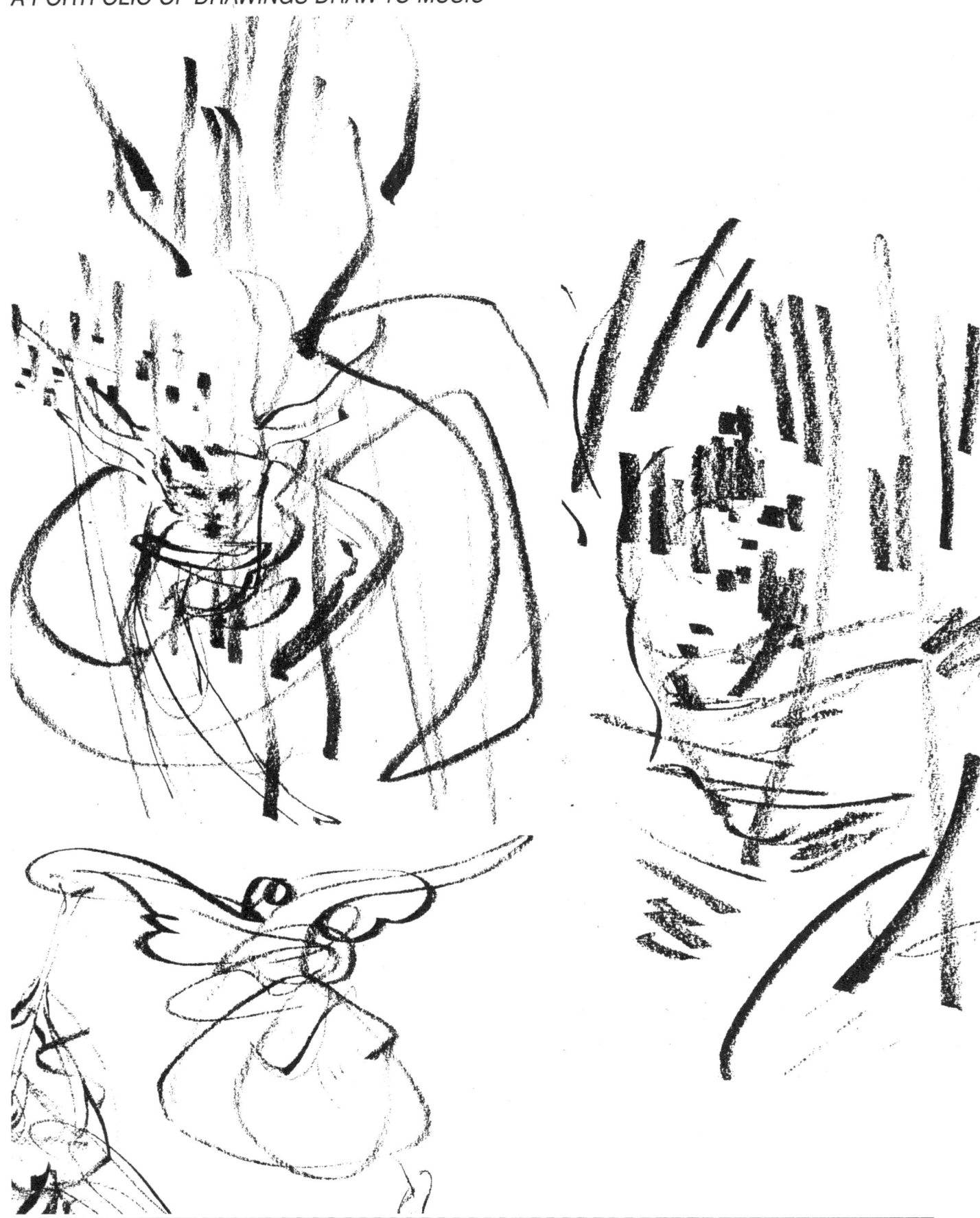

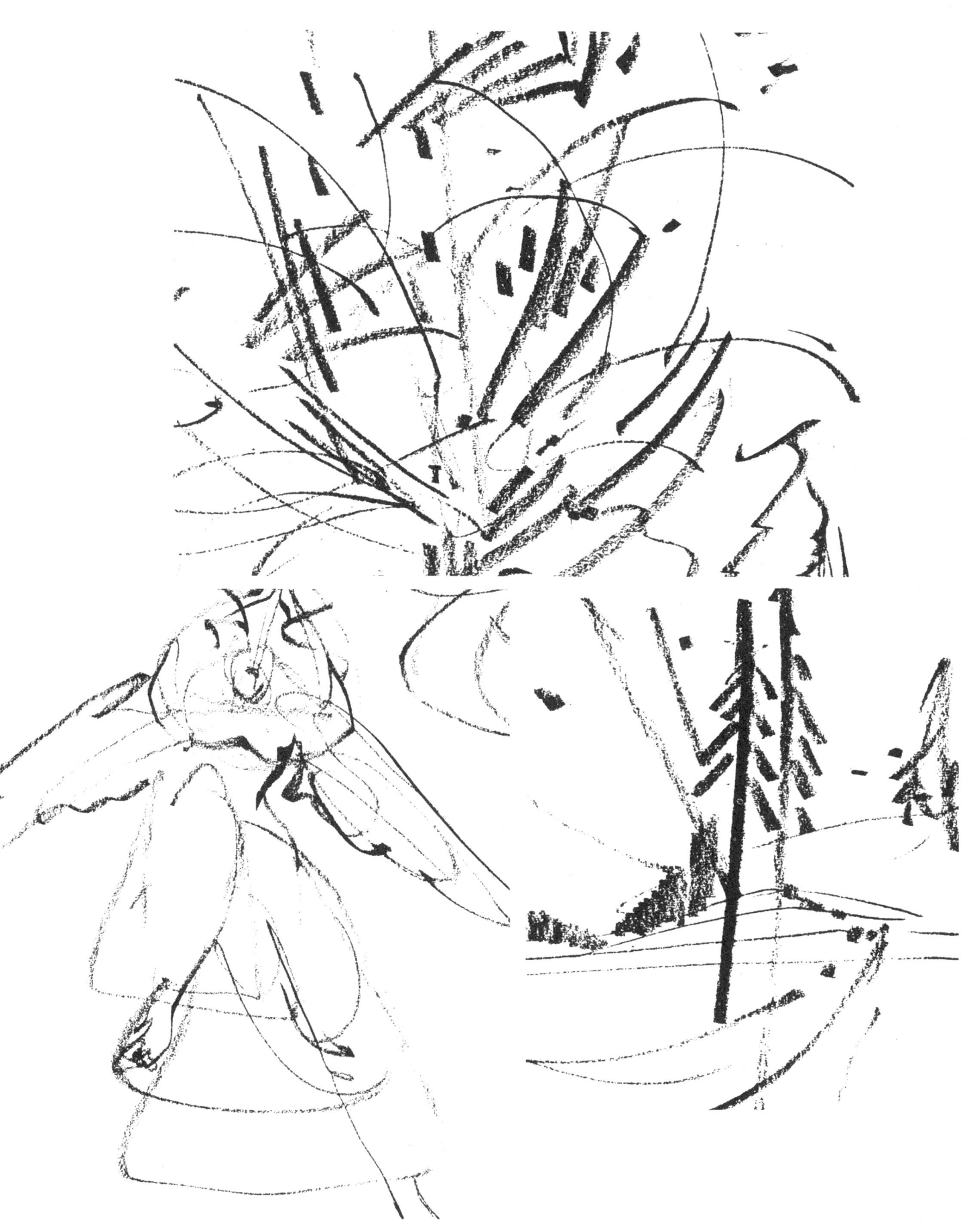

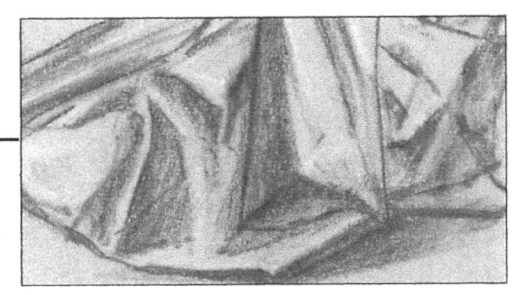

CHAPTER TWENTY-TWO

DRAPERY

INTRODUCTION

It is important to know how to draw drapery well for it serves many purposes. Think of drapery as a package which protects, beautifies, seduces and deceives, a package which *explains the form underneath as well as the action of the figure.*

I find in many drawings and paintings of today that while the head and hands may be well drawn that the rendering of drapery is rather weak and lacking. This may be due to the fact that the student spends most of his time in art school drawing and painting heads and figures – only dashing in the drapery at the last few moments and this without knowledge or concept. Another reason is that you cannot or rather should not copy drapery. To do so in almost all cases will result in a drawing that lacks form, action and the proper light and shade.

In the past the artist first made drawings of the nude figure. Next they would pose the model in the same pose only this time adding drapery. The drapery would conform to the form underneath. Folds which did not explain or confused the basic form were omitted and sometimes it would be necessary to invent a fold which explained the form or action of the figure more clearly. These principles were adhered to by the ancient Greeks and Romans whose statues showed simple, flowing lines of drapery. The Academic Artists at the turn of the century as well as the Victorian and pre-Raphaelite painters proceeded in much the same way.

Each era following the decline of Greek and Roman art had its own outlook on how to represent drapery. This was due to narrow provincialism in some cases and or guilds which set the standards that had to be adhered to. In Pre-Renaissance times the drapery folds were stiff and angular, possible due to the limitations of the commonly used tempera paint which did not allow the freedom of drawing and the brushwork of oil paint.

You should study the drapery of many different artists for they all had their own unique way of representing the same thing. Study the drapery drawings and paintings of Holbein, Durer, Tintoretto, Rubens, Ingres, Raeburn, Lord Leighton, Leonardo, Michelangelo, Fragonard, El Greco and J. S. Sargeant to name a few diverse artists.

Today too many artists copy what is before them without having a proper concept or much knowledge of the subject. The result is that there is neither form, action or correct light and shade in

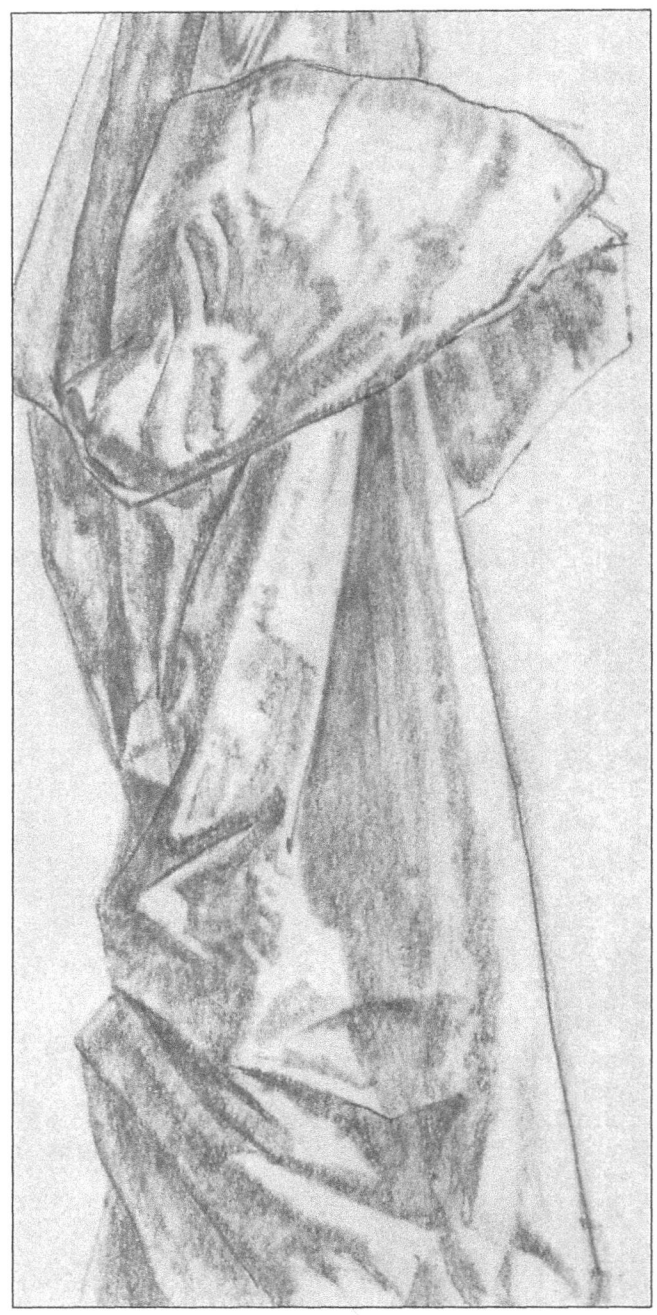

their drawings.

One sees many folds but one should not copy folds that do not explain the form underneath nor explain the action of the figure. It is perfectly legitimate to leave them out or put a fold in if it helps. One should not make dark folds in light areas or light folds in dark areas. They appear as such because of the values they're surrounded by and are therefore illusionary. To copy the values as you see them will destroy the largeness of the form and the lighting. Smaller folds and wrinkles can likewise be left out or underplayed for the same reason.

Drapery should be first drawn as realism and secondly as design. As realism its biggest idea is to explain what the model is and what the model is doing. As drapery rests on form it reveals what the form is beneath it. The folds that hang are due to gravity or by being pulled or twisted from two or more points of support. As realism we also have to show tailoring, folds, and the texture of the material.

Drapery is also used to set the figure off, to be used as a foil or to give the figure impact and emphasis. As such you should always be aware of its overall outside shape and make it interesting and decorative.

DRAWING DRAPERY

The following ideas are useful in the execution of good drawing of drapery. Of first concern is the outside pattern. This can be achieved by observing outside shapes, inside shapes and the relating of their lines. "Pointing off" is also useful. Place a dot where the line is to start, another one where you think it should end, and connect the two with a line.

The lines of drapery are mostly straight, seldom rounded. The patterns within the drape are never round and never square but always some kind of triangle.

Textures are to be considered. They are basically of three kinds. First there is silk which is thin and shiny. The folds will be sharp, angular and straight lined. The highlight is no lighter than the ridge light of a fold. Second is a medium textured material such as a muslin or cotton broadcloth. It is a flat matte texture and has angular folds but the folds are not as sharp as those of silk. Velvet is the thickest material and because it has a nap surface reflects very little light. With velvet the eyes and folds take more of a rounded shape. Radiations from the pull points will die out quicker than in stiffer material. *The darkest shadow on velvet is the cast shadow, not the slope of the ridge.* This is because the cast shadow is less affected by reflected light than the regular shadow.

Of course one has to draw the forms and planes and put them in light and shade. One need not use the whole range of values when rendering drapery. Five values should be enough. When drawing on grey paper one can use even less value gradations but may have to use white chalk to heighten some areas.

Folds are usually going into some kind of perspective. A simple way to think of them is to first imagine a pipe going into perspective and then draw the folds going around the pipe.

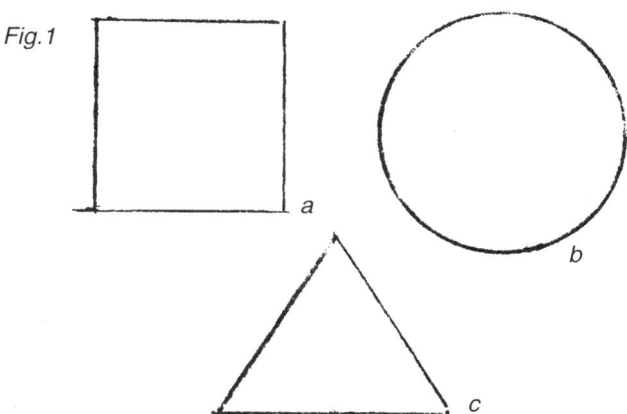

Figs. 1a.b.c. Shapes of drapery are never round or square but some kind of triangle

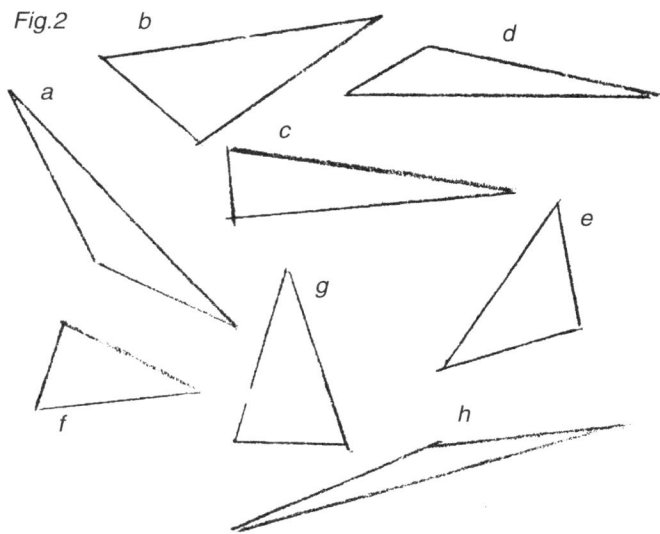

Figs. 2a.b.c.d.e.f.g.h.i. Some examples of triangular drapery shapes. There will be an infinite variety of these

Fig. 3. This is a drawing of the planes you will find in drapery. You can view it as it appears vertically or horizontally. Number **1** is a top slant plane, in this case receiving the most light. Number **2** is a shadow plane but since it is receiving light from the plane below it is not so dark. Number **3** is a top plane with a cast shadow on it. Number **4** is an upright plane which is dark and number **5** is another shadow underplane, darker than number **2**. It is receiving reflected light towards the rear which gives the illusion of projection and recession.

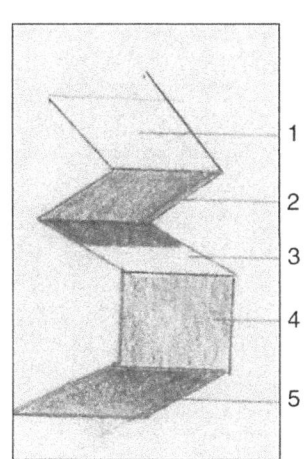

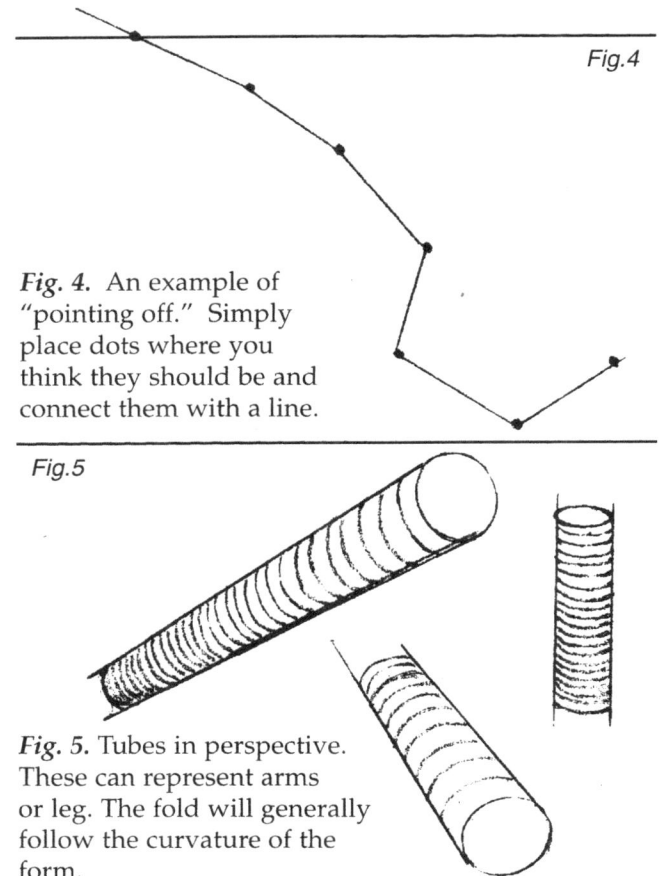

Fig.4

Fig. 4. An example of "pointing off." Simply place dots where you think they should be and connect them with a line.

Fig.5

Fig. 5. Tubes in perspective. These can represent arms or leg. The fold will generally follow the curvature of the form.

Fig.6

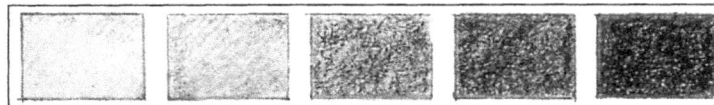

Fig. 6. One can get by by using only five different values as shown here. They can also be in a lighter key or darker key.

Fig. 7a. Drapery should follow the action line or the form lines of the figure. The arrow shows the direction of the action that the large folds should follow.

Fig. b. Here the folds are following the form lines of the chest and neck.

Fig. c. Folds following the form at the shoulder, elbows, chest, waist and crotch. Action folds start at pull points of the knee.

There are many points to observe and be aware of when drawing drapery. Among them are what are called "eyes," the system of radiation, the points of pull, points of support, piping, busy spaces, blank spaces between folds and forms between forms.

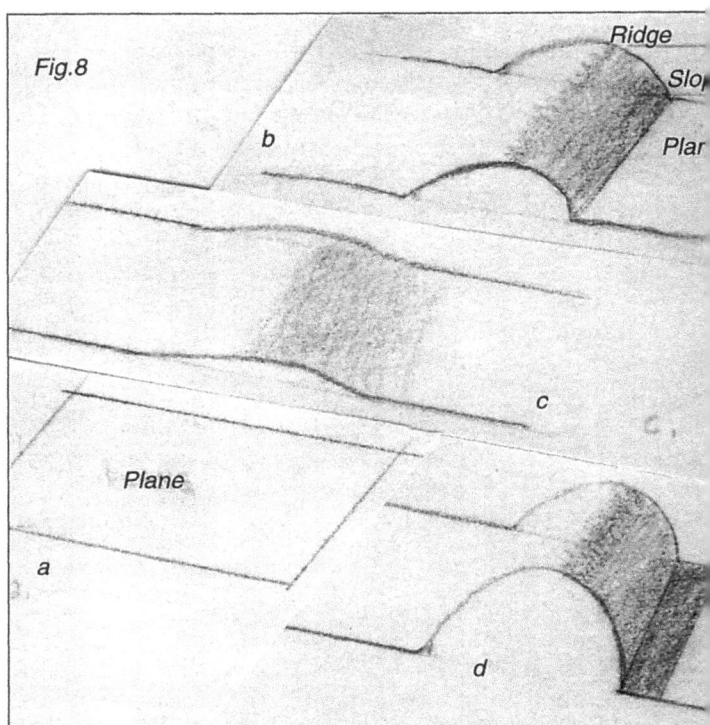

Fig.8

Let us start at the beginning, with a flat piece of material as shown in **Fig. 8a.** This is called a plane. By pushing the material together slightly we cause what is called a ridge. The side of the ridge is called the slope and the flat part is called a plane. When there is a light and shade on the ridge as shown in **Fig. 8b.** the light side transition is a soft edge and fairly hard edged where the shadow ends.

Fig. 8c. shows a very slight ridge, a shallow fold. In this case the shading will be soft edged on both sides of the ridge. In **Fig. 8d.** the ridge is very high, a deep fold, causing a cast shadow on the plane. The start of the shadow on the light side of the ridge is soft edged. The end of the cast shadow has a hard edge.

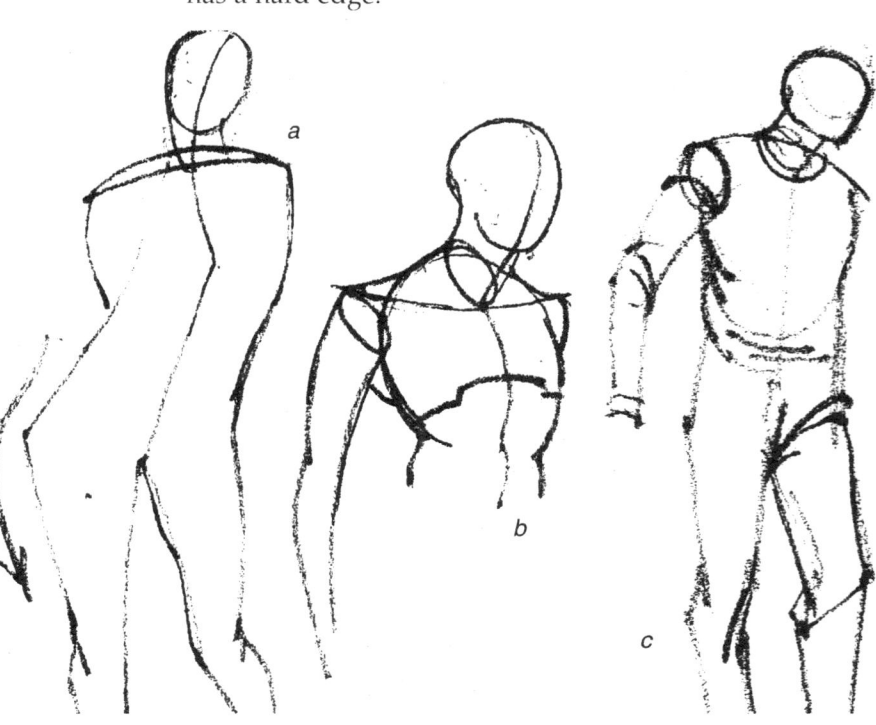

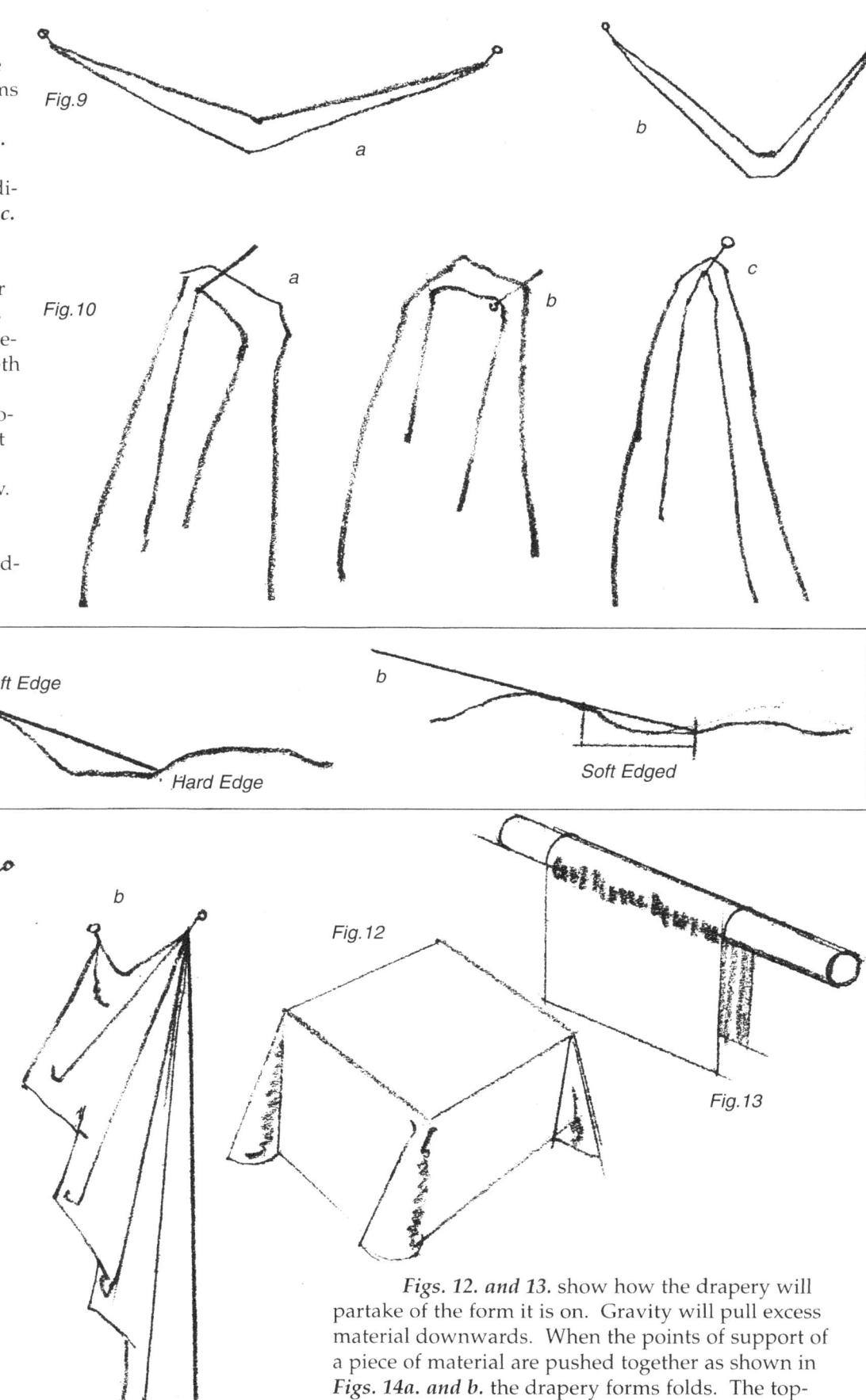

As material is bunched it has no place to go and therefore forms an "eye." This is illustrated in *Figs. 9a. and b.* "Eyes" are secondary points of support or radiation. *Figs. 10a. b. and c.* show three different types of "eyes."

The hardness or softness of the shadows or cast shadows on material depends on the depth of the folds. *Figs. 11a. and b.* show folds in profile. In *Fig. 11a.* the first ridge is high causing a hard edged cast shadow. In *Fig. b.* the folds are low so both the beginning and end of the shadows will be soft edged

Fig.9

Fig.10

Fig.11

Soft Edge

Hard Edge

Soft Edged

Fig.14

Fig.12

Fig.13

Figs. 12. and 13. show how the drapery will partake of the form it is on. Gravity will pull excess material downwards. When the points of support of a piece of material are pushed together as shown in *Figs. 14a. and b.* the drapery forms folds. The topmost fold will be the largest, the second fold will be smaller, the third one even smaller and so on.

231

Folds radiate from points of support in a certain manner. *Fig. 15a.* is a flat piece of cloth. *Fig. b.* shows one point of support with the folds radiating from it. Notice how the folds aim towards the other three corners.

Fig. c. Showing two points of support. The radiating folds curve now and try to go to the opposite corners.

Fig. d. Three points of support. Similar to the previous. In all cases the folds will originate at the points of support. This also applies to the folds on the drapery covering the figure.

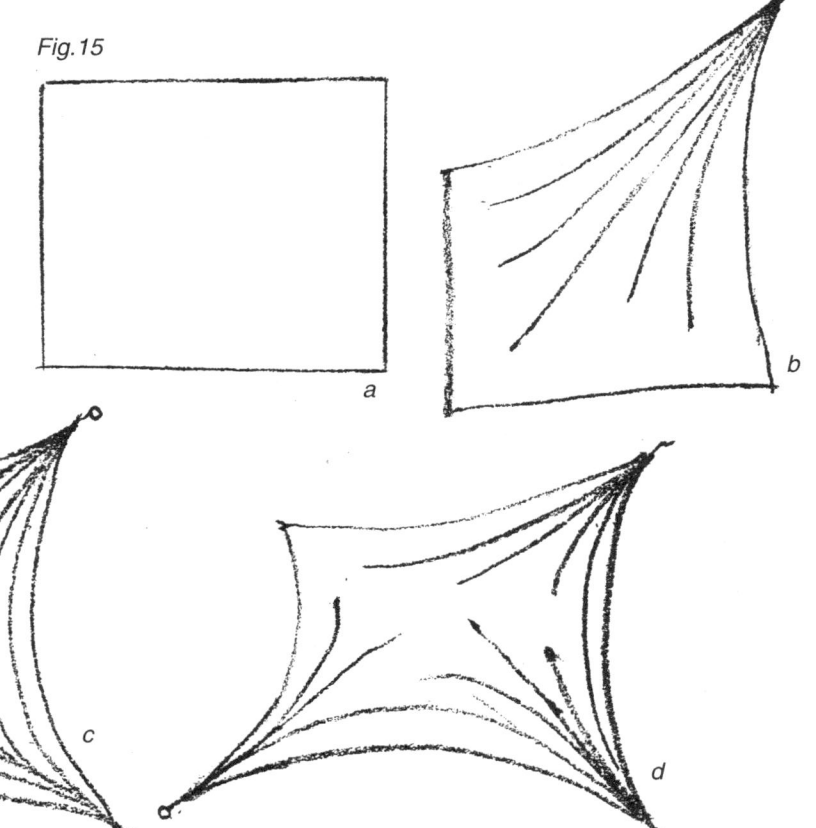

Fig.15

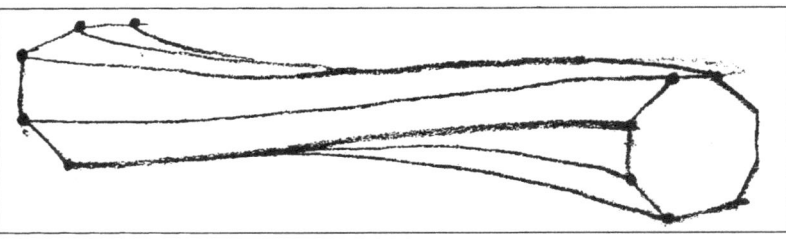

Fig. 16. Twisting folds going from one point of support to another.

Fig.16

Fig. 17. When the points of support are pushed closer folds will form. It is important to note that these folds fall alternately off center.

Fig. 18a.b. The top fold is the largest. The back part of this fold lies flat on the surface. Gravity takes over with the bulk of the material.

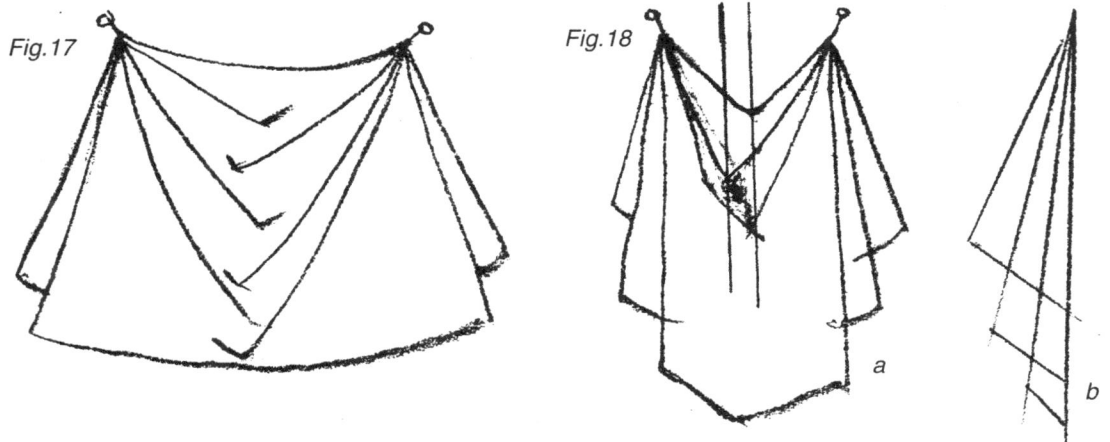

Fig.17

Fig.18

THE STRUCTURE OF DRAPERY

The drawings on this page illustrate folds that are caused by either pushing material together or by gravity. Since material is commonly on cylindrical forms it usually forms bands or rings that can touch or overlap.

Fig. 19. An example of crush folds formed by pushing material together on a cylindrical form.

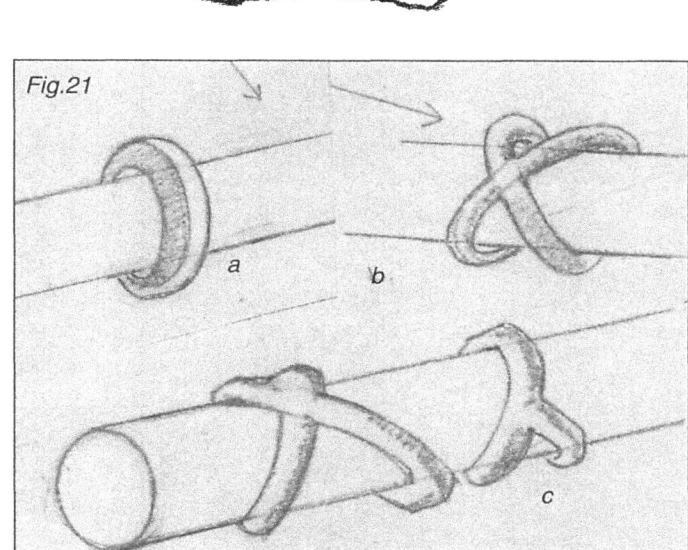

Fig.19

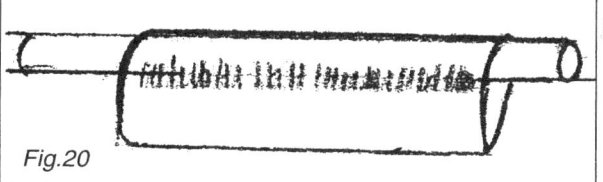

Fig.20

Fig. 20. A piece of material hanging freely on a form.

Fig. 21a.b.c. When this material is pushed together "rings" will form. These drawings are stylized to more clearly express the nature of the folds. **Fig. a.** is a single ring. **Fig. b.** shows two overlapping rings, and **Fig. c.** shows differences in the size of the rings. Any and all of these variations can be found together on drapery of the figure.

Fig. 22. The previous principles of rings applied to a suede or leather boot. The drawing of these rings is stressed – in actuality they will be softened and blended into the surrounding areas.

Figs. 23a.b. Two examples of twisting folds.

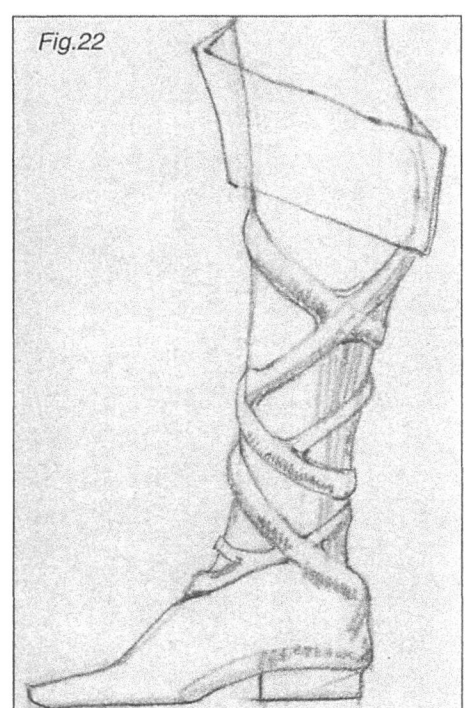

Fig.22

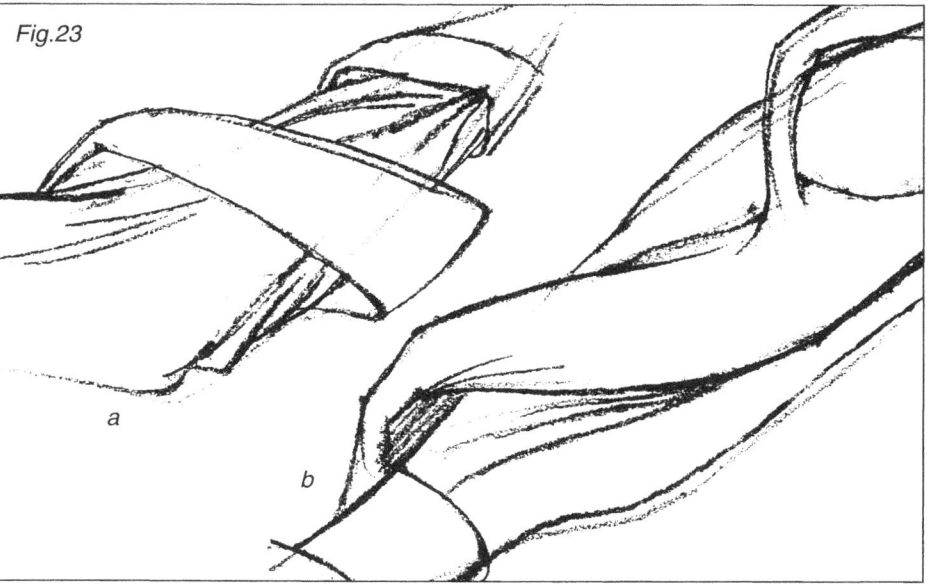

Fig.23

233

LYING ON, HANGING AND PULLING FOLDS

There are three basic kinds of folds.
1. Lying on. The drape takes the shape of the form it is on or draws the form underneath.
2. Hanging. Here gravity takes over. The drape pulls from a point or points of support. Basically there will be straight lines.
3. Pulling. Pulling folds convey action. They are frequently twisted and involve lines that are more curved. There are also folds that tunnel through and lock and interlock with other folds.

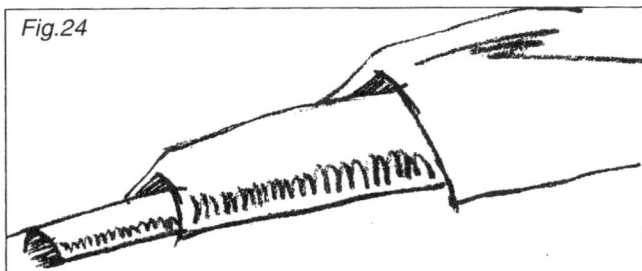

Fig. 24. An example of tunneling folds.

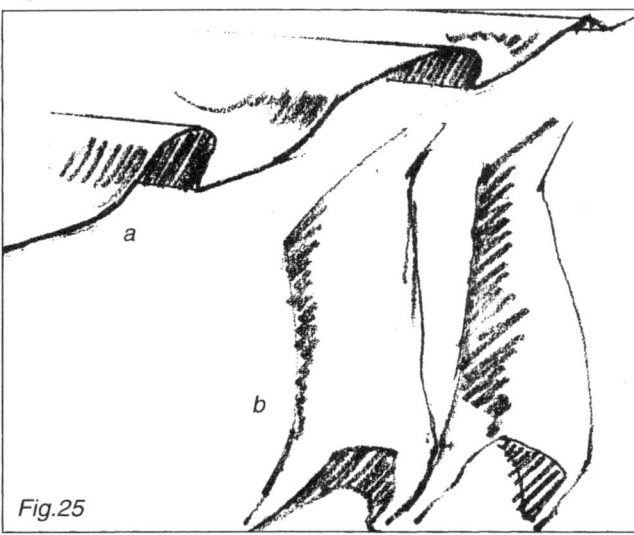

Figs. 25a.b. Examples of "pipes" caused by folded material.

Fig. a. shows pipes that are lying down.
Fig. b. An example of hanging pipes.

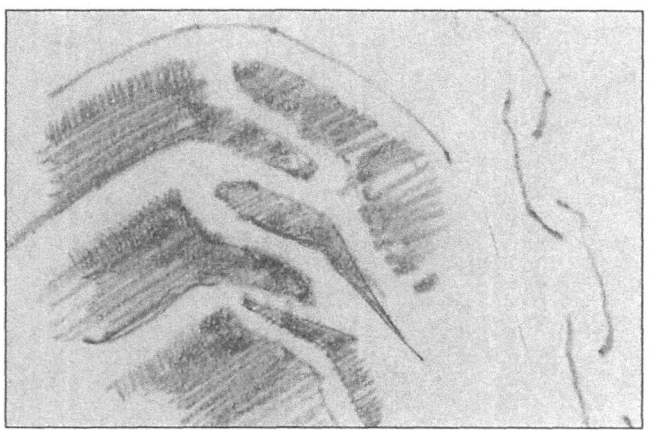

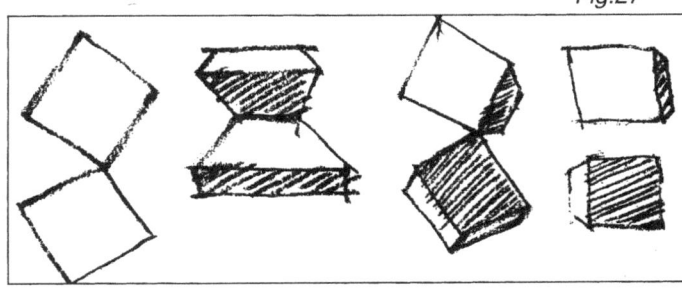

Fig. 27. Pulling and twisting folds that convey action are caused by the imbalance of the major masses represented by squares and cubes.

Figs. 28a.b. A measure of cloth hanging on a rounded form will always *follow the roundness of the form fractionally before it drops vertically due to gravity.*

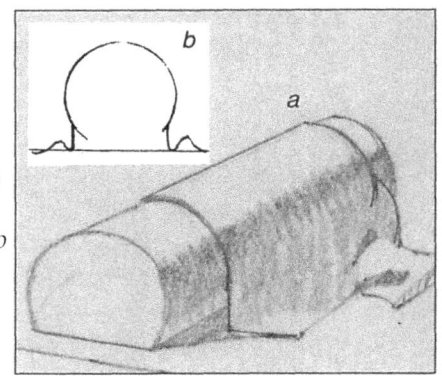

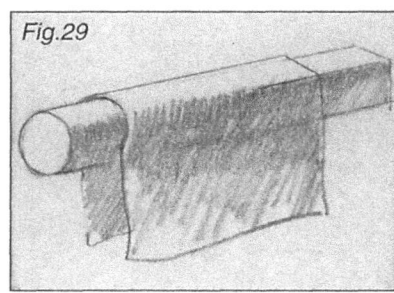

Fig. 29. A transition from a rounded to a square form. Notice the soft transition on the rounded part and the sharp transition on the square part.

Fig. 30. A very fat rounded form narrowing to a slimmer rounded form.

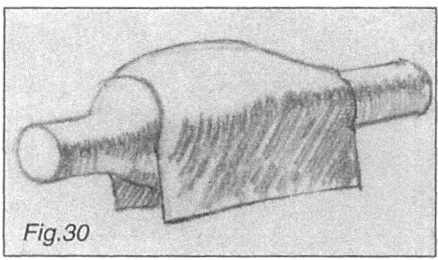

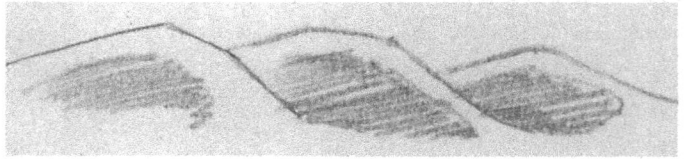

Figs. 26a.b. Two examples of interlocking folds.

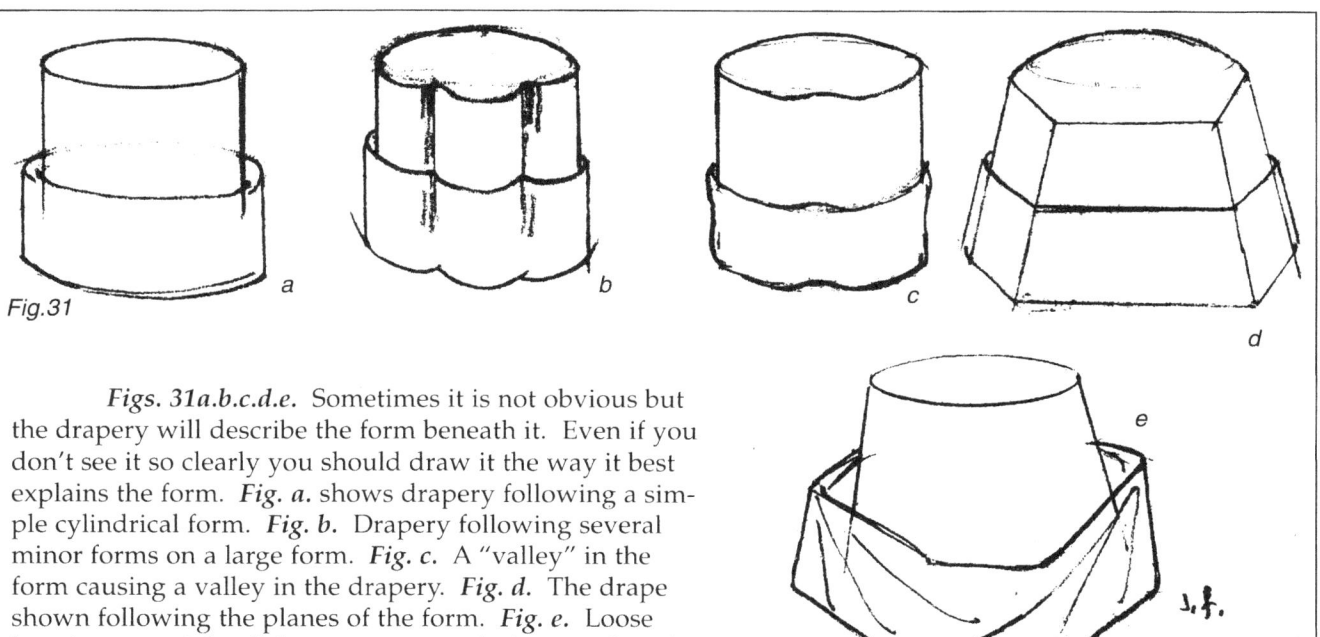

Fig.31

Figs. 31a.b.c.d.e. Sometimes it is not obvious but the drapery will describe the form beneath it. Even if you don't see it so clearly you should draw it the way it best explains the form. **Fig. a.** shows drapery following a simple cylindrical form. **Fig. b.** Drapery following several minor forms on a large form. **Fig. c.** A "valley" in the form causing a valley in the drapery. **Fig. d.** The drape shown following the planes of the form. **Fig. e.** Loose hanging material will form many straight lines and angles.

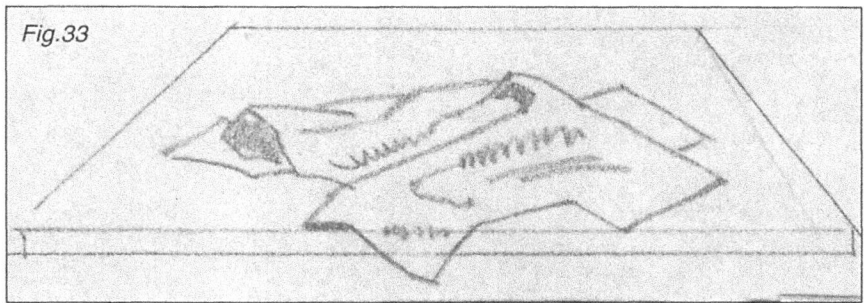

Fig.32

Fig.33

Fig. 32. Dropped drapery takes the shape of the plane it is on. The excess material can take many forms and shapes, such as pipes, ridges, eyes, etc. that lock and interlock with each other. In this instance the material is on a flat plane.

Fig. 33. Another example. Notice the straight lines at the base of the drape where it lies flat on the surface.

Fig. 34. Material on a rounded surface. Again, watch for the line at the base of the material which follows the curvature of the form.

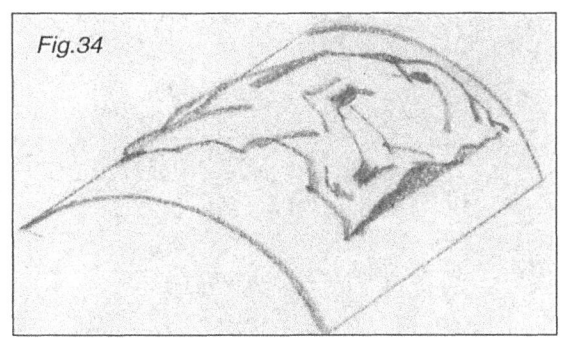

Fig.34

Fig. 35. Drapery over a compound form – in this instance a sphere and a box. The main folds will pull from the sphere to the corners of the box. Folds also will pull from the corners of the box.

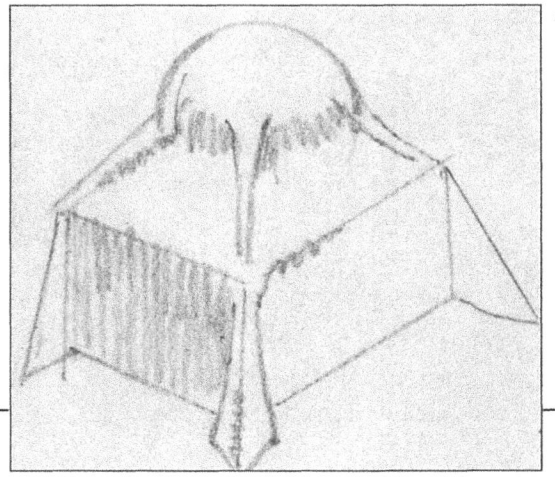

Fig.35

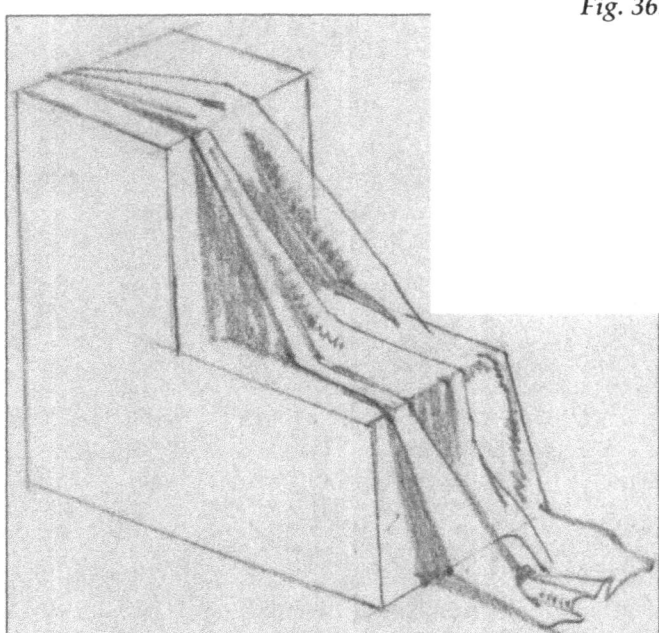

Fig. 36.

HANGING FOLDS

Figs. 39a.b.c. If material is fully stretched between two points of support there will be no folds but if we were to suspend it on one point of support as shown in *Fig. b.* then we will get folds. The folds will be small and close at top and large on the bottom as shown in *Figs. b. and c.*

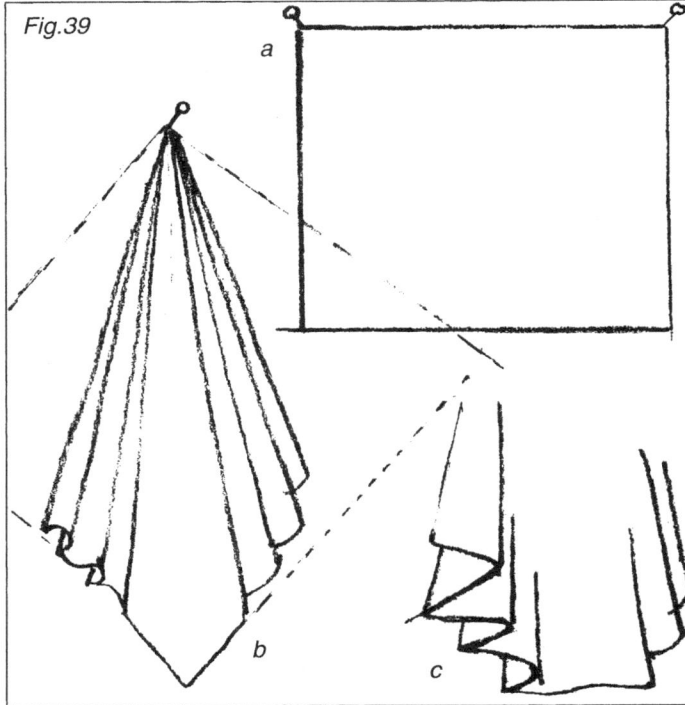

Fig. 37.
Loose material placed over a sphere will produce folds as shown here. *It is important to draw a light line encircling the sphere at the place where all the folds will start –* and they all will start at that line.

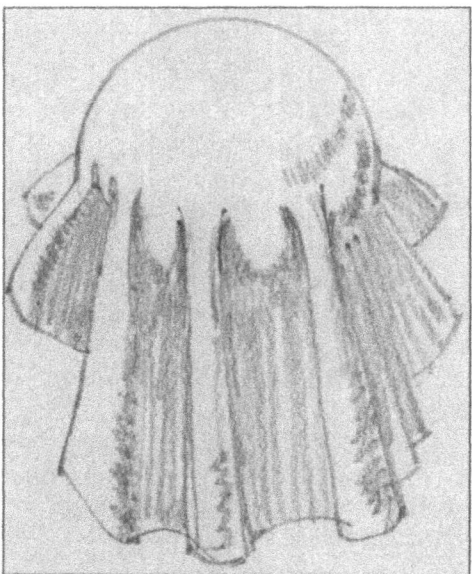

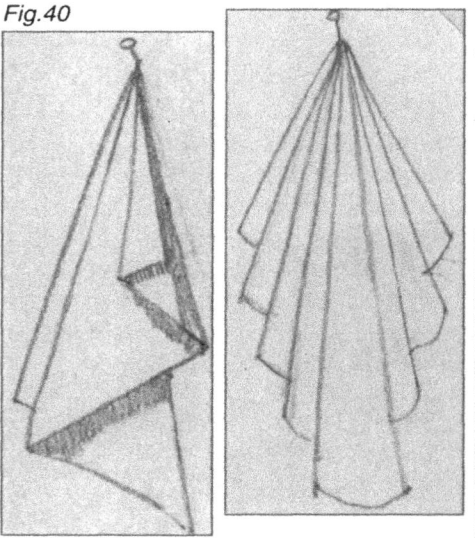

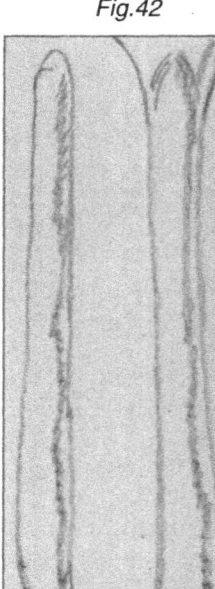

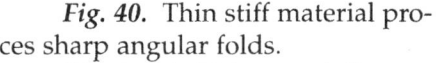

Fig. 40. Thin stiff material produces sharp angular folds.

Fig. 41. A thick material hanging from one point will produce folds that are rounded and of an overall greater width.

Fig. 42. Certain folds should be thought of as tubes, tubes that blend into a flat surface.

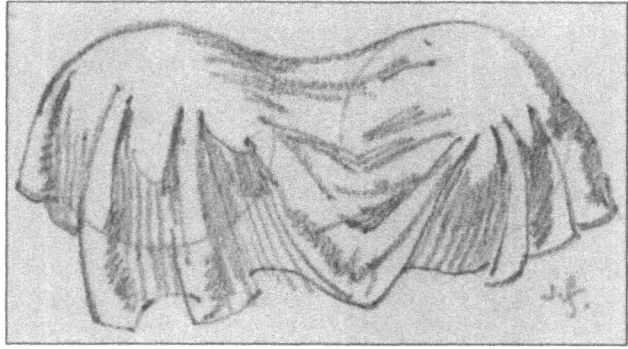

Fig. 38. Drapery covering two spheres. Again, draw a light circular line around the sphere where the folds will begin connecting folds between the folds as needed. Shading should be used on the sides of the spheres to show form.

Fig. 43. The width of the line at the bottom of a fold shows the thickness of the material. It should not be overlooked.

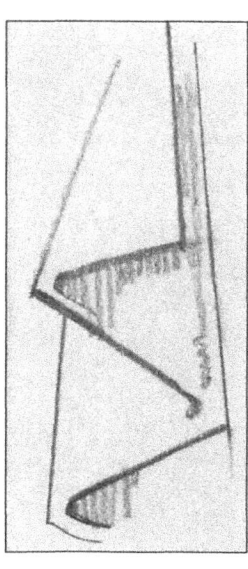

Figs. 44a.b. Two examples of "eyes." There is much angularity of line within the eye of the drape.

Fig. 45. An example of a drape hanging from one point of support. The folds are very narrow at the top and very wide at the bottom.

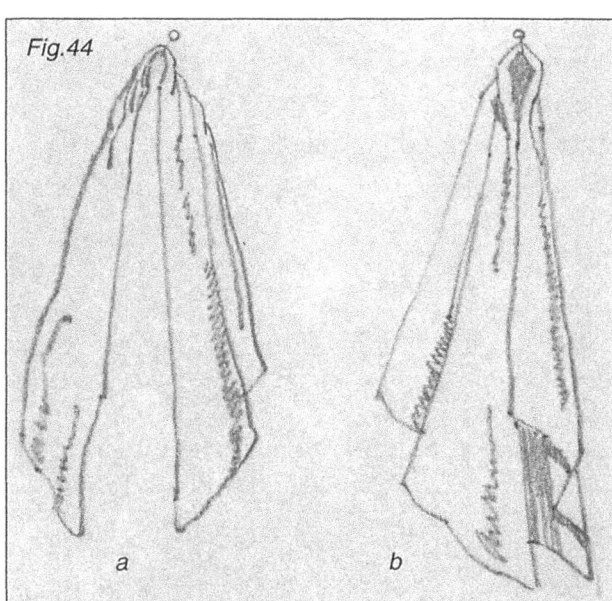

Fig.44

a   b

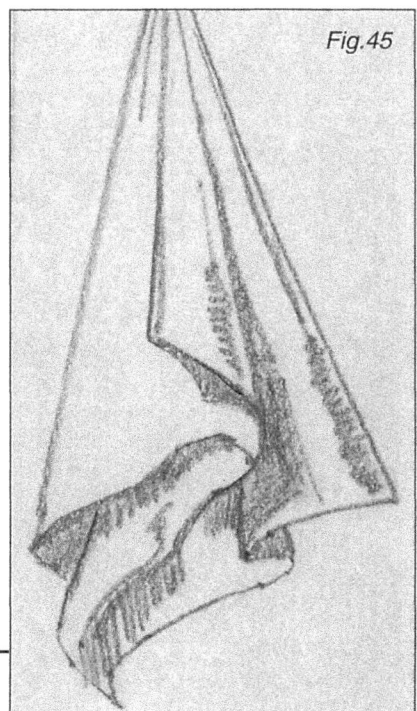

Fig.45

Fig. 46. A drape supported by two points of support. This will produce large deep folds mostly of the tubular kind. Careful attention should be paid to the cast shadows which describe the shape of the folds.

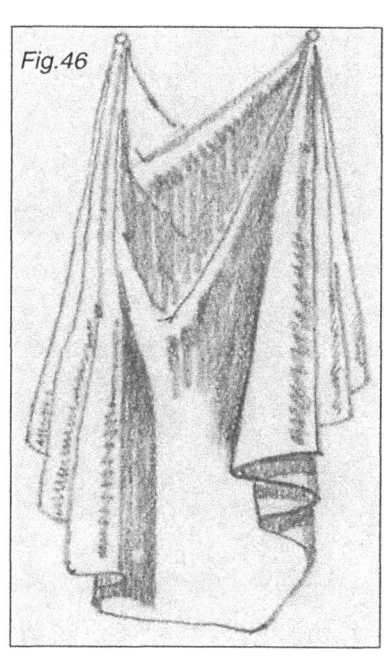

Fig.46

Fig. 47. Try to align the inside and outside corners of folds as shown in this example.

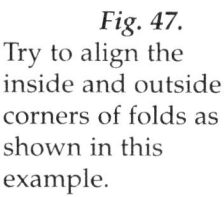

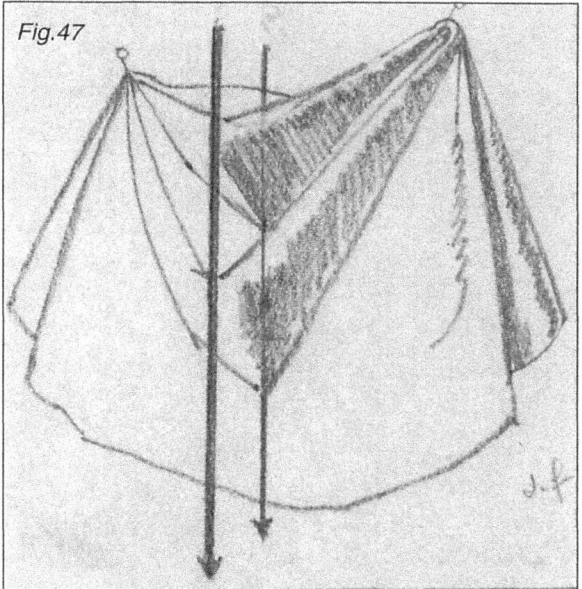

Fig.47

Fig. 48. The uppermost fold protrudes the most. This is also shown in profile in **Fig. 49.**

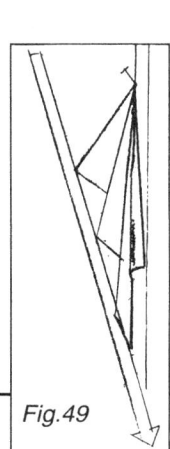

Fig.49

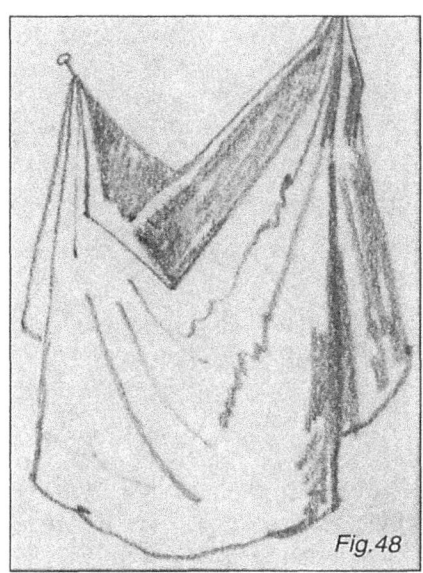

Fig.48

237

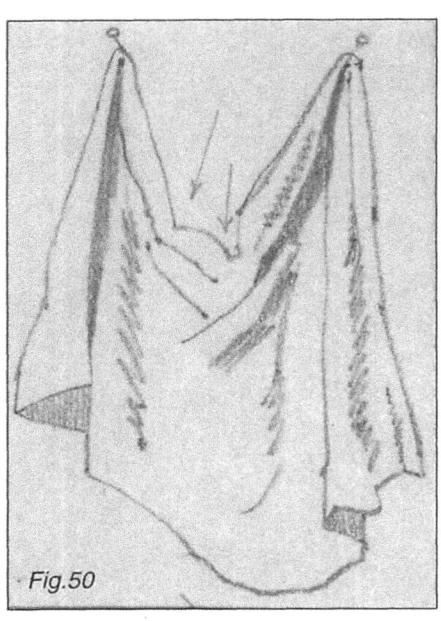

Fig. 50. A heavy material such as velvet showing deep fold breaks and long corners.

Fig. 51. Drapery either has long corners or short corners. This drawing shows long corners at the points of support.

Fig.50

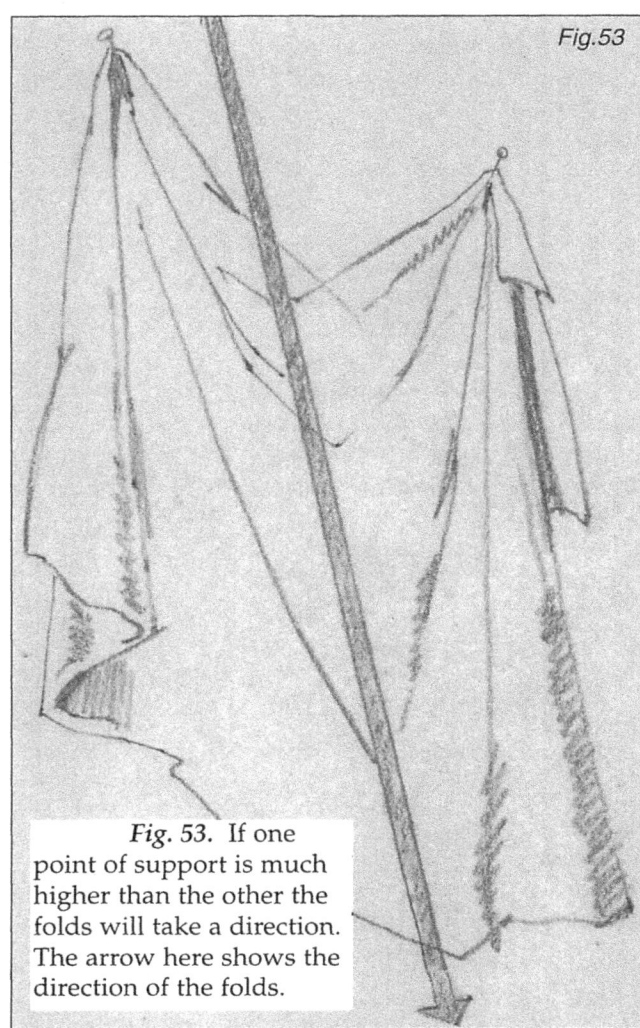

Fig.53

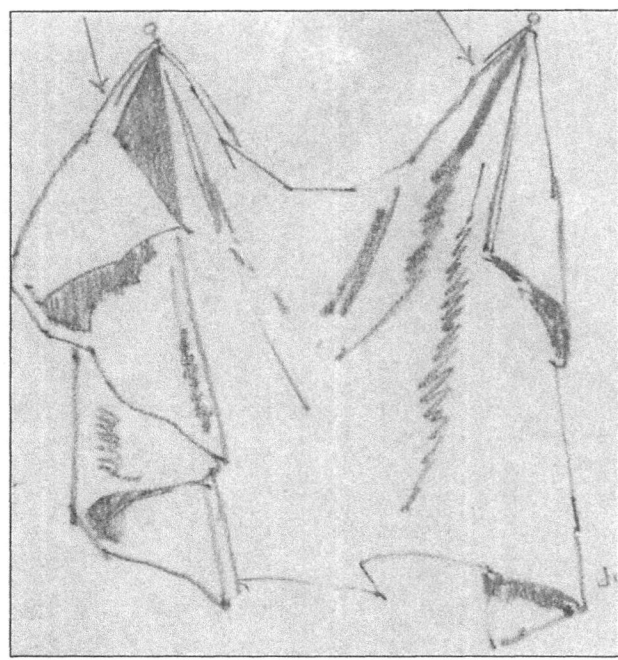

Fig.51

Fig.52

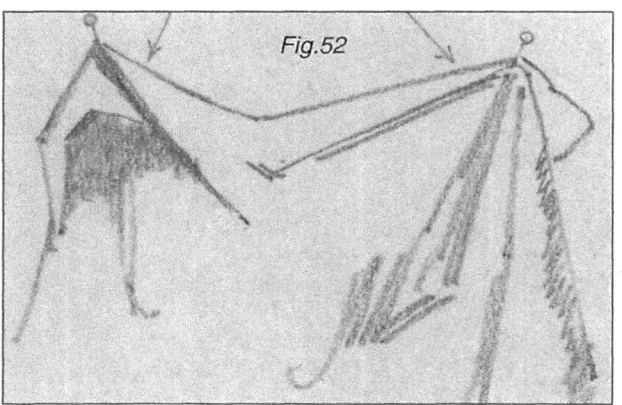

Fig. 52. An example of short corners at the points of support.

Fig. 53. If one point of support is much higher than the other the folds will take a direction. The arrow here shows the direction of the folds.

Fig. 54. Another example. The high side will have more folds than the lower side which becomes bulky. There is usually a sharp break at the bottom of the drape.

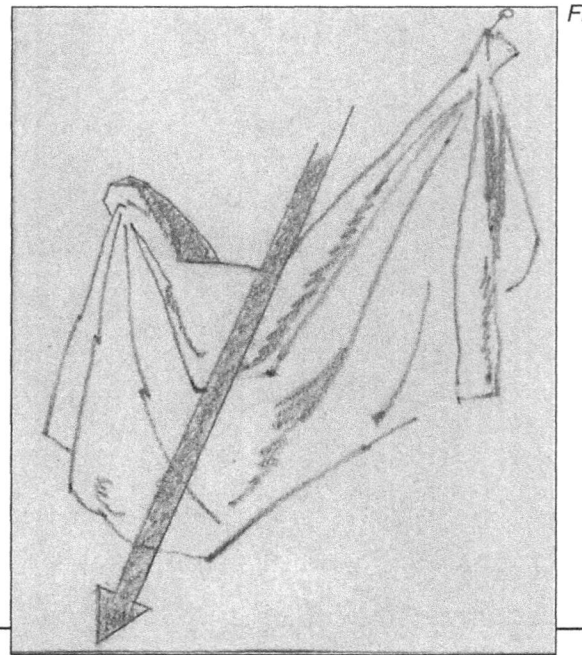

Fig.54

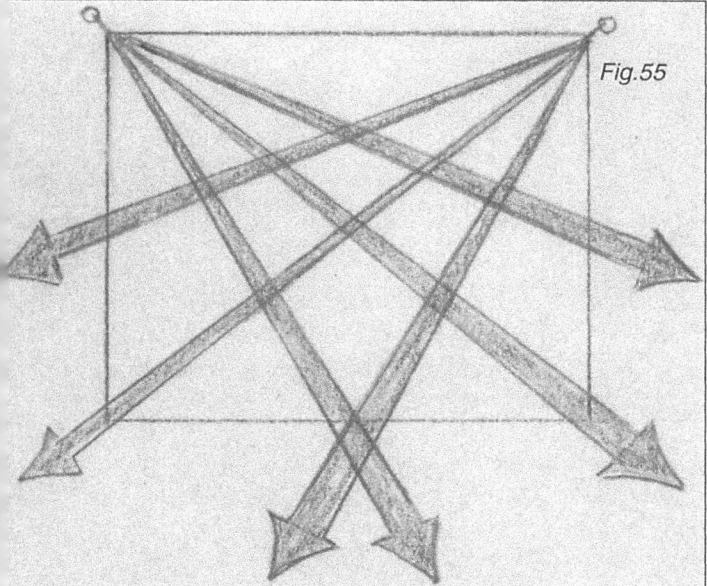

Fig. 55.

Fig. 55. Arrows show folds radiating from two support points going in two different directions.

Figs. 58a.b. Observe the zigzag effect of the apexes of the folds. *Fig. b.* shows a profile of *Fig. 58a.* Note that the top fold protrudes the most.

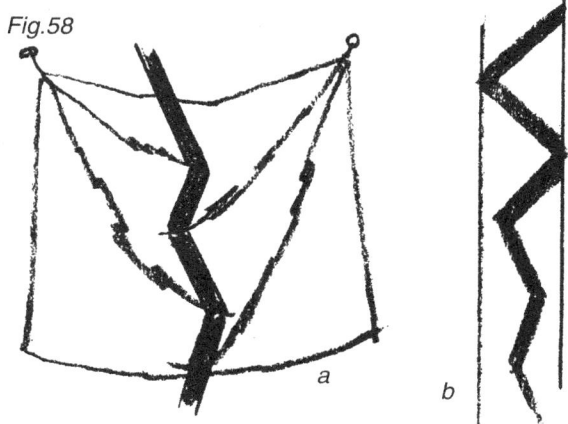

Fig.58

a

b

~~Fig. 59.~~ An example of tubular folds.
Fig. 59.

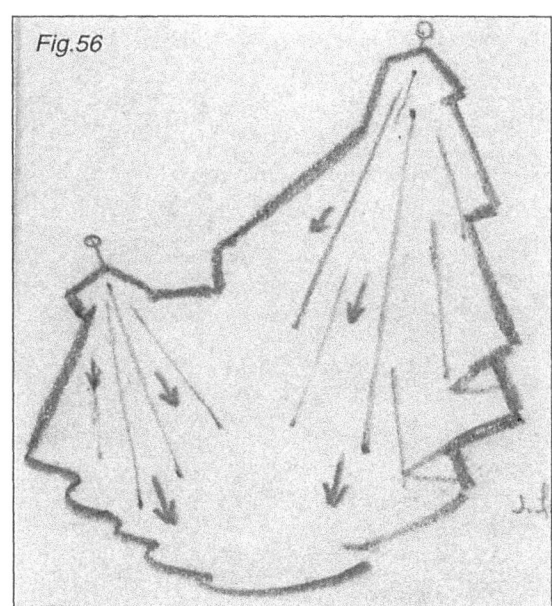

Fig.56

Fig. 56. Diagram showing how folds radiate from two support points.

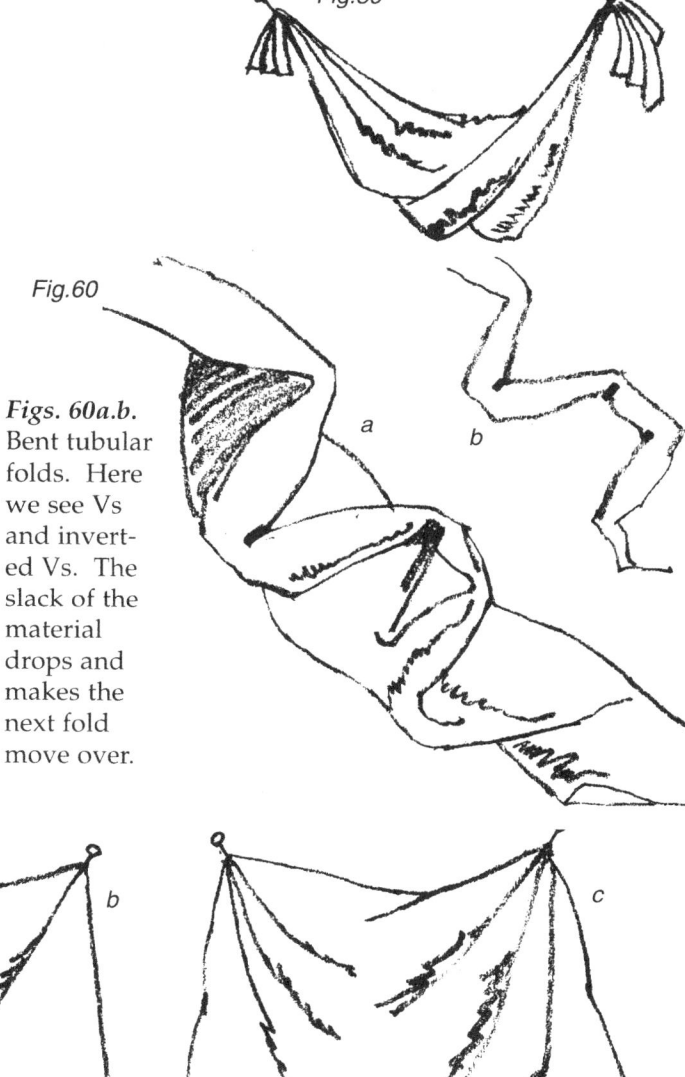

Fig.59

Fig.60

a

b

Figs. 60a.b. Bent tubular folds. Here we see Vs and inverted Vs. The slack of the material drops and makes the next fold move over.

Figs. 57a.b.c. Fig. 57a. shows folds that are very faint when the points of support are far apart. When we move the points closer the folds become more and more pronounced as shown in *Fig. b. and c.* Folds radiate from these points thus producing hanging folds and tubular folds.

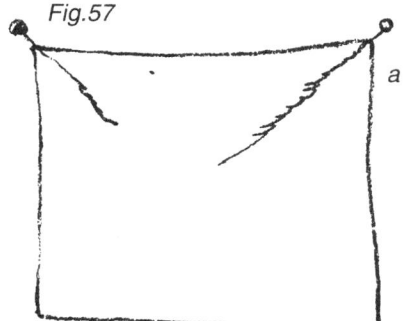

Fig.57

a

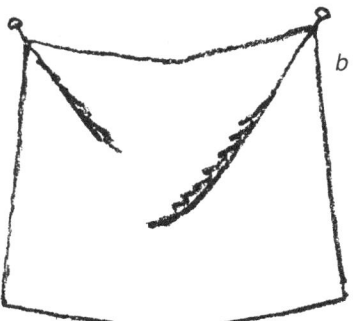

b

c

239

Fig. 61. The drape always takes the shape of the form it is on. Here the material is conforming to a cylinder.

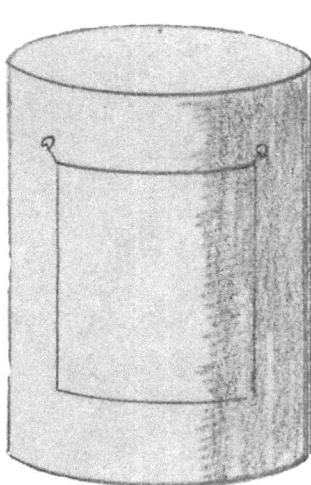

Fig.61

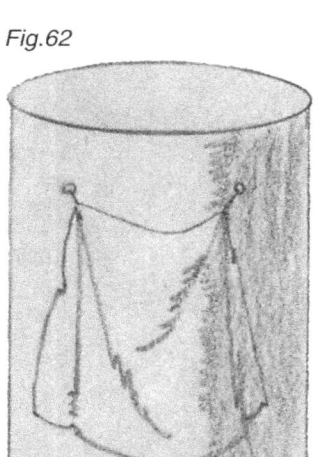

Fig.62

Fig. 62. By bringing the support points closer the folds round out at the bottom.

Fig. 63. One point of support high. Note now the directions of the folds. The folds still must appear to go around the big form however.

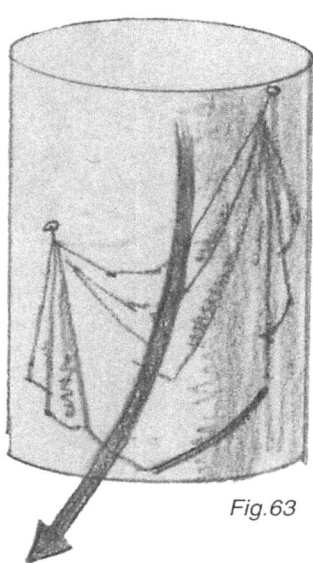

Fig.63

Fig. 64. Hanging folds going to a flat surface. This stylized drawing shows how one should think of a drape hanging on a vertical form and going to a flat surface.

Fig. 65. Realistically drawn folds guided by the previously shown structural diagram.

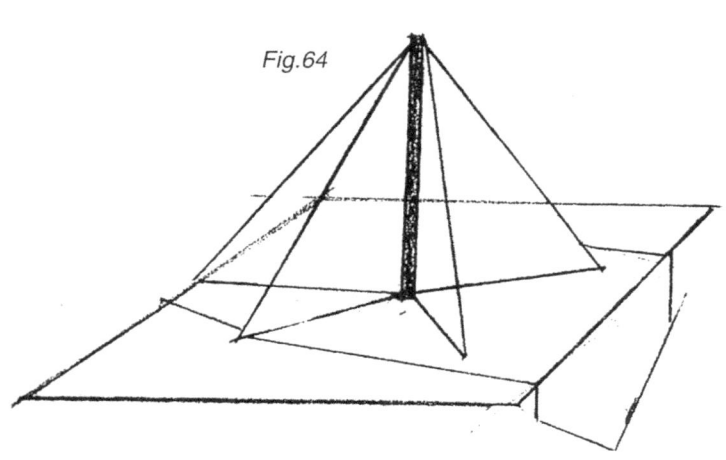

Fig.64

Fig. 66. Light and shade on seemingly complex drapery is accomplished by putting everything in a geometric shape, in this case a cone, and then adding shading to conform to the large pattern.

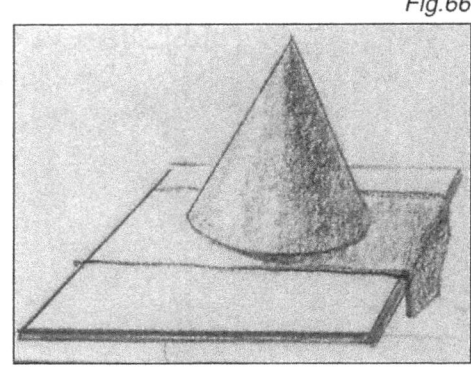

Fig.66

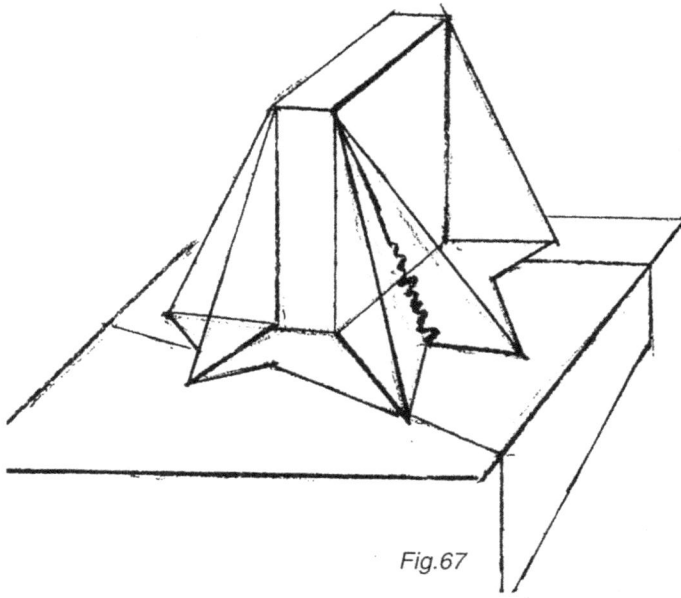

Fig.67

Fig. 67. Material covering a rectangular box resting on a platform. Draw the box or whatever form it may be first. Extend lines of the folds from the corners of the form to the flat surface of the platform. Notice the straight lines at the base of the drape on the platform designating flatness.

Fig.65

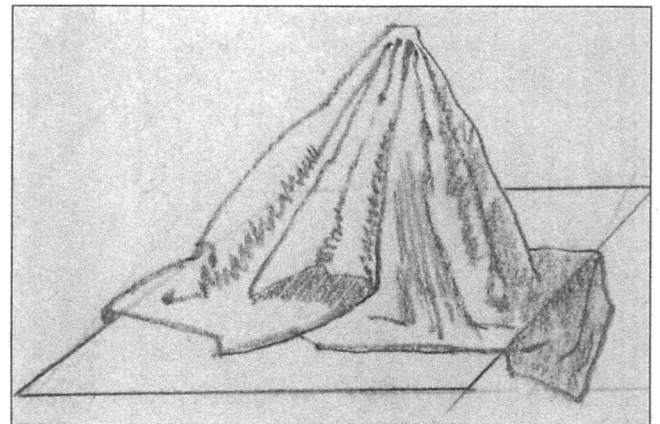

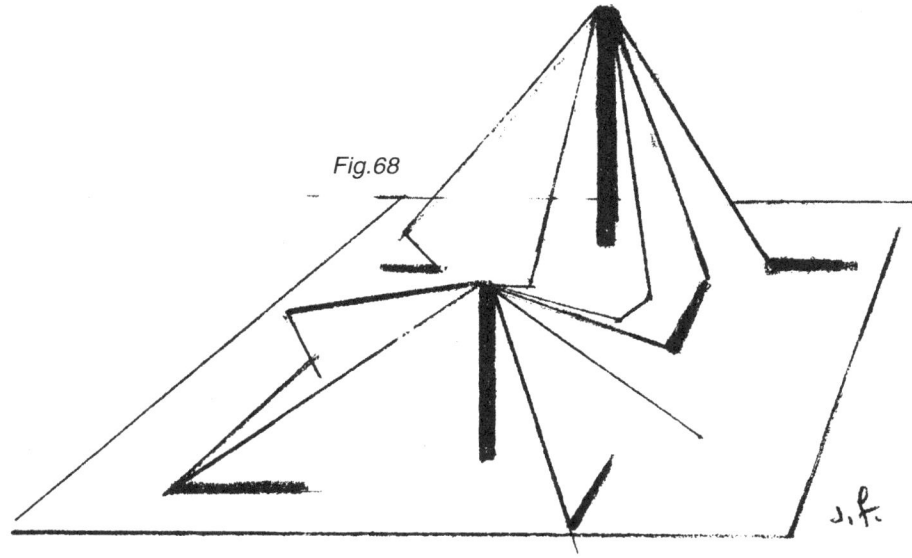

Fig.68

Fig. 68. The folds of the material will always go from the point of support to the flat of the surface. Keep looking for where the drape touches the platform and emphasize the straightness of that line. The drape should not appear that it dips into and below the flat surface.

PULLING FOLDS, BENDING, TILTING, TWISTING

Folds are called tubes. Tubes that flare are hanging folds. Tubes that tighten are called pulling folds.

A lying fold has no point of support – it just shows the shape of what it's on. A hanging fold has one supporting point. The folds are straight. A pulling fold has at least two points of pull and quite often three points.

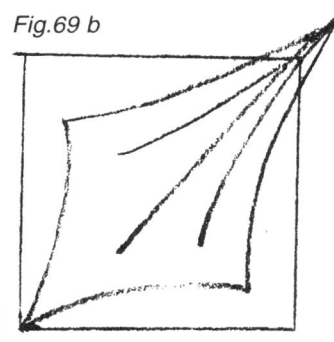

Fig.69 b

Figs. 69a.b. When radiating from one point of pull the main fold is straight, the secondary ones are curved.

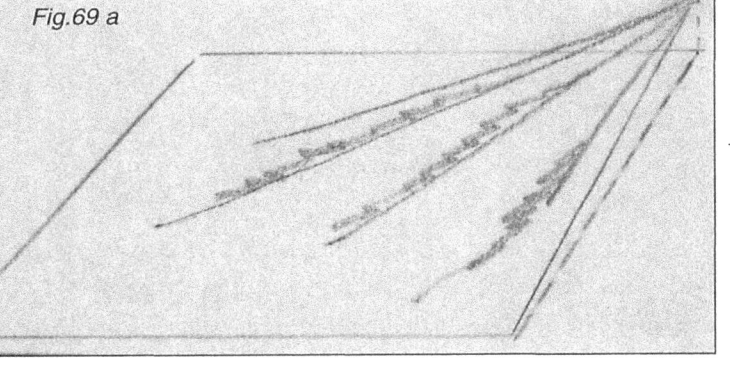

Fig.69 a

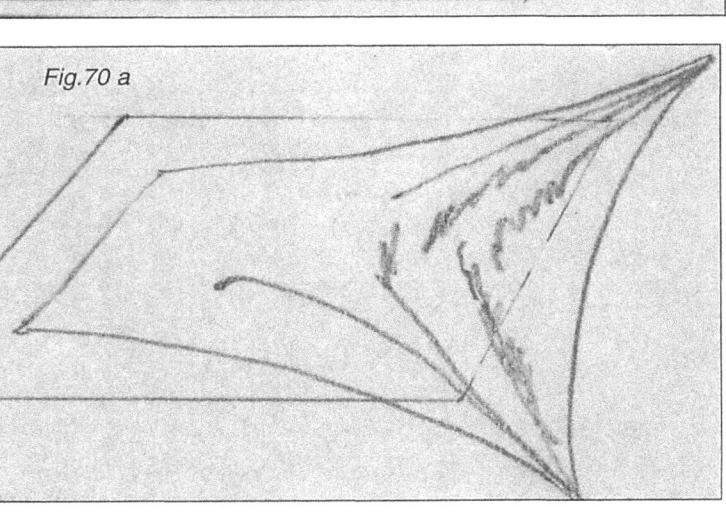

Fig.70 a

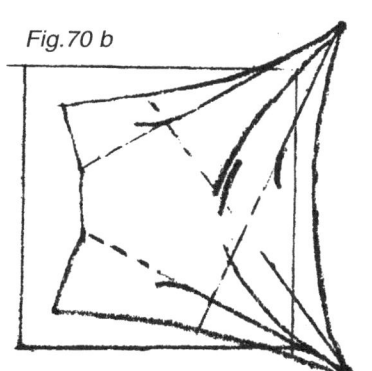

Fig.70 b

Figs. 70a.b. When radiating from two points of pull the main pull folds curve and try to connect whereas the secondary ones are straight.

Fig. 71. In a situation with three points of pull the main pulls connect and are curved. The center pull is straight.

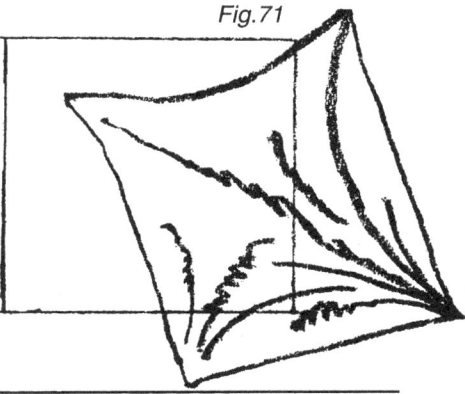

Fig.71

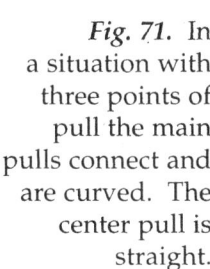

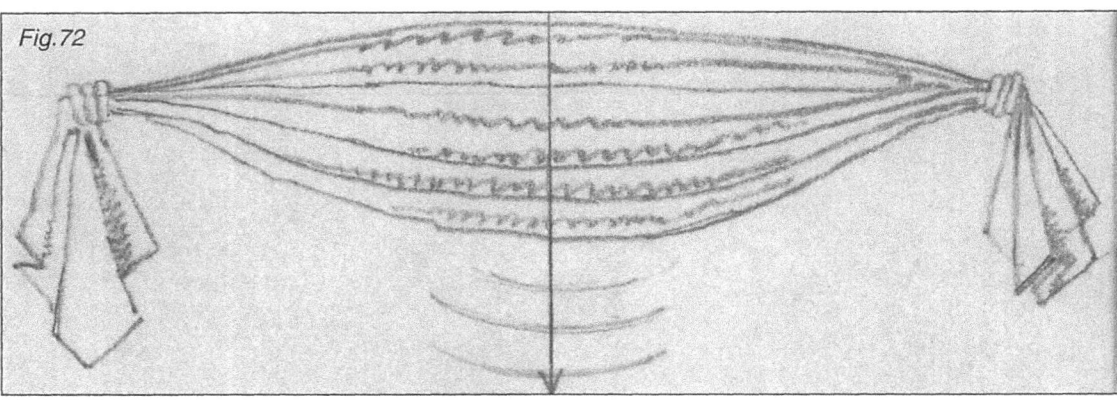

Fig. 72. A series of tubular pulls supported loosely at both ends will bulge at the center due to gravity.

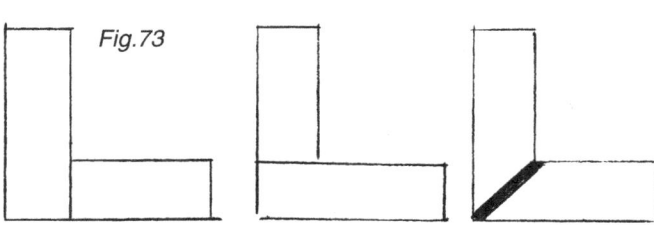

Figs. 73. These three diagrams can represent an arm, leg or torso. There will always be a break fold at the bend that goes diagonally to the opposite corner.

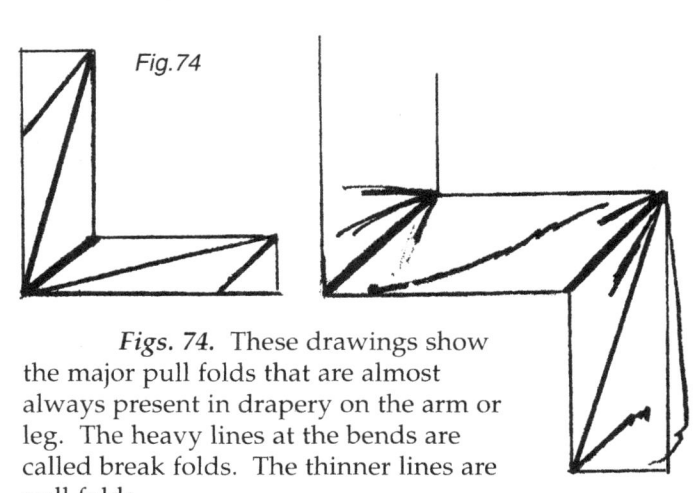

Figs. 74. These drawings show the major pull folds that are almost always present in drapery on the arm or leg. The heavy lines at the bends are called break folds. The thinner lines are pull folds.

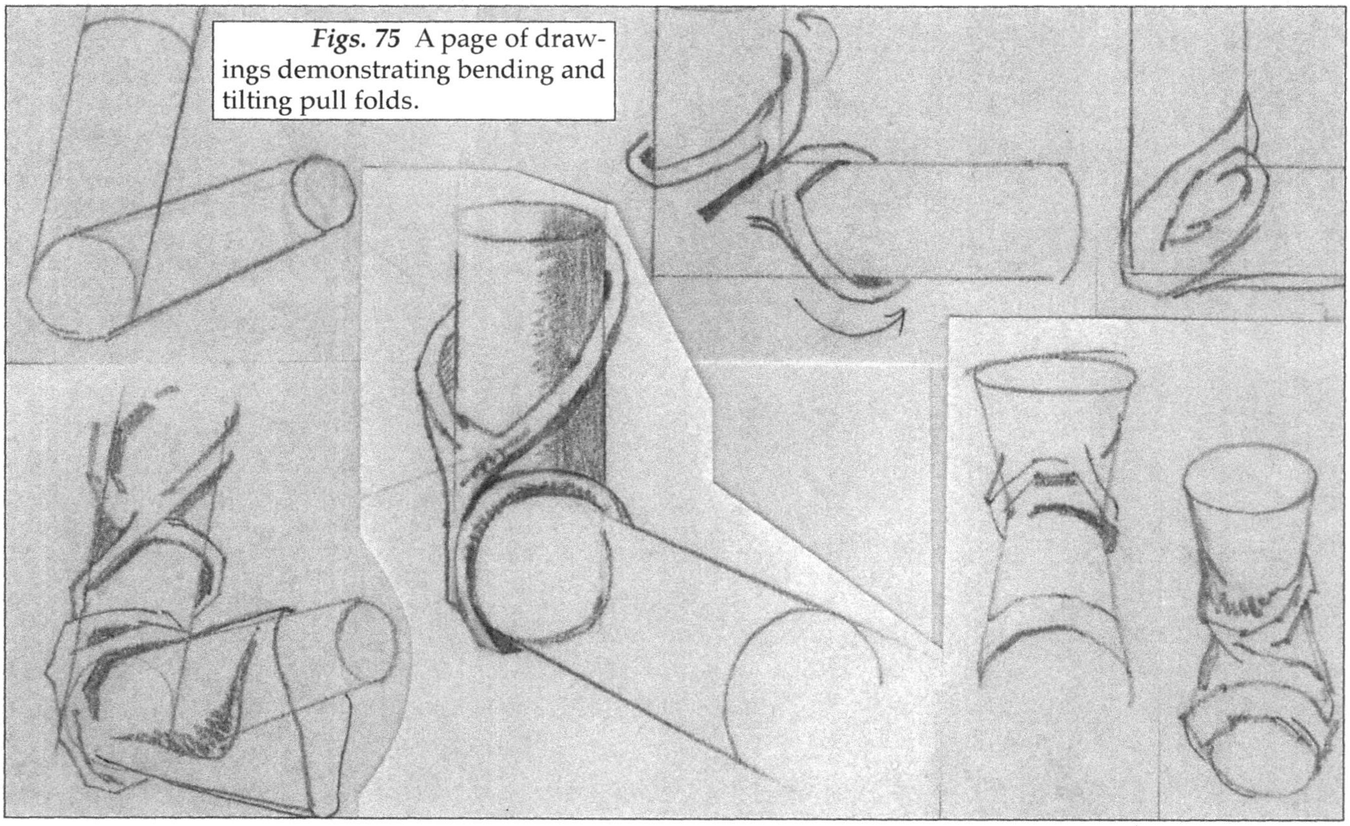

Figs. 75 A page of drawings demonstrating bending and tilting pull folds.

Figs. 76a.b. Twisting folds. Get the concept of the drape twisting around a form before you make a detailed drawing. In the case of a flat form visualizing it twisting first as shown in *Fig. a.*

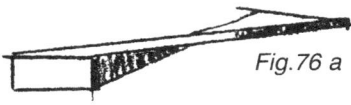
Fig.76 a

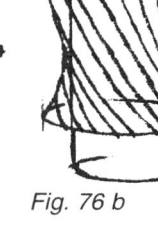
Fig. 76 b

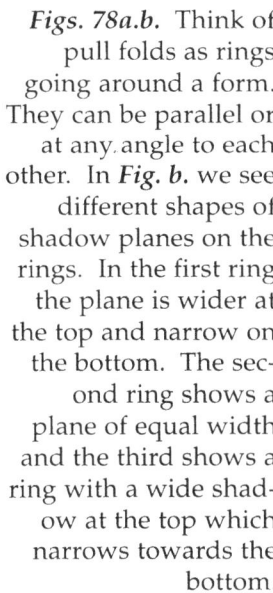
Fig,77

Fig. 77. An example of twisting folds.

Figs. 78a.b. Think of pull folds as rings going around a form. They can be parallel or at any angle to each other. In *Fig. b.* we see different shapes of shadow planes on the rings. In the first ring the plane is wider at the top and narrow on the bottom. The second ring shows a plane of equal width and the third shows a ring with a wide shadow at the top which narrows towards the bottom.

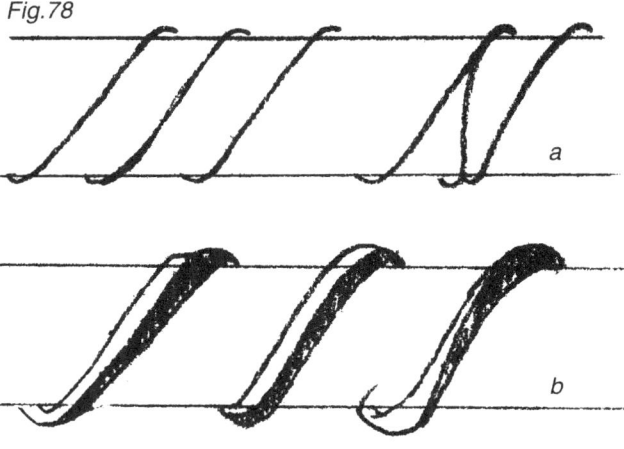
Fig.78

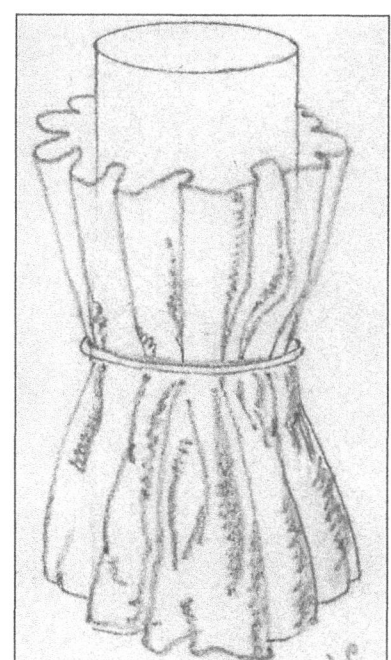
Fig.79

An example of loose material wrapped around a cylinder producing crushed folds (*see Fig. 95a.b.c.*)

EXCESS MATERIAL

Fig. 80. Shown here is loose material wrapping around a form. There are no ring-like folds in this situation.

Fig. 81. The excess material is compressed into a small area creating folds that take the shape of the form they are on.

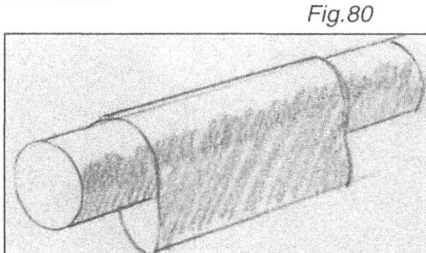
Fig.80

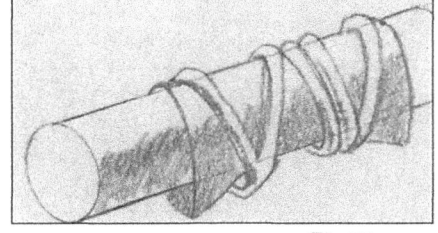
Fig.81

Fig. 82. Think of these folds as curtain rings.

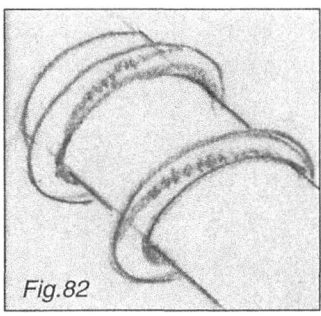
Fig.82

Fig. 83. Full rings. They can be many different angles to each other.

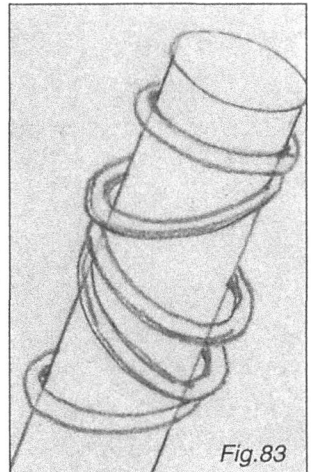
Fig.83

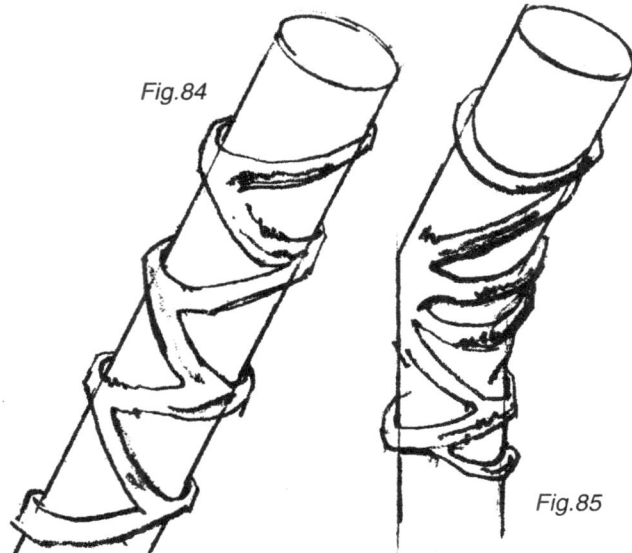

Fig.84

Fig.85

Fig. 84. An example of partial rings intersecting full rings.

Fig. 85. An example of half rings and full rings. All three of these types of rings can occur on one form.

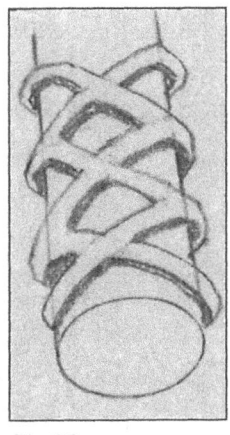

Fig.86a

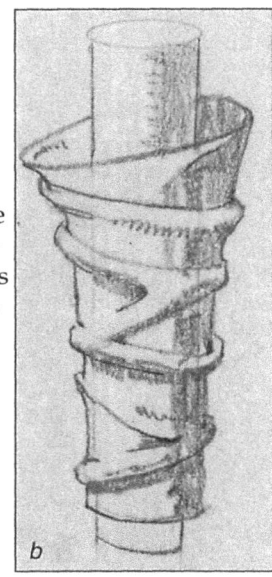

Figs. 86a.b.c.d. Four examples of how the curvature of the rings change to conform with the form and the perspective of the form.

b

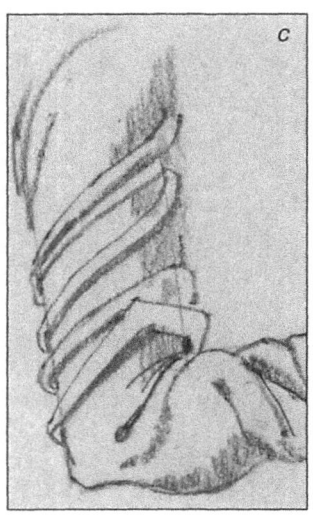

c

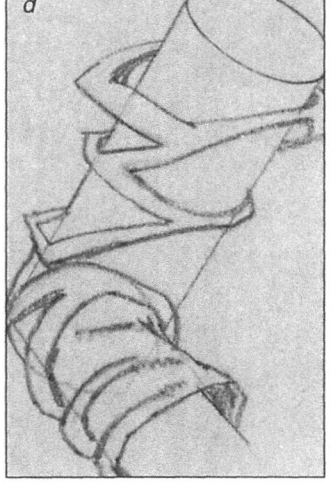

d

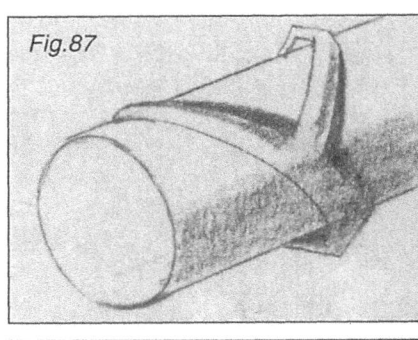

Fig.87

Fig. 87. Light and shade on a full ring and a half ring. Note the darkness of the cast shadow and how it follows the curvature of the form

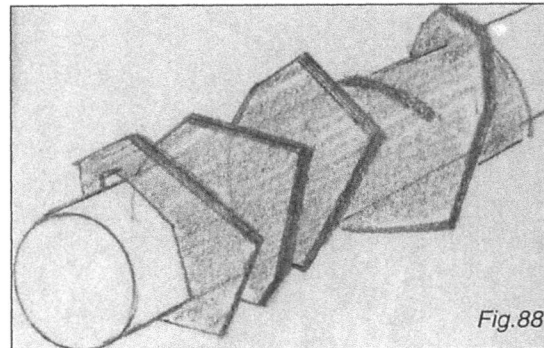

Fig. 88. An abstract conception of shapes and folds caused by pushing material together.

Fig.88

Figs. 89a.b. Two examples of tunneling folds. Example **89a.** is more abstract in concept than **Fig. b.**

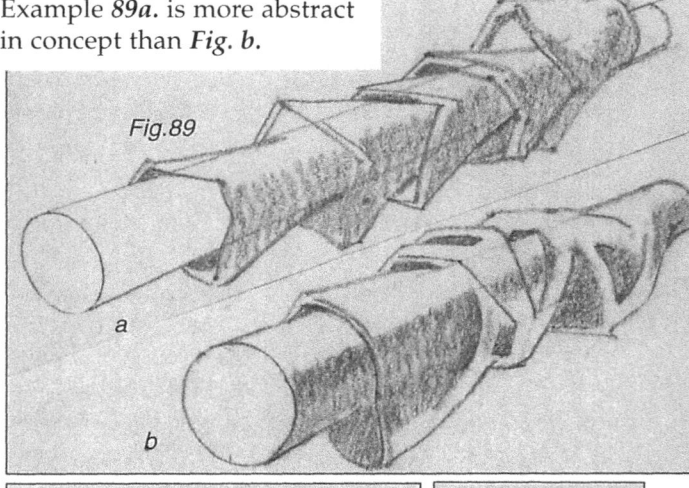

Fig.89

a

b

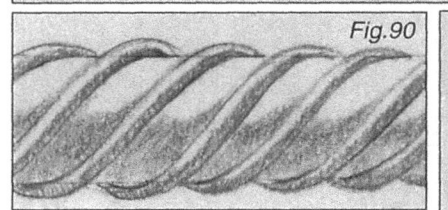

Fig.90

Fig. 90. Twisting folds around a cylindrical form.

Fig. 91. A drawing showing many different kinds of folds. The fold in the center coming off the ring fold is called a *bridge fold*. Notice that all the folds explain the form underneath.

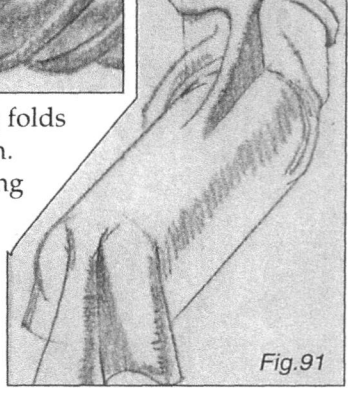

Fig.91

A bridge fold connecting two forms

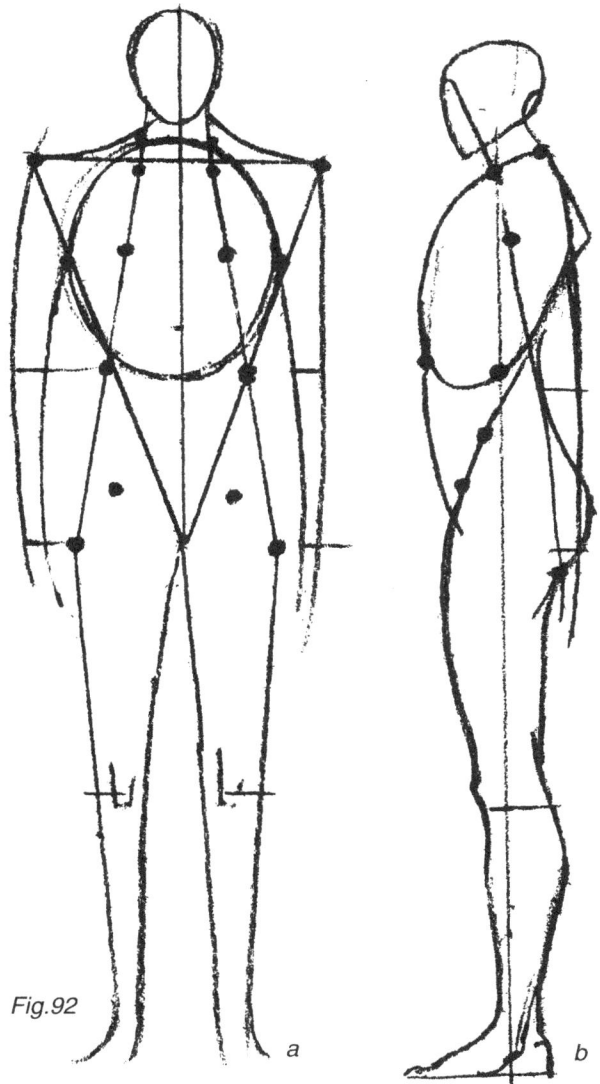

Fig.92

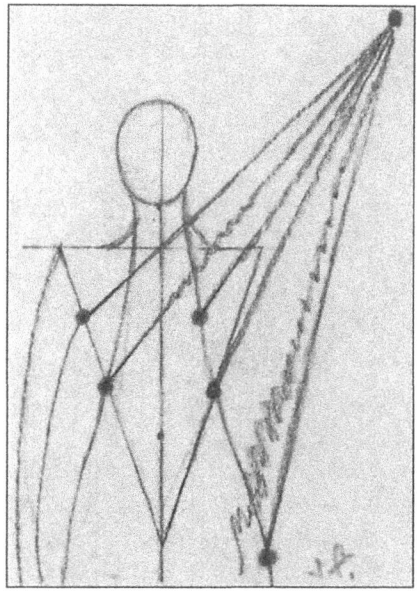

Fig. 93. A simplified drawing showing folds pulling from pull points to the top of the left hand, which incidentally serves as a pull point.

Fig.93

DRAPERY ON THE FIGURE

The drawings and diagrams on the following pages along with what has been previously discussed should give the artist enough information on how to properly think of and draw the clothing on the figure.

Two of the most important things to keep in mind are where the pull points are on the figure and which are the main planes of support.

Figs. 92a.b. The dots shown on the figure abstractions of the front and side views are the major pull points. The horizontal lines shown at the elbows, wrists and knees can also be pull points depending on the action. Pull folds can also originate on the surface of the figure and clothing such as where buttons are.

Fig.94

Figs. 94. The shaded areas on the front, back and side views of the figure represent the main planes of support of the drapery. Any top surface made by an action would also be a plane of support. It is from these surfaces that folds will pull from. These top surfaces are also generally lighter in value than the rest of the surfaces as they receive more light.

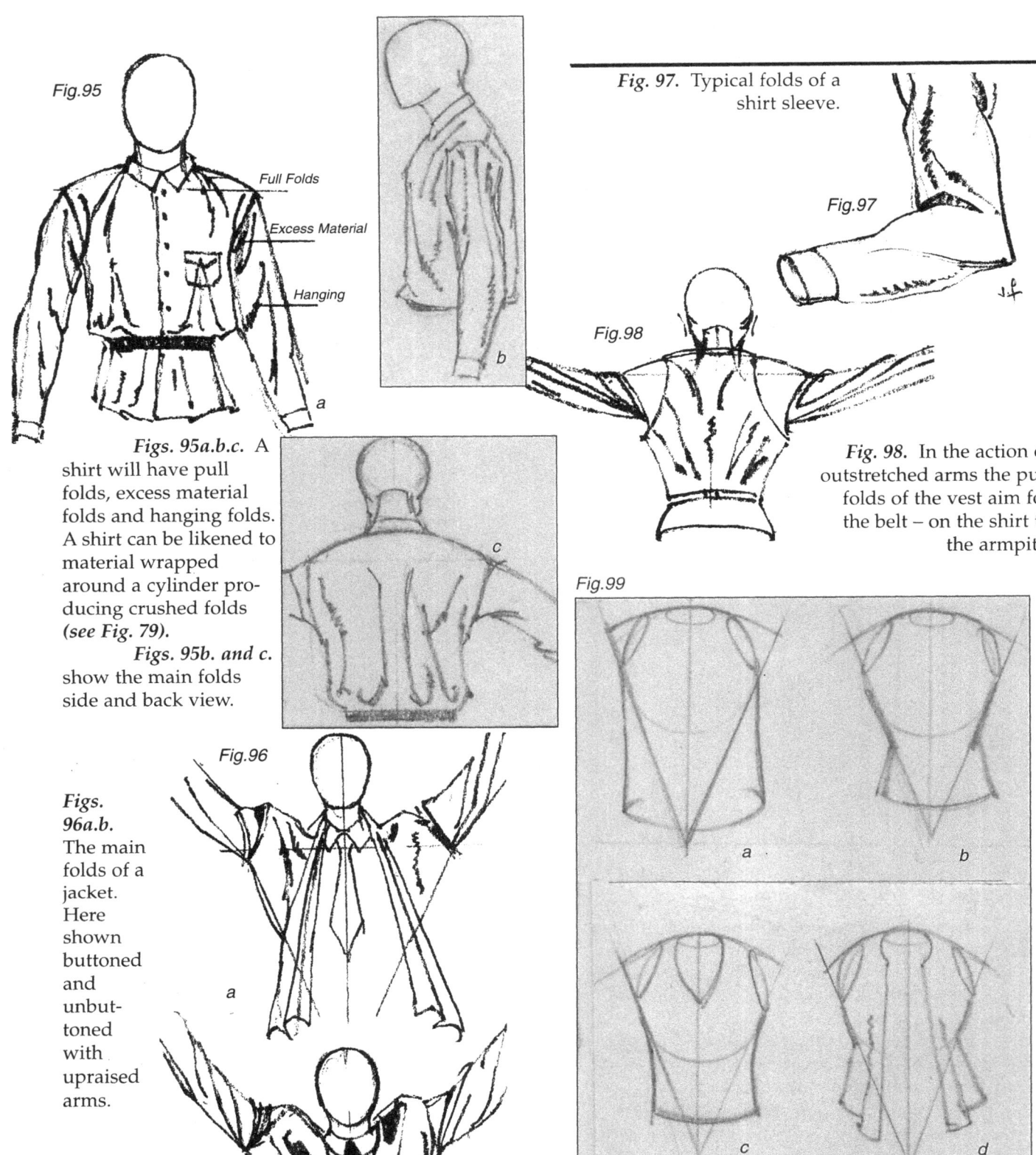

Fig.95

Full Folds

Excess Material

Hanging

a

b

c

Figs. 95a.b.c. A shirt will have pull folds, excess material folds and hanging folds. A shirt can be likened to material wrapped around a cylinder producing crushed folds *(see Fig. 79).*

Figs. 95b. and c. show the main folds side and back view.

Fig.96

Figs. 96a.b. The main folds of a jacket. Here shown buttoned and unbuttoned with upraised arms.

a

b

Fig. 97. Typical folds of a shirt sleeve.

Fig.97

Fig.98

Fig. 98. In the action of outstretched arms the pull folds of the vest aim for the belt – on the shirt to the armpits.

Fig.99

a

b

c

d

Figs. 99a.b.c.d. These four drawings show the major differences of vests or sweaters and how they relate to the rib cage within the figure abstraction. *Fig. a.* is a loose fit. *Fig. b.* is form fitting. *Fig. c.* is a normal fit with a low V neck, and *Fig. d.* shows an open front.

246

Figs. 100a.b.c. Different types of excess material on the sleeve of a shirt, front, back and side.

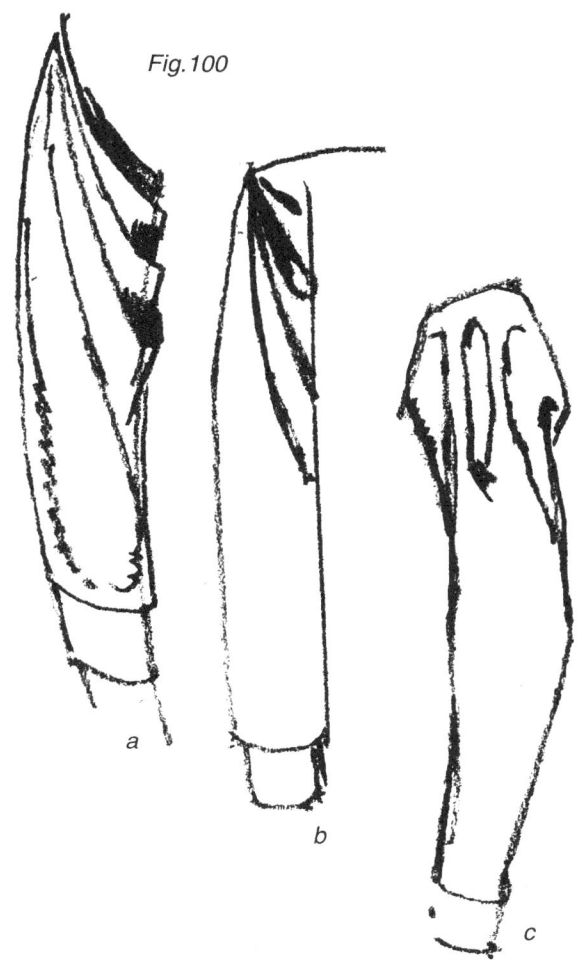

Fig.100

a

b

c

Figs. 101a.b. Two types of scarves. They consist of basically wrap around folds.

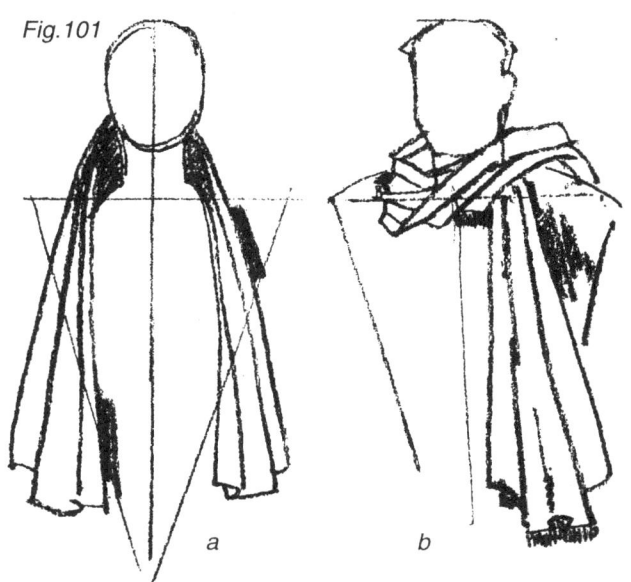

Fig.101

a

b

DRAWINGS SHOWING PULL FOLDS GOING WITH THE ACTION.

A series of drawings showing pull folds expressing the action of the figure.

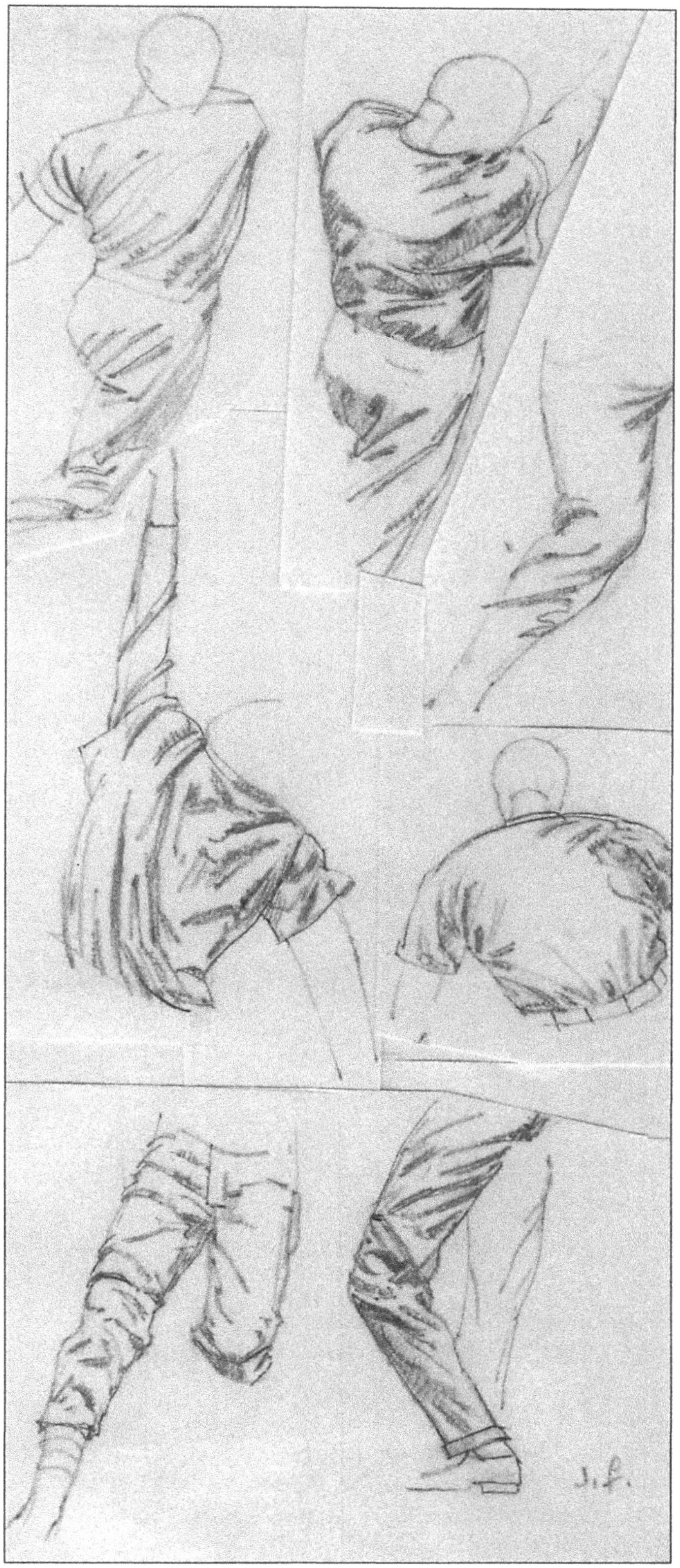

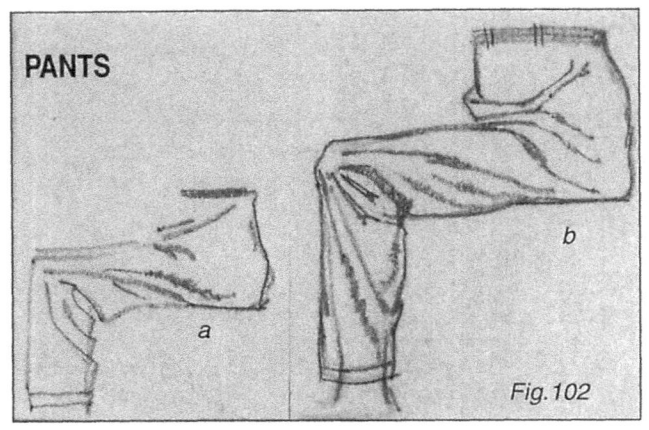

PANTS

Fig. 102

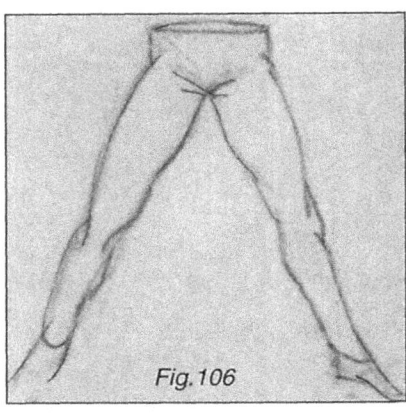

Fig. 106. Garments that are tailored to fit the form tightly have very few pull points.

Fig. 106

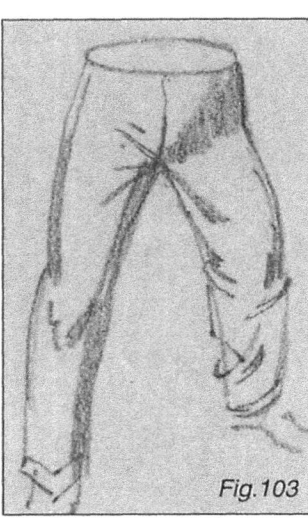

Fig.103

Figs. 102 a.b. The folds shown are almost always present providing the material is fairly loose.

Fig. 103. The right leg shows large folds going with the action while the folds on the left leg convey foreshortening.

Fig. 104. A seated figure showing the symmetry and relating of the major folds. The few folds shown are enough to fully explain the form underneath.

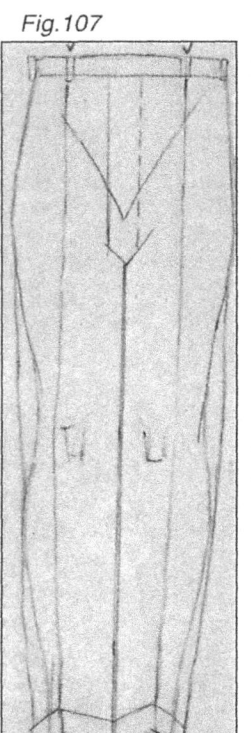

Fig.107

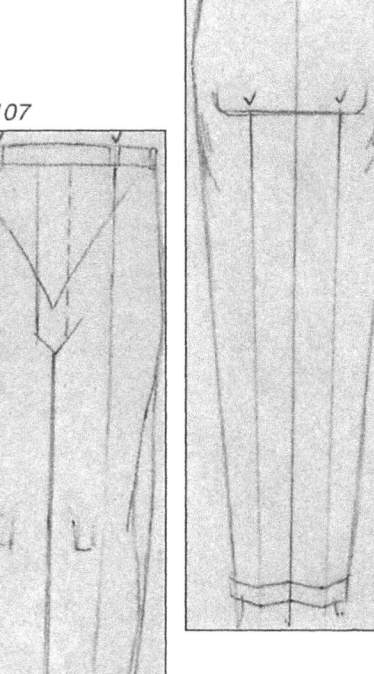

Fig.108

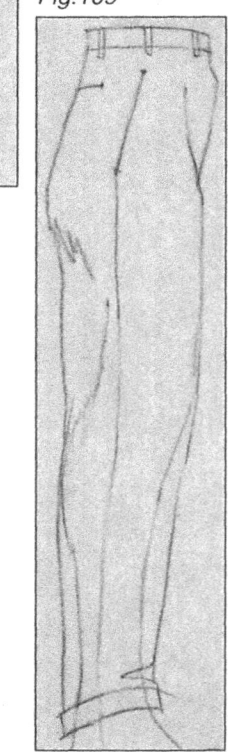

Fig.109

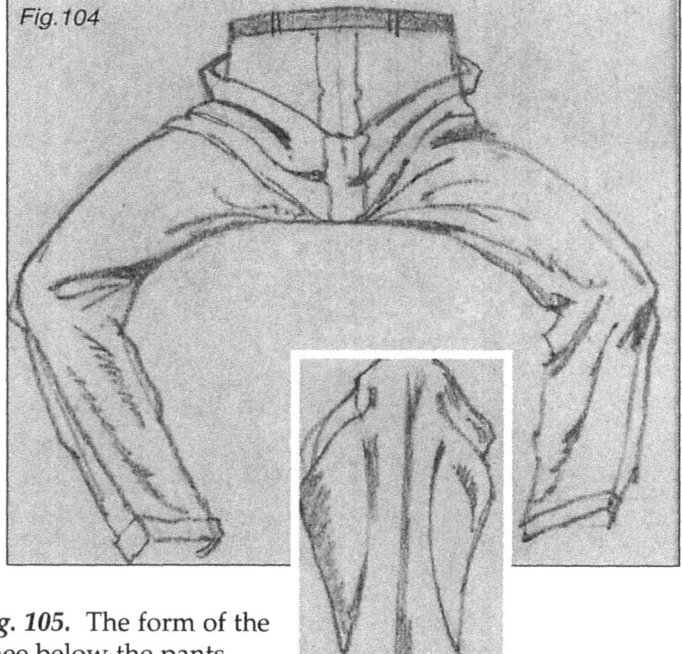

Fig.104

Fig.105

Fig. 105. The form of the knee below the pants material is the focal point of the folds and crease.

Fig. 107. Front view, creases hang from the waist shown at arrows.

Fig. 108. Back view, creases start at the buttocks shown by arrows.

Fig. 109. Side view showing seam and ankle break. The seam continues onto the cuff.

248

Fig. 110

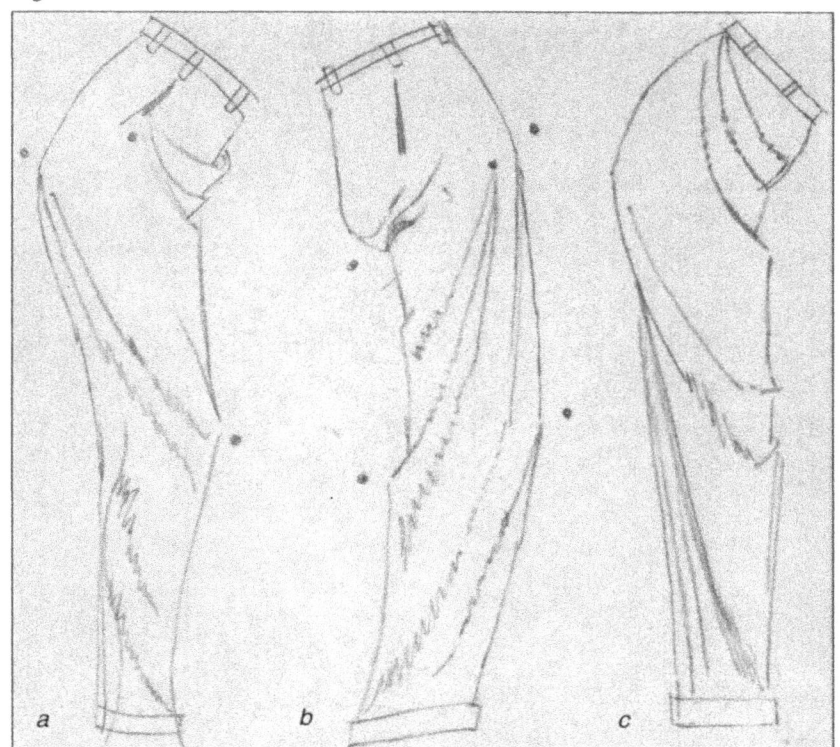

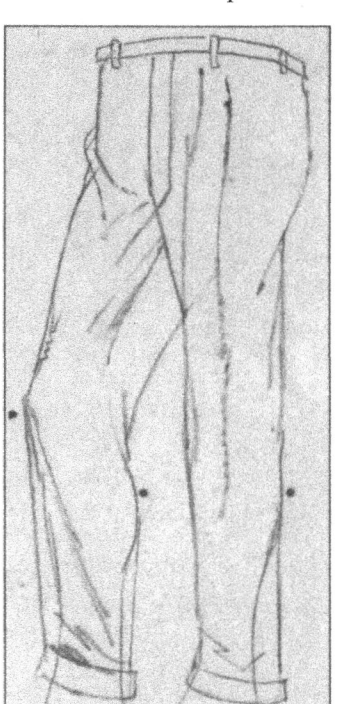

Fig. 111. Draw a simplified figure beneath the pants first. Note how the folds pull from the knees and the top back of the gastrocnemius forms.

Fig. 111

Figs. 110a.b.c. Folds originate at the pull points designated by dots when the body leans forwards or backwards.

SKIRT

Figs. 112a.b.c. Front, side and back view of the skirt. Arrows show where the material leaves the form and where the major folds originate.

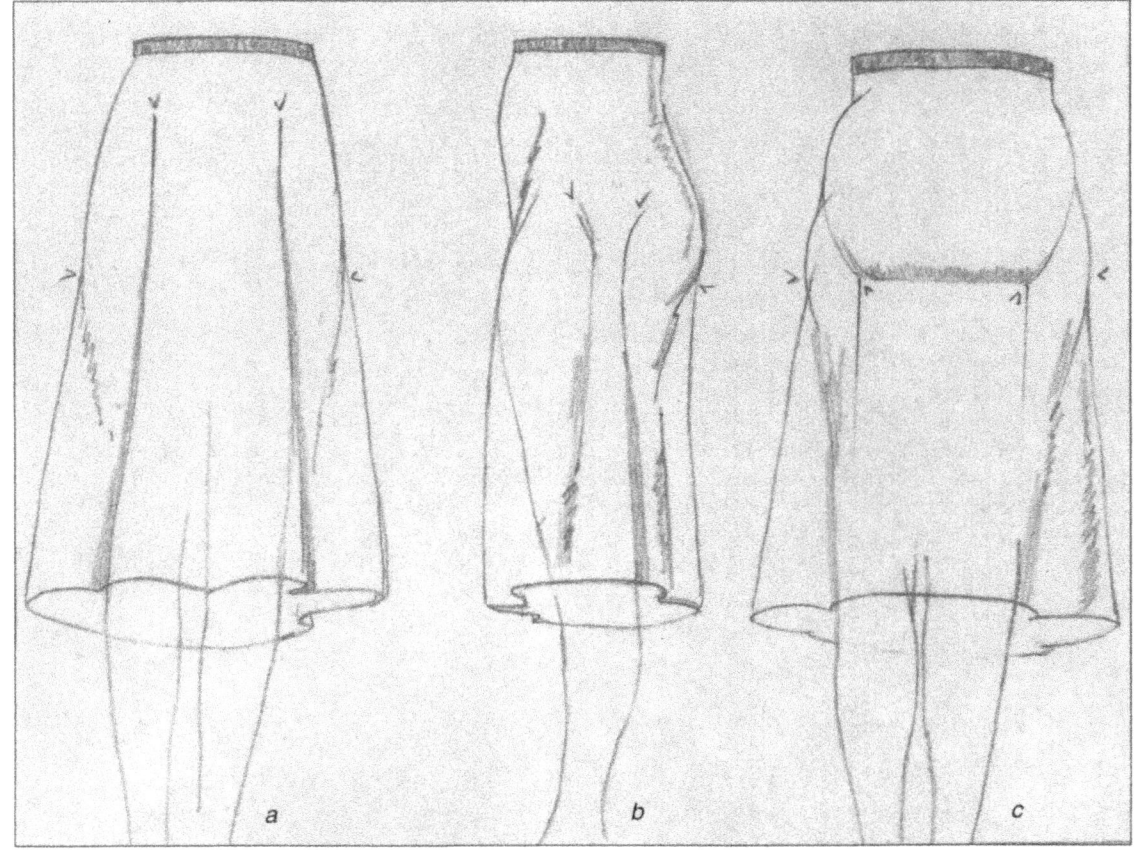

Fig. 112

249

Fig.113

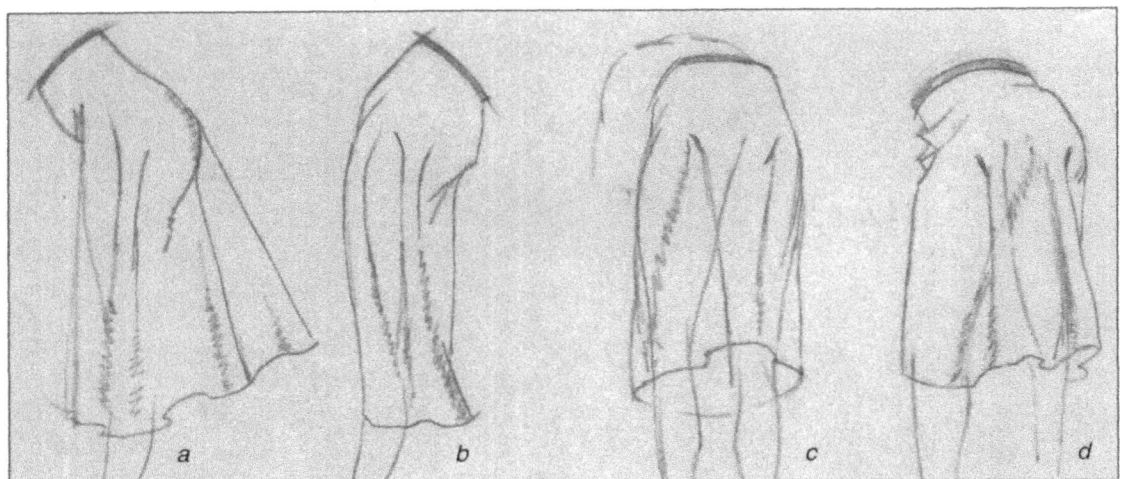

a   b   c   d

Figs. 113a.b.c.d. showing the origination of the major folds of a skirt when the body bends forwards, backwards and when bending over.

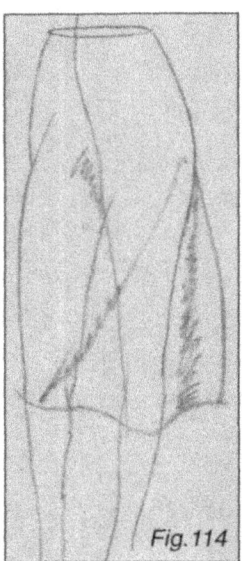

Fig.114

Fig. 114. One hip high. The major folds pull from that hip downwards and across to the opposite leg.

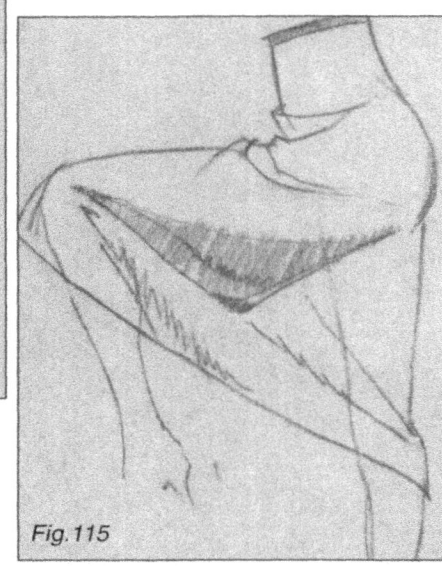

Fig.115

Fig. 117. Crossed legs. Lines showing the projecting knee and leg should be emphasized. Other horizontal folds should show perspective and explain the form underneath.

Fig. 118. Shown are the main folds on a skirt with one leg raised and bent.

Fig. 119. A tight fitting garment will have no pull folds.

Fig. 117

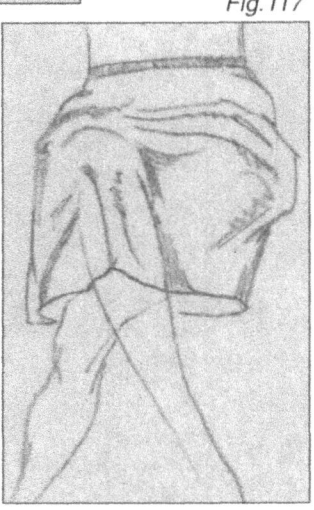

Fig. 115. The main pulling fold is from the kneecap to the back of the gastrocnemius form of the opposite leg. Notice the folds of the skirt at the waist where the leg meets the torso.

Fig. 116. The almost ever present standard folds of a skirt on a seated figure.

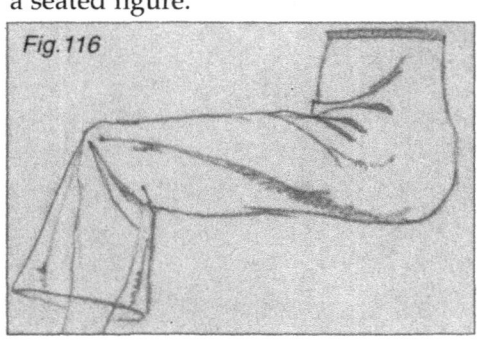

Fig.116

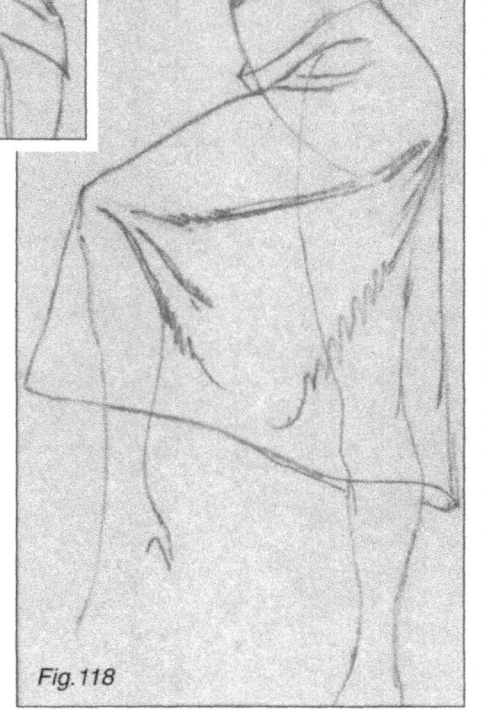

Fig.118

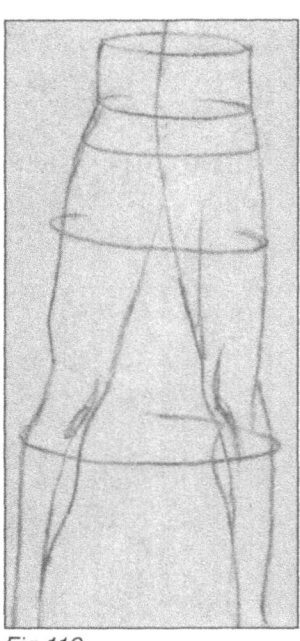

Fig.119

250

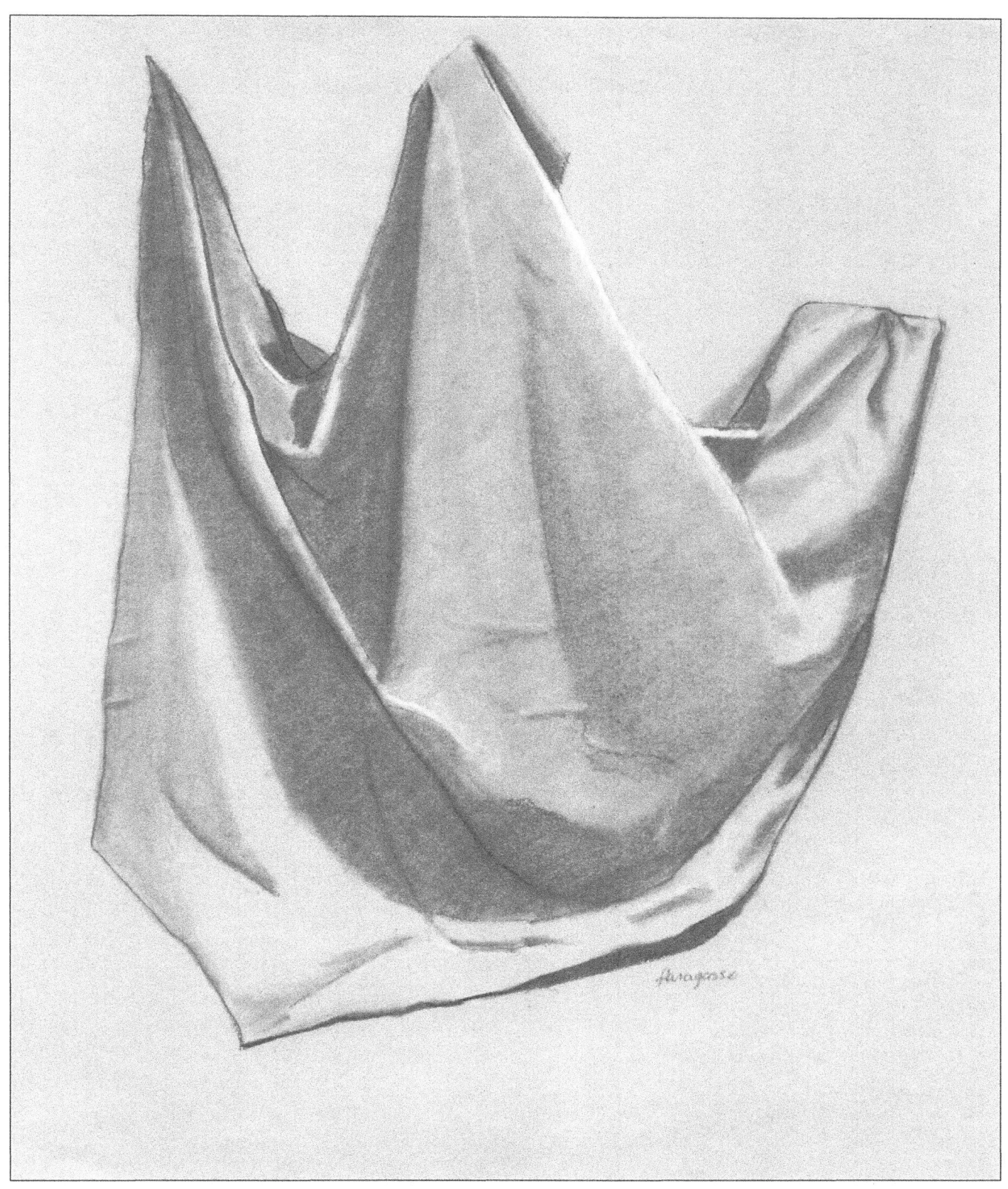

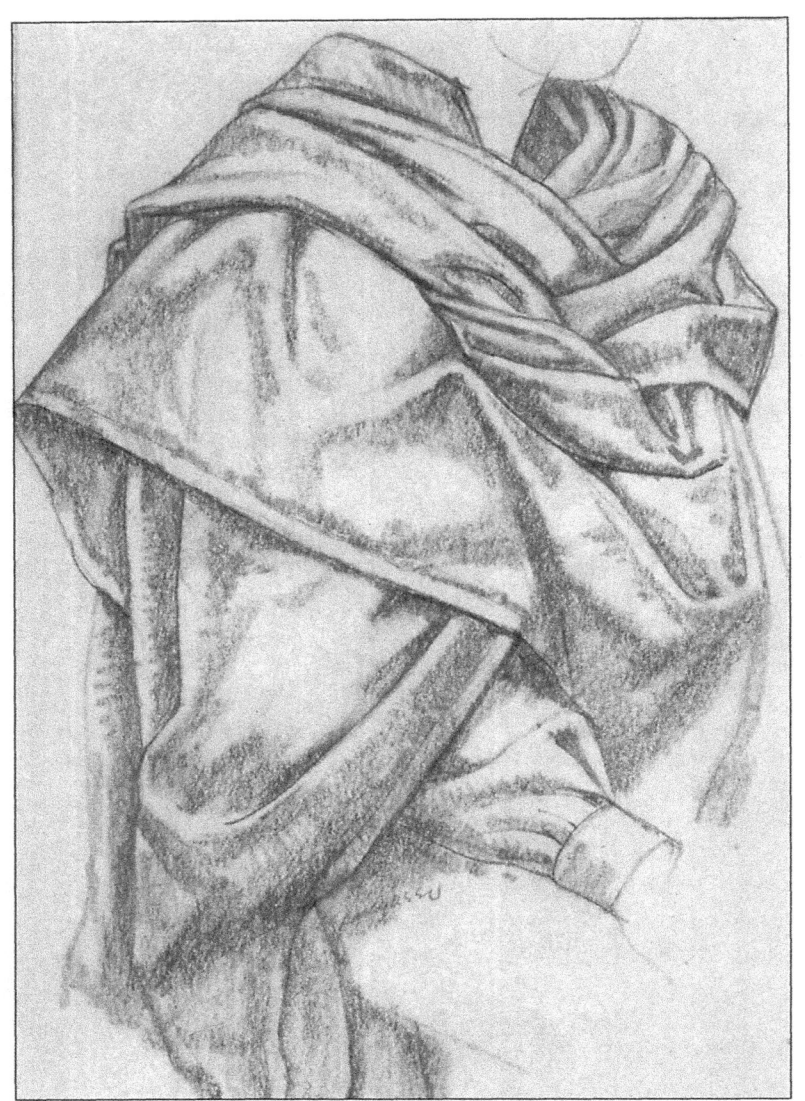

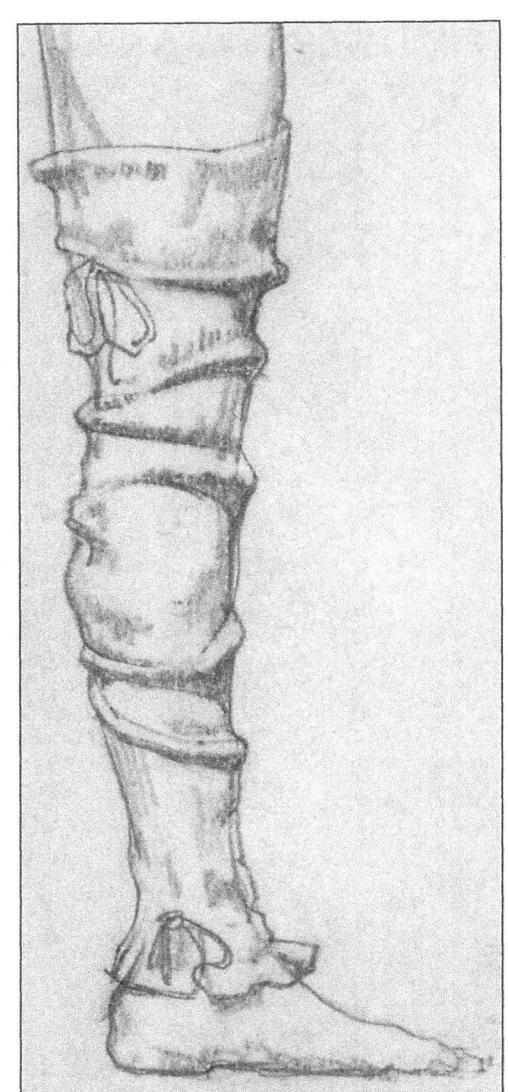

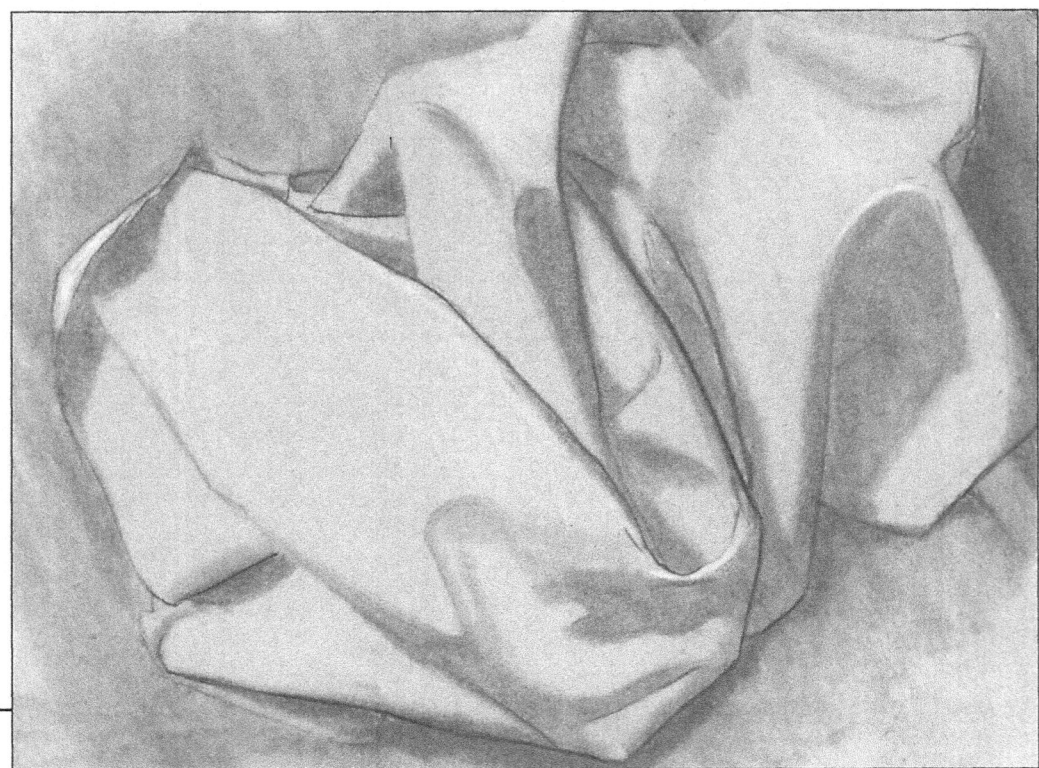

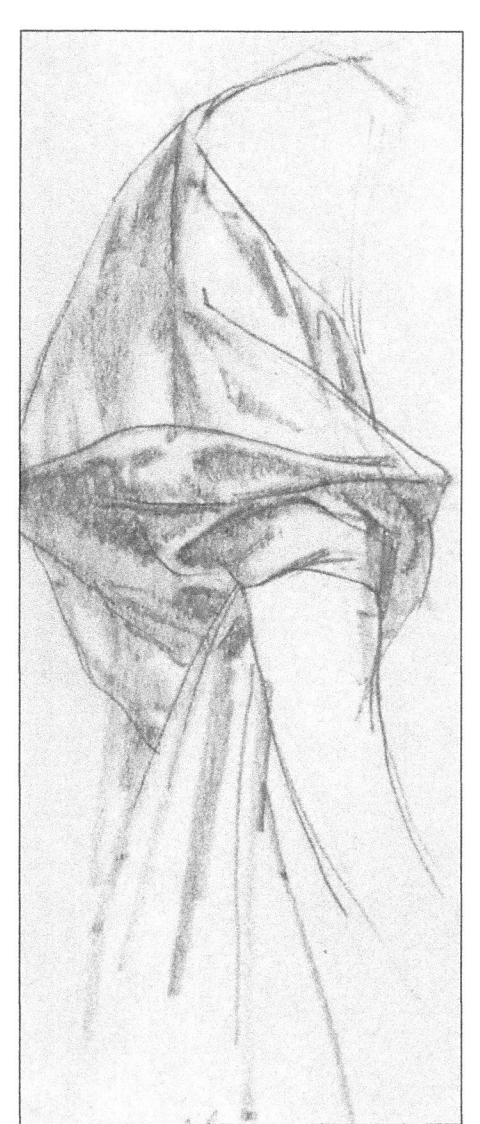

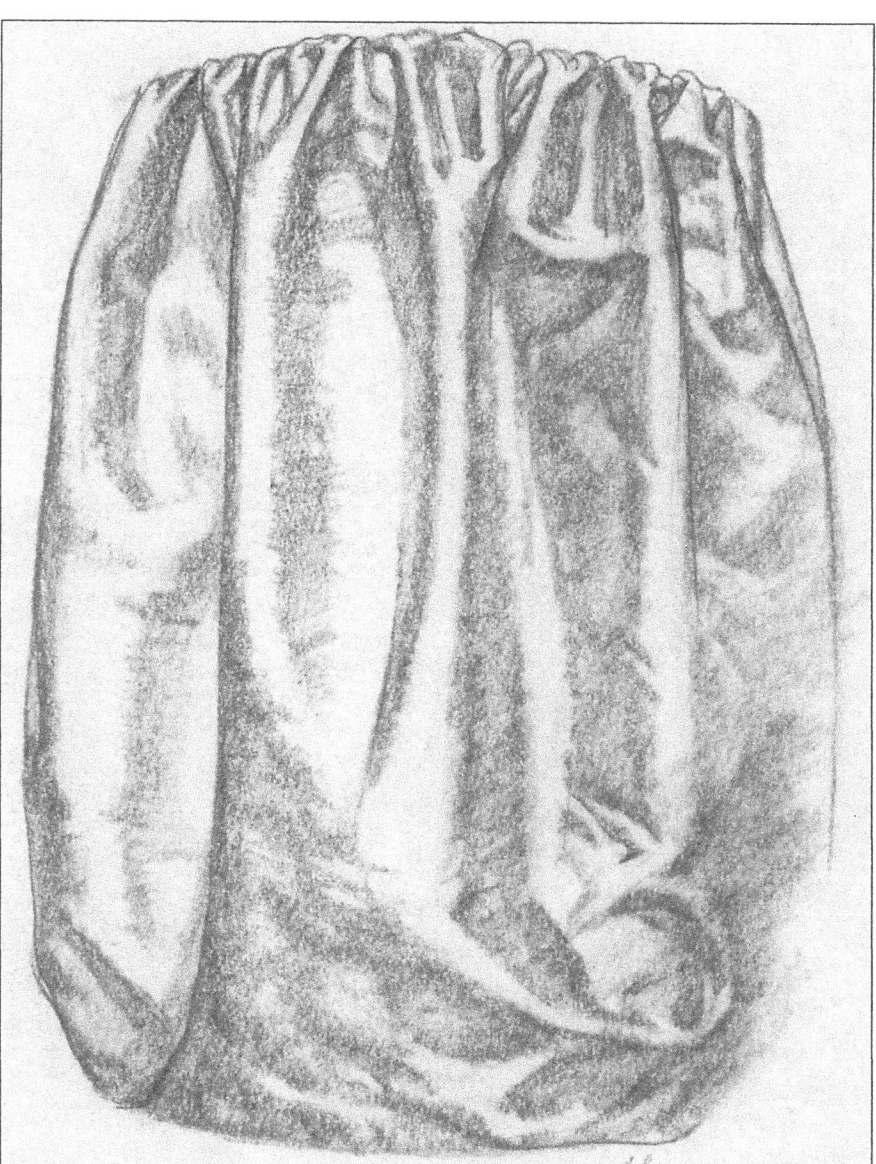

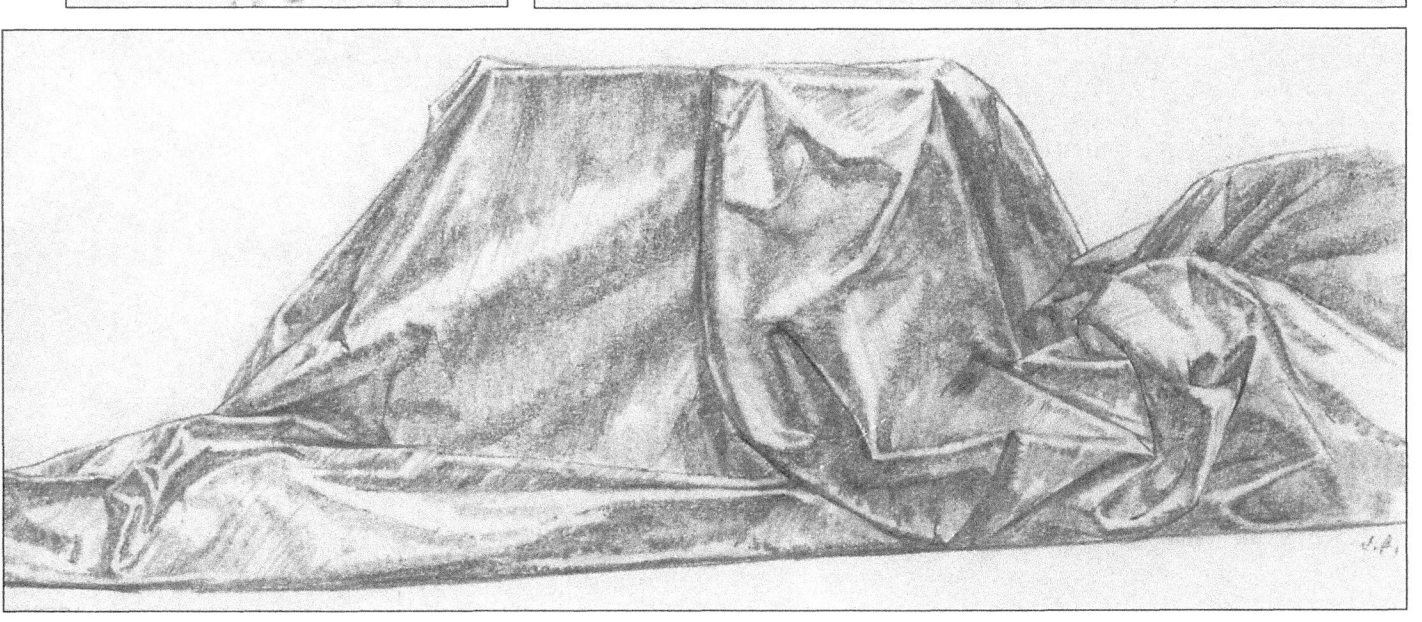

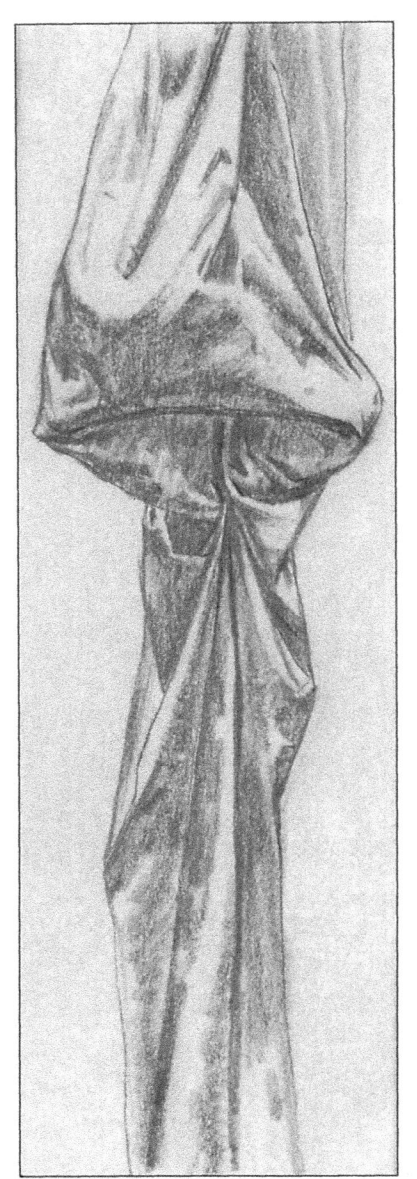

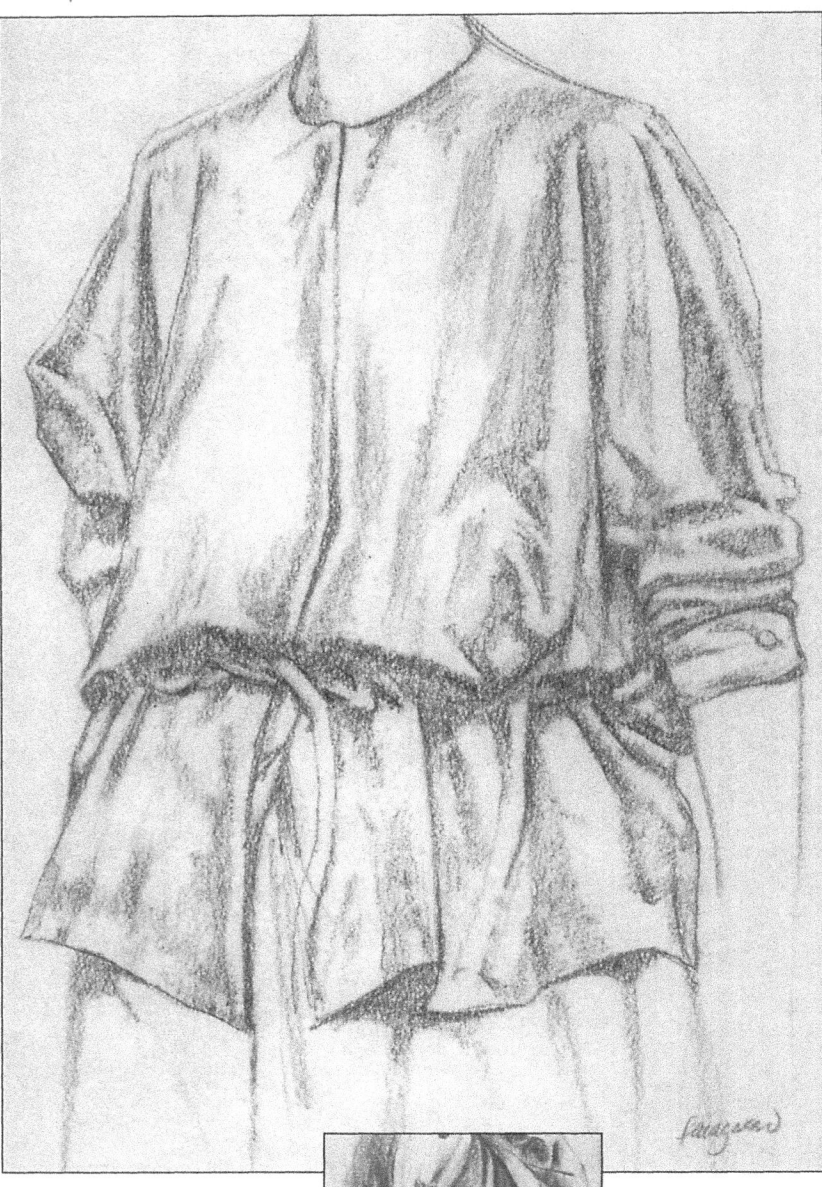

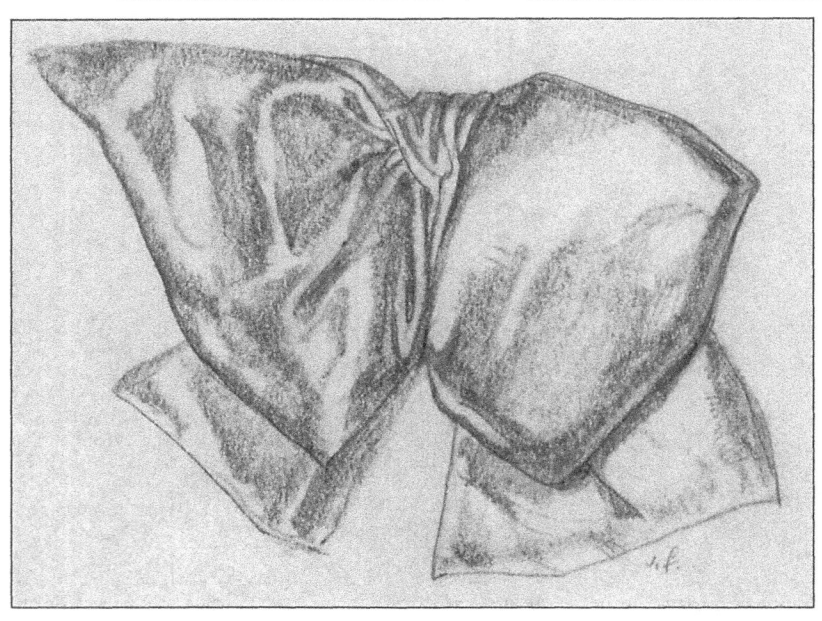

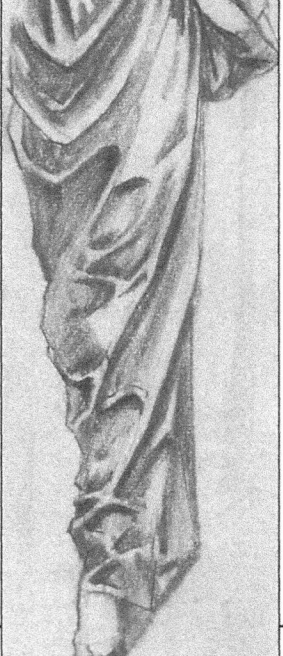

254

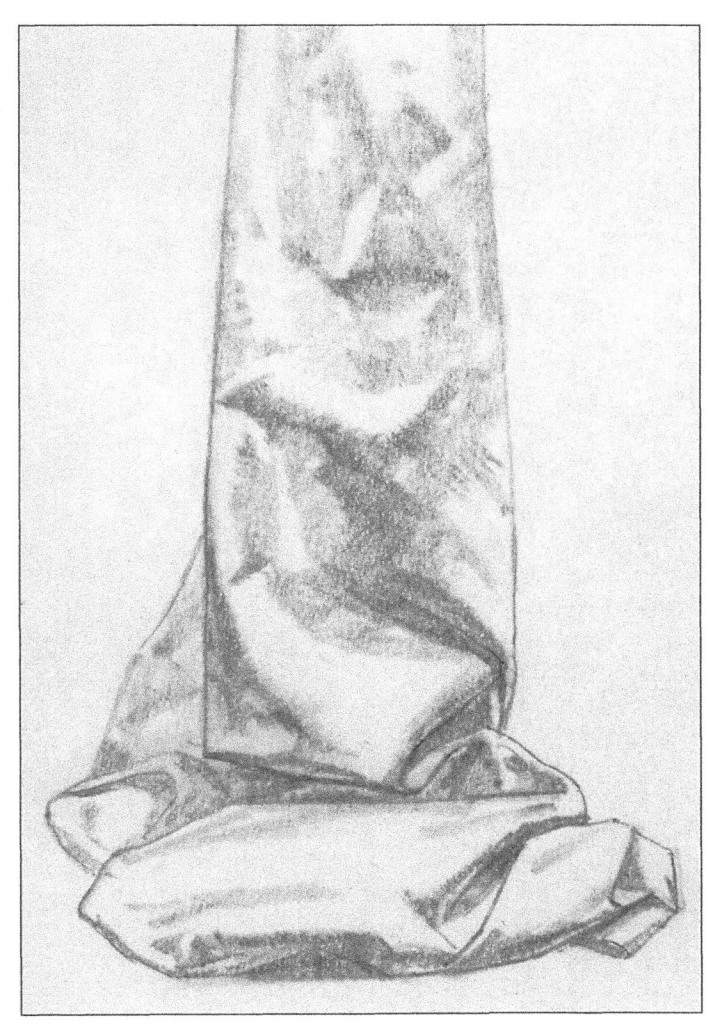

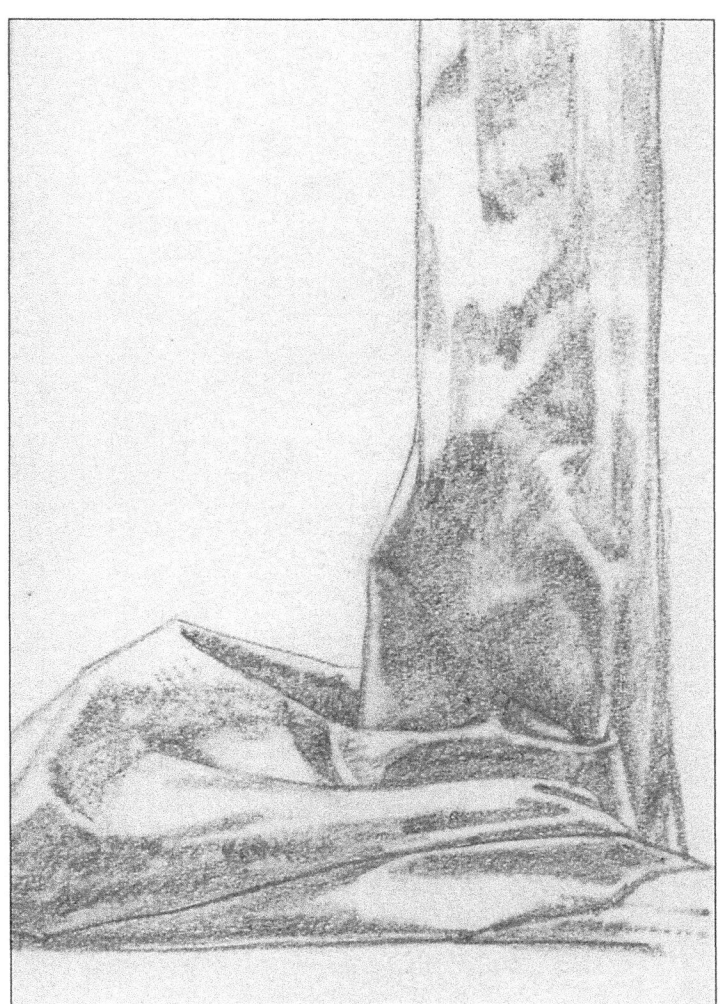

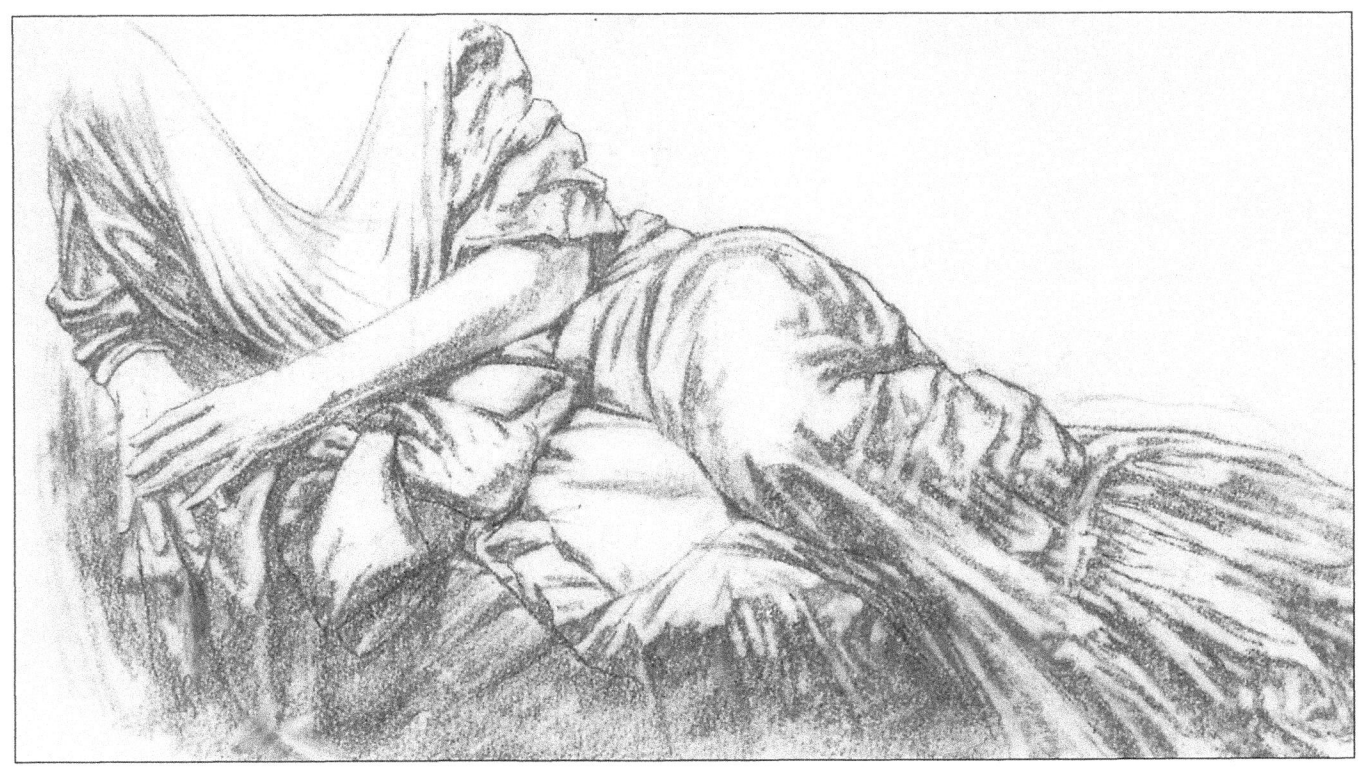

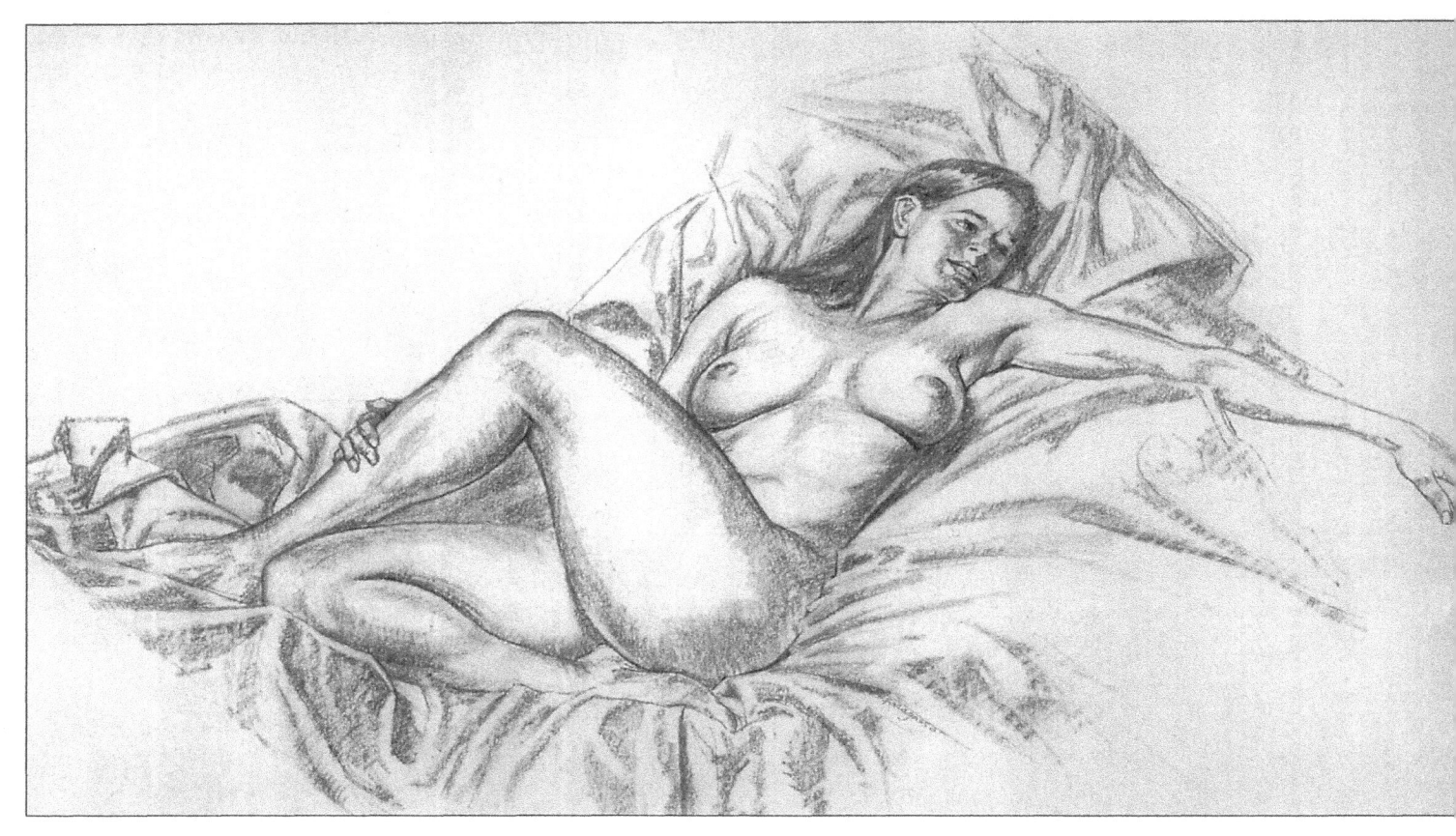

This book was written to foster the creative spirit of the artist and to aid in the development and the continuation of realistic representational art. It is my fondest hope that what is contained in these pages will expand your skill, perception and knowledge of drawing and that you may pass it on to future generations.

Jack Faragasso